WORKING HOLIDAYS 1993

CENTRAL BUREAU
FOR EDUCATIONAL VISITS & EXCHANGES

LONDON EDINBURGH BELFAST

41st edition

© Central Bureau for Educational Visits & Exchanges

ISBN 0 900087 91 9

Published by the Central Bureau for Educational Visits & Exchanges, Seymour Mews House, Seymour Mews, London W1H 9PE
℃ 071-486 5101   *Fax* 071-935 5741

Distributed to the book trade by Kuperard (London) Ltd, No 9, Hampstead West, 224 Iverson Road, West Hampstead, London NW6 2HL
℃ 071-372 4722   *Fax* 071-372 4599

Also available from the following organisations:
France: Eurovac ℃ 47 20 20 57
Germany: GIJK ℃ (0228) 95 25 0
Italy: The Reporter ℃ 055 257 8346
Spain: IZV ℃ (1) 542 10 89
United States: IIE ℃ (212) 894 5412

Cover illustration: Liz Pichon/Image Bank

Working Holidays 1993 was compiled and edited by the Print, Marketing & IT Unit, Central Bureau for Educational Visits & Exchanges, London

Typographic imaging and print production by the Print, Marketing & IT Unit, Central Bureau for Educational Visits & Exchanges, London

Printed and bound by BPCC Hazells

CONTENTS

A - Z

Practical advice and information to provide you with all you need to know to help you make your working holiday go smoothly.

WORK PROFILES

Details on the categories of work available, enabling you to decide where, when and how your skills and enthusiasms may be best employed.

JOBS INDEX

All the details on over 500 employers and 99,000 opportunities, paid and voluntary, from au pair work to workcamps, from Australia to Zaire, and in periods of from 3-365 days long.

INDEX & REPORT FORM

APPLYING FOR A JOB

Before applying, read carefully all the information given. Unless otherwise indicated, applications should be made in writing. Check in particular:

- skills, qualifications or experience required

- the full period of employment expected

- any restrictions of age, sex or nationality

- application deadlines

- any other points, particularly details of insurance cover, and other costs you may have to bear such as travel and accommodation.

When writing to any organisation it is **essential** to mention **Working Holidays 1993** and to enclose a large, stamped, self-addressed envelope, or if overseas, a large addressed envelope and at least two International Reply Coupons (available at Post Offices). When applying be sure to include the following:

- name, address, date of birth, nationality, sex

- education, qualifications, relevant experience, skills, languages spoken

- period of availability

- a passport-size photo, particularly if you are to have contact with the public

- anything else asked for, eg a *cv*

USING THIS GUIDE

The opportunities in **Working Holidays 1993** are given alphabetically by country, and are arranged into various categories depending on the type of work offered (the **Work Profiles** section at the front of the book goes into each category in detail). The **Information** section under each country lists addresses of embassies, consulates, tourist offices and youth and student travel centres - all useful sources of help and advice as you plan your working holiday and travel around. As a rule, tourist offices and embassies cannot help you to find employment, but they may be able to provide useful details, for example of hotels that may employ temporary staff, or information about the country you plan to visit. The **Information** section also details entry and work permit regulations, possibilities for budget travel and accommodation, relevant publications and information centres. The available jobs and voluntary opportunities are then listed under each recruiting organisation; a description is given of the work available, any skills or qualifications required, general conditions, wages and application procedures.

To apply for work, you must contact the recruiting organisations direct, and not the Central Bureau. Unless otherwise indicated, applications should be made in writing. Before applying, read carefully all the information given. Pay particular attention to:

✐ skills, qualifications or experience required

✐ the full period of employment expected

✐ any restrictions of age, sex or nationality

✐ application deadlines

✐ any other points, particularly details of insurance cover, and other costs you may have to bear such as travel and accommodation.

When writing to any organisation it is **essential** to mention **Working Holidays 1993** and to enclose a large, stamped, self-addressed envelope, or if overseas, a large addressed envelope and at least two International Reply Coupons (available at post offices). Be sure to also include the following:

✐ name, address, date of birth, nationality, sex

✐ education, qualifications, relevant experience, skills, languages spoken

✐ period of availability

✐ a passport-size photo, particularly if you are to have contact with the public

✐ anything else asked for, eg *cv*

Your letter will probably be acknowledged and they may either tell you straight away whether or not you have a job, or they may send you an official application form and further details. Any membership or registration fee should be sent to them only when you return the application form. In busy periods you may have to wait some time before your letter is acknowledged, so remember to apply well in advance of application deadlines.

Certain organisations provide facilities for, or will consider applications from those with handicaps. Those services and opportunities that are open to those with restricted ability are indicated by:

B Blind/partially sighted

D Deaf/hard of hearing

PH Physically handicapped

W Wheelchairs

Prices and wages are given either in £ Sterling or in the currency of the host country. The approximate exchange rates when this guide was compiled were (all rates = £ Sterling):

Australia 2.57 AU$	Israel 4.65 NIS
Austria 19.40 AS	Italy 2.10 L
Belgium 56.75 BF	Japan 245.72 ¥
Canada 2.22 Can$	Malta 0.55 LM
Czechoslovakia 53.10 Kcs	Netherlands 3.12 Fl
Denmark 10.66 DKr	New Zealand 3.47 NZ$
Finland 7.55 FIM	Norway 10.91 NKr
France 9.32 FF	Portugal 236.00 Esc
Germany 2.77 DM	Spain 175.00 Pt
Greece 336.00 Dr	Sweden 10.12 SKr
Hungary 135.00 Ft	Switzerland 2.48 SF
Iceland 100.00 ISK	Turkey 13120.00 TL
Ireland 1.04 IR£	United States 1.88 $

A - Z

A - Z

The main section of this guide, the **Jobs Index**, not only gives full details on the thousands of paid and voluntary work opportunities around the world, but also gives sources of information that can help in planning your working holiday, including advice on accommodation, travel and on getting to know the area and country in which you will be working.
This **A-Z** of practical advice and information provides virtually everything else you need to know to make your working holiday a success.

A

ADVERTISING This guide lists thousands of job opportunities. However, only employers offering a number of vacancies are included. Where one-off and short-notice opportunities exist, the places where they may be advertised, such as youth information centres, newspapers and magazines are detailed. In some instances it may be useful to advertise yourself for a job, and details of British representatives that can place advertisements in the *Situations Wanted* sections of foreign publications can be found in the **Job advertising** heading under the respective countries. Before taking on any job obtained in this way, however, the *bona fide* status of the employer must be ascertained. The following directories may be consulted in reference libraries:

Benn's Media Directories are comprehensive sources of information for anyone wishing to consult or advertise in foreign or British media. In three editions: *UK*, *Europe* and *World*. Published by Benn Business Information Services Ltd, PO Box 20, Sovereign Way, Tonbridge, Kent TN9 1RQ ℂ Tonbridge (0732) 362666.

Willings Press Guide provides information on over 24,000 publications worldwide, listing newspapers, periodicals and annuals in the UK, and details of major overseas newspapers and periodicals in over 116 countries. Published by Reed Information Services Ltd, Windsor Court, East Grinstead House, East Grinstead, West Sussex RH19 1XA ℂ (0342) 326972.

B

BAGGAGE What to include or exclude from your suitcase or rucksack can make or break your working holiday. The basic list of what to take may already be drawn up for you by virtue of the job you are going to. If you are having to take your own tent, sleeping bag, equipment and work clothes, then you are unlikely to have room for much else. Even where accommodation is provided, your own sleeping bag will allow you some flexibility in accommodation if you are going to travel around afterwards.
If you propose to do a fair amount of travelling, think carefully about the method of carrying your load, possibly investing in a good frame rucksack. Travel light, consider whether one pair of jeans or shoes, for example, would suffice, rather than two. Some companies will provide work clothes, from basic overalls to complete uniforms, allowing you the space to pack more casual and social clothes. However, if you are providing your own work clothes, consider how much free time you will have either during or after the working period, and whether you really will need a change of clothes for those occasions.
Try to get as much background information as you can on the area or country you are visiting, investigate the climate and weather patterns so that you will be taking the right sort of clothes, particularly if you will be involved in much outdoor work.

C

CUSTOMS If you are going to work in another country you should be fully aware of the Customs regulations governing all the countries you will be visiting. Full details of UK Customs regulations are given in the various Customs Public Notices obtainable from Customs & Excise local offices or from Customs at ports and airports in the UK. There are prohibitions and restrictions on the importation of certain goods including controlled drugs, firearms, ammunition, explosives, flick knives and certain other offensive weapons, horror comics, indecent or obscene books, magazines, video tapes, meat, poultry, plants, vegetables, fruit, certain radio transmitters and cordless telephones, animals and birds, articles derived from endangered species, goods bearing a false or misleading indication of origin, and certain counterfeit goods. Further information may be obtained from local customs enquiry offices (in the phone book under Customs and Excise) or from HM Customs & Excise, General Information Branch, New King's Beam House, 22 Upper Ground, London SE1 9PJ © 071-620 1313.

D

DRUGS If you are taking prescribed drugs it is advisable to carry a doctor's letter giving details of the medical condition and the medication, avoiding the possibility of confusion. It will also be useful to find out the generic rather than the brand name of the medicine, so that if need arises further supplies can be obtained abroad. If you are given any tablets or medicine when overseas it may not be legal to bring them back into your own country; if in doubt, declare the drugs at Customs when you return.

Some community service projects and workcamps involve working with ex-drug abusers, and participants will be asked to refrain from the use of tobacco, alcohol and other drugs whilst working on these projects. Those who feel that they will be unable to cope with this should not apply; conversely, those who have drug-related problems themselves should also think very carefully about participating in such work.

The social and legal conditions relating to the use of controlled drugs in the country you are visiting should be understood, particularly in relation to importation and usage. Further details on health precautions and treatment can be found in the **Health** and **Jabs** headings.

E

EMBASSIES Addresses and telephone numbers of embassies/consulates are given under each country throughout this guide. It should be noted that they cannot help in finding work, cannot provide money (except in certain specific emergencies), telex or telephone facilities, interpreting or legal advice services, or pay bills, whether legal, medical, hotel, travel or any other debts, though in an emergency they may help with repatriation. British citizens should note that there are consular offices at British Embassies in foreign capitals and at Consulates in some provincial cities. Consuls maintain a list of English-speaking doctors and will advise or help in cases of serious difficulty or distress.

As a last resort a consul can arrange for a direct return to the UK by the cheapest possible passage, providing the person concerned agrees to have his passport withdrawn and gives written confirmation that he will pay the travel expenses involved.

If the consul's urgent help is needed you should telephone or telegraph. The telegraphic address of all British Embassies is *Prodrome* and of all British Consulates *Britain*, followed in each case by the name of the appropriate town.

F

FOOD One of the joys of any holiday abroad is sampling the local food. This is no exception on a working holiday, though depending on the job being undertaken, such as working in a holiday centre, regular access to authentic local cuisine may be somewhat difficult.

Local tourist offices are good sources of information on shopping for local produce and in identifying good, cheap ethnic restaurants.

In many instances the working holiday will involve cooking for yourself. Given that you may be involved in heavy manual labour you should ensure that you are eating well, and consider resolving any conflict you may have if the best you have achieved in home cooking relies on the freezer contents. On some workcamps catering is undertaken on a rota basis; before you inflict your culinary skills on yourself, let alone others, you may care to buy a basic but practical cookery guide.

The Coordinating Committee for International Voluntary Service, UNESCO, 1 rue Miollis, 75015 Paris, France publish *Cookbook for Workcamps* which contains a variety of nutritious recipes and tips on cooking cheaply for large numbers. Cost FF15 or 15 IRCs.

G

GUIDES Under the **Publications** heading for each country **Working Holidays 1993** details a number of down-to-earth guides to areas and countries in which you will find yourself working and travelling. A good traveller's guidebook and map can make all the difference between a missed opportunity and a memorable experience. Forward planning and advance reading can give you a flavour of the country and some idea of sights worth seeing. Your local library should give you the opportunity to compare the available guides before buying your own copies. Tourist offices are a good initial source of free maps and guides. A good map of the area can help you make the most of your free time; locally available maps, for example those issued free at petrol stations, can be invaluable.

H

HEALTH Changes in food and climate may cause minor illnesses and, especially when visiting the hotter countries of southern Europe, North Africa, Latin America and the Far East, it is wise to take extra care in your hygiene, eating and drinking habits. Native bacteria, to which local inhabitants are immune, may cause the visitor stomach upsets, so it is worth avoiding tap water and doing without ice in your drinks. In a hot climate never underestimate the strength of the sun, nor overestimate your own strength. Drink plenty of fluid, make sure there is enough salt in your diet, wear loose-fitting cotton clothes, even a hat, and guard against heat exhaustion, heat stroke and sunburn, especially if you are working outdoors. See the section on **Jabs**, below, for further information on health precautions.

In the UK the Department of Health issues leaflet *T4 Health Advice for Travellers*, available from post offices, travel agents, libraries and doctors' surgeries, or by phoning 0800 555777. This includes details of compulsory and recommended vaccinations, other measures that can be taken to protect one's health, information on rabies, AIDS, malaria and other diseases. There is also advice on types of food and on water supplies which may be a source of infection.

A person is only covered by the NHS while in the UK, and will usually have to pay the full costs of any treatment abroad. However, there are health care arrangements between all EC countries (Belgium, Britain, Denmark, France, Germany, Greece, Ireland, Italy, Luxembourg, the Netherlands, Portugal and Spain). British citizens resident in the UK will receive free or reduced cost emergency treatment in other EC countries on production of form *E111* which is included inside leaflet *T4*, see above. Leaflet *T4* also explains who is covered by the arrangements, what treatment is free or at reduced cost, and gives the procedures which must be followed to get treatment in countries where form *E111* is not needed (usually Denmark, Ireland and Portugal). Form *E111* must be taken abroad and, if emergency treatment is needed, the correct procedures must be followed. There are also reciprocal health care arrangements between Britain and Australia, Austria, Barbados, Bulgaria, Channel Islands, Czechoslovakia, Finland, Gibraltar, Hong Kong, Hungary, Iceland, Isle of Man, Malta, New Zealand, Norway, Poland, Romania, Sweden, former republics of the USSR, Yugoslavia and the British Dependent Territories of Anguilla, British Virgin Islands, Falkland Islands, Montserrat, St Helena, and Turks and Caicos Islands. However, private health insurance may still be needed in these countries; leaflet *T4* gives full details. Despite reciprocal health arrangements it is still **essential** to take out full medical insurance whenever travelling overseas. The health treatment available in other countries may not be as comprehensive as in the UK, and **none** of the arrangements listed above cover the cost of repatriation in the event of illness. See the section on **Insurance**, below.

I

INSURANCE All workers should ensure that they have full insurance cover against risk of accident, illness and possible disability. Most large insurance companies offer comprehensive policies at reasonable cost, and workcamp organisations are sometimes able to arrange full cover for participants in their programmes. However, the insurance cover provided automatically by many employers is often solely against third party risks and accidents. You are therefore strongly advised to obtain precise details on this point and, if necessary, to take out individual policies.

The International Student Insurance Service (ISIS) policy provides, at competitive rates, a wide range of benefits covering death, disablement, medical and other personal expenses, loss of luggage, personal liability and cancellation, loss of deposits or curtailment. An advantage of this policy is that medical expenses can be settled on the spot in many countries by student organisations cooperating with ISIS; the medical limit for these expenses relates to each claim and therefore the cover is, in effect, limitless. A 24-hour assistance service is provided to handle all medical emergencies. Details in the UK from local Endsleigh Insurance centres.

J

JABS In addition to the compulsory vaccinations required for foreign travel, anyone about to undertake any sort of manual work is strongly advised to have an anti-tetanus injection. A certificate of vaccination against certain diseases is an entry requirement for some countries, and it is wise to consult embassies on this point, since requirements are continually subject to review. As a general rule it is wise to make sure that your protection against typhoid, polio and tetanus is up-to-date if you are travelling outside Europe, North America or Australasia.

Printouts indicating the immunisations and malaria tablets appropriate for any specific journey are available at a cost of £5, payable by credit card, from the Medical Advisory Service to Travellers Abroad (MASTA) ✆ 071-631 4408 or 0705 511420. Be prepared to give the countries to be visited in a journey (up to 6) in sequence, the month of arrival in each and the living conditions (rural, towns, cities, business, tourist), and the required information will be sent by return. MASTA printouts are also available without charge for those attending British Airways Travel Clinics for their immunisations; for details of the clinic nearest to you ✆ 071-831 5333.

Remember that protection against some diseases takes the form of a course of injections over several weeks, so allow plenty of time. Whilst abroad it is unwise to have your skin pierced by acupuncture, tattooing or ear piercing, for example, unless you can be sure that the equipment is sterile. A major cause of the spread of viruses, including AIDS, is the use of infected needles and equipment. In some countries blood for transfusions is not screened for the presence of the AIDS virus, but there may be arrangements for obtaining screened blood. The doctor treating you, or the nearest consulate or embassy may be able to offer advice. If you are concerned about the availability of sterile equipment whilst abroad, emergency medical travel kits are available through MASTA, see above, and other suppliers, and can be ordered through retail pharmacists. They contain a variety of sterilised and sealed items such as syringes and needles for use in emergencies. MASTA also has a range of health care items such as mosquito nets and water purifiers, available on mail order by calling the numbers given above.

K

KNOWLEDGE This edition of **Working Holidays** builds on over forty years of our knowledge in gathering together information on opportunities to experience life through a period of work in another environment. Every employer listed in this guide has been selected as offering a genuine working holiday; that is, you may be on holiday, but you will be expected to do a real job of work. Those employers who we feel cannot offer an authentic experience are not included; neither are those who can offer only one or two vacancies.

However, we need your help in monitoring that the jobs on offer live up to their promises. To this end we include a report form at the end of this guide; when you have been on your working holiday we would value your comments. Completed report forms enable us to continually improve on the information and advice we offer.

L

LANGUAGE Fluency in another language will increase the range of work opportunities open to you; in addition it will make your time in another country that much more enjoyable. Local education authority evening classes offer a range of classes to develop foreign language skills. The vocabulary and confidence gained will stand you in good stead when you find yourself abroad, even if, unless tuition is undertaken well in advance, you are unlikely to be totally fluent in the new language.

Study Holidays £8.95 including UK postage, is a comprehensive guide to hundreds of organisations offering courses in 26 European languages, from 1 week to 12 months. Detailed practical information on language resources and sources for grants is also given. Published by the Central Bureau for Educational Visits & Exchanges, Seymour Mews, London W1H 9PE.

While you are abroad, even the best phrase books will have limited use; if you are keen to develop your vocabulary a pocket dictionary will prove better value.

M

MONEY It's important that you work out how much money you'll need. The exact amount will depend on a variety of factors, including the location, the country itself, the total length of time you will be away, including what proportion of this period will be spent travelling rather than working, and the type of work you are undertaking. You will need some money to live on until your first pay day; this need only be pocket money if food and accommodation are being found for you. On the other hand, you may have to pay for your board, lodging and other needs, and you may be paid monthly, not weekly. If you're undertaking voluntary work in a remote location, with food and accommodation provided, pocket money may be enough to cover your needs, and you may even find difficulty in finding somewhere to spend that! A good guide as to how much to take is to make sure you've got enough to pay for at least two nights' accommodation and food, a long-distance telephone call, and return travel, if not already accounted for. If you do run out of funds it is possible to arrange for money to be transferred to a bank abroad, provided of course that you have the necessary funds available back home.

Large amounts of money are best taken as travellers' cheques; when obtaining these from a bank or travel agency you'll generally need to give a few days notice, and produce your passport. Shop around beforehand to compare commission rates charged. Read carefully any instructions given, particularly with regard to signing cheques and keeping a note of the numbers. Some travellers' cheques can be replaced while you're still abroad; others will be honoured by the issuing bank on your return. If you have a current bank account you will probably be able to obtain a supply of Eurocheques and a cheque card. These can be cashed abroad at banks where the Eurocheque sign is displayed, and in many cases are accepted by shops and restaurants. You'll also need to carry some foreign currency; you can get this at major travel agents and banks. Again, shop around for the best exchange and commission rates. Don't forget to take some of your own currency with you, for use on outward and return journeys.

N

NATIONALITY The information given in this guide particularly with reference to entry, work and health regulations, applies to British citizens and, as applicable, European Community (EC) citizens. Where possible full details on work opportunities and on employment regulations for other nationalities have been given, but applicants should check out job availability, entry and work permit regulations with employers and the consular sections of the appropriate embassies. In the main, voluntary work opportunities are open to all nationalities, with a letter of invitation acting as an entry permit; paid jobs usually require work permits, which depending on the country may be issued only for the job in question, and may not be available to certain nationalities.

O

OPPORTUNITIES The opportunities to undertake paid and voluntary work, from as short as one weekend up to 52 weeks, are all detailed under the **Jobs Index** section of this guide. Before this, the **Work Profiles** section details the categories of work on offer, and if you are in any doubt as to what type of work will be best suited to your needs, these profiles will enable you to decide where your skills and enthusiasms may be best employed. They will also answer some of the basic questions like where and when does the grape harvest take place, what is involved in being an au pair, exactly what is a kibbutz, where can I literally dig up the past, and how can I contribute practically to the conservation of this planet?

P

PASSPORTS/VISAS If you intend to work abroad and are not in possession of a valid passport, application for one should be made at least three months in advance. In most countries you will need to hold a full passport in order to undertake work. If a passport is lost or stolen while abroad the local police should be notified immediately; if necessary your nearest embassy or consulate will issue a substitute. It is therefore wise to keep a separate note of your passport number.

Within western Europe and certain other specified countries, British citizens can travel on a British Visitor's Passport; however, those travelling for purposes of work should obtain a full passport. Application forms for BVPs, valid for 12 months, are obtainable from any main UK post office, Monday-Saturday; they are not obtainable from passport offices other than the Passport Office, Belfast, and are only available to British citizens, British Dependent Territories citizens, and British Overseas citizens for holiday purposes of up to 3 months. Full UK passports, valid for 10 years, can be obtained from the regional offices listed below.

Passport Office, Clive House, 70-78 Petty France, London SW1H 9HD ✆ 071-279 3434 (personal callers only).

Passport Office, 5th Floor, India Buildings, Water Street, Liverpool L2 0QZ ✆ 051-237 3010

Passport Office, Olympia House, Upper Dock Street, Newport, Gwent NP9 1XA ✆ Newport (0633) 244500

Passport Office, Aragon Court, Northminster Road, Peterborough, Cambridgeshire PE1 1QG ✆ Peterborough (0733) 895555

Passport Office, 3 Northgate, 96 Milton Street, Cowcaddens, Glasgow G4 0BT ✆ 041-332 0271

Passport Office, Hampton House, 47-53 High Street, Belfast BT1 2QS ✆ Belfast (0232) 232371

The *Essential Information* booklet contains notes on illness or injury while abroad, insurance, vaccinations, NHS medical cards, consular assistance overseas, British Customs and other useful advice, and is available from all passport offices.

Nationals of other countries will need to consult their own passport-issuing authorities as to the issuing and validity of passports, and should read carefully details given under the **Information** and other headings for each country in this guide, so they are aware of the restrictions governing certain nationalities and their freedom to take certain jobs, particularly where the work is paid.

For entry to some countries a visa or visitor's pass is required, and in many a work and/or residence permit will be required. Requirements and regulations are noted in this guide under the **Entry regulations** headings for each country. Entry and work regulation requirements vary considerably, particularly outside the EC, and it is advisable to apply early to the relevant embassy or consulate as it may take some time to obtain the necessary documentation.

Q

QUALIFICATIONS Although this guide has a large number of opportunities for those with no particular qualifications other than enthusiasm and a willingness to be fully involved with the job in hand, before applying for any job check that you fully meet any credentials required. These need not be formal requirements either: for example, it's no use opting for farmwork if you suffer from hayfever; it's no use settling for a volunteer post if you must cover all your expenses; and it's no use choosing a workcamp if you don't like working hard and mixing with an international group. On the formal side, the more you can offer as regards language skills, teaching or training certificates, formal education or previous experience, then the wider range of options you will have, and consequently the better chance of being selected. It is always worthwhile listing relevant qualifications and experience when applying for any job; the competition for many of these jobs is strong, and employers can afford to be very selective.

R

REDUCTIONS Youth and student cards offer a range of reductions on travel, accommodation, restaurants, shopping and entry to cultural sites, and if you are eligible it is worth getting one of the available cards. The International Student Identity Card (ISIC) scheme is operated by the International Student Travel Confederation, a group of major official student travel bodies worldwide. ISIC provides internationally accepted proof of student status and consequently ensures that students may enjoy many special facilities, including fare reductions, cheap accommodation, reduced rate or free entry to museums, art galleries and historic sites. Obtainable from official student travel offices, students' unions and by mail order, the card is available to all full-time students, along with a free copy of the *Student Traveller* which details the discounts and facilities available worldwide. The card costs £5 and is valid for up to 16 months (1 September-31 December of the following year). Details in the UK from ISIC Administration, NUS Services Ltd, Bleaklow House, Howard Town Mills, Mill Street, Glossop SK13 8PT ℗ Glossop (0457) 868003.

The Federation of International Youth Travel Organisations (FIYTO) aims to promote educational, cultural and social travel among young people. The FIYTO International Youth Card is a recognised card offering concessions to young travellers including transport, accommodation, restaurants, excursions, cultural events and reduced rates or free entry to many museums, art galleries, theatres and cinemas. The card costs £4 and is valid for one year from date of issue. Available to all those between the ages of 12 and 26, together with a booklet giving details of concessions. Available in the UK from Campus Travel offices (London office: 52 Grosvenor Gardens, London SW1W 0AG ℗ 071-730 3402).

European Youth Cards are concessionary cards issued by a number of European youth agencies, entitling holders to a range of discounts and special offers on travel, cultural events and goods in high street shops in 18 European countries. Cards are renewable annually, and holders receive a directory of discounters and a regular magazine informing them of new discounts and activities available to card holders.

England and Wales: Under 26 Card available from the National Youth Agency, 17-23 Albion Street, Leicester LE1 6GD ℗ Leicester (0533) 471200. Cost £6.

Scotland: Young Scot Card available from the Scottish Community Education Council, West Coates House, 90 Haymarket Terrace, Edinburgh EH12 5LQ ℗ 031-313 2488. Cost £6.

Northern Ireland: European Youth Card available from USIT, Fountain Centre, Belfast BT1 6ET ℗ Belfast (0232) 324073, and other USIT offices. Cost £5.

Ireland: European Youth Card available from USIT, Aston Quay, O'Connell Bridge, Dublin 2 ℗ Dublin (1) 778117, and other USIT offices. Cost IR£5.

S

SOCIAL SECURITY If a person undertakes paid employment abroad in a country having reciprocal social security arrangements, advice as to their position should be sought from their social security authority.

The UK has reciprocal agreements with Australia, Austria, Barbados, Bermuda, Canada, Croatia, Cyprus, Finland, Iceland, Israel, Jamaica, Jersey and Guernsey, Malta, Mauritius, New Zealand, Norway, Philippines, Slovenia, Sweden, Switzerland, Turkey, United States and the Federal Republic of Yugoslavia. Leaflets explaining these agreements and how they affect UK nationals are available from the Contributions Agency, Overseas Contributions (RA), see below.

Leaflet SA29 gives details of the social security rights available to UK nationals working in the EC and how to claim them. Separate booklets are available describing the social security schemes (including health services) in certain EC countries. Leaflet NI38 Social Security Abroad is a guide to National Insurance contributions and social security benefits in non-EC and non-reciprocal agreement countries.

For copies of these leaflets and any further information contact the Contributions Agency, Overseas Contributions (EC/RA), Longbenton, Newcastle upon Tyne NE98 1YX ✆ 091-225 3002. See also the sections on **Health**, above and **Unemployment Benefit**, below.

T

TRAINING *Job Book 1993* £22.45, lists jobs and training schemes offered by over 1,200 UK employers. Editorial guidance identifies the job and training opportunities on offer, indexes help pin-point the employers who match individual needs and employer profiles give a more in-depth view on each organisation. Available in careers offices and libraries or from CRAC Publications, Hobsons Publishing plc, Bateman Street, Cambridge CB2 1LZ ✆ Cambridge (0223) 323154.

U

UNEMPLOYMENT BENEFIT If you are an EC citizen and unemployed and want to look for work in another EC country you may be able to get unemployment benefit there for up to 3 months. Claimants must have registered at an unemployment benefit office or a careers office

in their own country, normally for at least 4 weeks, and must be getting benefit when they leave. They must immediately register for work and also for benefit in all the countries they go to but may encounter problems if they cannot speak the languages of the countries they visit. Unemployed British citizens should ask for leaflet UBL22, or contact the Department of Employment, the Employment Service, St Vincent House, 30 Orange Street, London WC2H 7HT ✆ 071-839 5600.

Those who qualify for benefit, and are staying temporarily at workcamps away from their home areas in Great Britain, Northern Ireland or the Isle of Man run by charities or local authorities and providing a service to the community, may receive unemployment benefit for one period of up to 14 days in a calendar year provided they continue to be available for work during this period. They will not be required to attend the unemployment office during the workcamp. On return, their claims will be considered to see whether they continued to satisfy the conditions for the payment of unemployment benefit. It is essential, however, that they give the office details of the workcamp in advance. Unemployed people may earn up to £2 per day when working for voluntary groups, charities or the community, without having to forfeit their unemployment benefit, providing that they also remain available for work. However, if a person earns more than £52 in any week, benefit is forfeited for that week. See also the section on **Social Security**, above.

V

VOLUNTARY SERVICE Opportunities for short-term voluntary work are listed under the **Conservation, Community work, Peace camps** and **Workcamps** headings throughout this guide. The Central Bureau also publishes **Volunteer Work**, £8.99 including UK postage, an authoritative guide to agencies recruiting volunteers for medium and long-term service. Information on each agency covers its background and objectives, countries of operation, projects, experience and personal qualities required of the volunteer, and details of orientation and debriefing. Practical information includes details on preparation and training, understanding development, advisory bodies, insurance, travel, social security and health requirements.

The International Directory of Voluntary Work £8.95 is a guide to short and long term volunteer opportunities in Britain and abroad. *The Directory of Work and Study in Developing Countries* £7.95 is a guide to employment, voluntary work and academic opportunities in the Third World for those who wish to experience life there not just as a tourist. Both available from Vacation Work, 9 Park End Street, Oxford OX1 1HJ ✆ Oxford (0865) 241978.

Community Service Volunteers, 237 Pentonville Road, London N1 9NJ ✆ 071-278 6601 is the UK national volunteer agency which aims to involve young people as full time volunteers in the community and to encourage social change. Anyone aged between 16 and 35 who can be away from home for 4-12 months can volunteer and work with people in need: physically disabled and elderly people; people with learning difficulties; homeless people; young offenders and children in care. Volunteers go where their help is most needed in the UK, and work alongside professionals for 4+ months, receiving accommodation, food, pocket money and some travel expenses. Also places overseas volunteers, aged 18-35, with good English and able to meet British visa requirements. Overseas volunteers pay a £440 placement fee and work on the same projects as UK volunteers, receiving pocket money, food, accommodation, and some travel costs within Britain.

W

WORKING FULL TIME This guide does not attempt to cover regular paid employment abroad; those interested in finding such employment should apply through normal channels and advertisements. From time to time employment offices receive details of overseas vacancies, mainly in the EC. The majority of vacancies are for skilled persons aged 18+ with a good working knowledge of the language of the country chosen; applicants must be

prepared to work abroad for 6 months or more. In Britain contact the Training Agency, Employment Service Division, through your local Jobcentre or employment office, for further information.

Professionally qualified people wishing to work in their particular field should send a SAE/IRCs and a £2 postal order to the Federation of Recruitment and Employment Services Ltd, 36/38 Mortimer Street, London W1N 7RB for a list of member agencies dealing in overseas recruitment. Knowledge of a foreign language is usually preferred.

The Directory of Jobs and Careers Abroad £9.95, is a guide to permanent career opportunities worldwide, and outlines methods of finding work. Includes information on jobs in computer services, oil, mining and engineering, medicine and nursing, journalism, banking and accountancy, transport and tourism, and also includes information on work permits, visas, taxes and social security. Published by Vacation Work, 9 Park End Street, Oxford OX1 1HJ ✆ Oxford (0865) 241978.

The booklet *Working Abroad* gives broad guidelines relevant to working abroad, with useful information for UK nationals on how to apply for an overseas job. Published by the Employment Service, Overseas Placing Unit, Steel City House, c/o Rockingham House, 123 West Street, Sheffield S1 4ER and available from Jobcentres and employment offices. Also publish a series of booklets on working in EC countries.

X

XENOPHOBIA If you suffer from this condition, then a working holiday in another country, experiencing a different life and culture, and speaking another language, could prove to be just the cure. Even in your own country, taking part in an international workcamp could provide relief from some of the more extreme symptoms of xenophobia. However, if the condition has persisted for some time, then a working holiday, where international teamwork, shared experiences, opportunities to make and develop new friendships, and the challenges of new situations in far away environments are just some of the highlights, is probably not for you!

Y

YEAR BETWEEN A number of options are open to those who choose to widen their experience by taking a year off between school and higher education, school and work, or higher education and a career. Like a working holiday, this time is a valuable opportunity to develop personal skills, become more self- reliant and achieve an understanding of your own strengths and weaknesses. The opportunities listed in **Working Holidays 1993** are mainly geared towards the short-term. Whilst these are bound to be of interest to those who would like to spend a year doing a variety of short projects, details of medium-term voluntary projects, work placements and adventure opportunities specifically aimed at those taking a year out can be found in the Central Bureau's latest publication **A Year Between**. Carefully researched with the aspirations of school leavers and graduates in mind, **A Year Between**, price £8.99 including UK postage, offers authoritative advice and guidance, as well relating the experiences of people who have taken a year out.

Jobs in the Gap Year £5.95 is a booklet for those intending to work during their year between. It details opportunities for voluntary work, teaching, office work, engineering and science, attachment to the armed forces, and the leisure industry. Available from the Independent Schools Careers Organisation, 12a-18a Princess Way, Camberley, Surrey GU15 3SP ℗ Camberley (0276) 21188.

Z

Z As in algebra, so in a working holiday, Z is the third unknown quantity. Having decided on a job and the country in which you want to work, the third variable is **you** yourself. No matter that this guide lists thousands of opportunities all over the world, and provides a wealth of advice and information, at the end of the day you will need to use your own initiative, determination and imagination in order to obtain the job you want. Those with faint hearts will never get that opportunity to work their way round the world, undertaking for example, courier work on the Côte d'Azur in France, working in the orchard groves of a moshavim in Israel, picking pears in the Murray Valley in Australia, teaching sports at an American summer camp, and doing conservation work in Iceland. On the other hand, those lacking in wanderlust will find a host of opportunities nearer home. To all, the best of luck.

When writing to any organisation it is essential to mention Working Holidays 1993 and enclose a large stamped, self-addressed envelope, or if overseas, a large addressed envelope and at least two International Reply Coupons.

Working Holidays 1993 is published by the Central Bureau for Educational Visits & Exchanges, the UK national office responsible for the provision of information and advice on all forms of educational visits and exchanges; the development and administration of a wide range of curriculum-related pre-service and in-service exchange programmes; the linking of educational establishments and local education authorities with counterparts abroad; and the organisation of meetings, workshops and conferences related to professional international experience. Its information and advisory services extend throughout the educational field. In addition, over 25,000 individual enquiries are answered each year. Publications cater for the needs of people of all ages seeking information on the various opportunities available for educational contacts and travel abroad.

The Central Bureau was established in 1948 by the British government and is funded in the UK by the Department for Education, the Scottish Office Education Department, and the Department of Education for Northern Ireland.

Chairman of the Board: JA Carter
Director: AH Male
Deputy Directors: WE Musk, GJ Davey

Seymour Mews House, Seymour Mews, London W1H 9PE
℗ 071-486 5101
Telex 21368 CBEVEX
Dialcom 87:WQQ 383
Fax 071-935 5741

3 Bruntsfield Crescent
Edinburgh EH10 4HD
℗ 031-447 8024
Dialcom 87:WCP 034
Fax 031-452 8569

16 Malone Road
Belfast BT9 5BN
℗ 0232-664418/9
Fax 0232-661275

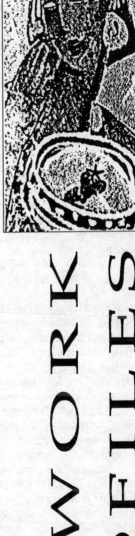

WORK PROFILES

The following profiles on the categories of work detailed in this guide may enable applicants to decide where their skills and enthusiasms may best be employed. More detailed information will be found in the **Jobs Index** under the respective categories for individual countries, and with particular employers, but these profiles outline the wide range of jobs on offer throughout **WORKING HOLIDAYS 1993**, and highlight the main opportunities available, with general details on age limits, requirements and periods of work.

ARCHAEOLOGY

Sitting in the bottom of a trench for hours on end, carefully brushing away decades of deposits is not everyone's idea of pleasure, but involvement in a project that may discover important finds of Palaeolithic, Bronze Age or Roman habitation has particular rewards. The range of archaeological projects available to participants is immense.

Typical opportunities include studying the life of Magdalenian reindeer hunters through the excavation of Upper Palaeolithic sites in France; working on Roman, Anglo-Saxon and medieval city sites in Britain; excavations of a castle and village with Crusader, Mamluk and Ottoman remains in Israel; and uncovering the skeletons of bison killed by Native Americans over 9,000 years ago in Nebraska. Although complete beginners are welcome on many excavation sites, applicants for archaeological work are often expected to have a formal interest in history or the classics, or to be studying archaeology at college or university level. It is also important to realise that on most excavations overseas, the site directors prefer to recruit those with experience; this is best first acquired on sites in your own country.

Archaeological work can be hard and may continue in almost all weathers, and participants should be prepared accordingly. Any relevant skills should be made clear when applying; those with graphic, topographic or photographic skills are often particularly welcome. Beginners will usually receive board and lodging in return for their labours. Wages and/or travelling expenses may be offered to more experienced volunteers. Basic accommodation is normally provided, but volunteers may have to take their own tents and cooking equipment. The minimum age for participants is usually 18; those under 18 may be welcome provided they can produce a letter giving parental consent or if they are accompanied by a participating adult. Families may also participate on some projects. Work may be available almost all year round, but owing to the nature of the work, projects are most often undertaken in the summer season. Anyone involved in excavation work is strongly advised to have an anti-tetanus injection beforehand.

AU PAIR/CHILDCARE

Working as an au pair can be an economic way to spend some time learning the language and experiencing the way of life in another country. It can be an invaluable way to widen your experience, particularly in the year between school and college/university or starting a career, for example, or in taking a break between job moves. Although au pair positions in most countries are now usually open to both sexes, many families traditionally specify females and as agencies recruit accordingly, male applicants will find opportunities more limited. One exception is the au pair programme in the United States, see below and in the **United States** section. Government regulations give an au pair the status of that of a member of a family, not that of a domestic. In return for board, lodging and pocket money au pairs are expected to help with light household duties including simple cooking and the care of any children, for a maximum of 30 hours per week. This should allow sufficient time to meet friends, go sightseeing and to take a part-time course in the language. Unfortunately, there is no guarantee that these conditions will be met as arrangements depend almost totally on goodwill and cooperation between the host family and the au pair, and au pairs should be aware of these potential problems before accepting a post. However, if an au pair post is found through one of the reputable agencies listed in this guide, most of these problems can be avoided as both family and au pair should be fully briefed.

Au pair positions outside the UK are open to those aged 17-27/30; stays are usually for a minimum of six months. There may be a limited number of short-term summer stays of 2/3 months, depending on the country. The work involves general household chores such as ironing, bedmaking, dusting, vacuuming, sewing, washing up, preparing simple meals and taking the children to and from school, plus general childcare duties.

A typical working day is of 5/6 hours, with 3/4 evenings babysitting in a 6 day week. The remainder of the evening, 1 full day and 3 afternoons per week are usually free. In addition to board and lodging approx £30-£35 per week pocket money is provided. There is usually an agency service charge, and applicants are responsible for their travel and insurance costs, although most agencies can provide information and advice. In some cases, normally after a stay of 12 months or more, the host family will pay a single or return fare. Under current regulations au pair agencies in the UK must be licensed by the Department of Employment, and can charge up to a maximum of £40 (VAT may be added) for finding an au pair position provided that they use an agent abroad as an intermediary. This fee is payable only after the applicant has been offered and accepted a position.

The au pair programme in the United States is open equally to males as well as females, with the emphasis as much on community involvement as on childcare. To be eligible you must be a citizen of a western European country with at least a fair degree of fluency in English. Character references and a medical certificate are required, and you will also need to have some childcare experience and, particularly as some of the communities are rural, be able to drive.

Au pairs work up to 45 hours per week spread over a maximum of 5½ days, with 1 full weekend free each month. Work involves active duties including feeding and playing with children, passive supervision such as babysitting. Ages 18-25. The positions last 12 months. The return flight plus approx $100 per week pocket money, board and accommodation, medical insurance, $300 for a course of study, 2 weeks holiday, and opportunities to travel are provided.

Au pair posts in Britain are open to those aged 17-27, unmarried and without dependants, who wish to learn English while living as a member of an English-speaking family. Only EC nationals (both sexes) and female nationals of Andorra, Austria, Cyprus, Czechoslovakia, the Faroes, Finland, Greenland, Hungary, Iceland, Liechtenstein, Malta, Monaco, Norway, San Marino, Sweden, Switzerland, Turkey and Yugoslavia are eligible. As a general rule au pairs in Britain can expect to work up to 5 hours per day with one fixed day per week free. They should have their own room and receive approximately £20-£30 per week pocket money.

It is the responsibility of the au pair agency to ensure that the correct arrangements are made for entry into the chosen country; however it is wise for applicants to check these requirements themselves with the relevant consulates, and details are given in this guide under the respective headings. Applicants should ascertain who is responsible for making travel arrangements and paying the fares; usually agencies will give advice on travel, but applicants make their own arrangements and pay the costs. It is essential to have sufficient funds to pay the fare home in case of emergency. Before leaving au pairs should make sure they have a valid passport, a visa/work permit as necessary, and a letter of invitation from the host family, setting out details of the arrangements that have been made, including details of pocket money and any contributions that may be payable to national insurance or other schemes in the destination country.

Au pair posts should not be confused with regular domestic employment, posts as nannies or mother's helps, or posts advertised as demi-pair or au pair plus, which are covered by different employment and entry regulations. Nannies usually have to have formal training, such as NNEB qualifications. They have sole charge of any children, and as a rule, they live with the family, working full-time. Mother's helps work alongside mothers, caring for children, and perhaps doing some cooking and housekeeping. They generally work a 8 hour day, 5/6 day week. Whereas au pair posts have the learning of a foreign language and the experience of life in another country as their basis, which means that au pairs cannot be placed in their home countries or countries where their own language is the native tongue (except the United States), these restrictions do not apply to other childcare and domestic posts.

For those with an interest in working with children but who are unavailable for the minimum periods of service of au pair and other childcare posts, or who do not possess the relevant qualifications or experience, a variety of less formal opportunities exist, particularly in the areas of community work, courier work and working as leaders or monitors; see below and under the respective headings for each country throughout this guide.

The Au Pair and Nanny's Guide to Working Abroad £7.95, is a comprehensive guide for those considering au pair, nanny or domestic work. Published by Vacation Work, 9 Park End Street, Oxford OX1 1HJ ℗ Oxford (0865) 241978.

COMMUNITY WORK

There are many opportunities in Britain and abroad to take part in projects dedicated to community service. Such an experience can be very valuable, particularly for those contemplating a career in social services and the caring professions. Applicants should be aware that any type of community work involves a high degree of commitment. The ideas and attitudes of voluntary service which used to be expressed as *helping those less fortunate than ourselves* or as *giving benefit to people in need* are inappropriate and patronising in society today. Working to overcome the effects of poverty, homelessness, illiteracy, high unemployment, and discrimination against an immigrant population are worthwhile challenges in themselves. The work can be undertaken in a variety of forms; for example construction, carpentry, painting and decorating work in community centres and homes can be equal in value to helping directly in the care of homeless, disadvantaged or disabled members of society.
Typical projects include helping to run playschemes for able-bodied or handicapped children; working in day centres/night shelters

for ex-drug addicts, alcoholics or the homeless; nursing and entertaining the elderly or physically handicapped; working with immigrant communities; and taking children from deprived inner city areas on holidays in the countryside. Examples include helping with fundraising, teaching first aid and on preparation for disasters, in New Delhi; supervising activities at an adventure centre for needy children in Lille, France; helping in youth clubs for Forces' children in Germany; working in night shelters, reception and community houses for the homeless, the isolated and unemployable, in London; working with residents on manual projects and organising activities at training centres for those with mental disabilities, in Torino, Italy; helping run youth camps, projects and family weeks for children and families under stress and from troubled areas, in Northern Ireland; and working with Sioux Indians on reservations in South Dakota, developing recreational and educational activities for children.

Applicants for community work schemes will need a good command of the host language, but formal skills or experience are not always necessary. The minimum age is 18, although younger applicants may be accepted on the basis of interests, experience and individual maturity.

Many community work projects can be particularly physically and emotionally draining, and potential applicants should read carefully all the literature provided on the project and consider their own strengths and weaknesses before formally applying. The ability to take initiatives within the framework of the project team, to cope with crises, to exert discipline without being authoritarian, and to maintain a sense of humour and perspective, is essential.

CONSERVATION

The Earth is 4,600 million years old; over the last 150 years we have come close to upsetting the ecological balance that has developed since the planet's creation. Earth's inhabitants have raided the planet for fuels, used the land, sea and air as rubbish tips, and caused the extinction of over 500 species of animals. For those who believe and care about the future of planet Earth, and who would like to make some contribution, no matter how small, towards its health and management, a variety of conservation work projects in Britain and around the world offer the opportunity to turn concerns into practical use. Volunteers can contribute to the conservation of the natural environment, from the coasts of Britain to the cloud forests of Costa Rica, and in the protection and restoration of neglected buildings of historic or environmental interest.

Work can be undertaken on a wide range of tasks: carrying out surveys to determine current population levels, habits or optimum environment of different species; building trails through forests and nature reserves; cleaning polluted rivers, ponds and lakes; stabilising sand dunes; or acting as environmental interpreter in a nature centre. There are also plenty of opportunities to preserve the built environment, including the restoration of railways, canals and other aspects of our industrial heritage; conserving churches, castles and monuments; renovating stately homes and gardens; rebuilding abandoned hamlets; preserving archaeological remains; and building drystone walls.

Typical opportunities include collecting seed for revegetation programmes in the Murray-Darling river catchment area of Australia; leading environmental conservation and study camps focusing on species protection, waste recycling and action against sea pollution, in Belgium; environmental protection work on islands in the Baltic; sand dune stabilisation and urban conservation in France's Northern Regional Park; restoration work on the British canal network; the restoration of an 11th century convent in Tuscany; biological and geological studies in natural caves in Portalegre, Portugal; trail routing and maintenance in a rare tropical white oak cloud forest in the mountains of Costa Rica; and radio-tracking endangered red wolves in the Great Smokey Mountains, United States. Those with relevant skills are particularly welcome, but many projects will include training on particular aspects of conservation

work. All tasks involve work which could not be achieved without volunteer assistance. The minimum age is usually 16 but can be as low as 13, and families with younger children will often be welcome. The projects are normally undertaken during the summer months, though opportunities exist at other times, and sometimes all year round. Basic accommodation is provided in church or village halls, schools, farm buildings or hostels, depending on the situation. Food is usually provided on a self-catering basis, with volunteers taking it in turns to cook. Volunteers contribute towards the cost of food and pay their own travel costs. Work can be strenuous; all volunteers should be fit and are strongly advised to have an anti-tetanus injection before joining any project.

COURIERS/REPS

The holiday market, particularly the package holiday sector, is a vast business, and provides a great number of seasonal work opportunities. Around 14 million Britons annually take a package holiday overseas, 5 million of them in Spain. However, for a variety of reasons there has been a recent drop of 10% in these numbers, with a further drop of 10% predicted for coming years. These statistics, coupled with an anticipated increase in holiday costs and the recent collapse of a major tour operator may well mean a corresponding reduction in the number of opportunities for seasonal employment, particularly outside the UK. Many holiday companies employ couriers to escort groups on holiday, between holiday areas, or from Britain to destinations overseas, in both the winter and summer seasons, December-April and May-August/September. Couriers are also required on a number of European campsites, acting as resident representatives, setting up and cleaning tents and mobile homes, responding to problems and emergencies, maintaining equipment, and arranging both children's and adult entertainment programmes. Other representatives are needed at hotels and holiday centres in resorts worldwide, providing client information and looking after welfare and other needs. Applicants will need to be 18/21+, mature, reliable, and with a good knowledge of both the clients' and local languages. The ability to be adaptable, independent, efficient, sensible, tactful, patient and sociable is essential. Previous experience in either courier work or in dealing with the public in similar situations also desirable. Many holiday operators will prefer to employ a courier or representative for the whole of the season, and consequently will give preference to those applicants available for long periods. Salaries and accommodation will vary according to qualifications, experience, resorts and seasons worked. There will usually be enough free time to make use of the hotel or centre's facilities, such as skiing or watersports.

There are courses for those interested in working as couriers/representatives. Sight and Sound Education Ltd, 118/120 Charing Cross Road, London WC2H 0JR © 071-379 0961 run an Employment Training course for those currently unemployed and receiving benefit. Another course is run at Westminster College, Peter Street, London W1V 3RR © 071-437 8536.

DOMESTIC WORK

Hotels and holiday centres take on extra kitchen assistants, waiters, waitresses, bar staff, cleaners, chambermaids and other domestic staff during the holiday seasons. However the comments made above under **Couriers/reps** with regard to the future volume of work generated by the package holiday industry should be noted. Domestic work can be very hard with long, unsocial hours. The ability to work as part of a team is essential. Knowledge of the local language may be needed, particularly where contact with the public is made, and relevant skills or experience are an advantage. Salaries, living conditions, tips or bonuses vary according to placement. Often the facilities open to clients will be available for staff use during free time. The minimum age is usually 17/18, and those with experience or relevant qualifications are particularly sought, although there are posts such as kitchen assistants and porters where previous experience is not necessary. Preference will usually be given to those able to work the whole of either the winter or summer season, usually December-April/May and April-July/ September respectively.

The Federation of Recruitment and Employment Services, 36/38 Mortimer Street, London W1N 7RB, is the UK trade association for the private recruitment service and produces a list of members who recruit domestic, catering and hotel staff in Britain and overseas, available on receipt of a SAE and a £2 postal order made payable to FRES, or equivalent value in IRCs. In Britain Jobcentres and employment offices often receive details of summer jobs in the hotel and catering industries.

FARMWORK/ GRAPE PICKING

A variety of work is available on international farmcamps, on agricultural establishments, including organic and bee farms, and in vineyards in a number of European countries and as far afield as Australia and Canada. Participants must be fit and ready to undertake whatever picking or other agricultural work they are required to do. The work is often very hard and patience is required; hours can be long and it is often necessary to work weekends. As most picking jobs are paid at piece-work rates, it is important to remember that bad weather can affect ripening, the amount of crops to be picked and thus the wages; if no work is available due to bad weather or for any other reason, no wages will be paid. The wage is normally enough to cover food, accommodation and other charges and leave a small net gain, varying according to the efficiency of the picker, the weather, and the quality and quantity of the harvest. Living conditions are often simple, with self-catering accommodation in dormitory huts or tents. On farmcamps participants may have to provide their own tents and cooking equipment, and a registration fee will be payable. Some international farmcamps provide facilities for sports and other leisure activities and may arrange excursions to places of interest.

Summer farmwork in Britain includes general farm labouring as well as vegetable harvesting and fruit picking. The work is mainly in Scotland, East Anglia, the South, the West Country and Kent, where it includes the traditional English working holiday of hop picking. Other crops to be picked include cherries, raspberries, strawberries, blackcurrants, loganberries, blackberries, plums, gooseberries, apples, pears, potatoes, courgettes and beans. A range of ancillary work such as strawing, weeding, irrigation, fruit inspection, packing, indoor processing, tractor driving or working in oast houses may also be available.

The work can be on individual, often family-run farms, on smallholdings or with cooperatives, or on international farmcamps. The general number of hours worked are 40-45 per week and 5-6 days. The length of the working season varies, depending on the crop being harvested, the weather and the location of the farm. The harvesting of soft fruit is normally undertaken between mid June and August, although in some areas picking may start as early as May. The picking of hops, apples and other crops runs from late August to October.

Work is also available on community and alternative farming projects. It can include assisting in the breeding of rare domestic animals; working with underprivileged children on farmsteads during their summer holidays; helping organic farmers, whose work is often labour-intensive as it does not rely on the use of artificial fertilisers or pesticides; helping on city farms and community garden projects; and working with the handicapped, disabled and disadvantaged on rehabilitation projects on the basis of a common interest in plants and animals.

Hop picking has traditionally been undertaken as a working holiday by many of the families of London's East End and their counterparts in the Black Country, once England's industrial heart. Although this tradition is still carried on today, the majority of the several hundred pickers working annually in the hop gardens of Hampshire, Kent, Sussex and Worcestershire are overseas students, local workers and Travellers. Hops are climbing bines, their bitter cones used in the flavouring of beer. At one time there were over 1,000 hop farms in southern England, supplying cones to brewers all over the world. However, since mainland

Europe and the United States began plantations to provide for most of their own needs, and since drinking fashion turned to lighter beers and lagers, the number of English hop producers has dwindled to around 250. Consequently the number of seasonal workers taken on is now substantially less than it once was. Generally a flat rate of pay, up to £25 per day, is paid rather than piece-work rates.

On farmcamps the emphasis is as much on living and working in an international community, with sports and social activities, as on earning money. The wages paid may only be sufficient to cover food and accommodation costs and to provide a little pocket money. The social and sports facilities provided can include swimming pools, tennis courts, games fields, games and television rooms, video, bars, discos and dances. The majority of workers will be in the 17-30 age range, and families are often welcome. On some camps English language tuition may be available for overseas workers during free time. Work permits are not required by those from outside Britain wanting to work on approved farmcamps, but workers from countries outside the EC subject to immigration control must be in full-time education, between the ages of 18 and 25 and have a Home Office card issued by an approved scheme operator. This card allows entry into Britain but does not entitle the visitor to take paid work of any other kind during the visit.

Most soft fruit picking is a slow and painstaking job, and workers will often be required to pick to a very high standard. Poor weather at the time of setting or harvesting can mean, as in 1991, that the number of pickers needed will be limited. In addition, the market competition of soft fruit from East Europe may well mean some decline in the number of farms, and consequently the number of opportunities available. All agricultural work is physically demanding and can involve long hours in all weathers. The living conditions offered are often simple, with self-catering accommodation in farm cottages, caravans, dormitory huts or tents. In some instances participants may have to take their sleeping bags, if not their own tents and camping equipment. Insurance cover is usually provided against accidents or illness, but personal insurance cover will normally be necessary. Community and alternative farmwork projects are generally of a voluntary nature, and some financial contribution towards board and accommodation may be required. The work can include hedging, ditching, pond and scrub clearance, haymaking, fruit and vegetable cropping, dairy work, bee keeping, stone walling, sheep shearing, animal rearing, building renovation, peat cutting, scything and compost making.

Grape picking under the sun in the south of France, tasting the product, living at the vineyard, taking *déjeuner sur l'herbe* with the grower and his family may conjure a colourful and idyllic scene. It certainly can be with proper planning, a genuine job awaiting you, and the true picture of what grape picking involves clearly defined. If not, then the reality can be very different. The hours of work are long, you need to be fit as the work is hard, the accommodation may be basic and often, during bad weather, only those hours actually worked will be paid. The decreasing need for manual labour owing to mechanisation together with the regular army of seasonal workers being swelled by the numbers of unemployed has also led to increased competition for jobs. Despite this, and providing you have a realistic assessment of just what a grape picking holiday involves, the grape harvest can provide an enjoyable summer job, as you toil away alongside the locals and workers from all over the world.

The main opportunities available, with brief details on age limits, requirements and periods of work are given under the different countries in the **Jobs Index**. The dates of the harvest should be regarded as approximate; they may vary by two weeks either way. Changes in the weather may also mean that you are given as little as 48 hours notice before work is due to commence. The quality and quantity of the harvests can vary enormously. 1986 was a good harvest, swelling the European wine lake to 6,070 million litres; 1987 was not indifferent in quality but was far from generous in quantity; the late and hard frosts of 1991 resulted in a substantially reduced crop. The effects of a good year can make for lower production in subsequent years, and in any case, wine consumption in the main wine producing areas is falling. Also, since the dollar weakened, the United States has lost some of its taste for European wines, and Australian and New Zealand wines have become increasingly popular. CIS/Russia, which has traditionally absorbed some of the European wine surplus is now increasing its own production capacity and planted 25% more vines over the last decade. Many EC farmers are taking advantage of subsidies to turn their land over to more lucrative forms of agriculture, and in France the total vineyard area has decreased from 3 million acres to 2.4 million in the last ten years. Nevertheless France, Italy and Portugal have an 80 litres per head, per year, wine consumption rate, compared to Britain's 10 litres per head. The net result, at least as far as summer workers are concerned, is that in France the quality areas such as Burgundy, Beaujolais and Bordeaux are where grape picking will prove to be most fruitful.

For those looking further afield for farmwork, in addition to opportunities on **Kibbutzim/ Moshavim**, see below, the fruitgrowing regions of the Goulbourn/Murray Valley in Australia, offer fruitpicking jobs from late January to April each year. These regions are situated approximately 300 miles south west of Sydney, and 100 miles due north of Melbourne; they are one of the most productive fruit growing regions of Australia, producing an annual crop of around 200,000 tonnes of fruit. The season starts in January with the harvesting of Bartletts pears, used mainly for canning. Other pear varieties and peaches extend the season through March and into April, finishing with apple harvesting. Piece-work rates apply, and although accommodation is offered on many orchards, those with rucksack and tent will find the climate conducive.

KIBBUTZIM/ MOSHAVIM

There are hundreds of kibbutzim and moshavim all over Israel, offering the opportunity to experience the challenge of living and working in a small, independent community. This in itself is potentially rewarding, as is living in a country whose society and culture are so different from one's own. The first kibbutz was established in 1909 by a group of individuals who wanted to form a community where there was no exploitation and no drive to accumulate individual wealth. The desire to establish a just society is the basic principle guiding kibbutz life, together with a commitment to undertake tasks important to the development of Israel and the Jewish people. There are now 250 kibbutzim throughout Israel providing a way of life for nearly 100,000, in which all means of production are owned by the community as a whole. The workforce consists of all members and any volunteers, who receive no wages but give their labour according to ability and in return receive in accordance with their needs. Kibbutzim are democratic societies and all members have a voice in determining how the kibbutz is run. A general assembly meets weekly and a number of committees discuss and resolve specialist problems. Kibbutzim welcome volunteers who are prepared to live and work within the community and abide by the kibbutz way of life. Volunteers share all communal facilities with kibbutz members, and should be capable of adapting to a totally new society.

The majority of work for volunteers is in the communal dining room, the laundry and possibly in children's houses. On most kibbutzim children live in houses apart from their parents, spending only part of the afternoons and evenings with them. This allows mothers to become active in the life of the kibbutz, and ensures an equality of education where the community as a whole is responsible for the care and education of the children. Some of the work during summer months includes citrus, melon and soft fruit harvesting, and volunteers may also be involved in haymaking, gardening or working in the fish ponds, cow sheds or chicken houses. Part of the time is also likely to spent in non-specialist, light industrial work. Volunteers work approximately an 8 hour day, 6 day week with Saturdays free and 2 additional days off at the end of each month. Work outdoors often starts at 05.00 and finishes at 14.00, the hottest part of the afternoon being free. Volunteers live together in wood cabins, 2-4 to a room, with food provided in the communal dining room.

Moshavim are collective settlements of from 10-100 individual smallholders. Each family works and develops its own area of land or farm while sharing the capital costs of equipment, marketing and necessary services. There are almost 1,000 moshavim where volunteers can live and work as a member of an Israeli family, mainly in the Jordan valley, the Arava and the western Negev. Most of the work is on the land, particularly in flower growing, market gardening and specialist fruit farming.

Kibbutzim or moshavim volunteers should be aged between 18 and 32, in good physical and mental health, and will need references, a medical certificate and a special entry visa. Pregnant women or families with young children will not be accepted. Prospective volunteers should bear in mind that the work is often physically arduous, that conditions can be uncomfortable, and the hours long. The effect of living in relatively close confinement with a group of fellow volunteers is also something that should not be underestimated. Working holidays on kibbutzim and moshavim can last from 5 weeks up to one year.

LEADERS & GUIDES

A wide range of opportunities exist for those with organising and leadership skills. They include leading a range of adventure holidays and expeditions, including those by truck or foot, in countries in Africa, Asia and South America; organising welfare and entertainment activities for groups of young people and adults on activity holidays throughout Europe; organising and running sports and activities at adventure holiday centres in a number of countries including France and Britain; acting as ski guide for school groups in alpine resorts; cooking and leading canoeing and hillwalking outings; and looking after children on holiday in Spanish coastal resorts, arranging entertainments, competitions and parties.

Depending to some extent on the individual job, applicants will need at least some of the following qualities: to be energetic, reliable and mature, self-motivated, resourceful, adaptable, with good stamina, tolerance, flexibility, initiative and a sense of humour. Previous travel experience and a knowledge of foreign languages will be an advantage. The minimum age is normally 21, and the period of work from 8 weeks-6 months. It is often necessary to attend a short training course, and previous experience in working with children is a definite advantage.

MONITORS, TEACHERS & INSTRUCTORS

For those with some teaching or instructing skills and qualifications there are a number of posts in a wide range of countries. Most of the opportunities will require formal qualifications, although a number will be open to those with at least relevant experience.

Monitors and teachers are required to teach English at English language camps for young people in Austria, Hungary, Poland and Turkey. Applicants should be native English speakers and have experience in working with or teaching children; organisational ability in sports, music and crafts an advantage.
Camp counsellors are needed on North American summer camps, and on similarly run day and residential camps in Britain and other European countries. General counsellors are responsible for the care and supervision of a group of 8-10 children aged 6-16. The work involves playing and living with the children 24 hours a day, and duties include supervising the camp, helping to maintain a high level of morale, supervising rest hours and conducting activities. Specialist counsellors are responsible for instructing the children in specific activities such as sports, watersports, sciences, arts and crafts, pioneering and performing arts.
Applicants are normally aged 18-35, and must be flexible, cooperative and adaptable, like and actively get on with children, and be prepared to work with young people intensively in an outdoor environment.

A variety of instructor posts are available including those for ski instructors, usually with BASI or ASSI qualifications, working the winter season, December-April. Qualified sports, watersports and other activity instructors are also required in a number of countries, usually

in the summer seasons, April or May-August or September. Instructors must have the ability to teach to a good basic level and impart their knowledge in an imaginative, interesting way, particularly as many of the posts involve work with children. On many holiday centres the emphasis is on informality and enjoyment; safety, fun and participation is often the main aim, rather than just pure sports teaching. To this end the ability to manage and organise, and to work within a team, is as important as technical abilities.

For those lucky enough to be native speakers of English, already the language of air traffic, international business, pop music, science and technology, opportunities to teach English exist not just in Britain and Ireland but also in Italy, Spain, Sweden and Japan. To work in language schools, applicants should be aged 20+; many of the openings are for graduates with a recognised TEFL qualification and/or experience. Many schools in Britain offer TEFL training and their own qualifications, however the most widely recognised qualifications are the RSA/Cambridge and TESOL certificates.

International House, 106 Piccadilly, London W1V 9FL ✆ 071-491 2598 runs courses leading to the RSA/Cambridge certificate.

Teaching English Abroad £8.95, is a guide to short and long term opportunities abroad in the field of teaching English as a foreign language. Available from Vacation Work, 9 Park End Street, Oxford OX1 1HJ ✆ Oxford (0865) 241978.

PEACE CAMPS

Forty five million people worldwide lost their lives in the Second World War. If this statistic was not troubling enough in itself, over two thirds of those killed were civilians, innocent bystanders killed not on the field of war, but in cities and concentration camps. In order that we may not simply forget the horrors of the Second World War or previous or subsequent conflicts, a number of organisations run peace camps in several countries, particularly in Germany. Their aim is through the understanding of events and history to prevent the repetition of the savageries of war. The work on peace camps often involves the maintenance of Second World War concentration camps as monuments, warning symbols and as a means of raising awareness of history. The camps also support peace information and activity centres, promote international discussion of the nuclear threat, alternative security policies and non-violence, and bring together peace movements in different countries. Volunteers should be aware that they may be confronted with disturbing situations and they should give a lot of thought to the subject of war and peace, before participating. Equally, volunteers should also be aware that they have the potential to make an important contribution to promoting tolerance and justice. Discussion forums and educational and cultural activities form an integral part of all peace camp activities. Ages 18+. Applicants should be interested in peace work, and have some knowledge of the political background of the host country.

WORKCAMPS

International workcamps are a form of short-term voluntary service, providing an opportunity for people of different racial, cultural and religious backgrounds to live and work together on a common project providing a constructive service to the community. By bringing together a variety of skills, talents and experiences from different nations, volunteers not only provide a service to others but also receive an opportunity for personal growth and greater awareness of their responsibility to the society in which they live and work. Workcamp participants have an opportunity to learn about the history, culture and social conditions of the host country and to partake in the life of the local community.

Workcamps generally run for periods of 2-4 weeks, April-October; some organisations also arrange camps at Christmas, Easter and at other times throughout the year. Young people participating in workcamps need to be mature enough not to require adult supervision and should be prepared to take responsibility for the successful running of the projects, group recreation activities and discussions. The minimum age is 17/18, with the exception of a number of youth projects, usually with a minimum age of 13.

The type of work undertaken varies considerably depending on both the area and the country in which the camp is being held. The work can include building, gardening and decorating, providing roads and water supplies to rural villages or constructing adventure playgrounds, and is within the capacity of normally fit volunteers. Virtually all workcamp organisers will consider volunteers with disabilities providing the nature of the work allows their active participation. Any manual work undertaken is usually for 7-8 hours a day, 5 or 6 days a week.

Workcamps can also involve community or conservation projects with work other than that of a manual nature. A few camps have shorter working hours and an organised study programme concerned with social problems or dealing with wider international issues. Accommodation is provided in a variety of building such as schools, community centres or hostels, and may sometimes be under canvas. Living conditions and sanitation vary considerably and can be very basic; in some cases running water may not be readily available. Food is generally provided, although it is often self-catering, with volunteers preparing and cooking their own meals, sometimes on a rota basis. In many camps food will be vegetarian.

Most workcamps consist of 10-30 volunteers from several countries. English is in common use as the working language, especially in Europe; the other principal working language is French. A knowledge of the host country's language is sometimes essential, especially for community work.

Workcamp applicants will generally pay a registration fee and arrange and pay for their own travel and possibly insurance. Most workcamp organisers operate on an exchange basis with organisers in other countries. In some cases, especially with regard to workcamps in eastern Europe, the registration fee is higher in order to support the cost of the exchange. Volunteers may occasionally be expected to make a contribution towards the cost of their board and lodging, and should take pocket money to cover basic needs. Although many organisations provide insurance cover for their volunteers, this is often solely against third party risks and accidents. Volunteers are strongly advised to obtain precise details on this and, where necessary, take out individual policies against illness, disablement and loss or damage to personal belongings. In addition to the compulsory vaccinations required for foreign travel, anyone joining a manual workcamp programme is strongly advised to have an anti-tetanus injection.

It is quite usual for workcamp organisations to hold day or weekend orientation seminars prior to volunteers going abroad. In some cases, especially for workcamps held in eastern Europe or Third World countries, attendance at these seminars is essential and volunteers should make every effort to attend. They will be able to learn a lot about aspects of voluntary work in the relevant countries as well as gaining practical background information on politics, culture and way of life.

Workcamp leaders are volunteers, usually in their early 20s, selected for general suitability and experience, and briefly trained. They have no special privileges on the camp, are expected to work as much as everyone else and can only be distinguished from their fellow volunteers by their extra responsibilities; most workcamps have two co-leaders of equal status. Domestic affairs are the responsibility of the group; the key function of the leaders is to enable the volunteers to form a cohesive group within which each volunteer feels expected and able to contribute fully to the work and life of the camp. An important function of the leaders is to act as the link between people professionally concerned with social need and volunteers whose willingness to help may not be matched, at least initially, with enough understanding of the problems involved and how to meet them. Besides basic training regarding the functions of leadership, workcamp organisations run special courses to prepare leaders for particular types of projects, such as children's playgroup leadership or the care of the mentally handicapped. Anyone interested in attending leadership training courses in Britain should contact one of the major UK workcamp organisations, details below.

Workcamp Organisers lists nearly 280 national and international voluntary service

organisations sponsoring workcamps in approx 90 countries. It includes the duration of the camps, months in which they take place, type of work, financial conditions and other details. Published every 3 years in cooperation with the Youth Division of UNESCO by the Coordinating Committee for International Voluntary Service, UNESCO, 1 rue Miollis, 75015 Paris, France. Cost FF12 or 14 IRCs. Also publish a *Camp Leader's Handbook*, cost FF12 or 14 IRCs.

When applying to join a workcamp in your own country it is essential to include a large stamped self-addressed envelope when you write to the organisers. If you would like to join a workcamp overseas, you should usually apply through the recruiting organisation in your own country, and not direct. The UK organisations that cooperate in the recruitment of volunteers on international workcamps are given at the end of each workcamp entry, and information on their registration/membership fees is given below. If no cooperating organisation is listed, or you need to write direct to an overseas workcamp organiser for any other reason, it is essential that you enclose a large self-addressed envelope and at least two International Reply Coupons (IRCs), available from post offices.

A major network of workcamp organisers is **Service Civil International (SCI)**. Those wishing to take part in an SCI workcamp abroad must apply through the SCI branch in their own country. In Britain, apply to **International Voluntary Service (IVS)**, Old Hall, East Bergholt, Colchester, Essex CO7 6TQ. *Registration fees (1992): £40 unwaged, £45 student, £55 waged (camps in Britain); £60 unwaged, £70 student, £75 waged (camps in western Europe and Northern Ireland); £70 unwaged, £75 student, £80 waged (camps in eastern Europe, Serbia, Slovenia and Turkey).*

The addresses of Service Civil International (SCI) branches in other countries are as follows:

Australia SCI, 121 Cascade Street, Katoomba 2780

Austria SCI, Schottengasse 3a 1/59, 1010 Vienna

Bangladesh SCI, GPO Box 3254, Dhaka 1000

Belgium SCI, rue Van Elewijk 35, 1050 Brussels

VIA, Draakstraat 37, 2018 Antwerp

Denmark SCI, Kyndbyvej 4, 3630 Jaegerspris

France SCI, 2 rue Eugène Fournière, 75018 Paris

Finland KVT, Rauhanasema, Veturitori, 00520 Helsinki

Germany SCI, Blücherstraße 14, W-5300 Bonn 1

Greece SCI, 43 Avlonos Street, 10443 Athens

Hungary SCI, Olasiget utca 28, 1103 Budapest

India SCI, K5 Green Park, New Delhi 110016

Ireland VSI, 37 North Great George's Street, Dublin 1

Italy SCI, via dei Laterani 28, 00184 Rome

Malaysia SCI, 4 Jalan Phillips, 11600 Pulau Pinang

Mauritius SVI, c/o Amicale, Arcade Rambour, Route Royale, Rose Hill

Nepal SCI, Jhochhen, DPO Box 4582, Kathmandu

Netherlands VIA, Pesthuislaan 25, 1054 RH Amsterdam

Northern Ireland IVS, 122 Great Victoria Street, Belfast BT2 7BG

Norway ID, Langesgate 6, 0165 Oslo

Slovenia MOST, Breg 12, PP 279, 61101 Ljubljana

Spain SCI-SCCT, Rambla Catalunya 5, pral 2, 08007 Barcelona

SCI-Madrid, Calle Colon 14, 1er Piso, 28020 Madrid

Sri Lanka SCI, 37 Mulgampola Road, Kandy

Sweden IAL, Barnängsgatan 23, 11641 Stockholm

Switzerland SCI, Postfach 228, 3000 Bern 9

United States SCI, Innisfree Village, Route 2, Box 506, Crozet, Virginia 22932

International Voluntary Service also cooperates with a number of workcamp organisers in other countries, who are not members of SCI. Further details are given below, and under the entries in the **Jobs Index**.

Christian Movement for Peace (CMP) is another international network of workcamp organisers. Those wishing to take part in a workcamp abroad must apply through the CMP/MCP branch in their own country. In Britain, CMP is based at Bethnal Green United Reformed Church, Pott Street, London E2 20F © 071-729 7985. *Registration fee: £30-£45.*

The addresses of CMP/MCP branches in other countries are given below. If there is no branch in your country, apply to the European headquarters: Mouvement Chrétien pour la Paix, Secrétariat Européen, 92 rue Stévin, 1040 Brussels, Belgium.

Belgium Carrefour Chantiers, 25 Boulevard de l'Empereur, 1000 Brussels

Canada Chantiers Jeunesse, 4545 avenue Pierre-de-Coubertin, Case Postale 1000, Succursale M, Montreal, Quebec H1V 3RZ

Chile CADESUR, c/o Calle Serrano nº 347, Casilla 109, Castro

Estonia CMP, c/o Tiit Pridel, Akademia Tee 22-31, 200 00 26 Tallin

France MCP, 38 rue du Faubourg St Denis, 75010 Paris

Germany CFD, Rendelerstraße 9-11, W-6000 Frankfurt-Bornheim 60

Hungary CMP, European House, Deszö utca 3, 1395 Budapest

Italy MCP, Via Marco Dino Rossi 12/C, 00173 Rome

Latvia CMP, c/o Latvijas Studentu Serviss, Jauniela 14, 226050 Riga

Malta CMP, John XXIII Peace Lab, Hal Far

Netherlands ICVD, Pesthuislaan 25, 1054 RF Amsterdam

Portugal MCP, rua António José Almeida nº 210, Sub-Cave Esq, 3000 Coimbra

Switzerland CFD, Falkenhöhleweg 8, 3001 Bern

The following British organisations recruit volunteers for workcamps in Britain and abroad, cooperating with a variety of different partners:

Concordia (Youth Service Volunteers) (CYSV) 8 Brunswick Place, Hove, Sussex BN3 1ET ✆ Brighton (0273) 772086. *Registration fee: £25-£70*

Quaker International Social Projects (QISP) Friends House, Euston Road, London NW1 2BJ ✆ 071-387 3601. Applicants for QISP workcamps abroad must be over 18 with previous experience of workcamps or voluntary service. *Registration fees (1992): £8 unwaged, £15 low waged, £25 waged (UK camps) or £15 unwaged, £20 student, £30 waged (overseas).*

United Nations Association (UNA) International Youth Service, Temple of Peace, Cathays Park, Cardiff CF1 3AP ✆ Cardiff (0222) 223088. *Registration fees: £45 (UK camps) or from £50 (overseas). Membership fees: £5 unwaged/student, £10 waged.*

The main workcamp organisers worldwide outside the SCI/CMP networks, together with their recruiting/partner organisations (CYSV, IVS, QISP or UNA) are given below:

Algeria ACAAEJ, Centre Culturel, Nacira 35250, W-Boumerdes **QISP UNA**

Austria Österreichischer Bauorden, PO Box 186, Hornesgasse 3, 1031 Vienna

Bangladesh BWCA, 289/2 Work Camps Road, North Shahjahanpur, Dhaka 17

Belgium Compagnons Bâtisseurs, 63 rue Notre Dame des Graces, 5400 March-en-Famenne **QISP UNA**

Bouworde VZW, Tiensesteenweg 145, 3010 Kessel-Lo

Bolivia VEA, PO Box 3556, La Paz

Bulgaria Argo-M, Boulevard Stamboliski 2A, Sofia 1000 **QISP**

Cameroon UCJG, BP 89, Foyer de Jeunesse Protestant, Douala **UNA**

Canada CBIE, 85 Albert Street, 14th Floor, Ottawa, Ontario K1P 6A4 **UNA**

Côte d'Ivoire AICV, 04 BP 714, Abidjan **UNA**

Czechoslovakia INEX, Gorkeho nam. 24, 116 47 Prague 1 **IVS QISP UNA**

KMC, Malostranske nabrezi 1, 118 00 Prague 1 **CYSV IVS QISP UNA**

Denmark MS, Borgergade 10-14, 1300 Copenhagen K **QISP UNA**

France Concordia, 38 rue du Faubourg St Denis, 75010 Paris **QISP UNA**

Jeunesse et Reconstruction, 10 rue de Trévise, 75009 Paris **CYSV**

UNAREC, 33 rue Campagne Première, 75014 Paris **QISP UNA**

Germany IBG, Schlosserstraße 28, W-7000 Stuttgart 1, Germany **QISP UNA**

IBO, Liebigstraße 23, PO Box 1438, W-6520 Worms-Horchheim

IJGD, Kaiserstraße 43, W-5300 Bonn 1 **CYSV QISP UNA**

NDF, Auf der Körnerwiese 5, W-6000 Frankfurt-am-Main 1 **UNA**

NIG, Universitätsplatz 1, O-2500 Rostock
QISP UNA

Pro International, zur Kalkkaute 21, W-3550
Marburg/Lahn CYSV

VJF, Unter den Linden 36-38, O-1086 Berlin
IVS QISP UNA

Ghana VOLU, PO Box 1540, Accra UNA

Greece ECVG, 15 Omirou Street, 14562
Kifissia UNA

Hungary UNIO, Kun B. pkp 37-38, 1138
Budapest QISP UNA

India JAC, H-65, South Extension 1, New
Delhi 11049

Italy AISC/IBO, via Cesare Battisti 3, 20071
Casalpusterlengo, Milano

Japan NICE, 501 Viewcity, 2-2-1 Shinjuku,
Shinjuku-ku, Tokyo 160 UNA

Kenya KVDA, PO Box 48902, Nairobi UNA

Lesotho LWA, PO Box 6, Maseru 100 UNA

Latvia IEC, 2 Republic Square, 226168 Riga
CYSV

Lithuania CSA, K Donelaicio 73-113, Kaunas,
LT-3006 UNA

Mexico AMISTOUR, Versalles 35-502, Mexico
DF 06-600 UNA

VIMEX, Alfredo Elizando #69, CP 15450,
Mexico DF UNA

Morocco ACIM, PO Box 8, Meknes

CJM, CCP Rabat No 1234, PO Box 566, Rabat
Chellah QISP UNA

CSM, BP 456, Rabat RP QISP

Pensée et Chantiers, 26 rue de Pakistan, BP
1423, Rabat RP

Netherlands SIW, Willemstraat 7, 3511 RJ
Utrecht IVS QISP UNA

Nigeria VWAN, PO Box 2189, Lagos UNA

Poland FIYE, ul Grzybowska 79, 00-844
Warsaw IVS QISP UNA

Portugal ATEJ, PO Box 4586, 4009 Porto Codex

Instituto da Juventude, Avenida da Liberdade
194, 1200 Lisbon CYSV IVS QISP UNA

Russia Cooperation Project, PO Box 52, Bratsk
- 18, Irkutsk Region 665718 QISP UNA

YVS, 7/8 Bol. Komsomolski per., Moscow
103982 UNA

Sierra Leone VWASL, PO Box 1205, Freetown
UNA

Spain Instituto de la Juventud, José Ortega y
Gasset 71, 28006 Madrid QISP UNA

Swaziland SWA, PO Box A, 129 Swazi Plaza,
Mbabane UNA

Togo ASTOVOCT, BP 97, Kpalime UNA

Tunisia ATAV, Maison du RCD, boulevard du
9 avril, La Kasbah, 1002 Tunis CYSV UNA

Turkey Gençtur, Yerebatan Caddesi 15/3,
Sultanahmet, 34410 Istanbul CYSV IVS QISP
UNA

GSM, Yüksel Caddesi 44/6, 06420 Kizilay,
Ankara UNA

Ukraine Students Forum/UFIYC Lviv
Polytechnic Institute, Mira St 12, 290646 Lviv
QISP UNA

United States CIEE, 205 East 42nd Street, New
York, NY 10017 UNA

VFP, 43 Tiffany Road, Belmont, Vermont 05730
IVS UNA

✐ In addition to **WORKING HOLIDAYS**, the Central Bureau for Educational Visits & Exchanges publishes a range of information guides covering the opportunities available for educational contacts and travel worldwide. Full details are given in *Information in Print*, produced annually and available by sending a stamped self-addressed envelope or two International Reply Coupons to the Print & Marketing Unit, Central Bureau for Educational Visits & Exchanges, Seymour Mews, London W1H 9PE. The main titles include:

VOLUNTEER WORK A period of voluntary work can be enriching and rewarding, involving you in improving the quality of community life and environment. A wide range of opportunities exist in developed and developing countries for a positive contribution to be made by recent graduates, skilled professionals, those unemployed or taking early retirement, and others with relevant qualifications or experience. Valuable information and guidance is given in **VOLUNTEER WORK**, £7.99, with comprehensive details on over 100 organisations recruiting volunteers for medium and long-term projects in Britain and 150 countries worldwide. The guide also provides a personal checklist to evaluate potential and Details practical information on preparation and training, medical requirements, insurance, social security, travel, advisory bodies and help for returning volunteers.

A YEAR BETWEEN is a complete guide for those taking a year out between school and higher education or work, or higher education and a career. A year out is a rare chance to stand back, assess where life has brought you so far, and seize the freedom offered to learn new skills and develop existing ones. **A YEAR BETWEEN**, £7.99, provides full details on over 100 organisations offering placements in industry, research, business, teaching, community/social service and youth work in Britain and overseas as well as opportunities for discovery, leadership, conservation projects and further study. Authoritative advice and information is included together with practical hints, discussions of the pros and cons, and details on planning and preparation. In fact, all you need to make the most of a year out.

STUDY HOLIDAYS If you need to brush up language skills in preparation for exams, want to learn another language for enjoyment or to further knowledge of the country and culture, then **STUDY HOLIDAYS**, £7.95, has details of a European language course that can provide just what you are looking for. Actually being in another country, learning formally and informally, is an ideal way to become confident and fluent in a second language. **STUDY HOLIDAYS** has just about all the information you need on holiday courses in twenty six European languages where you can receive expert tuition and stay in an area where you can put your language skills into practice. There is also practical information on accommodation, travel, sources for bursaries, grants and scholarships and language teaching resources.

HOME FROM HOME is an authoritative guide to over 120 bona fide organisations arranging homestays, exchanges, home exchanges, farm stays and term stays in more than 50 countries. Have you ever wished there was a way of really finding out what makes another country tick? Do you want to improve your language skills, make lasting friendships? Then **HOME FROM HOME**, £6.99, has all the right answers. At a time when travellers are turning away from the alienation of mass tourism **HOME FROM HOME** offers a wide selection of responsible alternatives in over 50 countries, from staying with a French family in the heart of Paris, discovering Ashanti traditions in Ghana to teaching English to a family in Japan.

All titles are available direct from the Print & Marketing Unit at the Central Bureau London, see above, by mail order (please add £1 per title for postage within the UK, £2.50 to mainland Europe and £5 worldwide) or from good bookshops.

An information pack containing twenty leaflets outlining opportunities for broadening educational horizons through voluntary service, seasonal work, exchanges, homestays, work placements, teaching, language learning and overseas study is available by sending two first-class stamps or three International Reply Coupons, to the Print & Marketing Unit, Central Bureau London, see above.

JOBS INDEX

INFORMATION

Algerian Embassy
54 Holland Park, London W11 3RS
☏ 071-221 7800

Kenya High Commission
45 Portland Place, London W1N 4AS
☏ 071-636 2371/5

Lesotho High Commission
10 Collingham Road, London SW5 0NR
☏ 071-373 8581/2

Nigeria High Commission
Nigeria House, 9 Northumberland Avenue,
London WC2N 5BX ☏ 071-839 1244

Sierra Leone High Commission
33 Portland Place, London W1N 3AG
☏ 071-636 6483

South African Embassy
South Africa House, Trafalgar Square, WC2N
5DP ☏ 071-930 4488

Tanzania High Commission
43 Hertford Street, London W1Y 8DB
☏ 071-499 8951

Tunisian Embassy
29 Prince's Gate, London SW7 1QG
☏ 071-584 8117

Zaïre Embassy
26 Chesham Place, London SW1X 8HH
☏ 071-235 6137

Zimbabwe High Commission
Zimbabwe House, 429 Strand, London WC2R
0SA ☏ 071-836 7755

Entry regulations Details of work permits and
entry requirements can be obtained in Britain
from the embassies/high commissions above.

Travel Campus Travel, 52 Grosvenor Gardens,
London SW1W 0AG ☏ 071-730 8111 (offices
throughout the UK) offers low-cost student/
youth airfares to destinations throughout
Africa.

North-South Travel, Moulsham Mill, Parkway, Chelmsford CM2 7PX ✆ Chelmsford (0245) 492882 arranges competitively priced, reliably planned flights to all parts of Africa. Profits are paid into a trust fund for the assignment of aid to projects in the poorest areas of the South.

STA Travel, 74 Old Brompton Road, London SW7 3LQ/117 Euston Road, London NW1 2SX ✆ 071-937 9962 (offices also in Birmingham, Bristol, Cambridge, Leeds, Manchester and Oxford) operates flexible, low-cost flights with open jaw facility - enter one country, leave by another - to destinations throughout Africa. Internal flights, accommodation and tours also available, plus advice from STA Travel's Africa Desk ✆ 071-465 0486.

Publications Lonely Planet's travel guides offer practical, down-to-earth information for those wanting to explore beyond the usual tourist routes. Titles include *Africa on a Shoestring* £14.95, for the low-budget independent traveller in Africa, and *Travel Survival Kits* to *Egypt & the Sudan* £8.95, *Kenya* £8.95, *Morocco, Algeria & Tunisia* £10.95, *South Africa, Lesotho & Swaziland* £10.95, *Zimbabwe, Botswana & Namibia* £10.95, *Central Africa* £6.95, *East Africa* £9.95 and *West Africa* £7.95.
Rough Guides provide comprehensive background information on cities and countries worldwide, plus details on getting there, getting around, places to explore and cheap places to stay. Titles include *Egypt* £9.99, *Kenya* £7.99, *West Africa* £10.99 and *Zimbabwe & Botswana* £8.99.
All the above are available from good bookshops and larger travel agents.

CONSERVATION

EARTHWATCH EUROPE Belsyre Court, 57 Woodstock Road, Oxford OX2 6HU ✆ **Oxford (0865) 311600**
Aims to support field research in a wide range of disciplines including archaeology, ornithology, animal behaviour and nature conservation. Support is given to researchers as a grant and in the form of volunteer assistance. Recent projects have included pinpointing groundwater sites in Nigeria's drought-plagued Sahel region; studying the problem of

a drop in the water level of Lake Navaisha, one of Kenya's largest freshwater lakes; studying the behaviour of small mammals in one of Zimbabwe's crowded wildlife parks; and assisting at an archaeological excavation investigating traces left by early man in Zaïre.

Ages 16-80. No special skills are required although each expedition may, because of its nature, demand some talent or quality of fitness. Volunteers should be generally fit, able to cope with new situations and work with people of different ages and backgrounds, and a sense of humour will help. 2-3 weeks, all year. Members share the costs of the expedition, from £500-£1200, which includes meals, transport and all necessary field equipment, but not travel to the staging area, although assistance may be given with travel arrangements. Membership fee £22 entitles members to join an expedition and receive magazines and newsletters providing all the information necessary to choose a project. **B D PH W** depending on project.

FARMWORK

GORMORGOR AGRICULTURAL DEVELOPMENT ORGANISATION ℅ Njala University College, Private Mail Bag, Freetown, Sierra Leone
Volunteers are needed throughout the year to help upgrade subsistence farming on cash-crop enterprises in Kenema-Vaogboi and surrounding villages, Dasse Chiefdom Moyamba district, Sierra Leone. Volunteers help with, and supervise, projects such as the production of rice, maize, bananas, pineapples and a variety of vegetables.

Ages 15+. Experience usually necessary. Volunteers should have commonsense, be independent, willing to live in an isolated village, physically and mentally fit and socially and culturally adaptable. They should also be flexible and prepared to participate in other activities such as town planning, accounting, report writing, health education courses, handicrafts, primary and adult education, and cultural activities on days when there are no supervisory duties. The working week will vary according to the season and the projects in operation. Half board accommodation in village staff house provided, and native entertainments arranged on some evenings. Volunteers arrange and pay their own travel and insurance, and contribute towards food. Orientation course arranged upon arrival. English-speaking volunteers preferred. Applications should be typed and include a *cv*, passport photo and 50p postal order.

LEADERS & GUIDES

EXODUS EXPEDITIONS 9 Weir Road, London SW12 0LT ✆ 081-675 7996
Operates a large range of expeditions including those by truck to Africa plus foot treks and shorter adventure holidays to Kenya, Morocco and Tanzania. Expedition leaders are needed to lead and drive expeditions; each expedition lasts 4-6 months, but leaders can expect to be out of the country for up to 12 months at a time. The work involves driving, servicing and when necessary repairing the vehicle; controlling and accounting for expedition expenditure; dealing with border formalities and other official procedures; helping clients with any problems that may arise and informing them on points of interest in the countries visited.

Ages 25-30. Applicants must be single and unattached, and able to commit themselves for at least 2 years. For this reason, and because of the amount of travelling and flexibility involved, applicants should have no personal or financial commitments. Driving experience of large vehicles plus HGV/PSV licence and a good basic knowledge of mechanics preferred. Applicants must be resourceful, adaptable and have leadership qualities and a good sense of humour. Previous travel experience and a knowledge of foreign languages an advantage. Basic training given to suitable candidates; trainees spend 2 months in the company's Wiltshire workshop, then go on an expedition with an experienced leader before leading on their own. Salary £50 per week with food and accommodation provided on site when training and £20 salary and £28 expenses per week plus food and accommodation on first expedition. Salary £80-£115 per week for a full expedition leader plus food and accommodation.

WORKCAMPS

AFRICA VOLUNTARY SERVICE OF SIERRA LEONE Private Mail Bag 717, Freetown, Sierra Leone
Aims to take part in development projects and to enhance international peace, understanding and cooperation. Volunteers are needed for agricultural, medical or renovation work in rural areas. Previous experience not always necessary.

Ages 15+. Good spoken English essential. 35 hour week, end July-end August. Food and accommodation provided; some excursions and discussions organised. Volunteers pay own insurance and travel. Placement fee US$300. Medium and long-term placements (4-12 months) also available for those with qualifications and/or experience.

ASSOCIATION CULTURELLE DES ACTIVITÉS D'AMITIÉ ET D'ÉCHANGES ENTRE JEUNES (ACAAEJ) Centre Culturel, Naciria 35250, W-Boumerdes, Algeria
A national association grouping five regional organisations in Algeria with the aim of promoting volunteering and development, improving international cooperation and understanding, protecting the environment, combatting illiteracy and encouraging humanitarian action. Volunteers are invited to take part in international workcamps. Recent projects have included construction work at an international peace centre in Kabylie; environmental work in the forest of Bainem near Algiers; and creating a play area for children at a crèche in Boumerdes.
Ages 18-30. Conversational level French or Arabic essential. 2-3 weeks, July-September. Food, accommodation and insurance during workcamp provided; volunteers pay their own travel costs.

Apply through partner organisation in country of residence. In the UK: Quaker International Social Projects, Friends House, Euston Road, London NW1 2BJ (experienced volunteers only) or United Nations Association, International Youth Service, Temple of Peace, Cathays Park, Cardiff CF1 3AP ✆ Cardiff (0222) 223088.

Outside the UK: please see information on page 30.

ASSOCIATION TUNISIENNE D'ACTION VOLONTAIRE (ATAV) Maison du RCD, Boulevard 9 Avril 1938, La Kasbah, 1002 Tunis, Tunisia

Volunteers are invited to take part in international workcamps, carrying out community development work. Recent projects have included restoring historic monuments, creating parks and children's playgrounds, and helping to construct or renovate youth centres and schools in various towns throughout Tunisia. Study themes include youth participation in national development, peace and solidarity. Sports, cultural activities and excursions arranged. Ages 18-35. Applicants must be in good health, with a good knowledge of French/Arabic and a background knowledge of Africa. Previous workcamp experience essential. 30 hour, 6 day week. Hours of work usually 06.00/07.00-12.00. 2/3 weeks, June-September. Food, accommodation with basic facilities and insurance provided, but volunteers pay own travel costs.

Apply through partner organisation in country of residence. In the UK: Concordia (Youth Service Volunteers) Ltd, Recruitment Secretary, 8 Brunswick Place, Hove, Sussex BN3 1ET © Brighton (0273) 772086 or United Nations Association, International Youth Service, Temple Of Peace, Cathays Park, Cardiff CF1 3AP © Cardiff (0222) 223088

Outside the UK: please see information on page 30.

CHRISTIAN STUDENTS' COUNCIL OF KENYA Ufungamano House, State House, Mamlaka Road, PO Box 54579, Nairobi, Kenya

Promotes cooperation and Christian unity, and organises workcamps, exchanges, afforestation, refugee awareness and women's programmes. Organises rural and urban projects providing an opportunity to participate directly in the work of churches and social welfare agencies in an attempt to meet the needs and relieve the suffering of local people. Architects, agriculturists, poultry farmers, carpenters and those with experience in building are especially needed. Knowledge of English necessary. April, August and December. 8 hour day. Visits arranged to self-sufficiency farms and tree nursery. Accommodation provided, but volunteers pay for travel and insurance.

HELP (SCOTLAND) 60 The Pleasance, Edinburgh EH8 9JT © 031-556 9497

HELP (Humanitarian Education & Long-term Projects) is a charity run by students from Edinburgh University, sending volunteers to communities in need around the world. Workcamps are intended to assist in the relief of poverty as well as to provide an educational experience. Projects have been set up in South African townships, including one based around the site of Mahatma Gandhi's first ashram in Bambayi, near Durban.

Work is varied and may include helping with adult education programmes, supporting a crèche, making toys, restoring buildings, gardening and playing with children. No experience or qualifications required; most applicants are students but there is no upper age limit. 40 hour, 5-6 day week for 4-6 weeks during the summer. Basic dormitory accommodation with simple food provided. Participants contribute £100 towards the project to cover board, lodging and equipment, and pay their own travel and insurance. **B D PH W** *Write for application form; apply by end February.*

KENYA VOLUNTARY DEVELOPMENT ASSOCIATION The Director, PO Box 48902, Nairobi, Kenya

Offers young people from Africa and overseas the opportunity to serve the country's rural or needy areas during their free time or holidays. Volunteers work alongside members of the local community helping with rural development projects such as irrigation schemes, tree planting, food growing, tilling, goat and hen rearing; and the construction of schools and clinics, helping with roofing and foundation digging. Discussions, games and other entertainments arranged, often involving the community. Working languages are English and Swahili. Emergency projects are also organised in times of catastrophe or disaster.

Ages 18+. Volunteers are expected to participate in all activities and to adapt fully to the local way of life. 6 hour day, 6 day week. Each workcamp lasts 2-3 weeks, April, July, August and December. Food and accommodation in local schools provided. Volunteers arrange and pay their own travel. Registration fee $160 for 1 camp or $210 for 2 camps; $2 postage costs.

Apply through partner organisation in country of residence. In the UK: United Nations Association, International Youth Service, Temple of Peace, Cathays Park, Cardiff CF1 3AP ℂ Cardiff (0222) 223088.

Outside the UK: please see information on page 30.

LESOTHO WORKCAMPS ASSOCIATION
PO Box MS6, Maseru 100, Lesotho
International workcamps are organised in rural areas throughout Lesotho, for which a small number of overseas volunteers are recruited to work alongside local people. Projects are in the field of rural development and involve manual work such as building roads, schools and clinics, tree-planting, and laying water supplies. 40+ hours per week for 2-3 weeks, June-July (winter season) and December-January (summer season). Ages 18+. Applicants must be physically fit; previous relevant experience preferred. Board and lodging provided, but conditions can be quite primitive. Excursions and entertainments organised. Registration fee payable.

Apply through partner organisation in country of residence. In the UK: United Nations Association, International Youth Service, Temple of Peace, Cathays Park, Cardiff CF1 3AP ℂ Cardiff (0222) 223088

Outside the UK: please see information on page 30.

NIGERIA VOLUNTARY SERVICE ASSOCIATION (NIVOSA) General
Secretary, GPO Box 11837, Ibadan, Nigeria
Brings together Nigerian and other nationals interested in promoting voluntary service. Organises international workcamps and promotes understanding and cooperation among communities. Projects include workcamps in the states of the Federation (Lagos, Oyo, Ogun and Ondo) involving the construction of hospitals, post offices, markets and schools. Tasks include site clearance, making and laying blocks, plastering, carpentry and digging, all with the help of community artisans. Volunteers live and work in villages, cooking in groups. Ages 18+. 6 hour day, 2 weeks, July-September. Volunteers pay own insurance and travel. Excursions, lectures and debates. Workcamps are usually preceded by

2/3 day leadership courses which include an orientation programme for new volunteers. Participation fee $5.

GENERAL

THE AFRICAN-AMERICAN INSTITUTE 833 United Nations Plaza, New York, NY 10017, United States
Can provide information on opportunities in Africa for employment in technical assistance positions, teaching posts and volunteer work experience.

See also opportunities under **Morocco** and **Worldwide**

When writing to any organisation it is essential to mention Working Holidays 1993 and enclose a large stamped, self-addressed envelope, or if overseas, a large addressed envelope and at least two International Reply Coupons.

ASIA

INFORMATION

Bangladesh High Commission
28 Queen's Gate, London SW7 5JA
℗ 071-584 0081

Embassy of the People's Republic of China
49-51 Portland Place, London W1N 3AH
℗ 071-636 9375/5726

India High Commission
India House, Aldwych, London WC2B 4NA
℗ 071-836 8484

Indonesian Embassy
38 Grosvenor Square, London W1X 9AD
℗ 071-499 7661

Korean Embassy
4 Palace Gate, London W8 5NF
℗ 071-581 0247

Royal Nepalese Embassy
12a Kensington Palace Gardens, London W8
4QU ℗ 071-229 1594/6231

Pakistan High Commission
35 Lowndes Square, London SW1X 9JN
℗ 071-235 2044

Vietnamese Embassy
12-14 Victoria Road, London W8
℗ 071-937 1912/8564

Entry regulations Details of work permits and
entry requirements can be obtained in Great
Britain from the embassies/high commissions
above.

Travel SD Enterprises Ltd, 103 Wembley Park
Drive, Wembley, Middlesex HA9 8HG ℗ 081-
903 3411 issues the Indrail Pass which allows
unlimited travel on all trains throughout India,
with no charge for night sleepers or
reservations. Available for periods of 1, 7, 15,
21, 30, 60 or 90 days. Cost from $15.

Indian Airlines operate a youth fare scheme
entitling those aged 12-30 to a discount of 25%
off the normal fare, all year. Also Discover
India scheme entitling the holder to unlimited

air travel within India. 21 days, all year. Cost $400. Further information from the Government of India Tourist Office, 7 Cork Street, London W1X 1PB ℭ 071-437 3677.

Campus Travel, 52 Grosvenor Gardens, London SW1W 0AG ℭ 071-730 8111 (offices throughout the UK) offers low-cost student/youth airfares to destinations throughout Asia.

North-South Travel, Moulsham Mill, Parkway, Chelmsford CM2 7PX ℭ Chelmsford (0245) 492882 arranges competitively priced, reliably planned flights to all parts of Asia. Profits are paid into a trust fund for the assignment of aid to projects in the poorest areas of the South.

STA Travel, 74 Old Brompton Road, London SW7 3LQ/117 Euston Road, London NW1 2SX ℭ 071-937 9962 (offices also in Birmingham, Bristol, Cambridge, Leeds, Manchester and Oxford) operates flexible, low-cost flights with open jaw facility - enter one country, leave by another - to destinations throughout Asia. Internal flights, accommodation and tours also available.

Trailfinders Travel Centre, 42-50 Earls Court Road, London W8 6EJ ℭ 071-938 3366 and Trailfinders, 194 Kensington High Street, London W8 7RG ℭ 071-938 3939 operate low-cost flights between London and destinations throughout Asia. Also arrange a Bangkok-Bali Rover, which provides the opportunity to travel east via Thailand, Malaysia, Singapore and Indonesia by road, rail and air. 20 days, departures all year. Cost £599, flight extra. Also have a travellers' library and information centre, an immunisation centre for overseas travel vaccinations, a travel goods shop and map/bookshop.

Publications Lonely Planet's travel guides offer practical, down-to-earth information for those wanting to explore beyond the usual tourist routes. Titles include *North East Asia on a Shoestring* £9.95, *South East Asia on a Shoestring* £12.95 and *West Asia on a Shoestring* £8.95 for the low-budget independent traveller in Asia. Also *Travel Survival Kits* to *Bangladesh* £5.95, *Burma* £5.95, *China* £12.95, *Hong Kong, Macau & Canton* £8.95, *India* £13.95, *Indonesia* £12.95, *Korea* £6.95, *Malaysia, Singapore & Brunei* £8.95,

Nepal £7.95, *Pakistan* £5.95, *Philippines* £8.95, *Sri Lanka* £5.95, *Taiwan* £6.95, *Thailand* £8.95, *Tibet* £7.95 and *Vietnam, Laos & Cambodia* £9.95.
Rough Guides provide comprehensive background information on cities and countries worldwide, plus details on getting there, getting around, places to explore and cheap places to stay. Titles include *Thailand* £8.99, *Nepal* £6.95 and *Hong Kong* £6.99.
Culture Shock! is a series of cultural guides written for international travellers of any background. The reader is introduced to the people, customs, ceremonies, food and culture of a country, with checklists of dos and don'ts. All guides cost £6.95 and countries in the series include China, India, Indonesia, Korea, Malaysia, Nepal, Pakistan, the Philippines, Singapore, Sri Lanka and Thailand.
Travellers Survival Kit to the East £6.95, is a practical guide to travelling between Turkey and Indonesia, following the overland route from Europe that remains accessible. Advice on preparations, transport and route planning, hitch hiking, frontier regulations, medical facilities, plus useful addresses. Published by Vacation Work, 9 Park End Street, Oxford OX1 1HJ ℭ Oxford (0865) 241978.
All the above are available from good bookshops and larger travel agents.

Bangladesh Today - A Profile contains essential information on the geography, climate, culture and wildlife of Bangladesh plus details of entry and exit regulations, currency, events, festivals, places to visit, accommodation, transport and other facilities. Available from the Bangladesh High Commission, Press Division, 28 Queen's Gate, London SW7 5JA ℭ 071-584 0081.

Travel Information provides information on accommodation, currency, climate, customs, health/entry regulations, inland travel and languages in India. Available from the Government of India Tourist Office, see above.

Pakistan Tourist Guide is a small booklet containing details of the history, people and language, plus information on travel, where to stay, sport and recreation, visa/health regulations and places of interest. Available from the Pakistan Development Corporation, 52-54 High Holborn, London WC1V 6RB ℭ 071-242 3131.

Accommodation The Government of India Tourist Office, see above, issues a booklet *Accommodation* containing information on hostels set up and run by the Department of Tourism in 25 states/Union territories.

COMMUNITY WORK

INDIAN VOLUNTEERS FOR COMMUNITY SERVICE 12 Eastleigh Avenue, Harrow, Middlesex HA2 OUF ✆ 081-864 4740
Aims to educate the public in the UK about rural culture and voluntary rural development in India. Operates a Project Visitors' scheme open to anyone who would like to visit a rural development project. Up to 2 weeks' orientation available in any project. Longer visits, with the possibility of voluntary work often available in many parts of India. Ages 18+. No special qualifications necessary. Basic board and vegetarian food provided for £2 per day. Visitors pay their own travel expenses and insurance.

CONSERVATION

EARTHWATCH EUROPE Belsyre Court, 57 Woodstock Road, Oxford OX2 6HU ✆ Oxford (0865) 311600
Aims to support field research in a wide range of disciplines including archaeology, ornithology, animal behaviour, nature conservation and ecology. Support is given to researchers as a grant and in the form of volunteer assistance. Recent projects have included caring for baby orang-utans and tracking wild adults in the rainforest of Borneo; assessing the habitat needs of the endangered sloth bear in the lowlands of Nepal; saving a rare species of crane in Vietnam; and documenting the behaviour of macaque monkeys in Bali. Ages 16-80. No special skills required although each expedition may, because of its nature, demand some talent or quality of fitness. Volunteers should be generally fit, able to cope with new situations and work with people of different ages and backgrounds, and a sense of humour will help. 2-3 weeks, all year. Members share the costs of the expedition, from £500-£1200, which includes meals, transport and all necessary field

equipment, but not travel to the staging area, although assistance may be given with arrangements. Membership fee £22 entitles members to join expeditions and receive magazines and newsletters providing all the information necessary to choose a project. **B D PH W** depending on project.

FARMWORK

INTERNATIONAL FARM EXPERIENCE PROGRAMME YFC Centre, National Agricultural Centre, Stoneleigh Park, Kenilworth CV8 2LG ✆ Coventry (0203) 696584
Provides assistance to young farmers and nurserymen by finding places in farms/nurseries abroad enabling them to broaden their knowledge of agricultural methods. Opportunities available on farms on the outskirts of Beijing, People's Republic of China. 1-3 months, beginning May or September. Board and lodging provided, plus 100 RMB pocket money per month. Optional 4-week course in Mandarin. Participants pay own fares and insurance; help given in obtaining visa. Ages 18-26. Applicants must have at least 2 years' practical experience, 1 year of which may be at agricultural college, and intend to make a career in agriculture. Registration fee £70. *Apply at least 3 months in advance; UK nationals only.*

LEADERS & GUIDES

EXODUS EXPEDITIONS 9 Weir Road, London SW12 0LT ✆ 081-675 7996
Operates a large range of expeditions including those by truck to Asia plus foot treks and shorter adventure holidays to Nepal, Pakistan, India, Indonesia and China. Expedition leaders are needed to lead and drive expeditions; each expedition lasts 4-6 months, but leaders can expect to be out of the country for up to 12 months at a time. The work involves driving, servicing and when necessary repairing the vehicle; controlling and accounting for expedition expenditure; dealing with border formalities and other official procedures; helping clients with any problems that may arise and informing them on points of interest

in the countries visited. Ages 25-30. Applicants must be single and unattached, and able to commit themselves for at least 2 years. For this reason, and because of the amount of travelling and flexibility involved, applicants should have no personal or financial commitments. Driving experience of large vehicles plus HGV/PSV licence and a good basic knowledge of mechanics preferred. Applicants must be resourceful, adaptable and have leadership qualities and a good sense of humour. Previous travel experience and a knowledge of foreign languages an advantage. Basic training will be given to suitable candidates; trainees spend 2 months in the company's Wiltshire workshop and then go on an expedition with an experienced leader before leading on their own. Salary £50 per week with food and accommodation provided on site when training and £20 salary and £28 expenses per week plus food and accommodation on the first expedition. Salary £80-£115 per week for a full expedition leader plus food and accommodation.

TEACHERS

English in Asia US$9.95 + $3 airmail is a useful guide for anyone interested in teaching English as a foreign language in Asia. Includes sections on teaching methods, common student errors, ideas for games and classroom activities, together with the addresses of private English language schools in Japan, Korea and Taiwan, and tips on visas and living in these countries. Published by Global Press, 697 College Parkway, Rockville, MD 20850, United States and available in the UK from Vacation Work, 9 Park End Street, Oxford OX1 1HJ ☎ Oxford (0865) 241978.

WORKCAMPS

BANGLADESH WORK CAMPS ASSOCIATION (BWCA) 289/2 Work Camps Road, North Shahjahanpur, Dhaka 17, Bangladesh
Promotes international development and peace through voluntary activities, and organises workcamps in urban and rural areas of Bangladesh. Projects include afforestation,

construction work, digging water tanks, health education and community work. Working language is English. Ages 16-45. 30 hour week, 1-6 weeks, October-April. Volunteers pay own insurance and travel. Participation fee US$30 per day. *Apply at least 3 months in advance enclosing US$25 application fee.*

HELP (SCOTLAND) 60 The Pleasance, Edinburgh EH8 9JT ☎ 031-556 9497
HELP (Humanitarian Education & Long-term Projects) is a charity run by students from Edinburgh University, sending volunteers to communities in need around the world. Workcamps are intended to assist in the relief of poverty as well as to provide an educational experience. Recent projects have included teaching English at a leprosy clinic in Pakistan and helping to construct a rural education centre in India. No experience or qualifications required; most applicants are students but there is no upper age limit. 40 hour, 5-6 day week for 4-6 weeks during the summer. Basic dormitory accommodation with simple food provided. Participants contribute £100 towards the project to cover board, lodging and equipment, and pay their own travel and insurance. **B D PH W** *Write for application form; apply by end February.*

JOINT ASSISTANCE CENTRE H-65, South Extension 1, New Delhi 110049, India
A voluntary action group for disaster assistance invites volunteers to help on workcamps throughout India. Projects include construction, environmental work, land reclamation, health and sanitation work, fundraising, teaching first aid, preparedness training for disasters and educational resource management. 2-3 weeks, all year. Also opportunities to help in the office, editing the journal and working in the library. Volunteers with at least 3 month commitment required to teach English, organise exhibitions and campaigns, help with administration and work on a community development project on the outskirts of Delhi. Also organises short visits/ stays on projects all over India, with opportunities to meet and work with local people, and to learn yoga, nature cures and Hindi. Ages 18+. All nationalities welcome, no experience necessary. Cost £60 per month covers shared camping accommodation with

self-catering facilities. Conditions are primitive and the summer is very hot. No travel, insurance or pocket money provided. *Enclose 3 IRCs if applying direct. Registration fee £10 to be sent by cheque or international money order.*

UK application forms from Friends of JAC, c/o 15 Burkes Road, Beaconsfield, Buckinghamshire HP9 1PB. Registration fee £10.

US & Canada application forms from Friends of JAC, c/o K Gopalan, Post Box 14481, Santa Rosa, CA 95402, United States. Registration fee US$20.

France application forms from Nathalie Marnier, 36 Bis, rue Henri Barbusse, 92110 Clichy, France. Registration fee FF100.

UNESCO YOUTH CENTRE Korean National Commission for UNESCO, PO Box Central 64, Seoul, Korea 100

Organises an international youth camp with a work project prepared by the Work Committee during the camp period. Discussions, lectures and workshops are held on international problems such as development and cultural identity. Recreational activities, including involvement with local villagers, are organised. Volunteers learn about the history and culture of Korea through a 3 day study tour. Official languages English and Korean. Volunteers live in 5 camps of various nationalities. 10 days, July. Accommodation, food, transport within Korea and medical expenses provided. Participation fee US$90. *Apply by 20 June.*

GENERAL

INVOLVEMENT VOLUNTEERS ASSOCIATION INC PO Box 218, Port Melbourne, Victoria 3207, Australia ℂ/Fax Melbourne (3) 646 5504

A non-profitmaking organisation set up to find volunteer placements in Australia and a number of countries en route, including Fiji, India and Thailand. Volunteers of all ages can take part in individual placements or team tasks. Placements are in community-based organisations involved in conservation, research, restoration or social welfare programmes. Recent projects have included planting fruit trees at an ecologically sustainable development programme in Fiji; assisting village people in northern Thailand to restore their hillsides after environmentally harmful forest practices; and providing administrative and caring assistance at a pavement clinic in Calcutta.

Volunteers must be able to speak English, arrange their own visitor visas, and organise their own international travel and insurance. Some paid work placements can be found in Australia for volunteers with suitable visas. Involvement Volunteers provides advice, placements, itinerary planning, meeting on arrival, initial accommodation, introductions to banking, taxation and a communications base in Australia. Cost AU$300 (approx £125/$225/DM400). B D

In Europe, apply to Involvement Volunteers-Deutschland, Postfach 110224, W-3400 Göttingen, Germany ℂ/Fax (551) 33 765.

In North America, apply to Involvement Corps Inc, 15515 Sunset Boulevard Suite 108, Pacific Palisades, California 90272, United States ℂ/Fax (310) 459 1022.

See also opportunities under **Japan** and **Worldwide**

When writing to any organisation it is essential to mention Working Holidays 1993 and enclose a large stamped, self-addressed envelope, or if overseas, a large addressed envelope and at least two International Reply Coupons.

INFORMATION

Australian High Commission
Australia House, Strand, London WC2B 4LA
© 071-379 4334

British High Commission
Commonwealth Avenue, Yarralumla, Canberra,
ACT 2600

Tourist office
Australian Tourist Commission, Gemini House,
10-18 Putney Hill, Putney, London SW15 6AA
© 081-780 1424

Youth hostels
Australian YHA, Level 3, 10 Mallett Street,
Camperdown, NSW 2050

Youth & student information
Australian Union of Students, 97 Drummond
Street, Carlton, Victoria 3053

Entry regulations A visa is required for a
working holiday, and will be granted subject to
certain conditions. The prime purpose of the
visit must be a temporary stay for a holiday of
specific duration and the applicant must have a
return ticket, or sufficient funds to pay for this,
plus sufficient funds to cover maintenance for a
substantial part of the holiday period;
employment must be incidental to the holiday
and only to supplement holiday funds;
employment in Australia must not be pre-
arranged except on a private basis and on the
applicant's own initiative; there should be
reasonable prospects of obtaining temporary
employment; full-time employment of more
than 3 months with the same employer should
not be undertaken; departure should be at the
expiration of the authorised period of
temporary entry; and applicants must meet
normal health and character standards. If all
these conditions are met the visa will be valid
for a period of 13 months from the date of
issue. A period of up to 2 weeks should be
allowed to obtain a working holiday visa and
travel tickets should not be purchased before a
visa is obtained. Applicants should be single
people or married couples without children
who are aged between 18 and 25 inclusive

(exceptionally ages up to 30 will be considered) and holders of valid UK, Canadian, Dutch, Irish or Japanese passports. Visa applications should be made to the nearest Migration Office, together with passport and a processing fee of AU$130 (£55 in the UK). There are offices in Britain at Australia House, see above, the Australian Consulate, Chatsworth House, Lever Street, Manchester M1 2DL and at the Australian Consulate, Hobart House, 80 Hanover Street, Edinburgh EH2 2DL.
The objective of the working holiday scheme is essentially to provide young people with opportunities for cultural exchange, the work undertaken being part-time or of a casual nature. Personal qualities such as initiative, self-reliance, adaptability, resourcefulness and open-mindedness are the important attributes, enabling the participant to profit from the experience and to provide Australia with an insight into cultural differences.

Travel Travellers are recommended to obtain relevant inoculations for their own personal protection during their journey to Australia depending on the route they take and the countries in which they stay.

Campus Travel, 52 Grosvenor Gardens, London SW1W 0AG © 071-730 8111 (offices throughout the UK) offers competitive fares to destinations in Australia with open jaw facility which allows travel out to one destination and return from another. Special student fares available to ISIC cardholders.

Council Travel, 28A Poland Street, London W1V 3DB © 071-437-7767 (offices also in Paris, Lyon, Düsseldorf, Tokyo and throughout the US) offers low-cost student/youth airfares to destinations throughout Australia, and can issue rail and bus passes. Accommodation, tours and travel insurance also available.

North-South Travel, Moulsham Mill, Parkway, Chelmsford CM2 7PX © Chelmsford (0245) 492882 arranges competitively priced, reliably planned flights to all parts of Australia. Profits are paid into a trust fund for the assignment of aid to projects in the poorest areas of the South.

STA Travel, 74 Old Brompton Road, London SW7 3LQ/117 Euston Road, London NW1 2SX

© 071-937 9962 (offices also in Birmingham, Bristol, Cambridge, Leeds, Manchester and Oxford) operates flexible, low-cost flights with open jaw facility to destinations throughout Australia. Internal flights, accommodation and tours also available.

Blue Roo Fares provide discounts of 55% on domestic jet routes. Details from Australian Airlines, 7 Swallow Street, London W1R 8DU © 071-434 3864.

The Greyhound Australia Bus-Pass offers unlimited bus travel on Australia's largest express route, with discounts on sightseeing, accommodation and car rental. Cost AU$300 (7 days) or AU$485 (15 days). Details from Greyhound International Travel, Sussex House, London Road, East Grinstead, West Sussex © East Grinstead (0342) 317317.

Austrailpass entitles the holder to unlimited travel on Railways of Australia. 14-90 days, cost from £189. Details from Compass, GSA, PO Box 113, Peterborough, Cambridgeshire PE1 1LE ©Peterborough (0733) 51780.

Publications *Traveller's Guide* is a free booklet which includes all the facts to plan a trip: travel, where to stay, general information on seasons, climate, time zones, currency, health services, customs, entry/visa requirements and useful addresses. Available from the Australian Tourist Commission, see above.

Lonely Planet's guide *Australia - A Travel Survival Kit* £13.95 is an essential handbook for travellers in Australia, offering practical, down-to-earth information for people wanting to explore beyond the usual tourist routes. *Culture Shock! Australia* £6.95 introduces the reader to the people, customs, ceremonies, food and culture of Australia, with checklists of dos and don'ts.
Travellers Survival Kit Australia & New Zealand £8.95, is a complete handbook for those going down under, giving information on travelling cheaply, local culture, pubs and restaurants, beaches and reefs, flora and fauna. Published by Vacation Work, 9 Park End Street, Oxford OX1 1HJ © Oxford (0865) 241978.
All the above are available from good bookshops.

CHILDCARE

Au pair arrangements are not common in Australia; however, childcare placements are available through the following agencies:

ACADEMY AU PAIR AGENCY LTD Glenlea, Dulwich Common, London SE21 7ES ✆ 081-299 4599
Can place nannies and mothers' helps throughout the year. 12+ months. Ages 18+. Applicants must have at least 6 months' childcare experience and full driving licence. Salary approx £100-£150 per week plus board and lodging provided. Travel, insurance and visa costs paid by applicants. Administration charge £40.

ANGLIA AGENCY 70 Southsea Avenue Southend-on-Sea, Essex ✆ Southend (0702) 471648
Positions for mothers' helps and nannies arranged throughout the year. Salary, board and lodging provided. Ages 18+. Travel costs paid by applicants. Service charge £40.

COMMUNITY WORK

INVOLVEMENT VOLUNTEERS ASSOCIATION INC PO Box 218, Port Melbourne, Victoria 3207 ✆/Fax Melbourne (3) 646 5504
A non-profitmaking organisation set up to find volunteer placements in Australia or countries en route. Volunteers of all ages can take part in a variety of individual placements including assisting teachers at special schools; acting as recreation officers at homes for older adults; and working as back up staff at disaster prevention organisations or rehabilitation care institutes for children or adults.
Placements available all year. Discounted internal travel to placement sites or discounted Scuba diving courses on the Barrier Reef available. Volunteers must be able to speak English, arrange their own visitor visas, and organise their own international travel and insurance. Some itinerant paid work placements can be found for volunteers with suitable visas. Involvement Volunteers provides advice, placements, itinerary

planning, meeting on arrival, initial accommodation, introductions to banking, taxation and a communications base in Australia. Cost AU$300 (approx £125/$225/DM400). **B D**

In Europe, apply to Involvement Volunteers-Deutschland, Postfach 110224, W-3400 Göttingen, Germany ✆/Fax (551) 33 765.

In North America, apply to Involvement Corps Inc, 15515 Sunset Boulevard Suite 108, Pacific Palisades, California 90272, United States ✆/Fax (310) 459 1022.

CONSERVATION

AUSTRALIAN TRUST FOR CONSERVATION VOLUNTEERS National Director, PO Box 423, Ballarat, Victoria 3350 ✆ (053) 331 483
A non-profitmaking, non-political, community-based organisation undertaking conservation projects including tree planting, erosion and salinity control schemes, and building and maintaining bush walking tracks.
Recent projects have included working with fisheries' researchers in Kakadu National Park and the Jabiru mining site in Northern Territory; constructing part of the Hume and Hovell walking track in New South Wales; and collecting seed for revegetation programmes in the Murray-Darling river catchment area.
Ages 17+. Experience and qualifications relating to the environment welcome, but not essential. Applicants should be fit, willing to work and mix with people from many nations in teams of 8-10. A sound knowledge of English essential. Food, accommodation and travel whilst working provided; volunteers must take a sleeping bag. Cost AU$550 for 6 weeks (1992). Applicants pay their own airfares. *Overseas volunteers welcome.*

EARTHWATCH EUROPE Belsyre Court, 57 Woodstock Road, Oxford OX2 6HU ✆ Oxford (0865) 311600
Aims to support field research in a wide range of disciplines including archaeology, nature conservation and ecology. Support is given to researchers as a grant and in the form of volunteer assistance. Recent projects have

included studying the tiny honey possum in Western Australia; determining the optimum habitat of locally threatened koalas in Queensland; monitoring skink lizards on the Junian Islands; and preserving and documenting aboriginal rock paintings in the Northern Territory. Ages 16-80. No special skills required although each expedition may, because of its nature, demand some talent or quality of fitness. Volunteers should be generally fit, able to cope with new situations and work with people of different ages and backgrounds, and a sense of humour would help. 2-3 weeks, all year. Members share the costs of the expedition, from £500-£1200, which includes meals, transport and all necessary field equipment, but does not include the cost of travel to the staging area, although assistance may be given with arrangements. Membership fee £22 entitles members to join an expedition and receive magazines and newsletters providing all the information necessary to choose a project. **B D PH W** depending on project.

INVOLVEMENT VOLUNTEERS ASSOCIATION INC PO Box 218, Port Melbourne, Victoria 3207, Australia ✆/Fax Melbourne (3) 646 5504

A non-profitmaking organisation set up to find volunteer placements in Australia or countries en route. Volunteers of all ages can take part in individual placements or team tasks. Placements relate to conservation in urban or rural areas: farm tree planting programmes; marine archaeology or zoology research; bird observatory operations; researching, restoring or maintaining historic sites, gardens or covenanted areas; and developing National Parks.
Placements available all year. Discounted internal travel to placement sites or discounted Scuba diving courses on the Barrier Reef available. Volunteers must be able to speak English, arrange their own visitor visas, and organise their own international travel and insurance. Some itinerant paid work placements can be found for volunteers with suitable visas. Involvement Volunteers provides advice, placements, itinerary planning, meeting on arrival, initial accommodation, introductions to banking, taxation and a communications base in

Australia. Cost AU$300 (approx £125/$225/ DM400). **B D**

In Europe, apply to Involvement Volunteers-Deutschland, Postfach 110224, W-3400 Göttingen, Germany ✆/Fax (551) 33 765.

In North America, apply to Involvement Corps Inc, 15515 Sunset Boulevard Suite 108, Pacific Palisades, California 90272, United States ✆/Fax (310) 459 1022.

FARMWORK

INTERNATIONAL AGRICULTURAL EXCHANGE ASSOCIATION YFC Centre, National Agricultural Centre, Stoneleigh Park, Kenilworth, Warwickshire CV8 2LG ✆ Coventry (0203) 696578

Provides opportunities for young people involved in agriculture, horticulture or home management to acquire practical work experience and improve their knowledge and understanding of the way of life in other countries. Types of farm include cattle and sheep; mixed (cattle, sheep and field crops); dairy; beef and crops; sheep and crops; plus a limited number of pig, horse and horticultural enterprises. Participants undertake paid work on the farm, approx 40 hours per week, and live as a member of the host family. Full board, lodging, insurance cover and minimum net weekly wage of £50-£60 provided. All programmes include 3/8 weeks unpaid holiday. 3 day orientation courses held at agricultural colleges and universities throughout Australia. Stopovers (2-3 days) in Singapore/Thailand arranged en route. Ages 18-30. Applicants should be single, and have good practical experience in the chosen training category, plus a valid driving licence. 9 months (departing April), 8 months (departing August), 7 or 9 months (departing September), 14 months - 7 in Australia plus 7 in Canada/US (departing September) or 14 months - 7 in New Zealand plus 7 in Australia (departing August). Cost from £2125. £200 deposit payable. Costs cover airfare, work permit, administration fee and orientation seminar, information meetings, insurance, supervision, placement with a host family and travel costs to placement. *Apply at least 4 months in advance; UK or Irish passport holders only.* **B D** if handicap is not severe.

Australian applicants requiring an exchange should apply to IAEA, 50 Oxford Street, Paddington, NSW 2021.

NORTHERN VICTORIA FRUITGROWERS' ASSOCIATION PO Box 394, Shepparton, Victoria 3630

VICTORIAN PEACH AND APRICOT GROWERS' ASSOCIATION PO Box 39, Cobram, Victoria 3644

Fruit picking jobs available under the Working Holidaymakers scheme. The Associations represent the 500 orchards in the Goulburn/ Murray Valley, Victoria. Season commences in late January with the harvesting of Bartlett pears, used mainly for canning, and continues into March and April when crops include other pear varieties, peaches, and apples. Piece-work rates apply. Accommodation often available; participants may camp in the orchards if they take their own equipment. For latest details on location and availability of work, contact either of the Associations on arrival.

Addresses for personal callers: Northern Victoria Fruitgrowers' Association Ltd, 21 Nixon Street, Shepparton, Victoria © (058) 21 5844/Victorian Peach and Apricot Growers' Association, 21 Station Street, Cobram, Victoria © (058) 72 1729

WILLING WORKERS ON ORGANIC FARMS (WWOOF) W Tree, Buchan, Victoria 3885
A non-profitmaking organisation which aims to help organic farmers and smallholders whose work is often labour-intensive as it does not rely on the use of artificial fertilisers or pesticides. Provides volunteers with first hand experience of organic farming and gardening; approx 230 host farms all over Australia especially in the eastern and southern coastal areas. Volunteers learn by doing, working in exchange for their keep. All types of farmwork, field work, animal care and building. Placements of up to 6 months can be arranged for agricultural students. Ages 17+. Full board and lodging provided in the farmhouse or outbuildings; volunteers should take a sleeping bag. No wages paid, and helpers must pay their own travel. Insurance and anti-tetanus vaccination recommended. Membership fee £10. **PH**

GENERAL

BRITISH UNIVERSITIES NORTH AMERICA CLUB (BUNAC) 16 Bowling Green Lane, London EC1R 0BD © 071-251 3472
A non-profit, non-political educational student club venture which aims to encourage interest and understanding between students. Administers a Work Australia programme for those who wish to work and travel in Australia. Jobs do not have to be organised in advance, but advice is offered to those wishing to do so. Orientation programmes on arrival give advice on finding a job, obtaining a visa, income tax, accommodation, travel, food and budgeting. Ages 18-25. Cost depends on route and stopovers, but includes return flight and registration, two nights' accommodation followed by orientation, and the help of Student Services Australia. In order to obtain a visa, applicants must have evidence of £2000 in personal funds (but round-trip transportation costs can be deducted from this). *UK, Irish, Canadian or Dutch nationals only.*

INFORMATION

Austrian Embassy
18 Belgrave Mews West, London SW1X 8HU
✆ 071-235 3731

British Embassy
Jaurèsgasse 12, 1030 Vienna

Tourist office
Austrian National Tourist Office, 30 St George
Street, London W1R 9FA ✆ 071-629 0461

Youth hostels
Österreichischer Jugendherbergsverband,
Gonzagagasse 22, 1010 Vienna

Youth & student information
Austrian Foreign Students' Service,
Rooseveltplatz 13, 1090 Vienna

Austrian Institute, 28 Rutland Gate, London
SW7 1PQ ✆ 071-584 8653

Büro für Studentenreisen, Schreyvogelgasse 3,
1010 Vienna

ÖKISTA (Austrian Committee for International
Educational Exchange), Garnisongasse 7, 1090
Vienna

Jugendinformationszentrum, Kalvarienberg-
straße 2, 4560 Kirchdorf

Jugendinformationszentrum, Info-Center,
Dambockgasse 1, 1060 Vienna

Entry regulations Work permits are required
for all kinds of employment including au pair
positions. When a job has been found the
prospective employer must obtain a permit;
employees are not allowed to apply for a work
permit themselves. The number of work
permits issued to foreign nationals is limited
and a permit will only be granted if there is no
Austrian national to fill the post; this applies
particularly to clerical and secretarial work.
Permits will not be granted to foreign passport
holders while on a visit to Austria. Students
who find holiday work through one of the
official student exchange agencies can obtain an

equivalent certificate from them. The work permit or equivalent should be submitted to the Consular Section of the Austrian Embassy, together with a valid passport, who will then issue the necessary visa. Holders of British passports do not require a visa for a work period of less than 6 months.

These regulations may change as of January 1993 subject to the European Economic Space agreement, and a work permit may no longer be required by UK and other EC nationals.

Social security All employed persons except au pairs must contribute to the health and social security scheme, which covers most medical expenses.

Employment offices The Austrian Embassy, see above, can supply a list of provincial employment offices. When applying to one of the offices the following details should be supplied in a letter typed in German: name, address, date of birth, education, profession, type of present employment, knowledge of foreign languages, length of intended stay, and type of job required. Applications for au pair positions, however, cannot be accepted.

Addresses of some provincial employment offices are:

Landesarbeitsamt für das Burgenland, Permayerstraße 10, 7001 Eisenstadt

Landesarbeitsamt für Kärnten, Kumpfgasse 25, 9010 Klagenfurt

Landesarbeitsamt für Niederösterreich, Hohenstaufengasse 2, 1013 Vienna

Landesarbeitsamt für Oberösterreich, Grüberstraße 63, 4010 Linz

Landesarbeitsamt für Salzburg, Auerspergstraße 67, 5020 Salzburg

Landesarbeitsamt für Steiermark, Bahnhofgürtel 85, 8021 Graz

Landesarbeitsamt für Tirol, Schopfstraße 5, 6010 Innsbruck

Landesarbeitsamt für Vorarlberg, Rheinstraße 32, 6903 Bregenz

Landesarbeitsamt für Wien, Weihburggasse 30, 1011 Vienna

For further information see *Working in Austria* available from the Austrian Embassy.

Applications for work can also be made under the International Clearing of Vacancies scheme; for further details contact the Training Agency.

Job advertising Publicitas, 517/523 Fulham Road, London SW6 1HD ✆ 071-385 7723 can accept job advertisements for a number of Austrian newspapers.

Travel Budget airfares are available from the Anglo-Austrian Society, 46 Queen Anne's Gate, London SW1H 9AU ✆ 071-222 0366.

Campus Travel, 52 Grosvenor Gardens, London SW1W 0AG ✆ 071-730 3402 (offices throughout the UK) and Council Travel, 28A Poland Street, London W1V 3DB ✆ 071-437 7767 (offices also in Paris, Lyon, Düsseldorf, Tokyo and throughout the US) offer Eurotrain under 26 reduced fares and student/youth airfares to destinations in Austria.

Accommodation Youth hostel accommodation in Vienna and hotel accommodation in Vienna, Innsbruck, Graz and Salzburg is available through the Anglo-Austrian Society, see above.

For accommodation in hotels, pensions and student hostels in Vienna, contact Büro für Studentenreisen, Schreyvogelgasse 3, 1010 Vienna.

ÖKISTA (Austrian Committee for International Educational Exchange), Garnisongasse 7, 1090 Vienna can provide all kinds of accommodation throughout Austria.

When writing to any organisation it is essential to mention Working Holidays 1993 and enclose a large stamped, self-addressed envelope, or if overseas, a large addressed envelope and at least two International Reply Coupons.

AU PAIR / CHILDCARE

Work permits for au pair positions are obtained by the host family from the local employment office and must be issued before the au pair arrives in Austria. The application should be accompanied by an agreement signed by the au pair, the host family and the au pair agency. Au pairs must be girls at least 18 years old, and can expect to receive board, lodging and a minimum of AS700 per week in exchange for looking after the children and helping with light housework and simple cooking.

Au pairs do not pay income tax and no contributions to the health and social security scheme can be made, so it is essential to join a private health insurance scheme. Evidence of this must be produced by the host family when applying for the work permit. Au pairs must give an undertaking to return home at the end of their stay, and prove that they have sufficient funds for the journey.

The following agencies can arrange au pair and childcare placements in Austria:

ACADEMY AU PAIR AGENCY LTD Glenlea, Dulwich Common, London SE21 7ES ℗ 081-299 4599
Can place au pairs. Ages 18-27. Some knowledge of German essential. Pocket money approx £30-£35 per week. Administration charge £40. Positions as nannies and mothers' helps also available for those with qualifications/experience.

ARBEITSGEMEINSCHAFT AUSLANDS-SOZIALDIENST Au-Pair-Vermittlung, Johannesgasse 16/1, 1010 Vienna
Can place au pairs in Vienna and other areas. Ages 18-25. Pocket money from AS700 per week. Registration fee AS600. Limited number of summer positions with families outside Vienna for 8+ weeks, without language classes.

HELPING HANDS AU PAIR & DOMESTIC AGENCY 39 Rutland Avenue, Thorpe Bay, Essex SS1 2XJ ℗ Southend-on-Sea (0702) 60206710
Can place au pairs and mothers' helps. Ages 18-27. Pocket money approx £30 per week for au pairs, higher for mothers' helps. Introduction fee £40 on acceptance of a family. *UK nationals only.*

INTERNATIONAL CATHOLIC SOCIETY FOR GIRLS (ACISJF) St Patrick's International Youth Centre, 24 Great Chapel Street, London W1V 3AF ℗ 071-734 2156
Au pair posts arranged for 9+ months. Ages 18+. Mainly for UK and Irish nationals.

LANGTRAIN INTERNATIONAL Torquay Road, Foxrock, Dublin 18, Ireland ℗ Dublin (1) 289 3876
Can place au pairs with Austrian families. Ages 18+. Pocket money £25-£40 per week. Placement fee £55.

MONDIAL AGENCY 32 Links Road, West Wickham, Kent BR4 0QW ℗ 071-777 0510
Can place au pairs in Vienna or the provinces. Ages 18-27. Pocket money approx £30 per week. Service charge £40.

ÖKISTA (Austrian Committee for International Educational Exchange), Au Pair Department, Garnisongasse 7, 1090 Vienna
Can place au pairs in Vienna, main cities and country areas. Ages 18-28. Pocket money approx AS700 per week. Registration fee AS500.

STUDENTS ABROAD LTD 11 Milton View, Hitchin, Hertfordshire SG4 0QD ℗ Hitchin (0462) 438909
Can place au pairs and occasionally mothers' helps. Ages 18-27 for au pairs. Basic knowledge of German helpful but there are opportunities for placements with British families in Vienna. Pocket money approx £30-£35 per week. Service charge £40.

UNIVERSAL CARE Chester House, 9 Windsor End, Beaconsfield, Buckinghamshire HP9 2JJ ℗ Beaconsfield (0494) 678811
Can place au pairs in Vienna, main cities and country areas. Ages 18-27. Knowledge of German essential. Pocket money approx £25 per week. Service charge £47. *Apply 2 months before work period desired. EC nationals only.*
PH

COURIERS / REPS

BLADON LINES Personnel Department, 56-58 Putney High Street, London SW15 1SF ℗ 081-785 2200

Opportunities for representatives to work in the ski resorts of St Anton, Lech and Obergurgl. Work involves welcoming and looking after guests, providing information, helping with coach transfers, managing chalet staff and ensuring everything is running smoothly. Ages 24+. Relevant experience an advantage, and good spoken German essential. Applicants must be prepared to work hard but will get time to ski. Season lasts December-May. Salary £50-£100 per week, depending on the size of the resort. Board, lodging, return travel, insurance, ski pass, ski hire and uniform provided. Training week held before departure.

There are also a few places in each resort for ski guides who act as assistant reps and whose work involves showing guests around the slopes, helping with coach transfers and organising *après ski*. Ages 22+ with good spoken German. Applicants should have good leadership qualities and be proficient skiers (minimum 20 weeks experience). Salary approx £50 per week. A week's training held in Val d'Isère before the season starts. *EC passport holders only*. PH depending on ability.

CANVAS HOLIDAYS LTD 12 Abbey Park Place, Dunfermline, Fife KY12 7PD

Provides accommodation for holiday families in ready-erected fully equipped tents and cabins on campsites. Positions available as resident campsite couriers, children's couriers, nannies and water sports couriers. The work involves a daily routine of tent cleaning as customers arrive and depart, providing information and advice on the local attractions and essential services, helping to sort out problems that might arise and organising activities for the children and get-togethers for the families. 7 day week with no fixed hours; the workload varies from day to day. At the beginning and end of the season there is a period of physical work when tents are put up and prepared or taken down and stored for the winter. Other tasks include administration, book keeping and stock control. Working knowledge of German

essential. Ages 18-25. Applicants should be those with a year between school and further education, undergraduates or graduates. They need to be enthusiastic, practical, reliable, self-motivated, able to turn their hand to new and varied tasks, and with a sense of humour. 6 months, April-October. Return travel (dependent on successful completion of contract), accommodation in frame tents and bicycle for use on site provided. Salary £80 per week (1992). *Applications accepted anytime; interviews commence early November for the following season. UK nationals only.*

CRYSTAL HOLIDAYS Crystal House, The Courtyard, Arlington Road, Surbiton, Surrey KT6 6BW ℗ 081-390 8737

Tour operator arranging year-round air, rail, coach and self-drive holidays throughout Austria. Representatives are required to meet and greet clients and be responsible for their welfare during their holiday. Ski guides also needed during winter season. Ages 20-35. Previous experience desirable and fluent German essential. Approx 60 hour, 7 day week, May-October and December-April. Basic salary plus commission; board, lodging, insurance, travel costs and uniform provided. 1 week training seminar held at beginning of each season. *Apply January/February for summer season, April/May for winter season.*

EUROCAMP Summer Jobs, (Ref WH), PO Box 170, Liverpool L70 1ES

One of Europe's leading tour operators, specialising in providing quality camping and mobile home holidays for families throughout Europe. Campsite couriers are required: work involves cleaning tents and equipment prior to the arrival of new customers; checking, replacing and making repairs on equipment; replenishing gas supplies; keeping basic accounts and reporting on a weekly basis to England. Couriers are also expected to meet new arrivals and assist holidaymakers with any problems that arise; organise activities and parties; provide information on local tourist attractions and maintain an information noticeboard. At the beginning and end of the season couriers are also expected to help in erecting and dismantling tents. Couriers need to be flexible to meet the needs of customers and be on hand where necessary;

they will be able to organise their own free time as the workload allows.

Ages 18+. Applicants should be independent, adaptable, reliable, physically fit, have plenty of initiative and relish a challenging and responsible position. Good working knowledge of German also necessary. Preference given to those able to work the whole season, April-September/October; contracts also available for first half season, April-mid July and second half season, mid July-September/October.

Children's couriers are also required, with the energy and enthusiasm to organise a wide range of exciting activities for groups of children aged 4-13. Experience of working with children within this age range is essential, but language ability is not a requirement. Ages 20+. Children's couriers must be available for the whole season, May-September.

For both positions the salary is £91.50 per week. Training is provided together with accommodation in frame tent with cooking facilities, insurance and return travel.

UK and EC passport-holders only. Early application advisable; interviews start September/ October.

SCHOOL WORLD The Coach House, Tyn-y-Coed Place, Roath Park, Cardiff CF2 4TX ✆ Cardiff (0222) 470077
Organises skiing holidays for school groups at a wide range of Austrian resorts. Requires representatives to prepare for the groups' arrival, operate quality and safety control, deal with any problems, arrange après ski programmes and generally ensure that clients enjoy their holiday. Season lasts from late December-mid April depending on school holiday dates. Hours worked vary but representatives are on call at all times. Ages 19-30. Experience of working with the public and a good knowledge of German essential; applicants must also be friendly and outgoing with a high level of common sense and personal organisation. Salary £35 per week, with a £15 bonus for each group looked after, depending on completion of contract. Full board accommodation, insurance and reasonable travel costs provided. 4-5 day residential training course held before departure. Recruitment begins July for following winter season. *Applicants must have UK National Insurance number.*

SEASUN SCHOOL TOURS Ski Department, Seasun House, 4 East Street, Colchester, Essex CO1 2XW
Provides skiing holidays in the Austrian Alps for school groups during peak school holiday dates at New Year, February and Easter. Requires resort representatives to spend weeks with groups coordinating their tour. Ages 20+. Applicants must be diplomatic, affable, fun, hardworking skiers, with experience of working with children and fluent German. Salary according to responsibility. Accommodation, travel, personal insurance and partial uniform provided. *Write for application form.*

SKIBOUND Olivier House, 18 Marine Parade, Brighton, East Sussex BN2 1TL
Specialises in winter sports tours for schools and adults and in activity tours and excursions in spring/summer. Area managers, representatives and hotel/chalet managers required for the winter and spring/summer seasons, December-April and May-August, in the Austrian Alps. Posts involve a considerable amount of client contact, and applicants must be presentable and keen to work hard. Ages 21+. Good knowledge of French/German required for representatives and preferably for managers; previous experience an advantage. Insurance, travel and full board accommodation provided. Wages dependent on position.

TRAVELSPHERE LTD Compass House, Rockingham Road, Market Harborough, Leicestershire LE16 7QD ✆ Market Harborough (0858) 410456
Couriers required to escort groups of adult and elderly passengers on coaching holidays throughout Austria. Work involves checking into accommodation, organising welcome meetings, guiding excursions and generally looking after the well-being of passengers to ensure they have an enjoyable holiday.

Ages 20-35. Previous experience of courier work not essential but applicants must have a friendly, outgoing personality and an ability to deal with the general public. Experience of travelling in Europe useful. Good spoken English and a knowledge of German required. 4 months, May-October. Couriers work long hours, but work is rewarding. Pay is at daily rate plus commission on sale of excursions. Half board accommodation generally provided, plus full insurance and travel costs. 3 day training course in the UK followed by additional training abroad. *Apply in writing between 1 November and 31 January enclosing a photograph.*

DOMESTIC

BLADON LINES Personnel Department, 56-58 Putney High Street, London SW15 1SF ✆ 081-785 2200
Opportunities for chalet girls to work in the ski resorts of St Anton, Lech and Obergurgl. Work involves cleaning chalets, making beds, caring for guests, shopping and preparing meals. Ages 20+. Experience and/or qualifications in catering or domestic work essential. Also positions for hostesses to work in larger chalets where no cooking experience is required. Hours very variable; applicants must be prepared to work hard but will get time to ski. Season lasts December-May. Salary approx £40 per week. Board, lodging, return travel, insurance, ski pass, ski hire and company ski jacket provided. One day briefing in London held before departure. *EC passport holders only.* PH depending on ability.

CRYSTAL HOLIDAYS Crystal House, The Courtyard, Arlington Road, Surbiton, Surrey KT6 6BW ✆ 081-390 8737
Tour operator arranging skiing holidays at resorts throughout Austria. Chalet staff are required to cook daily breakfast, afternoon tea and 3-course evening meal for clients, and keep chalets clean and tidy. Ages 20-35. Catering qualifications, experience and fluent German essential. Approx 60 hour, 6½ day week, December-April. Basic salary plus commission; board, lodging, insurance, travel costs and uniform provided. 1 week training seminar held at beginning of each season. *Apply April/May.*

FARMWORK

INTERNATIONAL FARM EXPERIENCE PROGRAMME YFC Centre, National Agricultural Centre, Stoneleigh Park, Kenilworth, Warwickshire CV8 2LG ✆ **Coventry (0203) 696584**
Provides assistance to young farmers and nurserymen by finding places in farms/ nurseries abroad, enabling them to broaden their knowledge of agricultural methods. Opportunities for practical horticultural and agricultural work usually on mixed farms. Applicants live and work with a farmer and his family and the work is matched as far as possible with the applicant's requirements. The work is physically hard. 8-10 hour day, 6 day week; every other weekend free. 3-12 months. Positions mostly available in spring and summer. Wages approx £30 plus board and lodging. Ages 18-26. Applicants must have at least 2 years practical experience, 1 year of which may be at an agricultural college, and intend to make a career in agriculture/ horticulture. Valid driving licence necessary. Applicants pay own fares. Registration fee £70. *UK applicants only.*

Austrian applicants seeking an exchange should apply to Präsidentenkonferenz der Landwirtschaftskammern Österreichs, I Löwelstraße Nr 12, Postfach 124, 1014 Vienna.

LEADERS & GUIDES

SEASUN SCHOOL TOURS Ski Department, Seasun House, 4 East Street, Colchester, Essex CO1 2XW
Provides skiing holidays in the Austrian Alps for school groups during peak school holiday dates at New Year, February and Easter. Requires reliable and conscientious ski guides to excort and supervise groups both on the mountain and in the evenings. Ages 20+. Applicants must be qualified to at least ASSI part 1. Experience with young beginners and a willingness to integrate with the group essential. Salary according to responsibility. Accommodation, travel, personal insurance and partial uniform provided. *Write for application form.*

MONITORS & INSTRUCTORS

SKI EUROPE Brentham House, 45c High Street, Hampton Wick, Kingston-upon-Thames, Surrey KT1 4DG © 081-977 7755
Operates holidays for groups and school parties. Part-time ski instructors are required for winter sports centres in the Tyrol and Salzburgland. BASI or full ASSI qualifications essential. Knowledge of foreign languages useful but not essential; fluent English a prerequisite. 6 hours teaching per day, 1-4 week periods over the New Year, February and April. Wages approx £75 per week, according to qualifications. Full board hotel accommodation and ski pass plus travel from London/resort. Access to the same facilities as the clients. *Interviews held May-November.*

YOUNG AUSTRIA Alpenstraße 108a, 5020 Salzburg
Opportunities available for monitors and EFL teachers at English language camps for Austrian and German children. The camps are based at holiday centre chalets in the Salzburg region, and are organised for children aged 10-19 who are studying English at school. The aim is to improve their knowledge of the English language and the British way of life. Monitors and teachers are responsible for the daily welfare of a group of approx 10-15 children, for the organisation of indoor and outdoor activities, including sports, music and crafts, excursions and for helping the children with English conversation. Teachers are responsible for the daily tuition (3½ hours) of English but also have to act as monitors. The language of the camps is English and a knowledge of German is not compulsory. Ages 21-35. Applicants should be native English speakers and have experience in working with or teaching children. Qualified teachers will be given priority for teaching posts. Applicant's ability and organisational skills in sports, music and crafts will be taken into consideration. 3 or 6 weeks, end June-beginning September. Board, accommodation, insurance and sports clothes provided. Pay from AS4200, monitors or AS5200, teachers, per 3 week

session, plus lump sum of AS2000 for travel expenses. Compulsory interviews and briefing held in London in June. *UK residents preferred; apply by February.*

WORKCAMPS

ÖSTERREICHISCHER BAUORDEN PO Box 186, Hornesgasse 3, 1031 Vienna
Austrian branch of International Building Companions, a volunteers' association with the aims of fighting misery and distress, and making a contribution towards a better understanding between nations. Volunteers are invited to work on international workcamps which take place throughout Austria. Projects have included construction, cleaning and renovation work at youth/social centres, churches, hostels, homes for the aged, kindergartens, schools, community centres and refugee resettlements; and housing for socially deprived families. Ages 18+. Applicants should have previous workcamp experience. 40 hour week, 3-4 weeks, July and August. Food, prepared by the volunteers, tent, family, school or centre accommodation, insurance and travel in Austria provided, but volunteers should take sleeping bags. Participation fee DM110. *Apply 2 months in advance.*

SERVICE CIVIL INTERNATIONAL Schottengasse 3a/1/59, 1010 Vienna
Service Civil International promotes international reconciliation through work projects. Volunteers are invited to live and work in international teams on workcamps. Recent projects have included working with Croats (a minority group in Austria) to develop their centre and prepare their annual local festival in the Burgenland; organising a fundraising fleamarket for a young people's advice centre in Innsbruck; helping with the harvest at an organic farm in Wartburg; working with children at a women's refuge in Vienna; and renovating a house and garden near Graz for use as an alternative school. Camps are linked to study themes. Workcamp languages are English and German. Ages 18+. Experience not essential but applicants should be highly motivated and prepared to work hard as part of a team. 35-40 hour week, 2-4 weeks, May-September. Food, accommodation and

insurance provided, but not travel. Volunteers prepare and cook their own meals. **B D PH W** *Apply through partner organisation in country of residence. In the UK: International Voluntary Service, Old Hall, East Bergholt, Colchester, Essex CO7 6TQ*

Outside the UK: please see information on page 30.

GENERAL

CANVAS HOLIDAYS LTD 12 Abbey Park Place, Dunfermline, Fife KY12 7PD
Provides ready-erected fully equipped tents for family holidays. Require applicants to form flying squads, teams of 5/6 people who help set up and equip 200-250 6 berth frame tents in an area containing approx 12 campsites. Similar work is also available taking down tents and cleaning and storing equipment. Ages 18-25. Knowledge of German not required, but is an advantage as flying squad members sometimes have the opportunity to continue as couriers. Applicants must be sociable in order to work in a small community, fit and able to work hard for long hours under pressure, work without supervision and cope with living out of a rucksack. April-mid June, possibly longer to set up the tents, and September to dismantle them. Valid international driving licence an advantage. Salary approx £80 per week. Tented accommodation and self-catering facilities provided. Outward travel paid by the company; return travel dependent on the completion of contract dates. *UK nationals only.*

EUROYOUTH LTD 301 Westborough Road, Westcliff, Southend-on-Sea, Essex SS0 9PT
℗ **Southend-on-Sea (0702) 341434**
Holiday stays arranged where guests are offered board and lodging in return for an agreed number of hours English conversation with hosts or their children. Time also available for guests to practise German if desired. Mainly ages 15-25, but sometimes opportunities for ages 13-16 and for older applicants. The scheme is open to anyone born and educated in the UK, interested in visiting Austria and living with a local family. 2-3 weeks, June-August. Travel and insurance paid by applicants. Registration fee approx £70. *Apply at least 12 weeks prior to scheduled departure date.*

BALTIC STATES

INFORMATION

Latvian Embassy 72 Queensborough Terrace, London W2 3SP ✆ 071-727 1698

Lithuanian Embassy 17 Essex Villas, London W8 7BP ✆ 071-937 1588

Entry regulations Details of work permits and entry requirements can be obtained in Britain from the embassies listed above.

Publications Lonely Planet's *Scandinavian and Baltic Europe on a Shoestring* £10.95 offers practical, down-to-earth information for the low-budget, independent traveller in Latvia and Lithuania.

AU PAIR / CHILDCARE

INTERNATIONAL EXCHANGE CENTER 2 Republic Square, 226168 Riga, Latvia ✆ Riga (0132) 327476
A non-governmental, non-profitmaking organisation working to promote peace and understanding through contacts between people of different nationalities. Can arrange au pair placements for females only in families throughout Latvia. Previous experience of working with children desirable but not essential. Basic knowledge of Russian or Latvian useful. Ages 17+. 30 hours per week. 2+ months, all year. Board, lodging and pocket money provided. Travel costs paid by applicants. Basic medical insurance arranged on request, and help given with obtaining a visa. Administration fee US$95. Host families arrange excursions to local places of interest. Language courses and sightseeing to major cities arranged at extra cost. *Apply at least 1 month in advance.*

When writing to any organisation it is essential to mention Working Holidays 1993 and enclose a large stamped, self-addressed envelope, or if overseas, a large addressed envelope and at least two International Reply Coupons.

FARMWORK

INTERNATIONAL EXCHANGE CENTER
2 Republic Square, 226168 Riga, Latvia
℃ Riga (0132) 327476
A non-governmental, non-profitmaking organisation working to promote peace and understanding through contacts between people of different nationalities. Volunteers are required to work on farmcamps based on or near the Baltic coast in Latvia. Work involves acting as group leader to a unit of approx 25 high school students doing harvesting and fruitpicking as part of their school practice. Ages 18-30. No previous experience necessary. Basic knowledge of Russian or Latvian useful. 6 day week for 1, 2 or 3 months, June-August. Board, lodging and pocket money equivalent to local workers provided, but no fares paid.
UK applicants apply through Concordia (Youth Service Volunteers) Ltd, Recruitment Secretary, 8 Brunswick Place, Hove, Sussex BN3 1ET ℃ Brighton (0273) 772086. Registration fee £30; administration fee £5.

MONITORS & INSTRUCTORS

INTERNATIONAL EXCHANGE CENTER
2 Republic Square, 226168 Riga, Latvia
℃ Riga (0132) 327476
A non-governmental, non-profitmaking organisation working to promote peace and understanding through contacts between people of different nationalities. Can place applicants as counsellors and instructors on children's summer camps based on or near the Baltic coast in Latvia. Work involves supervising a group of 20-25 children in conjunction with another counsellor, or providing instruction in sports, arts and crafts, outdoor pursuits, watersports, drama or music. Previous experience of working with children desirable. Basic knowledge of Russian or Latvian useful. Ages 18-30. 6 day week for 1, 2 or 3 months, June-August. Board, lodging and pocket money equivalent to local workers provided, but no fares paid.

UK applicants apply through Concordia (Youth Service Volunteers) Ltd, Recruitment Secretary, 8 Brunswick Place, Hove, Sussex BN3 1ET ℃ Brighton (0273) 772086. Registration fee £30; administration fee £5.

WORKCAMPS

CENTRE OF STUDENT ACTIVITIES (CSA) K Donelaicio 73-113, Kaunas, LT-3006, Lithuania
An independent, non-political, non-profit organisation formed from a union of student clubs at the Kaunas University of Technology, Lithuania. Volunteers are invited to take part in international workcamps. Recent projects have included restoring huts, fencing and roof repairs plus some summer haymaking at the Lithuanian museum of folk architecture in Rumsiskes; and construction and cultivation work at a centre for alternative technology and ecology in Marcinkanys. Discussion programmes and cultural excursions organised. Ages 18+. Applicants must be highly motivated and prepared to work hard as part of a team. 2 weeks, July-August. Food and accommodation provided, but volunteers pay their own travel and insurance costs.

Apply through partner organisation in country of residence. In the UK: United Nations Association, International Youth Service, Temple of Peace, Cathays Park, Cardiff CF1 3AP ℃ Cardiff (0222) 223088

Outside the UK: please see information on page 30.

INTERNATIONAL VOLUNTARY SERVICE
Old Hall, East Bergholt, Colchester, Essex CO7 6TQ
The British branch of Service Civil International, which promotes international reconciliation through work projects. Cooperates with workcamp organisations based in Latvia and Lithuania. Recent projects have included restoring castle walls in the medieval towns of Rauna and Sigulda; caring for pre-school children at a playscheme in Dobele; cleaning the shoreline and studying the environmental problems of the Baltic in the coastal town of Ronis and helping at an archaeological excavation in Vilnius. Study programmes cover a wide range of topics, and

visits are organised to local places of interest.
Ages 18+. Applicants must have previous
workcamp/voluntary work experience, and be
prepared to work hard and contribute to team
life. 35-40 hour week. 2-3 weeks, July-August.
Food, accommodation and insurance provided,
but not travel. Registration fee £85 (students
£75, unwaged £70) plus extra fee of £30 to
support exchange programme. Orientation
held in Edinburgh/London prior to departure.
B D PH

*Apply through partner organisation in country of
residence; see information on page 30.*

**QUAKER INTERNATIONAL SOCIAL
PROJECTS Friends House, Euston Road,
London NW1 2BJ**
Volunteers are invited to take part in
international workcamps organised by
SPEKTRAS in Lithuania. Recent projects have
included working as assistants to group leaders
in a childrens' summer camp, looking after the
children, helping them with their English and
organising activities. Ages 18+. Applicants
must have previous workcamp/voluntary work
experience and be prepared to work hard as
part of a team. Knowledge of Russian or
Lithuanian very useful, although interpreters
are available. 5 day week for 3 weeks, July-
August. Excursions arranged to places of
interest. Food and accommodation provided,
but volunteers pay their own travel and
insurance costs.

*Apply through partner organisation in country of
residence; see information on page 30.*

APPLYING FOR A JOB

Before applying, read carefully all the information
given. Unless otherwise indicated, applications
should be made in writing. Check in particular:

✐ skills, qualifications or experience required

✐ the full period of employment expected

✐ any restrictions of age, sex or nationality

✐ application deadlines

✐ any other points, particularly details of
insurance cover, and other costs you may have
to bear such as travel and accommodation.

When writing to any organisation it is **essential** to
mention **Working Holidays 1993** and to enclose a
large, stamped, self-addressed envelope, or if
overseas, a large addressed envelope and at least
two International Reply Coupons (available at
Post Offices). When applying be sure to include
the following:

✐ name, address, date of birth, nationality, sex

✐ education, qualifications, relevant
experience, skills, languages spoken

✐ period of availability

✐ a passport-size photo, particularly if you are
to have contact with the public

✐ anything else asked for, eg a *cv*

INFORMATION

Belgian Embassy
103-105 Eaton Square, London SW1W 9AB
✆ 071-235 5422

British Embassy
Rue d'Arlon 85, 1040 Brussels

Tourist office
Belgian National Tourist Office, Premier House,
2 Gayton Road, Harrow, Middlesex HA1 2XU
✆ 081-861 3300

Youth hostels
Centrale Wallonne des Auberges de la Jeunesse,
rue Van Oost 52, 1030 Brussels

Vlaamse Jeugdherbergcentrale, Van
Stralenstraat 40, 2008 Antwerp

Youth & student information
Centre National d'Information des Jeunes,
10 rue Jean Volders 1060 Brussels

Nationaal Informatiecentrum voor Jongeren,
Prinsstraat 15, 2000 Antwerp

Caravanes de Jeunesse Belge, 216 chaussée
d'Ixelles, 1050 Brussels

Accueil Jeunes, 79 rue Gillon, 1030 Brussels

Centre Jeunesse Liège, rue Ste Marguerite,
4000 Liège

Entry regulations UK citizens intending to
work in Belgium should have a full passport.
They must register at the nearest town hall
within 8 days and bring along a certificate of
good conduct. EC nationals may stay in
Belgium for up to 3 months in order to seek
employment. The number of opportunities
available to foreign students is, however,
extremely limited. The Belgian Embassy can
supply a list of job centres for temporary work
(T-Service).

Job advertising Advertisements for job
vacancies, situations wanted, services offered
and domestic help are included in the weekly

news magazine for English-speaking residents in Belgium, *The Bulletin*, avenue Molière 329, 1060 Brussels.

Publicitas Ltd, 517-523 Fulham Road, London SW6 1HD ✆ 071-385 7723 can place job advertisements in 12 Belgian newspapers and 17 magazines.

Travel Belgian National Railways, 10 Greycoat Place, London SW1P 1SB ✆ 071-233 0360 operates a scheme where a bike can be hired at one of 60 Belgian stations and returned to any one of 90. Advisable to reserve bikes in advance; cost approx £4.50 per day (£2.50 for rail ticket holders)

The Benelux Tourrail Card is available for 5 days within a period of 17 days, allowing unlimited travel on the national rail networks of Belgium, the Netherlands and Luxembourg. March-October; cost from £51. Details from Netherlands Railways, 25/28 Buckingham Gate, London SW1E 6LD ✆ 071-630 1735.

Euro-Domino is a pass allowing 5 or 10 days unlimited rail travel in 1 month on the railways of Belgium. Cost from £29/£53 (ages under 26) or £37/£66 (ages 26+), 5/10 days. Available from British Rail International Rail Centre, Victoria Station, London SW1V 1JY ✆ 071-928 5151.

Campus Travel, 52 Grosvenor Gardens, London SW1W 0AG ✆ 071-730 3402 (offices throughout the UK) and Council Travel, 28A Poland Street, London, W1V 3DB ✆ 071-437 7767 (offices also in Paris, Lyon, Düsseldorf, Tokyo and throughout the US) offer Eurotrain under 26 rail fares to all main destinations in Belgium, plus youth and student airfares.

Information centres ACOTRA World Ltd, rue de la Madeleine 51, 1000 Brussels arranges youth and student travel and is able to give advice and make reservations for accommodation. Also books tours and excursions, cultural and activity holidays, and issues youth/student reduction and youth hostel cards. The ACOTRA Welcome Desk at Brussels airport provides information and reservations for accommodation and transport, including BIJ train tickets for those under 26.

Brussels Welcome Open Door, rue de Tabora 6, 1000 Brussels ✆ Brussels (2) 511 8178 is a Catholic information service for visitors, residents, workers, immigrants, refugees and students, providing advice on education, language classes, social services, legal aid and religion. Free interpreting and translation service. Open Monday-Saturday, 10.00-18.00.

Centre National Infor Jeunes, impasse des Capucins 2/8, 5000 Namur ✆ Namur (81) 22 08 72 is the head office of the youth information service that has 12 centres throughout Belgium open to the public. Information is available on legal rights, study, leisure, holidays, in fact anything that particularly affects young people.

Publications *The Rough Guide to Holland, Belgium and Luxembourg* £6.95 provides comprehensive background information on Belgium, plus details on getting there, getting around, places to explore and cheap places to stay. Available from good bookshops.

Live & Work in Belgium, The Netherlands & Luxembourg £8.95 is a guide for those interested in finding temporary or permanent work, starting a business or buying a home in the Benelux countries. Published by Vacation Work, 9 Park End Street, Oxford OX1 1HJ ✆ Oxford (0865) 241978.

Accommodation *Camping*, a leaflet listing by province all camping sites and their facilities, is available from the Belgian National Tourist Office, see above.

Le CHAB, Hôtel de Jeunes, rue Traversière 8, 1030 Brussels is an inexpensive international accommodation centre, with 1-8 bedded rooms or dormitories. Cost from BF290 for bed and breakfast plus BF80 linen charge. Garden, bar-restaurant, TV, left luggage lockers and laundry service. Walking tours organised in summer.

Cheap accommodation for young people is available at Maison Internationale, chaussée de Wavre 205, 1040 Brussels, based in a former monastery. Cost from BF450 per night includes shower and breakfast. TV room, small restaurant and laundry service. Also youth camping site for cyclists situated in a large park, BF220 per night including breakfast.

Rijksuniversiteit Gent, Mrs K Van Den Broeck, Department of Guest Accommodation, Home A Vermeylen, Stalhof 6, 9000 Gent has cheap accommodation in single rooms in 2 halls of residence, 15 July-15 September. Bed and breakfast BF500 per night. Restaurant available.

The Youth Hostel Jacques Brel, 30 rue de la Sablonnière, 1000 Brussels ✆ Brussels (2) 218 0187, is centrally placed and offers cheap short stay accommodation for young people.

AU PAIR/CHILDCARE

Au pair posts are open to men and women aged 16-30. They are expected to work a maximum of 4 hours per day in return for pocket money, board and lodging, and must follow a language course in a recognised school.
On arrival in Belgium au pairs who are EC nationals must register with the local Communal Administration within 8 days, submitting proof of having enroled at a language school. They must also ensure that they are adequately covered in case of accident or illness, either by being in possession of an E111 form or by being included in the host family's health insurance scheme.
Prospective au pairs who are not EC nationals must apply for an *autorisation de séjour provisoire (ASP)* through the Belgian embassy in their country of residence, and, on arrival in Belgium must apply for a work permit. The host family must also draw up and sign a contract of employment, to be approved by the local Communal Administration.

The following agencies can arrange au pair and childcare placements in Belgium:

ACADEMY AU PAIR AGENCY LTD Glenlea, Dulwich Common, London SE21 7ES ✆ 081-299 4599
Can place au pairs. Ages 18-27. Some knowledge of French or Dutch essential. Pocket money approx £30-£35 per week.
Administration charge £40. Positions as nannies and mothers' helps also available for those with qualifications/experience.

ANGLIA AGENCY 70 Southsea Avenue, Leigh-on-Sea, Essex ✆ Southend-on-Sea (0702) 471648
Can place au pairs, mothers' helps and nannies. Ages 17+. Pocket money £30+ per week. Service charge £40.

HELPING HANDS AU PAIR & DOMESTIC AGENCY 39 Rutland Avenue, Thorpe Bay, Essex SS1 2XJ ✆ Southend-on-Sea (0702) 602067
Can place au pairs and mothers' helps. Ages 18-27. Pocket money approx £30 per week au pairs, higher for mothers' helps. Introduction fee £40 on acceptance of a family. *UK nationals only.*

INTERNATIONAL CATHOLIC SOCIETY FOR GIRLS (ACISJF) St Patrick's International Youth Centre, 24 Great Chapel Street, London W1V 3AF ✆ 071-734 2156
Au pair posts arranged for 9+ months. Ages 18+. Mainly for UK and Irish nationals.

LANGTRAIN INTERNATIONAL Torquay Road, Foxrock, Dublin 18, Ireland ✆ Dublin (1) 289 3876
Can place au pairs in Belgian families. Ages 18+. Pocket money approx £25-£40 per week. Placement fee £55.

PROBLEMS UNLIMITED AGENCY 86 Alexandra Road, Windsor, Berkshire SL4 1HU ✆ Windsor (0753) 830101
Can place au pairs. Ages 18-27. Pocket money £30-£35 per week. Service charge £40.

STUDENTS ABROAD LTD 11 Milton View, Hitchin, Hertfordshire SG4 0QD ✆ Hitchin (0462) 438909
Can place au pairs and mothers' helps. Ages 18-27 for au pairs. Basic knowledge of French preferred. Pocket money £30-£35 per week; higher for mothers' helps. Service charge £40.

UNIVERSAL CARE Chester House, 9 Windsor End, Beaconsfield, Buckinghamshire HP9 2JJ ✆ Beaconsfield (0494) 678811
Can place au pairs and mothers' helps. Ages 17-27 (au pairs) or 18-30 (mothers' helps). Basic knowledge of French essential. Pocket money £25 per week, higher for mothers' helps. Service charge £47. PH *Apply 2 months before work period desired. EC nationals only.*

COMMUNITY WORK

ATD QUART MONDE Avenue Victor Jacobs 12, 1040 Brussels ✆ Brussels (2) 6479900
Strives to protect and guarantee the fundamental rights of the poorest and most disadvantaged and excluded families, which constitute the Fourth World. These rights include the right to family life, to education and training, and to representation.

Volunteers are required to undertake varied manual and construction work on two centres in Brussels, under the direction of permanent, trained volunteers. Work includes masonry, carpentry, painting, roof and floor tiling. Ages 18+. No experience necessary but applicants should be interested in better understanding the causes and effects of persistent poverty and willing to work hard with others as a team. Approx 30 hour week. 2/3 weeks, July. Dormitory accommodation and insurance provided, but not travel. Volunteers take it in turns to cook. Participants should take a sleeping bag and all-weather working clothes. Cost BF800.

CONSERVATION

BRITISH TRUST FOR CONSERVATION VOLUNTEERS Room IWH, 36 St Mary's Street, Wallingford, Oxfordshire OX10 0EU
The largest charitable organisation in Britain to involve people in practical conservation work. Following the success of the Natural Break programme in the UK, BTCV is now developing a series of international working holidays with the aim of introducing volunteers to practical conservation projects abroad. It is hoped that the British volunteers will adapt to and learn from local lifestyles as well as participate in the community.

Projects last for 2-3 weeks and are based at the Château Braive. Work is on the management of the estate, a nature reserve being adapted for disabled access. Ages 18-70. Cost from £50 per week includes food and accommodation; everyone shares in domestic chores. Membership fee £12. No fares or wages paid.

NATUUR 2000 Flemish Youth Federation for the Study of Nature & Environmental Conservation, Bervoetstraat 33, 2000 Antwerp
Organises conservation activities such as management of nature reserves and smaller landscape elements, species protection, waste recycling, campaigns against sea pollution and solidarity campaigns on acid rain, tropical rain forests, pesticides and Arctic/Antarctic problems. Arranges nature study and conservation camps in Dutch-speaking areas of Belgium. Volunteers, preferably with experience in field biology are required to help lead the study camps which have recently included monitoring a bat reserve in an old fortress near Antwerp. Ages 15+. Knowledge of Dutch, French or English needed. July and August. Food, accommodation, insurance and travel from Antwerp to site provided. Visas/work permits arranged if necessary. Cost from BF1000, depending on type of camp, duration and location. Help is also needed in the office, 40 hour week, all year. Experience preferred.

COURIERS/REPS

EUROCAMP Summer Jobs, (Ref WH), PO Box 170, Liverpool L70 1ES
One of Europe's leading tour operators, specialising in providing quality camping and mobile home holidays for families throughout Europe. Campsite couriers are required: work involves cleaning tents and equipment prior to the arrival of new customers; checking, replacing and making repairs on equipment; replenishing gas supplies; keeping basic accounts and reporting on a weekly basis to England. Couriers are also expected to meet new arrivals and assist holidaymakers with any problems that arise; organise activities and parties; provide information on local tourist attractions and maintain an information noticeboard. At the beginning and end of the season couriers are also expected to help in erecting and dismantling tents.
Couriers need to be flexible to meet the needs of customers and be on hand where necessary; they will be able to organise their own free time as the workload allows.
Ages 18+. Applicants should be independent, adaptable, reliable, physically fit, have plenty of initiative and relish a challenging and

responsible position. Good working knowledge of French/Dutch also necessary. Preference given to those able to work the whole season, April-September/October; contracts also available for first half season, April-mid July and second half season, mid July-September/October.

Children's couriers are also required, with the energy and enthusiasm to organise a wide range of exciting activities for groups of children aged 4-13. Experience of working with children within this age range is essential, but language ability is not a requirement. Ages 20+. Children's couriers must be available for the whole season, May-September.

For both positions the salary is £91.50 per week. Training is provided together with accommodation in frame tent with cooking facilities, insurance and return travel.
UK/EC passport-holders only. Early application advisable; interviews start September/October.

TEACHERS

BELGIAN EMBASSY 103 Eaton Square, London SW1W 9AB ✆ 071-235 5422
Publish *Posts for Foreign Teachers in Belgium,* a list giving the addresses of international English-speaking schools that may be able to offer teaching posts.

WORKCAMPS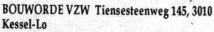

BOUWORDE VZW Tiensesteenweg 145, 3010 Kessel-Lo
A Catholic organisation which expresses solidarity with people in distress through creating better living environments. Volunteers undertake construction work under the guidance of experienced leaders. Recent projects have included painting doors and window-frames at a crisis centre in Antwerp; laying concrete at a youth centre in Vlezenbeek; painting and decorating in the Brussels offices of an organisation running projects in the Third World; and working in the grounds of a home for autistic people in Vollezele.
Ages 18+. No experience required but a keen attitude necessary. 8 hour day, 5 day week. 2-3

weeks, July-September. Full board, lodging and insurance provided. Volunteers pay their own travel. Registration fee BF1500.

CARREFOUR CHANTIERS 25 boulevard de l'Empereur, 1000 Brussels
An international movement open to all who share a common concern for lasting peace and justice in the world. Volunteers are needed to work in international teams on summer projects aimed at offering a service in an area of need and promoting self-help within the community, promoting international understanding and the discussion of social problems, and offering young people the chance to live as a group and take these experiences into the context of daily life. Recent projects have included demolition and renovation work for various youth and ecology movements; gardening work for a religious community which acts as a place of retreat for young people with problems; helping in a centre for the physically handicapped; and working with Spanish and Arabic immigrant families. Ages 18-30. Knowledge of French required on some camps. 6 hour day, 30-36 hour week. 2-4 weeks, July, August and October. Food, school, centre or tent accommodation and insurance provided; participants pay own travel costs.

Apply through partner organisation in country of residence. In the UK: Christian Movement for Peace, Bethnal Green United Reformed Church, Pott Street, London E2 0EF

Outside the UK: please see information on page 30.

SERVICE CIVIL INTERNATIONAL (SCI) rue Van Elewyck 35, 1050 Brussels
VRIJWILLIGE INTERNATIONALE AKTIE (VIA) Draakstraat 37, 2018 Antwerp
Service Civil International promotes international reconciliation through work projects. Volunteers are invited to work on workcamps organised by these two branches in Belgium. Recent projects organised by SCI include building a mini North-South village reflecting world cultural differences for children in Cuesmes; repairing toys and restoring the buildings of a toy museum in Brussels; and building solar collectors and a waterwheel at a biological farm near Namur. Recent projects organised by VIA include

preparing for an annual music festival featuring African and Latin American bands in Boechout; rebuilding an old watermill in Dworp; and gardening and indoor renovation work alongside residents of a home for elderly people in Eindhout-Laakdal. Good knowledge of French/Dutch needed for some camps. Ages 18+. Applicants should be highly motivated and prepared to work hard as part of a team. 35-40 hour week; 2-4 weeks, June-September. Food, accommodation and insurance provided. Volunteers pay their own travel costs **B D PH W** depending on project.

Apply through partner organisation in country of residence. In the UK: International Voluntary Service, Old Hall, East Bergholt, Colchester, Essex CO7 6TQ.

Outside the UK: please see information on page 30.

GENERAL

EUROYOUTH LTD 301 Westborough Road, Westcliff, Southend-on-Sea, Essex SS0 9PT
C **Southend-on-Sea (0702) 341434**
Holiday stays arranged where guests are offered board and lodging in return for an agreed number of hours English conversation with hosts or their children. Time is also available for guests to practise the host language if desired. Mainly ages 15-25, but sometimes opportunities for ages 13-16 and for older applicants. 2-3 weeks, June-August. Travel and insurance arranged by applicants. Registration fee approx £70. Number of places limited. *Apply at least 12 weeks prior to scheduled departure date. UK nationals only.*

APPLYING FOR A JOB

Before applying, read carefully all the information given. Unless otherwise indicated, applications should be made in writing. Check in particular:

✐ skills, qualifications or experience required

✐ the full period of employment expected

✐ any restrictions of age, sex or nationality

✐ application deadlines

✐ any other points, particularly details of insurance cover, and other costs you may have to bear such as travel and accommodation.

When writing to any organisation it is **essential** to mention **Working Holidays 1993** and to enclose a large, stamped, self-addressed envelope, or if overseas, a large addressed envelope and at least two International Reply Coupons (available at Post Offices). When applying be sure to include the following:

✐ name, address, date of birth, nationality, sex

✐ education, qualifications, relevant experience, skills, languages spoken

✐ period of availability

✐ a passport-size photo, particularly if you are to have contact with the public

✐ anything else asked for, eg a *cv*

INFORMATION

Bulgarian Embassy
186-188 Queen's Gate, London SW7 5HL
✆ 071-584 9400/9433

British Embassy
Boulevard Vassil Levski 65-67, Sofia 1000

Tourist office
Bulgarian National Tourist Office, 18 Princes
Street, London W1R 7RE ✆ 071-499 6988

Youth hostels
Union Bulgare de Tourisme, Boulevard Vassil
Levski 18, Sofia 1000

Youth & student information
Orbita Chain for Youth Tourism, Boulevard
Alexander Stamboliski 45a, Sofia

Entry regulations Details of entry
requirements can be obtained from the Visa
Section of the Bulgarian Embassy.
Employers/workcamp organisers recruiting for
work in Bulgaria will usually assist with
arranging a visa.

Travel Campus Travel, 52 Grosvenor Gardens,
London SW1 0AG ✆ 071-730 3402 (offices
throughout the UK) offer Eurotrain under 26
fares and youth and student airfares to
Bulgaria.

Accommodation Orbita Chain for Youth
Tourism, see above, offer accommodation at
student hostels in Sofia, Varna, Veliko Turnovo,
and in the Rhodope Mountains during July and
August. Also maintain international youth
centres for recreation and study.

Lonely Planet's *Eastern Europe on a Shoestring*
£13.95 provides practical information on
budget travel in Bulgaria and most other east
European countries.
The Rough Guide to Eastern Europe £7.95 is a
practical handbook covering Bulgaria, Hungary
and Romania, packed with useful and unusual
information.
Both books are available from all good
bookshops.

COURIERS/REPS

CRYSTAL HOLIDAYS Crystal House, The Courtyard, Arlington Road, Surbiton, Surrey KT6 6BW ✆ 081-390 8737
Tour operator arranging skiing holidays in Borovets and Pamporova. Representatives are required to meet and greet clients and be responsible for their welfare during their holiday. Ski guides and chalet staff also required. Ages 20-35. Previous experience and fluent Bulgarian desirable. Chalet staff must have catering qualifications and experience. Approx 60 hour, 6½ or 7 day week, December-April. Basic salary plus commission; board, lodging, insurance, travel costs and uniform provided. 1 week training seminar held at beginning of each season. *Apply April/May.*

LEADERS

SKI ARDMORE 11-15 High Street, Marlow, Buckinghamshire SL7 1AU ✆ Marlow (0628) 890060
Organise skiing holidays for school groups in the resort of Borovets, 70km south of Sofia. Ski leaders are required to supervise groups of up to 10 children and help run evening activities. Applicants must be good skiers with experience of working with youngsters. First aid qualification required. Ages 20+. Hours flexible, approx 60 hours per week. 1-8 weeks, December-April. Wages from £50 per week, full board hotel accommodation, insurance and travel costs provided. Training day held in December.

WORKCAMPS

ARGO-M Boulevard Stamboliski 2A, Sofia 1000
Volunteers are invited to participate on international workcamps with more than 100 volunteers from over 35 countries. Recent projects have included archaeological excavations in Plovdiv and Russe; renovating a children's theatre in Ravda; and environmental work around the lakes of the Rila Plateau. Also discussions on voluntary youth service for peace, detente and disarmament, East/West friendship, plus solidarity and cultural/sports events. Ages 18-30. Previous workcamp/community work experience and an interest in East/West relations essential. Knowledge of Russian or German useful. 8 hour day, 5 day week. 3 weeks, August. Board, lodging, working clothes and travel within Bulgaria provided. 5 day educational tour of cultural and historical sites arranged after the workcamp, for which a small fee may be charged.

Apply through partner organisation in country of residence. In the UK: Quaker International Social Projects, Friends House, Euston Road, London NW1 2BJ.

Outside the UK: please see information on page 30.

INFORMATION

Canadian High Commission
Macdonald House, 1 Grosvenor Square, London
W1X 0AB ✆ 071-629 9492

Immigration Section: 38 Grosvenor Street,
London W1X 0AA ✆ 071-409 2071

British High Commission
80 Elgin Street, Ottawa, Ontario K1P 5K7

Tourist office
Tourism Programme, Canadian High
Commission, Canada House, Trafalgar Square,
London SW1Y 5BJ ✆ 071-629 9492

Youth hostels
Canadian Hostelling Association, National
Office, 33 River Road, Tower A-3, Vanier,
Ottawa, Ontario K1L 8H9

Youth & student information
Association of Student Councils (Canada),
171 College Street, Toronto, Ontario M5T 1P7

Canadian Bureau for International Education,
85 Albert Street, Ottawa, Ontario K1P 6A4

Tourbec (1979) inc, 1178 Avenue Cartier,
Quebec City, Quebec G1R 2S7

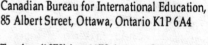

Entry regulations Employment Authorisation
is required for all types of employment, and
application should be made to the Canadian
Immigration Division Office. Authorisation
cannot be issued until the prospective employer
has obtained certification from a Canadian
employment centre to say that no qualified
Canadian citizen or landed immigrant is
available to fill the job in question. An
Authorisation only becomes valid when
stamped at the port of entry. Employment
opportunities for visitors are therefore
extremely restricted.
However, a limited number of foreign students
are admitted to Canada each year under an
international student summer employment
programme. Under this programme,
authorisation is granted to students who have
been offered employment in Canada, without

the vacancy first having been advertised to Canadian nationals. Applicants must obtain an offer of employment by their own means and having done so, produce written proof of the offer, showing position, salary, and working conditions. Authorisation is issued only for the job specified in the application, and is normally valid for a maximum of 20 weeks.

UK applicants must produce written proof that they are British citizens, and bona fide full-time students of British or Irish universities or similar institutions (including students who have been accepted for admission in the current year), and that they will be returning after the vacation period to continue their course of study. A number of organisations in the UK operate Exchange Visitor Programmes which help students to find employment in Canada. As the number of places is limited, applications should be made as early as possible. An additional student programme is now available whereby an offer of pre-arranged employment is not required, but evidence of funds needs to be produced along with a medical certificate and evidence of student status.

Those travelling to Canada and planning to remain there for an extended period may be required to prove at the time of entry that they have sufficient means to maintain themselves and have evidence of onward reservations. Those under 18 not accompanied by an adult should have a letter from a parent/guardian giving them permission to travel to Canada. Those wishing to work or study in Canada should contact the High Commission for further information before seeking admission. Information sheets *Do You Want to Work Temporarily in Canada?* and *Do You Want to Visit Canada?* can be obtained from the Immigration Section of the Canadian High Commission.

Travel Campus Travel, 52 Grosvenor Gardens, London SW1W 0AG ℂ 071-730 8111 (offices throughout the UK) and Council Travel, 28A Poland Street, London W1V 3DB ℂ 071-437 7767 (offices also in Paris, Lyon, Düsseldorf, Tokyo and throughout the US) offer low-cost student/youth airfares to destinations in Canada and issues rail and bus passes. Accommodation, tours and travel insurance also available.

North-South Travel, Moulsham Mill, Parkway, Chelmsford CM2 7PX ℂ Chelmsford (0245) 492882 arranges competitively priced, reliably planned flights to all parts of Canada. Profits are paid into a trust fund for the assignment of aid to projects in the poorest areas of the South.

STA Travel, 74 Old Brompton Road, London SW7 3LQ/117 Euston Road, London NW1 2SX ℂ 071-937 9971 (offices also in Birmingham, Bristol, Cambridge, Leeds, Manchester and Oxford), operates flexible, low-cost flights to destinations throughout Canada.

The Canrailpass provides unlimited travel at a fixed cost over the entire rail network or over any of 3 designated territories. Cost from Can$220, 30 days nationwide. Greyhound Bus passes also available from £65 (7 days low season). Details from Compass GSA, PO Box 113, Peterborough, Cambridgeshire PE1 1LE ℂ Peterborough (0733) 51780.

Publications Lonely Planet's *Canada - A Travel Survival Kit* £12.95 offers practical, down-to-earth information for independent travellers wanting to explore beyond the usual tourist routes.
The Rough Guide to Canada £9.99 provides comprehensive background information on Canada plus details on getting there, getting around, places to explore and cheap places to stay.
Culture Shock! Canada £6.95 introduces the reader to the people, customs, ceremonies, food and culture of Canada, with checklists of dos and don'ts.
Travellers Survival Kit USA and Canada £9.95, is a down-to-earth, entertaining guide for travellers to North America. Describes how to cope with the inhabitants, officialdom and way of life in Canada and the US. Published by Vacation Work Publications, 9 Park End Street, Oxford OX1 1HJ ℂ Oxford (0865) 241978.

All the above are available from good bookshops.

Canada Travel Information provides helpful practical hints covering health, climate, travel and accommodation. Available from Tourism Programme, Canadian High Commission, see above.

The Moneywise Guide to North America £11.10 including postage, provides essential information for anyone travelling on a budget in Canada, the US and Mexico, with useful information on getting around, where to stay, what to eat and places to visit. Published by BUNAC, 16 Bowling Green Lane, London EC1R OBD ✆ 071-251 3472.

Information centres The Canadian Bureau for International Education, 85 Albert Street, 14th floor, Ottawa, Ontario K1P 6A4 provides information and publications on international work, study and exchange, and a reception service for incoming students at Canadian international airports, August and September.

Accommodation No-frills accommodation available in a hostel in the heart of Old Quebec. Cost Can$13.75-$15.75 per night, plus membership fee. 4-8 bedded rooms, washing facilities, TV lounge and baggage check-in. Cafeteria on premises. No age limits. Apply to Centre International de Séjour de Quebec, 19 rue Ste-Ursule, Quebec G1R 4E1. PH W

The YMCA of Greater New York operates the Ys Way International, 356 West 34th Street, New York, NY 10001, United States. This programme offers inexpensive accommodation at YMCAs in major cities in Canada and the US. Average cost US$30 per night includes use of sports facilities. Details in Britain from Travel Cuts UK, 295A Regent Street, London W1R 7YA ✆ 071-637 3161.

CHILDCARE/ DOMESTIC

At present there is no au pair scheme in Canada, although similar employment for foreign nationals exists under the Live-in Caregiver Program. To qualify, applicants must be over 18, with at least 6 months experience of childcare or similar work; or professional qualifications in childcare such as NNEB, Scotvec or City & Guilds. Applications for temporary entry into Canada under the Live-in Caregiver Program must be made to the Immigration Section of the Canadian High Commission once an offer of employment has been made. Applicants may have to attend an interview, and a medical examination is required, after which applications take 4-6 weeks to process. Processing fee Can$75.

ACADEMY AU PAIR AGENCY LTD Glenlea, Dulwich Common, London SE21 7ES ✆ 081-299 4599
Can place nannies and mothers' helps throughout the year. 12 months minimum. Ages 18+. Applicants must have at least 6 months' childcare experience and full driving licence. Salary approx £100-£150 per week plus board and lodging. Travel, insurance and visa costs paid by applicants. Administration charge £40.

ANGLIA AGENCY 70 Southsea Avenue, Leigh-on-Sea, Essex ✆ Southend-on-Sea (0702) 471648
Positions for mothers' helps and nannies arranged throughout the year. Salary, board and lodging provided. 6+ months. Ages 18+. Travel costs paid by applicants. Service charge £40.

ANGLO PAIR AGENCY 40 Wavertree Road, Streatham Hill, London SW2 3SP ✆ 081-674 3605
Arranges childcare posts in Canada. Applicants must have at least 6 months' experience and a qualification in childcare. 5-6 hour day, plus limited babysitting with one full day free and time to study if required. Ages 18-27. 12 month stay usually required. Pocket money approx Can$5 per hour. Agency fee £40. Advice given on travel and insurance.

AVALON AGENCY Thursley House, 53 Station Road, Shalford, Guildford, Surrey GU4 8HA ✆ Guildford (0483) 63640
Positions available for mothers' helps, nannies and housekeepers. Ages 18+. Applicants should be single females, preferably with NNEB, minimum 1 year experience, and a valid driving licence; non-smokers preferred. Salary varies according to family and area; usually over Can$350 per month with full board. West Canada is approx Can$100 per month higher than the east. Contract is for 11½ months; 1½ days per week free. Travel paid by applicants, but return fare may be paid. Medical insurance essential, approx Can$30-$40 per month.

NANNIES UNLIMITED INC PO Box 5864, Station A, Calgary, Alberta T2H 1X4
Can place nannies and domestics in Calgary, Edmonton, Toronto, Regina, Vancouver and the North West Territories. Ages 18+. Applicants must speak English or French, have six months' related childcare/elderly training, and at least 5 O levels/GCSEs. 47½ hour week. Salary from Can$614 per month and accommodation with family in own room. Medical insurance available at nominal cost. Assistance given with obtaining a visa.

STUDENTS ABROAD LTD 11 Milton View, Hitchin, Hertfordshire SG4 0QD ✆ Hitchin (0462) 438909
Can place mothers' helps and nannies for a minimum of 1 year. Ages 18+. Applicants should be NNEB qualified or equivalent, or with a minimum of 1 year's live-in experience. References essential; drivers preferred. Board and lodging provided. Salary, dependent on experience and qualifications, approx Can$600 per month after deductions. Applicants pay their own fare. Service charge £40, including advice on formalities. *Allow minimum of 3 months to obtain work permit.*

CONSERVATION

CANADIAN PARKS SERVICE National Volunteer Coordinator, 25 Eddy Street, Ottawa, Ontario K1A 0H3 ✆ Hull (819) 994 5127
The federal agency responsible for protected examples of Canada's natural and cultural heritage. Aims to encourage public understanding, appreciation and enjoyment of this heritage in ways which will leave it unimpaired for future generations. Workers are needed in national parks, historic sites and canals across Canada. Voluntary positions exist to assist and enhance new programmes in natural resource management, cultural resource management, interpretation, visitor services and maintenance. Volunteers may serve as assistants interpreting or animating the history of a park, hosting in a campground, collecting data on flora and fauna in a park, maintaining or building trails, designing posters, photographing historic artefacts or wildlife, or keeping library files. Experience essential for applicants from outside Canada; degrees desirable for some positions. No age restrictions. Working languages English and French; bilingual applicants particularly welcome; fluency in Japanese or German an advantage. 2-40 hour week, depending on project. Direct expenses reimbursed; general liability insurance provided. Volunteers pay travel, accommodation and food costs. *Apply before January for summer and autumn positions; before July for winter and spring.*

FARMWORK

INTERNATIONAL AGRICULTURAL EXCHANGE ASSOCIATION YFC Centre, National Agricultural Centre, Stoneleigh Park, Kenilworth, Warwickshire CV8 2LG ✆ Coventry (0203) 696578
Operates opportunities for young people involved in agriculture, horticulture or home management to acquire practical work experience, and to strengthen and improve their knowledge and understanding of the way of life in other countries. Participants are given an opportunity to study practical methods on approved training farms, and work as trainees, gaining further experience in their chosen field. Types of farm include mixed (grain production and livestock); grain; dairy and crop; beef; poultry; plus a limited number of bee, horse and horticultural enterprises. Participants undertake paid work on the farm, approx 45 hours per week, and live as a member of the host family. Full board, lodging, insurance cover and minimum net weekly wage of £50-£60 provided. All programmes include 3/4 weeks unpaid holiday. 4 day orientation seminar held at agricultural colleges and universities throughout Canada. Stopovers (2-4 days) in Singapore/Thailand and Hawaii arranged for participants en route for the 14 month programme. Ages 18-30. Applicants should be single, and have good practical experience in the chosen training category, plus a valid driving licence. 9 months (departing February); 7 months (departing April); 14 months - 7 in Australia/New Zealand plus 7 in Canada (departing September). Cost from £1575 covers airfare, work permit, placement with a host family, travel costs to placement, administration fee, orientation seminar,

information meetings, and supervision. £200 deposit payable. *Apply at least 4 months in advance. UK or Irish passport-holders only.*

Canadian applicants requiring an exchange should apply to IAEA, 206-1501-17 Avenue SW, Calgary, Alberta T2T 0E2.

WILLING WORKERS ON ORGANIC FARMS (WWOOF CANADA) RR 2, Carlson Road S18 C9, Nelson, British Columbia V1L 5P5

A non-profitmaking organisation which aims to help organic farmers and smallholders whose work is often labour intensive, as it does not rely on artificial fertilisers or pesticides. Provides voluntary workers with first hand experience of organic farming and gardening on approx 60 host farms throughout Canada, on homesteads on the East Coast (Nova Scotia and New Brunswick), in Quebec, Ontario, Alberta and British Columbia. The work can include weeding, milking cows, apple picking and cleaning out stalls. Members receive a detailed farm description and address list of places needing help. Ages 16+. Hours vary from one farm to another. Integration into the farm family is valued, including recreational possibilities. Work available all year but especially between early spring and late autumn. Full board and lodging in own room, cabin or tent provided, but volunteers should take a sleeping bag. Opportunity on some farms to learn skills. Insurance and anti-tetanus vaccination recommended. Membership fee Can$20 and 2 IRCs. *EC nationals only.*

MONITORS &
TEACHERS

BRITISH UNIVERSITIES NORTH AMERICA CLUB (BUNAC) 16 Bowling Green Lane, London EC1R 0BD ✆ 071-251 3472

A non-profit, non-political educational student club which aims to encourage interest and understanding between students in Britain and North America. A very limited number of opportunities available for young people to work as Counselors on summer camps in Canada. The camps are permanent sites and cater for 40-600 children at a time. Camps can be organised privately, by the YMCA, Girl Scouts or Salvation Army, or they can be institutional camps for the physically, socially or mentally handicapped. Work involves living, working and playing with groups of 3-8 children aged 6-16. General Counselors are responsible for the full-time supervision of their group, ensuring that the children follow the set routine and providing counsel and friendship. They must therefore have fairly general experience and aptitude in the handling of children. Specialist Counselors must have a sporting/craft interest, qualifications or skills plus ability and enthusiasm to organise or teach specific activities. These include sports, watersports, music, arts and crafts, science, pioneering, entertainments and dance. Counselors with secretarial skills are also needed for office work. Ages 19½ (by 1 July)-35. Applicants must be resident in the UK, single, hard working as hours are long, with a genuine love of children and relevant experience. They should be able to show firm, fair leadership and be flexible, cooperative, energetic, conscientious, cheerful, patient, positive, able to adapt to new situations, and to function enthusiastically in a structured setting. 8/9+ weeks, with 1 day off most weeks, mid June-end August, followed by 1-6 weeks free for travel after the camp. Return flight, overnight hostel accommodation, transfer to camp, orientation and training, guide to North America plus board and lodging at the camp provided. Counselors live with the children in log cabins or tents. Registration fee £50 (1992). Insurance fee approx £84. Salary approx US$370 (US$430 for those aged 21+). Suitable for students, teachers, social workers and those with other relevant qualifications. Interviews held throughout the UK, mid November-early May. Compulsory orientation programme held at Easter. Membership fee £3. *Early application advisable; places limited.*

Irish applicants should apply to USIT, Aston Quay, O'Connell Bridge, Dublin 2 ✆ Dublin (1) 778117.

When writing to any organisation it is essential to mention Working Holidays 1993 and enclose a large stamped, self-addressed envelope, or if overseas, a large addressed envelope and at least two International Reply Coupons.

WORKCAMPS

CANADIAN BUREAU FOR INTERNATIONAL EDUCATION 85 Albert Street, 14th floor, Ottawa, Ontario K1P 6A4
Volunteers are invited to work on international workcamps. Recent projects have included building a garden for the blind and helping at a summer camp for mentally handicapped children in British Columbia; building an ocean adventure park for disabled children at Victoria; and helping handicapped visitors with activities at a holiday centre on Lake Joseph. Ages 18+. 2-4 weeks, July-September. Opportunities for hiking, swimming, biking and canoeing. Food, accommodation in tents or cabins, and insurance provided, but not travel. **B D**

Apply through partner organisation in country of residence. In the UK: United Nations Association, International Youth Service, Temple of Peace, Cathays Park, Cardiff CF1 3AP © Cardiff (0222) 223088.

Outside the UK: please see information on page 30.

FRONTIERS FOUNDATION INC Operation Beaver, 2615 Danforth Avenue, Suite 203, Toronto, Ontario M4C 1L6 © Toronto (416) 690 3930
Frontiers Foundation is a community development voluntary service organisation which works in partnership with requesting communities in low-income, rural areas across Canada. Projects help to provide and improve adequate housing, training and recreational activities in developing regions. Ages 18+. Volunteers must be available for a minimum of 12 weeks. Skills in carpentry, plumbing and electrical work are preferred for construction projects; previous social service and experience with children are preferred for recreation projects. Projects run all year; new volunteers are recruited between April and November. All accommodation, food and travel inside Canada provided. Travel outside Canada paid by applicants. Long-term projects of up to 18 months also available, provided that the volunteer's work is satisfactory after the initial 12 week period. Application kits and forms available upon request.

GENERAL

BRITISH UNIVERSITIES NORTH AMERICA CLUB (BUNAC) 16 Bowling Green Lane, London EC1R 0BD © 071-251 3472
Aims to encourage interest and understanding between students in Britain and North America; a non-profit, non-political educational student club which has enabled many thousands of students to enjoy self-financing working vacations in North America. As well as arranging employment on children's summer camps through the BUNACAMP programme, BUNAC can also assist with an unlimited variety of jobs through their Work Canada programme organised in cooperation with the Canadian Federation of Students. The job does not have to be organised in advance, and participants are able to change jobs once in Canada, if necessary. Those who wish to organise jobs before arrival in Canada will be offered advice on how to do so, and may use BUNAC's own job directory. There are also places outside the summer season, for secondary students in their year between.

The summer programme involves a compulsory orientation in Britain, return transatlantic flight, one night's accommodation followed by an orientation in Canada, work authorisation papers, a guidebook, and the services of BUNAC and CFS in North America. In order to obtain a visa, applicants must have evidence of student status, an orientation course certificate and proof of round-trip transportation. They must also provide evidence that they can support themselves whilst in Canada in one of the following three ways: definite evidence of a job, plus proof that they are taking at least Can$500 with them; definite evidence of sponsorship, plus proof that they are taking at least Can$500 with them; or proof that they are taking at least Can$1000 with them and can thus support themselves with their own funds until they get a job. Ages 18-29. 8/9+ weeks-6 months. Registration fee £65, return flight (1992) £360-£460, and insurance fee £84. A medical in Britain may be necessary, at participant's own expense. Membership fee £3. *Full British passport-holders only. Apply from October/November; closing date end April. Job directory available from January.*

INFORMATION

Embassy of the Russian Federation
13 Kensington Palace Gardens, London W8 4QX
✆ 071-229 3628

Consular section: 5 Kensington Palace Gardens,
London W8 4QS ✆ 071-229 80 27

British Embassy
Naberezhnaya Morisa Toreza 14, Moscow 72

Tourist office
Intourist Travel Limited, 219 Marsh Wall, Isle
of Dogs, London E14 9JF ✆ 071-538 8600

Youth & student information
Sputnik, Youth & Student Tourist Bureau, 15
Kosygin Street, Moscow 117946

Entry regulations The organisations listed here
will all assist participants on their programmes
to obtain the necessary visa for entry into
Russia and/or the republics of the
Commonwealth of Independent States. As a
general rule, participants are sent an official
invitation which they must take along to the
Consulate of the Russian Federation (along
with official documents such as a passport) in
order to obtain a visa. In the UK, visas take at
least 2 weeks to process. Visas for Ukraine are
available on the border only.

Travel Campus Travel, 52 Grosvenor Gardens,
London SW1W 0AG ✆ 071-730 3402 (offices
throughout the UK) and Council Travel, 28A
Poland Street, London W1V 3DB ✆ 071-437
7767 (offices also in Paris, Lyon, Düsseldorf,
Tokyo and throughout the USA) offer low-cost
student/youth airfares to Moscow and St
Petersburg.

Publications Lonely Planet's *USSR - A Travel
Survival Kit* £13.95 offers practical, down-to-
earth information for independent and group
travellers wanting to explore beyond the usual
tourist routes. Available from good bookshops.

*The Travellers Survival Kit Soviet Union &
Eastern Europe* £8.95, is an invaluable guide for
travellers. Contains information including

advice on where to go, travel bargains, budget accommodation and dealing with bureaucracy. Published by Vacation Work, 9 Park End Street, Oxford OX1 1HJ ✆ Oxford (0865) 241978.

TEACHERS

BRIT-POL HEALTH CARE FOUNDATION Gerrard House, Suite 14, Worthing Road, East Preston, West Sussex BN16 1AW ✆ (0903) 859222
Small number of teachers required to work on summer camps for children in the Ukraine. Applicants must be of English mother tongue and have an ability to communicate with children. Ages 20-50. 20-25 hours per week, 3 weeks, July and August. Board and lodging provided in local family, or in self-contained flat with food allowance paid. Return travel provided but not insurance. Also opportunities for qualified and experienced teachers, ages 25+, to teach English, management or administration for 3+ months, all year.
Applications can take up to 3 months to process. UK nationals only.

WORKCAMPS

THE COOPERATION PROJECT Foundation for Ecological Cooperation, Postbus 13844, 2501 EV The Hague, Netherlands THE COOPERATION PROJECT Mir Initiative, PO Box 28183, Washington, DC 20038-8183, United States ✆ (202) 857-8037
An international association of non-governmental organisations committed to promoting multinational perspectives on ecological and social issues. They have been organising international workcamps together since 1989, based at a campsite on the shores of the Bratsk reservoir. Volunteers work as a group, choosing a project of service to the community, for example planting trees and forestry work, maintaining an open-air museum of Russian settlers' homes or helping to build the first church in modern Bratsk. No experience necessary, but applicants should have an interest in cultural exchange, peace work and ecological issues. Knowledge of Russian useful but not essential; English is the working language. Ages 18+; those under 18

may be accepted if it is felt the project is appropriate to them. Approx 6 hour day, 5 day week. 2-3 weeks, July and August. Food and accommodation provided; volunteers should take a sleeping bag. Excursions also organised to Bratsk and Lake Baikal to study the region's history, industry and ecological problems. Cost US$330 (1992) covers board, accommodation, local transportation and emergency medical care under the Russian medical system. Volunteers pay their own fares, visa costs and any extra insurance. Help given in obtaining a visa and inexpensive tickets on the Trans-Siberian Railway. B D PH
Organised by The Cooperation Project, Baikal Foundation, Bratsk Branch, PO Box 52, Bratsk - 18, Irkutsk Region 665718.

Apply through partner organisation in country of residence. In the UK: Quaker International Social Projects, Friends House, Euston Road, London NW1 2BJ (experienced volunteers only) or United Nations Association, International Youth Service, Temple of Peace, Cathays Park, Cardiff CF1 3AP ✆ Cardiff (0222) 223088

Outside the UK: please see information on page 30.

INTERNATIONAL VOLUNTARY SERVICE Old Hall, East Bergholt, Colchester, Essex CO7 6TQ
The British branch of Service Civil International, which promotes international reconciliation through work projects. Cooperates with workcamp organisations based in various CIS republics. Recent projects have included helping with an archaeological dig in Samarkand; cleaning the River Don and practical work at the zoo in Rostov; helping staff at an old people's home in Moscow; restoring the 18th century Stanislav Cathedral in Mogilev; and making toys and repairing the playgrounds at a children's home in Minsk. Study programmes cover a wide range of topics, and visits are organised to local places of interest. Ages 18+. Applicants must have previous workcamp/voluntary work experience, and be prepared to work hard and contribute to team life. 35-40 hour week. 3 weeks, May-August. Food, accommodation and insurance provided, but not travel. Registration fee £85 (students £75, unwaged £70) plus extra fee of £30 to support exchange

programme. Orientation held in Edinburgh/ London prior to departure. **B D PH**

Apply through partner organisation in country of residence; see information on page 30.

STUDENTS FORUM/UFIYC Lviv Polytechnic Institute, Mira St 12, 290646 Lviv, Ukraine
The student organisation of Lviv Polytechnic in the Western Ukraine and the Lviv section of the Ukrainian Foundation for International Youth Cooperation invite volunteers to take part in international workcamps. Recent projects have included working together with the Red Cross Society on a playscheme for physically handicapped children in Tabir; renovating the interior of the 18th century Zolochiv Castle, east of Lviv; and a trip along the Dniepr river, carrying out environmental surveys. Ages 18+. Applicants must be highly motivated and prepared to work hard and contribute to team life. Knowledge of Russian very useful. 2-3 weeks, June-August. Food and accommodation provided, but volunteers pay their own travel and insurance costs.

Apply through partner organisation in country of residence. In the UK: Quaker International Social Projects, Friends House, Euston Road, London NW1 2BJ (experienced volunteers only) or United Nations Association, International Youth Service, Temple of Peace, Cathays Park, Cardiff CF1 3AP © Cardiff (0222) 223088

Outside the UK: please see information on page 30.

YOUTH VOLUNTARY SERVICE (YVS) 7/8 Bol Komsomolski per, Moscow 103982, Russia
Volunteers are invited to take part in international workcamps organised mainly in Russia. Recent projects have included restoring churches and monasteries in Kostroma, Upper Volga; conservation work removing diseased trees in the regional park of Nugush in Bashkira; building a summer house at an orphanage next door to Tolstoy's last home in Tula; and assisting at an archaeological dig at Saray Batu, the ancient city of the Golden Horde in Astrakhan. Study and discussion programmes related to camp themes; visits organised to local places of interest. Ages 18+. Applicants must be highly motivated and prepared to work hard as part of a team.

35-40 hour week. 2 weeks, July-August. Food and accommodation provided, but volunteers must pay their own travel and insurance costs. Camp language usually Russian, sometimes English.

Apply through partner organisation in country of residence. In the UK: United Nations Association, International Youth Service, Temple of Peace, Cathays Park, Cardiff CF1 3AP © Cardiff (0222) 223088

Outside the UK: please see information on page 30.

CZECHOSLOVAKIA

INFORMATION

Czechoslovak Embassy
25 Kensington Palace Gardens, London W8 4QY
© 071-229 1255
Visa section: 28 Kensington Palace Gardens,
London W8 4QY © 071-727 3966-7

British Embassy
Thunovská 14, 12550 Prague 1

Tourist office
Cedok, 17-18 Old Bond Street, London W1X
3DA © 071-629 6058

Youth & student information
Czechoslovak Youth and Students Travel
Bureau (KMC), Zitna ulice 12, 12105 Prague 2

Entry regulations UK and Irish nationals, and
nationals of almost all other European countries
do not require a visa to enter Czechoslovakia.
US nationals do not need a visa for stays of up
to 30 days. Other nationals should check visa
requirements and procedures with the Visa
Section of the Czechoslovak Embassy.
Workcamp organisations will inform
volunteers how to obtain the necessary visa/
permit and hold orientation days, giving
information on all aspects of the work covered
together with some political background and
practical information.

Travel Campus Travel, 52 Grosvenor Gardens,
London SW1W 0AG © 071-730 3402 (offices
throughout the UK) and Council Travel, 28A
Poland Street, London W1V 3DB © 071-437
7767 (offices also in Paris, Lyon, Düsseldorf,
Tokyo and throughout the US) offer Eurotrain
under 26 fares and youth and student airfares
to Czechoslovakia.

STA Travel, 74 Old Brompton Road, London
SW7 3LQ/117 Euston Road, London NW1 2SX
© 071-937 9921 (offices also in Birmingham,
Bristol, Cambridge, Leeds, Manchester and
Oxford) operates low-cost flights to Prague.

Publications Lonely Planet's *Eastern Europe on
a Shoestring* £13.95 provides practical
information on budget travel in Czechoslovakia

and most other east European countries.
The Rough Guide to Czechoslovakia £7.99 and
The Rough Guide to Prague £6.99 are practical
handbooks with concise, up-to-date information
on getting around Czechoslovakia.
All the above are available from good
bookshops.

CONSERVATION

**BRONTOSAURUS MOVEMENT Kancelar
Brontosaura, Bubenska 6, 170 00 Prague 7
✆ Prague (2) 80 29 10**
An independent movement open to anyone
wishing to improve the state of the
environment. Volunteers are invited to take
part in workcamps throughout Czechoslovakia.
Projects include nature conservation,
environmental education and the restoration of
historic monuments. No age limits and no
experience required; camp languages include
English and German. 1-3 weeks, during the
summer. Board and lodging provided in return
for approx 28 hours work per week. Ecological
excursions and training programmes held.
Volunteers pay own travel and insurance.
Apply April-May. **PH**

INEX Gorkeho nam 24, 116 47 Prague 1
A recently established workcamp organisation
aimed at promoting international
understanding, cooperation and leisure
activities through international exchange.
Volunteers are invited to take part in
international workcamps which contribute to
environmental and historical conservation.
Recent projects have included building wooden
paths across peat bogs at a nature reserve in
western Bohemia; track maintenance and
improvement at a steam railway restoration
project in central Slovakia; and cleaning and
restoring Gothic and Renaissance buildings in
the historic city of Znojmo, southern Moravia.
Ages 18+. English is the working language on
all projects. 2 weeks, July-August. Food and
accommodation in schools, tents or dormitories
provided; volunteers arrange their own travel
and insurance. **B D PH**

*Apply through partner organisation in country of
residence. In the UK: International Voluntary
Service, Old Hall, East Bergholt, Colchester, Essex*

CO7 6TQ *or Quaker International Social Projects,
Friends House, Euston Road, London NW1 2BJ
(experienced applicants only) or
United Nations Association, International Youth
Service, Temple of Peace, Cathays Park, Cardiff CF1
3AP ✆ Cardiff (0222) 223088.*

Outside the UK: please see information on page 30.

TEACHERS

**BRIT-POL HEALTH CARE FOUNDATION
Gerrard House, Suite 14, Worthing Road, East
Preston, West Sussex BN16 1AW ✆ (0903)
859222**
Small number of teachers required to work on
summer camps for children in Czechoslovakia.
Applicants must be of English mother tongue
and have an ability to communicate with
children. Ages 20-50. 20-25 hours per week for
3 weeks, July and August. Board and lodging
provided in local family, or in self-contained
flat with food allowance paid. Return travel
provided but not insurance. Also opportunities
for qualified and experienced teachers, ages
25+, to teach English, management or
administration for 3+ months, all year.
*Applications can take up to 3 months to process.
UK nationals only.*

WORKCAMPS

**KLUB MALDYCH CESTOVATELU (KMC)
Malostranske nabrezi 1, 118 00 Prague 1**
Volunteers are invited to take part in
international workcamps concerned with
conservation, construction and agricultural
work. Recent projects have included
environmental protection work in forests and
mountains, historic gardens and castles;
helping at the zoo; teaching English;
agricultural work on cooperative farms; and
building and repair work at youth hostels,
sports centres, camps, monasteries, old people's
homes and cooperatives. Also work/study/
peace camps. Excursions, lectures and
discussions linked to projects, meetings with
youth groups and visits to local places of
interest arranged. Ages 18-35. Previous
workcamp experience or similar voluntary
work experience useful. 40 hour, 5 day week.

2-3 weeks, May-September. Full board and simple lodging provided, but not pocket money. Anti-tetanus injection required. Volunteers pay their own travel. Working language usually English. **B D**

Apply through partner organisation in country of residence. In the UK: Concordia (Youth Service Volunteers) Ltd, Recruitment Secretary, 8 Brunswick Place, Hove, Sussex BN3 1ET ☏ Brighton (0273) 772086 or International Voluntary Service, Old Hall, East Bergholt, Colchester, Essex CO7 6TQ or Quaker International Social Projects, Friends House, Euston Road, London NW1 2BJ (experienced applicants only) or United Nations Association, International Youth Service, Temple of Peace, Cathays Park, Cardiff CF1 3AP ☏ Cardiff (0222) 223088.

Outside the UK: please see information on page 30.

APPLYING FOR A JOB

Before applying, read carefully all the information given. Unless otherwise indicated, applications should be made in writing. Check in particular:

✎ skills, qualifications or experience required

✎ the full period of employment expected

✎ any restrictions of age, sex or nationality

✎ application deadlines

✎ any other points, particularly details of insurance cover, and other costs you may have to bear such as travel and accommodation.

When writing to any organisation it is **essential** to mention **Working Holidays 1993** and to enclose a large, stamped, self-addressed envelope, or if overseas, a large addressed envelope and at least two International Reply Coupons (available at Post Offices). When applying be sure to include the following:

✎ name, address, date of birth, nationality, sex

✎ education, qualifications, relevant experience, skills, languages spoken

✎ period of availability

✎ a passport-size photo, particularly if you are to have contact with the public

✎ anything else asked for, eg a *cv*

DENMARK

INFORMATION

Royal Danish Embassy
55 Sloane Street, London SW1X 9SR ℂ 071-333 0200

British Embassy
Kastelsvej 36/38/40, 2100 Copenhagen 0

Tourist office
Danish Tourist Board, PO Box 2LT, London W1A 2LT ℂ 071-734 2637 *(open 11.00-16.00)*

Youth hostels
Landsforeningen Danmarks Vandrerhjem, Vesterbrogade 39, 1620 Copenhagen V

Youth & student information
Danmarks Internationale Studenterkomite, Skindergade 36, 1159 Copenhagen K

Informationskontoret/Huset, Vester Alle 15, 8000 Århus C

Entry regulations A UK citizen intending to work in Denmark should have a full passport. EC nationals may stay for up to 3 months in order to seek employment. If employment is obtained within this period, the residence permit will be granted automatically. To qualify for a residence permit the job must fulfil certain conditions such as working hours, salary and membership of an employment fund.

Once a job has been found it is necessary to obtain a personal registration number and social security certificate within 5 days by taking personal identification and a statement from the employer to the nearest *Folkeregisteret*. This entitles the employee to use the national health service.

There are no Danish offices operating exclusively as labour exchanges for foreigners; it is practically impossible to get a job without some knowledge of Danish, unless the work is in a restaurant or hotel where English is usually required. Permission to stay for more than 3 months must be obtained from the Department for Supervision of Aliens; for EC citizens this is a formality if they have a job.

Job advertising Frank L Crane (London) Ltd, International Press Representatives, 5/15 Cromer Street, Grays Inn Road, London WC1H 8LS ✆ 071-837 3330 can place job advertisements in *Berlingske Tidende* and *Metropol*, both leading Danish newspapers.

Travel The Nordic Tourist Ticket entitles the holder to unlimited travel on trains in Denmark, Finland, Norway and Sweden, and is also valid on some inter-Scandinavian ferries. Valid for 21 days, cost £115 for ages under 26, and £155 for ages over 26. Available from Norwegian State Railways, 21-24 Cockspur Street, London SW1Y 5DA ✆ 071-930 6666.

Campus Travel, 52 Grosvenor Gardens, London SW1W 0AG ✆ 071-730 3402 (offices throughout the UK) and Council Travel, 28A Poland Street, London W1V 3DB ✆ 071-437 7767 (offices also in Paris, Lyon, Düsseldorf, Tokyo and throughout the US) offer Eurotrain under 26 fares and youth and student airfares to Denmark.

Publications Lonely Planet's *Scandinavian and Baltic Europe on a Shoestring* £10.95 offers practical, down-to-earth information for the low-budget, independent traveller in Denmark and the Faroe Islands.
The Rough Guide to Scandinavia £8.95 provides comprehensive background information on Denmark and the Faroe Islands, with details on getting there, getting around, places to explore and cheap places to stay.
Michael's Guide to Scandinavia £10.95 is detailed and concise, providing invaluable practical advice for all kinds of travellers. Published by Inbal Travel.
All the above are available from good bookshops.

Map and General Travel Information leaflet provides information on travel, customs and entry formalities, residence and employment, the health service and other practical information. Available from the Danish Tourist Board, see above, price £1.50.

Information centres The Use-It Youth Information Centre Copenhagen, Rådhusstraede 13, 1466 Copenhagen K issue an information pack including *Working in Denmark*, a leaflet outlining help in looking for employment. Also produce *Playtime*, a newspaper intended as an alternative guide to Copenhagen for low-budget visitors, with advice on travel, food and accommodation, cultural attractions, practical information and a list of alternative organisations. Also provide poste restante and travel help/hitch hiking link services, plus free locker facilities.

Accommodation The Danish Tourist Board, see above, publish *Camping*, a list of 500 officially approved camping sites. Free brochures also available on youth hostels and hotels.

Bellahoj Camping, Hvidekildevej, 2400 Copenhagen NV is a campsite 5 km from the centre of Copenhagen, open 1 June-1 September, cost DKr34 per night. A camping pass is required on all campsites in Copenhagen, obtainable from campsite wardens, price DKr24, and valid all year.

The Use-It Youth Information Centre Copenhagen, see above, publish *Housing in Copenhagen* giving information on private rooms for rent, flats, bedsits, student halls and communes.

Copenhagen Sleep-In, Per Henrik Lings Allé 6, 2100 Copenhagen 0, is a hostel with 452 beds in 4-bedded rooms. Free hot showers. Open mid June-end August. Cost DKr85 per night, bed and breakfast; take your own sleeping bag.

A hostel within walking distance from Central Station is the City Public Hostel, Absalonsgade 8, 1658 Copenhagen V, with 209 beds; cost DKr120 per night, bed and breakfast. Open early May-end August.

AU PAIR / CHILDCARE

The following agencies can arrange au pair and childcare placements in Denmark:

ACADEMY AU PAIR AGENCY LTD Glenlea, Dulwich Common, London SE21 7ES ✆ 081-299 4599
Can place au pairs. Ages 18-27. Some knowledge of Danish useful. Pocket money approx £30-£35 per week. Administration

charge £40. Positions as nannies and mothers' helps also available for those with qualifications/experience.

ANGLIA AGENCY 70 Southsea Avenue, Leigh-on-Sea, Essex ✆ Southend-on-Sea (0702) 471648
Can place au pairs, mothers' helps and nannies. Ages 17+. Pocket money £30+ per week. Service charge £40.

HELPING HANDS AU PAIR & DOMESTIC AGENCY 39 Rutland Avenue, Thorpe Bay, Essex SS1 2XJ ✆ Southend-on-Sea (0702) 602067
Can place au pairs and mothers' helps. Ages 18-27. Pocket money approx £30 per week for au pairs, higher for mothers' helps. Introduction fee £40 on acceptance of a family. *UK nationals only.*

LANGTRAIN INTERNATIONAL Torquay Road, Foxrock, Dublin 18, Ireland ✆ Dublin (1) 289 3876
Can place au pairs in Danish families. Ages 18+. Pocket money approx £25-£40 per week. Placement fee £55.

UNIVERSAL CARE Chester House, 9 Windsor End, Beaconsfield, Buckinghamshire HP9 2JJ ✆ Beaconsfield (0494) 678811
Can place au pairs and mothers' helps. Ages 17-27. Knowledge of Danish and previous experience useful. Pocket money approx £25 per week, higher for those with experience. Service charge £47. PH *Apply 2 months before work period desired.*

CONSERVATION

MELLEMFOLKELIGT SAMVIRKE (Danish Association for International Coooperation), Borgerade 10-14, 1300 Copenhagen K
Mellemfolkeligt Samvirke international workcamps gather young people from different countries to cooperate on a project which benefits the local community or works towards conservation of the environment. Recent conservation projects have included forestry work in Stenlose; restoring an old farmhouse in South Sealand for use as a children's arts centre; carrying out water research tests in

Koge; and beach conservation work on the island of Avernakoe, south of Funen. Ages 18+. 30-40 hour week. 2-3 weeks, June-September. Board and lodging in community houses, Scout huts, farms, youth centres or schools and insurance provided. Volunteers pay own travel costs. Mentally or physically handicapped volunteers welcome on most camps; places also available for families. B D PH

Apply through partner organisation in country of residence. In the UK: International Voluntary Service Old Hall, East Bergholt, Colchester, Essex CO7 6TQ or
Quaker International Social Projects, Friends House, Euston Road, London NW1 2BJ (experienced volunteers only) or
United Nations Association, International Youth Service, Temple of Peace, Cathays Park, Cardiff CF1 3AP ✆ Cardiff (0222) 223088.

Outside the UK: please see information on page 30.

FARMWORK

GRAEVLERUPGAARD FRUGTPLANTAGE Egsgyden 38, Horne, 5600 Fåborg ✆ 62 60 22 31
Fruit pickers are needed to pick strawberries, 3-4 weeks, June-July. 30-40 hours per week. Piece-work rates paid. Ages 18+. Pickers should take their own food and camping equipment; insurance and travel not provided. *Apply by 1 May. EC nationals only.*

INTERNATIONAL FARM EXPERIENCE PROGRAMME YFC Centre, National Agricultural Centre, Stoneleigh Park, Kenilworth, Warwickshire CV8 2LG ✆ Coventry (0203) 696584
Provides assistance to young farmers and nurserymen by finding places in farms/nurseries abroad enabling them to broaden their knowledge of agricultural methods. Opportunities for practical agricultural work, usually on mixed farms throughout Denmark. Applicants live and work with a farmer and his family and the work is matched as far as possible with the applicant's requirements. Physically hard work, 3-12 months. Positions available throughout the year, with the exception of the winter months. Wages approx

£30 per week; board and lodging provided. Applicants pay own fares. Ages 18-26. Applicants must have at least 2 years practical experience, 1 year of which may be at agricultural college, and intend to make a career in agriculture. Valid driving licence necessary. Registration fee £70. *Apply at least 3 months in advance; UK applicants only.*

VI HJAELPER HINANDEN Inga Nielsen, Asenvej 35, 9881 Bindslev ℂ 98 93 86 07
A non-profitmaking organisation which aims to help organic farmers and smallholders whose work is often labour-intensive as it does not rely on artificial fertilisers or pesticides. Provides unskilled voluntary workers with first hand experience of organic farming and gardening, and a chance to spend some time in the country. Places exist on organic farms, smallholdings and gardens throughout Denmark. An address list giving details of people who require help can be obtained by sending a large self-addressed envelope plus Dkr50 or equivalent. Most people on the list speak English. Ages 16+. 3-4 hours per day; 3+ days, all year. Full board and lodging provided in the farmhouse or outbuildings; volunteers should take a sleeping bag. No wages paid, and helpers must pay their own travel costs. Insurance and anti-tetanus vaccination recommended.

WORKCAMPS

MELLEMFOLKELIGT SAMVIRKE (Danish Association for International Coooperation), Borgergade 10-14, 1300 Copenhagen K
Mellemfolkeligt Samvirke international workcamps gather young people from different countries to cooperate on a project which benefits the local community. This provides an opportunity to come into contact with the social problems found in every society and to help volunteers become more actively involved in the creation of a more just society. Recent projects have included arranging and supporting a big rock music festival in Skanderborg; building a summer house in the grounds of a Folk High School in Funen; and organising summer sports and activities for schoolchildren on the island of Bornholm. Projects are also run in Greenland and have

included reconstructing a Viking village and restoring an open-air museum.
Ages 18+. 30-40 hour week. 2-3 weeks, June-September. Board and lodging in schools, youth centres, community houses, Scout huts or inns and insurance provided. Volunteers pay own travel costs. Mentally or physically handicapped volunteers welcome on most camps, but camps on Greenland cannot take wheelchairs; places also available for families. **B D PH**

Apply through partner organisation in country of residence. In the UK: International Voluntary Service, Old Hall, East Bergholt, Colchester, Essex CO7 6TQ or
Quaker International Social Projects, Friends House, Euston Road, London NW1 2BJ (experienced volunteers only) or
United Nations Association, International Youth Service, Temple of Peace, Cathays Park, Cardiff CF1 3AP ℂ Cardiff (0222) 223088.

Outside the UK: please see information on page 30.

When writing to any organisation it is essential to mention Working Holidays 1993 and enclose a large stamped, self-addressed envelope, or if overseas, a large addressed envelope and at least two International Reply Coupons.

INFORMATION

Finnish Embassy
38 Chesham Place, London SW1X 8HW
℗ 071-838 6200

British Embassy
Itainen Puistotie 17, 00140 Helsinki

Tourist office
Finnish Tourist Board, 66/68 Haymarket,
London SW1Y 4RF ℗ 071-839 4048

Youth hostels
Suomen Retkeilymajajarjesto ry, Yrjonkatu 38B,
00100 Helsinki 10

Youth & student information
Travela-FSTS, Mannerheimintie 5C, 00100
Helsinki 10

Hotel Booking, Central Station, Asema-Aukio 3,
Helsinki

Entry regulations A work permit and a permit
of residence are required for all kinds of
employment, except for nationals of Denmark,
Iceland, Norway and Sweden. Applications for
a permit may not be made until an offer of
work has been received and the prospective
employer has provided a certificate giving
details of salary, type and duration of work,
plus personal information and a letter of
recommendation. Once this has been received,
a Labour Permit Application form, available
from the Finnish Embassy, should be completed
and returned, together with the certificate.
These will be sent to the Office of Alien Affairs
of the Finnish Ministry of the Interior in
Helsinki who will consult the Ministry of
Labour and reject or accept the application
accordingly; this takes about 4 weeks. The
applicants will then be notified of the decision
by the Embassy. A work permit is only valid
for the specific job for which it has been issued.
It is usually granted for 3 months, after which it
may or may not be extended. It is strongly
emphasised that anyone intending to work in
Finland should not enter the country before the
necessary formalities have been completed.
Foreign nationals may not apply for a permit

whilst on holiday in Finland.

These regulations may change as of January 1993 subject to the European Economic Space agreement, and a work permit may no longer be required by UK and EC nationals.

A booklet entitled *Working in Finland* outlining legal aspects of employment in Finland is available from Finnish Embassies.

Travel The Finnrailpass entitles the holder to unlimited travel on Finnish State Railways, cost from £63, 8 days. Available from Finlandia Travel, 223 Regent Street, London W1R 7DB ✆ 071-409 7334.

The Nordic Tourist Ticket entitles the holder to unlimited travel on trains in Finland, Denmark, Norway and Sweden, and is also valid on some ferries. Valid for 21 days, cost £115 for ages under 26, £155 for ages over 26. Available from Norwegian State Railways, 21-24 Cockspur Street, London SW1Y 5DA ✆ 071-930 6666.

Campus Travel, 52 Grosvenor Gardens, London SW1W 0AG ✆ 071-730 3402 (offices throughout the UK) and Council Travel, 28A Poland Street, London W1V 3DB ✆ 071-437 7767 (offices also in Paris, Lyon, Düsseldorf, Tokyo and throughout the US) offer Eurotrain under 26 fares and youth and student airfares to destinations in Finland.

Publications Lonely Planet's *Finland - a Travel Survival Kit* £9.95 and *Scandinavian and Baltic Europe on a Shoestring* £10.95 offer practical, down-to-earth information for the low-budget independent traveller in Finland.

The Rough Guide to Scandinavia £8.95 provides comprehensive background information on Finland, with details on getting there, getting around, places to explore and cheap places to stay.

Michael's Guide to Scandinavia £10.95 is detailed and concise, providing invaluable practical advice for all kinds of travellers. Published by Inbal Travel.

All the above are available from good bookshops.

Finland Facts and Map covers travel to and within Finland, accommodation, customs and other useful information, available from the Finnish Tourist Board, see above.

Accommodation The Finnish Tourist Board, see above, publish *Camping and Youth Hostels* listing campsites and youth hostels with their facilities and a map, and also *Hotels* which includes a section on hostels.

DOMESTIC

FINNISH FAMILY PROGRAMME Centre for International Mobility, PB 343, 00531 Helsinki ✆ Helsinki (0) 774 77033

Offers native speakers of English, French or German an opportunity to get acquainted with the Finnish way of life, living as a member of a family whilst speaking their own language. Host families include both farming and urban or suburban families who may move into the country for the summer. Applicants are expected to help with household chores and/or childcare. On farms the work also involves helping with haymaking, milking, gardening and fruit picking. Approx 25 hour, 5 day week. Board and lodging provided plus pocket money. Ages 18-23. 1-12 months, mostly June-August. *Applications for summer positions should reach the Centre for International Mobility by 31 March; for other positions apply at least 3 months in advance.*

UK applications to Central Bureau for Educational Visits & Exchanges, Vocational & Technical Education Department, Seymour Mews House, Seymour Mews, London W1H 9PE ✆ 071-486 5101.

FARMWORK

INTERNATIONAL FARM EXPERIENCE PROGRAMME YFC Centre, National Agricultural Centre, Stoneleigh Park, Kenilworth, Warwickshire CV8 2LG ✆ Coventry (0203) 696584

Provides assistance to young farmers and nurserymen by finding places in farms/nurseries abroad, enabling them to broaden their knowledge of agricultural methods. Opportunities for practical horticultural or agricultural work, usually on mixed farms. Applicants live and work with a farmer and his family and the work is matched as far as possible with the applicant's requirements.

8 hour day, 5 day week. 2-12 months. Positions are mostly available in spring and summer. Wages approx £55 per week; board and lodging provided. Ages 18-30. Some practical experience required. Applicants pay own fares and insurance. Registration fee £70. *Apply at least 3 months in advance; UK applicants only.*

Finnish applicants requiring an exchange should apply to the Centre for International Mobility, PB 343, 00531 Helsinki © Helsinki (0) 774 77033.

WORKCAMPS

KANSAINVÄLINEN VAPAAEHTOISTYÖ RY (KVT) Rauhanasema, Veturitori, 00520 Helsinki 52

KVT is the Finnish branch of Service Civil International which promotes international reconciliation through work projects. Volunteers are invited to work in international teams on workcamps organised throughout Finland. The workcamps aim to make people realise their responsibility and to work for constructive changes in the unjust areas of society. Projects are of a combined manual and social nature, with the aim of supporting communities either in remote depressed areas of Finland or those practising alternative methods of treating handicapped or underprivileged people.

Recent projects have included constructing a wilderness campsite and cleaning forest huts in Lapland; repairing hiking paths and nature trails at a youth centre in Rautavaara; reconstructing a summer house for use by the adult homeless on an island off the Helsinki coast; gardening and household work at a home for the disabled and able-bodied in Jyväskylä; and repairing tools, household equipment and farm machinery in Iisalmi to send to Third World countries. Most of the camps have a study element, which involves the discussion of questions and folk traditions relevant to the community and work for peace. The main language of the camps is English. Ages 18+. Applicants should be highly motivated and prepared to work hard as part of a team. 35-40 hour week. 2-4 weeks, June-September. Food, accommodation in schools, barns, tents or log cabins and work accident insurance provided.

Participants pay their own travel costs. Places also available for families. B D PH W depending on project.

Apply through partner organisation in country of residence. In the UK: International Voluntary Service, Old Hall, East Bergholt, Colchester, Essex C07 6TQ or Quaker International Social Projects, Friends House, Euston Road, London NW1 2BJ (experienced volunteers only).

Outside the UK: please see information on page 30.

Outside the UK: please see information on page 30.

GENERAL

MONASTERY OF VALAMO 79850 Uusi - Valamo

An ancient Eastern Orthodox religious community, whose history dates back to the 12th century. A popular pilgrimage site, it also serves as a meeting place for Christians of differing traditions and nationalities. Volunteers are invited to help with different tasks such as working in the monastery kitchen and garden; collecting brushwood, mushrooms and berries in the forest; and other common domestic chores which community living involves. Ages 18+. 34 hour week, all year. There is ample time for relaxation, traditional recreations such as sauna, and daily worship. In free time volunteers may also participate in courses or lectures at the Valamo Lay Academy. Full board and hostel accommodation provided, but no fares or wages paid. *All nationalities welcome.*

FRANCE

INFORMATION

French Embassy
58 Knightsbridge, London SW1X 7JT ℗ 071-235 8080
Visa Section: Consulate General, 6A Cromwell Place, London SW7 2EW ℗ 071-823 5292

British Embassy
35 rue du Faubourg St Honoré, 75383 Paris Cedex 08

Tourist office
French Government Tourist Office, 178 Piccadilly, London W1V 0AL ℗ 071-491 7622

Youth hostels
Fédération Unie des Auberges de Jeunesse, 6 rue Mesnil, 75016 Paris

Ligue Française pour les Auberges de la Jeunesse, 38 boulevard Raspail, 75007 Paris

Youth & student information
Accueil des Jeunes en France, 12 rue des Barres, 75004 Paris *(for correspondence)*
16 rue du Pont Philippe/119 rue Saint-Martin, 75004 Paris *(for personal callers)*

Centre d'Information et de Documentation Jeunesse (CIDJ), 101 quai Branly, 75740 Paris Cedex 15

Organisation pour le Tourisme Universitaire, 137 boulevard St Michel, 75005 Paris

Entry regulations UK citizens intending to work in France should have full passports. EC nationals may stay for up to 3 months to find a job; once a job has been found a residence permit, *carte de séjour de ressortissant d'un état membre de la CEE,* must be applied for. Application forms are available from the Prefecture de Police in Paris, or from the local police station or town hall elsewhere. The permit is valid for the period of employment, if this is less than 12 months. Those under 18 should have written parental consent and are not allowed to work in bars. Details of particular regulations applying to au pair posts and seasonal agricultural work are given under the respective headings, below. Non-EC nationals are not allowed to take up any form of employment in France unless they have been granted a permit before arrival. Several agreements exist between France and some African and South East Asian countries, Poland and Lebanon, and nationals of these countries are allowed to work in specific cases. Those studying in France can work after their first year.

Employment Offices The French equivalent of a British Jobcentre is the Agence Nationale pour l'Emploi (ANPE). There are ANPE offices throughout France and EC nationals can use their services. A list of all regional offices can be obtained from the head office, ANPE, Le Galilee, 4 rue Galilee, 93198 Noisy-le-Grand, France or from the Social Service at the Consular Section of the French Embassy. The Embassy also issues a leaflet *Employment in France of British nationals and nationals of other EC countries*, available from the Visa Section, PO Box 57, 6A Cromwell Place, London SW7 2EW.

Job advertising The French Publishing Group, Agencefrance Ltd, 4 Wendle Court, 131-137 Wandsworth Road, London SW8 2LL ℗ 071-498 2333 can place advertisements in most French newspapers and magazines.

Travel Rent-a-bike scheme available at 241 stations, bookable in advance; FF1000 deposit, cost FF44 per day, decreasing as the number of rental days increases. Carrismo card available in France only for ages 12-25 offers up to 50% reduction on 4 or 8 journeys, valid 1 year. Holiday Return (Séjour) Ticket gives concession of 25% if the journey covers more than 1000 km; valid two months. France Vacances Pass gives unlimited travel on 4 days during a period of 15 or on any 9 days during a period of 1 month, all year, plus, amongst other concessions, a £12.50 cross-Channel fare by Hoverspeed. Cost from £86. For further information and tickets, contact a continental rail agent or a principal British Rail Travel Centre.

Euro-Domino is a pass allowing 3, 5 or 10 days unlimited rail travel in 1 month on the railways of France. Cost from £76/£113/£176 (ages under 26) or £93/£128/£200 (ages 26+), 3/5/10

days. Available from British Rail International Rail Centre, Victoria Station, London SW1V 1JY ℗ 071-928 5151.

Campus Travel, 52 Grosvenor Gardens, London SW1W 0AG ℗ 071-730 3402 (offices throughout the UK) and Council Travel, 28A Poland Street, London W1V 3DB ℗ 071-437 7767 (offices also in Paris, Lyon, Düsseldorf, Tokyo and throughout the US) offer flexible youth and student charter flights to destinations throughout France. Also Eurotrain under 26 fares.

Information centres Accueil des Jeunes en France, 12 rue des Barres, 75004 Paris is a general information and advisory service for young travellers. Can provide vouchers for low-cost restaurants and arrange cheap accommodation, see below, and also supply cheap air, rail and coach tickets.

Centre d'Information et de Documentation Jeunesse (CIDJ), 101 quai Branly, 75740 Paris Cedex 15 provides a comprehensive information service for young people, with branches throughout France. Practical help can be provided in finding work. Information is also available on accommodation, social, cultural, artistic, scientific and sports facilities, activities and holidays plus practical information on staying, travelling and studying in France and facilities for the disabled. The centre also acts as the local branch of the ANPE and career advice/social security office. Publish a wide range of booklets and information sheets including *Recherche d'un Emploi Temporaire ou Occasionel; Séjour et Emploi des Étudiants Étrangers en France; Entrée, Séjour et Emploi des Étrangers en France* and *Réductions de Transports pour les Jeunes*. PH

Publications *Rough Guide to France* £9.99 and *Rough Guide to Paris* £6.99 provide comprehensive background information on France and the French capital, plus details on getting there, getting around, places to explore and cheap places to stay.
Culture Shock! France £6.95 introduces the reader to the people, customs, ceremonies, food and culture of France, with checklists of dos and don'ts.
All the above available from good bookshops.

Emplois d'Été en France 1993 lists thousands of vacancies including waiting and bar staff, au pairs, sports instructors, receptionists, work in factories, shops, language schools and offices and on farms and children's summer camps. Also includes special information for foreign students, with details of authorisation on working in France. Published by Vac-job, 4 rue d'Alesia, 75014 Paris. Distributed in the UK by Vacation Work, 9 Park End Street, Oxford OX1 1HJ © Oxford (0865) 241978, price £7.95. Vacation Work also publish *Live and Work in France* £6.95, a guide for those interested in finding temporary or permanent work, starting a business or buying a home in France.

1000 Pistes de Jobs FF110 including postage, is a comprehensive guide giving 1000 ideas and different ways of finding a holiday job, with practical advice and useful addresses. Although the book is primarily a guide for young French people, it is an invaluable source of reference for anyone wanting to work in France, providing that they speak fluent French. Available from L'Étudiant, 27 rue du Chemin Vert, 75011 Paris.

Accommodation Centre d'Information et de Documentation Jeunesse (CIDJ), 101 quai Branly, 75740 Paris Cedex 15 publish information sheets providing addresses of reasonable accommodation in youth centres, university halls and pensions, mainly in the Paris region: *Centres d'Hébergement Temporaires Paris et Région Parisienne; Hôtels Bon Marché et Pensions de Famille à Paris; Logement des Jeunes Travailleurs;* and *Le Logement de L'Étudiant.*

Accueil des Jeunes en France, 12 rue des Barres, 75004 Paris is a central booking office for youth accommodation with access to 11000 beds in the summer. Has 4 offices which guarantee to find any young traveller decent, cheap accommodation in Paris, with immediate reservation. Cost approx FF90 per night. Contact AJF Beaubourg, 119 rue St-Martin, 75004 Paris; AJF Hôtel de Ville, 16 rue du Pont Louis-Philippe, 75004 Paris; AJF Quartier Latin, 139 boulevard Saint-Michel, 75005 Paris; or AJF Gare du Nord, 75010 Paris.

Accommodation available for young people at a modern residential centre where facilities include restaurant, bar, art, theatre and music studios and language courses. Maximum 2 weeks, all year. Cost from FF115 per night, bed and breakfast; meals available from FF55. Reservations possible from 30 days in advance to Foyer International d'Accueil de Paris, 30 rue Cabanis, 75014 Paris. **PH**

Union des Centres de Rencontres Internationales de France (UCRIF), 104 rue de Vaugirard, 75006 Paris publish a list of 63 youth accommodation centres and hostels, each providing a comprehensive tourist service in a friendly atmosphere. Facilities include swimming, riding, sports grounds, cycling, skating, skiing, sailing and language courses. **PH**

ARCHAEOLOGY

ASSOCIATION DE RECHERCHES ET D'ÉTUDES D'HISTOIRE RURALE Serge Grappin, Maison du Patrimoine, 21190 Saint-Romain

Volunteers are required to work on two excavations in the Burgundy village of Saint-Romain. At Le Verger excavations have revealed 16 layers of occupation dating back to neolithic times; Le Vieux Château is the site of a 12th century castle and a Merovingian cemetery. Ages 18+. No experience necessary, but volunteers should be able to speak French. 40 hours per week, 15+ days, late July-September. No fares or wages paid. Food and village accommodation provided for FF15 per day; volunteers should take a sleeping bag. FF20 fee covers registration and insurance. Weekly visits arranged to local museums and sites of archaeological interest; training, conferences and courses organised on site.

ASSOCIATION POUR LE DÉVELOPPEMENT DE L'ARCHÉOLOGIE URBAINE A CHARTRES 16 rue Saint Pierre, 28000 Chartres

Volunteers are needed for urban rescue excavation work on sites in Chartres. The project is a long-term research programme on the archaeological and historical development of Chartres, covering its economic, cultural and social evolution from Roman to medieval times. Sites include Gallo-Roman buildings and constructions including amphitheatre, roads, houses, metal and pottery workshops, plus sites dating from the High Middle Ages. Talks/slides will be given on a variety of related subjects during July-September. Volunteers should be prepared for hard, physical work in all weathers. Punctuality is expected. Volunteers also work in the laboratory, washing, classifying, repairing and drawing finds. Ages 18+. Previous experience desirable and if possible applicants should enclose an archaeological *cv*. 8 hour day, 5 day week, with weekends free. 3+ weeks, preferably 4+, June-September. Food, accommodation and insurance provided, but no fares or wages paid. Volunteers should take their own sleeping bags. Registration fee FF200. *Apply 4 weeks in advance.*

CENTRE DE RECHERCHES ARCHÉOLOGIQUES F Audouze, Centre National de la Recherche Scientifique, 1 place Aristide Briand, 92195 Meudon Cedex

Experienced volunteers are required for the excavation of the Upper Palaeolithic site of Verberie on the river Oise, 80km north of Paris. The aim of the excavation is to study the everyday life of Magdalenian reindeer hunters. Work involves the digging of a living floor covered with flint tools and chips, bones and stones, plus mapping and restoring artefacts. Ages 18+. Some knowledge of French preferred. 8 hour day, 6 day week, 1 July-31 August. Food, camping accommodation and insurance provided. No fares or wages paid. Occasional visits to places of interest in the Oise area may be arranged. *Apply by end May.*

CERCLE ARCHÉOLOGIQUE DE BRAY/SEINE Claude & Daniel Mordant, rue du Tour de l'Église, Dannemoine, 89700 Tonnerre

Volunteers are required for the excavation of a late Bronze Age settlement at Grisy and Neolithic causewayed enclosures at Balloy. The aim is a study of the paleo-environment in the Upper Seine Valley. Work involves excavating and cleaning pottery and bones, with lectures and visits to other sites. Volunteers should preferably have a knowledge of the periods involved. 8 hour day, 6 day week. 2-4 weeks June-September. Food and camping accommodation provided but participants should take their own tents and sleeping bags.

No fares or wages paid. Registration fee FF30 includes insurance. *Apply by May/August.*

CHANTIERS D'ÉTUDES MEDIÉVALES Centre d'Archéologie Mediévale de Strasbourg, 4 rue du Tonnelet Rouge, 67000 Strasbourg

Organise international workcamps devoted to the study, restoration and maintenance of monuments or sites dating back to the Middle Ages. Restoration and excavation work is being carried out on various sites throughout Alsace, including medieval castles and houses, and the Maginot line. Beginners welcome. Teams of specialists in history, architecture, ceramics and archaeology accompany the participants on both restoration and excavation projects. Excavation techniques are taught and there are opportunities to study finds and draw conclusions. Ages 16+. Those under 18 require parental consent. Applicants are accepted from all countries, as long as they are fit and willing to adapt to a community lifestyle. 36 hour, 6 day week. 12/15 days, July-September. Cost from FF380 includes food and very basic accommodation in schools, houses, barracks, tents or hostels with self-catering facilities, plus insurance. Participants should take sleeping bags and work clothes. *Apply by May; applications may take several weeks to process.*

DEPARTMENT OF PREHISTORY & ARCHAEOLOGY Prof J Collis, The University, Sheffield S10 2TN

Volunteers are required for excavating, processing finds and surveying at Iron Age-Roman sites near Mirefleurs, Clermont-Ferrand, in conjunction with the Service des Fouilles Historiques de l'Auvergne. This is a long-term project studying the impact of urbanisation on a rural settlement, 2nd century BC and 2nd century AD. Experience not necessary. 12 weeks, July-September. Campsite accommodation with meals provided at a nearby house. Cost approx FF40-FF45 per day. No fares or wages paid. *Apply by 31 March.*

GROUPE ARCHÉOLOGIQUE DU MEMONTOIS M Louis Roussel, Directeur des Fouilles, 52 rue des Forges, 21000 Dijon

Volunteers are needed for excavation work at Malain on the Côte d'Or. The site consists of the Gallic and Roman town including roads, temples, squares, caves, houses and fields as well as a medieval castle and prehistoric earthworks. The object is to study the development of the town from its origins and explore its later development.

The camp is based on a collective lifestyle, and volunteers share in supervising digs, discussions on finds, taking charge of exhibitions and preparing meals. Work involves documenting, classifying, washing, collecting, drawing and photographing finds, and restoration work on ruins. Lectures and excursions organised. 7 hour day, 5½ day week. 4 weeks, July-August. Camping accommodation provided; food at a cost of FF100 per week. Volunteers should preferably be experienced, and can take their own camping equipment. No wages or fares paid. *Apply by May.* D

LABORATOIRE D'ANTHROPOLOGIE PRÉHISTORIQUE Université de Rennes I, Campus de Beaulieu, 35042 Rennes Cedex

Volunteers are required for excavations on prehistoric and protohistoric remains in Brittany. Ages 18+. 3-4 weeks, summer. Food and campsite accommodation provided but volunteers must take their own camping equipment. No fares or wages paid. *Apply in April for further details.*

MINISTERE DE LA CULTURE Circonscription des Antiquités Historiques et Préhistoriques de Bretagne, 6 rue du Chapitre, 35044 Rennes Cedex

Volunteers are needed to work on archaeological sites all over Brittany, ranging from Palaeolithic to medieval periods. Recent projects have included work on megalithic monuments and sites in Locmariaquer, St Laurent sur Oust and Monteneuf; the excavation of a Gallic/Gallo-Roman site prior to the building of a new road near Rennes; work on Iron Age and Dark Ages sites at Locronan and Quimper; and uncovering the ancient area of shops near the site of the forum in the Gallo-Roman capital at Corseul. Ages 18+. Volunteers should be prepared for hard physical work. Archaeological experience useful but not essential; basic French necessary. Approx 40 hour week. 1+ weeks, April-September. Board and lodging provided, varying from campsites to university halls of residence depending on the location. Cost FF50

per week plus travel to site. Participants should take a sleeping bag. Insurance provided. Anti-tetanus vaccination required. Excursions sometimes arranged. *Detailed list of sites available in March.*

MUSÉE DES ANTIQUITÉS NATIONALES Henri Delporte, Directeur, PO Box 30, 78103 Saint-Germain-en-Laye

Volunteers are required for the excavation of an upper Palaeolithic limestone cave site at Brassempouy in the Landes region. Tasks involve establishing precise date of female statuettes found. 15 days, July and August. Volunteers should be students of archaeology, preferably with some experience. Food and accommodation under canvas provided, but no fares or wages paid. *Apply in May/June.*

MUSÉE DES SCIENCES NATURELLES ET D'ARCHÉOLOGIE Service Archéologique du Musée de la Chartreuse, Pierre Demolon, Conservateur de Musée, 191 rue St-Albin, 59500 Douai

Beginners and experienced volunteers are required to help with urban rescue excavation in an area of Douai. The object is to trace the origins and development of the town from the 11th-16th century, concentrating on the medieval houses. Ages 18+. Preference will be given to those sufficiently experienced to take over sections of the excavation. Knowledge of French useful. 7½ hour day. 2+ weeks, July-September. Food and accommodation provided. No fares paid, but wages may be offered to specialists. Participants should take their own sleeping bag. Anti-tetanus vaccination compulsory. Registration fee FF100 covers insurance. *Apply by 15 June.*

MUSEUM NATIONAL D'HISTOIRE NATURELLE Laboratoire de Préhistoire, Institut de Paléontologie Humaine, Professeur Henry de Lumley, 1 rue René Panhard, 75013 Paris

Volunteers are required to work on various sites and caves in south east and south west France. Projects include investigating Acheulian and Tayacian industries, fauna, pre-Neanderthal human remains and dwelling structures at the Grotte du Lazaret in Nice and at Tautavel near Perpignan; studying and recording protohistoric rock engravings at a research centre in the Vallée des Merveilles in Tende; excavation at the Palaeolithic site of La Baume Bonne, Alpes de Haute Provence and at Les Eyzies, Dordogne. Opportunities to study finds. Specialists and amateurs welcome. 15+ days in March/April or 1 month, June-August. Board provided at local campsites, but participants should take their own tents and equipment. No fares or wages paid.

REMPART (Union des Associations pour la Réhabilitation et l'Entretien des Monuments et du Patrimoine Artistique), 1 rue des Guillemites, 75004 Paris
Aims to improve the way of life through a better understanding of and a greater respect for the archaeological, architectural and natural heritage and environment through the restoration of endangered buildings and monuments. Consists of a grouping of more than 140 local, departmental or regional associations, providing a wide variety of projects.
Volunteers are needed for archaeological work on sites in Auvergne, Centre, Ile de France, Languedoc-Roussillon, Lorraine, Midi-Pyrénées, Normandie, Poitou-Charentes, Provence-Alpes-Côte d'Azur and Corsica. Sites include medieval towns and villages, châteaux, fortresses, abbeys and churches, prehistoric and Gallo-Roman towns, early Christian sites, amphitheatres and villas, and post-medieval fortresses and castles. Work involves excavation, cleaning and restoration.
Participants are usually accompanied by experienced archaeologists and are involved in carrying out surveys, drawing plans, technical photography and learning archaeological methods and site history. Opportunities for swimming, tennis, riding, cycling, rambling, exploring the region, crafts and taking part in local festivities.
Ages 14/18+. There is no upper age limit, anyone feeling young is welcome. Some knowledge of French needed. 30-35 hour week. 2-4 weeks, Easter and June-September; a few camps are open throughout the year. Cost FF20-FF45 per day includes food and accommodation in huts, old buildings and tents, with self-catering facilities; a few camps are free. Volunteers help with camp duties, pay their own fares, and should take a sleeping bag. Applicants can choose which project they would like to work on in the workcamp programme and contact addresses are given. Registration fee FF200 includes insurance. Also arrange archaeology courses. D PH but no wheelchair access. *Enclose 3 IRCs.*

SERVICE ARCHÉOLOGIQUE - VILLE D'ARRAS Alain Jacques, 22 rue Paul Doumer, 62000 Arras
Volunteers needed to work on an excavation in Arras which includes the remains of the Roman town of Nemetacum and a 4th century barracks. No experience necessary. Ages 18+. 40 hour week, 15+ days, July and August. No fares or wages paid, but food, accommodation and insurance provided. Registration fee FF25. *Apply by 30 May.*

SOCIÉTÉ ALPINE DE DOCUMENTATION ET DE RECHERCHE EN ARCHÉOLOGIE HISTORIQUE (SADRAH) 11 montée de Chalemont, 38000 Grenoble
Volunteers are required to help at several archaeological excavations in the Isère region, including an 11th century deserted village, a site in the old quarter of Grenoble and earthworks dating back to the year 1000. No experience necessary. Ages 18+. 2+ weeks, all year, with one day off each week. Food, accommodation and insurance provided. No fares or wages paid. Membership fee FF80.

UNITÉ DE RECHERCHE ARCHÉOLOGIQUE The Director, No 12, Centre National de la Recherche Scientifique, 3 rue Michelet, 75006 Paris
Volunteers are needed for excavation work in the Vallée de l'Aisne. The project, organised in conjunction with the Université de Paris, involves the rescue of sites threatened by urban expansion, gravel extraction and motorway or canal construction, and the study of changes in settlement, subsistence and material culture within the valley over a 5000 year period. Recent work has been undertaken on a number of Neolithic and early Iron Age settlement sites.

Ages 18+. Archaeology students or experienced excavators preferred. 2+ weeks, late June-early September. Good food, dormitory accommodation in old farm buildings or camping space and hot showers provided, but no fares or wages paid. *Apply by 15 June.*

UNITÉ MUNICIPALE D'ARCHÉOLOGIE
Hôtel-Dieu, Avenue Joussaume Latour, 02400 Château-Thierry
Volunteers required at an excavation of the old castle in Château-Thierry, a site which has been inhabited since the 5th century and gives much valuable information about the daily life of people living there during the Medieval and Modern periods. Ages 18+. No experience necessary as training will be given. Knowledge of French essential. Approx 40 hours per week, 3+ weeks, June-October. Accident insurance and full board accommodation provided; volunteers should take a sleeping bag. Excursions organised to Soissons, Reims and other local places of interest, and training given in laboratory techniques such as cleaning and restoration. No fares or wages paid.

UNIVERSITÉ DU MAINE Annie Renoux,
Département d'Histoire, Avenue Olivier Messiaen, BP 535, 72017 Le Mans
Volunteers are required for excavation work at the site of the Château Comtal at Chavôt, Epernay, Champagne. Recent work has concentrated on the 10th-13th century castle of the Count of Champagne and involves excavating, cleaning, marking and recording finds. Lectures on excavation techniques. Ages 18+. Experience not necessary. 8 hour day, 5½ day week. 15+ days, July and August. Lunch and accommodation in stone building provided, but no fares or wages paid. Volunteers should take a sleeping bag. Qualified volunteers staying more than 3 weeks may be offered full expenses. *Early application advisable.*

AU PAIR/CHILDCARE

Certain conditions apply to anyone working as an au pair in France, regardless of the organisation through which they apply. Both sexes can apply, and must be aged between 18 and 30. Work is for a minimum of 3 months and a maximum of 12 months, with the possibility of an extension to 18 months. As a rule applicants should reach an agreement with the host family before leaving for France. It is then up to the host family or the organisation which arranged the placing to obtain, from the Direction Départementale du Travail et de l'Emploi (in Paris: Service de la Main-d'Oeuvre Etrangère, 80 rue de la Croix-Nivert, 75732 Paris Cedex 15), the form *Accord de placement au pair d'un stagiaire aide-familial.* This has to be signed by the family and returned together with a certificate of registration at a school in France specialising in teaching foreign students, proof of academic studies, and a current medical certificate. If the Direction Départementale are satisfied with the information supplied, they will stamp the *Accord de placement* and a copy will be sent to the applicant.

On arrival in France, an au pair from an EC country must obtain a *carte de séjour* from the local Commissariat de Police. Non EC passport-holders must apply for a long stay visa from the French Consulate in their country of residence before going to France, and on arrival in France must obtain a *carte de séjour* and *autorisation provisoire de travail* from the Direction Départementale, on production of the *Accord de placement.* The host family must register the au pair with the national insurance scheme and pay quarterly contributions which cover the au pair for accidents at work, sickness and maternity. Au pairs can expect to live as a member of the family and to have sufficient free time for recreation and to attend language classes. Work involves light household tasks including simple cooking, hand washing, cleaning, washing up, shopping, helping to prepare simple meals and childcare for up to 5 hours a day, plus 2 nights' baby-sitting per week. At least 1 day per week free, including at least 1 Sunday per month. Pocket money average FF1300 per month.

An information sheet, *Au Pair Posts in France,* giving details of conditions and formalities governing au pair posts is available from the Visa Section of the French Embassy.

Séjour Au Pair en France (Stagiaire Aide-Familial) is an information sheet including details of regulations and formalities for those applying to be au pairs, a list of organisations placing au pairs, plus addresses of Préfectures de Police in Paris. Also *Garde d'Enfants Temporaire et Baby-Sitting (Paris et Région Parisienne).* Both published by the Centre d'Information et de Documentation Jeunesse (CIDJ), 101 quai Branly, 75740 Paris Cedex 15.

The following agencies can arrange au pair and childcare placements in France:

ABOUT AU PAIRS 3 Garston Park, Godstone, Surrey RH9 8NE ✆ **Godstone (0883) 743735**
Can place au pairs. Single females only, ages 18-27. Pocket money £30 per week. Registration fee £25.

ACADEMY AU PAIR AGENCY LTD Glenlea, Dulwich Common, London SE21 7ES ✆ **081-299 4599**
Can place au pairs. Ages 18-27. Some knowledge of French essential. Pocket money approx £30-£35 per week. Administration charge £40. Positions as nannies and mothers' helps also available for those with qualifications/experience.

ANGLIA AGENCY 70 Southsea Avenue, Leigh-on-Sea, Essex ✆ **Southend-on-Sea (0702) 471648**
Can place au pairs, mothers' helps and nannies. Ages 18+. Pocket money £30+ per week. Service charge £40.

ANGLO PAIR AGENCY 40 Wavertree Road, Streatham Hill, London SW2 3SP ✆ **081-674 3605**
Can place au pairs and au pairs plus. Ages 18-27. Pocket money £30-£50 per week. Also placements for experienced nannies and mothers' helps; salary up to £100 per week. Agency fee £40.

AVALON AGENCY Thursley House, 53 Station Road, Shalford, Guildford, Surrey GU4 8HA ✆ **Guildford (0483) 63640**
Can place au pairs. Ages 18-30. Basic knowledge of French needed. Pocket money FF750 per months (2 month summer positions) or FF900 per month (6+ months). Insurance provided. Also positions for mothers' helps and nannies. Service charge £40.

HELPING HANDS AU PAIR & DOMESTIC AGENCY 39 Rutland Avenue, Thorpe Bay, Essex SS1 2XJ ✆ **Southend-on-Sea (0702) 602067**
Can place au pairs and mothers' helps. Ages 18-27. Pocket money approx £30 per week for au pairs, higher for mothers' helps. Introduction fee £40. *UK nationals only.*

HOME FROM HOME Walnut Orchard, Chearsley, Aylesbury, Buckinghamshire HP18 0DA ✆ **/Fax Aylesbury (0844) 208561**
Can place au pairs. Ages 18+. Reasonable level of French essential. Pocket money £25 per week. Placement fee £40. *UK nationals only.*

INTER-SÉJOURS 179 rue de Courcelles, 75017 Paris ✆ **Paris (1) 47 63 06 81**
Can place au pairs in Paris and the provinces. Ages 18-26. Pocket money FF1500 per month. Registration fee FF600.

INTERNATIONAL CATHOLIC SOCIETY FOR GIRLS (ACISJF) St Patrick's International Youth Centre, 24 Great Chapel Street, London W1V 3AF ✆ **01-734 2156**
Au pair posts arranged for 9+ months. Ages 18+. Mainly for UK and Irish nationals.

JOLAINE AGENCY 18 Escot Way, Barnet, Hertfordshire EN5 3AN ✆ **081-449 1334**
Can place au pairs and mothers' helps. Ages 18+. Weekly pocket money approx £25 (au pairs) or £30 (mothers' helps). Placement fee £40.

JUST THE JOB EMPLOYMENT AGENCY 8 Musters Road, West Bridgford, Nottingham NG2 5PL ✆ **Nottingham (0602) 813224**
Can place au pairs, mothers' helps and nannies. Ages 18+. Weekly pocket money £30-£40 (au pairs) or £75-£140 (other positions). *UK nationals only.*

LANGTRAIN INTERNATIONAL Torquay Road, Foxrock, Dublin 18, Ireland ✆ **Dublin (1) 289 3876**
Can place au pairs in French families. Ages 18+. Pocket money approx £25-£40 per week. Placement fee £50.

MONDIAL AGENCY 32 Links Road, West Wickham, Kent BR4 0QW ✆ **081-777 0510**
Can place au pairs in Paris or Nice. Ages 18-27. Pocket money approx £30 per week. Service charge £40.

PROBLEMS UNLIMITED AGENCY 86 Alexandra Road, Windsor, Berkshire SL4 1HU ✆ **Windsor (0753) 830101**
Can place au pairs. Ages 18-27. Pocket money £30-£35 per week. Service charge £40.

SÉJOURS INTERNATIONAUX LINGUISTIQUES ET CULTURELS
32 Rempart de l'Est, 16022 Angoulême Cedex ✆ 45 95 83 56
Can place au pairs all over France. Ages 18+. Pocket money approx FF300 per week. Registration fee FF750. *Apply by March for summer placements, by end June for placements starting September.*

STUDENTS ABROAD LTD **11 Milton View, Hitchin, Herts, SG4 0QD ✆ Hitchin (0462) 438909**
Can place au pairs, mothers' helps and nannies. Ages 18-27 for au pairs. Basic knowledge of French preferred. Pocket money approx FF1500 per month; higher for mothers' helps and nannies. Service charge £40. *Apply early for short-term summer placements and winter ski resort positions.*

UNIVERSAL CARE **Chester House, 9 Windsor End, Beaconsfield, Buckinghamshire HP9 2JJ ✆ Beaconsfield (0494) 678811**
Can place au pairs and mothers' helps. Ages 18-27 (au pairs), 18-35 (mothers' helps). Most families require a minimum knowledge of French. Monthly salary from FF1300 (au pairs), FF1500 (mothers' helps). Service charge £47. *Apply 2 months before work period desired. EC nationals only.* **PH**

COMMUNITY WORK

LES AMIS DE PAX CHRISTI **58 avenue de Breteuil, 75007 Paris**
An international Catholic movement for peace, organising centres for international encounters during the summer which attempt to encourage dialogue between different nations, races and religions, to give a living witness that peace is possible. Volunteers are needed to work in Lourdes. Hostels are set up in school buildings, to provide meals and accommodation. The aim is for the volunteers to form a lively international community. Work involves reception duties, cleaning, cooking, shopping, laundry, publicity and the setting up and dismantling of beds. Volunteers also invite the visitors to join them in reflection, dialogue and prayer. The work is hard but often rewarding. Duties and free time are allocated on a rota basis as far as possible so that everyone shares menial as well as more enjoyable aspects of the work. Ages 18-30. Volunteers must have a real commitment to peace. 3 weeks, July-early September. Food, dormitory accommodation and insurance provided. Volunteers pay their own travel costs.

ASSOCIATION DES PARALYSÉS DE FRANCE **Service-Vacances, 17 boulevard Auguste-Blanqui, 75013 Paris**
A non-profitmaking organisation recruiting volunteers to help physically handicapped adults on holiday all over France. Participants give aid and share their time with the handicapped as appropriate, so there are no fixed hours of work. July and August. Ages 18+. Males are in greater demand; no experience necessary. Full board youth centre accommodation and insurance provided, plus travel expenses from the French border. Social activities and excursions arranged are available to the volunteers.

CONSERVATION

LES ALPES DE LUMIERE **Prieuré de Salagon, Mane, 04300 Forcalquier**
Arranges conservation workcamps throughout Haute-Provence. Recent projects have included renovating medieval fortifications in Castellane; restoring the tower of a castle in Selonnet; tidying up the site of the ruined village of Méthamis; and laying out a nursery garden in Mane. Ages 18+. 15+ days, July-September, approx 30 hour week with afternoons free for leisure activities. Countryside excursions arranged. Volunteers should take a sleeping bag, working clothes, rucksack and walking shoes. Food, camping accommodation and insurance provided. Volunteers pay own travel and FF300-FF500 registration fee depending on length of stay. **D PH** but no access for wheelchairs.

ASSOCIATION CHANTIERS HISTOIRE ET ARCHITECTURE MEDIÉVALES (CHAM) **5 & 7 rue Guilleminot, 75014 Paris**
Founded in 1980 with the aim of rescuing and restoring historic French medieval buildings and monuments. Workcamps are organised at sites in Brittany, Burgundy, Centre, Nord-Pas

de Calais, Pays-de-Loire and Upper Normandy for groups of 15-40 volunteers. The work involves clearing sites, improving, rebuilding and stabilising, restoration work on masonry and archaeological excavations. Recent projects have included clearing the subterranean vaults of a 12th century château in Morbihan; repairing the masonry of a Roman Abbey in Ille-et-Vilaine; and restoring the ramparts around a village in Loir-et-Cher. Visits arranged to local sites of historic interest; talks are given on medieval history and architecture. Ages 15+. No experience necessary, but volunteers must be fit, motivated and able to adapt to communal life. Good knowledge of French needed. Approx 35 hour week, 1-10 weeks, July-September. Cost FF50 per day covers food and camping accommodation. Volunteers take turns to prepare food, pay their own travel expenses and should take a sleeping bag, practical clothes and sturdy footwear. Registration fee FF100 includes insurance. Also run training courses in restoration techniques. D PH depending on ability.

ASSOCIATION DROMOISE CHANTIERS ANIMATION ET VIE LOCALE (ADCAVL) Le Château, 26460 Le Poët-Celard ☎ 75 53 32 11
An association organising workcamps in villages throughout the department of Drôme, south of Lyon. Volunteers are invited to take part in projects aimed at restoring and allowing access to sites of historic and cultural interest. Recent projects have included restoration work on a dungeon in the medieval village of Pontaix; creating a riverside walk along the banks of the Isère in the town of Romans; preparing an exhibition area at a museum in Montguers illustrating the traditions of the local perfume industry; restoring the ramparts of the town of Die situated in the Vercors National Park; and repaving steep and narrow streets in the mountain village of Arpavon. Ages 18+. No experience necessary, but knowledge of French helpful. 25 hour week for 2-3 weeks, April-September. Afternoons are devoted to sports such as rock climbing, canoeing or horse riding; or craft workshops such as pottery, sculpture or painting. Cultural activities, walks and excursions organised at weekends, with opportunities to attend local festivals. Insurance, food and basic accommodation in tents, schools or village halls

provided, with volunteers taking it in turns to cook. Tools and materials provided, but volunteers should take work clothes, walking boots, rucksack and sleeping bag. All-inclusive participation fee FF980 (1992). No fares or wages paid. *UK applicants apply direct.*

In Belgium, apply through VZW De Kolk, 152 Tiensestraat, 3000 Leuven

In Germany, apply through Pro International, Bahnhofstraße 26B, W-3550 Marburg/Lahn

In the Netherlands, apply through Activity International, Bieslookstraat 31, 9731 HH Groningen

ASSOCIATION LE MAT Le Viel Audon, Balazuc, 07120 Ruoms
Volunteers needed to help in restoring a village in the Ardèche, developing its resources to create new jobs. Twenty years of workcamps have resulted in the creation of a farm and a youth hostel, and educational courses are also held. Work involves masonry, carpentry, cooking, baking bread and general care of the environment. Sports and social activities can also be organised. Ages 17-25. 6 hour day. Easter, July and August. Basic accommodation and communal meals provided. FF47 per day covers board. Volunteers pay own travel costs. Registration fee FF70 includes insurance.

ASSOCIATION POUR LA PARTICIPATION A L'ACTION RÉGIONALE (APARE) 41 cours Jean Jaurès, 84000 Avignon
Offers participants the opportunity to discover Provence through projects aimed at protecting the region's environment and heritage. Recent projects have included restoring a Roman chapel in Vaucluse; cleaning up the rivers Recluse and Pesquier; helping to preserve cultivated terraces north of Avignon; and repairing a Roman bridge in Var. Ages 14-16 or 18+. 3 or 4 weeks, June-November. Approx 30 hour week, with afternoons and weekends free for discovering the region on foot, by bike or canoe. Opportunities to attend local festivals, plays and poetry workshops. Volunteers should take a sleeping bag, working clothes, rucksack and walking shoes. Accommodation, food and insurance provided. Volunteers pay own travel. FF600 registration fee.

BRITISH TRUST FOR CONSERVATION VOLUNTEERS Room IWH, 36 St Mary's Street, Wallingford, Oxfordshire OX10 0EU
The Trust is Britain's leading organisation for the promotion of practical conservation work for protecting the environment. Since 1983 volunteers have worked alongside French environmental groups to carry out conservation tasks. Recent projects have included drystone walling in the Pyrénées; constructing a board walk through reedbeds near St Amand les Eaux; building a bird hide in a nature reserve in Le Quesnoy; and fencing work at a tortoise village built to protect the Hermanns Tortoise in Corsica. Ages 18-70. Cost £50 per week includes food and camping or dormitory accommodation. Everyone shares in the cooking. Membership fee £12. No fares or wages paid.

CENTRE PERMANENT D'INITIATION A LA FORET PROVENÇALE (ASSODEF) Hôtel de Ville, Chemin du Loubatas, 13860 Peyrolles
Each year large areas of forest in the South of France, Greece, Italy and Portugal fall victim to forest fires, due to carelessness and ignorance. For 10 years ASSODEF has been teaching young people about the dangers of forest fires and involving them in forest protection work. Volunteers are invited to take part in summer workcamps. Recent projects have included helping to build a forest information centre based on solar energy; setting up observation posts and information boards; building a concrete tank to hold rainwater in case of fire; footpath maintenance, coppicing, clearing undergrowth, and working to prevent forest fire. Ages 18+. No special skills or techniques required, but knowledge of French essential. 1/3 weeks, July-early September. Approx 30 hour week, with afternoons free for arranged leisure activities. Accommodation, food and insurance provided. Volunteers pay own travel and FF550 registration fee. PH

CLUB DU VIEUX MANOIR 10 rue de la Cossonnerie, 75001 Paris ℗ Paris (1) 45 08 80 40
A national movement which brings together young people willing to devote time to the restoration and upkeep of historic and endangered monuments and sites and to the protection of the natural environment. Recent projects have included laying a traditional stone pavement in the medieval town centre of Le Bugue in the Dordogne; restoring old buildings, including a 17th century chapel, 18th century fortresses, a 16th century church, and village sundials at Briançon in the Hautes-Alpes; helping with archaeological work at Philippe le Bel's 13th century château in Oise; and restoring a 16th century wooden coaching inn with dovecotes at Casteljaloux in Lot-et-Garonne. Three permanent sites at Guise, Argy and Pontpoint serve as centres for introduction to the environment, architectural heritage and for specialised research and instruction on materials, techniques and tools. Some sites also run special programmes/festivals. All volunteers receive manual and technical tuition in archaeology, building techniques, restoration of buildings, architecture, history and handicrafts. Ages 14/15+, depending on site chosen. Minimum age for specialised instruction is 16. 15+ days, Easter, July-September, Christmas and during the year. Simple self-catering accommodation provided in tents (summer) or under shelter (winter), sometimes without running water. Participants share in the day to day organisation of the camp, and discipline is strict. Cost FF60 per day includes board and lodging. Participants should take a sleeping bag. Volunteers aged 17+ staying for an extended period, other than during the summer, receive free board and lodging after a trial period of 15 days. Registration fee FF70 covers membership and insurance.

LES COMPAGNONS DU CAP, Pratcoustals, Arphy, 30120 Le Vigan ℗ 67 81 82 22
Volunteers are invited to help restore the abandoned village of Pratcoustals, situated high above the Arphy valley in the Cévennes region. Every summer renovation workcamps help make the site into a permanent centre, adding a museum and restaurant to existing holiday facilities. Work involves re-roofing with traditional tiles, masonry, drystone-walling, rebuilding stone steps and general improvements to the village. There is also environmental work in the surrounding chestnut forest and the chance to do research into the village's history. Weekend and evening activities include hiking, mountain-biking, swimming in mountain streams, sports,

social and musical events. Ages 18+. No experience necessary, but volunteers should be able to speak French and interested in living and working as a group. 2 weeks, June-September. Approx 30 hours work per week. FF58 per day covers dormitory/tent accommodation and meals; volunteers should take a sleeping bag. Registration fee FF70 covers accident insurance. D

CONCORDIA 38 rue du Faubourg St Denis, 75010 Paris

Volunteers are needed on approx 60 international workcamps which aim to help in the development of small communities in mountainous and isolated rural areas including Auvergne, Bourgogne, Champagne, Midi-Pyrénées, Picardy and Alpes, giving participants the chance to get to know their natural, political, economic and social environment.

Typical conservation projects include restoring houses, chapels, churches, feudal châteaux and forts, fountains, wells and wash-houses in villages and abandoned hamlets; clearing and signposting footpaths and hiking tracks; creating gardens and green spaces, observatories and bird hides; repairing traditional bread ovens, sheepfolds and mountain huts; restoring paintings and frescoes; and environmental protection in the Parc Naturel de la Vanoise. Volunteers are taught traditional building techniques by local craftsmen. Sports, crafts, theatre, festivals and other cultural and social activities arranged. Ages 18-25. Good knowledge of French needed for some camps. Applicants should preferably have previous workcamp experience. 35 hour week. 3 weeks, June-November and 2 weeks, Easter and Christmas. Also camps for ages 15-17; 25 hour week. Projects include cleaning rivers, laying out paths for walkers, working in the forest and restoration work on endangered monuments. Full board accommodation in schools, huts or community buildings and insurance provided. Volunteers pay their own travel costs. Registration fee FF550, FF1510 for ages 15-17. B D PH

Walking/cycling holidays organised to introduce the type of projects undertaken on workcamps and to discover the natural environment. Participants should be able to carry a rucksack and walk/cycle for 3-6 hours a day. Also arrange leader training seminars during the holidays.

Apply through partner organisation in country of residence. In the UK: Quaker International Social Projects, Friends House, Euston Road, London NW1 2BJ (experienced volunteers only; ages 18+) or United Nations Association, International Youth Service, Temple of Peace, Cathays Park, Cardiff CF1 3AP © Cardiff (0222) 223088.

Outside the UK: please see information on page 30.

ENFANTS ET AMIS DE BEAUCHASTEL Christian Coulet, 33 rue de France, 69100 Villeurbanne

Volunteers are needed to help in the restoration of an abandoned medieval village in the Ardèche, developing its resources to create new jobs. Work involves masonry, carpentry, roof and floor tiling, paving and cooking. Ages 18+. No experience necessary, but knowledge of French useful. Approx 30 hour week, 1-15 August. Accommodation in village schoolhouse and meals provided; sports and social activities organised. Volunteers pay own travel costs. Cost FF350 for 2 weeks includes insurance. Anti-tetanus vaccination advisable.

ÉTUDES ET CHANTIERS INTERNATIONAL (UNAREC) 33 rue Campagne Première, 75014 Paris

Founded to encourage and promote the participation of young people and adults in the redevelopment of rural communities, the conservation of the environment and the rehabilitation of old town areas. Workcamps organised in many areas of France for groups of 15-20 volunteers.

The work includes clearing silt and debris from rivers and streams, stabilising banks and clearing vegetation; clearing and maintaining footpaths and constructing new ones to give access to rural sites; restoring old buildings and converting them into meeting or sports centres; rebuilding villages or buildings which have been abandoned or fallen into disrepair; and creating environmental education centres in existing green spaces or laying out playgrounds in towns. Technical help and advice given by local craftsmen. Sports and social activities include festivals, concerts, exhibitions, evenings with the villagers, discovery of the region, crafts, sailing and windsurfing. Ages 13-17 (25 hour week) and 17+ (35 hour week). Food and lodging in *gîtes*, tents or schools provided. Cost FF100 per day for ages 13-17, free for ages 17+. Volunteers prepare their own food and help with chores and pay their own travel costs. Registration fee FF700. Long-term work also available.

Apply through partner organisation in country of residence. In the UK: Quaker International Social Projects, Friends House, Euston Road, London, NW1 2BJ (experienced volunteers only; ages 18+) or United Nations Association, International Youth Service, Temple of Peace, Cathays Park, Cardiff CF1 3AP ✆ Cardiff (0222) 223088.

Outside the UK: please see information on page 30.

JEUNESSE ET RECONSTRUCTION 10 rue de Trévise, 75009 Paris ✆ Paris (1) 47 70 15 88
Aims to provide short-term practical aid towards the redevelopment of small rural communities, the understanding of the environment and to encourage local inhabitants to continue with the work. Recent projects have included clearing brushwood and cleaning riverbanks, repaving village streets, restoring ancient ramparts, castles and churches in Drôme; restoring a Roman road and medieval tower in Hautes-Alpes; restoring a 14th century château, a watermill and a bread oven in Haute-Loire; and thatching a summer house, cleaning and renovating a stone bridge, replanting grass on ski slopes and clearing rivers in Puy-de-Dome. Tasks involve masonry, woodwork, carpentry, painting, electrical work, roofing and other manual work. Discussions held in the evenings and at weekends, centring on environmental problems. Camps are run on a democratic basis; volunteers decide how to go about the project, when to work, rest, shop and cook. Ages 17-35. Parental consent needed for those under 18. Applicants should preferably have previous workcamp experience. 7 hour day, 5 day week. 2/3+ weeks, April-September. Basic accommodation provided in schools, dormitories, tents, mills or barns. Volunteers should take a sleeping bag. Food, prepared by the volunteers, and insurance provided. Volunteers pay their own travel costs. Registration fee FF425.

Apply through partner organisation in country of residence. In the UK: British Trust for Conservation Volunteers, Room IWH, 36 St Mary's Street, Wallingford, Oxfordshire OX10 0EU or Concordia (Youth Service Volunteers) Ltd, Recruitment Secretary, 8 Brunswick Place, Hove, Sussex BN3 1ET ✆ Brighton (0273) 772086.

Outside the UK: please see information on page 30.

KLAUS & JEAN ERHARDT Bardou, 34390 Olargues ✆ 67 97 72 43
The village of Bardou is a living museum of medieval farming life and a retreat for artists and writers. Volunteers are required to help in the restoration of 16th century stone houses, plus farm maintenance and the care of a flock of 200 prizewinning Bizet sheep. Ages 20+. No experience necessary. 16 hour week. May-June and September-November. French useful but not essential. Accommodation in the village and social activities provided. Volunteers pay own food, insurance and travel costs.

THE MONTAURIOL TRUST Le Berger, 11410 Montauriol, Aude ✆ 68 60 34 30
Volunteers are required to help with the restoration of farm buildings and village houses in the Aude region, south of Castelnaudray. Ages 18-30. No special skills or experience required, but applicants should be English-speaking. 35 hour, 5 day week. 10 days minimum, May-September. Basic full board accommodation provided, but no fares, wages or insurance paid. Transport provided from Toulouse. *Apply at least 2 weeks in advance.*

MOUVEMENT CHRÉTIEN POUR LA PAIX 38 rue du Faubourg St Denis, 75010 Paris
An international movement open to all who share a common concern for lasting peace and justice in the world. Volunteers are required to work in international teams on summer projects aimed at offering a service in an area of need and promoting self-help within the community; promoting international understanding and the discussion of social problems; and offering young people the chance to live as a group and take these experiences into the context of daily life. Volunteers are needed to help in small rural communities, preserving their heritage by carrying out restoration and salvage work on old buildings and the environment. Recent

projects have included restoring the ruins of a monument and organising a sound and light show to display the tower during a village festival; clearing and repairing footpaths, and restoring an old village in the Drôme region; renovating medieval castles, churches, chapels and traditional country houses; clearing moats; renovating an old train and railway in the Gironde; clearing canals in the Cévennes, and repairing the banks of the river Hérault; studying the medicinal and nutritional values of forgotten plants, and creating a nature reserve. Sports, social activities and village festivities organised. Ages 15-17 and 18+. 6 hour day, 30-36 hour week. 2-3 weeks, July-August. Food, accommodation in tents or barns and insurance provided, but participants pay their own travel costs, and sometimes contribute towards food expenses. D PH but unsuitable for wheelchairs.

Apply through partner organisation in country of residence. In the UK: Christian Movement for Peace, Bethnal Green United Reformed Church, Pott Street, London E2 0EF

Outside the UK: please see information on page 30.

PIERRES SECHES EN VAUCLUSE
La Cornette, 84800 Saumane
Arranges workcamps mainly based on drystone-walling techniques. Recent projects have included restoring an 18th century wall built across the plateau of Vaucluse during the time of the last Plague. Ages 18+. 2 weeks, July-August. Approx 30 hour week with afternoons free for leisure activities. Country walks, swimming and canoeing arranged. Food and camping accommodation provided. Volunteers pay own travel and FF450 to cover registration, membership and insurance.

PIERRES VIVES BP 19, 04300 Forcalquier
Small number of volunteers required to help in the renovation of a large 16th century farmhouse overlooking a valley in the Alpes de Haute Provence. Repairs were begun in August 1990 and major work has since been undertaken on the ceilings and roofs. As well as manual construction work, help is also required with gardening, cooking, maintenance, and caring for horses. Ages 18-32. Experience of similar work essential; knowledge of French, English or Spanish preferred. 33 hour week with weekends free; 1-3 months, all year. Accommodation provided in the farmhouse, plus breakfast and lunch on working days. Some work clothes can be supplied but volunteers should take a sleeping bag, and must pay their own travel expenses. Courses held in building techniques; excursions organised to the surrounding region.

REMPART (Union des Associations pour la Réhabilitation et l'Entretien des Monuments et du Patrimoine Artistique), 1 rue des Guillemites, 75004 Paris
Aims to improve the way of life through a better understanding of and a greater respect for the archaeological, architectural and natural heritage and environment through the restoration of endangered buildings and monuments. REMPART consists of a grouping of more than 140 autonomous associations, providing a wide variety of work projects involving the restoration of medieval towns, cities, châteaux, fortresses, religious buildings, farms, ancient villages, roads, forges, walls, wind/watermills, Gallo-Roman amphitheatres and baths, churches and post-medieval fortresses, houses, villages and castles, old industrial sites plus contemporary murals, ramparts, churches, underground passages, paths, ski runs and steam engines. Work includes masonry, woodwork, carpentry, roofing, interior decorating, restoration and clearance work, plus carrying out surveys, technical photography and filing. Opportunities for sports, exploring the region, crafts, music, cinema and taking part in local festivities. Ages 14/18+. There is no upper age limit, anyone feeling young is welcome, and some camps accept families. Previous experience not necessary. Some knowledge of French needed. 30-35 hour week. 2-4 weeks, Easter and June-September; a few camps are open throughout the year. Cost FF20-FF45 per day (average FF30) for food and accommodation in huts, old buildings or tents, with self-catering facilities; a few camps are free. Volunteers help with camp duties, pay their own fares, and should take a sleeping bag. Applicants can choose which project they would like to work on from the workcamp programme and contact addresses are given. Registration fee FF200 includes insurance. Also

arranges courses in restoration techniques, artistic activities and environmental studies. *Enclose 3 IRCs.* D PH but no wheelchair access.

RESTANQUES ET MURETS DE VENASQUE
Mairie, 84210 Venasque
Volunteers required for workcamps with an environmental theme in the village of Venasque, near Avignon. Work involves environmental management and the restoration of ancient monuments. Ages 18+. No experience necessary. 25-30 hours per week, July-August. Board, lodging and insurance provided, and excursions arranged to local places of interest. Cost FF400-FF500 covers membership fee and registration. Volunteers pay their own travel costs. *Apply by 30 June.*

LA SABRANENQUE CENTRE
INTERNATIONAL rue de la Tour de l'Oume, 30290 Saint Victor la Coste
A small, non-profitmaking organisation that has been working since 1969 to preserve, restore and reconstruct abandoned rural sites, and bring them back to life. Aims to give volunteers the chance to discover the pleasure of working directly on genuine rural restoration projects while being part of a cooperative team. After completing the reconstruction of the medieval village of Saint Victor la Coste, 25km north of Avignon, La Sabranenque now works on several sites in nearby villages. Volunteers work in small teams, learning traditional construction techniques on-the-job from experienced leaders. Work can include masonry, stone cutting, floor or roof tiling, interior restoration, drystone walling, path paving and planting trees. 1 day per session spent visiting the region, which is rich in ancient monuments. Ages 18+. No experience necessary. 2+ weeks, 1 June-30 August. Cost FF100 per day includes full board accommodation in restored houses. Registration fee FF200.

SOLIDARITÉS JEUNESSES 38 rue du
Faubourg St Denis, 75010 Paris
Originally took over, saved and restored old mills in the Creuse region, with the help of volunteers, which now form the basis of international workcamps. Projects include the continuing restoration of old mills and other old buildings for conversion into international

meeting centres along the Creuse rivers, plus a feudal fortress in the Pyrénées-Atlantiques and the protection of their environment including cleaning rivers and banks, gardening, upkeep of footpaths, nature trails and open spaces, plus flora and fauna. Camps involve working mornings with cultural activities in the afternoons, including workshops and courses covering pottery, photography, carpentry, painting, ecology, wood carving, weaving and ironwork. Also courses in French and Esperanto. Opportunities exist for discovering the region and sports.
Ages 13+. 2 weeks, Easter, Christmas and June-September. Cost FF90 per day includes board, insurance and tent, dormitory or pension accommodation. Membership fee FF100. Participants should take a sleeping bag and work clothes. Courses last approx 2 weeks, July and August; cost FF1800 includes board, lodging, tuition and materials. D PH unsuitable for wheelchairs.

COURIERS / REPS

BELLE FRANCE Bayham Abbey, Lamberhurst, Kent TN3 8BG ✆ Lamberhurst (0892) 890885
Organise bicycle and walking holidays in Provence, the Loire Valley, Brittany and the Auvergne. Limited number of positions available for representatives. Applicants must have a thorough knowledge of French, good manual dexterity, a clean driving licence and two years driving experience. Training given. Ages 19+. 2½-3 months minimum, mid May-end September. Salary £175 per month plus allowance for food. Accommodation provided in studio, house or caravan, as well as personal insurance and return travel costs from London. Applicants should note that areas are very rural and there is likely to be little in the way of night life. Interviews held prior to appointment. *UK nationals only.*

BLADON LINES Personnel Department, 56-58 Putney High Street, London SW15 1SF ✆ 081-785 2200
Opportunities for representatives to work in French ski resorts. Work involves looking after guests, providing information, helping with coach transfers and ensuring everything is

running smoothly. Ages 24+. Relevant experience an advantage, and good spoken French essential. Applicants must be prepared to work hard but will get time to ski. Season lasts December-May. Salary £50-£100 per week, depending on the size of the resort. Board, lodging, return travel, insurance, ski pass, ski hire and company ski jacket provided. Training week held in London before departure.

CANVAS HOLIDAYS LTD 12 Abbey Park Place, Dunfermline, Fife KY12 7PD

Provides accommodation for families in ready-erected fully equipped tents and cabins. Positions available as resident couriers, children's couriers, nannies and watersports couriers. The work involves a daily routine of cleaning as customers arrive and depart, providing information and advice on the local attractions and essential services and helping to sort out any problems that might arise. 7 day week job with no fixed hours; the workload varies from day to day. At the beginning and end of the season there is a period of physical work when tents are put up and prepared for the customers or taken down and stored for the winter. Other tasks include administration, book-keeping and stock control.

Children's couriers are responsible for a number of children during various periods of the day or evening, and are expected to organise a variety of games, activities and competitions within the limitations of the campsite, and be flexible to cope with weather, varying numbers and limited preparation time. Applicants should have previous experience with children, through nursing, teacher training or group playschemes, and be able to use their initiative to develop ideas for activities.

Ages 18-25. Applicants are normally those with a year between school and further education, undergraduates or graduates. They need to be enthusiastic, practical, reliable, self-motivated, able to turn their hand to new and varied tasks, and with a sense of humour. 6 months, April-October. Return travel, dependent on successful completion of contract, accommodation in frame tents and moped or bicycle for use on site provided. Salary £80 per week (1992).
Applications accepted anytime; interviews commence November for the following season.

CARISMA HOLIDAYS Bethel House, Heronsgate Road, Chorleywood, Hertfordshire WD3 5BB ② Chorleywood (0923) 284235

Organises holidays in tents and mobile homes on beach sites along the west coast of France. Managers and couriers are required to be responsible for client families. Work involves welcoming families, providing information and advice, cleaning and maintaining tents and mobile homes, and babysitting for clients when necessary. Applicants should have a helpful and friendly disposition and experience of dealing with people. Good spoken French and English essential. Ages 17+. Working hours vary; couriers are expected to work early May-end September or late June-early September. Salary £65-£80 per week depending on responsibility and experience. Self-catering accommodation provided in tents or mobile homes. Full training given on site at start of season. Travel costs paid. *EC nationals only.*

CLUB CANTABRICA HOLIDAYS LTD Overseas Department, Holiday House, 146-148 London Road, St Albans, Hertfordshire AL1 1PQ

Organises camping holidays, providing fully equipped tents, caravans and mobile homes. Vacancies exist for couriers and maintenance staff to work the whole summer season, mid May-early October, in Port Grimaud, Cavalaire and Canet. 6 day week. Ages 21+. Salary from £45 per week, plus bonus at end of season. Experience an advantage, as is a good knowledge of French. Self-catering accommodation in tents or caravans, travel costs from Watford and insurance provided. *Apply enclosing cv. EC nationals only.*

CRYSTAL HOLIDAYS Crystal House, The Courtyard, Arlington Road, Surbiton, Surrey KT6 6BW ② 081-390 8737

Tour operator arranging year-round air, rail and self-drive holidays throughout France, and winter skiing holidays in the French Alps. Representatives are required to meet and greet clients and be responsible for their welfare during their holiday. Ski guides also needed during winter season. Ages 20-35. Previous experience desirable and fluent French essential. Approx 60 hour, 7 day week, May-October and December-April. Basic salary plus commission; board, lodging, insurance, travel costs and uniform provided. 1 week training seminar held at beginning of each season. *Apply January/February for summer season, April/ May for winter season.*

EUROCAMP Summer Jobs, (Ref WH), PO Box 170, Liverpool L70 1ES
One of Europe's leading tour operators, specialising in providing quality camping and mobile home holidays for families throughout Europe. Campsite couriers are required: work involves cleaning tents and equipment prior to the arrival of new customers; checking, replacing and making repairs on equipment; replenishing gas supplies; keeping basic accounts and reporting on a weekly basis to England. Couriers are also expected to meet new arrivals and assist holidaymakers with any problems that arise; organise activities and parties; provide information on local tourist attractions and maintain an information noticeboard. At the beginning and end of the season couriers are also expected to help in erecting and dismantling tents. Couriers need to be flexible to meet the needs of customers and be on hand where necessary; they will be able to organise their own free time as the workload allows.

Ages 18+. Applicants should be independent, adaptable, reliable, physically fit, have plenty of initiative and relish a challenging and responsible position. Good working knowledge of French also necessary. Preference given to those able to work the whole season, April-September/October; contracts also available for first half season, April-mid July and second half season, mid July-September/ October.

Children's couriers are also required, with the energy and enthusiasm to organise a wide range of exciting activities for groups of children aged 4-13. Experience of working with children within this age range is essential, but language ability is not a requirement. Ages 20+. Children's couriers must be available for the whole season, May-September.

For both positions the salary is £91.50 per week. Training is provided together with accommodation in frame tent with cooking

facilities, insurance and return travel.

UK/EC passport-holders only. Early application advisable; interviews start September/October.

FREEDOM OF FRANCE Personnel Department, Alton Court, Penyard Lane (878), Ross-on-Wye, Herefordshire HR9 5NR
✆ Ross-on-Wye (0989) 767833
Provides luxury self-drive, self-catering holidays at campsites throughout France. Campsite couriers are required to work from Brittany through to the Bordeaux coast and down to the Mediterranean. The work involves ensuring that tents are clean and tidy, meeting and greeting families on arrival, and lending a sympathetic ear to clients' requirements. Children's couriers are required to run entertainment programmes for children who will be divided into different age groups. April-September. Ages 20+. Good command of French preferred. Salary £80 per week. Self-catering accommodation in large tents, full liability and medical insurance and travel from UK port provided.

FRENCH COUNTRY CAMPING Assistant Operations Manager, 126 Hempstead Road, Kings Langley, Hertfordshire WD4 8AL
✆ Watford (0923) 261316
Operates self-drive family holidays providing fully furnished and equipped tents and mobile homes. Vacancies exist for operations team members plus a limited number of campsite couriers. Operations teams consist of 3-5 members and a supervisor travelling around France, responsible for setting up or closing down campsites. 3-4 days are spent at each site and the work involves long car journeys and heavy lifting work so applicants must be fit and capable of working long hours, maybe in poor weather. They will be expected to show initiative and an ability to work without supervision. 3-4 weeks, May or September, depending on unpredictable factors such as weather.

Applicants should have sound organisational ability and a mature, outgoing personality. French language ability essential for courier posts, useful for other positions. End May-beginning September. Work as campsite couriers entails preparing tents or mobile homes, welcoming clients, occasionally organising social activities, and dealing with any problems which may arise. Mid May-mid July or mid July-mid September. Ages 19+ (operations team members) or 21+ (couriers). Salary approx £90 per week. Accommodation in tents with cooking facilities and insurance provided. Travel expenses paid, provided company transport is used when available. *EC nationals only.*

FRENCH LIFE MOTORING HOLIDAYS
Overseas Personnel Manager, 26 Church Road, Horsforth, Leeds LS18 5LG ✆ Leeds (0532) 390077
Organises self-drive holidays with fully equipped tents and caravans on campsites, and requires site representatives. Work involves welcoming clients and looking after them during their holiday, cleaning and maintaining tents and caravans, organising excursions, caring for and entertaining children, providing a babysitting service, and running evening entertainment activities such as barbecues, wine and cheese and fancy dress parties. Representatives are on call 24 hours a day, usually 6 days a week. Ages 21+. Applicants should have experience of dealing with people, and be used to hard physical work. They should be dynamic, reliable, hard working, conscientious and loyal with the ability to work as part of a team, plus the staying power to last the whole season. Working knowledge of French essential. April-October, with some positions available for students only in June/July. Accommodation in shared frame tents with own bedroom area, self-catering cooking facilities and return travel provided. Salary approx £85 per week. All staff are required to take part in a training programme in April. *UK or French nationals only. Early application advisable - recruitment starts December, interviews commence mid-January.*

HAVEN FRANCE & SPAIN **Northney Marina, Northney Road, Hayling Island, Hampshire PO11 0NL**
Tour operator organising self-drive package holidays, with accommodation in luxury mobile homes and tents. Seasonal park managers are required to work on sites in coastal and inland regions of France. Work involves preparing accommodation, welcoming guests and sorting

out any problems that may arise. Tiger Club couriers also required, to work with children and organise entertainment. Experience preferred but not essential, as training is given. Knowledge of French essential. Ages 18+. 40+ hour week, although hours vary. May-September. Salary approx £95 per week, but varies according to workload. Self-catering accommodation in mobile homes or tents, insurance and travel expenses provided. *UK nationals only.*

KEYCAMP HOLIDAYS **92-96 Lind Road, Sutton, Surrey SM1 4PL ✆ 081-395 8170**
One of the UK's largest self-drive camping and mobile home tour operators, offering holidays on over 75 campsites in Europe. Campsite couriers are required to work for 3-6 months in an outdoor environment. Main duties include providing clients with information, organising social and sporting activities, cleaning mobile homes and tents, and providing activities for children. 3+ months, March-July or July-September. Ages 18+. Knowledge of French desirable. Accommodation, uniform, training and competitive salary provided. *Applications welcome from September. Phone for application form.*

LOTUS SUPERTRAVEL **Alpine Operations Department, Mobbs Court, 2 Jacob Street, London SE1 2BT ✆ 071-962 9933**
Arranges skiing holidays in the French alpine resorts of Méribel, Courchevel, Val d'Isère, Tignes, Avoriaz, La Plagne and Les Deux Alpes. Opportunities for resort representatives, responsible for looking after guests and supervising staff. Ages 24-34. Work involves travelling to the airport each weekend to welcome guests; organising their ski passes, ski hire and ski school; informing them of local events; overseeing the work of chalet girls and ensuring that chalets are kept in perfect running order. There are also opportunities for managers in the jumbo chalets (24-60 beds) who are responsible for the smooth running of their chalet and should be experienced in hotel work. Applicants must be available for the whole season, early December-end April. Approx 40+ hours per week. Board, lodging, ski pass, ski and boot hire and return travel provided; also insurance in return for approx £35 contribution. Salary £55-£85 per week, paid in local currency.

Training course held in London before departure, plus individual session to learn about the resort. *UK/EC passport holders only.*

MATTHEWS HOLIDAYS LTD
8 Bishopsmead Parade, East Horsley, Surrey KT24 6RP © **East Horsley (048 65) 4044**
Operates holidays in mobile homes on campsites mainly in Normandy, Brittany and on the Atlantic coast. Representatives are required to work on sites, welcoming clients, maintaining good relations, providing information and advice and cleaning mobile homes. No experience necessary, but fluent French essential. Ages 20+. 35 hour week; reps are expected to work the whole season, early May-end September. Salary FF850 per week (1992). Self-catering accommodation in caravans/mobile homes, medical insurance and travel costs provided. *UK nationals only.*

NSS RIVIERA HOLIDAYS 199 Marlborough Avenue, Hull HU15 3LG
Owns 29 chalets, cottages and mobile homes on a 4 star holiday village complex situated halfway between St Tropez and Cannes. Couple or two friends required to act as representatives, May-September. Work involves greeting clients, helping with all problems, organising a weekly party, cleaning and maintaining accommodation and keeping the gardens weeded and watered. Applicants should be active, reliable, well-adjusted non-smokers with a sense of humour, own car and extensive experience of DIY, gardening, plumbing, working with people and caring. Character and work references essential. Ages 40+. Hours are unsocial, but there is enormous job satisfaction; time off is arranged between the two representatives. Accommodation provided in 2 berth caravan with patio, mains hot shower and WC. Electricity, water, local tax, expenses and £150 per week provided; help given with ferry tickets and insurance. *Apply in writing with full background information as soon as possible.*

PGL YOUNG ADVENTURE LTD Personnel Department, Alton Court, Penyard Lane (878), Ross-On-Wye, Herefordshire HR9 5NR
© **Ross-on-Wye (0989) 767833**
Organises outdoor adventure holidays for young people and adults in the Ardèche and on the Mediterranean. Activities include canoeing, sailing, windsurfing and caving. Couriers/group leaders are required, accompanying children aged 12-17, starting and finishing in Manchester, Birmingham and London. The position involves complete responsibility for the group whilst travelling and at the centre, dealing with pocket money, illness and general coordination, including lights out, and helping with the evening programme. Ages 21+. Applicants should have a strong sense of responsibility, total commitment, enjoy the company of young people, be self-motivated, tolerant, flexible, positive, mature, with vitality, a good sense of humour, stamina, energy, enthusiasm, and a fairly extrovert personality. Good spoken French essential; experience in working with groups of young people, preferably abroad, in informal or formal settings, and ability to cope with demands on one's time needed. July-September. Couriers accompany groups on 10-day trips, and usually take 2/3 trips during the season. Return travel from the UK, full board accommodation in frame tents and health insurance provided. Sports and social facilities available, plus participation in programmed activities. Pocket money from £75 per 10-day trip. *Applications should ideally be made November-April.*

SCHOOL WORLD The Coach House, Tyn-y-Coed Place, Roath Park, Cardiff CF2 4TX
© **Cardiff (0222) 470077**
Organises skiing holidays for school groups at Pra Loup, Vars/Risoul, Les Deux Alpes, La Clusaz, Morzine, Les Gets, Chatel and Les Carroz. Requires representatives to prepare for the groups' arrival, operate quality and safety control, deal with any problems, arrange après ski programmes and generally ensure that clients enjoy their holiday. Season lasts from late December-mid April depending on school holiday dates. Hours worked vary but representatives are on call at all times. Ages 19-30. Experience of working with the public and a good knowledge of French essential; applicants must also be friendly and outgoing with a high level of common sense and personal organisation. Salary £35 per week, with a £15 bonus for each group looked after, depending on completion of contract. Full board accommodation, insurance and reasonable

travel costs provided. 4-5 day residential training course held. Recruitment begins July for following winter season. *Applicants must have UK National Insurance number.*

SEASUN SCHOOL TOURS Ski Department, Seasun House, 4 East Street, Colchester, Essex CO1 2XW
Provides skiing holidays in the French Alps for school groups during peak school holiday dates at New Year, February and Easter. Requires resort representatives to spend weeks with groups coordinating their tour. Ages 20+. Applicants must be diplomatic, affable, fun, hardworking skiers, with experience of working with children and fluent French. Salary according to responsibility. Accommodation, travel, personal insurance and partial uniform provided. *Write for application form.*

SEASUN/TENTREK HOLIDAYS 71/72 East Hill, Colchester, Essex CO1 2QW
✆ **Colchester (0206) 861886**
Provides self-catering family holidays in apartments, mobile homes and tents plus activity holidays for schools and groups. Requires representatives for the summer season, early April-mid November, in Marseillan Plage, Canet Plage and Benodet (Brittany). 50/60 hour week. Ages 19+. Applicants should be independent and resourceful with good communication skills and commitment. Knowledge of French an advantage, but not essential. Training provided. Salary and subsistence £240 per month; £40 per month extra paid on successful completion of contract. Accommodation, travel, personal insurance and partial uniform provided. B D PH depending on ability.

SIMPLY TRAVEL LTD 8 Chiswick Terrace, Acton Lane, London W4 5LY *✆* **081-995 3883**
Offer winter skiing holidays in the Savoie region of the French Alps; also summer programmes in self-catering villas/apartments and hotels in Corsica. Representatives are required to look after clients and ensure they have everything they need to enjoy their stay. Work also available for chalet maids, watersports instructors, handymen, odd jobs people, cooks and operations staff. Winter season from December-April; summer season

from April-October. 6 day week, with flexible hours. Ages 18+. Preference given to those with previous experience and good spoken French. Salary £30-£200 per week, depending on job. Accommodation, insurance and travel costs provided, plus food during winter only. Training given before start of season.

SKIBOUND Olivier House, 18 Marine Parade, Brighton, East Sussex BN2 1TL
Specialises in winter sports tours for schools and adults, and in activity tours and excursions in spring/summer. Area managers, hotel/chalet managers and representatives are required for the winter and spring/summer seasons, December-April and May-August in the French Alps. Posts involve a considerable amount of client contact, and applicants must be presentable and keen to work hard. Ages 21+. Good knowledge of French required for representatives and preferably for managers; previous experience an advantage. Insurance, travel and full board accommodation provided. Wages dependent on position.

SNOWTIME LTD 96 Belsize Lane, Hampstead, London NW3 5BE *✆* **071-433 3336**
Organises luxury winter skiing holidays in Méribel. Representatives required to ensure that standards are maintained and clients enjoy their holiday. Duties involve liaison with local companies, agents and suppliers; good command of French required. Applicants should be efficient, capable, friendly and outgoing, preferably with previous experience. Ages 24+. 30-50 hour week. December-May. Salary from £50 per week, plus return travel and insurance. *UK nationals only.*

SOLAIRE INTERNATIONAL HOLIDAYS 1158 Stratford Road, Hall Green, Birmingham B28 8AF *✆* **021-778 5061**
Organises camping and mobile home holidays in Normandy, Paris, Brittany, the Loire and Vendée, Dordogne, South West France and on the Mediterranean. Staff are required to prepare the tents and mobile homes at the beginning of the season in May and then close down at the end of the season in September/October. During the season staff act as couriers, ensuring the smooth running of the camps, and undertake some maintenance work. Children's couriers also required. No fixed hours. Ages

18+. No previous experience necessary. Fluency in French preferable but not essential. Wages £55-£80 per week. Accommodation in tents or mobile homes, insurance and travel provided.

SUSI MADRON'S CYCLING FOR SOFTIES 2 & 4 Birch Polygon, Rusholme, Manchester M14 5HX ✆ 061-248 8282

Organises a variety of cycling holidays in the regions of Beaujolais & Jura, Cognac & Charente, Dordogne & Garonne, Loire, Mayenne & Sarthe, Provence & Camargue, Rhône, Tarn and Venise Verte. Vacancies exist for regional assistants. The work includes maintaining cycles to a high standard, welcoming holidaymakers, helping in emergencies and providing on the spot information about the region. 2-3 months, 1 May-1 August, 1 June-1 August and 23 July-28 September. Ages 20+. Applicants should be mature, self-confident and adaptable; able to liaise with diverse groups from guests to hoteliers. Fluent English and French essential. Hours variable with one day off per week. Salary £75 per week plus bonus. Self-catering flat or house accommodation, travel and insurance provided. Full training given in all aspects of the job before work commences, and high level of support in place. *Apply November-January.*

VENUE HOLIDAYS 21 Christchurch Road, Ashford, Kent TN23 1XD ✆ Ashford (0233) 642505

Small family company offering self-drive holidays with fully-equipped tents on a campsite near Canet Plage in Roussillon. Representatives are required to assist with montage and demontage, clean and maintain accommodation, sort out any problems and organise social events for adults and children. Average 50 hours per week with one day off; daily workload varies considerably. Season lasts April-October; minimum requirement to work all of July and August. Ages 18-30. Previous experience of working with the public desirable, as is a working knowledge of French. Applicants should also be physically fit, able to work in hot conditions, mentally alert, with a pleasant, easygoing personality. Salary approx £45 per week, with possibility of bonus. Tented accommodation, communal meals, insurance and return fare provided.

DOMESTIC

ACORN VENTURE 137 Worcester Road, Hagley, Stourbridge, West Midlands DY9 0NW ✆ Hagley (0562) 882151

An activity holiday company catering for school groups at camping centres in Normandy and the Ardèche. Experienced catering staff required. Fluency in French an advantage. Ages 18+. 40-50 hour, 6 day week. Applicants are expected to work the full season, May-September. Salary approx £40-£45 per week. All meals and accommodation in tents provided, as well as insurance and cost of return travel from ferry ports. PH *Apply in writing with cv by end of January. If no reply within 28 days assume application unsuccessful.*

ALPOTELS AGENCY PO Box 388, London SW1X 8LX

Alpotels carries out aptitude tests at the request of French hotels, for 50 jobs as waitresses and chambermaids or night-porters, waiters and dishwashers. Ages 18+. Good knowledge of French needed. All jobs involve long hours and hard work as part of a professional team of French workers. 8 hour day with 1/1½ days free per week. December-April or June-September. Pay approx £120 per week; board, lodging and insurance provided. Interview fee £1 plus subscription to JITA Club. *Closing dates for interviews: 30 September (winter), 30 April (summer). EC nationals only.*

BLADON LINES Personnel Department, 56-58 Putney High Street, London SW15 1SF ✆ 081-785 2200

Opportunities for chalet girls to work in French ski resorts. Work involves cleaning chalets, making beds, looking after guests, shopping and preparing meals. Chefs, handymen and cleaners also needed. Limited amount of domestic work also available in Corsica, May-October. Ages 20+. Experience and/or qualifications in catering or domestic work essential. Hours are very variable; applicants must be prepared to work hard but will get time to ski. Season lasts December-May. Salary approx £40 per week. Board, lodging, return travel, insurance, ski pass, ski hire and company ski jacket provided. PH depending on ability. *EC nationals only.*

CAMPUS CENTRES Llangarron, Ross-on-Wye, Herefordshire HR9 6PG ✆ Ross-on-Wye (0989) 84701

Organise holidays for school groups at various centres in France. Bar, restaurant, kitchen and domestic staff required to work at a hotel in Trouville, Normandy, which is run as a schools' study centre and also open to the general public. Some experience preferred, although training is given on the job. Bar and restaurant staff must have fluent French. Ages 20+. 45-50 hour week. 4+ months, May-November; shorter contracts available during peak summer season. Wages £55-£60 per week. Accommodation provided in nearby apartment, plus all meals in hotel.

Also require chefs and domestic/kitchen assistants for activity centres on the Mediterranean. Fluent French useful. Chefs should be experienced and qualified (706/1 and 706/2 preferred); in-house training provided for other positions. Ages 18+. 50-60 hour, 6 day week, May-September. Wages £35-£50 per week; negotiable for chefs. Full board tented accommodation provided.

For both hotel and activity centre jobs medical/accident insurance and return travel from London provided. PH *UK nationals only.*

CRYSTAL HOLIDAYS Crystal House, The Courtyard, Arlington Road, Surbiton, Surrey KT6 6BW ✆ 081-390 8737

Tour operator arranging skiing holidays at resorts throughout the French alps. Chalet staff are required to cook daily breakfast, afternoon tea and 3-course evening meal for clients, and keep chalets clean and tidy. Ages 20-35. Catering qualifications, experience and fluent French essential. Approx 60 hour, 6½ day week, December-April. Basic salary plus commission; board, lodging, insurance, travel costs and uniform provided. 1 week training seminar held at beginning of each season. *Apply April/May.*

DISCOVER LIMITED Timbers, Oxted Road, Godstone, Surrey RH9 8AD ✆ Godstone (0883) 744392

Organises field trips and adventure holidays for young people. Small number of vacancies available for cooks, assistant cooks and general assistants at field study/activity centre in Mount Lozère. Experience useful but not essential; knowledge of French helpful. Non-smokers preferred.

Ages 18+. No fixed hours, April-October. Full board accommodation provided and travel costs paid. Salary £30-£60 per week. Friendly and relaxed working environment. Staff can usually take part in excursions with visiting groups. *UK nationals only.*

FLOT'HOME UK/BARGE FRANCE 25 Kingswood Creek, Wraybury, Staines, Middlesex

Operates floating holidays on French canals. Vacancies exist for Cordon Bleu chefs to work on hotel barges in Burgundy, Alsace-Lorraine and the Midi area of southern France. Experience and some knowledge of French or German essential.

Ages 21+. 50+ hours per week. 6+ months, throughout the year; peak season April-October. Salary £70-£125 per week, depending on experience; on-board accommodation, food and travel expenses provided, but not insurance. *UK nationals only.*

LOTUS SUPERTRAVEL Alpine Operations Department, Mobbs Court, 2 Jacob Street, London SE1 2BL ✆ 071-962 9933

Arranges skiing holidays in the French alpine resorts of Méribel, Courchevel and Val d'Isère. Opportunities for chalet staff responsible for looking after guests and keeping chalet clean and tidy. Ages 21-30. Work involves cooking, cleaning, acting as host/hostess, sitting down to dinner with guests, advising them on skiing areas and keeping them up to date with events in the resort. Chalet staff must work to a budget and account for expenditure.

Applicants must have cooking experience and preferably qualifications, be capable of running a chalet of approx 8 guests and have an outgoing and helpful personality.

In jumbo chalets (24-60 beds) there are opportunities for chalet girl helpers whose duties are similar to the chalet staff, but do not involve cooking, and also for chalet boy helpers who look after the heavier duties such as the cleaning of general areas, washing up, snow clearing, maintenance and sometimes bar work. Ages 21+. Applicants must be available for the whole season, early December-end April.

Approx 40+ hours per week. Board, lodging, ski pass, ski and boot hire and return travel provided; also insurance in return for approx £35 contribution. Salary £45 per week, paid in local currency. Briefings held in London before departure. *UK/EC passport-holders only.*

PGL YOUNG ADVENTURE LTD Personnel Department, Alton Court, Penyard Lane (878), Ross-on-Wye, Herefordshire HR9 5NR
✆ Ross-on-Wye (0989) 767833
Organises outdoor adventure holidays for young people and adults in the Ardèche and on the Mediterranean. Activities include canoeing, sailing, windsurfing and caving. Kitchen assistants, housemaids, caterers/cooks, chalet maids, bar/shop staff and organisers are required.
Ages 20+. Applicants should have relevant experience and be energetic and enthusiastic, reliable and mature, adaptable, friendly and efficient, with a sense of humour. May-September. Jobs are usually for approx 8 week periods but sometimes for the whole season. Staff also recruited for very short periods over the spring bank holiday.
Return travel from Dover, full board accommodation in frame tents and health insurance provided. 1 day free per week. Pocket money per week approx FF300 (housemaids, kitchen assistants, chalet maids, bar/shop staff and bar/shop organisers), or from £80 (cooks). Sports and social facilities available, plus participation in programmed activities.
Applicants available in May have a greater chance of selection. Applications should ideally be made November-April.

SKI ENTERPRISE (CHALETS) Groundstar House, London Road, Crawley, Sussex RH10 2TB ✆ Crawley (0293) 588260
Arranges chalet holidays in the Alps. Chalet staff are required to work in ski resorts. Work involves keeping chalets clean and tidy, making beds, cooking meals and acting as host/hostess.
Ages 21+. Cordon Bleu cookery qualifications and/or sound experience of catering essential. Applicants should also have a basic knowledge of accounts/budgeting, some knowledge of French or German, an outgoing, friendly personality with the ability to put people at ease. They also need enough stamina and sense of humour to last through the average 1,200

beds made and 3,500 meals cooked during the season.
Also positions for chalet helpers, for which not so much cooking experience is required. Hours variable; applicants must be prepared to work hard. 6 days per week, December-May. Wages up to £70 per week. Board, lodging, return travel, insurance and seasonal ski pass provided. *EC nationals only.*

SKIBOUND Olivier House, 18 Marine Parade, Brighton, East Sussex BN2 1TL
Specialises in winter tours for schools and adults, and in activity tours and excursions in spring/summer. Staff are required for all grades of hotel work in the winter and spring/summer seasons, December-April and May-August, in the French Alps. Posts involve client contact and applicants must be presentable and keen to work hard. Ages 18+. Previous experience useful; catering experience required for some posts. Insurance, travel and full board accommodation provided. Wages dependent on position.

SNOWTIME LTD 96 Belsize Lane, Hampstead, London NW3 5BE ✆ 071-433 3336
Organises luxury winter skiing holidays in Méribel. Chalet girls required to run chalets, either single-handedly or in pairs. Duties include cooking to a high standard, shopping, budgeting, housekeeping and acting as hostess. Applicants should be experienced cooks, preferably holding a recognised cooking diploma. They should have a friendly, easygoing personality, and the ability to mix well with clients.

Hotel girls also required to work in two-chalet hotels. Work involves cleaning, housekeeping and waitressing, with a few bar vacancies also available. Cooking skills not essential, but experience in catering industry an advantage.

Ages 18+. Knowledge of French useful. 30-50 hours per week. Girls work for the whole season, December-May. Salary from £35 per week, plus return travel and insurance.
Head and assistant chefs also required. Previous experience essential; working knowledge of French an advantage. Ages 18+. 40-50 hour week, December-May. Salary from £50 per week, plus return travel and insurance.

FARMWORK / GRAPE PICKING

A variety of seasonal farmwork is available, May-October. However those seeking this type of work will be competing against a large number of students as well as regular seasonal workers. This, added to the number of unemployed looking for work and to the decreasing need for manual labour due to mechanisation, often makes it difficult to find employment. Seasonal agricultural workers receive the national minimum wage, *le SMIC*, approx FF30 per hour. Accommodation and food are not always provided and workers should take their own camping and cooking equipment.

The grape harvest takes place between approx 20 September and 30 October in Beaujolais, Aquitaine, the Loire Valley, Central France, Burgundy, Languedoc, Midi-Pyrénées and Champagne. Three types of work are available: picking the grapes, collecting the baskets, or emptying baskets for which 20% more is paid. Work is generally for 8 hours a day and may include Sundays. Wages are usually slightly higher than *SMIC* rates, with board and lodging provided by the farmer and deducted from gross earnings. Workers generally pay their own travel costs.

All agricultural work is physically demanding and can involve working long hours in all-weather conditions; accommodation may be very basic. See under the **Farmwork/Grape picking** heading in the **Work Profiles** section for further information.

Those without a pre-arranged job are strongly advised to take enough money to cover the cost of their stay in France and their return fare should they be unable to find work.

Applications for employment can be made to the organisations listed below, or to local national employment agencies (ANPEs) in the relevant areas, listed at the end of this section. Applications should be written in French and sent a few months before work is due to start.

Applicants should state the type of work they are willing to undertake and the period for which they will be available. Due to the heavy demand for this type of work, many ANPEs may be reluctant to enter into correspondence. Applicants can call in person at an ANPE a few days before work is due to start, but the chances of finding employment at this stage are limited.

All applicants should have a working knowledge of French and a full passport. A birth certificate may be required by some employers in order for affiliation to the national insurance scheme.

Those interested in working on **organic farms** should check the classified section of the French bi-monthly review *Nature et Progrès*. To subscribe or place an advertisement, contact Nature et Progrès, Service Abonnement, BP6, 69921 Oullins Cedex. Also publish an annual list of some 1800 farmers, including those who take on trainees or seasonal workers.

With adjustments depending on the weather, the following periods represent the best opportunities for agricultural work and grape picking:

Mid May-mid June
Cherry and strawberry picking in the Rhône Valley, Central France and Perigord

June-August
Haymaking all over France

July-September
Harvesting gherkins, maize and raspberries in the Centre, Southwest, Auvergne and Aquitaine

August-September
Tomato and tobacco harvesting in the Southwest and East

Mid-September-end October
Apple picking in the Centre, grape picking in the Beaujolais region and plum picking in the Midi-Pyrénées

Throughout October
Grape picking in the Pays de la Loire, Centre, Burgundy, Aquitaine and Champagne regions

CLAUDE SIREJOL Le Castagné, 46170 St Paul de Loubressac, Montrutier ℂ 65 21 97 02 or 65 21 90 81 (recorded message)
A small number of volunteers interested in agriculture, organic farming, and tourism are needed to help with general farmwork throughout the year. Tasks include looking after livestock, crops and vegetables, and training in bread and yoghurt making. No experience necessary. Applicants under 18 must have parental consent. Full board and lodging in farmhouse or campsite and a small payment at the end of the work provided. Volunteers pay own travel and insurance costs.

FERME APICOLE DE SABLE Joseph Barale, 47400 Grateloup ℂ 53 88 80 23
Volunteers interested in beekeeping are required on this bee farm of 500 hives. The farm produces honey, pollen, queen bees and beeswax, and ensures pollenisation of surrounding orchards. Volunteers take part in all aspects of work necessary for the smooth running of the farm. Slide shows on various aspects of beekeeping, and excursions organised at weekends to places of apicultural or general interest. Applicants should be non-smokers aged 18+, who enjoy outdoor life and have no allergies to bees. Experience desirable, but not essential; knowledge of French required. Approx 50 hours per week, March-October. Midday meal, farm/camping accommodation and insurance provided, plus a small payment at end of work period. PH depending on ability. *UK nationals only.*

INTERNATIONAL FARM EXPERIENCE PROGRAMME YFC Centre, National Agricultural Centre, Stoneleigh Park, Kenilworth, Warwickshire CV8 2LG ℂ Coventry (0203) 696584
Provides assistance to young farmers and nurserymen by finding places in farms/nurseries abroad enabling them to broaden their knowledge of agricultural methods. Opportunities for applicants to live and work with a farmer and his family, the work being matched as far as possible with the applicant's requirements. Wages £35 per week; board and lodging provided plus some travel costs paid. Ages 18-26. Applicants must have a minimum of 2 years' practical experience, of which at least 1 year may be at agricultural college, and intend to make a career in agriculture or horticulture. Valid driving licence necessary. Registration fee £70. *EC nationals only; apply at least three months in advance.*

French applicants seeking an exchange should apply to Centre Nationale des Jeunes Agriculteurs, 14 rue la Boetie, 75382 Paris.

JEUNESSE ET RECONSTRUCTION 10 rue de Trévise, 75009 Paris ℂ Paris (1) 47 70 15 88
Offers a large number of places on grape picking camps during the wine harvest in Beaujolais, Champagne, Chablis, and Côte d'Or. Ages 16-30; those under 18 must have parental consent. All participants must supply a medical certificate. Up to 9 hour day, 7 day week. Applicants should be free to work anytime, for at least 8-10 days, and good harvests last 15-20 days, September and October. As little as 48 hours' notice may be given before work is due to start, so it is essential that applicants are prepared to leave for France at any time. Food and basic accommodation usually provided on the farm but participants should take a sleeping bag. Wages FF200-FF250 per day, from which board, lodging and national insurance are deducted. Participants arrange and pay their own travel. Membership fee FF125. *Enclose IRCs to the value of FF10.*

MAISON DES JEUNES ET DE LA CULTURE 25 rue Marat, 11200 Lézignan
Places young people on international camps throughout Languedoc to help with the wine harvest. Work involves either grape picking or carrying baskets, and is very strenuous. No experience necessary. Ages 16+. 8 hour day, 7 day week, September-October. 1-3 weeks, depending on placement; applicants must be prepared to be available for the full harvest. Wages approx FF230 per day for pickers, FF280 per day for carriers. Basic self-catering accommodation provided; participants should take a sleeping bag. Workers are insured against accidents. Registration fee FF100. *EC nationals only. Apply by 15 August.*

SERVICE DES ÉCHANGES ET DES STAGES AGRICOLES DANS LE MONDE (SESAME) 9 square Gabriel Fauré, 75017 Paris
Acts as an official clearing house for seasonal agricultural employment, working in

conjunction with local ANPEs. Receives notification of several hundred jobs, including fruit and vegetable picking, maize-topping and grape picking. Applications should be made by mail no earlier than 2 months before the proposed period of work. Successful applicants will be notified of a placement, often at short notice. Ages 18+. 8-10 hours per day, usually for 15-20 days, May-October. Wages are the *SMIC* or piece work rates; usually higher for grape picking. *French residents may apply through Minitel; access code 36-15 ESAME.*

ANPEs IN THE WINE PRODUCING AREAS
Aquitaine Tour 2000, terrasse Front-du-Médoc, 33706 Bordeaux Cedex

Bourgogne 7 rue des Corroyeurs, 21033 Dijon Cedex

6 rue Claude Debussy, 71000 Macon

Centre 3 passage des Albanais, 45000 Orléans

Cité Administrative, Champ Girault, PO Box 2510, 37025 Tours Cedex

Languedoc-Roussillon 44 avenue de Grande-Bretagne, 66000 Perpignan

Midi-Pyrénées 16 allée de Bellefontaine, 31081 Toulouse Cedex

16 rue Lavedan, 81004 Albi Cedex

Pays de la Loire 3 rue Celestin Frenet, 44000 Nantes Cedex

Square Lafayette, 49000 Angers

Poitou-Charentes 14 boulevard Chasseigne, Poitiers Cedex

Provence-Cote d'Azur 65 avenue Cantini, 13298 Marseille Cedex

Rhône-Alpes 87 rue de Seze, 69451 Lyon Cedex

ANPEs IN OTHER AGRICULTURAL AREAS
Alsace 8 rue de l'Auge, 68021 Colmar Cedex

18 rue Auguste-Larney, 67005 Strasbourg

Aquitaine Residence A Fallières, rue Diderot, 47015 Agen Cedex

2 rue Henri-Farbos, 4000 Mont-de-Marsan

45 rue Emile Guichene, 64016 Pau Cedex

17 rue Louis Blanc, 24016 Perigueux Cedex

Auvergne 70 rue Blatin, 63000 Clermont-Ferrand

Languedoc-Roussillon 76 allée d'Iéna, 11002 Carcassone

25 boulevard Renouvier, 34000 Montpellier

80 Avenue Jean-Jaurès, 30040 Nîmes Cedex

Rhône-Alpes 98/100 rue Boileau, 69455 Lyon Cedex 3

14 rue du Jeu de Paume, 26001 Valence Cedex

MONITORS & LEADERS

There are 23,000 holiday centres, *centres de vacances*, all over France, recruiting camp counsellors or monitors to supervise young people using the facilities during the summer holidays. Applicants must speak good French and will need to acquire a *Brevet d'aptitude aux fonctions d'animateur* (BAFA) certificate by undertaking a week's study of theory, a 50 hour specialisation course, and a week of practical application in a *centre*. The two training courses will cost approx FF2000, although in some cases the potential employer will offer reimbursement, but payment will be made for the practical training work. The training associations usually act as placement agencies. As a certified monitor the pay is approx FF4000 per month plus board and accommodation. Work is also available during other school holidays, and on Wednesdays during term time in *centres de loisirs*. The following five organisations offer preparation courses for the BAFA:

ASSOCIATION NATIONALE SCIENCES ET TECHNIQUES JEUNESSE (ANSTJ) 17 avenue Gambetta, 91130 Ris-Orangis ✆ 69 06 82 20

CENTRE D'ENTRAINMENT AUX
MÉTHODES D'ÉDUCATION ACTIVE
(CEMEA) 76 boulevard de la Villette, 75019
Paris ℭ Paris (1) 40 40 43 26

COMITÉ PROTESTANT DES CENTRES DE
VACANCES (CPCV) 47 rue de Clichy, 75009
Paris ℭ Paris (1) 42 80 06 99

UNION FRANÇAISE DES CENTRES DE
VACANCES (UFCV) 19 rue Dareau, 75014
Paris ℭ Paris (1) 45 35 25 26

UNION NATIONALE DES CENTRES
SPORTIFS ET DE PLEIN AIR (UCPA) 62 rue
de la Glacière, 75640 Paris Cedex 13 ℭ Paris
(1) 43 36 05 20

CLUB CANTABRICA HOLIDAYS LTD
Overseas Department, Holiday House, 146-148
London Road, St Albans, Hertfordshire
AL1 1PQ
Organises camping holidays, providing fully
equipped tents, caravans and mobile homes.
Kiddies representatives are required for the
summer season, mid May-early October, in
Cavalaire, Port Grimaud, and Canet. 6 day
week. Wages from £45 per week, plus bonus at
end of the season. Ages 21+. Nursing, teaching
or NNEB qualifications required; experience an
advantage. Self-catering accommodation in
tents or caravans, travel costs from Watford
and insurance provided. *Apply enclosing* cv.
EC nationals only.

PGL YOUNG ADVENTURE LTD **Personnel**
Department, Alton Court, Penyard Lane (878),
Ross-on-Wye, Herefordshire HR9 5NR
ℭ **Ross-on-Wye (0989) 767833**
Organises outdoor adventure holidays for
young people and adults in the Ardèche and on
the Mediterranean. Activities include canoeing,
sailing, windsurfing and caving. Group and
activity organisers are required. Group
organisers are responsible for group welfare
and for contributing to the entertainments
programme when not participating in the main
sports activities. Group organisers greet the
group of approx 45 on its arrival and are
responsible for them until their departure 3/4
days later. Entertainment organisers are
responsible for the organisation and running of

all evening activities and entertainments
including disco, games, talent contests and
competitive events for ages 12-18. Applicants
should be energetic and enthusiastic, reliable
and mature, self-motivated, with leadership
qualities, stamina, tolerance, flexibility,
initiative and a sense of humour. Experience in
working with children and handling young
people at leisure preferable.
Ages 20+. May-September. Jobs are usually for
8 week periods. Staff are also recruited for very
short periods over the spring bank holiday.
Return travel from Dover, full board
accommodation in frame tents and health
insurance provided. Sports and social facilities
available, plus participation in programmed
activities. 1 day free per week. Pocket money
approx FF350 per week. *Applications should
ideally be made between November and April.*

SEASUN SCHOOL TOURS **Ski Department,**
Seasun House, 4 East Street, Colchester, Essex
CO1 2XW
Provides skiing holidays in the French Alps for
school groups during peak school holiday dates
at New Year, February and Easter. Requires
reliable and conscientious ski guides to escort
and supervise groups both on the mountain and
in the evenings. Ages 20+. Applicants must be
qualified to at least ASSI part 1. Experience
with young beginners and a willingness to
integrate with the group essential. Salary
according to responsibility. Accommodation,
travel, personal insurance and partial uniform
provided. *Write for application form.*

TEACHERS &
INSTRUCTORS

ACORN VENTURE **137 Worcester Road,**
Hagley, Stourbridge, West Midlands DY9
0NW ℭ **Hagley (0562) 882151**
An activity holiday company catering for
school groups at camping centres in Normandy
and the Ardèche. Instructors required to
supervise activities such as watersports, target
sports, climbing, abseiling, orienteering, caving
and gorge walking. Previous experience and
qualifications such as BCU/RYA essential.
Fluency in French a distinct advantage. Ages
18+. 40-50 hour, 6 day week. Applicants are

expected to work the full season, May-September. Salary approx £40-£45 per week. All meals and accommodation in tents, insurance and cost of return travel from ferry ports provided. *Apply in writing with cv by end January. If no reply within 28 days assume application unsuccessful.* PH

CAMPUS CENTRES Llangarron, Ross-on-Wye, Herefordshire HR9 6PG ℗ Ross-on-Wye (0989) 84701

Organise holidays for school groups at various centres. Outdoor pursuits instructors required to work at centres in Languedoc and the Ardèche, teaching activities such as sailing, canoeing, windsurfing, climbing, abseiling, archery and rifle shooting. Applicants must be competent at their particular sport; previous experience in instructing and relevant qualifications such as BCU, RYA or MLTB an advantage. In-house training provided, as well as assistance towards training for relevant qualifications. Ages 18+; preference given to ages 20+. 50-60 hour, 6 day week, May-September. 1+ months; preference given to those able to work the whole season. Wages £35-£50 per week; negotiable for more senior staff. Full board tented accommodation, medical/accident insurance and return travel from London provided. PH considered.

CENTRE DE VOILE DE L'ABER WRAC'H, BP4, 29870 Landeda

Vacancies exist for qualified instructors to teach sailing and windsurfing at the centre situated in a small fishing village. Knowledge of French essential. Ages 19+. 40 hour week, June-September. Board, lodging and insurance provided. Salary FF600 per week. Excursions arranged to surrounding areas.

CENTRE RÉGIONAL DE NAUTISME DE GRANVILLE boulevard des Amiraux, Port de Herel, BP140, 50401 Granville Cedex

Staff are needed to teach and supervise sailing at all levels at a residential sailing school/youth centre, equipped with dinghies, sailboards, catamarans, sea kayaks and cruisers. Ages 19+. 36 hour week, July and August. Board and lodging provided. Salary FF145-FF165 per day according to level. Applicants must have good spoken French and a diploma awarded by the national sailing

federation of their country of origin. Travel paid by applicants.

FREEDOM OF FRANCE Personnel Department, Alton Court, Penyard Lane (878), Ross-on-Wye, Herefordshire HR9 5NR ℗ Ross-on-Wye (0989) 767833

Provides luxury self-drive, self-catering holidays at campsites throughout France. Activity instructors in canoeing, sailing and windsurfing are required to work at sites from Brittany through to the Bordeaux coast, and on the Mediterranean. Applicants should ideally have considerable experience, hold a RYA or BCU Certificate and have previously worked as an instructor. Good command of French useful. April-September, hours variable. Ages 20+. Salary £80 per week, self-catering tented accommodation, full liability and medical insurance, and travel from UK port provided.

FRENCH EMBASSY Cultural Service, 23 Cromwell Road, London SW7 2EL

Publishes an information sheet *Teaching Posts in France* giving details of how to obtain posts as *lecteurs* and assistants in state and private schools.

HEADWATER HOLIDAYS 146 London Road, Northwich, Cheshire CW9 5HH ℗ Northwich (0606) 48699

Operates activity holidays involving cycling, walking and Canadian canoeing throughout France. Requires canoeing instructors and cycling representatives with some experience of bicycle maintenance. The work includes briefing clients at the start of the holiday, helping with any queries or problems and canoe or bicycle familiarisation. Hours vary according to client's needs. Mid May-beginning October. Ages 20+. Driving licence and fluent French essential. Salary approximately £105 per week plus expenses, self-catering accommodation in village, travel and insurance provided. Training weekend held in UK before start of season.

PGL YOUNG ADVENTURE LTD Personnel Department, Alton Court, Penyard Lane (878), Ross-on-Wye, Herefordshire HR9 5NR ℗ Ross-on-Wye (0989) 767833

Organises outdoor adventure holidays for young people and adults in the Ardèche and on the Mediterranean. Activities include canoeing, sailing, windsurfing and caving. Experienced or qualified Canadian canoeists, sailors, windsurfers and cavers are required as instructors and river leaders at the centres. River leaders, senior sailors and their teams assist with the care and welfare and evening entertainment of the group, including total responsibility for their safety and enjoyment, as well as canoeing/sailing instruction.

Ages 20+, occasionally 18+ with relevant qualifications and experience. Applicants should ideally have considerable experience, hold a RYA or BCU Certificate, and have worked as an instructor. A good basic level of skill is important as well as the ability to impart to others with enthusiasm and interest. Applicants should also be able to adhere to strict safety standards, have the foresight to deal with emergencies, and recognise the limitations of each learner. The emphasis is on informality and enjoyment; the ability to manage and organise a team of staff is essential.
Applicants should be fit, energetic and enthusiastic, reliable and mature, with leadership qualities, initiative and a sense of humour; experience of working with young people preferable. May-September; jobs are usually for 8 week periods but are sometimes for the whole season. Staff are also recruited for short periods over the spring bank holiday. Return travel from Dover, full board accommodation in frame tents and health insurance provided. Sports and social facilities available, plus participation in programmed activities. Pocket money per week from FF350 (canoeists, sailors, windsurfers and cavers), from FF400 (river leaders), and from FF550 (senior watersports instructors in sailing, windsurfing and senior canoeists).
Applicants available in May and early June have a greater chance of selection. Applications should ideally be made between November and April.

SEASUN/TENTREK HOLIDAYS 71/72 East Hill, Colchester, Essex CO1 2QW
℃ **Colchester (0206) 861886**
Provides self-catering family holidays in apartments, mobile homes and tents plus activity holidays for schools and groups. Requires qualified watersports instructors and

senior instructors for the summer season, early April-mid November, in Marseillan Plage. 50/60 hour week.
Ages 19+. Applicants should be independent and resourceful with good communication skills and commitment. Knowledge of French an advantage, but not essential. Training provided.
Also require ski instructors to work with school holiday groups at resorts in the French Alps during the winter season. Ages 19+.
Applicants must have qualifications: BASI minimum, ASSI preferred.
Salary according to responsibility.
Accommodation, travel, personal insurance and partial uniform provided.

SKI ARDMORE 11-15 High Street, Marlow, Buckinghamshire SL7 1AU ℃ **Marlow (0628) 890060**
Organise skiing holidays for school groups in Alpe d'Huez, Serre Chevalier, Risoul, Pelvoux, Ovronnaz and Megève. Ski leaders are required to supervise groups of up to 10 children and help run evening activities. Applicants must be good skiers with experience of working with youngsters. First aid qualification required. Ages 20+. Hours flexible, approx 60 hours per week. 1-8 weeks, December-April. Wages from £50 per week, full board hotel accommodation, insurance and travel costs provided. Training day held in December.

SKI EUROPE Brentham House, 45c High Street, Hampton Wick, Kingston-upon-Thames, Surrey KT1 4DG ℃ **081-977 7755**
Operates holidays for groups and school parties. Part-time ski instructors are required for winter sports in Savoie, Vanoise and Hautes-Alpes. Work involves 6 hours teaching per day. BASI or full ASSI qualifications essential, together with a high level of teaching skill. A knowledge of foreign languages useful but not essential, however fluent English is a prerequisite. 1-2 week periods over Christmas, New Year, in February and April. Instructors receive full board hotel accommodation and ski pass plus travel expenses London/resort, and have access to the same facilities as the clients. Wages approx £75 per week, depending on qualifications. *Interviews take place May-November.*

WORKCAMPS

CENTRE DE LA FORMATION DE LA JEUNESSE DU QUART MONDE 29 rue du Stade, Champeaux, 77720 Mormant

Part of the ATD Fourth World Movement which aims to protect the fundamental rights of the poorest and most disadvantaged and excluded families, which constitute the Fourth World. These rights include the right to family life, to education and training, and to representation. Workcamps are organised at the youth centre, involving construction, carpentry, electrical installation, painting, gardening, office work and cooking. Evenings are reserved for discussions and the exchange of ideas about the fight against poverty, as well as sharing knowledge between young people of different social backgrounds. Ages 16-25. Volunteers should be concerned by persistent poverty and social exclusion, and fluent in French. 6 hours of manual work daily. 5/6 days, April, August/September and November. Full board accommodation provided. Volunteers pay their own travel and insurance and should take a sleeping bag. Cost FF250.

CENTRE D'INFORMATION ET DE DOCUMENTATION JEUNESSE (CIDJ) 101 Quai Branly, 75740 Paris Cedex 15

Publishes an information sheet *Chantiers de Travail Volontaire* which gives details on workcamps with a list of addresses, type of work and dates.

CHANTIERS DE JEUNES PROVENCE-COTE D'AZUR (CJPCA) 7 avenue Pierre de Coubertin, 06150 Cannes La Bocca

Arranges workcamps for young people all year round and especially during the summer. Recent projects have included environmental protection programmes and converting buildings to create outdoor pursuits centres or meeting places for young people including the restoration of a 17th century fort on the Ile Sainte-Marguerite. Ages 14-18. 2 weeks, July and August. Nature walks and watersports arranged. Volunteers pay own travel and FF1900 to cover membership, food, accommodation and insurance. Volunteers must have written parental consent, a medical certificate and a good knowledge of French.

COLLEGE LYCÉE CÉVENOL INTERNATIONAL Camp International de Travail, 43400 Le Chambon sur Lignon ℂ 71 59 72 52

An international school situated in 40 acres of wooded grounds high up in the heart of the Massif Central. The school was built through the help of volunteers, and an international workcamp is held every year to carry out renovation, decoration and repairs. Work is both indoor and outdoor, involving tasks such as painting, landscaping and paving. Evenings are time for discussion or relaxation. No experience necessary, but applicants should be fit enough for strenuous work. Ages 16-30. 30 hour week. 3 weeks, July-August. Full board accommodation provided, but no fares or wages paid. Participation fee FF815 (1992). Volunteers may take part, at a reduced rate, in a discovery trip around France organised by the Collège at the end of the workcamp.

CONCORDIA 38 rue du Faubourg St Denis, 75010 Paris

Volunteers are invited to work on a choice of approx 60 international workcamps which aim to help in the development of small communities in mountainous and isolated rural areas and give participants a chance to get to know their natural, political, economic, and social environment. Typical projects involve constructing community centres for use by villagers, children or handicapped people, and renovating or converting agricultural buildings, abbeys and schools. Work includes masonry, carpentry, flooring, painting, roofing, tiling, woodwork, plumbing, electrical and insulation work. Also equipping mountain huts with water and electricity, building rest *gîtes*, demolition, repair or maintenance work. Volunteers are taught traditional building techniques by local craftsmen. The camps provide an opportunity to discover a region, its traditions and inhabitants, and to become involved in the life of a village community. Sports, crafts, dance, music, theatre and other cultural activities arranged.

Ages 18-25. Good knowledge of French needed for some camps. Applicants should preferably have previous workcamp experience. 35 hour week. 3 weeks, June-November and 2 weeks, Easter and Christmas. Also camps for ages 15-

17; 25 hours per week. Projects include constructing a a sports field and renovating holiday, youth and watersports centres. Full board, accommodation in schools, huts or community buildings and insurance provided. Volunteers pay own travel. Registration fee FF550; FF1510 for ages 15-17. **B D PH**

Apply through partner organisation in country of residence. In the UK: Quaker International Social Projects, Friends House, Euston Road, London NW1 2BJ (experienced volunteers only; ages 18+) or United Nations Association, International Youth Service, Temple of Peace, Cathays Park, Cardiff CF1 3AP © Cardiff (0222) 223088.

Outside the UK: please see information on page 30.

INTERNATIONAL MOVEMENT ATD FOURTH WORLD 107 avenue du Général Leclerc, 95480 Pierrelaye

Strives to protect the fundamental rights of the poorest and most disadvantaged and excluded families, which constitute the Fourth World. These rights include the right to family life, to education and training, and to representation. Volunteers are needed, helping to build the international centre at Méry Sur Oise where training sessions take place. Work involves construction, carpentry, electrical installation, painting, plumbing, gardening, office work and cooking. Study preceding camp and during evenings arranged.

Ages 18+. Volunteers should be concerned by persistent poverty and social exclusion. All nationalities accepted. Knowledge of French helpful but not essential. 7 hour day. 2 weeks, July-September. Full board accommodation in tents and bungalows, and basic insurance provided. Volunteers should take a sleeping bag and work clothes. Cost FF400, 15 days. Volunteers pay their own travel costs. **B D**

MOUVEMENT CHRÉTIEN POUR LA PAIX 38 rue du Faubourg St Denis, 75010 Paris

An international movement open to all who share a common concern for lasting peace and justice in the world. Volunteers are needed to work in international teams on summer projects aimed at offering a service in an area of need and promoting self-help within the community, promoting international understanding and the discussion of social problems, and offering

young people the chance to live as a group and take these experiences into the context of daily life. Recent projects have included constructing a centre for meetings and group activities; building a new workshop in an educational centre; converting an old school into a rest centre in the Hautes-Alpes; creating a natural ice rink; restoring a 12th century chapel for use as a museum on provincial history and traditions; converting a 16th century chapel into a hiker's shelter; and putting on a play in a renovated monastery. Sports and social activities organised. International seminars also arranged. Ages 15-17 and 18+. 6 hour day, 30-36 hour week. 2-3 weeks, July-September. Food, accommodation and insurance provided, but participants pay their own travel costs and sometimes contribute towards expenses. **D PH** but unsuitable for wheelchairs.

Apply through partner organisation in country of residence. In the UK: Christian Movement for Peace, Bethnal Green United Reformed Church, Pott Street, London E2 0EF.

Outside the UK: please see information on page 30.

NEIGE ET MERVEILLES La Minière de Valluria, 06430 Saint Dalmas de Tende

Arranges sports, leisure and cultural activities, and youth meetings; workcamps are organised in the mountain hamlet where the centre is based. Recent projects have included rebuilding a mountain shelter surrounded by Bronze Age rock carvings; constructing a road; chopping and gathering wood; and conservation work on the site of a nearby fort. Ages 18+. 35 hour week. 2 weeks, April-September. Mountain walks and excursions arranged. Volunteers pay own travel and FF360 fee to cover costs.

SERVICE CIVIL INTERNATIONAL 2 rue Eugène Fournière, 75018 Paris

Service Civil International promotes international reconciliation through work projects. Volunteers are invited to take part in international workcamps organised throughout France. Recent projects have included accompanying adults with mental and physical handicaps on a holiday tour to the Grenoble area; working with children from disadvantaged backgrounds on a summer adventure project in Lille; wallpapering, painting and masonry work at a social housing project for elderly people; and ecological work on the natural wetlands of the Marais Poitevin. Projects are linked to study themes. Good knowledge of French needed on some camps. Walking holidays in the mountains also arranged, which provide fundraising and a workcamp atmosphere for those unable to attend other projects. Ages 18+. Applicants should be highly motivated and prepared to work hard as part of a team. 35-40 hour week. 2-4 weeks, July-September; a few places at Christmas, Easter and in the autumn. Food, accommodation, and insurance provided, but participants pay their own travel costs. B D PH

Apply through partner organisation in country of residence. In the UK: International Voluntary Service, Old Hall, East Bergholt, Colchester, Essex CO7 6TQ.

Outside the UK: please see information on page 30.

GENERAL

ACORN VENTURE 137 Worcester Road, Hagley, Stourbridge, West Midlands DY9 0NW ✆ Hagley (0562) 882151
An activity holiday company catering for school groups at camping centres in Normandy and the Ardèche. Centre managers required to coordinate activities, organise evening entertainments and make sure groups have all they need. General maintenance staff also required. Applicants should have some previous experience and fluency in French. Ages 18+. 40-50 hour, 6 day week. Applicants are expected to work the full season, May-September. Salary approx £40-£45 per week. All meals and accommodation in tents provided, as well as insurance and cost of return travel from ferry ports. PH *Apply in writing with cv by end January. If no reply within 28 days assume application unsuccessful.*

CAMPUS CENTRES Llangarron, Ross-on-Wye, Herefordshire HR9 6PG ✆ Ross-on-Wye (0989) 84701
Organise holidays for school groups at various centres in France. Group leaders, administrators, maintenance workers, drivers and nurses required to work at activity centres based in Languedoc and the Ardèche. Clean licence essential for drivers; nurses must have RGN qualification; administrators must have office experience and fluent French. No other qualifications or experience necessary; in-house training given. Ages 18+. 50-60 hour, 6 day week, May-September. Wages £35-£50 per week; negotiable for more senior staff. Full board tented accommodation, medical/accident insurance and return travel from London provided. *UK nationals only.* PH

CANVAS HOLIDAYS LTD 12 Abbey Park Place, Dunfermline, Fife KY12 7PD
Provides ready-erected fully equipped tents for holiday families. Requires applicants to form a flying squad, a team of 5/6 people who help set up and equip 200-250 6 berth frame tents in an area containing approx 12 campsites. Similar work is also available dismantling tents and cleaning and storing equipment. A knowledge of French is not required but it is an advantage as flying squads members sometimes have the opportunity to continue as couriers. Applicants must be sociable in order to work in a small community, fit, and able to work hard, long hours under pressure and without supervision, and to cope with living out of rucksack. Ages 18-25. End April-mid June, possibly longer, to set up tents, and September to dismantle them. Valid driving licence an advantage. Salary approx £80 per week plus tented accommodation and self-catering facilities. Outward travel paid; return travel dependent on the completion of contract dates.

CENTRE D'INFORMATION DE DOCUMENTATION JEUNESSE (CIDJ) 101 Quai Branly, 75740 Paris Cedex 15
Issues an information sheet listing branches throughout France which act as local branches of the Agence National pour l'Emploi (ANPE). Temporary jobs for young EC nationals, usually in offices, working with children, or as monitors in holiday camps, are put on the noticeboards.

EURO DISNEY Service du Recrutement-Casting, BP 100, 77777 Marne-la-Vallée ✆ Paris (1) 49 32 49 00
Over 12,000 cast members have contributed to the success of Euro Disney, situated 30km east of Paris, since its opening in April 1992. The

majority of the opportunities available are in the resort's restaurants (culinary service, housekeeping and custodial).
Ages 18+. Applicants must be able to communicate well in French and English. A friendly, cheerful and outgoing personality is essential, as the work will involve a lot of contact with visitors. Approx 39 hour week, June-September. Monthly gross salary between FF6000-FF7000. Staff covered by French social security and health insurance. No accommodation or travel costs provided. *EC nationals only.*

EUROYOUTH LTD 301 Westborough Road, Westcliff, Southend-on-Sea, Essex SS0 9PT ☎ Southend-on-Sea 341434
Holiday guest stays are arranged whereby guests are offered board and lodging in return for an agreed number of hours' English conversation with hosts or their children. Time is also available for guests to practise French if desired. Mainly ages 15-25, but sometimes opportunities for older applicants. The scheme is open to anyone who was born and educated in the UK, interested in visiting France and living with a local family for a short time. 2-3 weeks, June-August. Insurance and travel arranged by applicants, but tickets at reduced rates on request. Registration fee approx £80. *Apply at least 12 weeks prior to scheduled departure date. Limited places.*

FÉDÉRATION UNIE DES AUBERGES DE JEUNESSE (FUAJ) 27 rue Pajol, 75018 Paris
Variety of short-term work available at those youth hostels in France that organise sporting, cultural and educational activity programmes. Positions include cooks, dishwashers and kitchen assistants, receptionists, activity leaders and sports monitors.
Ages 18+. Good knowledge of French essential. Terms and conditions of work as agreed with employing Hostel. Those interested must apply to individual hostels direct and not to FUAJ, however FUAJ produce a guide to youth hostels in France which is available to personal callers.

Alternatively, addresses can be found in the *International Youth Hostel Handbook Vol I* sold at youth hostel outlets throughout Europe and the Mediterranean; see **Worldwide Information** section (page 297) for further details.

**FLOT'HOME UK/BARGE FRANCE
25 Kingswood Creek, Wraysbury, Staines Middlesex**
Operates floating holidays on French canals, using cabin cruisers and hotel barges. Vacancies exist for barge crews and boat yard assistants in Burgundy, Alsace-Lorraine and the Midi area of southern France. Crews consist of 4 members, including an experienced bargemaster, and positions range from deckhand to mechanic. Stewardesses are also required for hotel barges.
Ages 21+. 6+ months, throughout the year; peak season April-October. Crews work long hours, 50-80 per week, and must be fit. Previous experience of similar work preferred. Some knowledge of French and German essential. Salary £70-£125 per week, depending on experience; on-board accommodation and travel expenses provided. Applicants pay own insurance and food costs, except on hotel barges, where food is provided. *EC nationals only.*

**FREE TIME 9 bis boulevard des Italiens, 75002 Paris ☎ Paris (1) 42 96 95 87
MACDONALDS 11 boulevard Saint Denis, 75002 Paris ☎ Paris (1) 42 21 34 17**
Fast food franchises in major cities take on extra staff on a part-time contractual basis, particularly during holiday periods. Ages 18-25. Food, uniform and *le SMIC*, the national minimum wage provided. Applicants should either contact the managers of individual branches directly, or write to the main offices in Paris, addresses above.

FRENCH COUNTRY CAMPING Assistant Operations Manager, 126 Hempstead Road, Kings Langley, Hertfordshire WD4 8AL ☎ Watford (0923) 261316
Operates self-drive family holidays providing fully furnished and equipped tents and mobile homes. Vacancies exist for drivers and assistant drivers to deliver equipment to and from campsites immediately before and after the summer season. Applicants must have driving experience, preferably overseas and/or using vans. Good command of French desirable. Mid April-mid May or during September. Ages 21+. Salary approx £90 per week. Accommodation on sites, transport and insurance provided. *EC nationals only.*

HORIZON HPL LTD Southbank House, Black Prince Road, London SE1 7SJ ✆ 071-735 8171
A training organisation that can place candidates in hotels and companies in Paris in order to gain professional experience and improve French ability. Responsibilities depend on language level, ranging from general duties, waiter/waitress, reception and secretarial work to management and marketing placements. Ages 18-35. Experience not essential, but applicants must be highly motivated and have at least a basic knowledge of French. Language courses can be arranged to increase fluency. 40-45 hour, 5 day week for 3-6 months. Hotel trainees receive wages of £160 per month, 50% of transport costs within Paris and hotel/family accommodation; for company trainees remuneration and accommodation depend on placement. Trainees pay own travel expenses and must take out personal insurance. Placement fee £240 (hotels) or £300 (companies). Support provided by Paris office to ensure progress during placement and help with any problems. *EC nationals only; apply 2-3 months in advance.*

French candidates seeking hotel placements in Britain should apply to Horizon HPL sarl, 320 rue Saint Honoré, 75001 Paris, France ✆ *Paris (1) 43 70 34 90.*

NSS RIVIERA HOLIDAYS 199 Marlborough Avenue, Hull HU15 3LG
Owns 29 chalets, cottages and mobile homes on a 4 star holiday village complex situated halfway between St Tropez and Cannes. Couples required to act as helpers, working 3 days per week, mid March-mid May and mid September-early November. Two couples also required to act as caretakers, working own hours early November-April when the village site is closed. Work involves clearing and cleaning the interiors of the units and their contents, making any small repairs as required. Applicants should be active, reliable, well-adjusted non-smokers with a sense of humour, own car and extensive work experience, including a knowledge of DIY, gardening, plumbing, electrical work, painting and decorating. Character and work references essential. Ages 40+. Accommodation provided on site with private patio and parking. Electricity, water, site fees, local tax and expenses paid; help given with ferry tickets and insurance. *Apply in writing with full background information as soon as possible.*

PGL YOUNG ADVENTURE LTD Personnel Department, Alton Court, Penyard Lane (878), Ross-on-Wye, Herefordshire HR9 5NR ✆ **Ross-on-Wye (0989) 767833**
Organises outdoor adventure holidays for young people and adults in the Ardèche and on the Mediterranean. Activities include canoeing, sailing, windsurfing and caving. Staff required at the centres include: nurses, mainly responsible for the treatment of minor ailments, maintaining a medicine stock and also helping in administration and welfare; driver, site and stores assistants, responsible for transporting guests and staff, collecting and delivering food and equipment, ensuring the tidiness and keeping a close check on all the equipment; general maintenance assistants, work involves painting, labouring, carpentry, gardening, driving and errands, unloading and delivering goods; fibre glassers/canoe leaders to repair and maintain fibreglass canoes and accompany canoe pick-up trips; tent repairers, responsible for tent and sleeping bag repairs; LGV (previously HGV) drivers, responsible for delivering and collecting canoes; administrative assistants required for office work, public relations, costings, ordering, petty cash, wages, stock and giving information to the centres. Ages 20+. Applicants should be responsible, self-motivated, flexible, positive, energetic, and enthusiastic, reliable and mature, with a sense of humour; supplies and services staff also need to be very fit. Staff working with guests should preferably have experience of working with children. May-September; jobs are usually for 8 week periods but are sometimes for the whole season. Staff are also recruited for short periods over the spring bank holiday. Fibreglassers, tent repairers, LGV (previously HGV) drivers and general maintenance staff work March-October. Return travel from Dover, full board accommodation in frame tents and health insurance provided. Sports and social activities. 1 day free per week. Pocket money FF300-FF600 per week according to qualifications and position. *Applicants available in May have a greater chance of selection. Applications should ideally be made November-April.*

SKI ENTERPRISE (CHALET STAFF)
Groundstar House, London Road, Crawley,
Sussex RH10 2TB ✆ **Crawley (0293) 588260**
Arranges chalet holidays in the French Alps.
Handymen required to work in ski resorts in
the Alps and the Dolomites. Work is very
varied and can involve acting as van driver, log
chopper, wine merchant, impromptu cook and
snow shoveller. Ages 22+. Applicants must
hold a clean driving licence and have
experience in dealing with the general public,
flexibility and basic knowledge of French and
German. Good knowledge and experience in
plumbing, carpentry or electrical work also
helpful. Hours variable; applicants must be
prepared to work hard. 6 days per week,
December-May. Wages £60 per week. Board,
lodging, ski pass and hire, return travel and
medical insurance provided. *EC nationals only.*

SNOWTIME LTD 96 Belsize Lane,
Hampstead, London NW3 5BE ✆ **071-433 3336**
Organises luxury winter skiing holidays in
Méribel. Requires practical, mechanically
minded men to act as drivers and handymen.
As duties involve liaison with local companies,
agents and suppliers, a good command of
French is required. Applicants should be
efficient, capable, friendly and outgoing,
preferably with experience of this type of work.
Ages 25+. 30-50 hour week. Staff work the
whole season, December-May. Pay from £35 per
week, return travel and insurance provided.
Also require hotel and restaurant managers.
These positions involve a great deal of
responsibility, client contact and
administration. Previous experience in the
catering industry and a good command of
French is essential, as well as a friendly,
outgoing personality and good organisational
skills. Ages 24+ preferred. 40-50 hour week,
December-May. Salary from £50 per week, plus
return travel and insurance. *UK nationals only.*

When writing to any organisation it is
essential to mention Working Holidays 1993
and enclose a large stamped, self-addressed
envelope, or if overseas, a large addressed
envelope and at least two International Reply
Coupons.

APPLYING FOR A JOB

Before applying, read carefully all the information
given. Unless otherwise indicated, applications
should be made in writing. Check in particular:

✎ skills, qualifications or experience required

✎ the full period of employment expected

✎ any restrictions of age, sex or nationality

✎ application deadlines

✎ any other points, particularly details of
insurance cover, and other costs you may have
to bear such as travel and accommodation.

When writing to any organisation it is **essential** to
mention **Working Holidays 1993** and to enclose a
large, stamped, self-addressed envelope, or if
overseas, a large addressed envelope and at least
two International Reply Coupons (available at
Post Offices). When applying be sure to include
the following:

✎ name, address, date of birth, nationality, sex

✎ education, qualifications, relevant
experience, skills, languages spoken

✎ period of availability

✎ a passport-size photo, particularly if you are
to have contact with the public

✎ anything else asked for, eg a *cv*

GERMANY

INFORMATION

Embassy of the Federal Republic of Germany
23 Belgrave Square, 1 Chesham Place, London
SW1X 8PZ ✆ 071-235 5033

British Embassy
Friedrich-Ebert-Allee 77, W-5300 Bonn 1

Tourist office
German National Tourist Office, Nightingale
House, 65 Curzon Street, London W1Y 7PE
✆ 071-495 3990

Youth hostels
Deutsches Jugendherbergswerk,
Bismarckstraße 8, PO Box 220, W-4930 Detmold

Youth & student information
Artu Berliner Gesellschaft für Studenten und
Jugendaustausch GmbH, Hardenbergstraße 9,
W-1 Berlin 12 (Charlottenburg)

Youth Information Centre, Paul-Heyse-Straße
22, W-8000 Munich

Entry regulations A UK citizen intending to
work in Germany should have a full passport.
EC nationals may stay in Germany for up to
3 months in order to seek employment; a person
intending to stay longer than 3 months or who
is taking up employment must obtain a
residence permit from the local
Ausländerbehörde, no later than 3 months after
entry. Non-EC nationals wishing to enter
Germany require an entry visa which has to
have the approval of the destination's
Ausländerbehörde. This must be obtained prior
to entering and applicants should be resident in
an EC country for 12 months before their
application can be considered. Application
forms are obtainable from the German embassy
in the country where they are staying.
Clearance may take 6 weeks or more. If
employment is intended, written confirmation
of the job offer is required before an entry visa
will be granted.

The German Embassy distributes an
information booklet for non-resident workers
and emigrants returning to Germany,

containing background notes and details on all aspects of working and including entry requirements, employment regulations, social security and taxation. Also publish a leaflet, *Residence and Work in Germany* providing information needed on taking up employment.

Job advertising The Axel Springer Publishing Group, Unit 2, Princeton Court, 53/55 Felsham Road, London SW15 1BY ✆ 081-789 4929 is the UK office of a leading German publishing group which can place paid job advertisements in *Die Welt, Welt am Sonntag, Bild, Bild am Sonntag, Hamburger Abendblatt, Berliner Morgenpost, BZ* and approx 20 other national and local newspapers and magazines.

Publicitas Ltd, 517/523 Fulham Road, London SW6 1HD ✆ 071-385 7723 can place job advertisements in *Rheinische Post, Stuttgarter Zeitung, Süddeutsche Zeitung, Der Tagesspiegel* and *Frankfurter Neue Presse.*

Travel DB Rail Pass offers unlimited travel for 5, 10 or 15 days (within 1 month) on the Federal Railways network, and on certain coach services. Valid also for travel in the eastern Länder. Cost from £115. Also available to those under 26; cost from £80. Details from DER Travel Service, 18 Conduit Street, London W1R 9TD ✆ 071-499 0577/8

Euro-Domino is a pass allowing 3, 5 or 10 days unlimited rail travel in 1 month on the railways of Germany. Cost £81/£90/£134 (ages under 26) or £108/£121/£179 (ages 26+), 3/5/10 days. Available from British Rail International Rail Centre, Victoria Station, London SW1V 1JY ✆ 071-928 5151.

Campus Travel, 52 Grosvenor Gardens, London SW1W 0AG ✆ 071-730 3402 (offices throughout the UK) and Council Travel, 28A Poland Street, London W1V 3DB ✆ 071-437 7767 (offices also in Paris, Lyon, Düsseldorf, Tokyo and throughout the US) offer Eurotrain under 26 fares and youth/student airfares to Germany.

STA Travel, 74 Old Brompton Road, London SW7 3LQ/117 Euston Road, London NW1 2SX ✆ 071-937 9921 (offices also in Birmingham, Bristol, Cambridge, Leeds, Manchester and Oxford) operates flexible, low-cost flights

between London and destinations throughout Germany.

Publications *Young People's Guide to Munich* is an indispensable guide containing notes on where to stay, eating and drinking, public transport, maps, entertainment, places of interest, where to meet young people, special events and other useful information. Published by the Tourist Office of the City of Munich, Sendlinger Straße 1, W-8000 Munich 2, and available at tourist office counters.

International Youth Meetings in Germany 1991/92 lists services offered by German organisations to young visitors, and includes information on international workcamps, environmental protection programmes, youth work, language courses and social services. Available from Studienkreis für Tourismus, Dampschiffstraße 2, PO Box 1629, W-8130 Starnberg.

Live and Work in Germany £8.95 is a guide for those interested in finding temporary or permanent work, starting a business or buying a home in Germany. Published by Vacation Work, 9 Park End Street, Oxford OX1 1HJ ✆ Oxford (0865) 241978.

Rough Guide to Germany £11.99 and *Rough Guide to Berlin* £6.99 provide comprehensive background information on Germany and its future capital, plus details on getting there, getting around, places to explore and cheap places to stay. Available from good bookshops.

Accommodation *Camping in Germany* lists over 400 campsites with a map indicating the locations. Available from the German National Tourist Office, see above, who can also supply a comprehensive list of youth hostels.

Christlicher Verein Junger Menschen, Jugend-Gästehaus, Landwehrstraße 13, W-8000 Munich 2 offers YMCA accommodation in 1-3 bedded rooms for both sexes at a Christian centre situated close to the station. Cost from DM36 per night includes breakfast and shower. **D PH** but unsuitable for wheelchairs.

Haus International/Youth Hotel, Elisabeth-straße 87, W-8000 Munich 40 offers cheap, short-stay accommodation in 1-5 bedded rooms.

Facilities include swimming pool, games room, bar and restaurant. Cost from DM40 includes breakfast. Reservations should be made in advance. **PH**

Jugendlager am Kapuzinerhölzl, in den Kirschen, W-8000 Munich 19 is a large sleeping tent with space for 420, cooking area, canteen, showers, information bureau and recreation tent. Ages up to 23. Cost DM6 per night includes bedding and morning tea. Maximum stay 3 nights, end June-early September. Details from Kreisjugendring München, Paul-Heyse-Straße 22, W-8000 Munich 19.

The International Stuttgart Camp, Wiener Straße, 7000 Stuttgart 30 ℂ Stuttgart (711) 81 77 476 is a dormitory 15 minutes from the central station with room for up to 200 young people. Free showers and washrooms; cafeteria and self-catering facilities. Ages 16-27. Cost DM7 per night includes bedding. Maximum stay 3 nights, 10 July-6 September.

AU PAIR/CHILDCARE

Both males and females can be placed as au pairs with families in Germany provided they have experience of housework and childcare. Ages 18-28; 17 year old A level German students also accepted. Applicants must be single and without dependents and should get their own room, board and lodging, DM200-DM300 per month pocket money, plus a travel ticket in order to attend language classes. EC nationals should register with the local immigration office, *Ausländermeldeamt* during the first 3 days of their stay. A 3 month residence permit will be granted which can later be extended to the whole length of the stay. Non-EC nationals must obtain a special au pair visa, obtainable from the German Consulate of their home country on production of their current passport and a letter of invitation from the host family. Applications for visas take 2-3 months to process, so early application is advisable. On arrival the au pair must register at the local *Ausländeramt* within 3 days and will be issued with a 4 week residence permit. During this time they are required to undergo a medical examination at the local health department *Gesundheitsamt*, the fee being paid by the host family. After a satisfactory medical the residence permit will be extended for one year, and a work permit will be issued by the labour exchange. Before returning to their own country, all au pairs must inform the local *Ausländeramt*. The host family insures the au pair against illness and accident, but this only covers 50% of dental fees and does not cover chronic illness. It is customary for au pairs to have 2 weeks off after a 6 month stay. The following agencies can arrange au pair and childcare placements in Germany:

ACADEMY AU PAIR AGENCY LTD Glenlea, Dulwich Common, London SE21 7ES ℂ 081-299 4599
Can place au pairs. Ages 18-27. Some knowledge of German essential. Pocket money approx £30-£35 per week. Administration charge £40. Positions as nannies and mothers' helps also available for those with qualifications/experience.

ANGLIA AGENCY 70 Southsea Avenue, Leigh-on-Sea, Essex ℂ Southend-on-Sea (0702) 471648
Can place au pairs, mothers' helps and nannies. Ages 17+. Pocket money £30 per week. Service charge £40.

ANGLO PAIR AGENCY 40 Wavertree Road, Streatham Hill, London SW2 3SP ℂ 081-674 3605
Can place au pairs and au pairs plus. Ages 17-27. Pocket money £30-£50 per week. Also placements for experienced nannies and mothers' helps; salary up to £100 per week. Agency fee £40.

AVALON AGENCY Thursley House, 53 Station Road, Shalford, Guildford, Surrey GU4 8HA ℂ Guildford (0483) 63640
Can place au pairs. Ages 18-28. Basic knowledge of German needed. Pocket money £25 per week. Also positions for mothers' helps and nannies. Service charge £40.

HELPING HANDS AU PAIR & DOMESTIC AGENCY 39 Rutland Avenue, Thorpe Bay, Essex SS1 2XJ ℂ Southend-on-Sea (0702) 602067
Can place au pairs and mothers' helps. Ages 18-27. Pocket money approx £30 per week for au

pairs, higher for mothers' helps. Introduction fee £40. *UK nationals only.*

IN VIA Katholische Mädchensozialarbeit, Deutscher Verband eV, Karlstraße 40, Lorenz-Werthmann-Haus, Postfach 420, W-7800 Freiburg
Can place au pairs in towns throughout Germany. Ages 18-25. Knowledge of German essential. Pocket money DM350 per month. Branch offices in 20 major towns in Germany. *Enclose 4 IRCs.*

INTERNATIONAL CATHOLIC SOCIETY FOR GIRLS (ACISJF) St Patrick's International Youth Centre, 24 Great Chapel Street, London W1V 3AF ✆ 071-734 2156
Au pair posts arranged for 9+ months. Ages 18+. Mainly for UK and Irish nationals.

JOLAINE AGENCY 18 Escot Way, Barnet, Hertfordshire EN5 3AN ✆ 081-449 1334
Can place au pairs and mothers' helps. Ages 18-30. Weekly pocket money approx £25 (au pairs) or £30 (mothers' helps). Placement fee £40.

JUST THE JOB EMPLOYMENT AGENCY 8 Musters Road, West Bridgford, Nottingham NG2 5PL ✆ Nottingham (0602) 813224
Can place au pairs, mothers' helps and nannies. Ages 18+. Weekly pocket money £30-£40 (au pairs) or £75-£140 (other positions). *UK applicants only.*

LANGTRAIN INTERNATIONAL Torquay Road, Foxrock, Dublin 18, Ireland ✆ Dublin (1) 289 3876
Can place au pairs in families throughout Germany. Ages 18+. Pocket money approx £25-£40 per week. Placement fee £55.

PROBLEMS UNLIMITED AGENCY 86 Alexandra Road, Windsor, Berkshire SL4 1HU ✆ Windsor (0753) 830101
Can place au pairs. Ages 18-27. Pocket money £30-£35 per week. Service charge £40.

STUDENTS ABROAD LTD 11 Milton View, Hitchin, Hertfordshire SG4 0QD ✆ Hitchin (0462) 438909
Can place au pairs. Ages 18-27. Basic knowledge of German preferred. Pocket money approx £30-£35 per week. Service charge £40.

UNIVERSAL CARE Chester House, 9 Windsor End, Beaconsfield, Buckinghamshire HP9 2JJ ✆ Beaconsfield (0494) 678811
Can place au pairs in most major cities in Germany. Ages 17-27. Knowledge of German necessary. Pocket money approx DM300 per month. Service charge £47. PH *Apply 2 months before work period desired. EC nationals only.*

VEREIN FÜR INTERNATIONALE JUGENDARBEIT EV German YWCA/YMCA, 39 Craven Road, London W2 3BX ✆ 071-723 0216
Can place au pairs of both sexes in families all over Germany. Ages 18-25. Basic knowledge of German essential. Pocket money DM250-DM350 per month.

COMMUNITY WORK

BRITISH FORCES GERMANY Chief Youth Service Officer, BFG Youth Service, Education Branch, HQ, British Army of the Rhine, BFPO 140 ✆ (010 49) 2161-472 3176
Offers a voluntary service opportunity to UK nationals seeking practical experience in working informally with young people. Approx 30 student teachers/youth workers are recruited for the Summer Student Volunteers Scheme, to operate summer activity programmes in British Forces youth clubs located in major garrison towns and stations, and on RAF stations, in the northern part of Germany. Clubs have a mixed membership of 100-300 mainly in the 10-16 age group. 5-6 weeks, summer.
The Scheme involves considerable responsibility, and applicants should be socially mature, persuasive, outgoing individuals, capable of operating effectively on their own initiative but also able to work with other adults. Knowledge of German an advantage, but not essential. Travel, full board plus £35 per week pocket money provided. Applicants selected on the basis of relevant training and experience. *Apply by 1 February; interviews in April/May. UK nationals only.*

Also recruits leaders for youth clubs on a Trainee Youth Worker Scheme. Appointments are normally for 12 months. Travel, full board and honorarium provided. This Scheme is particularly suitable for mature young adults wishing to gain full-time professional training, and for newly-qualified youth workers. *UK nationals only.*

CAMPHILL SCHOOLS Heimsonderschule Brachenreuthe, W-7770 Überlingen-Bodensee ✆ (07551) 80070

Aims to provide a new and constructive way of life for mentally handicapped children, assisting them to achieve individual independence and social adjustment within Camphill Trust communities. Volunteers are needed to work alongside the residents in every aspect of life and also as helpers in school classes. As many of the children have severe handicaps they are in need of care such as bathing, dressing and other personal tasks. Volunteers must be willing to help wherever they are needed, and are encouraged not only to share in the responsibilities of living and working with the handicapped but also to participate in the cultural, recreational and social aspects of community life.
Ages 19+. 60-70 hours per week, all year round. Full board accommodation in single or double rooms and insurance provided, plus DM350 pocket money per month. Applicants pay their own travel expenses. Knowledge of German essential. Participants staying for one year have an opportunity to take part in the first year of a training course in curative education. D PH *Overseas applicants accepted.*

CHURCH ARMY Eastern Region, Independents Road, Blackheath, London SE3 9LG ✆ 081-318 1226

Founded to train and equip men and women to share their living experience of Jesus Christ in a relevant and caring way. Works in residential and field social care; parish deanery and diocesan missions; youth and children's work; Forces' hospitals and prison chaplaincies; and an increasing number of urban and rural projects. Volunteers who are committed Christians are needed to work on children's holiday clubs for Forces' families, end July-end August. Work involves looking after 7-11 year olds, leading Bible quizzes, stories and choruses, organising outings, picnics, visits and tours. Ages 18+. Board, accommodation, insurance and return flight provided. *Apply by 31 January. British passport-holders only.*

INTERNATIONALE JUGENDGEMEINSCHAFTSDIENSTE EV (IJGD) Kaiserstraße 43, W-5300 Bonn 1

A society for international and political education, organising approx 100 international workcamps each year, including 10-15 in Berlin. Recent projects have included organising games, excursions and theatre on a holiday scheme for handicapped people in Preußisch-Oldendorf; caring for the elderly at two homes in Berlin; preparing a fragrant Garden of the Senses at a nursing home for mentally handicapped people in Bedburg-Hau; and looking after and entertaining children on a camping holiday on the island of Norderney. On playschemes time for preparation and evaluation must be added to the normal 6 hour day. Ages 16-25. Good knowledge of German needed. 30 hour, 5 day week. 3 weeks, June-September. Simple accommodation provided in schools, youth centres, boarding houses, tents or barns. All meals, often self-catering, and insurance provided. Excursions arranged to sites of interest. Registration fee DM128. Volunteers pay own travel costs. B D PH

Apply through partner organisation in country of residence. In the UK: Concordia (Youth Service Volunteers) Ltd, 8 Brunswick Place, Hove, East Sussex BN3 1ET ✆ Brighton (0273) 772086 or Quaker International Social Projects, Friends House, Euston Road, London, NW1 2BJ (experienced volunteers only; ages 18+) or United Nations Association, International Youth Service, Temple of Peace, Cathays Park, Cardiff CF1 3AP ✆ Cardiff (0222) 223088.

Outside the UK: please see information on page 30.

CONSERVATION

BRITISH TRUST FOR CONSERVATION VOLUNTEERS Room IWH, 36 St Mary's Street, Wallingford, Oxfordshire OX10 0EU

The largest charitable organisation in Britain to involve people in practical conservation work. Following the success of the Natural Break programme in the UK, BTCV is now developing a series of international working holidays with the aim of introducing volunteers to practical conservation projects abroad. It is hoped that the British volunteers will adapt to and learn from local lifestyles as well as participate in the community. Projects last for 2-3 weeks and are based at the Ammersee Lake reserve, south of Munich. Work involves coppicing, harvesting hay meadows, and creating pools for breeding birds and amphibians. Ages 18-70. Cost from £50 per week includes accommodation and food; everyone shares domestic chores. Membership fee £12. No fares or wages paid.

CHRISTLICHER FRIEDENSDIENST EV, Rendelerstraße 9-11, W-6000 Frankfurt-Bornheim 60 ℂ (069) 459071-72

An international movement open to all who are concerned about violence, exploitation and injustice in society. Volunteers are needed to work in international teams on conservation projects. Recent projects have included helping to create protected areas for animals, plants and birds on sites near Germersheim and Landau; and building a biological sewage plant and a greenhouse on an organic farm near Fulda. Volunteers share in discussions centring on the host community and world problems. Ages 18+. 6 hour day, 30-36 hour week. 2-3 weeks, July-September. Food, accommodation and insurance provided, but participants pay their own travel. Registration fee DM150. B D PH

Apply through partner organisation in country of residence. In the UK: Christian Movement for Peace, Bethnal Green United Reformed Church, Pott Street, London E2 0EF

Outside the UK: please see information on page 30.

INTERNATIONALE BEGEGNUNG IN GEMEINSCHAFTSDIENSTEN EV (IBG) Schlosserstraße 28, W-7000 Stuttgart 1

Founded by Scout leaders to organise work projects of benefit to the community and to promote better international understanding. Volunteers are needed on international workcamps; each camp is made up of 15-20 participants from 6-8 countries who work together on a common project. Recent projects have included laying out an historical vineyard in Urbach; restoring an old city wall near Kassel, in the heart of Grimms' fairy tale country; protecting the winter habitat of bats in Kolbringen; and renovating the ruins of a 12th century fortress in the Diemel Valley. Ages 18-30. 30 hour week with weekends free. 3 weeks,

July-September. Food, simple accommodation in schools, youth hostels, empty buildings, forest or mountain huts with self-catering facilities and insurance provided, but not travel. Participants should take a sleeping bag. Registration fee DM120.

Apply through partner organisation in country of residence. In the UK: Quaker International Social Projects, Friends House, Euston Road, London, NW1 2BJ (experienced volunteers only) or United Nations Association, International Youth Service, Temple of Peace, Cathays Park, Cardiff CF1 3AP ℂ Cardiff (0222) 223088.

INTERNATIONALE JUGENDGEMEINSCHAFTSDIENSTE EV (IJGD) Kaiserstraße 43, W-5300 Bonn 1

A society for international and political education, organising approx 100 international workcamps each year, including 10-15 in Berlin. Recent projects have included restoring an 18th century lime-kiln in Saarfels; forestry work in Bavaria and Ostfriesland; cutting marshland grasses and removing non-native trees and bushes in Hessen; restoring a 200 year old half-timbered farmhouse in Mecklenburg-Vorpommern; and laying out a pond for frogs and newts in Hamburg's Elbmarschen. Ages 16-25. Basic knowledge of German needed, and previous workcamp experience preferable. 30 hour, 5 day week for 3 weeks, April and June-October. Simple accommodation provided in schools, youth centres, boarding houses, tents or barns. All meals, sometimes self-catering, and insurance provided. Volunteers pay their own travel costs. Excursions arranged to sites of interest. Registration fee DM128. Also arrange youth workshops linked to workcamp tasks on ecology themes. B D PH

Apply through partner organisation in country of residence. In the UK: Concordia (Youth Service Volunteers) Ltd, 8 Brunswick Place, Hove, East Sussex BN3 1ET ℂ Brighton (0273) 772086 or Quaker International Social Projects, Friends House, Euston Road, London NW1 2BJ (experienced volunteers only; ages 18+) or United Nations Association, International Youth Service, Temple of Peace, Cathays Park, Cardiff CF1 3AP ℂ Cardiff (0222) 223088.

Outside the UK: please see information on page 30.

SERVICE CIVIL INTERNATIONAL
Deutscher Zweig eV, Blücherstraße 14, W-5300 Bonn 1

Service Civil International promotes international reconciliation through work projects. Volunteers are invited to work in international teams on environmental and ecological workcamps. Recent projects have included digging ponds and laying footpaths at an environmental education centre in Hamburg; harvesting hay and doing environment management work in the wine-growing area of the Kaiserstuhl; cleaning a pond and building a refuge for amphibians at a holiday sailing centre in Hamburg; exploring alternative energy techniques at a youth education centre in Emlichheim; working to transform an old forest ranger's house into an ecological research base in Vorpommern; conservation work and studying ecological systems in the damaged alpine forests of Burgberg/Allgau; fighting natural and tourist-caused erosion at the popular nature reserve of Feldburg; and caring for endangered plants in protected meadows in the Swabian Alb. Opportunities to meet local members of ecological movements. All camps have a strong study element, linked to pollution, nature protection and ecological problems. Ecology cycle tours arranged. Knowledge of German needed on some camps. Ages 18+. No experience necessary, but applicants should be highly motivated and prepared to work hard as part of a team. 35-40 hour week. 2-4 weeks, April-October. Board, lodging and insurance provided, but not travel. **B D PH**

Apply through partner organisation in country of residence. In the UK: International Voluntary Service, Old Hall, East Bergholt, Colchester, Essex CO7 6TQ.

Outside the UK: please see information on page 30.

VEREINIGUNG JUNGER FREIWILLIGER
Unter den Linden 36-38, O-1086 Berlin

Founded as a voluntary service organisation in 1990 in what was then the GDR. Aims to promote solidarity, humanitarian and environmental action, and to combat racism and fascism. Volunteers are invited to join international workcamps with an environmental theme. Recent projects have

included protecting the unique dune-heathland environment of the Baltic island of Hiddensee; maintaining hiking trails through the Thuringian forest mountains near Ilmenau; helping to clean the polluted river Gera in Erfurt; and harvesting hay and caring for animals on an alternative farm in Langerwisch. Opportunities to meet ordinary people and talk about life in eastern Germany before and after unification. Ages 18-30. No experience necessary but applicants must be prepared to work hard and contribute to team life. Camp languages are English and German. 4-6 hour day, 5 day week. 2-3 weeks, July-September. Food, accommodation and insurance provided, but not travel. **B D PH**

Apply through partner organisation in country of residence. In the UK: International Voluntary Service, Old Hall, East Bergholt, Colchester, Essex CO7 6TQ or
United Nations Association, International Youth Service, Temple of Peace, Cathays Park, Cardiff CF1 3AP Ⓒ Cardiff (0222) 223088.

Outside the UK: please see information on page 30.

COURIERS / REPS

CANVAS HOLIDAYS LTD 12 Abbey Park Place, Dunfermline, Fife KY12 7PD

Resident couriers, children's couriers, nannies and watersports couriers are required to work on campsites for a holiday company providing accommodation for families in ready-erected fully equipped tents and mobile homes. The work involves a daily routine of tent cleaning as customers arrive and depart, providing information and advice on the local attractions and essential services, helping to sort out problems that might arise, and organising activities for the children and get-togethers for the families. 7 day week job with no fixed hours; the workload varies from day to day. At the beginning and end of the season there is a period of physical work when tents are put up and prepared for the customers or taken down and stored for the winter. Other tasks include administration, book keeping and stock control. Working knowledge of German essential. Ages 18-25. Applicants are normally those with a year between school and further education, undergraduates or graduates. They need to be enthusiastic, practical, reliable, self-motivated, able to turn their hand to new and varied tasks, and with a sense of humour. 6 months, April-October. Return travel, dependent on successful completion of contract, accommodation in frame tents, and moped or bicycle for use on site provided. Salary £80 per week (1992). *Applications accepted anytime; interviews commence early November for the following season.*

EUROCAMP Summer Jobs, (Ref WH), PO Box 170, Liverpool L70 1ES
One of Europe's leading tour operators, specialising in providing quality camping and mobile home holidays for families throughout Europe. Campsite couriers are required: work involves cleaning tents and equipment prior to the arrival of new customers; checking, replacing and making repairs on equipment; replenishing gas supplies; keeping basic accounts and reporting on a weekly basis to England. Couriers are also expected to meet new arrivals and assist holidaymakers with any problems that arise; organise activities and parties; provide information on local tourist attractions and maintain an information noticeboard. At the beginning and end of the season couriers are also expected to help in erecting and dismantling tents.
Couriers need to be flexible to meet the needs of customers and be on hand where necessary; they will be able to organise their own free time as the workload allows.
Ages 18+. Applicants should be independent, adaptable, reliable, physically fit, have plenty of initiative and relish a challenging and responsible position. Good working knowledge of German also necessary. Preference given to those able to work the whole season, April-September/October; contracts also available for first half season, April-mid July and second half season, mid July-September/October.

Children's couriers are also required, with the energy and enthusiasm to organise a wide range of exciting activities for groups of children aged 4-13. Experience of working with children within this age range is essential, but language ability is not a requirement. Ages 20+. Children's couriers must be available for the whole season, May-September.

For both positions the salary is £91.50 per week. Training is provided together with accommodation in frame tent with cooking facilities, insurance and return travel.

UK and EC passport-holders only. Early application advisable; interviews start September/October.

DOMESTIC

ALPOTELS AGENCY PO Box 388, London SW1X 8LX
Carries out aptitude tests at the request of German hotels for 30-50 jobs mainly as chambermaids or kitchen helpers. Ages 18+. Some knowledge of German useful but not essential. All jobs involve long hours and hard work in a professional team. 8 hours per day, with 2 days free per week. Jobs are available during two long seasons, December-May or June-November. Pay approx £85 per week. Board, lodging and insurance provided. Interview fee £1 plus subscription to JITA Club. *Closing dates for interviews: 30 September (winter) or 30 March/April (summer). EC nationals only.*

ARCADE HOTELS Mauritiusstraße 5-7, W-6200 Wiesbaden ✆ Wiesbaden (611) 3 93 61
Chambermaids and waiting staff required to work for this hotel chain operating in towns throughout Germany. Previous experience of hotel work and ability to speak German required. Ages 18+. 40 hour week. 6+ months, all year. Salary DM1800 per month. Bed and breakfast accommodation in hotel, insurance, and meals while on duty provided. *EC nationals only.*

FARMWORK

Since farms in Germany tend to be small and highly mechanised, the opportunities for seasonal agricultural work are limited. The main crops are flour and feed grains, potatoes, sugar beet, vegetables, fruit and wine. The likelihood of employment is higher grape picking in the south west than in any other sector, although the grape harvests are late, from mid October to mid November.

INTERNATIONAL FARM EXPERIENCE PROGRAMME YFC Centre, National Agricultural Centre, Stoneleigh Park, Kenilworth, Warwickshire CV8 2LG
℄ **Coventry (0203) 696584**
Provides assistance to young farmers and nurserymen by finding places in farms/nurseries abroad enabling them to broaden their knowledge of agricultural methods. Opportunities for practical horticultural/agricultural work, usually on mixed farms. Applicants live and work with a farmer and his family and the work is matched as far as possible with the applicant's requirements. The work is hard; 8-10 hour day, 6 day week, every other weekend free. 3-12 months throughout the year. Opportunities for farm and nursery work. Applicants pay own fares and insurance. Pocket money, board and lodging provided. Ages 18-26. Applicants must have a minimum 2 years' practical experience, of which 1 year may be at agricultural college, and intend to make a career in agriculture/horticulture. Valid driving licence necessary. Registration fee £70. *Apply at least 3 months in advance. EC nationals only.*

German applicants requiring an exchange should apply to Deutscher Bauernverband eV, Godesberger Allee 142-148, W-5300 Bonn 2.

WILLING WORKERS ON ORGANIC FARMS (WWOOF-DEUTSCHLAND) Stettiner Straße 3, W-6301 Pohlheim
A non-profitmaking organisation which aims to help organic farmers and smallholders whose work is often labour-intensive as it does not rely on the use of artificial fertilisers or pesticides. Provides unskilled voluntary workers with first hand experience of organic farming and gardening and a chance to spend some time in the country. Places exist on 75 farms throughout Germany. Work outside includes working in the fields, in the stable or on the market stall; indoor work includes spinning, weaving, cheesemaking, pottery and woodwork. Members receive a quarterly newsletter which details farms needing help. Ages 16+. 20-40 hour week. 1+ weeks. Full board and lodging provided in the farmhouse or in outbuildings; volunteers should take a sleeping bag. No wages paid, although long-term volunteers may receive small payment as

arranged with host. Helpers pay own travel costs. Insurance and anti-tetanus vaccination recommended. Families welcome. Membership fee DM15.

PEACE CAMPS

CHRISTLICHER FRIEDENSDIENST EV, Rendelerstraße 9-11, W-6000 Frankfurt-Bornheim 60 ℄ (069) 459071-72
An international movement open to all who share a common concern for lasting peace and justice in the world. Volunteers are needed to work in international teams on summer projects aimed at offering a service in an area of need and promoting self-help within the community, promoting international understanding and the discussion of social problems, and offering young people the chance to live as a group and take these experiences into the context of daily life. All workcamps are organised in cooperation with local groups to enable volunteers to gain an insight into the peace and anti-Fascist work being undertaken in Germany.
Recent peace projects have included repair work and gardening at a peace cottage in Herford; preparing an exhibition on the history of the international peace movement at a documentation centre and anti-war house at Sievershausen; and decorating a training centre for non-violent action in Wustrow. Activities include discussions on peace problems, visits to events and contacts with local peace groups. Ages 18+. 30-36 hour week, 2-4 weeks, June-September. Food, accommodation and insurance provided, but participants pay their own travel costs. Registration fee DM150. **B D PH**

Apply through partner organisation in country of residence. In the UK: Christian Movement for Peace, Bethnal Green United Reformed Church, Pott Street, London E2 0EF.

Outside the UK: please see information on page 30.

SERVICE CIVIL INTERNATIONAL Deutscher Zweig eV, Blücherstraße 14, W-5300 Bonn 1
Service Civil International promotes international reconciliation through work

projects. Volunteers are needed to work in international teams on peace camps run to support peace information and activity centres, to promote international discussion of the nuclear threat, alternative security policies and non-violence, and to bring together peace movements in different countries. Camps are linked to peace study themes and opportunities to meet local peace groups. Also organise anti-Fascist camps, helping to maintain concentration camps as monuments, warning symbols and means of raising awareness of history. Volunteers should be interested in and have some knowledge of the political background of this theme.

Recent projects have included repairing fences around mass graves at the Reinhorst evacuation camp; reconstructing the living and working spaces at the former labour/concentration camp of Neuengamme, near Hamburg, which has been turned into a documentation centre by former Resistance fighters; and gardening in the memorial grounds at Dachau. Study themes include history of the concentration camp and anti-Fascist resistance. Also international cycle and sailing tours for peace.

Ages 18+. Applicants should be highly motivated, committed to the camp theme and prepared to work hard as part of a team. Some camps require a knowledge of German. 35-40 hour week, 2-4 weeks, June-September, Christmas and Easter. Food and centre, tent or school accommodation plus insurance provided, but not travel. Volunteers prepare and cook their own meals. B D PH

Apply through partner organisation in country of residence. In the UK: International Voluntary Service, Old Hall, East Bergholt, Colchester, Essex CO7 6TQ.

Outside the UK: please see information on page 30.

WORKCAMPS

CHRISTLICHER FRIEDENSDIENST EV, Rendelerstraße 9-11, W-6000 Frankfurt-Bornheim 60 ℂ (069) 459071-72

An international movement open to all who share a common concern for lasting peace and justice in the world. Volunteers are required to work in international teams on summer projects aimed at offering a service in an area of need and promoting self-help within the community; promoting international understanding and the discussion of social problems; and offering young people the chance to live as a group and take these experiences into the context of daily life. All workcamps are organised in cooperation with local groups to enable volunteer teams to gain an insight into the peace, environmental and anti-Fascist work being undertaken in Germany.

Recent projects have included working in the garden of a home for refugees in Egelsbach/Dreieich; helping young unemployed people recycle old furniture and construct a children's playground in Hanau; and providing support for a group of young people with disabilities at an international youth meeting in Paderborn. All camps have a strong study element. Ages 18+. Some camps require a basic knowledge of German. 30-36 hour week, 2-4 weeks, July-September. Food, accommodation and insurance provided, but participants pay their own travel. Registration fee DM150. B D PH

Apply through partner organisation in country of residence. In the UK: Christian Movement for Peace, Bethnal Green United Reformed Church, Pott Street, London E2 0EF

Outside the UK: please see information on page 30.

INTERNATIONALE BEGEGNUNG IN GEMEINSCHAFTSDIENSTEN EV (IBG) Schlosserstraße 28, W-7000 Stuttgart 1

Founded by Scout leaders to organise work projects of benefit to the community, and to promote better international understanding. Volunteers are needed on international workcamps; each camp is made up of 15-20 participants from 6-8 countries who work together on common projects which have recently included maintaining a bicycle trail and building a barbecue hut in Wehrheim; taking part in an Indian Game to teach children about South American Indian culture at a playscheme in Schramberg; building a tent city for young travellers in Stuttgart; and helping with the harvest at a village rebuilt as it was 200 years ago in an open-air museum of Wackershofen. Ages 18-30. 30 hour week with free weekends. 3 weeks, July-September. Food, simple accommodation in schools, youth hostels, empty buildings, clubs or forest/ mountain huts with self-catering facilities, and insurance provided, but not travel. Participants should take a sleeping bag. Registration fee DM120.

Apply through partner organisation in country of residence. In the UK: Quaker International Social Projects, Friends House, Euston Road, London NW1 2BJ (experienced volunteers only) or United Nations Association, International Youth Service, Temple of Peace, Cathays Park, Cardiff CF1 3AP © Cardiff (0222) 223088.

Outside the UK: please see information on page 30.

INTERNATIONALE JUGENDGEMEINSCHAFTSDIENSTE EV (IJGD) Kaiserstraße 43, W-5300 Bonn 1

A society for international and political education, organising approx 100 international workcamps each year, including 10-15 in Berlin. Recent projects have included renovating an information centre on the Third World in Berlin Kreuzberg; gardening and building a footbridge at an artists' conference home in Schildow; renovating a former potash works in Hannover, which has been converted into a tram museum, and helping to guide visitors around the museum; constructing a theatre and laying a jogging path at a youth education centre in Bremen; and creating a playground at a small community school in Mecklenburg. Basic craftsmanship skills are taught for all projects. Parent/children and women only camps organised. Work/study camps also arranged on themes including Third World, peace and anti-Fascism. Ages 16-25. Basic knowledge of German needed. 30 hour, 5 day week. 3 weeks, June-September. Simple accommodation provided in schools, youth centres, flats, stations, boarding houses, tents or barns. All meals, often self-catering, and insurance provided. Volunteers pay own travel. Registration fee DM128.

Apply through partner organisation in country of residence. In the UK: Concordia (Youth Service Volunteers) Ltd, 8 Brunswick Place, Hove, East Sussex BN3 1ET © Brighton (0273) 772086 or Quaker International Social Projects, Friends House, Euston Road, London NW1 2BJ (experienced volunteers only; ages 18+) or

United Nations Association, International Youth Service, Temple of Peace, Cathays Park, Cardiff CF1 3AP © Cardiff (0222) 223088.

Outside the UK: please see information on page 30.

INTERNATIONALER BAUORDEN-DEUTSCHER ZWEIG EV Liebigstraße 23, PO Box 1438, W-6520 Worms-Horchheim

An international volunteers association with the aims of fighting misery and distress and making a contribution towards a better understanding between nations. Volunteers are needed to work in international teams for and together with the socially, mentally, economically and physically underprivileged. Recent projects have included painting and renovating an old people's home in Kirchheim; rebuilding abandoned houses using traditional methods in Quedlingburg; converting an old factory in Leuna into a workplace for severely handicapped adults; converting an old railway station into a leisure centre in Hasel; and renovating a Jewish cemetery in the eastern part of Berlin. Ages 18+. Some knowledge of German essential. 40 hour, 5 day week, 2-4 weeks. Easter and June-September. Food prepared by volunteers, tent, school or barrack accommodation and insurance provided, but volunteers should take a sleeping bag. Participants pay their own travel. *Apply 1 month in advance.*

NORDDEUTSCHE JUGEND IM INTERNATIONALEN GEMEINSCHAFTSDIENST EV (NIG) Universitätsplatz 1, O-2500 Rostock

A non-profitmaking organisation run by volunteers with the aim of promoting internationalism through voluntary projects. Volunteers are invited to take part in international workcamps in the Mecklenburg area of north-eastern Germany. Recent projects have included renovation and gardening work at an adult education centre in the tiny port of Lubmin; reconstructing the old manor house and historic village centre of Bansow; and organising children's activities at a holiday centre in Recknitzberg. Ages 18-30. English is usually the working language, although conversational German may be necessary on some projects. 2-3 weeks, July-September. Food, accommodation and insurance provided;

volunteers pay their own travel costs. **B D PH**

Apply through partner organisation in country of residence. In the UK: Quaker International Social Projects, Friends House, Euston Road, London NW1 2BJ (experienced volunteers only) or United Nations Association, International Youth Service, Temple of Peace, Cathays Park, Cardiff CF1 3AP © Cardiff (0222) 223088.

Outside the UK: please see information on page 30.

NOTHELFERGEMEINSCHAFT DER FREUNDE EV **Secretariat General, Auf der Körnerwiese 5, W-6000 Frankfurt-am-Main 1**

A fellowship founded on the conviction that peaceful coexistence is only possible if prejudices and differences between peoples are overcome. Aims to improve the situation of the needy and is working for a better understanding and reconciliation between peoples. Volunteers are needed on workcamps to help on projects which include manual and social work in homes for children, the elderly and the mentally handicapped, and in hospitals. Recent projects have included construction work, gardening and domestic work at centres for mentally handicapped people; path construction, farming and gardening at Camphill Village community farms for the handicapped; and repair work, painting and looking after elderly people at different homes throughout Germany. Ages 18-30. Junior camps arranged for ages 16-18. Volunteers must be willing to work hard, show tolerance, initiative and enthusiasm, and be prepared to participate in discussions and seminars during their free time. Good knowledge of German needed on some camps. 30-35 hour week, 3/4 weeks, March, April, May-December. Self-catering accommodation, food and insurance provided. Registration fee DM70. *Apply by mid May.*

ÖKUMENISCHER JUGENDDIENST **Planckstraße 20, O-1080 Berlin**

The Ecumenical Youth Council in Europe, the fellowship of national ecumenical youth councils or denominational bodies dealing with church youth work, offers young Christians from different countries and traditions the opportunity to meet and share their experiences and to discuss common issues and concerns.

Promotes workcamps in eastern Germany (formerly the GDR) where international teams live and work together on manual, social or study projects, offering an opportunity to share ideas on faith and life. Recent projects have included renovating churches and church centres in Walldorf, Schlabendorf and Rambow; environmental protection work in Storkow and Alt-Jabel; and working at centres for people with handicaps in Oschersleben and Klein-Wachau. All camps include a relevant theme for study and discussion. Basic knowledge of German usually necessary. Volunteers must be seriously motivated to contribute to the aims of the camp. Ages 18-30. 6 hour day, 2 weeks, July/August. Board and lodging usually provided. Volunteers pay their own travel and insurance costs. Registration fee approx £15. *Apply by 15 May. UK applications to the Ecumenical Youth Council in Europe, PO Box 464, Belfast BT4 2DE © Belfast (0232) 651134.*

PRO INTERNATIONAL **Bahnhofstraße 26A, W-3550 Marburg/Lahn**

Founded after the Second World War; aims to promote cooperation and understanding between people from all over the world by providing opportunities for them to meet and work together. The accent is on learning new skills and gaining experience in a practical field. Recent projects have included restoring an old railway carriage for a museum; renovating and gardening at homes for the handicapped and at youth centres; renovating and clearing paths, playgrounds and parks; looking after and playing with children; and coastal protection work, stabilising the dunes and planting grass on the East Frisian Islands. Ages 16-26. Previous workcamp experience preferable; knowledge of German useful. 30-35 hour, 5 day week. 2-3 weeks, Easter, and June-September. Board and accommodation provided in schools, old houses, youth hostels or tents. Volunteers help prepare meals and should take a sleeping bag. Travel extra. Registration fee DM100 includes insurance.

Apply through partner organisation in country of residence. In the UK: Concordia (Youth Service Volunteers) Ltd, 8 Brunswick Place, Hove, East Sussex BN3 1ET © Brighton (0273) 772086.

Outside the UK: please see information on page 30.

SERVICE CIVIL INTERNATIONAL
Deutscher Zweig eV, Blücherstraße 14, W-5300 Bonn 1

Service Civil International promotes international reconciliation through work projects. Volunteers are needed to work in international teams on social/manual projects in a variety of fields such as Third World solidarity and with self-help groups organised by young people facing long-term unemployment.

Recent projects have included constructing an environmental information centre in Berlin; looking after children from Byelorussia at a holiday camp in Weimar; converting the grounds of a building in Dresden which formally housed the East German secret police, taking account of the needs of disabled people who are now living there; establishing a park in the area formerly occupied by the Berlin Wall; organising a children's festival in Solingen; and joinery and renovation work at a centre for alternative education in Dransfeld. Solidarity camps are also organised, supporting Third World countries, helping organisations and projects involved in social, medical and educational work, by a combination of practical and educational assistance which includes providing materials for refugee camps and supporting self-reliant development and human rights. All camps include a strong study element. Also women's camps and East-West bicycle tour. Ages 18+. Applicants should be highly motivated and prepared to work hard as part of a team. Good German needed for some camps. 40 hour week, 2-3 weeks, July-September, Christmas and Easter. Board, lodging and insurance provided, but not travel. **B D PH**

Apply through partner organisation in country of residence. In the UK: International Voluntary Service, Old Hall, East Bergholt, Colchester, Essex CO7 6TQ.

Outside the UK: please see information on page 30.

VEREINIGUNG JUNGER FREIWILLIGER
Unter den Linden 36-38, O-1086 Berlin

Founded as a voluntary service organisation in 1990 in what was then the GDR. Aims to promote solidarity, humanitarian and environmental action, and to combat racism and fascism. Volunteers are invited to join international workcamps to help with a variety of construction and social projects. Recent projects have included reconstructing a traditional 200 year old cottage in Burg; building a play centre for children in Gräfenheinichen; restoring a medieval graveyard in Halle; and maintenance work on the antifascist/antistalinist memorial of Sachsenhausen. Opportunities to meet ordinary people and talk about life in eastern Germany before and after unification. Ages 18-30. No experience necessary but applicants must be prepared to work hard and contribute to team life. Camp languages are English and German. 4-6 hour day, 5 day week. 2-3 weeks, July-September. Food, accommodation and insurance provided, but not travel. **B D PH**

Apply through partner organisation in country of residence. In the UK: International Voluntary Service, Old Hall, East Bergholt, Colchester, Essex CO7 6TQ or
United Nations Association, International Youth Service, Temple of Peace, Cathays Park, Cardiff CF1 3AP © Cardiff (0222) 223088.

Outside the UK: please see information on page 30.

GENERAL

CANVAS HOLIDAYS LTD 12 Abbey Park Place, Dunfermline, Fife KY12 7PD

Provides ready-erected fully equipped tents for holiday families. Requires applicants to form flying squads, teams of 5/6 people who help set up and equip 200-250 6 berth frame tents in an area containing approx 12 campsites. Similar work is also available taking down tents and cleaning and storing equipment. Ages 18-25. Knowledge of German not required but is an advantage as flying squad members sometimes have the opportunity to continue as couriers. Applicants must be sociable in order to work in a small community, fit and able to work for long hours under pressure, work without supervision and cope with living out of a rucksack. Early April-mid June, possibly longer, to set up the tents, and September to dismantle them. Valid driving licence an advantage. Salary approx £80 per week, tented accommodation, self-catering facilities and outward travel provided. Return travel dependent on the completion of contract dates.

EUROYOUTH LTD 301 Westborough Road, Westcliff, Southend-on-Sea, Essex SS0 9PT ℂ Southend-on-Sea (0702) 341434
Holiday guest stays are arranged where guests are offered board and lodging in return for an agreed number of hours English conversation with hosts or their children. Time is also available for guests to practise German if desired. Mainly ages 15-25, but sometimes opportunities for older applicants. 2-3 weeks, June-August. Travel and insurance paid by applicants. Registration fee approx £70. *Apply at least 12 weeks prior to scheduled departure date; number of places limited. UK nationals only.*

INVOLVEMENT VOLUNTEERS-DEUTSCHLAND Postfach 110224, W-3400 Göttingen ℂ/Fax (551) 33 765
Works in association with the Involvement Volunteers network to find volunteer placements in Germany. Volunteers of all ages can take part in individual placements or team tasks. Placements relate to conservation in urban or rural areas; bird breeding/training operations; biological research; restoring or maintaining historic sites or gardens; developing National Parks; and assisting at special schools for disabled children. Volunteers must be able to speak English (German in special cases), arrange their own visitor visas where necessary, and organise their own international travel and insurance. Involvement Volunteers provides advice, placements, itinerary planning, introductions to banking, and a communications base in Germany. Cost DM400 (approx £125/$225/AU$300). **B D**

In Australia, New Zealand and Asia Pacific, apply to Involvement Volunteers Association Inc, PO Box 218, Port Melbourne, Victoria 3207, Australia ℂ/Fax Melbourne (3) 646 5504.

In North America, apply to Involvement Corps Inc., 15515 Sunset Boulevard Suite 108, Pacific Palisades, California 90272, United States ℂ/Fax (310) 459 1022.

TOC H National Projects Office, 1 Forest Close, Wendover, Aylesbury, Buckinghamshire HP22 6BT ℂ Aylesbury (0296) 623911
Requires volunteers for a variety of short-term residential projects throughout Germany. Projects may include working with people having different disabilities; work with underprivileged children; playschemes and camps; conservation and manual work. Ages 18+. Programmes giving further details of projects and application procedures are published in March and September. B D PH depending on project. *Early application advised.*

ZENTRALSTELLE FÜR ARBEITSVERMITTLUNG DER BUNDESANSTALT FÜR ARBEIT Feuerbachstraße 42-46, W-6000 Frankfurt-am-Main 1
The central placement office of the Federal Employment Services. Concerned with the recruitment of foreign workers, including the free placement of foreign students for temporary jobs of at least 2 months. Ages 18+. Applicants must speak good German.

GREAT BRITAIN

INFORMATION

Tourist offices
British Tourist Authority, Thames Tower, Black's Road, Hammersmith, London W6 9EL ✆ 081-846 9000. Offices in 19 countries and a network of information centres throughout Britain.

Scottish Tourist Board, 23 Ravelston Terrace, Edinburgh EH4 3EU ✆ 031-332 2433
London office: 19 Cockspur Street, London SW1Y 5BL ✆ 071-930 8661/2/3

Wales Tourist Board, Brunel House, 2 Fitzalan Road, Cardiff CF2 1UY ✆ Cardiff (0222) 499909
London office: 12 Lower Regent Street, London SW1 ✆ 071-409 0969

Youth hostels
YHA, Trevelyan House, 8 St Stephen's Hill, St Albans, Hertfordshire AL1 2DY

SYHA, 7 Glebe Crescent, Stirling FK8 2JA

Youth & student information
National Union of Students, 461 Holloway Road, London N7 6LJ ✆ 071-272 8900

UK Council for Overseas Students (UKCOSA), 60 Westbourne Grove, London W2 5SH ✆ 071-229 9268

Entry regulations Nationals of Belgium, Denmark, France, Germany, Gibraltar, Greece, Ireland, Italy, Luxembourg, the Netherlands, Portugal and Spain do not need a work permit to take up or seek employment in Great Britain. At the time of going to press it is expected that nationals of Austria, Finland, Iceland, Norway and Sweden (and subject to the detailed provisions of their special transitional arrangements, Liechtenstein and Switzerland) will also be able to come to the UK and seek work without a permit from 1 January 1993. Other nationals who are subject to immigration control need a work permit and will be refused entry if one cannot be produced at the port of entry. A work permit is not required for au pair posts or temporary employment at approved farmcamps, but an au pair must have a letter of invitation from the family and seasonal agricultural workers must be between the ages of 18 and 25 years inclusive, in full-time education and have a Home Office card issued by an approved scheme operator. Neither the letter of invitation nor the Home Office card provides entitlement to any other kind of paid work. Permits are not usually required for temporary voluntary work on international workcamps or other voluntary opportunities, but it is advisable to obtain prior entry clearance from a British diplomatic post abroad. Overseas students studying in Britain who wish to take paid work in their free time or during vacations do not require work permits but they must first obtain the consent of the Department of Employment through the local Jobcentre or employment office and provide evidence from their college that employment will not interfere with their studies. Further information on work permits may be obtained from the Overseas Labour Section of the Department of Employment, Caxton House, Tothill Street, London SW1H 9NF ℂ 071-273 5336/7 or in leaflets *WP1/5 notes* and *OW21* (WP notes) published by that Department and obtainable on ℂ Bristol (0272) 244780. Commonwealth citizens with proof of a grandparent's birth in the UK do not need a work permit provided that they obtain prior entry clearance from a British Consular post overseas. Other Commonwealth citizens aged 17-27 inclusive may enter Britain for up to 2 years during which they can take work incidental to their holiday. They must have the means to pay for their return journey and not fall a charge on public funds. Nationals from countries needing a visa to come to the UK must obtain one before travelling, whether coming for a temporary or longer stay. Applications for visas must be made to a British Diplomatic post overseas. Further information on concessions for Commonwealth citizens of UK ancestry, the provisions for Commonwealth working holidaymakers and immigration requirements generally may be obtained from the Home Office, Lunar House, Wellesley Road, Croydon, Surrey CR9 2BY ℂ 081-686 0688.

Job advertising Most newspapers in Britain carry classified advertising. There are several daily newspapers with national distribution and hundreds of local newspapers published on a daily or weekly basis. An evening daily newspaper circulating in London only is the *Evening Standard,* Classified Advertising, Northcliffe House, 2 Derry Street, London W8 5TT ℂ 071-938 3838. As well as accepting paid advertisements this paper also advertises many short-term job opportunities, especially in the Tuesday edition. *Time Out* is a weekly magazine aimed at young people in London, giving details of events in the capital; to advertise contact Classified Advertising, Time Out, Tower House, Southampton Street, London WC2E 7HA ℂ 071-836 5131.

Travel Anyone under 24 or a full-time student in the UK can buy a British Rail Young Person's Railcard, entitling the holder to 30% reduction on many tickets. Cost £15, valid 1 year. Further details and application forms are available from principal British Rail stations or most student travel offices. British Rail also offer a variety of discount tickets depending on age, time of day and distance to be travelled. Make sure you ask for the cheapest available ticket. Further information can be obtained from British Rail offices or agents in other countries, and from any British Rail station.

National Express operate extensive coach services to most major towns and cities throughout the UK. Full-time students can buy a Student Coach Card entitling them to approx 30% reduction on standard fares. Cost £6, valid 1 year. For further information contact National Express ℂ 081-770 7770.

Hitch-hikers' Manual Britain £3.95, is a comprehensive handbook including hints on techniques, route planning, legal matters, and how lifts can be found on boats, planes and hovercrafts. Contains descriptions of how to reach the best hitching points for 200 towns, plus a section on motorway hitching. Published by Vacation Work, 9 Park End Street, Oxford OX1 1HJ ℂ Oxford (0865) 241978.

Information centres International Travellers' Aid, The Kiosk, Platform 8, Victoria Station, London SW1V 1JT is an interdenominational voluntary organisation, helping and providing information to travellers, particularly if they have just arrived from overseas, are unfamiliar with English, need advice on accommodation, need to trace friends, relatives or lost possessions, or are in distress of any kind.

The National Association of Volunteer Bureaux, St Peter's College, College Road, Saltley, Birmingham B8 3TE ✆ 021-327 0265 was set up to serve and represent Britain's volunteer bureaux and to promote volunteering in general. Does not recruit volunteers, but can put enquirers in touch with their local volunteer bureau, who will be able to advise them of the entire range of voluntary work available locally.

The National Youth Agency, 17-23 Albion Street, Leicester LE1 6GD ✆ Leicester (0533) 471200 can provide information on community involvement and young volunteer organisations in England and Wales.

The Scottish Community Education Council (SCEC), West Coates House, 90 Haymarket Terrace, Edinburgh EH12 5LQ ✆ 031-313 2488 promotes community involvement and service by young people in Scotland. Although it does not recruit volunteers or find placements for them, it provides an information sheet giving details of volunteer projects in Scotland, including conservation work, workcamps, community projects, playschemes and some opportunities for long-term volunteers.

Publications *Vac Work* details vacation work, sandwich placements, training and other types of employment available to undergraduates during the vacations. The main issues are published in February and November and supplements are available during the academic year. Published by Central Services Unit for Graduate Careers Services. Available for consultation in university, polytechnic or college careers information rooms, or direct from CSU Publications, Armstrong House, Oxford Road, Manchester M1 7EQ price £1.50.

Directory of Summer Jobs in Britain 1993 £7.95, lists opportunities all over Britain with details of wages and hours, conditions of work, and qualifications required. Published by Vacation Work, 9 Park End Street, Oxford OX1 1HJ ✆ Oxford (0865) 241978.

Accommodation The International Friendship League, Peace Haven, 3 Creswick Road, Acton, London W3 9HE works to promote a spirit of mutual respect and friendship among the peoples of the world. Offers accommodation at residential centres in London and Gloucester, all year. Cost from £10 per night, bed and breakfast. Also offers a hospitality service throughout Britain of households prepared to provide accommodation at a reasonable charge and take visitors to places of interest. *Apply at least 8 weeks in advance enclosing 4 IRCs.*

Hackney Camping, Millfields Road, London E5 ✆ 081-985 7656 is a campsite for those taking their own tents/equipment. Open mid June-end August. Cost £4 per night, includes the use of hot showers, shop, snack bar and baggage store. From September-May contact Tent City Ltd (address below) ✆ 071-749 9074. **B D PH**

Tent City, Old Oak Common Lane, East Acton, London W3 7DP ✆ 081-743 5708 offers camping accommodation for young travellers at a football pavilion and park, with 450 beds in 14 large mixed or single sex tents. Bedding available; also space for those taking their own tents. Open early June-late September. Cost £5 per night including use of hot showers, snack bar and baggage store. **B D PH**

ARCHAEOLOGY

COUNCIL FOR BRITISH ARCHAEOLOGY 112 Kennington Road, London SE11 6RE ✆ 071-582 0494
Ensures the safeguarding of all kinds of archaeological material, stimulates an informed interest in the past and provides information on how volunteers can assist in archaeological excavations. Opportunities in all parts of Britain; hours and payment vary, but where the work is organised by the Government some form of allowance is normally paid and hostel or camping accommodation provided. 2/3+ weeks. Applicants must be over 16 and fit. Details published in *British Archaeological News*, bi-monthly; annual subscription £10.50 (UK) or £11.50 (Europe). Lists sites where volunteer helpers are needed, giving details of location, type and accommodation.

CRICKLEY HILL ARCHAEOLOGICAL TRUST c/o Department of Archaeology, The University, Nottingham NG7 2RD
℗ Nottingham (0602) 484848 ext 4519
One of the largest excavations in Europe, entirely staffed and run by unpaid volunteers and based on a hilltop in the Cotswolds. Remains of some 20 phases of occupation have been identified, ranging from the Neolithic to the sub-Roman period. Ages 16+. Experience not necessary. 48 hour week, early July-mid August. Full board accommodation provided, cost £35 per week; campers also welcome. Some grants available to experienced workers towards the cost of board and lodging. Insurance provided but no fares or wages paid. Weekend and short-term work available for experienced diggers. Optional training week organised, cost £135 includes lectures, field trips, full board accommodation and excursions. D PH some mobility necessary.

DORSET NATURAL HISTORY & ARCHAEOLOGICAL SOCIETY Dorset County Museum, Dorchester, Dorset DT1 1XA
℗ Dorchester (0305) 262735
Volunteers are required to help on rescue excavations all over Dorset; current excavations include prehistoric and Roman sites. Some training provided; experience preferable. Ages 16+. Volunteers must be fit, self-reliant and prepared for hard, disciplined work. 1+ weeks, April-September. Usually no wages paid. Volunteers should take tents and camping equipment if no other accommodation is provided. D *Full details available in March.*

UPPER NENE ARCHAEOLOGICAL SOCIETY Toad Hall, 86 Main Road, Hackleton, Northampton NN7 2AD ℗ Northampton (0604) 870312
Limited number of volunteers required to assist in the excavation of a large Romano-British villa. Work involves trowelling, digging, drawing, surveying, assisting with photography, processing and recording finds. Relevant qualifications and experience welcome but not essential. Ages 17+. 50 hours per week. 2 weeks, August, and Sundays all year. Campsite available nearby, cost £7.50 for 2 weeks; or bed and breakfast arranged with local families, cost from approx £7 per night. £16.50 fee for 2 weeks covers site running costs

and refreshments. Insurance provided, but no fares or wages paid. Occasional talks and an excursion to local excavation or place of interest arranged. D PH

AU PAIR / CHILDCARE

Au pair posts are intended only for those aged 17-27, unmarried and without dependants, wishing to visit Britain to learn English while living as a member of an English-speaking family. Only EC nationals (both sexes), female nationals of the former Yugoslavia, and female nationals of Andorra, Austria, Cyprus, Czechoslovakia, the Faroes, Finland, Greenland, Hungary, Iceland, Liechtenstein, Malta, Monaco, Norway, San Marino, Sweden, Switzerland and Turkey are eligible, and will be permitted to spend no more than a total of 2 years in Britain as an au pair. On arrival non-EC national au pairs should provide the immigration officer with a letter of invitation from the host family, giving precise details of the au pair arrangements, including the amount of pocket money, accommodation, free time, details of the host family, house and household, and exact nature of assistance expected, and may also be required to produce a return ticket or evidence of sufficient funds to pay for return travel. As a general rule au pairs can expect to work up to 5 hours per day with 1 fixed day per week free. An au pair should have his/her own room, receive approx £20-£30 per week pocket money, and may reasonably be asked to do light housework, cooking, childcare and occasional evening babysitting.

EC nationals wishing to stay longer than 6 months should apply to the Home Office for an extension of stay. Au pairs who are not EC nationals or Commonwealth citizens and who are staying longer than 6 months as au pairs will be required to register with the police, taking along their passport and two passport-sized photographs. Au pair posts should not be confused with regular childcare employment; *nannies* and *au pair plus* posts usually fall into this category. Information and advice on immigration matters can be obtained from British Embassies, Consulates and High Commissions or from the Home Office, Lunar House, Wellesley Road, Croydon, Surrey CR9

2BY ℂ 081-686 0688. The following agencies can arrange au pair and childcare placements in Great Britain:

ABOUT AU PAIRS 3 Garston Park, Godstone, Surrey RH9 8NE ℂ Godstone (0883) 743735 Can place au pairs throughout England. Single females only, ages 18-27. Pocket money £30 per week.

ACADEMY AU PAIR AGENCY LTD Glenlea, Dulwich Common, London SE21 7ES ℂ 081-299 4599 Can place au pairs. Ages 18-27. Some knowledge of English essential. Pocket money approx £30-£35 per week. Positions as nannies and mothers' helps also available for those with qualificaions/experience.

ANGLIA AGENCY 70 Southsea Avenue, Leigh-on-Sea, Essex ℂ Southend-on-Sea (0702) 471648 Can place au pairs, mothers' helps and nannies. Ages 17+. Pocket money £30 per week.

ANGLO PAIR AGENCY 40 Wavertree Road, Streatham Hill, London SW2 3SP ℂ 081-674 3605 Can place au pairs and au pairs plus in London. Ages 17-27. Weekly pocket money £30+ (au pairs) or £40+ (au pairs plus).

AVALON AGENCY Thursley House, 53 Station Road, Shalford, Guildford, Surrey GU4 8HA ℂ Guildford (0843) 63640 Can place au pairs and *aides de famille*. Ages 18-27. Pocket money £25-£35 per week (au pairs) or £35-£60 per week (*aides de famille*).

EUROYOUTH LTD 301 Westborough Road, Westcliff, Southend-on-Sea SSO 9PT ℂ Southend-on-Sea (0702) Can place au pairs. Ages 18+. Knowledge of English desirable. Pocket money £24-£27 per week. Also opportunities for mothers' helps and holiday helps. *Apply 9 weeks in advance.*

HELPING HANDS AU PAIR & DOMESTIC AGENCY 39 Rutland Avenue, Thorpe Bay, Essex SS1 2XJ ℂ Southend-on-Sea (0702) 602067 Can place au pairs, demi pairs, au pairs plus and mothers' helps, mainly in London suburbs, country areas and seaside towns. Ages 17-27. Pocket money £12-£70 per week depending on position.

HOME FROM HOME Walnut Orchard, Chearsley, Aylesbury, Buckinghamshire HP18 0DA ℂ/Fax Aylesbury (0844) 208561 Can place au pairs throughout Britain. Ages 18+. Pocket money £30 per week. Placement fee £40.

INTERNATIONAL CATHOLIC SOCIETY FOR GIRLS (ACISJF) St Patrick's International Youth Centre, 24 Great Chapel Street, London W1V 3AF ℂ 071-734 2156 Au pair posts arranged mostly for 9+ months; also some 3 month summer positions. Ages 18+.

JOLAINE AGENCY 18 Escot Way, Barnet, Hertfordshire EN5 3AN ℂ 081-449 1334 Can place au pairs, demi pairs and mothers' helps with families in the London area, on the coast and in the country. Ages 17+. Pocket money £10-£70 per week, depending on position.

JUST THE JOB EMPLOYMENT AGENCY 8 Musters Road, West Bridgford, Nottingham NG2 5PL ℂ Nottingham (0602) 813224 Can place au pairs and au pairs plus in Aberdeen, Blackpool, Cardiff, Derby, Glasgow, Leeds, Leicester, London, Manchester, Newcastle, Norwich, Nottingham and Sheffield. Ages 18+. Weekly pocket money £28-£30 (au pairs) or £40 (au pairs plus).

MONDIAL AGENCY 32 Links Road, West Wickham, Kent BR4 0QW ℂ 081-777 0510 Can place au pairs with families in the south of London and the Home Counties. Ages 18-27. Pocket money £30 per week. Service charge £40.

PROBLEMS UNLIMITED 86 Alexandra Road, Windsor, Berkshire SL4 1HU ℂ Windsor (0753) 830101 Can place au pairs and au pairs plus mainly in the South East, also Scotland and Wales. Ages 18-27. Basic conversational English and some experience in housework essential. Weekly pocket money £30-£35 (au pairs) or £40 (au pairs plus).

STUDENTS ABROAD LTD 11 Milton View, Hitchin, Hertfordshire SG4 0QD ✆ Hitchin (0462) 438909
Can place au pairs and mothers' helps with families in the London area and throughout the UK. Ages 18-27 for au pairs. Basic knowledge of English required. Pocket money £30-£35 per week; higher for mothers' helps.

UNIVERSAL CARE Chester House, 9 Windsor End, Beaconsfield, Buckinghamshire HP9 2JJ ✆ Beaconsfield (0494) 678811
Can place au pairs in London and throughout Britain. Ages 18-27. Pocket money £30 per week. Also mothers' helps in London and the South East. Pocket money £50-£80 per week. PH

CHILDREN'S PROJECTS

ASSOCIATION FOR ALL SPEECH IMPAIRED CHILDREN 347 Central Markets, Smithfield, London EC1A 9NH ✆ 071-236 6487/3632
Works to improve educational provision for children and young people with speech and/or language impairments, and gives support and advice to parents and professionals. Arranges adventure weeks for children aged 6-18+ covering a wide range of outdoor pursuits and indoor activities. The adventure weeks are held in centres in the countryside or at the seaside for the younger children; recent venues have included Kendal, Whitby, Southport, Broadstairs, Basingstoke, and Eyam. Committed volunteers with fluent English are needed, to spend a week devoting time and energy. Work involves being a friend and constant companion on a 1:1 basis throughout the week, helping to stimulate and give supportive help. Ages 18+, 1 week, all year. Full board accommodation in hostel or youth centre provided, but help towards cost welcomed. No wages or travel paid. B D PH depending on ability.

ATD FOURTH WORLD The General Secretary, 48 Addington Square, London SE5 7LB ✆ 071-703 3231
Works very closely with some of the most disadvantaged and marginalised families to help ensure they have a place in society. Street libraries are a recognition that social exclusion is inherited by children, and seek to combat this early by introducing learning, creativity and fun into some of the poorest estates. Permanent trained volunteers run the libraries, and their subsequent evaluation of the projects contributes understanding to further anti-poverty initiatives. Short-term volunteers should wish to share in the discoveries of the children, work hard in a lively team, and seek to better understand the experience of poverty. Approx 40 hour, 5½ day week. 1-4 weeks, during Easter, summer and half-term school holidays. Accommodation provided. Applicants asked to contribute to food costs.

BIRMINGHAM PHAB CAMPS Suzanne Webb, 3 Gresley Close, Four Oaks, Sutton Coldfield B75 5HT
Volunteers are needed to help on holidays which aim to integrate physically handicapped and able-bodied children aged 7+. Work involves being responsible for the children 24 hours a day, supervising, caring and organising activities including riding, watersports, excursions and evening activities such as discos and parties. Each camp has an experienced leader and qualified nurse; volunteers attend an informal training day when they meet their leader and learn a little more about the holidays and handicaps. Volunteers should have imagination, enthusiasm and the ability to get on with children. The holidays are informal and generally a lot of fun for all.
Ages 17+. Volunteers able to drive minibuses, ages 21+, particularly welcome, and qualified nurses also required. 7-10 days, July and August. Board and lodging provided. Insurance and travel between Birmingham and the holiday site arranged. B D PH

BIRMINGHAM YOUNG VOLUNTEERS ADVENTURE CAMPS 4th Floor, Smithfield House, Digbeth, Birmingham B5 6BS ✆ 021-622 2888
Volunteers are needed to help with holidays on the Pembrokeshire coast, near Malvern and in Atherstone for disadvantaged children from the Birmingham area. 1 week, July-September. Volunteer helpers encourage close personal contact which allows development of personalities through new relationships and experiences. Experience of drama, art, games organisation, music or cooking useful. Ages

17+. Also opportunities for minibus drivers, ages 21+. Training given. Full board hostel or camping accommodation, insurance cover and travel costs from Birmingham to the holiday provided. *Applicants from outside Britain are welcome, but due to the short length of the camps they would need to be already resident in Britain, at least during the summer.*

THE BLACKIE Duty Officer, Great Georges Project, Great George Street, Liverpool L1 5EW ✆ 051-709 5109
The Great Georges Community Cultural Project, known locally as The Blackie, is a centre for experimental work in the arts, sports, games and education of today. Housed in a former church in an area typical of the modern inner-city: multi-racial, relatively poor, with a high crime rate and a high energy level; sometimes a lot of fun.
Volunteers are needed to work with children/ adults on playschemes, special projects and outdoor events. The general work of running the Project is shared as fairly as possible, with everyone doing some administration, repairs, building work, cleaning, talking to visitors and playing games with the children. Ages normally 18+, although younger volunteers may be accepted. Applicants should have a good sense of humour, stamina, a readiness to learn, and a willingness to work hard and to share any skills they may have. The children and young people who visit the Project are tough, intelligent, friendly and regard newcomers as a fair target for jokes, so the ability to exert discipline without being authoritarian is essential. 12 hour day, 5½ day week, 4+ weeks; volunteers particularly needed at Christmas, Easter and summer.
Accommodation provided in shared rooms at staff house; volunteers should take a sleeping bag. Vegetarian breakfast and evening meal provided, cooking on a rota basis. Those who can afford to, contribute approx £17.50 per week to cover food and housekeeping. *Overseas applicants welcome; good working knowledge of English required.*

CHRISTIAN MOVEMENT FOR PEACE
Bethnal Green United Reformed Church, Pott Street, London E2 0EF ✆ 071-729 7985
An international movement open to all who share a common concern for lasting peace and justice in the world. Volunteers are required to work in international teams on summer projects aimed at offering a service in an area of need and promoting self-help within the community; promoting international understanding and the discussion of social problems; and offering young people the chance to live as a group and take these experiences into the context of daily life. Recent projects have included running playschemes in east London, Bradwell-on-Sea, Leicester and Tiverton, involving fundraising, arts and craft activities, music and movement, sports, camping and bus trips. Participants are encouraged to become involved in the life of the host community. Ages 17+, or 18+ for overseas volunteers, who must have good English. Volunteers must enjoy working with children, be able to contribute their own ideas to the schemes, show initiative in organising indoor and outdoor activities and be prepared to take a full part in all aspects of the project. 30-36 hour week. 2-3 weeks, July and August, and sometimes at Easter. Board, lodging and insurance provided, but participants pay their own travel costs. Registration fee £30.
Apply through partner organisation in country of residence; for further information see page 30.

COMMUNITY ACTION PROJECTS Camp Organiser, Goodricke College, University of York, Heslington, York YO1 5DD ✆ York (0904) 433133
Volunteers are needed to help on an annual camp for children with additional needs aged 6-13, who might not otherwise get a holiday. Many of the children are emotionally disturbed, hyperactive or come from unsettled backgrounds. The camp takes about 30 children per week and is usually held on the North Yorkshire Moors. Activities include drama, arts and crafts, horse-riding, ice-skating, going to the beach, excursions, games, shows and walks. Duties include supervising tents, playing with and looking after the children, dealing with emotional problems, taking responsibility for situations as they arise, driving the minibus, cooking and sharing camp duties/chores. 1-3 weeks during school summer holidays. The work is physically and emotionally tiring, so the maximum stay as a volunteer is 3 weeks, 2 weeks as a driver. Ages 18+, (drivers must be over 21 with 1 year's clean driving licence). Volunteers should

have initiative, enthusiasm, a sense of humour, lots of energy, the ability to take responsibility and participate fully in all camp activities, plus a liking for children, friendliness and tolerance. Skills in games, arts/crafts, cookery, wildlife, sports or first aid are very useful, as well as the ability to drive a minibus. References required. Smaller camps, catering for up to 20, are also run at Easter, based in village schools or similar buildings. Food and accommodation provided. Venture weeks are run for 14-16 year olds in August, involving backpacking, canoeing, rock-climbing, abseiling, setting up camp, orienteering and problem solving. Experience of camping and working with teenagers useful. A training day is arranged the day before each camp begins to give volunteers the opportunity to meet one another and discuss the running of the camp. B D PH depending on ability. *Overseas volunteers with a working knowledge of English accepted.*

EASTWOOD AREA COMMUNITY EDUCATION OFFICE 218 Ayr Road, Newton Mearns, Glasgow © 041-639 7160

Provides educational and recreational activities for all members of the community and needs volunteers to help on summer playschemes. Work involves supervising 5-16 year olds in sports, crafts, games, and taking them on outings or to special events. Ages 16+. No qualifications or experience required, but volunteers must be able to speak English. 25 hour week, July. Insurance provided, but not travel. Board and accommodation arranged in student halls of residence, cost approx £50 per week. B D PH W

FLYSHEET CAMPS SCOTLAND The Resident Organiser, Finniegill, Lockerbie, Dumfriesshire DG11 2LP

A remote farmstead situated high in the hills of southwest Scotland, providing wilderness camps for children, mainly from families in need. The aim is to provide a setting where people of all ages and backgrounds can come together and experience living and working in ways that are different from their everyday life. All aspects of a simple lifestyle are explored, and the experience is as important as the end-product. There is no telephone, no electricity and no amenities for 15 miles.
A limited number of dedicated volunteers are

needed, both for work on the 8 acres of woodland and on the children's camps. Ages 18+. 2-3+ weeks, Easter to late autumn. Primitive bothy or tent accommodation and insurance provided. Volunteers pay their own travel costs and contribute to the cost of food. D PH *Overseas applicants accepted; fluent English required for children's camp volunteers. No telephone enquiries.*

INTERNATIONAL VOLUNTARY SERVICE Old Hall, East Bergholt, Colchester, Essex CO7 6TQ

IVS is the British branch of Service Civil International which promotes international reconciliation through work projects. Volunteers are needed to work in international teams running children's projects throughout Britain. Recent projects have included helping to run summer playschemes in Liverpool, Birkenhead, Tiverton and Edinburgh; involving local children in a water safety project on a canal in Glasgow; working among children with mental and physical disabilities in the Broom Valley, south Yorkshire; and working with children on a recycling project in Newtown, mid-Wales.
Ages 18+. 35-40 hour week, 2-4 weeks, June-September, Christmas and Easter. Overseas volunteers must speak good English. Experience in working with children an advantage. Volunteers must be prepared to work hard and contribute actively to the work and team life, and be prepared for additional mental and emotional strain. Food, accommodation in village halls, houses, schools, homes, hospitals or community centres with self-catering facilities and insurance provided, but volunteers pay their own travel costs. Registration fee (1992) £55 (students £45, unwaged £40). B D PH

Apply through partner organisation in country of residence; for further information see page 30.

LEICESTER BOYS' & GIRLS' SUMMER CAMP & INSTITUTE Shaftesbury Hall, Holy Bones, Leicester LE1 4LJ © Leicester (0533) 519863

Seasonal staff are required at a holiday home in Mablethorpe which provides the poorest and most deserving children aged 7-11 from Leicester and its neighbourhood with a fortnight's holiday. The home is situated on the sandhills and the children have their own path to the beach. Work includes looking after the children, playing with them, taking them to the beach, and perhaps making beds and a little housework. Ages 18+. 1+ months, May-August. Preference given to applicants able to work the whole season. Board and lodging provided plus a salary of £43 per week. *UK nationals only. Apply to Leicester Children's Holiday Home, Quebec Road, Mablethorpe, Lincolnshire LN12 1QX* ✆ *Mablethorpe (0507) 472444.*

LIVERPOOL CHILDREN'S HOLIDAY ORGANISATION Wellington Road School, Wellington Road, Liverpool L8 4TX ✆ **051-727 7330**
Volunteers are needed to help run holidays for Merseyside children, particularly those from low income families who would not otherwise be able to afford one, at centres throughout Britain. Volunteers are responsible for looking after the happiness and safety of groups of 4-6 children aged 7-9, 9-11 and 12-14, providing them with a wide range of entertaining and stimulating activities. No experience necessary but volunteers must have plenty of energy and enthusiasm for being with children, and are on call 24 hours per day. All volunteers will be interviewed before attending a 1 week residential training course, usually at Easter.

Ages 18+. Holidays last 8 or 11 days. Full board dormitory accommodation shared with the children. Accommodation and expenses covered during the holiday period, and basic insurance and return travel from Liverpool to centre provided. Pocket money approx £30 per week. Participants pay nominal fee for training course. PH *UK residents only.*

LONDON CHILDREN'S CAMP Recruitment Officer, 105 Bevan Street West, Lowestoft, Suffolk NR32 2AF
Volunteers are required to provide a holiday for underprivileged children from London on a campsite in Kessingland, Suffolk. Leaders have pastoral care for a group of approx 6 children, aged 8-14, and are involved in inventing and organising different activities and in the day to day running of the camp. 11-13 days, July-end August.
Ages 18+. Applicants should be energetic,

prepared to work 16-17 hours per day, have a sense of humour, be innovative, fairly thick-skinned, tolerant, able to listen, confident, willing to keep order and cope with the children who are sometimes difficult and hard to motivate. Camping accommodation provided plus washing facilities, leaders' hut and a large dining room. Pocket money £25+ per camp. B if accompanied D PH but unsuitable for wheelchairs. *EC nationals only.*

LOTHIAN PLAY FORUM Regional Organising Secretary, Room 9, Dalry Primary School, Dalry Road, Edinburgh EH11 2BU
Organises over 130 playschemes for children in and around Edinburgh, dealing with over 10,000 children. Volunteers are needed to help with games, art, visits, camps and drama. Ages 18+. 4 weeks, July/August. Experience with children an advantage. No food or accommodation provided. *Apply by end April.*

MANSFIELD DISTRICT COUNCIL Play Officer, Leisure Services, Civic Centre, Chesterfield Road, Mansfield, Nottinghamshire NG19 9BT ✆ **Mansfield (0623) 663026**
Playleaders and assistants are required to work at various parks and community/leisure centres throughout the Mansfield area. Work involves organising a variety of play activities for both able-bodied and disabled children aged 5-14.
Applicants must have a good basic education, previous experience of working with groups of children and/or special skills in subjects such as arts, crafts, sports, dance, drama or music. Ages 18+. 20 hours per week; 1 week, Easter or 6 weeks, July-August. Pay £3.80 per hour (leaders), £3.24 per hour (assistants). No accommodation available, but full insurance cover and training provided. B D PH

TADWORTH COURT CHILDREN'S SERVICES Tadworth Court Trust, The Chief Executive, Tadworth, Surrey KT20 5RU ✆ **Burgh Heath (0737) 357171**
Requires volunteers for residential summer schemes for physically and mentally handicapped children, aged 4-16, who normally live at home. The services are provided in a children's hospital and at a residential school. Work involves acting as a friend to the

children, carrying out basic personal care, organising games, encouraging them to take an active part in daily activities, escorting them on outings, and organising evening activities. Previous experience with children or handicapped people preferable, but not essential. Creative skills, handicraft or musical ability welcomed. The work is very rewarding but can also be physically and emotionally tiring.

Ages 18+. 9 hour day, worked in shifts, with 2 days off per week. 4+ weeks, mid July-mid September. Lodging provided, plus a meal allowance of £38.50 per week. Travel expenses within Britain can be reimbursed. *Apply by 31 May*. D PH depending on ability; unsuitable for wheelchairs.

UNITED NATIONS ASSOCIATION
International Youth Service, Temple of Peace, Cathays Park, Cardiff CF1 3AP *✆ Cardiff (0222) 223088*
Aims to assist in community development by acting as a means to stimulate new ideas and projects, and encouraging the concept of voluntary work as a force in the common search for peace, equality, democracy and social justice. Volunteers are needed for community work on summer workcamps in various parts of Wales.

Recent projects have included helping to run playschemes in the south Wales valleys, organising indoor and outdoor activities for children, some of whom are mentally and physically handicapped; and taking groups of deprived or socially handicapped children on holiday, including walks, swimming, sports and excursions.

Ages 18+. Volunteers are expected to join in the activities of the local community and to create a happy and effective project. 40 hour week, 2-4 weeks, April-May and July-September. Accommodation in church halls, youth hostels, schools or community centres, food and insurance provided. Volunteers share the cooking, pay their own travel costs and should take a sleeping bag. Good command of English essential. Registration fee £45. B D PH on some projects.

Apply through partner organisation in country of residence; for further information see page 30.

COMMUNITY WORK

A Place for You in Britain? As a Volunteer is a free leaflet containing useful information on obtaining work as a volunteer and detailing opportunities available. *A Place for You in Britain? Working for World Development*, contains information on how to show concern for world development and the types of activities possible, plus organisations and resource centres to contact. Both published by Christians Abroad, 1 Stockwell Green, London SW9 9HP ✆ 071-737 7811.

Opportunities for Volunteers on Holiday Projects free on receipt of SAE/IRC and published annually, gives details of organisations needing volunteers to help physically disabled people on holiday. Published by RADAR (Royal Association for Disability and Rehabilitation), 25 Mortimer Street, London W1N 8AB ✆ 071-637 5400, which works to remove the barriers which separate disabled people from society.

Student Community Action (SCA) is a network of over 100 groups of volunteers based in colleges, polytechnics and universities throughout Britain, working in cooperation with community-based projects, or on their own projects in response to the needs of the local area. Projects include playschemes, work in women's refuges, caring for the elderly or disabled, and campaigning on welfare rights and homelessness. Most of the work is done during termtime, but some groups run projects during Easter and summer vacations, open to people not studying at the college. The SCA Development Unit (SCADU) publishes a list of summer volunteering opportunities in May each year, and can give details of local SCA groups. Write, stating where in Britain you would like to volunteer, to SCADU, Oxford House, Derbyshire Street, London E2 6HG.

ASHRAM COMMUNITY SERVICE PROJECT
23/25 Grantham Road, Sparkbrook, Birmingham B11 1LU ✆ 021-773 7061
A multi-purpose community development project in a multi-racial, inner city area, working for social, economic and environmental change. Its activities include bilingual training courses for the long-term

unemployed, a home care and safety project, organic gardening on derelict land, legal advice bureau and Credit Union. Volunteers invited to help with horticulture, domestic tasks and general administration, as well as helping at stalls and various events. Ages 21+. No experience necessary. Hours negotiable; usually 09.00-17.00. Insurance and accommodation provided in residential community on site, with opportunities to join in social events. Volunteers pay travel and board and lodging as far as possible. B D PH but unsuitable for wheelchairs. *Overseas applicants welcome.*

ASSOCIATION FOR SPINA BIFIDA AND HYDROCEPHALUS (ASBAH) Five Oaks Centre, Ben Rhydding Drive, Ilkley, West Yorkshire LS29 8BD *Ⓒ* Ilkley (0943) 603013/ 609468
A residential training centre for young people with spina bifida and/or hydrocephalus, running courses in driving, outdoor pursuits, conservation, fashion and independence training. Volunteers are required to accompany excursions, assist with cooking and personal needs of residents, and generally socialise with young disabled people at the centre. No experience necessary. Applicants must be cheerful, lively and mature. Overseas volunteers should have a reasonable standard of spoken English. Ages 18+. 30-35 hours per week. 1-4 weeks, all year. Bed and breakfast accommodation provided locally; all other meals taken at the centre. Insurance provided, and travel costs in some cases. B D PH

BREAK Mr G M Davison, 20 Hooks Hill Road, Sheringham, Norfolk NR26 8NL *Ⓒ* Sheringham (0263) 823170
Provides holidays and respite for unaccompanied mentally, physically and emotionally handicapped children and adults from pre-school age upwards, and for socially deprived children. Holiday and special care opportunities also exist for mentally handicapped adults and families with special needs. Volunteers are needed as care assistants for residential work at two holiday homes at Sheringham and Hunstanton. Work involves helping with the personal welfare of the guests, their recreational programme and with essential domestic duties. Placements involving work discussions and assessments

can be arranged for those seeking practical experience prior to or as part of an educational course. Ages 17/18+. Applicants should be stable, conscientious, patient and understanding. The work is physically and emotionally demanding. 40 hour week. 1-9 months, all year. Board, lodging and £22 per week pocket money provided, plus travel expenses within Britain. *Overseas volunteers accepted.*

CAMPHILL VILLAGE TRUST Loch Arthur Village Community, Beeswing, Dumfries DG2 8JQ *Ⓒ* Kirkgunzeon (038 776) 687
Aims to provide a new and constructive way of life for mentally handicapped adults, assisting them to achieve individual independence and social adjustment within Trust communities. Loch Arthur Community provides a home, work, further education and general care for approx 30 handicapped adults, and consists of 5 houses, a farm and an estate of 500 acres. Volunteers are needed to work alongside the residents in every aspect of life and main areas of work are on the farm and in the garden, houses and workshops. As many of the adults have fairly severe handicaps they are also in need of care such as bathing, dressing and other personal tasks. Ages 18+. Volunteers must be willing to help wherever they are needed, and are encouraged not only to share in the responsibilities of living and working with the handicapped but also to participate in the cultural, recreational and social aspects of Community life. 6 weeks minimum stay; 6-12 months preferred. Food and accommodation provided, plus pocket money for long-term volunteers. *Overseas applicants accepted.*

CECIL HOUSES INC 2/4 Priory Road, Kew, Richmond, Surrey TW9 3DG *Ⓒ* 081-940 9828
A housing association and charity providing hostels for homeless women, sheltered hostel-flats for active pensioners and residential care homes for the frail elderly. It aims to provide caring communities where individuals can mix with others in similar circumstances. Volunteers are needed to help staff caring for the residents; work includes helping with social activities, light domestic work and generally assisting in improving the residents' lifestyle. Ages 18+. No experience needed. 4+ months, all year. 39 hour week. Full board,

lodging and £21 per week pocket money provided. *Overseas volunteers with good English accepted.*

CROYDON COMMUNITY AND VOLUNTARY SERVICES Volunteer Organiser, Strand House, Zion Road, Thornton Heath, Surrey CR4 8RG © 081-684 2245/2210

Volunteers living in the London area are needed to accompany adults with physical or learning disabilities on holiday. Volunteers would be involved with escorting the holidaymakers to the venue and generally supporting them throughout the holiday. Holidays last 3-8 days and consist of a small group of adults with 1-2 volunteers. References will be taken up for all volunteers. Board, accommodation and return travel from Croydon to the holiday centre provided, plus pocket money. PH depending on ability.

EDINBURGH CYRENIANS 20 Broughton Place, Edinburgh EH1 3RX © 031-556 4971

A trust set up to develop and provide services to homeless single people, running a city community in central Edinburgh and a rural project on a small organic farm in West Lothian. Residents are a mix of young people referred by social workers, hospitals or other agencies. Volunteers live and work alongside residents and other volunteers, sharing the jobs involved in running a large household, with particular responsibility for managing household accounts, upholding the rules of the community, attending weekly meetings, forming helpful relationships with community members and offering assistance and support to residents. Community life is challenging, difficult and stressful, but can also be extremely rewarding.

Ages 18-30. Applicants should have personal commitment, an open mind, willingness to learn, a sense of responsibility, energy, enthusiasm and a sense of humour. Overseas volunteers should have a working knowledge of English. 5 day week with access to flat away from community on days off. 6 months, all year. Volunteers receive full board accommodation, £22 per week pocket money, £160 grant for 1 weeks' holiday after 3 months, £30 clothing allowance and £135 leaving grant after 6 months. Regular training given and

volunteers supervised by non-residential social workers. B D PH unsuitable for wheelchairs.

GLASGOW SIMON COMMUNITY 5 Finnieston Quay, Glasgow G3 8HN © 041-204 3715

Aims to offer time, friendship, practical help and supportive accommodation to men and women who have been homeless for some time. There is an outreach team and 4 small group homes in which residents and volunteers live together, sharing in the running and day-to-day life. Contact is made with homeless people, especially rough sleepers, and friendship and practical help is offered. Volunteers also maintain contact and good relations with relevant agencies. Ages 18+. No academic qualifications required but certain personal qualities essential, including a non-patronising attitude, the ability to accept people for what they are, and to cope with stress and emotional pressures. Recruitment takes place all year round. Informal training provided during the first month, with training visits to relevant agencies and regular opportunities to participate in training events. 5 day week, 24 hour day. 6 months, preferably longer. Allowance of £45 per week covers pocket money, compulsory savings and holiday allowance. Full board accommodation provided; separate accommodation for days off. Volunteers take their turn cooking along with the residents. Travel expenses paid during the time in the community; for interview up to £40 is paid. The work relies on commitment and involvement; first 3 weeks are an introductory/trial period. *All nationalities welcome, but applicants must have good spoken English.*

HELP THE HANDICAPPED HOLIDAY FUND 147A Camden Road, Tunbridge Wells, Kent TN1 2RA © Tunbridge Wells (0892) 547474

Aims to provide group holidays for physically handicapped people from the age of 11 upwards. Volunteers provide help and care during holiday visits in Cornwall, Dorset, Kent, Lancashire and Sussex. No experience necessary. Ages 18+. Hours depending on the guests' needs and level of care. Helpers must provide their own pocket money and a small contribution towards the cost of accommodation and insurance. B D PH depending on ability.

INDEPENDENT LIVING ALTERNATIVES

Fulton House, Fulton Road, Empire Way, Wembley, Middlesex HA9 0TF ✆ **081-902 8998 ext 228/9**

A non-profitmaking charity run by people with direct experience of disability, designed to promote independence to people disabled. Volunteers are needed to provide physical support in the form of partnership on a full-time basis. Ages 17+. 5 day week. Food, accommodation, £50 per week plus expenses provided. Training given on placement. B D PH depending on ability. *Overseas volunteers welcome, but must be completely fluent in English.*

INDEPENDENT LIVING SCHEMES (ILS)

Kenneth Smith & Dorothy Kendrick, Lewisham Social Services, Laurence House, 1 Catford Road, London SE6 4SW ✆ **081-695 6000 exts 8639/8638**

Aims to enable severely disabled people (all wheelchair users) to live in the community with help from volunteers, who will assist in personal care, including toileting and lifting, shopping, social and community activities. Ages 18-50, no experience necessary. Two 24 hour shifts per week, sleeping in. Weekly allowances include £30 pocket money and £30 for food. £12 per month provided for clothing and leisure. Shared accommodation provided and household bills paid. 6 month placement period preferred but other lengths can be negotiated. Obligatory interview in London; travel costs reimbursed from within the UK. Write or telephone for application form and information pack. B D PH depending on ability. *Overseas applications can only be accepted from those who have right of entry into the UK or who require no sponsorship.*

THE INTERNATIONAL FLAT

Mrs B Gandhi, 20 Glasgow Street, Glasgow G12 8JP ✆ **041-339 6118**

A voluntary organisation based in the Hillhead area of Glasgow, needing volunteers to help on a playscheme for children aged 6-12 from various ethnic backgrounds. Activities include puppet shows, films, indoor and outdoor games, arts and crafts and visits around Glasgow. Ages 18+. Experience preferred, but not essential. 30 hour week. 3 weeks, July. Self-catering accommodation provided. *Apply before mid April. Overseas volunteers accepted.*

INTERNATIONAL VOLUNTARY SERVICE

Old Hall, East Bergholt, Colchester CO7 6TQ

IVS is the British branch of Service Civil International, which promotes international reconciliation through work projects. Volunteers are needed for community work on international workcamps.

Recent projects have included building paths suitable for wheelchairs at a holiday centre for people with disabilities in Aviemore; planning language classes and activities at a centre for refugees from Africa and Sri Lanka in south London; living in a community of adults with mental disabilities in north Yorkshire, picking fruit, weeding and drystone-walling; and organising crafts, drama and outings for residents in a long-stay hospital in Birmingham. There are approx 80 international workcamps involving groups of 6-18 volunteers.

Ages 18+. Overseas volunteers must speak fluent English. Volunteers must be prepared to work hard and contribute actively to the work and team life, and be prepared for additional mental and emotional strain. 35-40 hour week, 2-4 weeks, June-September, and Christmas and Easter. Food, insurance and accommodation in village halls, houses, schools, homes, hospitals or community centres with self-catering facilities provided, but volunteers pay their own travel costs. Registration fee (1992) £55 (students £45, unwaged £40). B D PH

Apply through partner organisation in country of residence; for further information see page 30.

KITH & KIDS

404 Camden Road, Islington, London N7 0SJ ✆ **071-700 2755**

A self-help group providing support for the families of children who have a physical or learning disability. Volunteers are required to take part in social training schemes, working on a 2:1 basis with learning-disabled children and young adults, helping them with everyday skills and experiences within the community. No experience necessary, just enthusiasm. 2 days training provided before each project. Ages 16+. 2 weeks, August or 1 week, Christmas and Easter. Hours 09.30-17.00 daily. Lunch provided and all reasonable travel expenses paid. No accommodation is available so volunteers should be based in or around north London. PH depending on ability.

THE LEONARD CHESHIRE FOUNDATION
Secretary to the Personnel Adviser, Leonard Cheshire House, 26/29 Maunsel Street, London SW1P 2QN © 071-828 1822

Runs over 80 homes throughout the UK, mostly in country areas, for the care of severely handicapped people, mainly physically disabled adults. Cheshire Homes offer the affection and freedom of family life, and the residents are encouraged to lead the most active lives that their disabilities permit.
Volunteers are needed in many Homes to assist with the general care of residents who require help in personal matters, including washing, dressing and feeding, as well as with hobbies, letter writing, driving, going on outings or holidays and other recreational activities.

Ages 18-30. Preference generally given to those planning to take up medical or social work as a career. Volunteers must be adaptable, dedicated, hard working, punctual and willing to undertake a wide variety of tasks. Up to 39 hour, 5 day week, for periods of 3-12 months. Board, lodging and at least £25 per week pocket money provided. Travel costs paid by volunteers. *Overseas applicants must have a good working knowledge of English.*

LONDON CITY MISSION Youth
Department, 175 Tower Bridge Road, London SE1 2AH © 071-407 7585

Volunteers are needed to help with outreach work in evangelical churches and mission centres around London, working alongside experienced Christian workers. Work includes open-air meetings, helping with vagrants, street witnessing, some visiting, practical and tourist work and children's meetings. Knowledge of foreign languages helpful but not essential. Some in-service training given.

Ages 18-30. 2-8 weeks, July-September. Other short-term opportunities available throughout the year. Hours worked depend on the individual placements, but volunteers should be prepared for hard work and long hours. Basic accommodation and food provided. Expenses covered by the Mission, but participants are asked to donate towards the cost if possible. One year programme also available, beginning September. *Applicants must be practising evangelical Christians.*

MENCAP (Royal Society for Mentally Handicapped Children and Adults), Holiday
Services Office, 119 Drake Street, Rochdale, Lancashire OL16 1PZ © Rochdale (0706) 54111

Volunteer helpers are needed on adventure, guest house and special care holidays throughout England and Wales for unaccompanied people with a mental handicap. Work involves being responsible for the personal care of each guest, including washing, feeding and other essential tasks as well as stimulating and interesting them in activities, communicating and being a friend. Duties are shared on a rota basis and can include cooking, cleaning, making beds and night duty. Much time is also spent playing, talking and planning activities.

Ages 18+. No experience necessary, but volunteers need energy, enthusiasm and an interest in people with a mental handicap. Qualified nurses welcome. Maximum 14 hours work per day. 1-2 weeks, Easter-September. Board and accommodation provided. Travelling expenses up to £20 will be reimbursed. PH *Applications from outside Britain welcome.*

THE OCKENDEN VENTURE Personnel
Officer, Ockenden, Guildford Road, Woking, Surrey GU22 7UU © Woking (0483) 772012

A voluntary organisation providing home, health, education and rehabilitation for displaced persons, refugees and young people. There are Ockenden centres in North Wales, Yorkshire and Surrey. Volunteers are needed to assist in caring for refugee families, and a small group of physically and mentally handicapped refugees; and to help with driving, gardening, cooking, painting and maintenance. The communities are run on non-institutional lines in order to create homes, so volunteers are expected to accept a fair share of responsibility at all levels. The Venture aims to provide young volunteers with experience in community responsibility and awareness of social needs.

Ages 18+. Approx 14 places per year for graduates or mature school leavers. Limited number of placements for summer volunteers; most positions for 1 year. 5 day week. Full board and lodging plus £22 per week personal allowance.

OUTWARD BOUND CITY CHALLENGE
Roscoe House, Roscoe Street, Liverpool L1 9DW ✆ 051-707 0202
Provides residential personal development courses for young people, based around the social challenges of inner-city areas. Volunteers are needed to run group sessions and provide support and counselling for those taking part in intensive voluntary service placements with disabled people, the homeless, elderly or mentally ill. Based mainly around Liverpool, Coventry and Humberside. Volunteers need experience of working with the 16+ age group, group work or counselling skills. Teaching or youth work qualifications preferred as well as a clean driving licence. Ages 23+. 2-3 weeks, all year. Tutors are residential and fully committed for the duration of the course, which includes working weekends and evenings. All food, accommodation, insurance, travel expenses, honorarium of approx £350 for 2 weeks and weekend staff training course provided. B D PH W *Overseas applicants welcome; reasonable command of English essential.*

PETRUS COMMUNITY 82 Holt Road, Liverpool L7 2PR ✆ 051-263 4543
A voluntary organisation providing a variety of accommodation and support for homeless single people in inner-city Liverpool. Currently run 3 projects including hostels providing long-stay accommodation and a dry house for recovering alcoholics. Many of the residents have been unemployed for long periods, are socially isolated and some have chronic medical or psychiatric problems. Main tasks include housekeeping, dealing with enquiries and day to day problems. Ages 18+. Volunteers are expected to be capable and responsible, able to cope with the demands of the job. 40 hour working week with 2 free days. Average length of stay 6 months, all year. £30 per week plus full board and accommodation provided. One week's holiday after 3 months service plus leaving bonus. *UK nationals only.*

QUEEN ELIZABETH'S FOUNDATION FOR THE DISABLED Holiday Organiser, Lulworth Court, 25 Chalkwell Esplanade, Westcliff-on-Sea, Essex SS0 8JQ ✆ Southend-on-Sea (0702) 431725
Volunteers are required to help give lively informal holidays to severely physically disabled people at a holiday home on the seafront at Westcliff-on-Sea. Work involves assisting nursing staff to look after guests, many of whom are confined to wheelchairs and need complete help with all aspects of personal care as well as escorting on outings, shopping, theatre and pub trips. The work is hard but rewarding, requiring some heavy lifting. A sense of humour helps. Ages 18+. 1-2 weeks, all year except Christmas. Full board and accommodation provided, and contribution of £15 per week made towards travel expenses. *Overseas volunteers with a good working knowledge of English accepted.*

THE RICHARD CAVE MULTIPLE SCLEROSIS HOLIDAY HOME The Administrator, Servite Convent, Leuchie House, North Berwick, East Lothian EH39 5NY ✆ North Berwick (0620) 2864
Volunteers are needed at a holiday home for persons of all ages with multiple sclerosis. Male and female applicants accepted, although there are twice as many female guests as males. No nursing qualifications necessary. Ages 18-30. Board and accommodation plus pocket money provided. Fares occasionally paid within Britain.

RIDING FOR THE DISABLED ASSOCIATION Avenue R, National Agricultural Centre, Kenilworth, Warwickshire CV8 2LY ✆ Coventry (0203) 696510
Provides the opportunity of riding for disabled people who might benefit in their general health and well-being. Voluntary helpers are sometimes needed for riding holidays in the summer; a list is produced in January detailing the holidays available. Ages 17+. Experience with horses or disabled people useful. No set hours of work; volunteers will be expected to work a full week. Board and lodging plus travel expenses may be provided subject to the holiday organiser's discretion; helpers may be asked to contribute. No wages provided.

RITCHIE RUSSELL HOUSE The Churchill Hospital, Headington, Oxford OX3 7LJ ✆ Oxford (0865) 741841
A purpose-built unit designed for disabled adults, the majority of whom suffer from chronic or progressive neurological diseases,

such as multiple sclerosis, cerebro-vascular accidents, or the effects of head or spinal injury. Patients are intermittently resident, or attend daily, in a secure, lively, relaxed environment where patients and staff work together to improve the quality of life. Each patient is given the opportunity of an annual holiday and volunteers are needed, responsible with the help of staff for the total care of patients on a 1:1 basis, including washing, dressing, toileting and feeding. Ages 18+, fluent English necessary. Experience useful but not essential. All prospective carers are interviewed. 12 hour day, summer. Half board usually in hotel or chalet, insurance and some travel provided. Volunteers are asked to contribute £35-£40.

SHAD Support and Housing Assistance for People with Disabilities, Sue Denney, Winkfield Resource Centre, 33 Winkfield Road, London N22 5RP © 081-365 8528
A scheme which enables people with physical disabilities to live in their own homes, with full control over their lives. Volunteers are required to assist physically disabled adults with all aspects of daily living, including personal care, cooking, housework and going out. No experience necessary; volunteers will receive instruction. Driving licence useful. Ages 18-30. 3+ months, all year. Volunteers work full-time with one person, as part of a team of 2-3 volunteers on a rota basis. Pocket money £48 per week, fares, other expenses, separate accommodation and insurance provided. 4 days per fortnight and regular long weekends off. *Limited number of overseas applications accepted; EC nationals only.*

THE SHAFTESBURY SOCIETY Holiday Centre, New Hall, Low Road, Dovercourt, Harwich, Essex CO12 3TS © Harwich (0255) 504219
Provides holidays for elderly and handicapped guests, and requires volunteers to assist guests in various ways, such as escorting them to the beach, the shops or on outings, and helping with personal needs such as getting up, washing, dressing, toilet, eating, going to bed, bed making. No experience necessary. Ages 16+. 1-2 weeks, April-October. Hours variable, depending on requirements. Single or double room accommodation, food, insurance and travel from London provided.

THE SIMON COMMUNITY 129 Malden Road, PO Box 1187, London NW5 4HW © 071-485 6639
A small registered charity working with homeless people in central London. Founded in 1963 as a venture in care and as a body that would campaign for the plight of homeless people. Aims to work with those for whom no other adequate provision exists. Four houses, including a night shelter, comprise a tier structure enabling even the most difficult personalities to feel accepted and participate in the operation of the Community as far as they feel able.
Volunteers are needed to live and work with residents in the Community's houses. Activities include helping to obtain medical care and Social Security; making referrals to other organisations; talking to residents; cooking, campaigning, maintenance and administration; involvement and facilitation in group meetings; visiting people in hospital; and outreach work. The work is both physically and emotionally demanding. Workers and residents share in daily work and decision making. Volunteers must be caring, sensible, mature and stable enough to take on the burden of other people's problems whilst retaining their own balance. They must be capable of taking their own initiative within the framework of a team and learn to deal with crises. A sense of humour and confidence are valuable attributes. Accommodation is basic and conditions can be rough. Workers live in the project they are assigned to; full board and weekly pocket money provided. Minimum commitment 3 months. 1 day off per week; 10 days leave after 13 weeks. *All nationalities welcome; good knowledge of English essential.*

ST EBBA'S HOSPITAL Hook Road, Epsom, Surrey KT19 8QJ © Epsom (0372) 22212
Cares for the mentally/physically handicapped, with about 350 adult residents, and aims to give the extra care and attention needed, and so help them lead a more contented life. Volunteers are needed to help in various departments: sports, physiotherapy, music and drama, gardening, training, and with general care. No experience necessary, just a sensible, caring nature. Work available for different periods, all year. 32 hour week. Ages 16+. Accommodation and food provided.

ST PANCRAS HOSPITAL Voluntary Services Organiser, 4 St Pancras Way, London NW1 0PE © 071-387 4411 ext 368
A hospital specialising in elderly care and psychiatric rehabilitation. Volunteers are required to befriend elderly patients and assist with outings, shopping trips and home visits as well as spending time chatting, listening, playing games and other activities. Volunteers also needed to help run trolley shop, assist in groups run for psychiatric patients by the Occupational Therapy department, and help in the physiotherapy gym with elderly residents and patients. No experience necessary, just enthusiasm and a liking for the elderly. Volunteers should be punctual, reliable and able to converse in English.
Ages 18+. 10.00-16.30, 3 days a week for 6+ weeks. Insurance, local travel costs and meal vouchers provided, but no accommodation available.

THE SUE RYDER FOUNDATION Administration Officer, Sue Ryder Home, Cavendish, Sudbury, Suffolk CO10 8AY © Glemsford (0787) 280252
Founded to help relieve physical and psychological suffering, the Foundation has over 80 homes, primarily for the disabled and incurable but also admits sick people who, on discharge from hospital, still need care and attention. Aims to give adults and children a family sense with something to contribute, as an individual, to the common good. Helpers are needed at headquarters and the Sue Ryder Home, Cavendish, and on occasions at other Foundation Homes. The work is largely domestic and nursing under supervision, including making beds, serving meals, feeding, working in the kitchen, laundry and gardens and possibly some office and maintenance work. Volunteers should be flexible and adaptable and are expected to help with whatever needs doing. Helpers are also required with training or experience in housekeeping, nursing, physio or occupational therapy, secretarial work, decorating, carpentry, plumbing, engineering, electrical work and bricklaying, as well as site supervisors, surveyors, draughtsmen, talks representative and writers. Help is also needed in Sue Ryder gift and coffee shops, museum, and retreat houses.

Ages 18+. Preference given to students and graduates. 35 hour week for 2+ months, all year. Board and lodging provided, plus approx £10 pocket money per week. *Overseas volunteers with good command of spoken English accepted.*

UNIVERSITY COLLEGE HOSPITAL Voluntary Services Department, Gower Street, London WC1E 6AU © 071-388 6866
Volunteers are required to assist in the general, children's and elderly wards. Work involves befriending long stay and acute patients of all ages, escorting patients with disabilities and helping with occupational and physio therapy. No experience or qualifications necessary; fluent English essential.
Ages 17+. 24 hour week for 6+ weeks, all year. Insurance and local travel costs provided, but no accommodation. Meals provided, depending on hours worked.

WINGED FELLOWSHIP TRUST Recruitment Officer, Angel House, 20-32 Pentonville Road, London N1 9XD © 071-833 2594
Aims to provide 1 or 2 week holidays for as many severely physically disabled people as possible, to give their families a break. Runs 5 holiday centres in Surrey, Essex, Hampshire, Merseyside and Nottinghamshire, each providing holidays for 30-36 disabled adults at a time.
Volunteers are needed to provide the guests with help, companionship and entertainment. This includes washing, dressing and feeding the guests, helping them to bed, writing postcards, playing cards and accompanying them on outings, plus a certain amount of domestic work. Some volunteers may also be asked to help on night duty. Special fortnights include music, drama, craft, fishing and photography, so volunteers with these skills are particularly welcome. Opportunity to take part in country day trips. The atmosphere at the centres is informal and friendly. Hard physical work with long hours.
Ages 16+. 1 or 2 weeks, almost all year round. Accommodation in 2-6 bunk bedded rooms, all meals, use of facilities and fares within Britain provided. Volunteers also required to help on overseas trips and adventure holidays for which a small contribution towards costs in required. *Overseas volunteers with a good standard of spoken English accepted.*

WOODLARKS CAMP SITE TRUST Honorary Secretary, Kathleen Marshall House, Tilford Road, Lower Bourne, Farnham, Surrey GU10 3RN ✆ Farnham (0252) 716279
Voluntary helpers are required on summer camps for severely physically handicapped adults and children at a 12 acre site of pinewoods and grassland on the Surrey/ Hampshire border. Emphasis is placed on the participants trying to do things they would not otherwise have the opportunity to do, and accomplishing things they had always thought impossible. Each week a different group goes to the camp from hospitals, special schools or private homes. Usually one volunteer for each disabled person, and they remain partners for the duration of the camp. Facilities include heated swimming pool, sports equipment, dining/recreation room and open wood fires for cooking. 1+ weeks, mid May-mid September.
Ages 12+. No experience needed, but commitment essential. A nominal fee is charged to help cover food costs. Camping equipment supplied. B D PH *Overseas volunteers accepted.*

YOUNG DISABLED ON HOLIDAY
33 Longfield Avenue, Heald Green, Cheadle, Cheshire SK8 3NH
Volunteers are needed to help on holidays for young physically disabled people. Activities include sightseeing, theatre visits, discos, shopping expeditions, and other adventure pastimes. Ages 18-35. Applicants should have a sense of fun and adventure. Each disabled person has at least 1 helper. 1 week, April-October. Volunteers are expected to contribute 25% of holiday costs.

CONSERVATION

BRITISH TRUST FOR CONSERVATION VOLUNTEERS Room WH, 36 St Mary's Street, Wallingford, Oxfordshire OX10 0EU ✆ Wallingford (0491) 39766
A charity promoting practical conservation work by volunteers; organises numerous conservation working holidays on sites including nature reserves, country estates, National Trust properties and in National Parks. Volunteers are given a chance to contribute in a practical way to the conservation of rural and urban areas. Over 600 projects are organised each year, and recent projects have included conserving the sensitive coastal habitats of orchids, natterjack toads and sand lizards in Merseyside; clearing reeds from a medieval moat in Worcestershire; excavating a secret water garden in Wales; and conserving floating acid bogs in Staffordshire. Instruction is given in the use of tools and equipment, traditional techniques and other conservation skills. Also provide slide shows, guided tours and talks on the conservation value of the work. Approx 12 volunteers work on each project with an experienced leader. Beginners welcome.

Ages 16-70. Overseas volunteers must be over 18, and speak reasonably good English. 1 or 2 weeks, all year, with 1 day off per week to explore surrounding area. Also offer weekend tasks when local groups will accept volunteers aged 12+. Food and accommodation in volunteer centres, youth hostels, estate cottages, village halls, farm buildings or basecamps provided. Volunteers should take a sleeping bag, waterproofs, boots and working clothes. Cost from £28.50 includes food and accommodation and everyone takes it in turns to prepare food. Two friends can apply to work on the same project. Travel paid by volunteers. Anti-tetanus vaccination essential. Projects qualify under the Duke of Edinburgh's Award Scheme. Weekend training courses in practical conservation skills and leadership arranged. It is necessary to become a member of BTCV before attending a working holiday. Cost £12 for ordinary membership (including overseas); £6.60 for unwaged, students or retired people; £17 for families. *Full programme available by Easter.*

CATHEDRAL CAMPS Manor House, High Birstwith, Harrogate, North Yorkshire HG3 2LG ✆ Harrogate (0423) 770385
Aims to preserve, conserve, restore and repair cathedrals and Christian buildings of the highest architectural significance. Volunteers can expect both spectacular and routine work, maintenance work, cleaning roof voids, towers, spiral staircases, wall memorials, traceried woodwork and drain culverts, vacuum cleaning nave walls, washing floors, painting iron railings, plus gardening and renewing path

areas, all under the guidance of craftsmen. At some cathedrals volunteers are also able to work with professional conservators on projects concerning external stonework, internal marble pillars and memorials. 36 hour week, 08.30-17.00 each day with Saturday afternoon, Sunday and evenings free. Food and self-catering accommodation provided, sometimes in hostels, although often in the cathedral hall; volunteers should usually take a sleeping bag.

Ages 16-30. Volunteers should be willing to do a fairly hard day's work, contribute to the social life of the camp, and help with domestic duties on a rota system. Each camp is run by a leader and 2 assistants. A letter of recommendation is required from anyone attending a camp for the first time; two friends may apply to work in the same camp. Anti-tetanus vaccination advised. Camps are held at different cathedrals and churches for 1 week, mid July-early September.
Travel and optional personal insurance paid by volunteers. Projects qualify under the Duke of Edinburgh's Award Scheme. All volunteers receive an admission card valid for 1 year for most English cathedrals. Camp fee approx £30 per week; bursaries available for those who are unwaged, except on vacation, and for volunteers who can show they cannot afford to join a camp. B D PH

THE CRAFT CENTRE St George's Island, Looe, Cornwall PL13 2AB ✆ (0836) 522919
St George's Island lies one mile off the south Cornish coast, and has been opened to day visitors by the present owners as a non-commercial, non-profitmaking project to conserve its unspoilt natural beauty and develop it as a nature reserve. Helpers are required to meet and assist day visitors, serve in the café/craft shop, help with gardening, track and beach clearing and plotting nature trails. No experience necessary.

Ages 16+ for unaccompanied volunteers; families also welcome. Approx 40 hour week. 1+ weeks, April-end September, weather permitting. Self-catering accommodation provided in chalet, cottage and huts. £10 booking fee covers gas/electricity charges and insurance. Volunteers pay own travel costs and

must take a sleeping bag, sensible clothing and adequate supplies for several days, as tides and weather restrict trips to the mainland and there are no shops on the island. Opportunities to learn organic gardening, recycling, shell and flower craft, jam-making and other crafts. B D PH welcome, but difficult terrain and access.

DERBYSHIRE INTERNATIONAL YOUTH CAMP Education Department, County Offices, Matlock, Derbyshire DE4 3AG ✆ Matlock (0629) 580000
Organises international workcamps at Elvaston Castle Country Park and Shipley Park, aimed at improving the environment and developing understanding between young people from different countries. Recent projects have included constructing woodland walks, rebuilding a footbridge, erecting fencing, improving drainage, scrub clearance, plus work on a children's adventure play area. As well as undertaking manual work, participants are encouraged to help on community service projects, helping with general meal preparation and cleaning duties. Full training for manual work will be given, with trained supervisors available at all times. Extensive leisure programme arranged.
Ages 16-21. 1/2 weeks, late July-mid August. Accommodation provided in a residential school with sports and recreational facilities. Cost approx £25 per week covers food and accommodation. 20 free places available for young Derbyshire people. Qualifies under the Duke of Edinburgh's Award Scheme. B D PH
Apply by 1 April.

DYFED WILDLIFE TRUST Islands Booking Officer, 7 Market Street, Haverfordwest, Dyfed SA61 1NF ✆ Haverfordwest (0437) 765462
Skomer Island is a 720 acre national nature reserve, renowned for the finest seabird colonies in the south west, with fulmars, guillemots, kittiwakes, oystercatchers, puffins, razorbills, large gulls and over 100,000 pairs of Manx shearwaters. In addition there are many land birds including buzzards, choughs, owls, skylarks, ravens and pheasants. Voluntary assistant wardens are required to help with a variety of tasks; the main work concerns the day visitors, helping to meet the boats, collect landing fees and giving general information

and advice. Also patrolling the island to ensure visitors keep to the footpaths, and possibly assisting with various management tasks such as repair and maintenance work, path clearance, driftwood collecting, and surveys and scientific work. Applicants should be fit and prepared for hard work and long hours. Experience useful but not essential. 1+ weeks, mid April-September. Boat passage to Skomer and simple bunk bed accommodation with cooking facilities provided. Volunteers should take a sleeping bag and food. *Apply in September to be sure of a place.*

FESTINIOG RAILWAY COMPANY
Volunteer Officer, Harbour Station, Porthmadog, Gwynedd LL49 9NF
© **Porthmadog (0766) 512340**
Volunteers are required to help in the maintenance and running of the 150 year old narrow gauge railway; wide variety of work available. Traffic and Commercial Department: working in booking offices, guard's vans, buffet cars, shops, cafes and small sales outlets; Locomotive Operating Department: cleaning locomotives, working on the footplate; Mechanical Department: turning, welding, machining, steam fitting, sheet metal work, joinery, upholstery and paintwork; Permanent Way/Civil Engineering Department: working on winter track relaying projects and summer siding work, helping to repair fences, bridges, culverts and heavy walling. The Active Parks and Gardens Department needs skilled and unskilled assistance with improving the appearance of station surrounds and picnic areas. Qualified and experienced electricians and builders also needed. Training given where necessary. Ages 16+, unless in a supervised party. Volunteers must be fit. All year. Qualifies under the Duke of Edinburgh's Award Scheme. Limited self-catering hostel accommodation for regulars, for which a small charge is made; food extra. Camping space and local accommodation list also available. *Overseas volunteers with a good understanding of, and ability to speak clear English accepted.*

FOREST SCHOOL CONSERVATION CAMPS
The Workcamps Secretary, 110 Burbage Road, London SE24 9HD
Conservation workcamps are arranged throughout the year. Recent projects have included traditional coppicing techniques and working with timber in Essex; maintenance and reconstruction on buildings in Cambridgeshire; and restoring an old manorial farm complex and woodlands in Berkshire. 1/2 weeks, Easter and summer, and at weekends. Ages 17/18+. Volunteers pay their own fares; arrangements sometimes made regarding food, but volunteers may be asked to contribute up to £2.20 per day towards food and expenses. Lightweight camping accommodation only. B D PH but unsuitable for wheelchairs. *Overseas volunteers accepted.*

GREAT WESTERN SOCIETY Didcot Railway Centre, Didcot, Oxfordshire OX11 7NJ
© **Didcot (0235) 817200**
A society dedicated to preserving the history of the Great Western Railway. Runs a 16 acre working museum at Didcot housing restored locomotives, rolling stock and other exhibits of a vanished age. Volunteers are invited to help out with restoration projects such as equipping the newly built locomotive works and the development of a new station area. Work may involve track work, maintenance of locomotives and coaches, gardening, signalling, painting, cleaning small relics or catering. No experience necessary as training or guidance is given. Ages 14+ unless accompanied by an adult. Work available weekends all year, or midweek April-October. Also 1 week during August when board and lodging is provided in train compartments. No fares or wages paid, but third party insurance cover provided. B D PH

INTERNATIONAL VOLUNTARY SERVICE
Old Hall, East Bergholt, Colchester, Essex CO7 6TQ
IVS is the British branch of Service Civil International, which promotes international reconciliation through work projects. Volunteers are needed to work in international teams on various conservation projects. Recent projects have included environmental work on heathland, beaches and a bird reserve in Suffolk; renovating and replanting the herb garden of a community for sustainable development near Aylesbury; coppicing and woodland management near the Irish sea coast in west Cumbria; replacing slates and restoration work in a church on the Shetland island of Papa Stour; and helping to restore the

natural beauty of Merthyr Tydfil's mining valleys.

Ages 18+. Applicants should be prepared to work hard and contribute actively to team life. 35-40 hour week. 2-4 weeks, June-September. Food, accommodation and insurance provided, but no travel. Registration fee (1992) £55 (students £45, unwaged £40) B D PH

Apply through partner organisation in country of residence; further information on page 30.

IRONBRIDGE GORGE MUSEUM TRUST
Volunteer Organiser, The Wharfage,
Ironbridge, Telford, Shropshire TF8 7AW
℗ **Ironbridge (0952) 433522**
Conserves, restores and interprets the rich industrial heritage of the Gorge, the birthplace of the Industrial Revolution. The Museum comprises six main sites and a number of smaller ones, and has been created around a unique series of industrial monuments concentrating on the iron and pottery industries, and spread over some 6 square miles. Volunteers are needed to work on various sites involving industrial archaeology, research, excavation, interpretation of exhibits and general site duties. At Blists Hill Open Air Museum demonstrators in Victorian costume are often needed to explain the site and its shops, works and houses to visitors. Training, costume, equipment and supervision provided as appropriate. Opportunities for talking to the public; those with good language skills particularly welcome.

Ages 18+. 36 hour week, March-October. Low-cost self-catering hostel accommodation on site, £1.15 per night, or youth hostel 3 miles away. Participants pay for their own food. Insurance provided. Own transport, bicycle or car, usually essential. Participants can enter sites free. *Overseas volunteers must have excellent standard of spoken English.*

THE MONKEY SANCTUARY Looe, **Cornwall, PL13 1NZ** *℗* **Looe (0503) 262532**
Has received worldwide recognition as the first place where a natural colony of Woolly Monkeys has survived and bred outside the South American rainforests. It is a centre both for conservation and for the education of the public, who visit at Easter and during the

summer months. Volunteers are required to help with various jobs including preparation of monkey foods; cleaning and maintenance of monkey enclosures and grounds; attending to visitors in the summer; and general maintenance work during the winter. They also spend time with monkeys in their territory. Summer volunteers with appropriate skills and an interest in conservation may contribute to talking with visitors and educational work.

Ages 18+. No experience necessary, but applicants should have an interest in the field, and practical skills are always welcome. 2+ weeks, all year. Full board and accommodation provided, but volunteers pay their own travel. Food is usually vegetarian, and volunteers share accommodation with the sanctuary team. Those with musical instruments should bring them along. Subsistence may be available to long-term volunteers. B D PH W applications considered on an individual basis.

NATIONAL TRUST ACORN PROJECTS
Volunteer Unit, PO Box 12, Westbury,
Wiltshire BA13 4NA *℗* **Westbury (0373)**
826826
The Trust was formed at the end of the 19th century for the preservation of places of historic interest and natural beauty. It owns and protects houses and gardens, parks and estates, mountains, moors, coastline, farms and nature reserves. Acorn Projects are organised at NT properties throughout England, Wales and Northern Ireland, providing an opportunity to carry out conservation work and to encourage an active and practical interest in the Trust's work. Volunteers carry out essential tasks on the estates which could not otherwise be done.

Recent projects have included improving and widening coastal footpaths, barn construction, botanical surveying, the repair of drystone walling; fenland conservation work, erosion control and scrub clearance to improve downland ecology; and archaeological digs. Majority of the work done outdoors, but there are occasionally wet weather tasks such as clearing out old buildings or cleaning, restoring or painting agricultural implements.
Mainly ages 17-30, 18+ for overseas volunteers. Instruction given by experts. 8 hour day, 5½

day week, evenings free. 1+ weeks, January-November. Accommodation provided in NT hostels, village halls, stable blocks, farmhouses, cottages or converted barns. Volunteers should take sleeping bags and contribute approx £34 per week towards the cost of food and accommodation. Help with kitchen duties expected; travel costs paid by volunteers. The projects qualify under the Duke of Edinburgh's Award Scheme. Two friends may apply to work on the same project. Anyone completing a full week's work qualifies for 1 year's free admission to NT properties. *Application forms and brochure available from January.*

NATIONAL TRUST REGIONAL OFFICE
Penny Rowe, Lanhydrock, Bodmin, Cornwall PL30 4DE ℘ Bodmin (0208) 74281
Volunteers are needed to help clear litter from Cornish beaches. Each morning volunteers spend 2-3 hours collecting litter from among rocks and sand dunes; once the task is completed the rest of the day is free to discover and explore miles of fine coastal scenery. Ages 16-20. 12 days, July and August. Cost £110 covers all meals and accommodation at Beach Head NT basecamp, a converted barn on a remote and beautiful part of the coast. Facilities include hot showers, drying room, common room with log fire and fully equipped kitchen. Minibus available for outings and expeditions. Volunteers help with cleaning, preparing meals and washing up. Participants pay own travel expenses and should take a sleeping bag.

OPERATION OSPREY The Royal Society for the Protection of Birds, c/o Richard Thaxton, Grianan, Nethy Bridge, Inverness-shire PH25 3EF ℘ Boat of Garten (047 983) 694
Volunteer wardens and cooks are needed at Loch Garten, part of the Abernethy Forest Nature Reserve in the ancient Caledonian Forest, Strathspey. Teams of volunteer wardens keep a 24 hour watch from the hide and are expected to maintain a log of the ospreys' activities and to spend time talking to visitors (60,000 in 1991) about the RSPB's work at Loch Garten, and acting as a guide.
Volunteers work on a shift basis, with every third day free, and also help with camp chores. Bicycles available on day off, but own transport useful. Interest in ornithology preferable. Volunteer cooks are responsible for preparing

meals for up to 18 people; after initial supervision they will be expected to cope on their own on a day on/day off basis. Ages 18+. 1+ weeks, 28 March-5 September. Full board and camping or caravan accommodation, washing facilities, kitchen/dining area and common room provided for a nominal charge of £10 per week. Volunteers should take a sleeping bag, warm clothing and walking boots. Volunteer cooks who stay 1 week will have single fare paid; for 2+ weeks return travel paid. Overseas volunteer cooks have rail fare paid, London-Aviemore.

THE ROYAL SOCIETY FOR THE PROTECTION OF BIRDS Reserves Management Department, The Lodge, Sandy, Bedfordshire SG19 2DL ℘ Sandy (0767) 680551
Protects wild birds and their threatened habitat by giving them a haven of 120 nature reserves all over Britain, publicising and enforcing bird protection laws, guarding rare breeding birds, studying environmental effects, protecting migratory birds and producing films, publications, lectures and displays. Volunteer wardens are needed on nature reserves, assisting the wardens by carrying out physical management work, helping to escort visitors around the reserve, helping in information centres, dealing with enquiries and keeping records of birds. Volunteers usually work in teams of 2-4. Ages 16+. An interest in, and knowledge of, birds an advantage. 1+ weeks, all year. Accommodation in chalets or cottages. Cooking facilities provided, but volunteers are responsible for their own food and transport, and should take a sleeping bag. *EC nationals only.*

THE SCOTTISH CONSERVATION PROJECTS TRUST Director, Balallan House, 24 Allan Park, Stirling FK8 2QG ℘ Stirling (0786) 79697
A charitable trust promoting the practical involvement of people in improving the quality of Scotland's environment. Work is carried out throughout Scotland, including the Western Isles, Orkney and Shetland. Recent projects have included improving habitat for otters by restoring and replanting the riverbank at Strathyre, near Balquhidder; creating dragonfly pools in Gordon Moss, a peat-bog in the

Borders designated a Site of Special Scientific Interest; installing kissing gates and signposts along the Colvend Coastal Path on the Solway; repairing drystane dykes at Armadale Castle on the Isle of Skye; tree-planting on Beinn Eighe National Nature Reserve, Ross-shire; and stabilising sand dunes at Dunnet Bay, Caithness. Instruction is given in the use of tools and equipment, traditional techniques and other conservation skills. Also slide shows, guided tours and talks on the conservation value of the work. Approx 12 volunteers work on each project; beginners welcome.

Ages 16-70. Some projects are more physically demanding than others and volunteers must be prepared to cope with working on remote and exposed sites. 8 hour day, 1 day off per week. 1-2 weeks, March-November. Food, insurance and accommodation in centres, tents, huts, youth hostels, cottages, village halls, farm buildings or basecamps provided. Volunteers should take a sleeping bag, waterproof clothing, boots and midge repellent. Anti-tetanus vaccination advisable. Everyone helps to prepare food, and volunteers contribute £4 per day (£3 for students/unwaged) towards food and accommodation costs. Two friends can apply to work on the same project. Projects qualify under the Duke of Edinburgh's Award Scheme. Weekend training courses in practical conservation skills and leadership arranged. Membership fee £12; £6 if unwaged or student, £15 for family, £10 for overseas members. PH depending on ability.

THISTLE CAMPS National Trust for Scotland, 5 Charlotte Square, Edinburgh EH2 4DU ✆ 031-226 5922 ext 257
Founded to promote the permanent preservation of countryside and buildings of historic interest or natural beauty. Thistle Camps are residential voluntary work projects organised by NTS to help in the conservation and practical management of properties in the care of the Trust. Recent projects have included sand dune stabilisation on the Isle of Iona; rhododendron clearance and upland footpath maintenance around the country park at Brodick Castle on the Isle of Arran; landscaping and scrub clearance on the Isle of Canna; improving wildlife habitats in the Old Wood of Drum; and upland footpath maintenance at

Glencoe. Work parties on Fair Isle, Britain's most remote inhabited island, help the islanders repair buildings, maintain the airstrip and help with all kinds of croft work such as fencing, drystane dyking, painting, crop-cleaning, ditching and haymaking.
Ages 16-70. Up to 2 friends can be placed together. Volunteers should be fit for hard, practical work. 8 hour day, 5 day week. 1-2 weeks, March-October. Similar weekend projects are carried out by local Conservation Volunteers groups on NTS properties in their area. An experienced leader and/or a Trust Ranger Naturalist supervises all practical work, and gives instruction in the safe use of tools. One day free for recreation and exploration in the area. Insurance, hostel-type or basecamp accommodation and food provided, but volunteers help with catering arrangements and other chores. Old clothes, waterproofs, a sleeping bag and boots or wellingtons should be taken to all camps. Qualifies under the Duke of Edinburgh's Award Scheme. Participants pay their own way to a central pick-up point, and make a contribution, either £10 or £20 depending on their circumstances. *Overseas volunteers with good English welcome: they should apply by March at the latest to be sure of a place.*

UNITED NATIONS ASSOCIATION
International Youth Service, Temple of Peace, Cathays Park, Cardiff CF1 3AP ✆ Cardiff (0222) 223088
Volunteers are needed to work in international teams on conservation workcamps in various parts of Wales. Recent projects have included protecting sand dunes and woodland in the Pembrokeshire National Park; clearing non-native plants and litter in the Great Orme country park; and constructing paths and cycle paths in the Afan Valley, West Glamorgan. Volunteers share in discussions centring on the host community and world problems, and are expected to take an active part in all aspects of the project. Ages 18+. 40 hour week. 2 weeks, June-August. Accommodation, food and insurance provided. Volunteers share the cooking, pay own travel costs and should take a sleeping bag. Registration fee £45. B D PH

Apply through partner organisation in country of residence; further information on page 30.

THE WATERWAY RECOVERY GROUP John Glock, 47 Melfort Drive, Leighton Buzzard, Bedfordshire LU7 7XN ℗ Leighton Buzzard (0525) 382311

The national coordinating body for voluntary labour on the inland waterways of Britain, the WRG promotes and coordinates local societies and travelling groups involved in restoring abandoned and derelict waterways to a navigable state. Volunteers are needed on workcamps to help with this work. There are over 30 active restoration projects which encompass tasks such as excavating and laying foundations for a new canal bridge, building retaining walls, dredging and banking, clearing vegetation, pile driving, bricklaying and demolition work. Canals currently being restored include the Huddersfield, Montgomery, Wey and Arun, Droitwich, Hereford and Gloucester, Wiltshire and Berkshire, and Pocklington. Ages 16+. Parental consent required for those under 18. Work is unpaid and mostly unskilled; full training is given and work is directed by local experts. Volunteers should be reasonably fit and willing to work hard in all weathers, with enthusiasm, a sense of humour and the ability to live harmoniously in fairly close contact with approx 20 volunteers at each camp. 1+ weeks, March-October and over the Christmas/New Year holiday. 8 hour day. Basic accommodation provided free in village halls, plus 3 good meals a day at charge of approx £21 per week. Volunteers should take a sleeping bag and old clothes and be prepared to help with domestic chores, although a camp cook is normally resident. Insurance provided. Qualifies under the Duke of Edinburgh's Award Scheme. Publish *Navvies* a bi-monthly journal which provides details of all activities including weekend working parties across the country and current restoration news. *Overseas volunteers with good command of English accepted.*

COURIERS / REPS

BUTLIN'S LTD Head Office, Bognor Regis, West Sussex PO21 1JJ

Provides family holidays and leisure facilities, encompassing accommodation, retailing, catering, amusement parks, professional entertainment and conferences, all on the same site. Vacancies exist for Redcoats, hosts/hostesses responsible for entertainments and organising children's programmes, at centres in Ayr, Bognor Regis, Minehead, Pwllheli and Skegness. Short and long term positions available virtually all year round, exact dates depending on each centre. Experience not normally necessary as training provided. 39-45 hour week. Ages 18+. Applicants should have enthusiasm, tact, attention to detail and the ability to integrate into a team. Salary, according to individual centres, accommodation in single or shared rooms, meals and uniform provided. Insurance and travel paid by applicants. Staff entertainment programmes, use of leisure facilities plus many of guest facilities, and holiday discounts available. *EC nationals only; apply direct to the preferred centre:*

Wonderwest World, Heads of Ayr, KA7 4LB, Scotland; Southcoast World, Bognor Regis, West Sussex PO21 1JJ; Somerwest World, Minehead, Somerset TA24 5SH; Starcoast World, Pwllheli, Gwynedd LL53 6HX, North Wales; Funcoast World, Skegness, Lincolnshire PE25 1NJ.

DOMESTIC

ACORN VENTURE 137 Worcester Road, Hagley, Stourbridge, West Midlands DY9 0NW ℗ Hagley (0562) 882151

Activity holiday company catering for school groups at camping centres in Tal-y-Bont and Shell Island in North Wales. Experienced catering staff required for the full season, May-September. Ages 18+. 40-50 hour, 6 day week. Salary approx £40-£45 per week. All meals, tent accommodation, insurance and cost of travel to centre provided. *Apply in writing with cv by end January; if no reply within 28 days assume application unsuccessful.*

ANGLIA AGENCY 70 Southsea Avenue, Leigh-on-Sea, Essex ℗ Southend-on-Sea (0702) 471648

Cook, housekeeper, daily help and hotel and catering positions arranged. Long and short term vacancies, all year. Board and lodging usually provided. Hours and wages vary according to type of work. Ages 17+. Travel costs paid by applicants.

BEAUMONT CAMPS LTD Personnel Department, The Kingswood Centre, Barn Lane, Near Albrighton, Wolverhampton WV7 3AW ✆ Wolverhampton (0902) 846141
Organises holidays for children in American-style day and residential camps. Staff are recruited for 18 camps throughout the country. Opportunities exist for caterers/head cooks, responsible for managing kitchen assistants, cooking meals for staff and campers, stock and portion control, and food ordering according to a strict budget. Back-up staff are also required as cleaners and kitchen assistants, which may also involve working as an assistant monitor looking after children at certain times of the day. Staff must be available for the whole season, 5-9 weeks, July and August, including compulsory day/weekend orientation course, setting up and clearing camps. Ages 18-35. Day camp staff: 45 hour week. Residential staff: 24 hour day, with 1 free day per week plus alternate nights off; wages £40-£100 per week. Board and accommodation provided. PH

BREAN LEISURE PARK/UNITY FARM Coast Road, Brean Sands, Somerset TA8 2RF ✆ Brean Down (0278) 751595
Vacancies available at two holiday centres on the north west coast of Somerset. Staff needed for a range of positions: bar work, catering, general ground and building maintenance. Experience not essential, but staff should be enthusiastic and committed. Ages 18+. 39 hour week, Easter-October. Salary £3.25 per hour. No accommodation provided; vacancies most suited to local students or applicants with local accommodation. Travel costs paid by applicants. D PH *UK nationals only.*

BRIGHSTONE HOLIDAY CENTRE The Personnel Manager, Brighstone, Isle of Wight PO30 4DB ✆ Isle of Wight (0983) 740537
Staff needed on a seasonal basis for a holiday centre catering for approx 300 guests. Work available for waiting staff, snack bar, service room, washing up and other catering assistants. 39 hour week, May-September. Full board and accommodation in single/twin bed chalet provided. Salary based on council rate. Ages 16+. No experience needed. Insurance and maximum of £12 towards return journey provided, if employment conditions are fulfilled. *EC nationals only.*

BUTLIN'S LTD Head Office, Bognor Regis, West Sussex PO21 1JJ
Provides family holidays and leisure facilities, encompassing accommodation, retailing, catering, amusement parks, professional entertainment and conferences, all on the same site. Catering and bar staff, waiters/waitresses, qualified chefs and cooks, cleaners and porters, are required at centres in Ayr, Bognor Regis, Minehead, Pwllheli and Skegness. Short and long term positions available virtually all year round, exact dates depending on each centre. Experience not normally necessary as training provided. 39-45 hour week. Ages 16+, local applicants, 18+ others. Applicants should have enthusiasm, tact, attention to detail and the ability to integrate into a team. Salary according to individual centres, accommodation, meals and uniform provided. Insurance and travel paid by applicants. Staff entertainment programmes, use of leisure facilities plus many of guest facilities, and holiday discounts available. *EC nationals only. Apply direct to the preferred centre:*

Wonderwest World, Heads of Ayr, KA7 4LB, Scotland; Southcoast World, Bognor Regis, West Sussex PO21 1JJ; Somerwest World, Minehead, Somerset TA24 5SH; Starcoast World, Pwllheli, Gwynedd LL53 6HX, North Wales; Funcoast World, Skegness, Lincolnshire PE25 1NJ.

CAMPUS CENTRES Llangarron, Ross-on-Wye, Herefordshire HR9 6PG ✆ Ross-on-Wye (0989) 84701
Organise activity holidays for school groups at a centre in Herefordshire. Chefs and domestic/kitchen assistants required. Chefs should be experienced and qualified (706/1 and 706/2 preferred); in-house training provided for other positions. Ages 18+. 50-60 hour, 6 day week, February-November. Wages £35-£50 per week; negotiable for more senior staff. Full board accommodation and medical/accident insurance provided, but no fares paid. PH

THE CEILIDH PLACE West Argyle Street, Ullapool, Ross & Cromarty IV26 2TY ✆ Ullapool (0854) 612103
An arts centre in the north west of Scotland providing a range of facilities including a clubhouse, hotel, restaurant, book and coffee

shop. A programme of arts events runs throughout the season, including poetry readings, concerts and exhibitions. Positions available for general assistants, cooks and domestic staff. Training given, but cooking staff must have qualifications and experience. Ages 18+. 40 hour week. 12+ weeks, March-December. Basic wages council rates apply: from £85 per week after deductions for board; other rates depending on skills and responsibility. *All nationalities welcome.*

FRIENDLY HOTELS PLC Premier House, 10 Greycoat Place, London SW1P 1SB ✆ 071-222 8866

Hotel group requires waitresses, room attendants and porters in hotels in Birmingham, Burnley, Eastbourne, Hull, London, Milton Keynes, Newcastle-under-Lyme, Newcastle-upon-Tyne, Nottingham, Walsall, Welwyn and in Scotland. Experience useful but not essential. Work available all year round, minimum 4 months. 39 hour week. Ages 18+. Salary approx £100 per week. Accommodation available in single or shared rooms, in or outside hotel. **PH** limited opportunities.

HATTON HOTELS GROUP SERVICES LTD Hatton Court, Upton Hill, Upton St Leonards, Gloucester GL4 8DE ✆ Gloucester (0452) 617412

A small, privately owned company running hotels in the English Cotswolds. Restaurant staff, bar staff and chambermaids are required. Preference given to those with previous catering experience. Ages 18+. 45 hour, 5 day week. Wages £75-£100 per week depending on position; full board and lodging provided.

HOTHORPE HALL Christian Conference Centre, Theddingworth, near Lutterworth, Leicestershire LE17 6QX ✆ Market Harborough (0858) 880257

Provides conference facilities for groups of up to 140 people, mainly from church groups. Volunteers are required to undertake a variety of duties, including kitchen assistance, serving and washing up, and general domestic work. Gardening and maintenance also involved. Ages 18+. Volunteers should have a Christian commitment, willingness to join in as a member of the community, and a responsible attitude to their work. 6 day week. 6+ weeks, all year. No

experience necessary. Pocket money £15 per week. Accommodation in shared rooms and all meals provided. *Overseas applicants with good spoken English accepted.*

HUNTSHAM COURT Huntsham Village, Near Tiverton, Devon EX16 7NA ✆ Clayhanger (039 86) 365

Staff required all through the year at country house hotel in the heart of Devon. Offers the opportunity to learn aspects of catering and hotel management in a warm, friendly atmosphere. Work is varied and interesting, and includes acting as waiter/waitress, catering and gardening.
Ages 18+. Willingness to learn more important than experience, though cooks require qualifications. Knowledge of English necessary. 15-40 hour week. Pay from £45 per week, plus insurance and full board accommodation. *EC nationals only.*

THE IONA COMMUNITY Staff Coordinator, Isle of Iona, Argyll, Strathclyde PA76 6SN ✆ Iona (068 17) 404

An ecumenical Christian community seeking new and radical ways of living the Gospel in today's world. On Iona the Community runs two centres, each welcoming up to 50 guests to a common life of work, worship, meals and recreation. Kitchen assistants and housekeeping assistants are required at both centres. Kitchen assistants help provide up to 90 meals, often vegetarian. Cooking skills not essential, but a willingness to learn is. Housekeeping assistants help with cleaning, washing and ironing, as well as supervising guests in household chores. Also require assistants to work in the Coffee House, baking, preparing food, serving, clearing tables and keeping the place clean and tidy. On the nearby Island of Mull the Camas centre welcomes up to 16 guests each week, mainly unemployed or disadvantaged young people, to a common life of work, worship, arts, crafts and outdoor activities. Requires a competent cook to provide up to 25 meals over the summer months.

Ages 18+. Most important is a willingness to join fully in the community life, which includes worship and social activities as well as work. The work is demanding but rewarding, and the hours flexible. 6 day week, February-December.

Full board, shared accommodation, pocket money of £15 per week and assistance with travel expenses provided within mainland Britain. *Applications received before 31 December given priority.*

KNOLL HOUSE HOTEL Staff Manager, Studland, Dorset BH19 3AH ✆ Studland (092 944) 251
Country house hotel with 80 rooms and 100 acres of gardens and grounds adjoining the beach. Chefs (with previous experience), waiters, waitresses and kitchen staff are required from April-October. Willingness to learn is more important than experience. 39 hour week, 2 days free. Ages 17+. Pay approx £90 per week, full board accommodation and insurance provided. *EC nationals only.*

LEICESTER BOYS' & GIRLS' SUMMER CAMP & INSTITUTE Shaftesbury Hall, Holy Bones, Leicester LE1 4LJ ✆ Leicester (0533) 519863
Seasonal domestic staff are required at a holiday home in Mablethorpe which provides the poorest and most deserving children aged 7-12 from Leicester and its neighbourhood with a fortnight's holiday. The home is situated on the sandhills and the children have their own path to the beach. Positions include cooks and kitchen assistants, catering staff and dining room attendants to supervise children at mealtimes.
Ages 18+. 1+ months, May-August. Preference given to applicants able to work the whole season. Board and lodging provided plus a salary of approx £43 per week. *UK nationals only. Apply to Leicester Children's Holiday Home, Quebec Road, Mablethorpe, Lincolnshire LN12 1QX ✆ Mablethorpe (0507) 472444.*

LITTLE CHEF Unit 2, Cartel Business Centre, Stroudley Road, Basingstoke, Hampshire RG24 0FW ✆ Basingstoke (0256) 812828
Catering assistants required for outlets throughout Great Britain. No previous experience needed. Duties include serving customers, cooking and cleaning on a rota/shared basis. Ages 16+. 39 hours per week. 10+ weeks, May-September. Hourly wages £2 (ages 16-17) or £2.65 (ages 18+). Applicants must find own accommodation; meals on duty provided. No travel costs paid.

LONDON HOSTELS ASSOCIATION LTD Personnel Manager, 54 Eccleston Square, London SW1V 1PG ✆ 071-834 1545
Part-time residential domestic work available in 10 London houses run mainly for young people in full-time employment or students. Female staff are employed as dining room assistants, serving meals, clearing tables and using washing up machines; also as junior housekeepers, involving normal housekeeping duties, cleaning public and residential rooms, changing linen and general evening duties once a week. Male staff are employed as kitchen or house porters, assisting in the preparation of food, cleaning the kitchen catering area and public utility rooms, washing up, and other manual duties. Ages 17+. 6+ months, possibly 3-4 months in summer, all year. 30-40 hour week. Working hours usually 07.00-11.00/17.00-19.30. 1½ days free per week. Board, accommodation and insurance provided. Salary approx £36-£50 per week, according to hours worked. *EC nationals only.*

MAYDAY STAFF SERVICES 21 Great Chapel Street, London W1V 3AQ ✆ 071-439 2056
An employment agency recruiting temporary and permanent catering staff of a high standard throughout central London and surrounding area. Can place experienced chefs, waiting and bar staff, as well as kitchen porters and general catering assistants with no experience. Catering assistants' work includes food preparation, serving food at counter, washing up, clearing tables, and general kitchen duties. Kitchen porters' work includes washing up both manually and with a machine, cleaning and vegetable preparation. 25-40 hour week, all year. Ages 16+. Catering assistants and kitchen porters wages £3.20-£3.60 per hour. Meals usually available when on duty and public liability insurance provided. D PH limited opportunities. *Overseas applicants must have good command of English, and work permit where applicable.*

MCTAVISH'S KITCHENS (OBAN) LTD 8 Argyll Square, Oban, Argyll
Two restaurants in Oban and Fort William, on the scenic west coast of Scotland, supplying traditional Scottish entertainment and food. Work available in general catering positions: kitchen assistants, cooks, waiting staff; also bar

work and cleaning. Experience not necessary. Ages 17+. 40 hour week, April to October. Salary from £75 per week. Full board accommodation provided. **PH** *Written applications only. EC nationals only.*

MONTPELIER EMPLOYMENT AGENCY 34 Montpelier Road, Brighton, Sussex BN1 2LQ ✆ Brighton (0273) 778686
Introduces staff of all categories to hotels throughout Britain. Previous experience essential. Applicants must be free of any work permit restrictions and already resident in Britain. Approx 39 hour week. Minimum 12 weeks during summer period. Ages 18+. Salary approx £80-£100 including accommodation; varies according to area, type of job, previous experience and whether accommodation is provided.

PGL YOUNG ADVENTURE LTD Personnel Department, Alton Court, Penyard Lane (878), Ross-on-Wye, Herefordshire HR9 5NR ✆ Ross-on-Wye (0989) 767833
Organises outdoor adventure holidays for young people and families in England, Scotland and Wales. Catering and domestic assistants, cooks and assistant cooks required. Most centres run a self-service system with cooked breakfast, packed lunch and full evening meal.

Ages 18+. Applicants should be fond of children, responsible, flexible, patient, energetic and enthusiastic, reliable and mature, with a sense of humour and the ability to cooperate with others as part of a team contributing fully to the life of the centre. 4+ weeks, February-September. Staff are also recruited for short periods at peak times such as Easter and the spring bank holiday. Catering staff generally work a split shift, with the middle hours of the day free. 1 day off per week. Full board accommodation provided. Pocket money £30-£42 per week depending on qualifications, responsibility and length of stay. Travel expenses paid by applicants.
All staff can join in the activities during free periods and are encouraged to take part in evening activities with the guests. Staff may sometimes be asked to help out in areas other than their own. *Early application advisable; the majority of positions are filled by end June.*

PORTH TOCYN HOTEL Abersoch, Gwynedd LL53 7BU ✆ Abersoch (075 881) 2966
A country house hotel, requiring staff for all aspects of front of house hotel work. No experience necessary, but languages an advantage. Easter-November, hours variable. Ages 17+. Salary £9.50-£10.50 per shift, accommodation in staff cottage, food, liability insurance, use of hotel facilities including tennis courts, swimming pool and windsurfers provided. *EC nationals only.*

RAASAY OUTDOOR CENTRE Isle of Raasay, By Kyle IV40 8PB ✆ Raasay (047 862) 266
Limited number of assistants needed for catering, cleaning and general maintenance work. Experience not essential. Ages 18+. 40-50 hour week, March-October. Wages according to age and experience. Full board accommodation with shared facilities provided. Applicants pay their own travel expenses and insurance. Opportunity to take part in sports activities organised at the centre and to explore surrounding areas.

SCATTERGOODS AGENCY Thursley House, 53 Station Road, Shalford, Guildford, Surrey GU4 8HA ✆ Guildford (0483) 33732
Arranges posts in hotels, restaurants and public houses as chambermaids, *plongeurs*, barpersons, waiting staff, cooks, kitchen assistants, porters and general assistants. Relevant experience preferable. Ages 18+. 40-50 hour week; 6 months minimum. Wages £75+ per week. Board, lodging and insurance provided. *EC nationals only.*

SCOTTISH FIELD STUDIES ASSOCIATION LTD Kindrogan Field Centre, Enochdhu, Blairgowrie, Perthshire PH10 7PG ✆ Strathardle (025 081) 286
Aims to create a greater awareness and understanding of the Scottish countryside. The Centre is a large country house in the Highlands and provides accommodation, laboratories and a library for up to 80 people with opportunities for all aspects of field studies. Seasonal staff are needed for domestic duties such as cleaning, washing up, general maintenance and gardening. Ages 18+. No experience needed. 40 hour week, all year. Wages £69 per week. Accommodation and meals provided. Participants pay own travel

and insurance costs. Staff may participate in field study courses when possible. *EC nationals only.*

STUDENTOURS 3 Harcourt Street, London W1H 1DS ℗ 071-402 5131 **or (0403) 891431**
Domestic staff are required to work at youth centres in Sussex. Ages 17+. 30 hour, 5 day week, in staggered morning and evening shifts. 2-6 months, all year. Board, lodging and £40 per week wages provided.

UNIVERSAL AUNTS PO Box 304, London SW4 0NN ℗ 071-738 8937
Vacancies are available for resident and non-resident housekeepers, nannies and mothers' helps. Also opportunities for cooks, waitresses, washers up, cleaners and drivers. Ages 18+. Permanent and temporary positions, all year. Salary according to qualifications.

FARMWORK / FRUIT PICKING

Summer farmwork in Britain includes general farm labouring as well as vegetable harvesting and soft fruit picking, often on international farmcamps. The work is mainly in Scotland, East Anglia, the South, the West Country and Kent, where it includes the traditional English working holiday of hop picking. Other crops to be picked include cherries, raspberries, strawberries, blackcurrants, loganberries, blackberries, plums, gooseberries, apples, pears, potatoes, courgettes and beans. A range of ancillary work such as strawing, weeding, irrigation, fruit inspection, packing, indoor processing, tractor driving or working in oast houses may also be available.
The work can be on individual, often family-run farms, on smallholdings or with cooperatives, or on international farmcamps. The general number of hours worked are 40-45 per week and 5-6 days. The length of the working season varies, depending on the crop being harvested, the weather and the location of the farm. The harvesting of soft fruit is normally undertaken between mid June and August, although in some areas picking may start as early as May. The picking of hops,

apples and other crops runs from late August to October. On farmcamps the emphasis is as much on living and working in an international community, with sports and social activities, as on earning money. The wages paid may only be sufficient to cover food and accommodation costs and to provide a little pocket money. The social and sports facilities provided can include swimming pools, tennis courts, games fields, games and television rooms, video, bars, discos and dances. The majority of workers will be in the 17-30 age range, and families are often welcome. On some camps English language tuition may be available for overseas workers during free time. Work permits are not required by those from outside Britain wanting to work on approved farmcamps, but workers from countries outside the EC subject to immigration control must be in full-time education, between the ages of 18 and 25 and have a Home Office card issued by an approved scheme operator. This card allows entry into Britain but does not entitle the visitor to take paid work of any other kind during the visit. Most fruit picking jobs are paid at piece-work rates so it is important to remember that bad weather can affect the ripening and amount of crops to be picked. While every effort is made to provide full-time employment, on occasion work may be temporarily limited; it is therefore essential that workers have enough money to cover basic living expenses throughout their stay.

ADRIAN SCRIPPS LTD Moat Farm, Five Oak Green, Tonbridge, Kent TN12 6RR ℗ **Paddock Wood (0892) 832406**
Apple, pear and hop pickers required on four farms in Kent. No experience necessary, but good English required. Ages 18+. 50+ hours per week, September-October. Wages approx £140 per week for hop pickers; piece-work rates paid to fruit pickers. Self-catering accommodation provided; workers should take sleeping bag and working clothes. *Non-EC nationals must have valid work permit.*

ASHRAM COMMUNITY SERVICE PROJECT 23/25 Grantham Road, Sparkbrook, Birmingham B11 1LU ℗ 021-773 7061
A multi-purpose community development project in a multi-racial, inner-city area, working for social, economic and environmental change. Volunteers are invited

to help with a land use project, Ashram Acres, which grows vegetables organically on previously derelict land. Asian vegetables are a speciality, and various animals are kept. Work involves organic gardening, caring for animals, building and maintenance work. Ages 21+. No experience necessary, training is usually given where required. Hours negotiable; usually 09.00-17.00, all year. Insurance and accommodation in residential community provided with opportunities to join social events. Volunteers pay own travel, and are expected to pay as far as possible for board and lodging. B D PH unsuitable for wheelchairs.

**SC & JH BERRY LTD Gushmere Court Farm, Selling, Faversham, Kent ME13 9RF
℃ Canterbury (0227) 795205**
Assistance needed with the harvest of hops, apples and pears. Work includes loading and unloading kilns and pressing hops in the oast house, cutting and loading bines in the hop garden, work on the hop picking machines, loading, sorting, clearing up, and picking apples and pears in the orchards. A few tractor-driving posts available for which instruction is given; UK or international driving licence required. Ages 18+. On the job training given. Basic 40 hour week plus 15 hours overtime, Saturday afternoon/Sunday off, end August-end September. Wages approx £150 per week. Caravan accommodation with all facilities available; workers will need to buy and cook their own food. Insurance not provided. Workers should provide their own clothing, including waterproofs and rubber boots, and sleeping bag and towels. *EC nationals only.*

**CAWLEY FARMS Ashton Fruit Farm, Ashton, Leominster, Herefordshire HR6 0DN
℃ Brimfield (058 472) 401**
Fruit pickers needed. Ages 16+. Hours variable, end June-early August. Piece-work rates paid. Campsite provided, but workers should take their own food and camping equipment. *EC nationals only.*

CONCORDIA (Youth Service Volunteers) Ltd, Recruitment Secretary, 8 Brunswick Place, Hove, Sussex BN3 1ET ℃ Brighton (0273) 772086
Aims to bring together the youth of all nations throughout the world, to promote a better

understanding between them of their ideas, beliefs and ways of living. Can place applicants on international farmcamps in the UK: hop picking in Kent; soft fruit picking in Scotland, Kent, Lincolnshire, Oxfordshire, Herefordshire, Sussex and Devon; apple picking in Hampshire and Kent; and vegetable picking in Cambridgeshire, Devon, Kent and Somerset. Volunteers must be prepared to work hard when and where required. Every effort will be made to find alternative work in the event of bad weather or crop failure, but it should be stressed that work cannot be guaranteed. Mainly ages 18-25. Season runs June-October; soft fruit June-August, hops and apples late August-October. Piece-work rates paid for soft fruit picking; hop/apple pickers receive wages as laid down by the Agricultural Wages Board. All workers subject to tax on their earnings. Conditions and costs of board and lodging vary according to location. Majority of accommodation provided in huts, caravans or farm cottages but workers are expected to take their own food and sleeping bags. In some camps workers provide own tents and cooking equipment. Registration fee £30. Travel paid by applicants. *Overseas applicants accepted.*

DOUGLAS COURTS Barnyards Farm, Beauly, Inverness-shire IV4 7AT ℃ Inverness (0463) 782866
A farm ¼ mile from Beauly on the route north to John O'Groats, close to Loch Ness. Raspberry picking work available, 6-7 weeks, July-August. 7.00-16.00, 6½ days per week, weather permitting, with optional evening work. Ages 17+. No experience necessary. Piece work rates paid. Campsite facilities and some caravans available; £10 deposit. Kitchen and hot showers free of charge to all pickers on site. Applicants should take their own tents, cooking equipment and suitable warm, waterproof clothing.

**FIVEWAYS FRUIT FARM Fiveways, Stanway, Colchester, Essex CO3 5LR
℃ Colchester (0206) 330244**
Strawberry and apple pickers required; semi-skilled orchard work also available. Ages 18+. No experience necessary. 40+ hours per week, May-October. Piece-work rates paid. Campsite accommodation provided with showers, toilets,

TV and cooking facilities; £7.50 per week charge payable in advance.

FORDE ABBEY FRUIT GARDENS c/o A R Davies, Prossers Cottage, Tatworth, Chard, Somerset TA20 2SG ℂ/Fax South Chard (0460) 20272
Fruit pickers required to work in fruit fields belonging to Forde Abbey in Dorset. Work is mainly strawberry picking, with possibility of administrative or supervisory work. No experience necessary. Ages 18+. 30-40 hours per week; 4+ weeks, mid June-mid August. Piece work/Agricultural Wages Board rates paid. Camping accommodation provided, cost £2.50 per night; self-contained cottages or caravans for early applicants. *Apply in writing enclosing SAE and photo. Early application advised. UK nationals only.*

FRIDAY BRIDGE INTERNATIONAL FARMCAMP LTD The Manager, March Road, Friday Bridge, Wisbech, Cambridgeshire PE14 0LR ℂ Wisbech (0945) 860255 (May-November) or Norwich (0603) 662052 (November-May)
A cooperative set in the heart of the Fen Country with local growers and farmers, needs seasonal workers to harvest its crops. Work involves weeding and strawing, and also picking gooseberries, strawberries, plums, apples, blackberries, pears, potatoes, courgettes and beans. Campers are collected from and returned to the camp daily by the farmer for whom they are working. Ages 16-30. 1+ weeks, approx 30 May-23 October. Hourly and piece-work rates normally paid. Indoor processing work also available. Many social and sports facilities available including swimming pool, tennis courts, games field, games/TV room, bar, discos and dances. Other facilities include hot showers, drying rooms and camp shop. Cost approx £50 per week covers full board accommodation in huts and facilities. Registration fee £30. *EC nationals only.*

GREAT HOLLANDEN FARM Mr B R Brooks, Mill Lane, Hildenborough, near Sevenoaks, Kent TN15 0SG ℂ Hildenborough (0732) 832276
Fruit pickers and agricultural workers are needed to pick and pack all types of soft fruit to a very high standard. Work is also available

harvesting and pruning raspberries at the end of the season. Ages 18+. Pickers are trained and should be hard working and conscientious. 2+ weeks, mid May-end October. Hours 06.00-15.00 with opportunities for evening work. Piece-work rates paid. Accommodation available in mobile homes, cost £9 per week; or those with tents may use campsite. Charge of £4 per week for use of facilities such as kitchens, mess room, showers. Farm shop offering food on site. *Early booking advised; notification of acceptance early May.*

GREENS OF DEREHAM Norwich Road, Dereham, Norfolk ℂ Dereham (0362) 692014
Fruit pickers are required throughout July to pick strawberries. Ages 17+. Work may take place until 16.00. Workers are paid in cash daily. Camping area provided. Applicants pay own insurance and travel costs. *UK nationals only.*

HARVESTING OPPORTUNITY PERMIT SCHEME (GB) YFC Centre, National Agricultural Centre, Stoneleigh Park, Kenilworth, Warwickshire CV8 2LG ℂ Coventry (0203) 696589
Issues work permits to university students, aged 19-25, from central and eastern Europe. Finds employment on fruit, vegetable and hops farms throughout Great Britain for full-time university students born in 1968-73. Students live and work on registered farm. 7-13 weeks, 1 May-30 November. No experience necessary, but the work is physically hard. Knowledge of English essential. British agricultural wage rates. Students from central and eastern Europe require Workcards; HOPS (GB) have a restricted number. EC students also welcome to apply for guaranteed farm placement. Agricultural/rural students preferred. *Application forms available from September; completed forms with £35 administration fee accepted November-January.*

HILL FARM ORCHARDS Droxford Road, Swanmore, Hampshire SO3 2PY ℂ Droxford (0489) 878616
Apple picking, soft fruit picking and general farm work available. No experience necessary; overseas applicants must have some knowledge of English. Ages 18+. 30-40 hours per week, July and September-October. Piece-work and

Agricultural Wages Board rates paid. Campsite accommodation and accident insurance provided. Those interested can learn about farming techniques and apple juice production.

HUDSON FARMS Badliss Hall, Ardleigh, Colchester, Essex ✆ Colchester (0206) 230306
Soft fruit production and plant raising farm; work includes picking and planting strawberries, raspberries and vegetables. June-October. 30 hour week, Monday-Friday with occasional weekend work. Ages 18+. Piece-work/Agricultural Wages Board rates paid. Work not guaranteed in bad weather and no wet weather equipment provided. Campsite facilities with cooking areas available, £7.50 per week; workers must take their own sleeping bags and tents.

INTERNATIONAL FARM CAMP The Organiser, Hall Road, Tiptree, Colchester, Essex CO5 0QS ✆ Tiptree (0621) 815496
Fruit picking work available. Ages 18-25. 35 hour, 5 day week. 2+ weeks, end May-September; few places available mid July-end August. Facilities include hot showers, drying and ironing rooms, shop, table tennis and TV. Piece-work rates paid. Cost approx £38 per week includes full board accommodation in huts. Workers must help with kitchen duties for at least 1 day during their stay. £25 deposit, £15 of which is refundable on completion of booked stay. *Students only.*

THE LANGHAM FRUIT FARMS LTD Malting Farm, Langham, Colchester, Essex CO4 5NW ✆ Colchester (0206) 272559
General fruit picking work available. Experience of agricultural work useful. Ages 18+. 30 hour week. 1+ months, July to October. Wages according to age and experience. No accommodation on farm, but camping facilities nearby. Workers pay their own travel expenses and insurance. *Due to large volume of applications replies only made if applicants are accepted.*

MARE HILL FRUIT FARM Mare Hill, Pulborough, West Sussex RH20 2EA
Fruit pickers are needed to pick strawberries, raspberries, blackcurrants and gooseberries on a farm 15 miles from the sea. Early June-mid August. Ages 18-24, mainly students. Piece-

work rates paid. Campsite provided; participants must take their own tent and cooking equipment. Facilities include community hut with showers, TV and radio. *Early booking necessary; EC nationals only.* D

NEWTON FRUIT FARMS Mudcroft Farm, Newton, Wisbech, Cambridgeshire PE13 5HF ✆ Wisbech (0945) 870254
Apple pickers are needed on a family-run farm in the Fens. Ages 20+. 40-50 hour week. 4/5 weeks, September/October. Piece-work or hourly rates with bonuses paid. Campsite and accommodation available in self-catering 4/5 berth caravans in orchard. Workers should take their own cooking equipment and bedding. Food can be bought from local tradesmen. Deposit payable. *EC nationals only.* D

OAK TREE FARM Mr R E S Stephenson, Hasketon, Woodbridge, Suffolk IP13 6JH ✆ Grundisburgh (0473) 735218
Strawberry pickers needed. Piece-work rates paid. Ages 18+, girls and couples only. 8 hour day, 6 day week excluding Saturday. 3+ weeks, approx 25 June-25 July. Self-catering hostel or camping accommodation approx £3 per week. Campers should take their own tents and equipment. *Apply by mid-March.*

A P & S M PARRIS Cutliffe Farm, Sherford, Taunton, Somerset TA1 3RQ ✆ Taunton (0823) 253808
Farm close to Exmoor National Park requires pickers for strawberries, raspberries, currants and runner beans. Work also available packing fruit for markets. Ages 18+. No experience necessary as training given. 45-50 hour week, beginning 05.30-06.00 during busy periods. 6-8 weeks, early June-August. Piece work rates paid. Self-catering accommodation in caravans for small weekly charge, or pickers can bring their own tents. *Apply by February.*

PERIMETER FARMS LTD Yeld Lane, Kelsall, Cheshire ✆ Kelsall (0829) 52583
Work available picking raspberries at an international farm camp near Inverness in Scotland. No experience required. Ages 17+. 1+ weeks, mid July-end August. Piece-work rates paid. Accommodation on campsite overlooking Beauly Firth; workers should take their own tents and cooking equipment. £20

paid towards travel costs for those who pick regularly. Shopping trips and excursions to Inverness arranged. Work packing frozen fruit at end of season also available. D PH

R & J M PLACE LTD **International Farm Camp, Church Farm, Tunstead, Norwich, Norfolk NR12 8RQ** ✆ **Smallburgh (0692) 536337**
Strawberry, raspberry and blackberry pickers and agricultural workers needed. Other work, such as crop irrigation, fruit inspection or packing, may also be available. Ages 17-25. 8 hour day, 5/6 day week. 29 May-13 September. Piece-work rates paid. Bed and breakfast provided from £32 per week in converted farm buildings; the remaining meals are self-catering. Workers should take a sleeping bag, and help with essential camp duties. Facilities include kitchen, dining hall, bar, showers, shop, laundry room, pool tables, table tennis, darts, volleyball, football and canoeing instruction. Registration fee £24 includes membership of social club. *Overseas applicants accepted.* D

SEGGAT FARMS **Seggat, Auchterless, Turriff, Aberdeenshire AB53 8DL** ✆ **Turriff (08884) 223**
Strawberry pickers and packers needed. No experience necessary. Ages 17+. 45 hour week, mid July-mid August. Piece-work rates paid. Self-catering accommodation in dormitory; workers should take own sleeping bags. Space for tents also available. Pickers pay own travel costs and insurance. *All nationalities welcome.*

SPELMONDEN ESTATE CO LTD **The Director, Spelmonden Farm, Goudhurst, Kent TN17 1HE** ✆ **Goudhurst (0580) 211400**
Hop pickers required, and also a very limited number of apple pickers. Ages 18+. 5 weeks, from 1 September. Hop pickers receive £2.69 per hour for up to 40 hour week, and £4.03 per hour overtime. Apple pickers paid at piece-work rates. Self-catering accommodation and facilities free of charge. *UK nationals only.*

G & B WALKER STRAWBERRY GROWERS **Newton of Lewesk, Old Rayne, Insch, Aberdeenshire AB52 6SW** ✆ **Insch (04645) 250**
Pickers wanted for strawberry season. No experience required. Ages 16+. 36 hour week. 4-6 weeks, July-August. Piece-work rates. Self-

catering dormitory accommodation on site. Workers pay for food, laundry and travel costs. *All nationalities welcome.*

WORKING WEEKENDS ON ORGANIC FARMS (WWOOF) **19 Bradford Road, Lewes, Sussex BN7 1RB** ✆ **Lewes (0273) 476286**
A non-profitmaking organisation which aims to help organic farmers and smallholders whose work is often labour-intensive as it does not rely on the use of artificial fertilisers or pesticides. Provides unskilled voluntary workers with first hand experience of organic farming and gardening, and a chance to spend an energetic weekend in the country. Working weekends are organised on organic farms, smallholdings and gardens throughout Britain. The work can include hedging, haymaking, fruit, vegetable and dairy work, beekeeping, sheep shearing, rearing kids and ducklings, building renovation, peat cutting, hooking and scything, seaweed spraying and compost making. Members receive a bi-monthly newsletter which details places needing help on specific weekends, and also lists job opportunities in the organic movement. After completing 2 scheduled weekends members may apply for their own copy of the complete list of WWOOF places, including some overseas, so that independent arrangements for longer periods can be made. Ages 16+. Families welcome on some farms. Opportunities to learn crafts. 8 hour day, weekends all year. Full board and lodging provided in the farmhouse or outbuildings; volunteers should take a sleeping bag. No wages paid, and helpers must pay their own travel costs. Insurance and anti-tetanus vaccination recommended. Membership fee £8. D

LEADERS & GUIDES

ADVENTURE & COMPUTER HOLIDAYS LTD **28 Gowrie Road, London SW11 5NR** ✆ **071-350 1896**
Adventure holiday camp leaders are required for day and residential courses at centres in Surrey and Cornwall. Ages 19+. Experience of working with children essential; preference given to teachers, student teachers and those with NNEB qualifications. 5-6 weeks, May-

August, with busiest periods during July-August. 35+ hours per week. Full board and lodging provided on residential courses. Weekly salary £120 (day courses) or £150 (residential courses). Free transport from London available, otherwise applicants pay own travel costs.

THE IONA COMMUNITY Staff Coordinator, Isle of Iona, Argyll, Strathclyde PA76 6SN *©* Iona (068 17) 404
An ecumenical Christian community seeking new and radical ways of living the Gospel in today's world. On Iona the Community runs two centres, each welcoming up to 50 guests to a common life of work, worship, meals and recreation. Volunteers are required to help run the children's programme for those staying at the centres. Some experience of working with children, flexibility and organisation essential, as is the willingness to work as part of a team. Also require guides to offer guided tours of the Abbey, a rebuilt Benedictine monastery, for guests and visitors, often many hundreds each day in the summer months. Duties include keeping the Abbey clean, preparation for worship and welcoming people to services. An interest in history, meeting people and worship essential.

On the nearby Island of Mull the Camas Centre welcomes up to 16 guests each week, mainly unemployed or disadvantaged young people, to a common life of work, worship, arts, crafts and outdoor activities. Requires programme workers and general assistants with experience and, if possible, qualifications in one or more of the following: outdoor skills (canoeing, walking, camping, abseiling), arts and crafts, working with groups of sometimes very demanding teenagers, games, driving and maintenance.

Ages 18+. All the work is demanding but rewarding, but most important is a willingness to join fully in the community life, which includes worship and social activities as well as work. 6 day week, February-December. Full board, shared accommodation, pocket money of £15 per week and assistance with travel expenses within mainland Britain provided. *Applications received before 31 December given priority.*

**LONDON SIGHTSEEING TOURS
3A Victoria House, South Lambeth Road, London SW8 *©* 071-582 2838**
Require guides for panoramic tours of London by double-decker bus. Applicants should be good communicators and have a flexible attitude. English must be first language; foreign languages useful but not vital. No experience necessary; full training provided. Work available throughout the summer, 3+ months. Hours are long and unsocial; applicants must be hard working. Ages 18+. Salary £3.50 per hour and uniform provided; generous tips can usually be expected. No accommodation or meals provided.

**NORD-ANGLIA INTERNATIONAL LTD
10 Eden Place, Cheadle, Cheshire SK8 1AT
© 061-491 4191**
Organises children's summer day camps in north west England, and English language courses for overseas students at centres throughout Britain. Social activity monitors are needed for supervision and courier duties, to liaise with the course director and help with the organisation, animation and supervision of sports. Mostly 5 afternoons per week. Ages 18+. No formal teaching qualifications required. 2-10 weeks, Easter and July/August. Most courses last 3 weeks, July. Wages £50-£105 per week depending on duties. Successful applicants are expected to attend a 1-day training and information session before commencing employment. Applicants must arrange own board, accommodation, travel and insurance. *Only native speakers of English should apply.*

**PGL YOUNG ADVENTURE LTD Personnel Department, Alton Court, Penyard Lane (878), Ross-on-Wye, Herefordshire HR9 5NR
© Ross-on-Wye (0989) 767883**
Organises outdoor adventure holidays for young people and families in England, Wales and Scotland. Activities include pony trekking, sailing, canoeing, archery, judo, windsurfing, fencing, rifle shooting, hill walking, orienteering, swimming and many others. Group leaders are required to take charge of a group of young people, joining in the activities and developing group identity, as well as planning and organising the evening programme of activities. They are responsible

for looking after the welfare of the group, and must expect to be fully involved with them throughout their stay, with the prime task of ensuring that the guests enjoy their holiday and get the most out of the experience. Ages 20+. Applicants should have a strong sense of responsibility and total commitment, be well organised, calm, patient, flexible and caring, have a wide range of skills, experience of working with children in informal or formal settings, an ability to cope with demands on their time, initiative, imagination, stamina, energy, enthusiasm, a good sense of humour and a strong personality. It is not necessary to be an extrovert - different types of personality will tackle the post in different ways, and all can be equally successful. Previous experience of working with young people useful. 4+ weeks, February-September. Staff also recruited for short periods, such as Easter and the spring bank holiday. 1 day off per week. Full board accommodation provided. Pocket money £30-£42 per week, depending on qualifications and length of stay. Applicants pay their own travel expenses. All staff are encouraged to take part in evening activities with the guests, and may sometimes be asked to help out in areas other than their own. *Early application advisable; majority of positions filled by end June.*

MONITORS & INSTRUCTORS

ACADEMIC TRAVEL (LOWESTOFT) LTD The Briar School of English, 8 Gunton Cliff, Lowestoft, Suffolk NR32 4PE *Ø* **Lowestoft (0502) 573781**
Aims to provide an educational and cultural experience for young people from overseas, providing sports, visits and social activities in addition to English lessons. Requires experienced teachers and instructors to teach English and sports. Appropriate qualifications necessary: TEFL English, LTA tennis, RYA sailing and BCU kayak/canoe. Knowledge of French, German, Italian and Spanish useful. End June-end August, average 25 hours per week. Ages 18+. Salaries according to position; insurance provided. Help given with accommodation. *UK nationals only.*

ACORN VENTURE 137 Worcester Road, Hagley, Stourbridge, West Midlands DY9 0NW *Ø* **Hagley (0562) 882151**
An activity holiday company catering for school groups at camping centres in Tal-y-Bont and Shell Island in North Wales and Chideock in Dorset. Instructors required to supervise activities such as watersports, target sports, climbing, abseiling, orienteering, caving and gorge-walking. Previous experience and qualifications such as BCU/RYA essential. Ages 18+. 40-50 hour, 6 day week. Applicants are expected to work the full season, May-September. Salary approx £40-£45 per week. All meals and accommodation in tents, insurance and cost of travel to centre provided. *Apply in writing with cv by end January. If no reply within 28 days assume application unsuccessful.*

ACTION HOLIDAYS LTD Windrush, Bexton Lane, Knutsford, Cheshire WA16 9BP *Ø* **Knutsford (0565) 654775**
Runs children's multi-activity holidays at centres in Cheshire, Hampshire and Surrey. Requires supervisors and instructors with considerable previous experience of working with children. Enthusiasm for the job and enjoyment of sports activities essential. Specialist activities include archery, go-karting and performing arts. 50+ hour week, 1 day off. Salary £45-£100 per week, depending on responsibility, shared accommodation and meals provided. Participants pay own travel expenses and insurance. *Overseas applicants will need to arrange their own work permit.*

ADVENTURE INTERNATIONAL Belle Vue, Bude, Cornwall EX23 8JP *Ø* **Bude (0288) 355551**
Aims to develop participants' respect for themselves, others, and the environment through a range of experience-based courses to be pursued within a framework of safety. Requires outdoor pursuits and development training instructors to take part in teaching a range of activities including surfing, canoeing, sailing, climbing, plus looking after young people's welfare. March-November. Up to 36 hour week. Ages 18+. Nationally recognised qualifications in outdoor pursuits preferred. Salary £30-£80 per week, depending on post, experience and qualifications; insurance, board and accommodation provided. B D PH

ANGLO-CONTINENTAL Director of Studies, 33 Wimborne Road, Bournemouth, Dorset BH2 6NA ✆ Bournemouth (0202) 557414
An English language school which, as part of a wide range of programmes, organises junior holiday courses for those aged 8-16, combining English language and creative leisure. Staff are required for sports coaching and residential supervision, with additional responsibility for recreational and social activities. The posts involve careful supervision of junior students in and out of school hours. Opportunities to teach and organise sports, lead educational excursions and to conduct other activities such as computer programming, arts and crafts, cookery and give talks on British life, literature and institutions. A number of administrative posts are also available in the areas of travel and social activities. Applicants should have organising ability, drive and enthusiasm plus wide sporting and cultural interests. Irregular working hours including evening activities. 6 day week, June-August. Staff may be required to attend brief training seminars in the week prior to the arrival of students. Residential accommodation provided at most centres in return for extra duties. Weekly salaries, paid according to qualifications and experience. All applicants must attend for interview; travel expenses refunded for successful candidates.

ARDMORE ADVENTURE 11-15 High Street, Marlow, Buckinghamshire SL7 1AU ✆ Marlow (0628) 890060
Organises activity holidays for young people at residential and day centres in the Thames Valley, Somerset and Wales. Specialist instructors with relevant experience and qualifications required to teach abseiling, aerobics, archery, arts and crafts, BMX bikes, canoeing, computing, fencing, gymnastics, horse riding, performing arts, pottery, rifle shooting, sailing, tennis, trampolining and windsurfing. Ages 18+. Applicants should preferably have experience of working with children. 2/3+ weeks, Easter and mid June-early September. Day centres 40 hours per week, residential centres 60 hours per week. Wages from £45 per week, depending on position. Full board, single or shared accommodation and insurance provided, but no travel. B D PH depending on ability. *UK nationals only.*

BEARSPORTS OUTDOOR CENTRES Personnel Department, Windy Gyle, Belford, Northumberland NE70 7QE ✆ Belford (0668) 213289
Voluntary and paid outdoor pursuits instructors required to lead a wide variety of activities including canoeing, rock climbing, windsurfing, hill walking, orienteering, cycling and wilderness survival. Domestic assistants also required. Applicants must be experienced and proficient in outdoor pursuits; for paid positions a clean driving licence and recognised qualifications are essential. Ages 17-35 (voluntary) or 21-35 (paid). 6 day week, with long hours of rewarding, enjoyable work. Appointments made at various times throughout the year. Full board accommodation provided. Salary for paid positions from £25-£50 per week depending on age and qualifications. Staff entitled to discounts on RYA, BCU and MLTB qualification courses run at the centres.

BEAUMONT CAMPS Personnel Department, The Kingswood Centre, Barn Lane, Near Albrighton, Wolverhampton WV7 3AW ✆ Wolverhampton (0902) 846141
Organises a wide range of holidays for children in American-style day and residential camps. Staff are recruited for 10 day and 8 residential camps throughout the country. Opportunities exist for general monitors, specialist instructors and group leaders. General monitors are chosen for their experience with children and their sports or activity skills. Activities include pioneering, waterfront, ball games, music, dance, arts and crafts. Each monitor is assigned to a group of 8-10 children, taking them to the activities and ensuring their safety throughout the day, and is responsible to a group leader. Day camp monitors accompany children daily by coach from pick-up points, and must live in the Greater London area.
Specialist instructors are needed to teach a limited number of activities where special caution is required; these include canoeing, sailing, archery, judo, fencing, trampolining, caving, subaqua, rifle shooting, horse riding, soccer, tennis, swimming, mini motorbikes and computing. Specialists assume total responsibility for the safety of both children and staff during the activity under instruction, and should have relevant qualifications or

experience. Group leaders liaise with the camp director, coordinate groups and organise monitor duties, timetables and catering arrangements. Also opportunities for waterfront, TEFL and computing staff. Residential staff are responsible for groups of children aged 8-17, during the day and in the evening. All staff must genuinely enjoy working with children, possess leadership ability, and be willing to work a long, hard exhausting day enthusiastically in a structured setting where regulations apply to all. Ages 18-35. Staff must be available for the whole season, July-September. 5-9 weeks, including compulsory day/weekend orientation course, setting up and clearing camps. 1 free day per week plus alternate nights off. Wages £40-£50 per week. Board and accommodation provided. PH

CAMP WINDERMERE Low Wray, Ambleside, Cumbria LA22 0JJ ✆ Ambleside (053 94) 32163
A full-time training centre for school parties and youth groups with the emphasis on training, safety and enjoyment. Recognised as an approved establishment by the Mountain Leadership Training Board, the British Canoe Union and the Royal Yachting Association. Volunteer assistant outdoor pursuits instructors are needed to teach walking, canoeing, sailing, camping and other activities in the Lake District. Experience useful but not essential. 24 hour day, 7 day week, May-September. Ages 18+. Full training to national standards in canoeing, sailing and walking, tent accommodation and catering provided.

CAMPUS CENTRES Llangarron, Ross-on-Wye, Herefordshire HR9 6PG ✆ Ross-on-Wye (0989) 84701
Organise activity holidays for school groups at a centre in Herefordshire. Outdoor pursuits instructors required to teach activities such as sailing, canoeing, windsurfing, climbing, abseiling, archery and rifle shooting. Applicants must be competent at their particular sport; previous experience in instructing and relevant qualifications such as BCU, RYA or MLTB an advantage. In-house training provided, as well as assistance towards training for relevant qualifications. Ages 18+; preference given to ages 20+. 50-60

hour, 6 day week. 1+ months, February-November; preference given to those able to work 4+ months. Wages £35-£50 per week; negotiable for more senior staff. Full board accommodation provided, but no fares paid. PH considered.

EDINBURGH SCHOOL OF ENGLISH (Junior Courses), 271 Canongate, The Royal Mile, Edinburgh EH8 8BQ ✆ 031-557 9200
Organise residential and non-residential English language classes for young people at schools in Edinburgh, Aberdeen, Dundee, Strathallan and Durham. Activity monitors required to supervise groups of up to 10 students and help organise their leisure programme of sports, cultural visits and social outings. Applicants must be fit, active, keen on sports, with a friendly, outgoing personality and a sound knowledge of the locality they will be working in. Experience of working with young people an advantage. Ages 21+. 3-12 weeks, Easter and mid June-September. Hours by agreement. Wages £100 per week. Full board university or school accommodation provided only if course is residential. One day briefing provided at start of course. *UK nationals only.*

ERA ADVENTURE HOLIDAYS LTD Director of Personnel, 2 Mays Road, Teddington, Middlesex TW11 0SQ
Aims to provide a memorable and stimulating holiday for ages 6-15. Children are given the opportunity to follow many activities including crafts, sports instruction, discos, competitions, trips and camping. Staff are required for various duties at a centre based at a school in the New Forest. Sports instructors in gymnastics, archery, judo, canoeing, tennis, motor sports, windsurfing, squash and badminton are required who must be prepared to take groups of youngsters of varying abilities and standards. Supervisors, teachers of English, nurses and drivers also required. Applicants must have a mature attitude, enjoy being with children and be willing to take the initiative by participating and involving the youngsters in all activities. The work can be at times very demanding and tiring but is enjoyable and rewarding. Ages 21+. Experience preferred. End July-end August. Hours of work variable; 1 day off per week plus set off-duty periods. Some residential duties are expected.

Full board accommodation and insurance provided. Wages £25-£100 per week.

EXTRAMURAL CENTRE Atlantic College, St Donats, Llantwit Major, South Glamorgan CF6 9WF ☎ (0446) 792711
Requires instructors to teach a variety of outdoor activities including canoeing, climbing, swimming and archery, on courses for disadvantaged young people. 6 hour day, 6 day week, June-August. Ages 18-25. Previous experience highly desirable, and national awards in the relevant sport an advantage. Salary £40 per week; on-the-job training, board and dormitory accommodation provided. *Apply by mid February. EC nationals only.*

HOTROCKS 97 Swineshead Road, Wyberton Fen, Boston, Lincolnshire PE12 7JG ☎ Boston (0205) 311700
Organises activity courses for school groups at centres in Derbyshire, Snowdonia and north Devon. Qualified and experienced instructors required to teach a variety of activities including canoeing, hillwalking, climbing, archery and watersports. Unqualified applicants also considered for kitchen and maintenance duties. Ages 18-30. Approx 50 hours per week, May-September. Staff training, full board and lodging provided, plus salary of approx £45 per week, depending on experience and qualifications. *Apply by end April.*

HYDE HOUSE ACTIVITY HOLIDAY CENTRE c/o 6 Kew Green, Richmond, Surrey ☎ 081-940 7782
Situated on a 50 acre estate 9 miles from Poole, organising outdoor multi-activity holidays and courses for schools and groups. Sports include windsurfing, water skiing, dinghy and longboat sailing, snorkelling, canoeing, climbing, abseiling, parascending, grass skiing, orienteering, riding and archery. Full and part-time instructors required; qualifications preferred. 6 day week. 8+ weeks, March-October. Full board accommodation provided. Salary £45 per week.

KIDS KLUB The Hall, Great Finborough, near Stowmarket, Suffolk IP14 3EF ☎ Stowmarket (0449) 675907
Provides activity holidays for 6-15 year olds at a country house. Staff are needed to organise and play with the children, creating a happy family atmosphere and holiday of a lifetime. Activities are many and varied. Staff are chosen for their enthusiasm and love of children. Knowledge of European languages an asset but not essential. Ages 18+. 48 hour week during Easter, and beginning July-end August. Wages negotiable; full board accommodation provided. Participants pay own travel and insurance costs.

MILLFIELD SCHOOL Village of Education, Street, Somerset BA16 0YD ☎ Street (0458) 45823
An independent school organising a range of special interest holidays for children and adults, with over 100 different activities and 350 courses to choose from. Instructors are needed to teach a wide variety of outdoor pursuits, sports, arts, crafts and cookery courses, plus EFL. Facilities include sports halls, games fields, swimming pool, dance/health studios and technology centre. Ages 20+. Degree or teaching qualifications and/or relevant sports coaching qualifications essential. 25 hour week. 4 weeks, July and August. Wages approx £100 per week. Small group accommodation and catering provided in exchange for evening or weekend supervisory duties. Staff pay own travel and insurance costs. PH

MOUNTAIN VENTURES LTD 120 Allerton Road, Liverpool L18 2DG ☎ 051-734 2477 Jobs at Bryn Du, Ty Du Road, Llanberis, Gwynedd ☎ Llanberis (0286) 870454
Assistant instructors required to work on a voluntary basis at a centre in Snowdonia running activity and adventure holidays for children and school groups, and outdoor development training programmes for young adults. Wide range of activities are covered, including watersports, hill walking, rock climbing, target sports, orienteering, campcraft and expeditions. Ages 17+. Previous experience and outdoor pursuits qualifications welcome but not essential; motivation and enthusiasm for outdoor activities are considered more important. Approx 40 hour week, March-October. Pocket money starts at £10 per week, increasing as volunteers stay longer. Full board accommodation and insurance provided; volunteers can also take part in in-house

training programmes when available. *Overseas volunteers should have a good command of English.* D

PGL YOUNG ADVENTURE LTD **Personnel Department, Alton Court, Penyard Lane (878), Ross-on-Wye, Herefordshire HR9 5NR** ✆ **Ross-on-Wye (0989) 767833**
Organises outdoor adventure holidays in England, Wales and Scotland. Instructors are needed for sailing, windsurfing, pony trekking, canoeing, hill walking, orienteering and archery. Staff are also needed with particular interest and skills in swimming, campcraft, caving, basketball, American football, aerobics, tennis, squash, badminton, volleyball, judo, fencing, cycling, drama, field studies, gymnastics, golf, rollerskating, climbing, abseiling, assault courses, nature trails and arts and crafts. At some centres instructors are needed who are proficient in a number of activities.

Ages 18+. Instructors should ideally have a qualification or previous experience of teaching with a good basic level of skill, but consideration will be given to candidates who are competent in the given activity. Training can be arranged. Enthusiasm and stamina essential, plus the ability to adhere to strict safety standards and the foresight to deal with emergency situations, and recognise the limitations of each child. Applicants should have a strong sense of responsibility and total commitment, enjoy the company of young people, be self-motivated, tolerant, flexible, positive, mature, with vitality and a good sense of humour. 4+ weeks, February-September.

Staff are also recruited for short periods such as Easter and the spring bank holiday. 1 day off per week. Full board accommodation provided. Pocket money from £32-£47 per week, depending on qualifications and length of stay. Senior activity instructors receive from £65 per week; senior watersports instructors and canoeists receive £60-£100 per week. Applicants pay own travel expenses. All staff are encouraged to take part in evening activities with the guests, and may sometimes be asked to help out in areas other than their own. *Early application advisable; majority of positions filled by end June.*

PRIME LEISURE ACTIVITY HOLIDAYS LTD **7 Streatfield House, Alvescot Road, Carterton, Oxfordshire** ✆ **Carterton (0993) 840192**
Organise multi-activity holiday camps for children aged 4-14 at day and residential centres in Surrey, Hampshire, Berkshire and Oxfordshire. Monitors are required to coach and supervise groups of up to 15 children in activities such as tennis, football, swimming, archery, gymnastics and basketball. Previous experience of teaching or working with children preferred, and applicants should have relevant awards or professional qualifications. Ages 18+. 50 hour week. 2-6 weeks during Easter and summer school holidays. Staff receive £85-£200 per week, plus full board accommodation on site. No travel costs provided.

RANK EDUCATION SERVICES LTD **Castle Mill, Lower Kings Road, Berkhamsted, Hertfordshire HP4 2AP** ✆ **Berkhamsted (0442) 876641**
Designed to help organisations concerned with the character development of young people, arranging a variety of residential activity holidays. Instructors are required for school venture and language weeks which cater for groups of children aged 8-14 in Cornwall, Kent, Somerset, Sussex, the Isle of Wight, Scotland and Wales. A wide range of crafts and outdoor activities are taught including judo, badminton, boating, fencing, swimming, ball games, abseiling, orienteering, gymnastics, aerobics, archery, art, crafts, drama and video-making. Qualifications or experience preferable but not always essential. For language weeks fluent French or German and English are required. Applicants must be friendly and enthusiastic, and have a genuine interest in working with children. October, November, January, February and March-May. Wages approx £80-£90 per week. Board and lodging provided.

ROB HASTINGS ADVENTURE LTD **25 Southcourt Avenue, Leighton Buzzard LU7 7QD** ✆ **Leighton Buzzard (0525) 379881**
Operate adventure, activity and creative holidays for all ages at a centre in north Wales. Wide range of activities organised, including sailing, white water canoeing, golf, archery, fencing, mountain biking, racquet sports, country walking, horse riding, rock climbing, arts and crafts. Instructors are required to

supervise and teach activities, help out with domestic duties and contribute to evening entertainment. Ages 18+. Specialist qualifications desirable and experience essential. Driving licence and experience of driving minibuses required for some positions. Applicants need to be out-going and enthusiastic, enjoy challenges, working in a team and doing a job well. Tolerance, flexibility, stamina, and a sense of fun combined with a responsible attitude also important. 6 day week, 6 weeks, July and August. Salary from £43 per week according to the type of job. Full board accommodation and travel costs provided. All staff take part in on-site training programme. PH *UK nationals only.*

ROCKLEY POINT SAILING SCHOOL Hamworthy, Poole, Dorset BH15 4LZ ✆ Poole (0202) 677272

Teaches sailing to individuals and groups in dinghies and yachts, and requires instructors with RYA qualifications. Those with the ability to achieve RYA qualifications within a short time may also apply. Some posts for house mothers, to look after the children when not sailing. Ages 18+. 40 hour week, March-October. Wages dependent on experience. Accommodation provided.

SPORTS EXPERIENCE 86 Dorset Road, Merton Park, London SW19 ✆ 081-543 4207

Organises multi-activity day and residential camps for children in London and south east England. Monitors are required to assist in the supervision of both sporting and non-sporting activities. Relevant sports qualifications and experience of working with children desirable but not essential; applicants should be young, enthusiastic people who have a positive ability to get on with children. Good spoken English essential. Ages 18+. Hours variable, mid July-end August. Salary £40-£75 per week depending on responsibility, qualifications and experience. Travel and meals provided; single self-catering accommodation in halls of residence can be arranged. *EC nationals only.*

ST JOSEPH'S HALL Junction Road, Oxford OX4 2UJ ✆ Oxford (0865) 711829

Social activity supervisors required to accompany excursions and organise sports and other activities at English language schools in

Oxford and Cambridge. Previous experience or qualifications preferred. Ages 18+. 4-12 weeks, June-August. Salary £130-£170 per week. Applicants arrange own accommodation. In-house training sessions arranged. *UK nationals only.*

STUDENTOURS 3 Harcourt Street, London W1H 1DS ✆ 071-402 5131 or (0403) 891431

Monitors are required to organise sports programmes and supervise children's activities at summer camps in Sussex. Ages 17+. 5+ hour day, 5 day week with evenings free. 2-6 months, all year. Board, lodging and insurance provided. Pocket money from £40 per week.

TASIS ENGLAND Coldharbour Lane, Thorpe, Surrey KT20 8TE ✆ (0932) 565252

Counsellors required to work at an American-style international summer school for 12-18 year-old students. Counsellors act as teachers' aides, sports coaches, evening activity organisers, excursion chaperons and also have some residential/dormitory duties. Ages 19+. Applicants should be students who have completed at least one year in higher education. An interest in sports and some relevant experience also desirable. 40 hour week. 8 weeks, end June-end August. Salary approx £1000 for 8 weeks. Full board dormitory accommodation provided. No travel costs paid. *EC nationals only.*

TIGHNABRUAICH SAILING SCHOOL Tighnabruaich, Argyll PA21 2BD

Instructors are needed to teach sailing and windsurfing to high standards in a relaxed holiday atmosphere. Appropriate sailing or windsurfing qualifications required. Approx 36 hour week, June-September. Ages 18+. Salary £60 per week and self-catering youth hostel accommodation provided.

THE WOODSIDE ADVENTURE CENTRE c/o 6 Kew Green, Richmond, Surrey ✆ 081-940 7782

The Centre is situated in Bideford and organises outdoor activity holidays and courses for all ages and levels. Sports include water skiing, canoeing, sailing, surfing, riding, abseiling, sand yachting, climbing, snorkelling, coastal/hill walking, orienteering, skate sailing, grass slope skiing and archery. Full or part-time instructors required. Qualifications preferred. 36 hour, 6 day week. 8+ weeks, March-October. Salary £45 per week. Full board centre accommodation provided.

YOUNG LEISURE ACTIVITY HOLIDAYS
Rock Park Centre, Llandrindod Wells, Powys LD1 6AE ✆ Llandrindod Wells (0597) 822021
Activity holiday centre situated in a rural area of mid-Wales. Requires a small number of instructors and assistant instructors to teach a range of activities including archery, abseiling, climbing, canoeing and mountain biking. Ages 18-40. Only those with experience and nationally recognised qualifications in the relevant sports should apply. First aid qualification also preferred. 40-50 hours per week for 2-6 weeks during the summer. Salary of £50-£60 per week and full board and lodging provided. *Apply in winter prior to summer season.*

TEACHERS

ANGLO-CONTINENTAL Director of Studies,
33 Wimborne Road, Bournemouth, Dorset BH2 6NA ✆ Bournemouth (0202) 557414
A group of schools situated in Bournemouth providing English language courses for overseas students. Qualified teachers and university graduates, preferably with EFL experience, required at international vacation centres (ages 14+) and at an international school for juniors (ages 8-16). English is taught at 6 levels, with emphasis on oral English; maximum class size 15. Junior school staff will also be expected to take part in out-of-class activities, including excursions, sports and social activities, and general student welfare. 30-40 hour week, June-August. Staff may be required to attend brief training seminars in the week prior to the arrival of the students. Residential accommodation provided in return for extra duties at junior school, but at some centres staff have to arrange their own accommodation. Weekly salary according to qualifications and experience. Vacation course teachers are carefully chosen for their skill and enthusiasm, and for a lively, interesting and entertaining approach. Applicants must attend for interview and successful candidates will have travelling expenses refunded.

ANGLO EUROPEAN STUDY TOURS LTD
8 Celbridge Mews, London W2 6EU ✆ 071-229 4435
Runs English language courses for foreign students during the summer at centres in Bristol, Edinburgh, London, Norwich, Swansea and Tunbridge Wells. Teachers with appropriate qualifications and experience required. Applicants should be of English mother tongue and preferably have an additional language. Vacancies from mid June-end August. Salary up to £192 per week for 17 contact hours. Applicants arrange their own accommodation and travel.

BEAUMONT CAMPS LTD Personnel
Department, The Kingswood Centre, Barn Lane, Near Albrighton, Wolverhampton WV7 3AW ✆ Wolverhampton (0902) 846141
Organises a wide range of holidays for children in American-style day and residential camps throughout the country, and runs Britannia language schools for 11-17 year olds in various towns in Kent. TEFL teachers and coordinators are required both for camps and schools. Applicants should preferably have TEFL qualifications and experience. Ages 18-35. Staff should be available for the whole season, June-September, including compulsory day/ weekend orientation course. 1 free day per week. Salary £100-£130 per week. Board and accommodation provided. PH

ELIZABETH JOHNSON ORGANISATION
Education Department, West House, 19/21 West Street, Haslemere, Surrey GU27 2AE ✆ Haslemere (0428) 652751
Arranges short-term holiday courses in English for young students, particularly from mainland Europe, the Middle East and Japan. Teachers are needed at more than 35 centres in the areas around Brighton, Bristol, Farnham, Reading, Southampton, Bournemouth, Portsmouth, Guildford, Cambridge and Chertsey. Work normally involves 4 mornings teaching per week, accompanying students on excursions and supervising activities in the afternoons and sometimes in the evenings; occasionally escorting between course centre and arrival/ departure point. Weekends normally free, although some programmes involve weekend activities. Applicants must be native English speakers and should be qualified and/or

experienced teachers, in particular those with TEFL experience, or graduates/final year students at colleges, especially those studying languages. Vacancies on some courses for those with qualifications to teach art, drama, riding, tennis and indoor sports. Flexibility and enthusiasm essential. All applicants should be capable of carrying out programmes in a lively and responsible way as a full-time commitment. 2-3 weeks, Easter and 2-8 weeks, June-September. Salary according to programme. No accommodation provided; preference given to local applicants. All new teachers attend 1 day briefing workshop.

EURO-ACADEMY 77A George Street, Croydon, Surrey CR0 1LD *C* 081-681 2905/6
Teachers required for 15 centres in the south of England, London and the Home Counties, to provide EFL tuition to classes of up to 15 students, supervise sports and accompany them on excursions. Applicants should be graduates with English as their mother tongue; TEFL RSA Preparatory certificate essential. 3 hours teaching per morning, plus afternoon and Saturday excursions, March-April and July-August. Wages £150-£180 per week depending on experience and qualifications. No insurance, travel costs or accommodation provided.

EUROYOUTH LTD 301 Westborough Road, Westcliff, Southend-on-Sea, Essex SS0 9PT *C* Southend-on-Sea (0702) 341434
Organises stays for overseas students which can be combined with language and activity courses. Part-time EFL teachers required for English language courses for students aged 14-17. 12 hour week, 3 weeks, Easter and July-August. Ages 20+. TEFL training or experience desirable, and knowledge of foreign languages useful. Salary approx £7 per hour depending on qualifications or experience. Apply giving personal particulars, experience, qualifications and availability dates. No accommodation provided. *UK nationals only.*

INTERLINK SCHOOL OF ENGLISH 126 Richmond Park Road, Bournemouth, Dorset BH8 8TH *C* Bournemouth (0202) 290983
Requires experienced teachers with degree and preferably TEFL qualification, to teach English to overseas students. 30 hour week, July-August. Ages 21+. Salary £160-£188 per week.

Applicants must arrange their own accommodation.

INTERNATIONAL STUDY PROGRAMMES The Manor, Hazleton, Cheltenham, Gloucestershire GL54 4EB *C* Cotswold (0451) 860379
Organises educational visits and arranges holiday language courses, international holiday camps, study tours and homestay programmes. EFL tutors required to teach on a wide variety of language programmes at approx 20 centres and camps throughout Britain. Work includes planning and carrying out tuition programmes (17 hours per week), supervising group activities, including sports sessions, excursions and evening activities. Ages 21+. Tutors must have TEFL experience and/or degree and PGCE or other teaching qualifications in English and modern languages. 2-6 weeks, June-August. Salary approx £175-£230 per week including camp, family or residential board and accommodation or £215-£270 per week if own accommodation provided. Tutors also receive £20 travel allowance per course. *Native English speakers only.*

Also French teachers (native speakers and British teachers who are fluent in French) required Easter and late July-late August to work on Fun with French non-residential courses for 5-12 year old British children in many locations throughout the UK. Work involves organising fun activities in French, such as language teaching, games, cookery, drama, singing, art and crafts, sports. Hours are 09.00-16.00, Monday-Friday. Salary £165-£230 if accommodation provided; £215-£280 with own accommodation.

LTC INTERNATIONAL COLLEGE OF ENGLISH Compton Park, Compton Place Road, Eastbourne, East Sussex BN21 1EH *C* Eastbourne (0323) 27755
Runs a residential college for overseas students. Experienced teachers, preferably with TEFL qualifications, required to teach English, supervise students and organise extracurricular activities. Ages 21+. Applicants must be native English speakers and candidates with qualifications such as a degree plus RSA/ UCLES TEFLA certificate preferred. 20 hour week plus 15-20 hours of supervision and

extracurricular activities. Mid June-end August. Salary £650+ per month. Residential accommodation in shared bedrooms, full board and National Insurance provided; applicants arrange their own travel. One-day induction programme. Also vacancies for residential or non-residential social organisers and welfare assistants. PH *Apply after 1 January.*

NORD-ANGLIA INTERNATIONAL LTD 10 Eden Place, Cheadle, Cheshire SK8 1AT ℂ 061-491-4191
Organises holidays, based on English language courses, for overseas students at up to 50 centres throughout Britain. Staff required to teach English and supervise social and cultural activity sessions.
Ages 21+. Applicants must be graduates, preferably with TEFL experience. 15+ hours teaching, plus up to 5 afternoon or evening activity sessions per week. Full day excursions count as 2 activity sessions. 2-10 weeks, Easter and July/August; most courses 3 weeks, July. Accommodation provided in some residential centres, where teachers have responsibility for supervising students in the evenings. Salary from £125 per week, depending on hours worked and accommodation. Successful applicants expected to attend 1 day training and information session before commencing employment. Applicants arrange own travel and insurance. *Only native speakers of English should apply.*

OXFORD INTENSIVE SCHOOL OF ENGLISH Unit 1, Kings Meadow, Ferry Hinksey Road, Oxford OX2 0DP ℂ Oxford (0865) 792799
Requires teachers for schools in the Midlands, East Anglia and the South West, to provide intensive EFL tuition for teenagers in their vacations, teaching English in small classes and supervising during leisure activities.

Applicants should be graduates with English as their mother tongue, preferably with a modern languages background; teaching experience advantageous, but not essential. 3/4 hours per weekday plus supervision during afternoons and at weekends. Easter and July/August. Wages £135+ per week and public liability insurance provided. Applicants will have to arrange their own board and lodging.

RICHARD LANGUAGE COLLEGE 43-45 Wimborne Road, Bournemouth, Dorset BH3 7AB ℂ Bournemouth (0202) 555932
Graduates are required to teach EFL to groups of 12-14 adults. Duties include teaching, correction of homework, and some participation in extracurricular activities on the extensive sports and social programme. Applicants should have a degree in English, French or German, and preferably RSA Cambridge Certificate in TEFL. Ages 22+. Maximum 30 x 45 minute lessons per week. Late June-mid September. Part board family accommodation can be arranged at cost of £50-£55 per week, full board at weekends. Salary according to qualifications and experience. Employer's public liability insurance and interview travel expenses provided.

ST JOSEPH'S HALL Junction Road, Oxford OX4 2UJ ℂ Oxford (0865) 711829
English language teachers required for centres in Oxford and Cambridge. Applicants should have a degree or equivalent, experience of teaching English as a foreign language, and preferably the RSA Prep Cert/Diploma in TEFL. Ages 20+. 15-30 hours per week. 4-12 weeks, June-August. Salary from £225 per week. No accommodation provided. In-house training sessions arranged. *UK nationals only.*

STUDIO SCHOOL OF ENGLISH 6 Salisbury Villas, Station Road, Cambridge CB1 2JF ℂ Cambridge (0223) 69701
Vacancies for high calibre EFL teachers. Applicants should have a degree/PGCE, and ideally a TEFL qualification. Native English speakers only. 15-30 hour week. June/July-August/September. Wages according to qualifications and experience. Board and accommodation not provided.

WORKCAMPS

ATD FOURTH WORLD The General Secretary, 48 Addington Square, London SE5 7LB ℂ 071-703 3231
Works very closely with some of the most disadvantaged and marginalised families to help ensure they have a place in society. Workcamps at the family centre in Surrey reflect the emphasis laid on working with

hands as well as minds, and the importance of basic skills for people to have any participation in society. The work, alongside permanent volunteers, is mainly manual, such as building, painting and landscaping, with some secretarial and translation work. All work undertaken contributes to the role of the family centre as a focus for exchange between the poorest, and the non-poor who work so hard in supporting them. Applicants should be willing to work hard in a team and go beyond a superficial understanding of poverty.

Ages 18+. Approx 40 hour, 5½ day week. 2 weeks, July. Also weekends, June-September and 3 month scheme. Accommodation provided. Applicants asked to contribute towards living expenses, to take a sleeping bag and all-weather working clothes.

CHRISTIAN MOVEMENT FOR PEACE
Bethnal Green United Reformed Church, Pott Street, London E2 0EF ✆ 071-729 7895
An international movement open to all who share a common concern for lasting peace and justice in the world. Volunteers are invited to work in international teams on summer projects aimed at offering a service in an area of need; promoting international understanding and the discussion of social problems; and offering young people the chance to live as a group and take these experiences into the context of daily life. Recent projects have included working on a children's mural project on the theme of One World, One Race; organising a holiday for children of Somali refugees; helping on a mobile playbus on council estates and outside benefit offices; and helping to organise One World Week in a community centre in Birmingham.
Ages 17+ (18+ overseas volunteers). Those with community/social work experience particularly welcome. Volunteers must be prepared to take a full part in all aspects of the camp. Overseas volunteers must have good English. 30-36 hour week. 2 weeks, usually during the summer. Board, lodging and insurance provided but volunteers pay their own travel costs and sometimes contribute towards living expenses. Registration fee £30. B D PH

Apply through partner organisation in country of residence; for further information see page 30.

INTERNATIONAL VOLUNTARY SERVICE
Old Hall, East Bergholt, Colchester, Essex CO7 6TQ
IVS is the British branch of Service Civil International, which promotes international reconciliation through workcamps. Recent projects have included working with local teenagers in Invergordon to create a sculpture or mural based on the theme of oil and water, the area's main industries; travelling by canal barge from Manchester to Liverpool, using street theatre to campaign for Latin American solidarity; helping crofters with weeding, drystone walling, fencing and clearing ditches on Fair Isle; and cleaning, sharpening and renovating old tools in Southampton to send to communities in the Third World. Projects combining manual and social work also arranged; these normally involve painting, converting, renovating, maintenance and conservation work, building and gardening at schools, homes and residential centres for the elderly and handicapped or emotionally disturbed children or adults, often working alongside the residents and joining in with the life of the community. Work/study camps also organised on specific themes such as anti-racism, Third World solidarity and East-West cooperation. Approx 80 international workcamps all over Britain involving groups of 6-18 volunteers.
Ages 18+. Volunteers must be fit and prepared to work hard, contributing actively to the work and team life. Overseas volunteers must speak fluent English. 35-40 hour week, 2-4 weeks, June-September. Food, accommodation and insurance provided, but not travel. Registration fee (1992) £55 (students £45, unwaged £40) B D PH

Apply through partner organisation in country of residence; for further information see page 30.

QUAKER INTERNATIONAL SOCIAL PROJECTS Volunteer Administrator, Friends House, Euston Road, London NW1 2BJ
Volunteers are invited to work on a variety of projects aimed at making life more positive for members of a community. Projects bring together 8-20 people of different nationalities, backgrounds and countries to work on a common task. Previous volunteers have been involved in organising general activities, crafts,

sports and music on a children's playscheme in Dudley; constructing a network of paths through the grounds of Paradise House, a Rudolf Steiner community in Painswick; sharing English and communication skills with first- and second-language speakers at a multicultural community centre in London's Docklands; and talking with elderly residents of a hospital in Lancaster about their memories of people and places in their lives. Work/study projects also organised on East-West relations. Most projects have a study element relevant to the work undertaken. Volunteers of all backgrounds and abilities welcome; relevant skills and experience an advantage. Overseas volunteers should have good English. Ages 18+; 16+ on some projects. 1-4 weeks, mainly during the summer. Food, accommodation and insurance provided; no fares or wages paid. Registration fee (1992) £25 (students/low waged £15, unwaged £8). B D PH welcome.

Apply through partner organisation in country of residence; for further information see page 30.

UNITED NATIONS ASSOCIATION International Youth Service, Temple of Peace, Cathays Park, Cardiff CF1 3AP ✆ Cardiff (0222) 223088
Aims to assist in community development by acting as a means to stimulate new ideas and projects, encouraging the concept of voluntary work as a force in the common search for peace, equality, democracy and social justice. Volunteers are invited to take part on international workcamps. Recent projects have included decorating and other tasks to help in the reconstruction of a Norwegian church in Cardiff; building a pagoda in the grounds of Ely hospital; and looking after handicapped children on holiday in Mid Glamorgan. Ages 18+. Volunteers are expected to join in the activities of the local community, and to create a happy and effective project. 40 hour week. 2-4 weeks, July-September. Accommodation in church halls, hospitals, homes or community centres, food and insurance provided. Some camps are self-catering. Volunteers pay their own travel costs and should take a sleeping bag. Registration fee £45. B D PH

Apply through partner organisation in country of residence; for further information see page 30.

GENERAL

ACORN VENTURE 137 Worcester Road, Hagley, Stourbridge, West Midlands DY9 0NW ✆ Hagley (0562) 882151
Activity holiday company catering for school groups at camping centres in Tal-y-Bont and Shell Island in North Wales. Centre managers required to coordinate activities, organise evening entertainments and make sure groups have all they need. General maintenance staff also required. Ages 18+. Applicants should have some previous experience. 40-50 hour, 6 day week. Applicants are expected to work the full season, May-September. Salary approx £40-£45 per week. All meals and accommodation in tents, insurance and cost of travel to centre provided. *Apply in writing with cv by end January. If no reply within 28 days assume application unsuccessful.*

ARDMORE ADVENTURE LTD 11-15 High Street, Marlow, Buckinghamshire SL7 1AV ✆ Marlow (0628) 890060
Organises activity holidays for young people at residential and day centres in the Thames Valley, Somerset and Wales. Centre directors and senior group leaders required. Ages 18+. Applicants should be English speakers, preferably with experience of working with children. 2/8+ weeks, Easter and mid June-early September. Day centres 40 hour week, residential centres 60 hour week. Wages £45+ per week, depending on position. Full board, single or shared accommodation and insurance provided, but not travel. B D PH depending on ability. *UK nationals only.*

BEAUMONT CAMPS LTD Personnel Department, The Kingswood Centre, Barn Lane, Near Albrighton, Wolverhampton WV7 3AW ✆ Wolverhampton (0902) 846141
Organises a wide range of holidays for children in American-style day and residential camps. Staff are recruited for 10 day and 8 residential camps throughout the country. Opportunities exist for NNEB qualified nursery leaders responsible for looking after and organising a programme for 3-5 year olds, SRN qualified camp nurses, administrative and book keeping staff, programme organisers, transport coordinators and PSV/HGV drivers. Staff at

residential camps are responsible for groups of children aged 8-17 during the day and evening. Fluent French required for administrative posts at some centres. All staff must genuinely enjoy working with children, possess leadership ability, and be willing to work a long, hard, exhausting day enthusiastically in a structured setting where regulations apply to all. Ages 18-35. Staff must be available for the whole season, July/September, including compulsory day/weekend orientation course, setting up and clearing camps. 1 free day per week plus alternate nights off. Salary £40-£100 per week. Board and accommodation provided. PH

BUTLIN'S LIMITED Head Office, Bognor Regis, West Sussex PO21 1JJ
Provides family holidays and leisure facilities, encompassing accommodation, retailing, catering, amusement parks, professional entertainment and conferences, all on the same site. Vacancies exist in the retail and leisure areas, and for lifeguards, nurses, nursery nurses, entertainers, security staff, electricians and technicians, at centres in Ayr, Bognor Regis, Minehead, Pwllheli and Skegness. Relevant qualifications such as RGN, NNEB useful. Short and long term positions almost all year, exact dates varying according to centre. 39-45 hour week. Ages 16+, local applicants, 18+ others. Salary dependent on individual centres, accommodation, meals, uniform and staff entertainment programme provided. Use of the leisure and guest facilities and holiday discounts available. Applicants pay own insurance and travel costs. *EC nationals only. Apply direct to the preferred centre:*

Wonderwest World, Heads of Ayr KA7 4LB; Southcoast World, Bognor Regis, West Sussex PO21 1JJ; Somerwest World, Minehead, Somerset TA24 5SH; Starcoast World, Pwllheli, Gwynedd, North Wales LL53 6HX; Funcoast World, Skegness, Lincolnshire PE25 1NJ.

CHESSINGTON WORLD OF ADVENTURES Leatherhead Road, Chessington, Surrey KT9 2NE ✆ Epsom (0372) 729560
A zoo and theme park, requiring seasonal staff to work as catering assistants, cashiers, ride operators, site cleaners, gardeners and shop assistants. No experience necessary as training given, but staff must be enthusiastic and enjoy

working as part of a team. 40 hour week, March-October. Ages 16+. Salary £2.50-£3.50 per hour, employers' liability insurance and subsidised staff canteen, but accommodation not provided. *Overseas applicants with work permits and good English welcome.*

COUNCIL ON INTERNATIONAL EDUCATIONAL EXCHANGE (CIEE) Work Exchanges Department, 205 East 42nd Street, New York NY 10017, United States
Work in Britain/Student Exchange Employment Programme (SEEP) enables American students to have an educational and cultural experience through a period of work in Britain of up to 6 months. Programme participants may enter Britain at any time of year, and work in any type of employment; most students work in the service industries, although many undertake career-oriented jobs. Ages 18+. Students must be residing and studying in the US at the time of application and enrolled as a matriculating student at an accredited college or university, taking at least 8 credit hours, or enrolled full-time. Applicants may either find a job before leaving the US or look for one on arrival. Advice on travel, accommodation, administrative procedures and finding a job provided prior to departure and at orientation session on arrival. *Work in Britain Handbook* includes information contacts for employment and a regional employment guide. Administration fee $125. B D PH W

THE GRAIL CENTRE 125 Waxwell Lane, Pinner, Middlesex HA5 3ER ✆ 081-866 2195
The Centre, set in 10 acres of grounds, is home to a Christian lay community of women. Conferences and courses are organised and the Centre is always open to friends and strangers alike. Volunteers are required, mainly to assist with household tasks and garden maintenance; possibility of other types of work such as administration, reception duties, office work, sewing and artwork. Any particular skills or experience volunteers may have are put to good use. Applicants are likely to be motivated by a desire to experience community life and offer service to the wider community. Ages 19/20+. Basic knowledge of spoken English necessary for volunteers to gain from their experience. 35-40 hour week, with 1½ days free. 3+ months, all year, except summer, where 2 month stay is

acceptable for students whose vacation time is limited. £12-£15 pocket money per week and full board accommodation in Centre provided. *Apply at least 6 months in advance.* D

HARRODS LTD Personnel Recruitment, Brompton Road, Knightsbridge, London SW1X 7XL ✆ 071-730 1234
London's famous department store requires seasonal staff for sales, administration, portering, driving and warehouse work. 41 hour week, July and January sales and pre-Christmas, September-December. Relevant previous experience essential. Good command of English also essential for sales work, as is excellent presentation. Ages 18+. Salary £160 per week for sales/administration; £150 per week for warehouse work. Insurance and subsidised staff restaurant provided. B D PH limited opportunities. *Overseas candidates must obtain their own work permits, where necessary.*

THE IONA COMMUNITY Staff Coordinator, Isle of Iona, Argyll, Strathclyde PA76 6SN ✆ Iona (068 17) 404
An ecumenical Christian community seeking new and radical ways of living the Gospel in today's world. On Iona the Community runs two centres, each welcoming up to 50 guests to a common life of work, worship, meals and recreation. Volunteers are needed to work in the Abbey shop. The work involves contact with a large number of people and includes till work, serving, stocking shelves and cleaning. The ability and willingness to serve and work quickly under pressure for prolonged periods is essential. Also require a driver/general assistant to take luggage and provisions between the centres and the jetty. Full driver's licence required, as is a willingness to work responsibly, often alone. Interest in meeting people useful: driver comes into contact with many staff, guests, day villagers and islanders. Ages 18+ (21+ for drivers). Most important is a willingness to join fully in the community life, which includes worship and social activities as well as work. The work is demanding but rewarding, and the hours flexible. 6 day week, February-December. Full board, shared accommodation, pocket money of £15 per week and assistance with travel expenses within mainland Britain provided. *Applications received before 31 December given priority.*

MADHYAMAKA BUDDHIST CENTRE Kilnwick Percy Hall, Pocklington, York YO4 2UF ✆ Pocklington (0759) 304832 (14.00-17.00)
A residential Buddhist community of lay and ordained people living and working together. Based in a Georgian hall situated in 40 acres of woodland, lakes and parkland. Volunteers are invited to help with the upkeep of the building and grounds, in return for board and lodging. Up to 6 volunteers required at any one time. Ages 16+. No experience necessary, but volunteers should speak English. The work is varied and can include sewing, cleaning painting and decorating, gardening, plastering, joinery and electrical work. 35 hour, 5 day week, usually for 1 week, all year. Opportunity to attend free teaching and meditation sessions. Volunteers pay own travel costs and are asked to abide by the Centre's code of discipline which includes not smoking, drinking, eating meat or playing loud music on the premises. B D PH but unsuitable for wheelchairs.
US applications to Saraha Buddhist Centres, 342 Liberty Street, San Francisco, California 94114.

PAX CHRISTI 9 Henry Road, London N4 2LH ✆ 081-800 4612
Promotes international exchanges, forming an international community spirit to spread the church's teaching on peace, and encourages Christian participation in social and political life. Volunteers are needed to work in international summer youth hostels in London and possibly other cities, usually set up in school buildings, and providing bed and breakfast and light refreshment in the evenings. Each hostel is run by a team of 15 volunteers; approx two-thirds are from overseas. The aim is for the volunteers to form a lively international community to provide a welcoming and friendly atmosphere. Work involves reception duties, cleaning, cooking, shopping, laundry, publicity, accounts and the setting up and dismantling of beds, and is hard but often rewarding. Duties and free time allocated on a rota basis so that everyone shares the menial as well as the more enjoyable aspects. Free time activities include picnics, sightseeing, sports, games, parties, theatre and cinema trips. Ages 19+. Approx 40 hour week. 4/5 weeks, July/August. Food, dormitory accommodation with self-catering facilities and insurance provided. Volunteers pay own travel costs.

PGL YOUNG ADVENTURE LTD Personnel Department, Alton Court, Penyard Lane (878), Ross-on-Wye, Herefordshire HR9 5NR ✆ Ross-on-Wye (0989) 767833
Organises outdoor adventure holidays in England, Wales and Scotland. Activities include pony trekking, sailing, canoeing, archery, hill walking, tennis, squash, arts and crafts, fencing, judo, rifle shooting, cycling, grass skiing, gymnastics, golf, badminton and many others. Staff are required for the following service and supplies positions:
Administrative Assistants, generally acting as assistants to the manager and responsible for petty cash, staff wage sheets, lost property, programme schedules, reception, telephone enquiries and correspondence; Stores and Site Maintenance staff, responsible for the general appearance and cleanliness of the centre, with duties including litter control, maintaining tents and equipment, cutting grass, cleaning, painting, looking after stores, and maintenance and repair work - carpentry, plumbing, electrical experience welcome; Nurses, preferably RGN/EGN qualified, with a driving licence and experience in child nursing; Drivers, including PCV and LGV, responsible for looking after passengers and maintenance of vehicles; Gardeners, with horticultural interest and ability; Coffee Bar/Tuck Shop staff, responsible for cleaning and organising the shop, displaying and selling the goods, stocktaking and taking charge of the money. Ages 18+, 21+ for drivers. Applicants should be fond of children, responsible, flexible, energetic and enthusiastic, patient, reliable and mature with a sense of humour, capable of working on their own initiative, and have the ability to cooperate with others as part of a team, contributing fully to the life of the centre. 4+ weeks, February-September. Staff are also recruited for short periods at Easter and the spring bank holiday. 1 day off per week. Full board accommodation provided. Pocket money from £34-£42 per week for general positions, from £75 for nurses and LGV/PCV drivers. Travel expenses paid by applicants. All staff can join in the activities during free periods and are encouraged to take part in evening activities with the guests. Staff may sometimes be asked to help out in areas other than their own. *Early application advisable; majority of positions filled by end June.*

STUDENTOURS 3 Harcourt Street, London W1H 1DS ✆ 071-402 5131 or (0403) 891431
Volunteers are required for various duties at youth centres in Sussex. Staff are needed to help on children's farms, looking after the animals plus maintenance of the nature study trails and assault course. Other duties involve gardening, maintenance of fences, restoring Victorian architecture and the Italian gardens. Workers also required for general maintenance work in the grounds of the centres, for painting, cementing, building, construction and driving work. Volunteers can participate in the sports and activities organised at the centres. Ages 17+. 5+ hour day, 5 day week with evenings free. 2-6 months, all year. Accommodation, insurance and meals whilst on duty provided. At other times workers are provided with food but must do their own cooking. Pocket money from £40 per week. All tools and equipment supplied.

TOC H National Projects Office, 1 Forest Close, Wendover, Aylesbury, Buckinghamshire HP22 6BT ✆ Aylesbury (0296) 623911
Requires volunteers for a variety of short-term residential projects throughout Great Britain. Projects include working with people having different disabilities; work with underprivileged children; playschemes and camps; conservation and manual work. Ages 16+. Programmes giving further details of projects and application procedures are published in March and September. B D PH W depending on project. *Early application advised.*

WINDSOR SAFARI PARK Personnel Department, Winkfield Road, Windsor, Berkshire SL4 4AY ✆ Windsor (0753) 830886
Seasonal workers required February-September to act as food and beverage assistants, rides and amusements operators, house and grounds maintenance staff and guest relations personnel in this leisure park with an African theme. No experience necessary; personality is considered more important than qualifications. Ages 16+. Salary dependent on age. Full costume provided; canteen facilities available. No accommodation provided. B D PH W *EC nationals only.*

INFORMATION

Greek Embassy
1a Holland Park, London W11 3TP
© 071-221 6467

British Embassy
1 Ploutarchou Street, 106 75 Athens

Tourist office
National Tourist Organisation of Greece,
4 Conduit Street, London W1R 0DJ
© 071-734 5997

Youth hostels
Greek YHA, 4 Dragatsaniou Street, Athens

Youth & student information
British Travel and Student Service, 10 Stadiou
Street, Athens

International Student and Youth Travel, 11
Nikis Street, Syntagma Square, 105 57 Athens

STS, 1 Felellindy Street, Syntagma Square,
Athens

Entry regulations A UK citizen intending to
work in Greece should have a full passport. EC
nationals may stay for up to 3 months in order
to look for or take up employment, after which
a residence permit will be required. To obtain a
residence permit, applicants should go to the
Aliens' Department of the Ministry of Public
Order in Athens, or outside Athens to the local
police station. Citizens of non-EC countries
require a work permit and a temporary
residence permit, which should be applied for
by the prospective employer from the local
prefecture. Applicants will be notified once
permission has been granted, and should take
their passport to the Greek Consulate in their
home country to be stamped. This entitles the
applicant to obtain a residence permit from the
Aliens' Department and a work permit from the
local prefecture, on arrival in Greece. During
the time of this procedure the applicant should
not be resident in Greece.
Job opportunities are extremely limited and
permits are only issued in cases where the work
necessitates the employment of a foreigner, and

in some professions of special interest. It is against immigration regulations to enter Greece as a tourist to seek and/or take up employment, and any persons so doing risk refusal of leave to enter Greece and/or deportation. An information sheet, *Residence and Employment*, is available from the Labour Counsellor Office at the Greek Embassy.

Job advertising Publicitas Ltd, 517/523 Fulham Road, London SW6 1HD ✆ 071-385 7723 can place job advertisements in various Greek morning and evening journals, weeklies, monthlies and magazines.

Travel STA Travel, 74 Old Brompton Road, London SW7 3LQ/117 Euston Road London NW1 2SX ✆ 071-937 9921 (offices also in Birmingham, Bristol, Cambridge, Leeds, Manchester and Oxford) operates flexible low-cost flights between London and Greece.

Campus Travel, 52 Grosvenor Gardens, London SW1W 0AG ✆ 071-730 3402 (offices throughout the UK) and Council Travel, 28A Poland Street, London W1V 3DB ✆ 071-437 7767 (offices also in Paris, Lyon, Düsseldorf, Tokyo and throughout the US) offer student/youth airfares and summer charter flights to Athens, plus Eurotrain under 26 fares.

Information centres International Student & Youth Travel Service (ISYTS/Eurotrain), 11 Nikis Street, 2nd Floor, Syntagma Square, 105 57 Athens ✆ Athens (1) 3221267/323 3767 is the official student and youth travel service specialising in tickets for domestic and international air, sea and land travel, plus information on cheap hotel accommodation, excursions, tours, cruises and festivals.

Also issues student cards and provides free welcome and poste restante service. Cannot offer information on job opportunities. Open Monday-Friday, 0900-1700 and Saturday, 0900-1300.

Publications *The Rough Guide to Greece* £9.99 and *The Rough Guide to Crete* £6.99 provide comprehensive background information on Greece and Crete, plus details on getting there, getting around, places to explore and cheap places to stay. Available from good bookshops.

Accommodation National Tourist Organisation of Greece, see above, issues *Camping*, a booklet listing sites run by them, situated by the sea and equipped with modern facilities.

Young Women's Christian Association of Greece, 11 Amerikis Street, 106 72 Athens offers accommodation at YWCA centre near Athens airport for females only. Can also provide bed and breakfast hostel accommodation in single and double bedded rooms for females only travelling through Athens or Salonika.

AU PAIR / CHILDCARE

There are no special regulations governing the employment of au pairs in Greece. EC nationals must obtain a medical certificate, and apply for a residence permit if staying for longer than 3 months.

ANGLIA AGENCY 70 Southsea Avenue, Leigh-on-Sea, Essex ✆ Southend-on-Sea (0702) 471648
Can place au pairs, mothers' helps and nannies. Ages 17+. Pocket money from £30 per week depending on position. Service charge £40.

GALENTINAS CHILDCARE CONSULTANCY PO Box 51181, 145 10 Kifissia ✆ Athens (1) 808 1005
Can place nannies, au pairs plus, mothers' helps and domestics. Males and females, ages 18-25. Pocket money Drs65000-Drs250000 depending on placement. Goodwill bond deposit equivalent of 2 months' pay refunded on completion of contract. *EC nationals only.*

STUDENTS ABROAD LTD 11 Milton View, Hitchin, Hertfordshire SG4 0QD ✆ Hitchin (0462) 438909
Can place au pairs, mothers' helps, nannies and domestic staff. Ages 18-27 for au pairs. Pocket money from £30 per month; higher for other positions. Service charge £40.

When writing to any organisation it is essential to mention Working Holidays 1993 and enclose a large stamped, self-addressed envelope, or if overseas, a large addressed envelope and at least two International Reply Coupons.

CONSERVATION

BRITISH TRUST FOR CONSERVATION VOLUNTEERS Room IWH, 36 St Mary's Street, Wallingford, Oxfordshire OX10 0EU
The largest charitable organisation in Britain to involve people in practical conservation work. Following the success of the Natural Break Programme in the UK, BTCV is now developing a series of international working holidays with the aim of introducing the volunteering ethic to communities abroad. It is hoped that British volunteers will adapt to and learn from local lifestyles as well as participate in the community. Recent projects have included paving and drystone walling in the courtyard of an old school in Zagori; and footpath construction in the Nestos Delta, one of the most important Mediterranean wetland sites. 2-3 weeks. Ages 18-70. Cost from £100 includes food and camping/dormitory accommodation. Everyone shares in the cooking. Membership fee £10. No fares or wages paid.

COURIERS/REPS

SIMPLY TRAVEL LTD 8 Chiswick Terrace, Acton Lane, London W4 5LY © 081-995 3883
Specialist tour operator offering summer programmes in self-catering villas and apartments on Crete. Representatives are required to look after clients and ensure they have everything they need to enjoy their stay. Work also available for maids, watersports instructors, handymen, odd jobs people, cooks and operations staff. Season lasts from April-October. 6 day week, with flexible hours. Ages 18+. Preference given to those with previous experience and spoken Greek. Salary £30-£200 per week, depending on job. Accommodation, insurance and travel costs provided. Training given before start of season.

WORKCAMPS

EUROPEAN CONSERVATION VOLUNTEERS GREECE 15 Omirou Street, 14562 Kifissia
A non-profitmaking, non-governmental organisation promoting intercultural exchanges and conservation. Volunteers are invited to take part in international workcamps. Projects have a strong emphasis on Greek culture and tend to take place in very remote parts of the country. Recent projects have included rebuilding a children's playground and carrying out maintenance work at an SOS village near Athens; reconstructing cobbled streets at a traditional village on Mount Pelion; and restoring an old mansion in Portaria for conversion into a cultural centre. Ages 18+. Applicants must be highly motivated. 2+ weeks, July-August. Volunteers pay $100 to cover food and accommodation, and pay their own travel and insurance costs. B D PH

Apply through partner organisation in country of residence. In the UK: United Nations Association, International Youth Service, Temple of Peace, Cathays Park, Cardiff CF1 3AP © Cardiff (0222) 223088.

Outside the UK: please see information on page 30.

SERVICE CIVIL INTERNATIONAL
43 Avlonos Street, 10443 Athens
Service Civil International promotes international reconciliation through work projects. Volunteers are needed to work in international teams on various workcamps. Recent projects have included helping to construct a road to join two villages on the island of Lefkada; constructing and restoring sea walls to prevent erosion on the island of Naxos; working with young handicapped people in Thessaloniki; preparing for the annual wine festival in Achala; and marking paths leading to a volcano in the centre of the island of Nisiros. Ages 18+. Volunteers should preferably have previous workcamp experience. Applicants should be prepared to work hard and contribute to team life. 35-40 hour week. 2-4 weeks, July-August. Food and basic accommodation provided but not travel. Volunteers prepare and cook their own meals. B D PH

Apply through partner organisation in country of residence. In the UK: International Voluntary Service Old Hall, East Bergholt, Colchester, Essex CO7 6TQ.

Outside the UK: please see information on page 30.

GENERAL

EUROYOUTH LTD 301 Westborough Road, Westcliff, Southend-on-Sea, Essex SS0 9PT
C Southend-on-Sea (0702) 341434
Arranges holiday guest stays where guests are offered board and lodging in return for an agreed number of hours English conversation with hosts or their children. Time is also available for guests to practise Greek if desired. Mainly ages 15-25, but there are sometimes opportunities for ages 13-16 and for older applicants. 2-3 weeks, June-August. Travel and insurance paid by applicants. Registration fee £70. *Apply at least 12 weeks prior to scheduled departure date. UK nationals only.*

INTERTOM HELLAS International Trust Office Mediators, 24-26 Halkondili Street, Athens 104 32 *C* Athens (1) 52 39 470
Can place hotel, bar, disco and office staff throughout Greece including Athens and a number of islands. Salaries from Dr40000-Dr65000 per month, plus board and lodging provided. Can also place housekeepers, mothers' helps, nannies and au pairs. Airport reception service.

PIONEER TOURS Working Holiday, 11 Nikis Street, Syntagma Square, Athens 105 57
C Athens (1) 32 24 321
Organises a variety of working holidays all over Greece, including hotel work, au pair work and fruit picking. Ages 18+. Relevant experience sometimes required, also knowledge of English. 8 hour day, 6 day week. Work available mainly in summer. Pay from Dr1500 per day, plus food and accommodation. Travel paid from Athens to place of work; return fare to Athens paid after 1+ month's work. Registration fee £20. *EC nationals only.*

SUNSAIL The Port House, Port Solent, Portsmouth PO6 4TH *C* Portsmouth (0705) 219847
Crew members required to work aboard cruising yachts sailing in flotillas around the Greek islands. Vacancies for experienced skippers to be responsible for the well-being of up to 13 cruising yachts and 60 holidaymakers, to give daily briefings on navigation, and provide sailing assistance where necessary.

Applicants must have considerable sailing experience, be cheerful, hardworking and able to deal with people of varying backgrounds and ages. Ages 23-30.

Also bosuns/mechanics needed, responsible to the skipper for maintaining the marine diesel engines and repairing any other items aboard. Must have excellent knowledge of marine diesels and practical ability to cope with all sorts of breakdowns and repairs. Ages 22-30.

Hostesses are required to look after laundry, accounting, and cleaning of boats, advising holidaymakers on shops and restaurants, and organising social events and barbecues. Sailing experience useful, but bright personality, patience and adaptability essential. Ages 22-30.

All staff should be prepared for very hard work and long hours. 12+ hour day, 1 free day per week. Knowledge of German advantageous but not essential. Staff must work for the whole season, mid March-November. Wages approx £85 per week, paid monthly. Accommodation on board, return travel and medical insurance provided.

INFORMATION

Hungarian Embassy
35 Eaton Place, London SW1X 8BV
℃ 071-235 4048/7179
Consular section: ℃ 071-235 2664

British Embassy
Harmincad Utca 6, Budapest V

Tourist office
Danube Travel Ltd, 6 Conduit Street, London
W1R 9TG ℃ 071-493 0263

Youth hostels
Hungarian YHA, Semmelweis utca 4, 1395
Budapest V

Youth & student information
International Bureau for Youth Tourism &
Exchange (BITEJ), Ady E utca 19, 1024 Budapest
Postal address: PO Box 147, 1389 Budapest

Express Youth & Student Travel Bureau,
Semmelweis utca 4, 1395 Budapest V

Entry regulations Nationals of EC member
states and of most western and eastern
European countries, Canada and the United
States do not need a visa to visit Hungary or to
take up voluntary work there. All other
nationalities should check visa requirements
with Hungarian embassies/consulates. Those
wishing to take up paid work in Hungary must
get their prospective employer to apply for a
work permit. With the exception of British
nationals, a work visa must also be applied for:
applicants must complete a visa form at the
Hungarian embassy and submit their passport,
2 photos and their work permit (forwarded to
them by the prospective employer), after which
the visa should take 24 hours to process.

Travel Campus Travel, 52 Grosvenor Gardens,
London SW1W 0AG ℃ 01-730 3402 (offices
throughout the UK) and Council Travel, 28A
Poland Street, London, W1V 3DB ℃ 071-437
7767 (offices also in Paris, Lyon, Düsseldorf,
Tokyo and throughout the US) offer Eurotrain
under 26 fares and student/youth flights to
Budapest.

Publications *Hungary Tourist Information* is a free annual booklet giving information on Hungary including travel, entry formalities, customs, insurance, transport, accommodation, historic monuments, entertainment, sports and other useful information and addresses. Available from Danube Travel Ltd, see above.

Lonely Planet's *Eastern Europe on a Shoestring* £13.95 provides practical information on budget travel in Hungary and most other east European countries.
The Rough Guide to Hungary £7.99 provides comprehensive background information on Hungary, plus details on getting there, getting around, places to explore and cheap places to stay.
Michael's Guide to Hungary £6.95 is detailed and concise, providing invaluable practical advice for all kinds of travellers. Published by Inbal Travel.
All the above are available from good bookshops.

Accommodation Elender Kft Youth Hostel, Istenhegyi utca 32, 1126 Budapest © Budapest (1) 1552928 has accommodation for young people with a splendid view over the city. Open 21 June-28 August. Cost Ft2000 per night.

CONSERVATION

BRITISH TRUST FOR CONSERVATION VOLUNTEERS Room IWH, 36 St Mary's Street, Wallingford, Oxfordshire OX10 0EU
The largest charitable organisation in Britain to involve people in practical conservation work. Following the success of the Natural Break Programme in the UK, BTCV is now developing a series of international working holidays with the aim of introducing the volunteering ethic to communities abroad. It is hoped that British volunteers will adapt to and learn from local lifestyles as well as participate in the community. Recent projects in Hungary have included restoring the Kelemer peat bogs, remnants of the last Ice Age 12,000 years ago; and restoring the original steppe mosaic ecosystem of Mount Tokaj. 10 days, June-September. Ages 18-70. Cost from £140 includes transport from Budapest Airport, food

and basic accommodation, with everyone sharing in domestic chores. Membership fee £12. No fares or wages paid.

FARMWORK

BIOKULTURA ASSOCIATION Mr Szabolcs Seléndy, Magyar Biogazdálkodók, Környezetkímélök és Egészségvédök Egyesülete, Török u. 7, Budapest 1023 © Budapest (1) 136 8852/115 0064
The Hungarian Association of Organic Growers may be able to help find placements for volunteers on organic farms and gardens in Hungary. Work can include weeding, animal husbandry and helping with the harvest. Experience not essential, but knowledge of Hungarian, German or Russian useful. Ages 18+. 30 hour week, March-September. No wages paid, and volunteers must pay their own travel. Insurance and anti-tetanus vaccination recommended.

MONITORS & TEACHERS

BRIT-POL HEALTH CARE FOUNDATION Gerrard House, Suite 14, Worthing Road, East Preston, West Sussex BN16 1AW © (0903) 859222
Small number of teachers required to work on summer camps for children in Hungary. Applicants must be of English mother tongue and have an ability to communicate with children. Ages 20-50. 20-25 hours per week for 3 weeks, July and August. Board and lodging provided in local family, or in self-contained flat with food allowance paid. Return travel provided but not insurance. Also opportunities for qualified and experienced teachers, ages 25+, to teach English, management or administration for 3+ months, all year.
Applications can take up to 3 months to process. UK nationals only.

CENTRAL BUREAU FOR EDUCATIONAL VISITS & EXCHANGES Schools Unit, Seymour Mews House, Seymour Mews, London W1H 9PE © 071-486 5101 ext 2411
Teachers and sixth formers are required at English language summer schools, the main objective of which is to provide Hungarian

pupils, aged 16-17, with the opportunity of practising English learnt in school, and by spending 3 weeks in the company of a group of British teachers and young people to acquire a deeper awareness of the British way of life. Duties include assisting with the teaching of English as a foreign language, running conversation classes and organising sporting, musical and social activities including drama, embroidery, folk dancing and singing workshops. Ages up to 45. Applicants should be native English speakers, sixth formers or those aged 16-19 and willing to assist the staff; or teachers qualified in the teaching of any discipline: EFL or ESL qualifications an advantage. Applicants should have a sense of responsibility, organisational skill, adaptability to new surroundings, a sociable nature and an ability and interest in sports and/or drama and music, plus experience in working with or teaching children.

Participants must fully commit themselves to the teaching of English and the organisation of various educational, outdoor and social activities. 3 weeks, July/August. Board and accommodation provided at school, sharing with the pupils. Excursions and visits to places of interest arranged by the host school and 3 day trip to visit places of interest on the return to Budapest. Applicants pay group travel cost of approx £230 (1992) including insurance. 1 day briefing session held in June. Organised by the Hungarian Ministry of Education under the auspices of the Hungarian Commission for UNESCO.

WORKCAMPS

HELP (SCOTLAND) 60 The Pleasance, Edinburgh EH8 9JT ✆ 031-556 9497
HELP (Humanitarian Education & Long-term Projects) is a charity run by students from Edinburgh University, sending volunteers to communities in need around the world. Workcamps are intended to assist in the relief of poverty as well as to provide an educational experience. Recently volunteers have been helping to establish a self-sufficient community near Pecs, working to set up a bio-region, build accommodation, plant crops and develop a horticultural programme. No experience or

qualifications required; most applicants are students but there is no upper age limit.
40 hour, 5-6 day week for 4-6 weeks during the summer. Basic dormitory accommodation with simple food provided. Participants contribute £100 towards the project to cover board, lodging and equipment, and pay their own travel and insurance. **B D PH W** *Write for application form; apply by end February.*

UNIO YOUTH WORKCAMPS ASSOCIATION International Relations Department, Kun B. pkp 37-38, 1138 Budapest
Volunteers are invited to take part in international workcamps at various locations in Hungary. Recent projects have included digging, planting and general maintenance work in the city parks of Miskolc; renovating the building and surrounding parkland of a 14th century monastery in Szeceny; clearing litter on the shore of Lake Balaton; and environmental work in the Pilis mountains north of Budapest. Leisure activities also arranged. Ages 18+. Applicants should have previous workcamp or voluntary service experience and be prepared to work hard and contribute to team life. Camp language is English, but German also useful. 2-3 weeks, June-August. Board and lodging provided in schools, huts or tents. Participants pay own insurance and travel costs.

Apply through partner organisation in country of residence. In the UK: Quaker International Social Projects Friends House, Euston Road, London NW1 2BJ or
United Nations Association International Youth Service, Temple Of Peace, Cathays Park, Cardiff CF1 3AP ✆ Cardiff (0222) 223088

Outside the UK: please see information on page 30.

When writing to any organisation it is essential to mention Working Holidays 1993 and enclose a large stamped, self-addressed envelope, or if overseas, a large addressed envelope and at least two International Reply Coupons.

ICELAND

INFORMATION

Icelandic Embassy
1 Eaton Terrace, London SW1W 8EY
© 071-730 5131

British Embassy
Laufasvegur 49, 101 Reykjavík

Tourist office
Icelandair, 172 Tottenham Court Road, London
W1P 9LG © 071-388 5599

Youth hostels
Icelandic YHA, Bandalag Islenskra Farfugla,
Laufasvegur 41, 101 Reykjavík

Youth & student information
Iceland Tourist Board, Laufasvegur 3, 101
Reykjavík

Entry regulations Foreign nationals may not
seek or accept employment in Iceland after their
arrival in the country unless they have a prior
working permit. This must be applied for from
the Ministry of Social Affairs by the
prospective employer on behalf of the foreign
national, and the employer must show
sufficient proof that the foreign national will
fill a position for which no skilled Icelander is
presently available. These regulations may
change as of January 1993 subject to the
European Economic Space agreement, and a
work permit may no longer be required by UK
and EC nationals.

British nationals do not need a visa to visit
Iceland, but must be in possession of a return
travel ticket, have a re-entry permit into their
country of origin, and show sufficient funds for
their support during their intended stay.
Provided these requirements are met, they may
stay in Iceland for a period of up to 3 months;
extensions may be granted by the nearest police
authority.

Information centres Dick Phillips Specialist
Icelandic Travel Service, Whitehall House,
Nenthead, Alston, Cumbria CA9 3PS © Alston
(0434) 381440 can give details on the physical
environment and general advice, and stocks

maps and most of the relevant English language publications including guides and books on Icelandic life, environment and history. Hostelling, walking, riding and motorised tours of Iceland organised. Can also book travel by ferry from Lerwick or Scrabster, from £136 single, June-August. 25% reduction to holders of ISIC cards. Sea passage from Aberdeen to Lerwick can be arranged. *Personal callers welcome October-June.*

Publications Lonely Planet's *Iceland, Greenland and the Faroe Islands - A Travel Survival Kit* £8.95 offers practical, down-to-earth information for the low-budget, independent traveller in Iceland.
The Rough Guide to Scandinavia £8.95 provides comprehensive background information on getting around Iceland, with details on getting there, places to explore and cheap places to stay.
Both are available from good bookshops.

CONSERVATION

BRITISH TRUST FOR CONSERVATION VOLUNTEERS Room IWH, 36 St Mary's Street, Wallingford, Oxfordshire OX10 0EU
The largest charitable organisation in Britain to involve people in practical conservation work. Since 1983 Trust members have been assisting the Icelandic Nature Conservancy Council with footpath maintenance work in the Skaftafell National Park, and more recently in the spectacular Jokulsár Canyon. Volunteers work alongside locals, and should be prepared for hard physical work. The constant daylight means that there are plenty of opportunities for walking, climbing and exploring the spectacular land- and ice-scape. Ages 18+. 10-14 days, June-July. Cost £360+ includes food and flight. Camping accommodation, cooking facilities and insurance provided.

IRELAND

INFORMATION

Irish Embassy
17 Grosvenor Place, London SW1X 7HR
✆ 071-235 2171

British Embassy
31/33 Merrion Road, Dublin 4
✆ Dublin (1) 269 5211

Tourist office
Irish Tourist Office, Ireland House, 150 New Bond Street, London W1Y 0AQ ✆ 071-493 3201

Youth hostels
An Oige Irish YHA, 39 Mountjoy Square, Dublin 1 ✆ Dublin (1) 363111

Youth & student information
Union of Students in Ireland, 16 North Great Georges Street, Dublin 1 ✆ Dublin (1) 786 366

Union of Students in Ireland Travel Service (USIT), Aston Quay, O'Connell Bridge, Dublin 2 ✆ Dublin (1) 778117

National Youth Council of Ireland, 3 Montague Street, Dublin 2 ✆ Dublin (1) 784122

Entry regulations UK citizens intending to work in Ireland do not need a passport, but should produce evidence of their place of birth; those born in Northern Ireland may claim Irish nationality. Citizens of other member states of the EC do not require work permits. Those interested in working in Ireland can consult the nearest office of FAS - Training and Employment Authority (Head office: 27-33 Upper Baggot Street, Dublin 4 ✆ Dublin (1) 685777), or consult recruitment advertisements in local newspapers. Those in the UK seeking work may complete form *ES13* at their local Jobcentre, which is then forwarded to FAS.

Information centres Community and Youth Information Centre, Sackville House, Sackville Place, Dublin 1 ✆ Dublin (1) 786844 offers information on a wide range of subjects including youth affairs, education, employment agencies, welfare rights, sports, travel and accommodation.

Travel Campus Travel, 52 Grosvenor Gardens, London SW1W 0AG ✆ 071-730 3402 (offices throughout the UK) and Council Travel, 28A Poland Street, London W1V 3DB ✆ 071-287 3337 (offices also in Paris, Lyon, Düsseldorf, Tokyo and throughout the US) offer student/ youth airfares, student coach fares and Eurotrain under 26 fares. Student/youth ferry fares for car travel also available.
Campus Travel also issues a £6 Travelsave stamp for ISIC cards, entitling holders to 50% discount on Irish rail, ferry and coach travel.

Publications *Irish Youth Handbook* £1.95 plus £1.50 postage, is a useful reference and resource aid which provides detailed information on voluntary youth organisations together with a comprehensive list of useful addresses, youth travel and accommodation. Published by and available from the National Youth Council of Ireland, 3 Montague Street, Dublin 2 ✆ Dublin (1) 784122.

The Rough Guide to Ireland £8.99, provides comprehensive background information on getting around Ireland, with details of getting there, places to explore and cheap places to stay. Available from good bookshops.

Accommodation Kinlay House, Christchurch, 2-12 Lord Edward Street, Dublin, owned and run by USIT, see above, provides low cost accommodation in the centre of Dublin.

Similarly, Kinlay House Shandon, Bob and Joan Walk, Shandon, Cork, provides low cost accommodation in the centre of Cork.

AU PAIR / CHILDCARE

LANGTRAIN INTERNATIONAL Torquay Road, Foxrock, Dublin 18 ✆ Dublin (1) 289 3876
Can place au pairs in Irish families. 30 hour week with one full day and some evenings off. Time off to attend language classes 2-3 mornings or afternoons per week. Experience desirable but not essential. 6+ months.
Ages 18+. £25-£40 per week pocket money, full board, lodging and insurance provided. Travel paid by applicants. Placement fee £55.

COMMUNITY WORK

SIMON COMMUNITY (NATIONAL OFFICE) PO Box 1022, Lower Sheriff Street, Dublin 1 ✆ Dublin (1) 711606/711319
A voluntary body offering support and accommodation to the long-term homeless at residential houses and night shelters in Cork, Dublin, Dundalk and Galway. Full-time workers required on a residential basis, living-in and sharing food with residents, taking responsibility for household chores and working to create an atmosphere of trust, acceptance and friendship by talking, listening and befriending residents.
Ages 18-35; older volunteers considered. No experience or qualifications necessary, but applicants should be mature, responsible individuals with an understanding of, and empathy for homeless people. Tolerance and an ability to get on with people and work as part of a team also essential qualities. 3-12 months, recruitment throughout the year; first month probationary period.
Volunteers work 3 days on and 2 days off, with 2 weeks holiday entitlement every 3 months. A flat away from the project is provided for workers on their days off. Allowance of IR£32 per week and insurance provided, but not travel costs. Training given by project leaders; formal training courses in aspects such as first aid may also be provided. *All nationalities welcome; overseas applicants must have a good standard of spoken English.*

VOLUNTARY SERVICE INTERNATIONAL 37 North Great George's Street, Dublin 1 ✆ Dublin (1) 788679
The Irish branch of Service Civil International, which promotes international reconciliation through work projects. Volunteers are needed to work in international teams on various community workcamps.
Recent projects have included helping to run the Navan Travellers Summer project in County Meath, with the aim of improving facilities for Travellers, organising sports, arts/crafts, games, discos and outings for Travellers' children and youth with talks on their life and culture; organising playschemes of creative, recreational and educational activities in Kilkenny and in inner city areas of Dublin; and

doing manual work alongside residents in the grounds of Camphill communities in Wexford, Kildare and Tipperary.

Ages 18+. Overseas volunteers should have good English. Volunteers must be highly motivated and prepared to work hard as part of a team. 35-40 hour week, 2-4 weeks, June-September. Food, accommodation and insurance provided, but not travel. B D PH

Apply through partner organisation in country of residence. In the UK: International Voluntary Service Old Hall, East Bergholt, Colchester, Essex CO7 6TQ.

Outside the UK: please see information on page 30.

CONSERVATION

BRITISH TRUST FOR CONSERVATION VOLUNTEERS Room IWH, 36 St Mary's Street, Wallingford, Oxfordshire OX10 0EU
The largest charitable organisation in Britain to involve people in practical conservation work. Following the success of the Natural Break Programme in the UK, BTCV is now developing a series of international working holidays with the aim of introducing the volunteering ethic to communities abroad. It is hoped that British volunteers will adapt to and learn from local lifestyles as well as participate in the community. Projects last 2 weeks, July-August and are run in conjunction with Conservation Volunteers Ireland. Recent projects have included woodland management and maintenance in the gardens of Shankhill Castle near Kilkenny and constructing a footpath through woodlands in County Cork.
Ages 18-70. Cost from £50 includes food and accommodation, with everyone sharing in domestic chores. Membership fee £12. No fares or wages paid.

FARMWORK

WILLING WORKERS ON ORGANIC FARMS (WWOOF) c/o Annie Sampson, Crowhill, Newgrove, Tulla, Clare
A non-profitmaking organisation which aims to help organic farmers and smallholders whose work may be labour-intensive as it does not rely on the use of artificial fertilisers or pesticides. Provides unskilled voluntary workers with first hand experience of organic farming and gardening, and a chance to spend some time on small or large holdings throughout Ireland. The work can include working with horses, cows, goats, sheep, pigs and various fowl; all aspects of organic gardening, cutting turf, preserving fruit and vegetables; making various cheeses and yoghurt, stonewalling, hedging and renovating. Members receive a current list of holdings together with a short description of each one. Length of stay can be weekend, week, month or longer by arrangement.
Ages 16+. Opportunities to learn crafts. Full board lodging provided in the farmhouse and outbuildings; volunteers should take a sleeping bag. No wages paid, and helpers must pay their own travel costs. Insurance and anti-tetanus vaccination recommended. Membership fee £4.

TEACHERS

ANGLO EUROPEAN STUDY TOURS LTD 8 Celbridge Mews, London W2 6EU ✆ 071-229 4435
Runs English language courses for foreign students during the summer at 3 centres in Dublin and one in Limerick. Teachers with appropriate qualifications and experience required. Applicants should be of English mother tongue and preferably have an additional language. Ages 24+. Vacancies from mid June-end August. Salary up to £192 per week for 17 contact hours. Applicants arrange own accommodation and travel.

WORKCAMPS

VOLUNTARY SERVICE INTERNATIONAL 37 North Great George's Street, Dublin 1 ✆ Dublin (1) 788679
The Irish branch of Service Civil International, which promotes international reconciliation through work projects. Volunteers are needed to work in international teams on various workcamps, which have recently included restoration and maintenance work on 200 year old buildings for use as housing in Dublin; creating nature pathways through a primeval

wood in Co Clare; and gardening, clearing paths and repairing stone walls on Inis Mor, the largest of the three Aran Islands, off the Galway coast.

Ages 18+. Overseas volunteers should speak good English. Volunteers must be highly motivated and prepared to work hard as part of a team. 35-40 hour week, 2-4 weeks, June-September. Food, accommodation and insurance provided, but not travel. B D PH

Apply through partner organisation in country of residence. In the UK: International Voluntary Service Old Hall, East Bergholt, Colchester, Essex CO7 6TQ.

Outside the UK: please see information on page 30.

When writing to any organisation it is essential to mention Working Holidays 1993 and enclose a large stamped, self-addressed envelope, or if overseas, a large addressed envelope and at least two International Reply Coupons.

ISRAEL

INFORMATION

Israeli Embassy
2 Palace Green, London W8 4QB
℃ 071-957 9500

British Embassy
192 Hayarkon Street, Tel Aviv 63405

Tourist office
Israel Government Tourist Office, 18 Great
Marlborough Street, London W1V 1AF
℃ 071-434 3651

Youth hostels
Israel Youth Hostels Association, Youth Travel
Bureau, PO Box 1075, 3 Dorot Rishonim Street,
Jerusalem

Youth & student information
Israel Students' Tourist Association (ISSTA),
109 Ben Yehuda Street, Tel Aviv 63401

The Public Council for Exchange of Youth and
Young Adults, 67 Pinsker Street, Tel Aviv

Entry regulations A work permit is required
for employment in Israel, and this should be
obtained by the prospective employer on
application to the Ministry of the Interior, who
will then authorise the issue of a visa. It is
important that a permit is obtained before
leaving for Israel. Volunteers on archaeological
digs, kibbutzim or moshavim will receive their
visas on arrival. Applicants should be aware
that it is now more difficult to find a place on a
kibbutz, and are strongly advised not to travel
to Israel hoping to be accepted if they have not
arranged a place prior to departure.
Immigration officials are making it very
difficult for one-way ticket holders to enter the
country; kibbutz and moshav volunteers should
be able to produce a return or open ticket plus
proof of sufficient means of support whilst in
the country, at the port of entry. The cost of
living is high and no volunteer should leave for
Israel with less than £100 spending and
emergency money. Employment opportunities
are limited and a work permit will only be
granted if a vacancy cannot be filled by local
manpower. British Visitors Passports are not

accepted for entry into Israel; British travellers must have full passports. All passports must be valid for 6+ months from the date of intended departure from Israel.

Travel Council Travel, 28A Poland Street, London, W1V 3DB ✆ 071-437 7767 (offices also in Paris, Lyon, Düsseldorf, Tokyo and throughout the US) offers low-cost student/ youth airfares to Tel Aviv.

North-South Travel Ltd, Moulsham Mill, Parkway, Chelmsford CM2 7PX ✆ Chelmsford (0245) 492882 arranges competitively priced, reliably planned flights to Israel. Profits are paid into a trust fund for the assignment of aid to projects in the poorest areas of the South.

STA Travel, 74 Old Brompton Road, London SW7 3LQ/117 Euston Road, London NW1 2SX ✆ 071-937 9921 (offices also in Birmingham, Bristol, Cambridge, Leeds, Manchester and Oxford) operates flexible low-cost flights between London and Tel Aviv.

Publications Lonely Planet's *Israel - A Travel Survival Kit* £7.95 offers practical, down-to-earth information for independent travellers wanting to explore beyond the usual tourist routes.
The Rough Guide to Israel £5.95 provides comprehensive background information on Israel, plus details on getting there, getting around, places to explore and cheap places to stay.
Culture Shock! Israel £6.95 introduces the reader to the people, customs, ceremonies, food and culture of Israel, with checklists of dos and don'ts.
All the above are available from good bookshops.

Israel: A Youth and Student Adventure is a comprehensive booklet with information on cheap accommodation, free tours, museums, home hospitality, sports facilities, events, study courses and volunteer work, plus medical aid, hitching and useful addresses. *Israel Destination Profile* is a free 34 page booklet containing a wealth of useful information covering entry regulations, climate, accommodation, travel, shopping, eating out, cultural activities, entertainment and sport. Both available from the Israel Government Tourist Office, see above.

Accommodation *Kibbutz Inns Guest Houses* lists 25 inns offering board and accommodation; facilities include private beaches, swimming pools and tennis courts. *Christian Hospices in Israel* lists approx 40 hospices offering board and accommodation, indicating denomination and prices. Both available from the Israel Government Tourist Office, see above.

ARCHAEOLOGY

AYALA TRAVEL 13 Hazvi Street, Jerusalem 94386 ✆ (02) 381233
Organises archaeological excavation holidays at various sites throughout Israel. Excavations include Tiberias, a Roman and Byzantine site at the Sea of Galilee; Zichron Ya'acov, a site covering Hellenistic through to early Roman periods; and the ancient port of Tel Dor with remains from Canaanite through to Crusader periods. Ages 17+. No experience necessary, but applicants should be in good physical condition and have medical and accident insurance. 2 weeks, April-May and July-January. 7 hour day, 5 day week. Cost from $450 includes airport transfer, full board accommodation in kibbutz/guest house and 1 day guided tour. Participants arrange their own travel and insurance. *UK applications to WST Charters, Priory House, Wrights Lane, London W8 6TA ✆ 071-938 4362. Cost from £279.*

DEPARTMENT OF CLASSICAL STUDIES Professor M Gichon, Division of Archaeology, Yad Avner, Ramat Aviv, 69978 Tel Aviv
Volunteers are required for excavations of town fortifications and public buildings at two sites at Horvat Eqed and Emmaus, dating from the Hellenistic to the Roman and Byzantine period, located in the Judaean foothills. 1+ weeks, June-September. 6½ hour day with 1 hour rest. Accommodation provided at a cost of US$30 per day. No charge for senior students, postgraduates in archaeology or experienced diggers, provided arrangements are made in advance. No fares, insurance or wages paid. Ages 16+. Lectures in history, archaeology and geography provided as well as trips and recreational activities. Also opportunities for

volunteers to work on processing of finds, under supervision, November-June. PH accepted under certain circumstances.

DOR/NAHSHOLIM CENTER OF NAUTICAL AND REGIONAL ARCHAEOLOGY Mr Kurt Raveh, Department of Antiquities & Museums Maritime Centre, PO Box 114, Kibbutz Nahsholim, Doar-Na Hof Carmel 30815
Located in a 19th century glass factory, the Dor Center is the home base for the Department's maritime inspection team, underwater archaeology and Tel Dor area excavations. Volunteers are needed throughout the year to help with rescue excavations, underwater survey and excavation, field work including diving, technical and restoration work, and in the museum for clerical and tour guide work. Reduced rate accommodation in kibbutz beach guest houses. Applicants arrange own insurance and pay travel costs.

THE HEBREW UNIVERSITY OF JERUSALEM The Director, Institute of Archaeology, Mount Scopus, Jerusalem 91905
Conducts excavations all over Israel, concerned with the prehistoric, Biblical and classical periods. Current excavations include a dig at Hazor in Galilee, with Bronze and Iron Age remains; a large Iron Age site at Miqne/Ekron, one of 5 Philistine capital cities; and Persian, Iron Age, Hellenistic and Roman period remains at Tel Dor. 2-6 weeks, June-August. Lectures on Biblical archaeology and visits to other sites. 7-9 hour day, starting early in the morning. Accommodation provided for small fee. Volunteers pay own travel and insurance. Volunteers should write, indicating the period and vicinity they are interested in, and the times and dates when they will be available.

ISRAEL ANTIQUITIES AUTHORITY PO Box 586, Rockefeller Museum, Jerusalem 91004 ✆ Jerusalem (2) 292607
Volunteers are needed to help on excavations dating from the prehistoric era through to Crusader times. Recent excavations have been carried out at over 30 sites and have included a major port on the Mediterranean coast dating back to the late Hellenistic and Islamic periods; a Roman water system near the Sea of Galilee; a castle and village with Crusader, Mamluk and Ottoman remains; remains of a Roman-

Byzantine city near Nazareth; Bronze Age remains of a fortified city near Naharriya; a Chalcolithic village in the Negev desert; a sanctuary of Pan-Hellenistic temples and grotto; and a prehistoric site in the northern Jordan Valley. Work includes digging, shovelling, and hauling baskets, with cleaning and sorting pottery in the afternoons. Excavations are conducted throughout the year, but the main season is May-September. 2+ weeks. The Authority also conducts rescue excavations and emergency surveys throughout the year on short notice. Ages 18+. Experience not needed, but volunteers should be highly motivated, fit and able to work long hours in very hot weather. Lectures and field trips organised. On some sites volunteers may have to pay a fee or provide a medical certificate. Insurance obligatory. Travel to Israel paid by volunteers. *Archaeological Excavations* published annually in January, gives details of digs arranged all over Israel. When applying it is helpful to indicate any previous studies or experience in archaeology, anthropology, geography, excavation work or related fields such as architecture, surveying, graphic arts, photography or pottery restoration.

JEWISH NATIONAL FUND Eli Shenhav, 11 Zvi Shapira Street, Tel Aviv 64538
Volunteers required to help excavate a Shuni Roman theatre at Binyamina. Ages 17+. 1+ weeks, July-August. Cost US$15 per day includes medical and accident insurance, meals and accommodation in tents at the youth summer camp. Lectures arranged. 5 day week. Hours of work 06.00-13.00; other work 17.00-19.00. Volunteers pay own travel costs and should take a sleeping bag.

PROJECT 67 LTD 10 Hatton Garden, London EC1N 8AH ✆ 071-831 7626
Organises digs at various sites in cooperation with the Antiquities Authority. The work consists of clearing away debris, shovelling, hauling baskets, cleaning fragments of pottery and other artefacts. Ages 18+; no maximum limit. Previous experience not necessary, but volunteers should be fit, enthusiastic and prepared for hard work in a hot climate. Hours of work 05.00-12.30. Afternoons usually free. Evening lectures and trips arranged to nearby sites and museums. 2 weeks, May-October. Cost

from £345 covers return flight, full board and insurance.

TEL AVIV UNIVERSITY Institute of Archaeology, Ramat Aviv, PO Box 39040, Tel Aviv 69978
Volunteers are required to excavate the remains of Bronze Age Tel Kabri near Nahariya. Excavations have revealed fortification systems and urban remains of a Canaanite city and a Phoenician town. 3 weeks, July-August. Classes and lectures arranged. Ages 18+. Campsite accommodation US$12 per day. Registration fee US$25. Hours of work 05.30-13.00 and 17.00-19.00. Volunteers pay own travel costs.

AU PAIR / CHILDCARE

The following agencies can arrange au pair and childcare placements in Israel:

ANGLIA AGENCY 70 Southsea Avenue, Leigh-on-Sea, Essex ✆ Southend-on-Sea (0702) 471648
Can place au pairs, mothers' helps and nannies. Ages 18+. Pocket money £30 per week. Service charge £40.

HELPING HANDS AU PAIR & DOMESTIC AGENCY 39 Rutland Avenue, Thorpe Bay, Essex SS1 2XJ ✆ Southend-on-Sea (0702) 602067
Can place au pairs and mothers' helps. Ages 18-27. Pocket money approx £30 per week au pairs, higher for mothers' helps. Introduction fee £40 on acceptance of a family. *UK nationals only.*

STAR AU PAIRS INTERNATIONAL 16 Michal Street, Tel Aviv 63261
Can place au pairs, mothers' helps and nannies, especially in Tel Aviv, Haifa and Jerusalem. Ages 18+. Previous experience preferred but not essential. Knowledge of English and driving licence an advantage. Pocket money US$600+ per month. Applicants receive return fare after completing 1 year's contract.

STUDENTS ABROAD LTD 11 Milton View, Hitchin, Hertfordshire SG4 0QD ✆ Hitchin (0462) 438909
Can place mothers' helps, nannies and housekeepers. Ages 19+. Some experience

essential. Pocket money from approx £300 per month; more for experienced nannies and housekeepers. Service charge £40.

KIBBUTZIM

A kibbutz is a communal society in which all the means of production are owned by the community as a whole. Members do not receive wages or salaries but give their labour in return for the provision of their basic needs. Kibbutzim welcome volunteers who are prepared to live and work within the community and abide by the kibbutz way of life. Volunteers share all communal facilities with kibbutz members and should be capable of adapting to a totally new society. Some of the work during the summer months is citrus, melon and soft fruit harvesting, and volunteers may also be involved in haymaking, gardening or working in the fish ponds, cow sheds or chicken houses. Work is also available in the kibbutz factory, helping in non-specialist, light industrial work. For those who find the heat uncomfortable, indoor work is usually available in the kitchens, dining rooms, laundries or factories. Volunteers work approx 8 hour day, 6 day week, with Saturdays free and 2 additional days off at the end of each month. Work often starts at 05.00 so that afternoons are free. Volunteers live together in wood cabins or stone houses with food provided in the communal dining room. Laundry, toilet requisites, entertainment, medical care and other basic needs, such as stamps and cigarettes, usually available as required, and some kibbutzim have bars and discos. A small amount of pocket money, approx £20 per month, may also be provided. Kibbutzim should not be regarded as holiday bases; volunteers can make arrangements for sightseeing at the end of their work period.

Kibbutz Volunteer £5.95 describes kibbutzim and how they function, conveying the atmosphere of the communities and explaining what to expect when working in one. There are details of 200 kibbutzim plus a map showing locations and how to apply. Also includes other short-term work opportunities in Israel, including the moshav movement, au pair work, social work, archaeological digs and fruit picking.

Published by Vacation-Work, 9 Park End Street, Oxford OX1 1HJ ✆ Oxford (0865) 241978.

GILTOURS (UK) LTD 16 Gloucester Place, London W1H 3AW ✆ 071-935 1701
Arranges kibbutz volunteer places throughout the year. 8+ weeks, maximum 1 year. Ages 18-35. 6-8 hour day, 6 day week, with 7 free days each month. Pocket money approx US£85 per month. Shared accommodation and meals provided. Registration fee £30. Open return flights from £199. Health insurance must be taken out at the volunteer office in Tel Aviv.

KIBBUTZ REPRESENTATIVES Volunteer Coordinator, 1a Accommodation Road, London NW11 8ED ✆ 081-458 9235
Operates a working visitor scheme throughout the year whereby volunteers spend 8-12 weeks on a kibbutz. Volunteers pay their own travel costs and must be in possession of a return ticket or adequate funds for the return journey. All applicants must supply a medical certificate and 2 character references, and attend an orientation interview. Ages 18-32. Registration fee £40. *Limited places during July and August; apply before Easter.*

PROJECT 67 LTD 10 Hatton Garden, London EC1N 8AH ✆ 071-831 7626
Arranges working holidays on kibbutzim for 5+ weeks, all year. Cost from £275 covers return flight, transfer to kibbutz and registration fee. Tel Aviv office assists with queries and onward travel. Ages 18-32. *All nationalities welcome.*

MOSHAVIM

A moshav is a collective of individual smallholders, based on the family unit. Each family works and develops its own plot of land/farm while sharing the capital costs of equipment and marketing. Moshavim are different from kibbutzim in that each family lives in its own house and makes its own living; there are some communal buildings and facilities such as a club house or swimming pool. Volunteers on moshavim live and work as a member of an Israeli family and are expected to share in the social and cultural activities of the family and village. In some cases a small group of volunteers may live in their own bungalow, but they will each be *adopted* by the family for whom they are working. Most of the work is on the land, with emphasis on flower growing, market gardening and specialist fruit farming. It should be stressed that work on a moshav is tougher and more demanding than on a kibbutz, and working hours may be long. Volunteers are expected to develop close relationships with the family, which demands a far greater personal effort than on a kibbutz. In return for their work volunteers receive board and lodging plus wages of approx £100 per month, more than the pocket money given on a kibbutz. Lectures, cultural activities and excursions arranged.

GILTOURS (UK) LTD 16 Gloucester Place, London W1H 3AW ✆ 071-935 1701
Arranges moshav volunteer places throughout the year. Ages 18-35. 8+ weeks, maximum 1 year. 8 hour day, 6 day week, 1 day free per month. Wages US$320 per month. Self-catering accommodation, food cost approx US$50 per month. Registration fee £30. Open return flights from £199. Health insurance must be taken out at the moshav volunteer office in Tel Aviv.

PROJECT 67 LTD 10 Hatton Garden, London EC1N 8AH ✆ 071-831 7626
Arranges working holidays in moshav families. 2+ months, all year. Ages 21-35. Wages approx US$400 per month. Cost to participants from £235 covers return flight and registration fee. *All nationalities welcome.*

GENERAL

FRIENDS OF ISRAEL EDUCATIONAL TRUST 25 Lyndale Avenue, London NW2 2QB ✆ 071-435 6803
Volunteers required to work in Jerusalem's 60-acre botanic garden, in the grounds of the Hebrew University. Work involves digging, weeding and seed maintenance. Ages 18+. Horticultural qualifications welcome but not essential; volunteers must have previous experience of long hours of manual work. 30-40 hours per week. 2 weeks, March and October. Cost £450 covers half-board hotel accommodation and travel, but not insurance. Tours and lectures organised for volunteers. *UK nationals only.* D

INFORMATION

Italian Embassy
14 Three Kings Yard, Davies Street, London
W1Y 2EH ✆ 071-629 8200

British Embassy
Via XX Settembre 80A, 00187 Rome

Tourist office
Italian State Tourist Office (ENIT), 1 Princes
Street, London W1R 8AY ✆ 071-408 1254

Youth hostels
Associazione Italiana Alberghi per la Gioventù,
via Cavour 44, 3rd floor, 00184 Rome

Youth & student information
Centro Turistico Studentesco et Giovanile CTS
(Student Travel), via Nazionale 66, 00184 Rome
and via Genova 16, 00184 Rome

Student Travel Service Florence, via Zanetti 18,
50123 Florence

ESTC, Largo Brancaccio 55, 00184 Rome

Intercultura, Piazza San Pantaleo 3, 00186 Rome

Entry regulations UK citizens intending to
work in Italy should have full passports. Police
registration is required within 3 days of
entering Italy. EC nationals may stay for up to
3 months, and those wishing to stay longer
must obtain an extension from the police. When
status changes from visitor to employee the
individual must immediately apply for a work
permit.

Job advertising Publicitas Ltd, 517/523 Fulham
Road, London SW6 1HD ✆ 071-385 7723 can
place job advertisements in a number of Italian
newspapers and magazines including *Il Giorno*
(Milan daily); *Il Gazzettino* (Venice daily); *Il
Tempo* (leading Rome newspaper); *La Sicilia*
(leading Sicilian newspaper), plus a number of
trade, technical and general interest magazines.

Travel Centro Turistico Studentesco UK Ltd, 33
Windmill Street, London W1P 1HH ✆ 071-580
4554 offers low-cost rail travel and charter

flights, and reductions on Mediterranean shipping lines, for students and young people.

CIT (England) Ltd, 3-5 Landsdowne Road, Croydon, Surrey CR9 1LL ✆ 081-686 0677 issues a Kilometric ticket valid for 3000 km (maximum 20 journeys) which can be shared by up to 5 people, the 3000 km being divided by the number of passengers. Valid 2 months; cost £90. Travel at Will ticket entitles the holder to unlimited travel on the Italian rail network. Valid for up to 30 days; cost from £88 (8 days).

Euro-Domino is a pass allowing 3, 5 or 10 days unlimited rail travel in 1 month on the railways of Italy. Cost from £68/£85/£142 (ages under 26) or £90/£113/£189 (ages 26+), 3/5/10 days. Includes fast train supplements. Available from British Rail International Rail Centre, Victoria Station, London SW1V 1JY ✆ 071-928 5151.

Campus Travel, 52 Grosvenor Gardens, London SW1W 0AG ✆ 071-730 3402 (offices throughout the UK) and Council Travel, 28A Poland Street, London, W1V 3DB ✆ 071-437 7767 (offices also in Paris, Lyon, Düsseldorf, Tokyo and throughout the US) offer Eurotrain under 26 fares and low-cost student/youth airfares.

STA Travel, 74 Old Brompton Road, London SW7 3LQ/117 Euston Road, London NW1 2SX ✆ 071-937 9921 (offices also in Birmingham, Bristol, Cambridge, Leeds, Manchester and Oxford) operates flexible, low-cost flights between London and destinations in Italy.

Information centres Servizio Turistico Sociale, Youth and Student Travel Service, via Zanetti 18, 50123 Florence provides a reception and information service. Arranges accommodation, discount travel and also gives information on au pair work and working abroad, tours, Italian courses and events. B D PH

Publications *The Rough Guide to Italy* £9.99 provides comprehensive background information on Italy, plus details on getting there, getting around, places to explore and cheap places to stay. *Culture Shock! Italy* £6.95 introduces the reader to the people, customs, ceremonies, food and culture of Italy, with checklists of dos and don'ts. Both available from good bookshops.

Live and Work in Italy £7.95 is a guide for those interested in finding temporary or permanent work, starting a business or buying a home in Italy. Published by Vacation Work, 9 Park End Street, Oxford OX1 1HJ ✆ Oxford (0865) 241978.

Italy, Travellers Handbook is a free booklet containing useful information for visitors with notes on accommodation, culture and leisure, sports and travel. Also includes general information, and the addresses of provincial and local tourist boards. Available from the Italian State Tourist Office, see above.

Accommodation Federazione Italiana del Campeggio e del Caravanning, via V Emanuele 11, PO Box 23, 50041 Calenzano, Florence ✆ Florence (55) 882391 operates an international campsite booking centre and publishes a list of member campsites which can accept bookings, with details of costs, opening dates and facilities. *Apply by 15 May.* Also publishes a map of all Italian campsites, available on receipt of 3 IRCs.

ARCHAEOLOGY

ARCHEOCLUB D'ITALIA Arco de' Banchi 8, 00186 Rome
Volunteers are required to assist on archaeological excavations arranged throughout Italy. Sites include Bronze Age remains, medieval monasteries and castles. Work involves research, excavating, gathering and cataloguing finds and drawing up plans of sites. Ages 16+; those under 18 will need parental consent. No experience necessary, but volunteers should have some knowledge of Italian. 2-3 weeks, August. Approx 24 hours per week, mornings only. Cultural/educational activities organised in afternoons, including one guided visit per week in nearby town. No wages or travel paid. Cost L250000 per week covers insurance and full board accommodation in local youth hostel, school or inn.

DIPARTIMENTO SCIENZE DELL'ANTICHITA Prof Francesco d'Andria, Università, 73100 Lecce
Volunteers are required for the excavation of a site at Otranto-Veste on the Adriatic coast of

Apilia, a long-term project to investigate the Messapian culture and its relations with Greece and Magna Graecia in the Archaic period. Experienced volunteers with knowledge of the period preferred. 4 weeks, July. Food and accommodation provided; no fares or wages paid. *Apply by 30 May.*

GRUPPI ARCHEOLOGICI D'ITALIA via Tacito 41, 00193 Rome ℂ (6) 687 4028/689 6981
Volunteers are required for the excavation and restoration of various sites. Recent projects have included excavation of an Etruscan necropolis and a Roman villa, and documentation and excavation of a 10th-15th century medieval town, near Tolfa; excavation of the Diana Nemorense Sanctuary, 1st century BC, in Nemi; excavation of the Appia Antica near Rome; excavation of a Roman villa of the Imperial period near Viterbo, in Ischia di Castro; and excavation of part of the walls of the 14th-16th century Fortezza da Basso in Florence. Ages 16+. Experience in excavation techniques preferable but not essential. 2+ weeks, July-September. 6 hour day. Cost L450000-L550000 for 2 weeks, includes full board hostel or centre accommodation and insurance. Lectures and excursions. No fares or wages paid. *Apply by 15 June.*

AU PAIR / CHILDCARE

Au pair posts in Italy are open to males and females, ages 18-30, for a maximum of 12 months. A written agreement must specify duties, which should not involve more than 5-6 hours of light housework per day, with two days and 2-3 evenings free each week. As well as full board accommodation the host family must provide private accident/health insurance and at least L50,000 pocket money per week.

The following agencies can arrange au pair and childcare placements in Italy:

ACADEMY AU PAIR AGENCY LTD Glenlea, Dulwich Common, London SE21 7ES ℂ 081-299 4599
Can place au pairs. Ages 18-27. Some knowledge of Italian essential. Pocket money approx £30-£35 per week. Administration charge £40. Positions as nannies and mothers'

helps also available for those with qualifications/experience.

ANGLIA AGENCY 70 Southsea Avenue, Leigh-on-Sea Essex ℂ **Southend-on-Sea (0702) 471648**
Can place au pairs, mothers' helps and nannies. Ages 18+. Pocket money £30 per week. Service charge £40.

ANGLO PAIR AGENCY 40 Wavertree Road, Streatham Hill, London SW2 3SP ℂ **081-674 3605**
Can place au pairs and au pairs plus. Ages 18-27. Pocket money £30-£50 per week. Also placements for experienced nannies and mothers' helps; salary up to £100 per week. Agency fee £40.

AU PAIRS-ITALY 46 The Rise, Sevenoaks, Kent TN13 1RJ
Can place au pairs, mothers' helps, nannies and governesses throughout Italy, including Sicily and Sardinia. Families include members of the nobility and some of Italy's most distinguished households. Ages 18+. Applicants must supply 3 references and a medical certificate. Monthly pocket money approx £140 (au pairs), £220 (mothers' helps), £300-£800 (nannies and governesses). *EC nationals only.*

AVALON AGENCY Thursley House, 53 Station Road, Shalford, Guildford, Surrey GU4 8HA ℂ **Guildford (0483) 63640**
Can place au pairs in all areas except Rome. Ages 18-30. Basic knowledge of Italian needed. Monthly pocket money and insurance provided. Service charge £40.

HELPING HANDS AU PAIR & DOMESTIC AGENCY 39 Rutland Avenue, Thorpe Bay, Essex SS1 2XJ ℂ **Southend-on-Sea (0702) 602067**
Can place au pairs and mothers' helps. Ages 18-27. Pocket money approx £30 per week for au pairs, higher for mothers' helps. Introduction fee £40. *UK nationals only.*

HOME FROM HOME Walnut Orchard, Chearsley, Aylesbury, Buckinghamshire HP18 0DA ℂ/Fax Aylesbury (0844) 208561
Can place au pairs. Ages 18+. Placement fee £40. Basic knowledge of Italian an advantage.

Pocket money £25 per week. Placement fee £40. UK *nationals only.*

JOLAINE AGENCY 18 Escot Way, Barnet, Hertfordshire EN5 3AN *✆* **081-449 1334**
Can place au pairs and mothers' helps. Ages 18-27. Pocket money from £30 per week. Placement fee £40.

JUST THE JOB EMPLOYMENT AGENCY 8 Musters Road, West Bridgford, Nottingham NG2 5PL *✆* **Nottingham (0602) 813224**
Can place au pairs, mothers' helps and nannies. Ages 18+. Weekly pocket money £30-£40 (au pairs) or £75-£140 (other positions). UK *nationals only.*

LANGTRAIN INTERNATIONAL Torquay Road, Foxrock, Dublin, Ireland 18 *✆* **Dublin (1) 289 3876**
Can place au pairs with Italian families. Ages 18+. Pocket money £25 per week. Placement fee £55.

STUDENTS ABROAD LTD 11 Milton View, Hitchin, Hertfordshire SG4 0QD *✆* **Hitchin (0462) 438909**
Can place au pairs, au pairs plus, mothers' helps and nannies. Ages 18-27 for au pairs. Basic knowledge of Italian useful but not essential. Pocket money from approx £30 per week (au pairs); higher for other positions. Service charge £40. *Apply early for temporary summer positions.*

UNIVERSAL CARE Chester House, 9 Windsor End, Beaconsfield, Buckinghamshire HP9 2JJ *✆* **Beaconsfield (0494) 678811**
Can place au pairs and mothers' helps. Ages 18-27. Knowledge of Italian not essential, but experience with children desirable and GCSE English preferred. Pocket money approx L300000 per month. Service charge £47. PH *Apply 2 months before work period desired. EC nationals only.*

COMMUNITY WORK

SERVIZIO CIVILE INTERNAZIONALE via dei Laterani 28, 00184 Rome
Service Civil International promotes international reconciliation through work projects. Volunteers are needed to work in international teams on various community workcamps. Recent projects have included organising games, cultural activities and visits for Saharawi children in a refugee camp in Livorno; gardening, painting and taking elderly people on excursions at a centre in Carpi Anziani; and organising beach activities for mentally handicapped children in Cagliari. Ages 18+. Knowledge of Italian necessary for some camps. Applicants should be highly motivated, fit and prepared to work hard as part of a team. 35-40 hour week. 1-3 weeks, June-September. Food, accommodation and insurance provided, but not travel. B D PH

Apply through partner organisation in country of residence. In the UK: International Voluntary Service, Old Hall, East Bergholt, Colchester, Essex CO7 6TQ.

Outside the UK: please see information on pages 30.

CONSERVATION

ALTERNATIVE TRAVEL GROUP LTD Restoration Project, 69-71 Banbury Road, Oxford OX2 6PE *✆* **Oxford (0865) 310399**
Volunteers are required to help with the restoration of an 11th century convent in the Tuscany countryside, and with its conversion into a staging post for those on walking holidays. Ages 16+. Applicants must be hard-working and reliable. 5+ weeks, January-November. 35 hour week. Knowledge of Italian not essential. £1.50 pocket money per day worked, full board accommodation in convent and return travel provided. Swimming pool nearby; bicycles available, and at least 1 excursion organised each week. Applicants must attend for interview in Oxford.

BRITISH TRUST FOR CONSERVATION VOLUNTEERS Room IWH, 36 St Mary's Street, Wallingford, Oxfordshire OX10 0EU
The largest charitable organisation in Britain to involve people in practical conservation work. Following the success of the Natural Break programme in the UK, BTCV is now developing a series of international working holidays with the aim of introducing volunteers to practical conservation projects abroad. It is hoped that

the British volunteers will adapt to and learn from local lifestyles as well as participate in the community. Projects last for 2-3 weeks and take place throughout Italy. Work is often in conjunction with WWF Italy on the management of their reserves. Ages 18-70. Cost from £50 per week includes food and accommodation; everyone shares in domestic chores. Membership fee £12. No fares or wages paid.

MOVIMENTO CRISTIANO PER LA PACE
via Marco Dino Rossi 12/C, 00173 Rome
Volunteers are invited to work in international teams on summer projects aimed at offering a service in an area of need and promoting self-help within the community; promoting international understanding and the discussion of social problems; and offering young people the chance to live as a group and take these experiences into the context of daily life. Recent conservation projects have included working with local groups to prevent fires in an area south of Rome; assisting with the garlic harvest together with members of an organic farming cooperative in Emilia Romagna; and clearing a beach and organising ecological awareness activities in Sicily. Ages 18+. A knowledge of Italian may be required. 6 hour day, 30-36 hour week. 2-4 weeks, July-August. Food, accommodation and insurance provided, but participants pay own travel costs.

Apply through partner organisation in country of residence. In the UK: Christian Movement for Peace, Bethnal Green United Reformed Church, Pott Street, London E2 0EF or United Nations Association, International Youth Service, Temple of Peace, Cathays Park, Cardiff, CF1 3AP ✆ Cardiff (0222) 223088.

Outside the UK: please see information on page 30.

LA SABRANENQUE CENTRE
INTERNATIONAL rue de la Tour de l'Oume, 30290 Saint Victor la Coste, France
A small, non-profitmaking organisation that has been working since 1969 to preserve, restore and reconstruct abandoned rural sites, and bring them back to life. Aims to give volunteers the chance to discover the interest and pleasure of working directly on genuine rural restoration projects while being part of a cooperative team. In collaboration with Italian preservation organisations, La Sabranenque supervises several conservation projects. Volunteers are needed in small teams in Gnallo, a hamlet in northern Italy, learning traditional construction techniques on-the-job from experienced leaders. Work includes masonry, stone cutting, floor or roof tiling, interior restoration, drystone walling, paving and planting trees. Ages 18+. No experience necessary. 3 weeks, August. Cost L15000 per day includes full board accommodation. Registration fee FF200.

SERVIZIO CIVILE INTERNAZIONALE
via dei Laterani 28, 00184 Rome
Service Civil International promotes international reconciliation through work projects. Volunteers are invited to take part in international workcamps on various conservation projects, which have recently included marking paths and organising an exhibition on turtles on the island of Asinara; building a path through the national park surrounding the Mount Etna volcano; planting trees around a monastery in San Luri; working in the fields, fruit picking and restoring old buildings in the almost deserted village of Mogliazze; and cleaning up a fountain in the castle grounds at Goriano Valli. Ages 18+. Applicants should be highly motivated and prepared to work hard as part of a team. 40 hour week. 2-4 weeks, June-September. Food, accommodation and insurance provided, but not travel. B D PH

Apply through partner organisation in country of residence. In the UK: International Voluntary Service Old Hall, East Bergholt, Colchester, Essex CO7 6TQ.

Outside the UK: please see information on page 30.

COURIERS / REPS

BLADON LINES Personnel Department,
56-58 Putney High Street, London SW15 1SF
✆ **081-785 2200**
Opportunities for representatives to work in the ski resort of Courmayeur. Ages 24+. Relevant experience an advantage, and good spoken Italian essential. Applicants must be

prepared to work hard but will get time to ski. December-May. Salary approx £50-£70 per week, board, lodging, return travel, insurance, ski pass, ski hire and company ski jacket provided. Training week held in London before departure. PH depending on ability. *EC nationals only.*

CANVAS HOLIDAYS LTD 12 Abbey Park Place, Dunfermline, Fife KY2 7PD

Resident couriers, children's couriers, nannies and watersports couriers are required to work on campsites for a holiday company providing accommodation for families in ready-erected fully equipped tents and mobile homes. The work involves a daily routine of tent cleaning as customers arrive and depart, providing information and advice on the local attractions and essential services, helping to sort out problems that might arise, and organising activities for the children and get-togethers for the families. 7 day week with no fixed hours; the workload varies from day to day. At the beginning and end of the season there is a period of physical work when tents are put up and prepared for the customers or taken down and stored for the winter. Other tasks include administration, book keeping and stock control. Ages 18-25. Working knowledge of Italian essential. Applicants are normally those with a year between school and further education, undergraduates or graduates. They need to be reliable, self-motivated, able to turn their hand to new and varied tasks, and with a sense of humour. 6 months, April-October. Return travel, dependent on successful completion of contract, and accommodation in frame tents provided. Salary £80 per week (1992). *UK nationals only. Applications accepted anytime; interviews commence early November.*

CLUB CANTABRICA HOLIDAYS LTD Personnel Department, Holiday House, 146-148 London Road, St Albans, Hertfordshire AL1 1PQ ✆ St Albans (0727) 833141

Organises holidays providing fully equipped tents and caravans. Requires couriers and maintenance staff to work from mid May-early October. Ages 21+. Previous experience an advantage, as is a good knowledge of Italian. 6 day week. Salary from £45 per week with bonus at end of the season. Self-catering accommodation in tents or caravans, travel costs from Watford and insurance provided. *Apply enclosing cv. EC nationals only.*

CRYSTAL HOLIDAYS Crystal House, The Courtyard, Arlington Road, Surbiton, Surrey KT6 6BW ✆ 081-390 8737

Tour operator arranging air, rail and self-drive holidays to the Italian Lakes and winter skiing holidays in the Italian Alps. Representatives are required to meet and greet clients and be responsible for their welfare during their holiday. Ski guides also needed during winter season. Ages 20-35. Previous experience desirable and fluent Italian essential. Approx 60 hour, 7 day week, May-October and December-April. Basic salary plus commission; board, lodging, insurance, travel costs and uniform provided. 1 week training seminar held at beginning of each season. *Apply January/ February for summer season, April/May for winter season.*

EUROCAMP Summer Jobs, (Ref WH), PO Box 170, Liverpool L70 1ES

One of Europe's leading tour operators, specialising in providing quality camping and mobile home holidays for families throughout Europe. Campsite couriers are required: work involves cleaning tents and equipment prior to the arrival of new customers; checking, replacing and making repairs on equipment; replenishing gas supplies; keeping basic accounts and reporting on a weekly basis to England. Couriers are also expected to meet new arrivals and assist holidaymakers with any problems that arise; organise activities and parties; provide information on local tourist attractions and maintain an information noticeboard. At the beginning and end of the season couriers are also expected to help in erecting and dismantling tents. Couriers need to be flexible to meet the needs of customers and be on hand where necessary; they will be able to organise their own free time as the workload allows.

Ages 18+. Applicants should be independent, adaptable, reliable, physically fit, have plenty of initiative and relish a challenging and responsible position. Good working knowledge of Italian also necessary. Preference given to those able to work the whole season, April-September/October; contracts also available for first half season, April-mid July and second half season, mid July-September/October.

Children's couriers are also required, with the energy and enthusiasm to organise a wide range of exciting activities for groups of children aged 4-13. Experience of working with children within this age range is essential, but language ability is not a requirement. Ages 20+. Children's couriers must be available for the whole season, May-September.

For both positions the salary is £91.50 per week. Training is provided together with accommodation in frame tent with cooking facilities, insurance and return travel. *UK and EC passport-holders only. Early application advisable; interviews start September/October.*

KEYCAMP HOLIDAYS 92-96 Lind Road, Sutton, Surrey SM1 4PL ℂ 081-395 8170
One of the UK's largest self-drive camping and mobile home tour operators, offering holidays on over 75 campsites in Europe. Campsite couriers are required to work for 3-6 months in an outdoor environment. Main duties include providing clients with information, organising social and sporting activities, cleaning mobile homes and tents, and providing activities for children. 3+ months, March-July or July-September. Ages 18+. Knowledge of Italian desirable. Accommodation, uniform, training and competitive salary provided. *Applications welcome from September. Phone for application form.*

SCHOOL WORLD The Coach House, Tyn-y-Coed Place, Roath Park, Cardiff CF2 4TX ℂ Cardiff (0222) 470077
Organises skiing holidays for school groups at Tonale, Marilleva, Folgarida, Andalo, Fonte di Pejo and Aprica. Requires representatives to prepare for the groups' arrival, operate quality and safety control, deal with any problems, arrange après ski programmes and generally ensure that clients enjoy their holiday. Ages 19-30. Experience of working with the public and a good knowledge of Italian essential; applicants must also be friendly and outgoing with a high level of common sense and personal organisation. Season lasts from late December-mid April depending on school holiday dates.

Hours worked vary but representatives are on call at all times. Salary £35 per week, with a £15 bonus for each group looked after, depending on completion of contract. Full board accommodation, insurance and reasonable travel costs provided. 4-5 day residential training course held. Recruitment begins July for following winter season. *Applicants must have UK National Insurance number.*

SEASUN/TENTREK HOLIDAYS 71/72 East Hill, Colchester, Essex CO1 2QW ℂ Colchester (0206) 861886
Provides self-catering family holidays in apartments, mobile homes and tents plus activity holidays for schools and groups. Requires representatives for the summer season, April-mid November in Venice. 50/60 hour week. Ages 19+. Applicants should be independent, resourceful with good communication skills and commitment. Knowledge of Italian an advantage, but not essential. Training provided. Salary and subsistence £240 per month; £40 per month extra paid on successful completion of contract. Accommodation, travel, personal insurance and partial uniform provided. B D PH depending on ability.

SKIBOUND Olivier House, 18 Marine Parade, Brighton, East Sussex BN2 1TL
Specialises in winter sports tours for schools and adults, and in activity tours and excursions in spring/summer. Area managers, hotel/chalet managers and representatives are required for the winter and spring/summer seasons, December-April and May-August in the Italian Alps. Posts involve a considerable amount of client contact, and applicants must be presentable and keen to work hard. Ages 21+. Good knowledge of Italian required for representatives and preferably for managers; previous experience an advantage. Insurance, travel and full board accommodation provided. Wages dependent on position.

VENUE HOLIDAYS 21 Christchurch Road, Ashford, Kent TN23 1XD ℂ Ashford (0233) 642505
Small family company offering self-drive holidays with fully-equipped tents, caravans and chalets at campsites in Tuscany and on the Venetian Riviera. Representatives are required

to assist with montage and demontage, clean and maintain accommodation, sort out any problems and organise social events for adults and children.
Ages 18-30. Previous experience of working with the public desirable, as is a working knowledge of Italian. Applicants should also be physically fit, able to work in hot conditions, mentally alert, with a pleasant, easygoing personality. Average 50 hours per week with one day off, but daily workload varies considerably. Season lasts April-October, with a minimum requirement to work all of July and August. Salary approx £45 per week, with possibility of bonus. Tented accommodation, communal meals, insurance and return fare provided.

DOMESTIC

BLADON LINES Personnel Department, 56-58 Putney High Street, London SW15 1SF *℘* 081-785 2200
Opportunities for chalet girls to work in the ski resort of Courmayeur. The work involves cleaning chalets, making beds, caring for guests, shopping and preparing meals. Ages 20+. Experience and/or qualifications in catering or domestic work essential, as is the ability to cook well. Hours are very variable; applicants must be prepared to work hard but will get time to ski. Season lasts December-May. Salary approx £40 per week, board, lodging, return travel, insurance, ski pass, ski hire and company ski jacket provided. One day briefing held in London before departure. PH depending on ability. *EC nationals only.*

CRYSTAL HOLIDAYS Crystal House, The Courtyard, Arlington Road, Surbiton, Surrey KT6 6BW *℘* 081-390 8737
Tour operator arranging winter skiing holidays in the Italian Alps. Chalet staff are required to cook daily breakfast, afternoon tea and 3-course evening meal for clients, and keep chalets clean and tidy. Ages 20-35. Catering qualifications, experience and fluent Italian essential. Approx 60 hour, 6½ day week, December-April. Basic salary plus commission; board, lodging, insurance, travel costs and uniform provided. 1 week training seminar held at beginning of each season. *Apply April/May.*

FARMWORK

Seasonal farmwork is available through local agricultural cooperatives, at *Ufficio di Collocamento* (job centres) or by applying direct to farms. Information on local cooperatives, job centres and farms is available by calling in person at *Centri Informazione Giovani* (youth information centres) which can be found in most major towns. The harvesting seasons are:

May-August
Strawberries, cherries, peaches and plums in Emilia Romagna

September-October
Apples and pears in Emilia Romagna, Piemonte and Trentino. Grapes in Emilia Romagna, Lazio, Piemonte, Puglia, Trentino, Veneto, Toscana

November-December
Olives in Puglia, Toscana, Liguria, Calabria, Sicilia. Flowers in Liguria, Toscana, Lazio, Puglia. Tobacco in Umbria, Puglia, Campania

MONITORS & INSTRUCTORS

CLUB CANTABRICA HOLIDAYS LTD Overseas Department, Holiday House, 146-148 London Road, St Albans, Hertfordshire AL1 1PQ *℘* St Albans (0727) 833141
Organises camping holidays, providing fully equipped tents, caravans and mobile homes. Kiddies club staff are required for the summer season, mid May-early October. Ages 21+. Nursing, teaching or NNEB qualifications required; experience an advantage. 6 day week. Salary from £45 per week, plus bonus at end of season. Self-catering accommodation in tents and caravans, travel costs from Watford and insurance provided. *Apply enclosing cv and SAE/IRCs. EC nationals only.*

SKI EUROPE Brentham House, 45c High Street, Hampton Wick, Kingston-upon-Thames, Surrey KT1 4DG *℘* 081-977 7755
A company with its own ski school operating holidays for groups and school parties. Part-

time ski instructors required for winter sports in Piemonte. Work involves 6 hours teaching per day. BASI or full ASSI qualifications essential, together with a high level of teaching skill. Knowledge of foreign languages useful but not essential; fluent English a prerequisite. 1-2 week periods over Christmas and the New Year, February and April. Instructors receive full board accommodation and ski pass plus travel expenses London/resort, and have access to the same facilities as the clients. Wages approx £75 per week, depending on qualifications. *Interviews take place May-November.*

SUMMER CAMPS (British Institutes), via Matteotti 34, 18038 San Remo ⊘ San Remo (184) 50 60 70
Organises English language courses combined with multi-activity holidays for Italian children under 16 at summer camps in the pine forests and mountain areas of northern Italy. Staff are needed to teach the children English, develop creative thinking and stimulate their appreciation of the natural environment. As well as teaching and supervising children, work involves organising evening entertainment, a gala day and participating in all aspects of camp duties. Activities include hill walking, sports, excursions, handicrafts and drama. Ages 19+. Applicants must have English as their mother tongue. TEFL qualifications and knowledge of Italian useful, but more importantly applicants must have a genuine interest in children, be fun loving, energetic, innovative and enthusiastic. Experience of working with children necessary. Also opportunities for actors and sports/ survival instructors. 65-75 hours per week, mid June-end August. Salary £330 per month, plus full board accommodation and insurance.

WORKCAMPS

ASSOCIAZIONE ITALIANA COSTRUTTORI via Cesare Battisti 3, 20071 Casalpusterlengo (MI)
An international volunteers association with the aims of fighting misery and distress and making a contribution towards a better understanding between nations. Volunteers are needed on workcamps; projects involve living and working in small communities, often rural, which are socially or economically underprivileged. Recent projects have included building, cleaning or renovating community centres, houses, kindergartens, playgrounds, centres for youth at risk and the handicapped, village schools, churches, rehabilitation centres or farm buildings such as granaries, sheep folds and cowsheds; harvesting grain and fruit, collecting firewood, fencing pastures and planting vines; or helping the disadvantaged and physically handicapped. Importance is given to volunteers understanding the significance and purpose of each project and realising the importance of their personal contribution. Ages 18+. 40-48 hour, 5 day week. 3 weeks, July/August. Food, prepared by the volunteers, and tent, family, school or centre accommodation provided, but volunteers should take sleeping bags. Volunteers pay own travel, 40% of which may be refunded. Registration fee L13000 includes insurance. *Apply 2 months in advance.*

COMUNITA EMMAUS Segretariato Campi di Lavoro, via la Luna 1, 52020 Pergine Valdarno, (AR)
Volunteers are needed to join international workcamps in various towns throughout Italy, organised by individual Emmaus communities which are self-supporting through recycling raw materials and old items. This involves collecting, sorting and selling paper, books, clothes, furniture, household apparatus, ironware and metals. Proceeds from the sale of items is often directed to development projects in the Third World. The camps aim to create a community in each place. Ages 18+. Volunteers should be committed to community living and solidarity. 8 hour day, 6 day week. 3+ weeks, June-September. Board, accommodation and accident insurance provided, but volunteers pay their own travel costs and should take a sleeping bag and work clothes.

MOVIMENTO CRISTIANO PER LA PACE via Marco Dino Rossi 12/C, 00173 Rome
Volunteers are invited to work in international teams on summer projects aimed at offering a service in an area of need and promoting self-help within the community; promoting international understanding and the discussion of social problems; and offering young people

the chance to live as a group and take these experiences into the context of daily life. Recent projects have included construction work on a peace pagoda; and building children's playgrounds in Sicily. Ages 18+. Knowledge of Italian may be required. 6 hour day, 5/6 day week. 2-4 weeks, July-August. Food, accommodation and insurance provided, but participants pay own travel costs.

Apply through partner organisation in country of residence. In the UK: Christian Movement for Peace, Bethnal Green United Reformed Church, Pott Street, London E2 0EF or United Nations Association, International Youth Service, Temple of Peace, Cathays Park, Cardiff CF1 3AP ℗ (0222) 223088.

Outside the UK: please see information on page 30.

SERVIZIO CIVILE INTERNATIONALE via dei Laterani 28, 00184 Rome

Service Civil International promotes international reconciliation through work projects. Volunteers are needed to work in international teams. Recent projects have included working at a centre for immigrants in Turin, preparing food, gardening and organising cultural activities; collecting old clothes and tools to raise money for projects in Africa and Asia; organising a photo-exhibition around the theme of peace in Carpi; and creating street theatre involving the local anti-racist movement in Romanengo. Most camps include a study element on ecology, peace and disarmament. Some camps include local volunteers who are recovering from drug-abuse problems, in an effort to help them readapt to social life, and volunteers should be sensitive to their need for a drug-free environment. Ages 18+. Applicants should be highly motivated and prepared to work hard as part of a team. Knowledge of Italian useful. 40 hour week. 2-4 weeks, June-September. Food, accommodation and insurance provided, but not travel. B D PH depending on project.

Apply through partner organisation in country of residence. In the UK: International Voluntary Service Old Hall, East Bergholt, Colchester, Essex CO7 6TQ.

Outside the UK: please see information on page 30.

GENERAL

CANVAS HOLIDAYS LTD 12 Abbey Park Place, Dunfermline, Fife KY2 7PD

A company providing ready-erected fully-equipped tents for family holidays, requires a number of applicants to form flying squads, teams of 5/6 people who help set up and equip 200-250 6 berth frame tents in an area containing approx 12 campsites. Similar work is also available dismantling tents and cleaning and storing equipment. Ages 18-25. Knowledge of Italian not required, but is an advantage as flying squad members sometimes have the opportunity to continue as couriers. Applicants must be sociable in order to work in a small community, fit and able to work hard for long hours under pressure, work without supervision and cope with living out of a rucksack. Driving licence an advantage. Early April-mid June, possibly longer to set up the tents, and September to dismantle them. Salary £80 per week. Tented accommodation, self-catering facilities and outward travel provided; return travel dependent on the completion of contract dates. *UK nationals only.*

COMUNITA' DI AGAPE Centro Ecumenico, Segreteria, 10060 Prali, Torino

An international ecumenical community centre in a remote part of the Italian Alps, constructed by workcamp volunteers in response to the need for reconciliation after the Second World War. Now used for national and international conferences, study camps, courses and other meetings on ecological, peace, Third World, political, cultural, theological and women's issues. A service group made up of volunteers from many countries works alongside the resident community during the summer months. The work is varied and can include kitchen duties, housework, cleaning, working in the coffee bar or laundry, babysitting, maintenance, construction or repair work. There are opportunities for volunteers to take part in the conferences. Knowledge of at least basic Italian useful. Applicants should be willing to make a contribution to the collective life of the community. Ages 18+. 36 hour, 6 day week. 1+ months, June-September. Volunteers are sometimes taken on outside the summer period. Full board accommodation and insurance provided. Volunteers pay own travel costs. Anti-tetanus vaccination advised. *Apply at least 2 months in advance; limited number of places.*

EUROYOUTH LTD 301 Westborough Road, Westcliff, Southend-on-Sea SS0 9PT
Ⓣ Southend-on-Sea (0702) 341434
Holiday guest stays arranged where guests are offered board and lodging in return for an agreed number of hours English conversation with hosts or their children. Time is also available for guests to practise Italian if desired. Mainly ages 15-25, but there are sometimes opportunities for older applicants. 2-3 weeks, mainly July/August. Travel and insurance paid by applicants. Registration fee approx £70. *Apply at least 12 weeks prior to scheduled departure date. UK nationals only.*

SUNSAIL The Port House, Port Solent, Portsmouth, Hampshire PO6 4TH
Ⓣ Portsmouth (0705) 370566
Crew members are required to work aboard cruising yachts flotilla sailing off Sardinia and Corsica. Vacancies for experienced skippers, responsible for the well-being of up to 13 cruising yachts and 60 holidaymakers, giving daily briefings on navigation and providing sailing assistance where necessary. Applicants must have considerable sailing experience, be cheerful, hardworking and able to deal with people of varying backgrounds and ages. Ages 23-30. Also bosuns/mechanics needed, responsible to the skipper for maintaining the marine diesel engines and repairing any other items aboard. Must have excellent knowledge of marine diesels and practical ability to cope with all sorts of breakdowns and repairs. Ages 22-30. Hostesses are required to look after laundry, accounting and cleaning of boats, advising holidaymakers on shops and restaurants, and organising social events and barbecues. Sailing experience useful, but bright personality, patience and adaptability essential. Ages 22-30. All staff should be prepared for very hard work and long hours. 12 hour day, 1 free day per week. Knowledge of German advantageous, but not essential. Staff must work the full season, mid March-November. Salary approx £85 per week, paid monthly. Accommodation on board, return travel and medical insurance provided.

INFORMATION

Japanese Embassy
101-104 Piccadilly, London W1V 9FN
✆ 071-465 6500

British Embassy
1 Ichiban-cho, Chiyoda-ku, Tokyo 102

Tourist office
Japan National Tourist Organisation, 167 Regent
Street, London W1R 7FD ✆ 071-734 9638

Youth hostels
International Youth Hostel Association, Hoken
Kai Kan, 1-2 Sado Hara-Cho, Ichigaya,
Shinjuku-ku, Tokyo 162

Youth & student information
International Student Association of Japan,
Tokyo Chapter, c/o Kokusai Kyoiku, Shinko-
kai, 1-21 Yotsu Ya, Shinjuku-ku, Tokyo 160

Entry regulations A visa is required for all
types of employment. This can only be obtained
once a job has been secured and application
must be made from outside Japan. Before
granting a visa the Japanese Embassy will
require various documents, including copies of
the contract or agreement made between the
applicant and the employer in Japan, details of
the applicant's personal history and proof of
qualifications, plus details of the company/
firm by whom the applicant will be employed; a
complete list of the documents required can be
obtained from the Embassy. If entering Japan
by the Polar Route via Moscow no vaccinations
are necessary; however, if any countries on the
Southern Hemisphere Route have been visited,
vaccination against cholera is strongly
recommended. For further details, contact the
Consular Section of the Embassy.

Job advertising Publicitas Ltd, 517/523 Fulham
Road, London SW6 1HD ✆ 071-385 7723 can
place job advertisements in *Nihon Keizai
Shimbun*, the leading financial business daily.

Travel Campus Travel, 52 Grosvenor Gardens,
London SW1V 0AG ✆ 071-730 8111 (offices
throughout the UK) and Council Travel, 28A

Poland Street, London W1V 3DB © 071-437 7767 (offices also in Paris, Lyon, Düsseldorf, Tokyo and throughout the US) offer low-cost student/youth airfares to Tokyo. Also sell the Japan Rail Pass, giving unlimited travel on Japan Rail Group trains, buses and ferries; cost from ¥27800 (7 days).

North-South Travel Ltd, Moulsham Mill, Parkway, Chelmsford CM2 7PX © Chelmsford (0245) 492882 arranges competitively priced, reliably planned flights to Japan. Profits are paid into a trust fund for the assignment of aid to projects in the poorest areas of the South.

Publications Lonely Planet's guide *Japan - A Travel Survival Kit* £13.95, is an essential handbook for travellers to Japan, offering practical, down-to-earth information for people wanting to explore beyond the usual tourist routes. *Culture Shock! Japan* £6.95 introduces the reader to the people, customs, ceremonies, food and culture of Japan, with checklists of dos and don'ts. Both are available from good bookshops.

Your Guide to Japan is a 35 page booklet containing notes on frontier formalities, climate, currency and travel to and within Japan, accommodation, places of interest, what to do, including festivals, arts and traditional sports plus general information. Available from the Japan National Tourist Organisation, see above. Maps, guides/pamphlets and a variety of other tourist literature also available.

Jobs in Japan US$14.95 + $3 airmail has information and advice for English-speakers wishing to work in Japan. Most opportunities are in the teaching field, but details of other possibilities are also given. Appendix includes list of employment sources, private English language schools, international schools and survival Japanese. Knowledge of Japanese and teaching credentials not essential. Published by Global Press, 697 College Parkway, Rockville, MD 20850, United States. Available in the UK from Vacation Work, 9 Park End Street, Oxford OX1 1HJ © Oxford (0865) 241978, price £9.95.

Information Centres Japan-Care Service/YAC Planning Inc, #902 Towa Shinjuku Co-op, 2-6-3 Shinjuku, Shinjuku-ku, Tokyo, Japan © Tokyo

(03) 3341 8689 Fax (03) 3352 6790 offers a variety of services to foreigners visiting Japan, including help with renting accommodation, advice on Japanese language schools and a talent bank introduction service to companies.

FARMWORK

INTERNATIONAL AGRICULTURAL EXCHANGE ASSOCIATION YFC Centre, National Agricultural Centre, Stoneleigh Park, Kenilworth, Warwickshire CV8 2LG © Coventry (0203) 696578
Operates opportunities for young people involved with agriculture, horticulture or home management to acquire practical work experience in the rural sector, and to strengthen and improve their knowledge and understanding of the way of life in other countries. Participants are given an opportunity to study practical methods on approved training farms and work as trainees, gaining further experience in their chosen field.

Types of farm include pig, dairy or beef farms, horticulture in apple orchards, or enterprises growing mixed vegetables or cucumbers. Participants undertake paid work on the farm, approx 48 hours per week, and live as a member of the host family. Full board and lodging, insurance cover and a minimum net weekly wage of £40 provided. All programmes include at least 3-4 weeks unpaid holiday. 10 day orientation seminar held at the beginning of each programme.

Ages 18-30. Applicants should be single, have good practical experience in the chosen training category, plus a valid driving licence. 8 and 12 months (departing April). Cost from £2350 covers airfare, work permit, administration fee, orientation seminar, information meetings, insurance, supervision, placement with a host family and travel costs to placement. £200 deposit payable. *Apply at least 6 months in advance. UK or Irish passport-holders only.*

Japanese applicants requiring an exchange should apply to Mr K Shimoda, 1293-9 Ishii, Fujimi, Seta, Gunma 371-01.

TEACHERS

English in Asia US$9.95 + $3 airmail is a useful guide for anyone interested in TEFL in Asia. Includes sections on teaching methods, ideas for games and classroom activities, together with the addresses of private English language schools in Japan and other Asian countries. Published by Global Press, 697 College Parkway, Rockville, MD 20850, United States; available in the UK from Vacation Work, 9 Park End Street, Oxford OX1 1HJ ✆ Oxford (0865) 241978, price £8.95.

JAPAN EXCHANGE AND TEACHING (JET) PROGRAMME JET Programme Officer, Council on International Educational Exchange, 33 Seymour Place, London W1H 6AT ✆ 071-224 8896
The Programme seeks to promote mutual understanding between Japan and other countries, and fosters international perspectives by promoting exchange at local levels, as well as intensifying foreign language education in Japan. Conducted under the co-sponsorship of local government authorities in Japan, and the Ministries of Foreign Affairs, Education, and Home Affairs. Vacancies for teaching assistants, carrying out coaching in English language and pronunciation, preparation of teaching materials and participation in extracurricular activities, under the guidance of Japanese academic staff. Placements are mostly in lower and upper secondary schools. Teaching experience or training an advantage. Knowledge of Japanese not essential, but candidates are expected to devote some effort to learning the language before they leave for Japan and whilst they are there. Before departure successful candidates will receive written materials on the programme and on basic Japanese. Further orientation provided on arrival in Tokyo. Contracts are for 1 year, commencing 1 August, and may be renewed in certain circumstances by mutual consent. Salary ¥3,600,000+ per year, tax free; paid holiday on similar terms to Japanese colleagues. Participants are expected to work an average of 40 hours a week. Return air ticket provided. Assistance given on finding accommodation. *British nationals only, under 35 and graduates of a British college or university*

holding at least a Bachelor's degree. Application forms available September. Closing date end November; interviews take place February/March in London or Edinburgh.

Nationals of Ireland, Canada, France, Germany, the United States, Australia and New Zealand should apply to the Japanese Embassy in their country.

YOUNG ABROAD CLUB Kowa Building, 4th floor, 2-3-12 Shinjuku, Shinjuku-ku, Tokyo 160
Cultivates international understanding by promoting youth abroad. Qualified English teachers are needed to work in local cities, for at least 1 year, starting at various times throughout the year. Contracts depend on qualifications and place of work. 5-7 hour day, 6 day week. Salary ¥200,000 per month. Lodging provided in company dormitory. Travel paid by applicants.

WORKCAMPS

NIPPON INTERNATIONAL CAMPING EMBASSADORS (NICE) 501 Viewcity, 2-2-1 Shinjuku, Shinjuku-ku, Tokyo 160
A relatively new workcamp organisation, established by young Japanese who have participated in projects in Europe and the United States over the past few years. Volunteers are invited to take part in international workcamps. Recent projects have included repairing equipment in a youth hostel at the foot of Mount Fuji; forestry work and work alongside people with learning difficulties in Hinode; and cleaning the beach and maintaining footpaths in the coastal town of Zushi. Ages 18+. 2 weeks, August-September. Food, accommodation and insurance provided, but volunteers may have to contribute US$50 towards the cost of each project, in addition to any registration fee levied by the organisation through which they apply. No fares or wages paid. **B D PH W**

Apply through partner organisation in country of residence. In the UK: United Nations Association, International Youth Service, Temple of Peace, Cathays Park, Cardiff CF1 3AP ✆ Cardiff (0222) 223088.

Outside the UK: please see information on page 30.

LATIN AMERICA & CARIBBEAN

INFORMATION

Argentine Embassy
53 Hans Place, London SW1X 0LA
✆ 071-584 6494

Belize High Commission
10 Harcourt House, 19a Cavendish Square,
London W1M 9AD ✆ 071-499 9728

Bolivian Embassy
106 Eaton Square, London SW1W 9AD
✆ 071-235 4248/2257

Brazilian Embassy
32 Green Street, Mayfair, London W1Y 4AT
✆ 071-499 0877

Chilean Embassy
12 Devonshire Street, London W1N 2DS
✆ 071-580 6392

Costa Rica Embassy
5 Harcourt House, 19a Cavendish Square,
London W1M 9AD ✆ 071-495 3985

Cuban Embassy
167 High Holborn, London WC1V 6PA
✆ 071-240 2488

Ecuador Embassy
Flat 3b, 3 Hans Crescent, Knightsbridge,
London SW1X 0LS ✆ 071-584 1367

Jamaican High Commission
1-2 Prince Consort Road, London SW7 2BZ
✆ 071-823 9911

Mexican Embassy
42 Hertford Street, Mayfair, London W1Y 7TF
✆ 071-499 8586

Nicaraguan Embassy
8 Gloucester Road, London SW7 4PP
✆ 071-584 4365

Paraguay Embassy
Braemar Lodge, Cornwall Gardens, London
SW7 4AQ ✆ 071-937 1253

Peruvian Embassy
52 Sloane Street, London SW1X 9SP
✆ 071-235 1917/2545

Entry regulations Details of work permits and entry requirements can be obtained in Britain from the embassies listed above.

Latin America: a guide to employment and opportunities for young people. Offers advice and contacts for those seeking long and short term teaching posts, office work, voluntary work, expeditions and cheap travel. Available from the Hispanic & Luso Brazilian Council, Canning House, 2 Belgrave Square, London SW1X 8PJ ✆ 071-235 2303; price £2 (free to members).

Travel North-South Travel Ltd, Moulsham Mill, Parkway, Chelmsford CM2 7PX ✆ Chelmsford (0245) 492882 arranges competitively priced, reliably planned flights to all parts of Latin America. Its profits are paid into a trust fund for the assignment of aid to projects in the poorest areas of the South.

STA Travel, 74 Old Brompton Road, London SW7 3LQ/117 Euston Road, London NW1 2SX ✆ 071-937 9962 (offices also in Birmingham, Bristol, Cambridge, Leeds, Manchester and Oxford) operates flexible, low-cost flights with open-jaw facility - enter via one country and leave by another - between London and destinations throughout Latin America. Internal flights, accommodation and tours also available.

Campus Travel, 52 Grosvenor Gardens, London SW1W 0AG ✆ 071-730 8111 (offices throughout the UK) and Council Travel, 28A Poland Street, London W1V 3DB ✆ 071-437 7767 (offices also in Paris, Lyon, Düsseldorf, Tokyo and throughout the US) offer low-cost student/ youth airfares to destinations throughout Latin America.

Publications Lonely Planet's travel guides offer practical, down-to-earth information for people wanting to explore beyond the usual tourist routes. Titles include *South America on a Shoestring* £12.95 and *Central America on a Shoestring* £10.95 for the low-budget independent traveller in Latin America, and *Travel Survival Kits* to *Argentina, Uruguay & Paraguay* £10.95, *Bolivia* £6.95, *Brazil* £10.95, *Chile & Easter Island* £6.95, *Colombia* £7.95, *Costa Rica* £6.95, *Ecuador & the Galapagos Islands* £8.95, *Mexico* £11.95 and *Peru* £8.95.

Rough Guides provide comprehensive background information on cities and countries worldwide, plus details on getting there, getting around, places to explore and cheap places to stay. Titles include *Brazil* £7.95, *Guatemala & Belize* £6.95, *Mexico* £6.95 and *Peru* £7.95.

The Traveller's Survival Kit Central America £8.95, and *The Traveller's Survival Kit South America* £10.95 are detailed handbooks containing information on where it's safe to go, travel bargains, budget accommodation and eating and drinking. *The Travellers Survival Kit Cuba* £9.95 gives full information for visitors to Cuba on how to get there, eating out, where to stay, how to get around, what to see and what to do, and includes a set of 20 maps. All published by Vacation Work, 9 Park End Street, Oxford OX1 1HJ ✆ Oxford (0865) 241978.

Michael's Guide to South America £13.95, is detailed and concise, providing invaluable practical advice for all kinds of travellers. Smaller *Michael's Guides* to various areas of Latin America also available, price £6.95. Each guide is illustrated throughout with colour photographs and maps. Published by Inbal Travel.

All the above are available from good bookshops and the larger travel chains.

ARCHAEOLOGY

EARTHWATCH EUROPE Belsyre Court, 57 Woodstock Road, Oxford ✆ Oxford (0865) 311600
Aims to support field research in a wide range of disciplines including archaeology, ornithology, animal behaviour, nature conservation and ecology. Support is given to researchers as a grant and in the form of volunteer assistance. Recent projects have included excavating shell middens in the dry Camarones Valley high in the Andes of northern Chile; uncovering the origins of Buenos Aires; and exploring jungle waterways in Belize to discover and excavate ancient Mayan architecture. 2-3 weeks, all year. Ages 16-80. No special skills required although each expedition may, because of its nature,

demand some talent or quality of fitness. Volunteers should be generally fit, able to cope with new situations, and work with people of different ages and backgrounds, and a sense of humour will help. Members share the costs of the expedition, from £500-£1200, which includes meals, transport and all necessary field equipment, but does not include the cost of travel to the staging area, although assistance may be given in arranging it. Membership fee £22 entitles members to join an expedition and receive magazines and newsletters providing all the information necessary to choose a project. B D PH W depending on project.

COMMUNITY WORK

AMERICAN FRIENDS SERVICE COMMITTEE INC Personnel Department, 1501 Cherry Street, Philadelphia, Pennsylvania 19102, United States
A Quaker organisation undertaking programmes of relief, service and education. Volunteers are needed for manual and educational work on community service projects in villages in Mexico and occasionally other Latin American countries, living and working with the community.
Projects involve constructing and repairing schools, irrigation systems, clinics, roads and houses destroyed by natural disasters. Other work includes reafforestation, gardening, nutrition and health. Project life follows the patterns of village life, and volunteers must fit into and respect local customs. Groups consist of about 15 volunteers; half of the project leaders and volunteers are Mexican.
Participants live as a group, sharing in work and maintenance tasks such as cooking, cleaning, carrying water and weekly market trips. Work can be physically and psychologically strenuous; each unit responds to its situation with creativity and flexibility, and each project develops from the initiatives and skills of the participants.
Ages 18-26. Applicants should be healthy, willing to adapt to group living, prepared to respond positively to the unexpected, be fluent in Spanish and have had some workcamp or community experience. Construction, gardening, arts, crafts, childcare or recreation experience useful. 7 weeks, July-August. Cost

approx US$700 includes orientation conferences, food, accommodation in schools or unused buildings and insurance. Travel and pocket money not provided. Registration fee US$75. *Limited scholarships available. Apply by 1 March.*

AMIGOS DE LAS AMERICAS 5618 Star Lane, Houston, Texas 77057, United States
An international non-profitmaking, private voluntary organisation that provides leadership development opportunities for young people, improved community health for the people of Latin America and better cross-cultural understanding on both American continents. Volunteers are needed to work in teams in schools, health clinics and house-to-house in Latin American countries including Brazil, Mexico, Costa Rica, the Dominican Republic, Paraguay and Ecuador. In addition to providing technical knowledge and supplies, volunteers assume leadership roles as health educators. Projects include animal health and rabies inoculation; human immunization; oral rehydration therapy; community sanitation; latrine construction and dental hygiene.

Ages 16+, no upper limit. Volunteers must complete a training programme. One year of secondary school Spanish required. 4-8 weeks, mid June-mid August. Volunteers live with families or in schools or clinics; food provided by the community. Cost US$2300-$2500, depending on the region visited, includes international travel, board, lodging, in-country transportation, supplies and training materials. Volunteers arrange and pay for domestic travel to point of departure, and are advised to take out health insurance.

VOLUNTARIOS EN ACCION (VEA) PO Box 3556, La Paz, Bolivia ✆ La Paz (2) 36 23 46
A voluntary service organisation aiming to aid rural education. Volunteers are required to help build furniture for schools in rural areas, at the carpentry shop at Huarina on the Bolivian high plateau. 40 hour week, all year round.
Ages 19+. Applicants must be fluent in Spanish; carpentry skills an asset. Food, accommodation and local travel provided, but no pocket money or insurance. Visits to neighbouring communities, local festivals and fairs arranged whenever possible. B D PH

CONSERVATION

CORAL CAY CONSERVATION LTD Sutton
Business Centre, Restmor Way, Wallington,
Surrey SM6 7AH ✆ 081-669 0011
Established in 1986 to assist the Belize
Government in managing and protecting
coastal resources threatened by recent booms in
tourism and fisheries. Volunteers are required
to assist scientific expeditions in surveying the
Belize Barrier Reef, which, second only in size
to the Great Barrier Reef of Australia, is unique
in the western hemisphere as regards its size
and variety of reef types and pristine corals. No
scientific background required as training in
survey techniques is given, but volunteers must
be members of the British Sub-Aqua Club or
have proof of diving ability through another
recognised training agency. Can provide
diving tuition through their branch of the Sub-
Aqua Club.
Ages 16+. 4-12 weeks, all year. Approx 60 hour
week. Subject to weather conditions, two
survey dives take place per day under the
supervision of qualified marine scientists.
Expedition members also share responsibility
for organising dive teams, preparing and
maintaining equipment, and domestic tasks.
Weekends are free for recreational diving,
watersports or visits to rainforests, Mayan
ruins or jaguar and howler monkey reserves.
Cost from £1600, 4 weeks, includes return
flight, transit hotel accommodation, full board
and basic accommodation on site, equipment
hire and scientific training. Volunteers must
take adequate medical precautions and supply
their own diving kit.

EARTHWATCH EUROPE Belsyre Court,
57 Woodstock Road, Oxford ✆ Oxford (0865)
311600
Aims to support field research in a wide range
of disciplines including archaeology,
ornithology, animal behaviour, nature
conservation and ecology. Support is given to
researchers as a grant and in the form of
volunteer assistance. Recent expeditions have
included recording the behaviour of katydids in
the Amazon rainforests of Peru; monitoring
tropical plants in Brazil; and analysing plant
data on the slope of a live volcano in Costa
Rica. Ages 16-75. No special skills are required

although each expedition may, because of its
nature, demand some talent or quality of
fitness. Volunteers should be generally fit, able
to cope with new situations, work with people
of different ages and backgrounds, and a sense
of humour will help. 2-3 weeks, all year.
Members share the costs of the expedition, from
£500-£1200, which includes meals, transport
and all necessary field equipment, but does not
include the cost of travel to staging area,
although assistance may be given in arranging
it. Membership fee £22 entitles members to join
an expedition and receive magazines and
newsletters providing all the information
necessary to choose a project. B D PH W
depending on project.

GENESIS II - TALAMANCA CLOUD FOREST
Apdo 655, 7.050 Cartago, Costa Rica
Volunteers are needed to help with new trail
routing, construction, maintenance and
upgrade work on existing trails, in a rare
tropical white oak cloud forest in the
mountains of Costa Rica. The forest is situated
at a height of 2360m and is being preserved for
academic research and recreational activities
such as bird-watching.
Ages 21+. Experience preferred, but not
essential as training can be given. All
nationalities welcome; some knowledge of
Spanish helpful. 30 hour week, for 4+ weeks, all
year. Volunteers contribute US$100 per week to
cover dormitory style accommodation, all meals
and laundry facilities, but make own travel and
insurance arrangements. *Only fully fit and
dedicated people need apply; competition for places
is strong.*

NICARAGUA SOLIDARITY CAMPAIGN
The Red Rose Club, 129 Seven Sisters Road,
London N7 7QG ✆ 071-272 9616
An organisation set up in 1978, dedicated to
building support for the FSLN (Sandinista
party) and popular organisations in Nicaragua.
Volunteers are invited to join environmental
brigades organised by the Nicaragua Solidarity
Campaign and Environmental Network for
Nicaragua. Work involves planting trees,
terracing and soil conserving. Skills in ecology
or biology welcome but not essential.
Ages 18+. Volunteers must be fit, ready to learn
and prepared to adapt to living and working in
very basic conditions. They should also be

committed to supporting the work being done in Nicaragua on their return. Activists in the labour and environmental movements and people from ethnic minorities particularly encouraged to apply. 30 hour week. Two brigades each summer: 4-6 weeks, July/August; and one in winter: 4 weeks, December/January. 3 day programme of visits and talks included. Cost approx £1100 covers air fare, insurance, local transport, food and accommodation. Advice given on fundraising and/or sponsorship. B D PH accepted, depending on ability. *Apply 3 months in advance. UK residents only.*

UNIVERSITY RESEARCH EXPEDITIONS PROGRAM University of California, Desk M11, Berkeley CA 94720, United States
Volunteers are needed to provide field assistance for research in the natural and social sciences. Projects include studying and documenting plants in the vanishing rainforests of Ecuador; and exploring the benefits of the relationship between plants and insects in the tropical rainforest on the Atlantic lowlands of Costa Rica.
Ages 16+. Applicants should be in good health, have a desire to learn, enthusiasm, a willingness to undertake rigourous but rewarding work, flexibility and sensitivity to other cultures. Skills such as sketching and photography, plus wilderness or camping experience, knowledge of animal behaviour, general ecology and botany useful. 2/3 weeks, all year. Contribution to costs from US$985 covers research equipment and supplies, meals, accommodation and ground transportation. Travel to site not provided but route guidance given. D PH depending on project. *Partial scholarships available. Apply at least 2 months before session.*

LEADERS & GUIDES

EXODUS EXPEDITIONS 9 Weir Road, London SW12 0LT ✆ 081-675 7996
Operates a large range of expeditions including those by truck to South America plus foot treks and shorter adventure holidays to Peru, Ecuador, Bolivia and Brazil. Expedition leaders are needed to lead and drive expeditions; each expedition lasts 4-6 months, but leaders can

expect to be out of the country for up to 24 months at a time. The work involves driving, servicing and when necessary repairing the vehicle; controlling and accounting for expedition expenditure; dealing with border formalities and other official procedures; helping clients with any problems that may arise and informing them on points of interest in the countries visited.
Ages 25-30. Applicants must be single and unattached, able to commit themselves for 2 years, with no personal or financial commitments. Driving experience of large vehicles plus HGV/PSV licence and a good basic knowledge of mechanics preferred. Applicants must have leadership qualities and be resourceful, adaptable and have a good sense of humour. Previous travel experience and a knowledge of foreign languages an advantage. Basic training will be given to suitable candidates; trainees spend 2 months in the company's Wiltshire workshop and then go on an expedition with an experienced leader before leading on their own. Salary £50 per week with food and accommodation provided on site when training and £20 per week plus food and accommodation with £28 per week expenses on the first expedition. Salary £80-£115 per week for a full expedition leader plus food and accommodation.

WORKCAMPS

CUBA SOLIDARITY CAMPAIGN José Marti International Work Brigade, Latin America House, Priory House, Kingsgate Place, London NW6 ✆ 071-388 1429
Offers western Europeans a unique way of seeing life in Cuba and of learning in detail how the people have organised their society since the beginning of the revolution in 1959. Volunteers are needed for agricultural and construction work in the Caimito area of Havana province. As well as tending and picking fruit, the Brigade has contributed to the construction of a polytechnic, a college for building workers and housing for textile workers.
Ages 17+. Volunteers must be fit. 4½ day, 35 hour week, July or September-October. Participants work for 2 weeks and spend the final week travelling around. If possible, 2 days

per week are spent visiting factories, schools, hospitals, industry, agriculture and seeing Havana and its surroundings. Full programme of activities organised including lectures, concerts and films. Applications encouraged from those who have undertaken active political work within ethnic groups, the women's movement, industry, the Labour movement and solidarity organisations. Cost to participants approx £650 covers airfare, food, hostel accommodation, insurance and travel within Cuba, allowing approx £100 for pocket money. Compulsory orientation weekends organised. *Apply by end March.* **B D**

Irish applications to Ireland-Cuba Friendship Society, c/o Margaret O'Leary, 93 Jamestown Road, Finglas East, Dublin 11.

GENERAL

BRITISH UNIVERSITIES NORTH AMERICA CLUB (BUNAC) 16 Bowling Green Lane, London EC1R OBD ✆ 071-251 3472
A non-profit, non-political educational student club venture which aims to encourage interest and understanding between students in Britain and the Americas. Operates a small programme in Jamaica for adventurous people for whom the unique experience gained is more important than the money earned.

The programme is open to full-time degree/ HND students aged 18+. Work is available for the summer months, from end June onwards. Orientation programmes held throughout Britain give advice on finding and choosing a job, obtaining a visa, income tax, accommodation, travel food and budgeting. Cost £634-£751 (1992), depending on departure date, includes administration fees, insurance and round trip flight to Montego Bay. Applicants will need to show proof of purchase of £150 travellers cheques. *EC nationals only. Application forms available January; apply by 30 April.*

APPLYING FOR A JOB

Before applying, read carefully all the information given. Unless otherwise indicated, applications should be made in writing. Check in particular:

✐ skills, qualifications or experience required

✐ the full period of employment expected

✐ any restrictions of age, sex or nationality

✐ application deadlines

✐ any other points, particularly details of insurance cover, and other costs you may have to bear such as travel and accommodation.

When writing to any organisation it is **essential** to mention **Working Holidays 1993** and to enclose a large, stamped, self-addressed envelope, or if overseas, a large addressed envelope and at least two International Reply Coupons (available at Post Offices). When applying be sure to include the following:

✐ name, address, date of birth, nationality, sex

✐ education, qualifications, relevant experience, skills, languages spoken

✐ period of availability

✐ a passport-size photo, particularly if you are to have contact with the public

✐ anything else asked for, eg a *cv*

INFORMATION

Luxembourg Embassy
27 Wilton Crescent, London SW1X 8SD
© 071-235 6961

British Embassy
14 boulevard Roosevelt, 2450 Luxembourg

Tourist office
Luxembourg Tourist Office, 122 Regent Street,
London W1R 5FE © 071-434 2800

Youth hostels
Centrale des Auberges de Jeunesse
Luxembourgeoises, 18 place d'Armes, 2346
Luxembourg

Youth & student information
Service National de la Jeunesse, 1 rue de la
Poste, BP707, 2346 Luxembourg

Union Nationale des Étudiants
Luxembourgeois, 20 avenue Marie-Thérèse,
2132 Luxembourg

Entry regulations UK citizens intending to
work in Luxembourg should have full
passports. EC nationals may stay in
Luxembourg for up to 3 months; those wishing
to stay longer must apply to the local police for
a residence permit. Non-EC nationals must
have a job and a work permit (*Déclaration
Patronale*), and have *Permis de Séjour* stamped in
their passport before entering Luxembourg.

French and German, in addition to the
Luxembourg language, are commonly used in
business and industry, and anyone seeking
employment should have a good knowledge of
at least one of these languages.

Job advertising *Letzeburger Journal*, rue
A Fischer 123, PO Box 2101, 1251 Luxembourg
is a leading daily newspaper which will accept
advertisements for jobs.

Luxemburger Wort, rue Christophe-Plantin 2,
2988 Gasperich-Luxembourg is the largest and
most important daily newspaper in
Luxembourg accepting job advertisements.

Travel Campus Travel, 52 Grosvenor Gardens, London SW1W 0AG © 071-730 3402 (offices throughout the UK) and Council Travel, 28A Poland Street, London W1V 3DB © 071-437 7767 (offices also in Paris, Lyon, Düsseldorf, Tokyo and throughout the US) offer Eurotrain under 26 fares and youth/student airfares to Luxembourg.

The Benelux Tourrail Card is available for 5 days within a period of 17, allowing unlimited rail travel on the national railway networks of Luxembourg, Belgium and the Netherlands. March-October; cost from £45. Details from Netherlands Railways, 25/28 Buckingham Gate, London SW1E 6LD © 071-630 1735.

Publications *The Rough Guide to Holland, Belgium and Luxembourg* £6.95 provides comprehensive background information on Luxembourg, plus details on getting there, getting around, places to explore and cheap places to stay. Available from good bookshops.

Live & Work in Belgium, The Netherlands & Luxembourg £8.95 is a guide for those interested in finding temporary or permanent work, starting a business or buying a home in the Benelux countries. Published by Vacation Work, 9 Park End Street, Oxford OX1 1HJ © Oxford (0865) 241978.

Grand Duchy of Luxembourg contains practical information for visitors covering entry requirements, climate, accommodation, transport, outdoor activities, museums, special events and places of interest. Available from the Luxembourg Tourist Office, see above.

Accommodation Gîtes d'Etape Luxembourgeois, Caritas, 29 rue Michel Welter, 2730 Luxembourg have rest houses and vacation homes available throughout Luxembourg. All year; cost approx FB120-FB180 per night, self-catering.

The Luxembourg Tourist Office, see above, can provide a booklet listing accommodation throughout the country. Also produce a leaflet *Camping* which lists all the authorised camping sites together with facilities available.

AU PAIR / CHILDCARE

There is no special agency for au pairs in Luxembourg; positions may be found through general employment agencies, through adverts in local newspapers/magazines or through the government employment bureau, Administration de l'Emploi, see below. The employer must obtain from this office an *Accord Placement Au Pair*, which is an agreement specifying the conditions and obligations governing the au pair's stay. This agreement must be filled in by the host family and forwarded to the au pair for signature. The agreement is then submitted for approval to the Administration de l'Emploi, which then forwards copies to the parties concerned. This contract must be concluded before the au pair leaves her country of residence. This is particularly important for non-EC nationals, as for them the contract serves as a work permit. The agreement stipulates that the host family is required to affiliate the au pair to all branches of the Luxembourg Social Security system. If the au pair falls ill, the host family must continue to provide board and lodging and guarantee all appropriate treatment until necessary arrangements have been made.

DOMESTIC

LUXEMBOURG EMBASSY 27 Wilton Crescent, London SW1X 8SD © 071-235 6961 Can supply a booklet *Hotels, Auberges, Restaurants, Pensions*, published annually, which includes detailed listings of establishments all over Luxembourg which often need seasonal domestic staff. *Available free on receipt of an A4 SAE. Those outside the UK should contact the Luxembourg Embassy in their country of residence.*

TEACHERS

LUXEMBOURG EMBASSY 27 Wilton Crescent, London SW1X 8SD © 071-235 6961 Publishes an information sheet on education in Luxembourg, listing English-speaking schools, language and secretarial schools, *lycées*, and *collèges d'enseignement* which may have vacancies for teachers. Opportunities in private schools only, as Luxembourg nationals only can teach in state schools. *Available free on receipt of an A4 SAE. Those outside the UK should contact the Luxembourg Embassy in their country of residence.*

GENERAL

ADMINISTRATION DE L'EMPLOI 38a rue Philippe II, BP 23, 2010 Luxembourg ℂ 47 68 55-1
The government employment office dealing with all employment enquiries, can provide information on the availability of work in Luxembourg.

AIDA LUXEMBOURG 70 Grand'rue, 1660 Luxembourg
Can provide information on temporary jobs for students.

BUREAU-SERVICE 2 allée Leopold Goebel, 1635 Luxembourg
Can provide information on temporary office jobs.

LUXEMBOURG EMBASSY 27 Wilton Crescent, London SW1X 8SD ℂ 071-235 6961
Can provide lists for those interested in working in Luxembourg; one gives the addresses of British and American firms, the other lists Luxembourg's major companies, classified according to their branch of activity. *Available free on receipt of an A4 SAE. Those outside the UK should contact the Luxembourg Embassy in their country of residence.*

MANPOWER-AIDE TEMPORAIRE 19 rue Glesener, 1631 Luxembourg
Can provide information on temporary jobs in all professions.

OFFICENTER 25 boulevard Royal, 2449 Luxembourg
Can provide information on temporary office jobs for students.

INFORMATION

Malta High Commission
16 Kensington Square, London W8 5HH
✆ 071-938 1712/6

British High Commission
7 St Anne Street, Floriana

Tourist office
Malta National Tourist Organisation, 4 Winsley Street, London W1N 7AR ✆ 071-323 0506

Youth hostels
Malta Youth Hostels Association, 17 Tal-Borg Street, Pawla

Youth & student information
Youth Service Organisation, c/o Director of Education, Floriana

NSTS, Student and Youth Travel, 220 St Paul Street, Valletta

Entry regulations Foreign nationals may not seek or accept employment after their arrival in Malta unless they have a prior work permit. Work permits must be applied for by the prospective employer on behalf of the foreign national; the employer must show sufficient proof that the foreign national will fill a position for which no skilled Maltese national is presently available. British nationals do not need a visa and may stay for up to 3 months.

Travel *Malta and Its Islands* is an information sheet giving brief details of history, climate, health, accommodation, food, shopping, places of interest, sport, festivals and other events. Available free from the Malta National Tourist Organisation, see above.

Campus Travel, 52 Grosvenor Gardens, London SW1W 0AG ✆ 071-730 3402 (offices throughout the UK) offers youth/student airfares to Malta.

When writing to any organisation it is essential to mention Working Holidays 1993 and enclose a large stamped, self-addressed envelope, or if overseas, a large addressed envelope and at least two International Reply Coupons.

GENERAL

BRITISH UNIVERSITIES NORTH AMERICA CLUB (BUNAC) 16 Bowling Green Lane, London EC1R 0BD ℂ 071-251 3472
A non-profit, non-political educational student club which aims to encourage interest and understanding between students. Administers a Work Malta programme for catering students who wish to gain course-related experience. Participants spend 3-6 months in accredited Maltese hotels or restaurants between April and October (start date is flexible). Students and their tutors are encouraged to set out work experience criteria so that a suitable position can be arranged. Cost £225 (1992) includes placement, working visa, round-trip flight, pre-booked accommodation for 2 nights and orientation on arrival, assessment (optional) and support from cooperators. Applicants must be British nationals who are enrolled in a full-time course of HND level or above in catering or hotel administration at a recognised college, polytechnic or university in the UK.

Organised in cooperation with NSTS Student and Youth Travel, Malta.

MALTA YOUTH HOSTELS ASSOCIATION 17 Triq Tal-Borg, Pawla
Volunteers motivated to help and work hard to develop Malta's tourist industry are needed to work as directed by the Malta Youth Hostels Association. This will mainly involve support work in Malta and Gozo's youth hostels, including office work and administration, renovation and construction work such as painting, plastering, building walls and repairing roofs. Ages 16-50; those under 18 must provide a letter giving parental consent. 21 hours per week. 2-12 weeks, all year, commencing the 1st and 15th of each month. Hostel accommodation provided with volunteers preparing their own meals. Participants pay own travel and insurance costs. Cost from £21 for 2 weeks covers cost of evening meals and deposit.

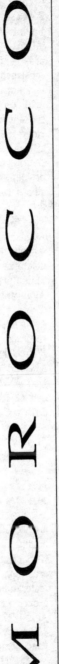

INFORMATION

Moroccan Embassy
49 Queen's Gate Gardens, London SW7 5NE
℡ 071-581 5001/4
Consular Section: Diamond House, 97/99 Praed
Street, London W2 ℡ 071-724 0719

British Embassy
17 boulevard de la Tour Hassan, BP45, Rabat

Tourist office
Moroccan Tourist Office, 205 Regent Street,
London W1R 7DE ℡ 071-437 0073

Youth hostels
Union Marocaine des Auberges de Jeunesse,
6 Place Amiral Philibert, Casablanca

Fédération Royale Marocaine des Auberges de
Jeunesse, avenue Oqba Ibn Nafii, Meknes

Entry regulations British nationals require a
full passport and a work permit before taking
up employment in Morocco and this will be
applied for by the prospective employer, and
issued by the Ministry of Labour. British
passport holders are free to travel without a
visa, but their passport must be valid for 6+
months on their day of entry into Morocco.
Those wishing to stay for over 3 months must
register with the police, justifying their stay
with a valid work permit. It should be noted
that it is difficult for foreigners to obtain
employment in Morocco. An information sheet,
Employment in Morocco, is available from the
Moroccan Consulate.

Travel Campus Travel, 52 Grosvenor Gardens,
London SW1W 0AG ℡ 071-730 8111 (offices
throughout the UK) and Council Travel, 28A
Poland Street, London W1V 3DB ℡ 071-437
7767 (offices also in Paris, Lyon, Düsseldorf,
Tokyo and throughout the US) offer Eurotrain
under 26 fares to destinations in Morocco.

Publications Lonely Planet's *Morocco, Algeria &
Tunisia - A Travel Survival Kit* £10.95 offers
practical, down-to-earth information for
independent travellers wanting to explore
beyond the usual tourist routes.

The Rough Guide to Morocco £7.99 provides comprehensive background information on Morocco, plus details on getting there, getting around, places to explore and cheap places to stay. Both the above are available from good bookshops.

WORKCAMPS

LES AMIS DES CHANTIERS INTERNATIONAUX DE MEKNES (ACIM) PO Box 8, Meknes

Volunteers are invited to take part in international workcamps. Projects generally include archaeological digs, agricultural and construction work. Excursions, cultural and social evenings arranged. Ages 18+. Applicants should have previous workcamp or voluntary work experience. 30-35 hour week, afternoons and weekends free. 3 weeks, July/August. Board, lodging and insurance provided, but no pocket money. Travel costs paid by volunteers.

CHANTIERS JEUNESSE MAROC BP 1351, Rabat RP

Volunteers invited to take part in international workcamps concerning the economic, social and cultural development of the people. Recent projects have included restoring arcades and the historical gates of the town of Essaouira; gardening and landscaping in the town parks of Fes; building, painting and cleaning to help in the reconstruction of a youth centre in Ahfir; and helping out with children at an orphanage in Rabat. Ages 18+. 35 hour week. 3 weeks, July and August. Food, school accommodation and some insurance cover provided, but not travel. Only basic accommodation is provided, sometimes with no running water. Applicants should have previous workcamp or voluntary work experience. Knowledge of French or Arabic an advantage.

Apply through partner organisation in country of residence. In the UK: Quaker International Social Projects, Friends House, Euston Road, London, NW1 2BJ (experienced volunteers only) or United Nations Association, International Youth Service, Temple of Peace, Cathays Park, Cardiff CF1 3AP ℗ Cardiff (0222) 223088.

Outside the UK: please see information on page 30.

CHANTIERS SOCIAUX MAROCAINS PO BOX 456, Rabat RP

Volunteers are required to work in international teams on manual and community projects. Recent projects have included construction work at children's centres in Benmim and Harhoura; renovation work at youth centres in Kenitra and Marakesh; and conservation and clearance work at Al Houcima, Sidi Kacem and other towns and villages. Volunteers share in discussions centring on the host community and world problems and are expected to take a full part in all aspects of the camp. Walks and excursions arranged.

Ages 18+. 35 hour week. 2-3 weeks, July and August. Food, accommodation in colleges, schools, centres or rural communes and insurance provided. Participants cook on a rota basis and should take a sleeping bag. Applicants pay their own travel costs.

Apply through partner organisation in country of residence. In the UK: Quaker International Social Projects, Friends House, Euston Road, London NW1 2BJ (experienced volunteers only) or United Nations Association International Youth Service, Temple of Peace, Cathays Park, Cardiff CF1 3AP ℗ Cardiff (0222) 223088.

Applications from outside the UK: please see information on page 30.

PENSÉE & CHANTIERS BP 1423, Rabat RP

Arranges various cultural and social activities, training schemes and workcamps. Volunteers are needed for a variety of workcamps aimed at helping community schemes. Projects include work on schools, youth clubs, social centres and green spaces, involving construction, restoration, painting and gardening tasks. No experience necessary.

Ages 17+. All nationalities accepted. 5 hour day, 6 day week. 3 weeks, July and August. Food, accommodation and insurance provided, but participants should take a sleeping bag and work clothes. Social and cultural activities organised, including excursions and discussions.

NETHERLANDS

INFORMATION

Royal Netherlands Embassy
38 Hyde Park Gate, London SW7 5DP
© 071-584 5040

British Embassy
Lange Voorhout 10, 2514 ED, The Hague

Tourist office
Netherlands Board of Tourism, 25-28
Buckingham Gate, London SW1E 6LD
© 071-630 0451

Youth hostels
Stichting Nederlandse Jeugdherberg Centrale
(NJHC), Prof Tulpplein 4, 1018 GX Amsterdam

Youth & student information
EXIS, Centre for International Youth Activities,
Prof Tulpstraat 2, 1018 HA Amsterdam/PO Box
15344, 1001 MH Amsterdam

Foreign Student Service, Oranje Nassaulaan 5,
1075 AH Amsterdam

Entry regulations UK citizens intending to
work in the Netherlands should have a full
passport. EC nationals may stay for up to 3
months; those wishing to stay longer should
contact the local police within 8 days of arrival
in order to apply for a residence permit.
Citizens of non-EC countries must possess a
work permit, which can be applied for by the
employer. Visitors may be asked to prove that
they have adequate means of self-support for
the duration of their proposed stay and that the
cost of the return journey can be covered.
Further details of the regulations governing
temporary employment, plus useful
information for those seeking a job, are
contained in an information sheet, *Information
about working and residence in the Netherlands*,
available from the Netherlands Embassy.

Job advertising Frank L Crane (London) Ltd,
International Press Representation, 5/15
Cromer Street, Grays Inn Road, London WC1H
8LS © 071-837 3330 can place job
advertisements in *Het Parool, De Volkskrant,
Trouw* and all leading Dutch newspapers.

Publicitas Ltd, 517/523 Fulham Road, London SW6 1HD ℂ 071-385 7723 can place job advertisements in *De Telegraaf* (largest morning daily) and numerous magazines.

Travel NBBS Travel, Informatiecentrum, Schipholweg 101, PO Box 360, 2300 AJ Leiden is the national office for youth and student travel. It administers 33 travel offices including 7 in Amsterdam, and can arrange cheap travel and hotel accommodation.

Rail Rovers entitle the holder to unlimited travel for 3/7 days on the Netherlands Railways network; cost approx £25/£39.50. A Public Transport Link Rover, for use in conjunction with the 7 day Rail Rover, entitles the holder to unlimited travel on Amsterdam and Rotterdam metro systems and on buses and trams throughout the Netherlands. Cost approx £7.50 for 7 days.
The Teenage Rover Ticket is available for 4 days within a period of 10 days, June-August, to those aged up to 19; cost approx £16.
The Benelux Tourrail Card is available for 5 days within a period of 17 days, allowing unlimited travel on the national railway networks of the Netherlands, Luxembourg and Belgium during March-October; cost from £51. Bicycle hire is available at reduced rates for rail ticket holders at many stations.
Details from Netherlands Railways, 25/28 Buckingham Gate, London SW1E 6LD & 071-630 1735.

Euro-Domino is a pass allowing 5 days unlimited rail travel in 1 month on the railways of the Netherlands. Cost from £29 (ages under 26) or £38 (ages 26+). Available from British Rail International Rail Centre, Victoria Station, London SW1V 1JY ℂ 071-928 5151.

Campus Travel, 52 Grosvenor Gardens, London SW1W 0AG ℂ 071-730 3402 (offices throughout the UK) and Council Travel, 28A Poland Street, London W1V 3DB ℂ 071-437 7767 (offices also in Paris, Lyon, Düsseldorf, Tokyo and throughout the US) offer Eurotrain under 26 fares and youth/student flights to destinations in the Netherlands.

Publications *The Rough Guide to Holland, Belgium, and Luxembourg* £6.95 and *The Rough*

Guide to Amsterdam £6.99 provide comprehensive background information on the Netherlands and Amsterdam plus details on getting around, places to explore and cheap places to stay. Available from good bookshops.

Live & Work in Belgium, The Netherlands & Luxembourg £8.95 is a guide for those interested in finding temporary or permanent work, starting a business or buying a home in the Benelux countries. Published by Vacation Work, 9 Park End Street, Oxford OX1 1HJ ℂ Oxford (0865) 241978.

Information centres EXIS, Centre for International Youth Activities, PO Box 15344, 1001 MH Amsterdam/Prof Tulpstraat 2, 1018 AH Amsterdam is the national centre fostering international contacts between young people. Provides information and advice, mainly to young Dutch people, on holidays, vacation work, au pair placements, language courses and exchanges.

Accommodation Ernst Sillem Hoeve, Soestdykerweg 10b, 3734 MH Den Dolder is an international YMCA conference and holiday centre with 100 beds. Open all year; all ages. Also YMCA camps with 25-60 beds in tents and dormitories, May-September; ages up to 24.

Hans Brinker Hotel, Kerkstraat 136-138, 1017 GR Amsterdam has budget accommodation in a variety of rooms from singles to dormitories of up to 12 beds. Facilities include restaurants, cafe, bar and tourist information. Open all year. Cost from Dfl 23 bed and breakfast, summer.

Netherlands Board of Tourism, see above, can provide information on virtually every type of accommodation available in the Netherlands.

AU PAIR / CHILDCARE

Au pair posts in the Netherlands are open to both males and females, aged between 18 and 30. In return for doing light housework and looking after children au pairs get board, lodging, insurance, a minimum of Dfl 450 per month and the opportunity to attend a language course. Posts are generally for a minimum of 6 months, maximum 1 year.

The following agencies can arrange au pair and childcare placements in the Netherlands:

ACADEMY AU PAIR AGENCY Glenlea, Dulwich Common, London SE21 7ES ✆ 081-299 4599
Can place au pairs. Ages 18-27. Applicants should have some knowledge of Dutch. Pocket money approx £30-£35 per week. Administration charge £40. Positions also available as nannies and mothers' helps for those with qualifications/experience.

ANGLO PAIR AGENCY 40 Wavertree Road, Streatham Hill, London SW2 3SP ✆ 081-674 3605
Can place au pairs and au pairs plus. Ages 18-27. Pocket money £30-£50 per week. Also placements for experienced nannies and mothers' helps; salary up to £100 per week. Agency fee £40.

AVALON AGENCY Thursley House, 53 Station Road, Shalford, Guildford, Surrey GU4 8HA ✆ Guildford (0483) 63640
Can place au pairs. Ages 18-30. 6+ months. Basic knowledge of Dutch needed. Pocket money paid. Service charge £40.

HELPING HANDS AU PAIR & DOMESTIC AGENCY 39 Rutland Avenue, Thorpe Bay, Essex SS1 2XJ ✆ Southend-on-Sea (0702) 602067
Can place au pairs and mothers' helps. Ages 18-27. Pocket money approx £30 per week for au pairs, higher for mothers' helps. Introduction fee £40 on acceptance of a family. *UK nationals only.*

HOME FROM HOME Walnut Orchard, Chearsley, Aylesbury, Buckinghamshire HP18 0DA ✆/Fax Aylesbury (0844) 208561
Can place au pairs. Ages 18+. Pocket money £25 per week. Placement fee £40.

JUST THE JOB EMPLOYMENT AGENCY 8 Musters Road, West Bridgford, Nottingham NG2 5PL ✆ Nottingham (0602) 813224
Can place au pairs, mothers' helps and nannies. Ages 18+. Weekly pocket money £30-£40 (au pairs) or £75-£140 (other positions). *UK nationals only.*

LANGTRAIN INTERNATIONAL Torquay Road, Foxrock, Dublin 18, Ireland ✆ Dublin (1) 289 3876
Can place au pairs with families throughout the Netherlands. Ages 18+. Pocket money £25-£40 per week. Placement fee £55.

PROBLEMS UNLIMITED AGENCY 86 Alexandra Road, Windsor, Berkshire SL4 1HU ✆ Windsor (0753) 830101
Can place au pairs. Ages 18-27. Pocket money £30-£35 per week. Service charge £40.

STUDENTS ABROAD LTD 11 Milton View, Hitchin, Hertfordshire SG4 0QD ✆ Hitchin (0462) 438909
Can place au pairs. Ages 18-27. Pocket money approx £30-£35 per week. Service charge £40.

CONSERVATION

SIW INTERNATIONALE VRIJWILLIGERS-PROJEKTEN Willemstraat 7, 3511 RJ Utrecht
Volunteers are invited to work in international teams on conservation projects. Recent projects have included haymaking, reed-cutting and ditch clearing in the fenland nature reserve of the Maarsseveense Plassen; and building and repairing alternative energy producing machines such as windmills, water pumps and solar panels in Twente. Study elements include environmental education, pollution and nature protection.
Ages 18-30. Volunteers with previous workcamp experience preferred. 30 hour, 5 day week, with weekends free. 2/3 weeks, July-August. Food, accommodation in schools, farms, tents or scout huts and insurance provided, but not travel. B D PH

Apply through partner organisation in country of residence. In the UK: International Voluntary Service, Old Hall, East Bergholt, Colchester, Essex CO7 6TQ or
Quaker International Social Projects, Friends House, Euston Road, London NW1 2BJ (experienced volunteers only) or
United Nations Association, International Youth Service, Temple of Peace, Cathays Park, Cardiff CF1 3AP ✆ Cardiff (0222) 223088.

Outside the UK: please see information on page 30.

COURIERS / REPS

KEYCAMP HOLIDAYS 92-96 Lind Road, Sutton, Surrey SM1 4PL ℗ 081-395 8170
One of the UK's largest self-drive camping and mobile home tour operators, offering holidays on over 75 campsites in Europe. Campsite couriers are required to work for 3-6 months in an outdoor environment. Main duties include providing clients with information, organising social and sporting activities, cleaning mobile homes and tents, and providing activities for children. 3+ months, March-July or July-September. Ages 18+. Knowledge of Dutch desirable. Accommodation, uniform, training and competitive salary provided. *Applications welcome from September; phone for application form.*

PGL YOUNG ADVENTURE LTD Personnel Department, Alton Court, Penyard Lane (878), Ross-on-Wye, Herefordshire HR9 5NR ℗ Ross-on-Wye (0989) 767833
Couriers are required to escort groups of young people on Dutch barge holidays, starting and finishing in London. Couriers are totally responsible for the welfare of their group, and for giving them an enjoyable holiday. The barge provides accommodation for up to 34 guests, and each group has 2 couriers. Holidays run for 10 days and the itinerary allows for frequent stops at centres of interest within easy access of the moorings. Ages 21+. Applicants should have skill and experience of working with children, and in controlling groups of teenagers aged 12-15 and 16-18. They should be committed, tolerant, flexible, enthusiastic and have stamina, energy and a sense of humour. Fairly demanding job, and preference will be given to those with maturity, resourcefulness, strong personality and a previous knowledge of the area. Couriers are employed for 1 or 2 trips, July-September. Pocket money £4 per day plus expenses, approx £75 per 10 day trip.

When writing to any organisation it is essential to mention Working Holidays 1993 and enclose a large stamped, self-addressed envelope, or if overseas, a large addressed envelope and at least two International Reply Coupons.

FARMWORK

CENTRAAL BUREAU ARBEIDSVOORZIENING Bureau Internationale Arbeidsbemiddeling en Stagiaires, PO Box 437, 2280 AK Rijswijk
Can assist those interested in holiday or seasonal farmwork by putting them in touch with potential employers. Most vacancies occur in the floriculture/flower bulb sector, in the provinces of Noord-Holland and Zuid-Holland. Work involves digging, peeling, sorting, counting and packing bulbs, and getting bulbs and flowers ready for transport. Also some vacancies in fruit/vegetable greenhouses of the Westland in Zuid-Holland, helping with the harvest, sorting and packing produce. Ages 16+. Applicants should be fit and prepared for hard, dirty work outdoors in all weathers and/or indoors in hot greenhouses. 8+ weeks, peak period October-December. Hours variable. Salary dependent on age, circumstances, hours worked and form of payment. Transport and accommodation usually arranged by applicants. *EC nationals only.*

INTERNATIONAL FARM EXPERIENCE PROGRAMME YFC Centre, National Agricultural Centre, Stoneleigh Park, Kenilworth, Warwickshire CV8 2LG ℗ Coventry (0203) 696584
Provides assistance to young farmers and nurserymen by finding places in farms and nurseries abroad to enable them to broaden their knowledge of agricultural methods. Opportunities to take part in practical training schemes, living and working on a farm, where the work is matched as far as possible with the applicant's requirements. 3-12 months, all year. Pocket money, board and lodging provided. The work is hard; 8-10 hour day, 6 day week, every other weekend free. Ages 18-26. Applicants must have a valid driving licence, at least 2 years practical experience, 1 year of which may be at an agricultural college, and intend to make a career in agriculture or horticulture. Registration fee £70. *UK nationals only; apply at least 4 months in advance.*

Dutch applicants requiring an exchange should apply to Stichting Uitwisseling, Postbus 97, 1860 AB Bergen NH.

WORKCAMPS

ICVD Pesthuislaan 25, 1054 RF Amsterdam
Volunteers are needed to work in international
teams on summer projects aimed at offering a
service in an area of need and generating self-
help within the community; promoting
international understanding and the discussion
of social problems; and offering young people
the chance to live as a group and take these
experiences into the context of daily life. Recent
projects have included repairing tools to be sent
to Nicaragua and Zimbabwe for the Dutch
branch of Tools for Self-Reliance; building and
renovation work; fruit picking and construction
work in a former monastery at De Weyst;
manual work at an organic mixed farm at
Beemster; and converting a farmhouse into a
centre for people who have had traumatic
experiences, in Giethoorn.
Ages 18+. 6 hour day, 30-36 hour week. 2-3
weeks, June-August. Food, accommodation and
insurance provided, but participants pay their
own travel costs.

Apply through partner organisation in country of
residence. In the UK: Christian Movement for
Peace, Bethnal Green United Reformed Church,
Pott Street, London E2 0EF.

Outside the UK: please see information on page 30.

**SIW INTERNATIONALE VRIJWILLIGERS-
PROJEKTEN Willemstraat 7, 3511 RJ Utrecht**
Volunteers are invited to work in international
teams on voluntary construction and social
projects. Recent projects have included
collecting and repairing bicycles, furniture and
clothes in Tilburg; organising holiday activities
for underprivileged children in Amersfoort;
repairing and painting items in a children's
playground in Enschede; and organising
handicraft activities for refugees in Goes. All
camps include a related study theme.
Excursions and films arranged.

Ages 18-30. Volunteers with previous
workcamp experience preferred. 30-35 hour, 5
day week, with weekends free. 2/3 weeks, July
and August. Food, accommodation in schools,
farms, tents or Scout huts and insurance
provided, but not travel. **B D PH**

Apply through partner organisation in country of
residence. In the UK: International Voluntary
Service, Old Hall, East Bergholt, Colchester, Essex
CO7 6TQ or
Quaker International Social Projects, Friends
House, Euston Road, London, NW1 2BJ
(experienced volunteers only) or
United Nations Association, International Youth
Service, Temple of Peace, Cathays Park, Cardiff CF1
3AP © (0223) 223088.

Outside the UK: please see information on page 30.

**VRIJWILLIGE INTERNATIONALE AKTIE
Pesthuislaan 25, 1054 RH Amsterdam**
VIA is the Dutch branch of Service Civil
International which promotes international
reconciliation through work projects. Recent
projects include repairing old tools to send to
refugee communities in Malawi and El
Salvador; harvesting potatoes, onions and
pumpkins on a biodynamic farm at a Camphill
community in Bosch en Duin; painting the
refectory and candle factory of a Benedictine
monastery in Egmond; and repairing bikes and
laying cycle paths at a centre for asylum
seekers in Stevensbeek. Study themes include
Third World problems, human rights, peace,
apartheid systems, women and violence. Ages
18+. Applicants should be highly motivated
and prepared to work hard as part of a team.
35-40 hour week. 2-4 weeks, June-September.
Food, accommodation and insurance provided,
but not travel. **B D PH W**

Apply through partner organisation in country of
residence. In the UK: International Voluntary
Service, Old Hall, East Bergholt, Colchester, Essex
CO7 6TQ.

Outside the UK: please see information on page 30.

GENERAL

**BAARTMAN & KONING BV PO Box 27,
2170 AA Sassenheim**
A horticultural organisation supplying flower
bulbs and roots for export. Vacancies available
for applicants interested in horticulture. Work
includes packing, handling and cleaning of
bulbs. Applicants should be hard working and
require stamina; experience in the flower bulb

industry preferred. 40 hour week with possibility of paid overtime, January-March and late July-late September. Ages 17+. Wages according to age and experience. Accommodation not provided although reasonable bed and breakfast/campsite facilities nearby. Travel costs paid by applicants. *EC nationals only.*

Applicants must register in person at the Baartman & Koning Factory, Teylingerlaan 7, Voorhout.

CENTRAAL BUREAU ARBEIDSVOORZIENING
Arbeidsbemiddeling en Stagiaires, PO Box 437, 2280 AR Rijswijk
May be able to assist young people in finding temporary employment for at least 8 weeks from mid October-end December.

ROYAL NETHERLANDS EMBASSY 38 Hyde Park Gate, London SW7 5DP ✆ 071-584 5040
Can provide a list of labour exchanges in some major towns in the Netherlands, as well as information sheets on social security and income tax.

NEW ZEALAND

INFORMATION

New Zealand High Commission
Immigration Service: New Zealand House,
Haymarket, London SW1Y 4TQ ℗ 071-973 0366

British High Commission
44 Hill Street/PO Box 1812, Wellington 1

Tourist office
New Zealand Tourist Board, 3rd floor, New
Zealand House, 80 Haymarket, London SW1Y
4TE ℗ 071-973 0360

Youth hostels
YHA of New Zealand Inc, PO Box 436,
Christchurch 1

Youth & student information
New Zealand University Students Association,
Student Travel Bureau, PO Box 6368, Te Aro,
Wellington

Entry regulations A Work Visa is required for
all types of employment. Those entering New
Zealand temporarily for full-time and pre-
arranged employment, as distinct from working
on a casual basis, should apply to the
Immigration Service at New Zealand House,
see above, at least 4 weeks before the intended
date of departure; earlier in the case of teachers,
doctors, nurses or other hospital staff.
An application for a Work Visa must be
supported by an offer of employment from a
New Zealand employer. Those who have been
accepted under an approved exchange scheme
or whose prospective employer has permission
to recruit from the New Zealand Immigration
Service may also be considered.

New Zealand does not have a Working Holiday
Visa arrangement. Those who are interested in
working on a casual basis in New Zealand
should apply for a work permit when they are
in the country itself. They should approach the
nearest Regional/Branch Office of the
Immigration Service in New Zealand with a
written offer of employment if they want a
permit to work. A fee will be charged for this
application. The Immigration Service will check
that the employment offered cannot be

undertaken by local jobseekers and will not restrict employment opportunities in New Zealand. Applicants must therefore understand that there is no guarantee that they will be able to secure permission to work.

Applicants must have a passport valid for at least 3 months beyond the last day of their proposed stay, a fully paid return or onward ticket, plus proof that they will have a minimum of NZ$1000 per month of stay on arrival or have made prior arrangements for their support while in the country. Permits are granted for an initial period of 3 months, 6 months for UK passport-holders. 9 months is the maximum period of stay for visitors.

Travel Campus Travel, 52 Grosvenor Gardens, London SW1W 0AG ✆ 071-730 8111 (offices throughout the UK) and Council Travel, 28A Poland Street, London W1V 3DB ✆ 071-437 7767 (offices also in Paris, Lyon, Düsseldorf, Tokyo and throughout the US) offer low-cost student/youth airfares to destinations in New Zealand.

Compass GSA, PO Box 113, Peterborough, Cambridgeshire PE1 1LE ✆Peterborough (0733) 51780 are agents for New Zealand railways. Travelpass provides unlimited travel on trains, buses and ferry. Cost from £138 (8 days).

Publications Lonely Planet's *New Zealand - A Travel Survival Kit* £9.95 offers practical, down-to-earth information for independent travellers wanting to explore beyond the usual tourist routes. Available from good bookshops.

Travellers Survival Kit Australia & New Zealand £8.95 is a handbook for those going down under, giving information on travelling, local culture, restaurants, beaches and reefs, flora and fauna. Published by Vacation Work, 9 Park End Street, Oxford OX1 1HJ ✆ Oxford (0865) 241978.

When writing to any organisation it is essential to mention Working Holidays 1993 and enclose a large stamped, self-addressed envelope, or if overseas, a large addressed envelope and at least two International Reply Coupons.

FARMWORK

INTERNATIONAL AGRICULTURAL EXCHANGE ASSOCIATION YFC Centre, National Agricultural Centre, Stoneleigh Park, Kenilworth, Warwickshire CV8 2LG ✆ Coventry (0203) 696578
Operates opportunities for young people involved with agriculture, horticulture or home management to acquire practical work experience in the rural sector, and to strengthen and improve their knowledge and understanding of the way of life in other countries. Participants are given an opportunity to study practical methods on approved training farms, and work as trainees, gaining further experience in their chosen field.

Types of farm include dairy, sheep, cropping or mixed farms (crops plus dairy/sheep/beef/ deer); sheep and beef; limited horticultural enterprises. Participants undertake paid work on the farm, approx 45 hours per week, and live as a member of the host family. Full board and lodging, insurance cover and a minimum net weekly wage of £50-£60 provided.
All programmes include 3/4 weeks unpaid holiday. 4 day orientation seminar held at the beginning of each programme at agricultural colleges and universities throughout New Zealand. Stopovers (2-4 days) in Singapore/ Thailand (on direct programmes) or Singapore/ Thailand and Hawaii (for 14 months programme) arranged en route.

Ages 18-30. Applicants should be single, and have good practical experience in the chosen training category, plus a valid driving licence. 8 months (departing August); 6 months (departing September); 14 months - 7 in New Zealand plus 7 in Australia (departing August). Cost from £2225 covers airfare, work permit, administration fee, orientation seminar, information meetings, insurance, supervision, placement with a host family and travel to placement. £200 deposit payable. B D if handicap is not severe. *Apply at least 4 months in advance. UK or Irish passport-holders only.*

New Zealand applicants seeking an exchange should apply to IAEA, Parklane Arcade, The Strand, PO Box 328, Whakatane, North Island.

WILLING WORKERS ON ORGANIC FARMS (WWOOF NZ) c/o Andrew and Jane Strange, PO Box 10-037, Palmerston North
✆ Palmerston North (63) 553 555
A non-profitmaking organisation which aims to help organic farmers and smallholders whose work is often labour-intensive as it does not rely on the use of artificial fertilisers or pesticides. Provides volunteers with first hand experience of organic farming and gardening, by spending some time on one of over 300 farms and smallholdings spread over both main islands.

Ages 17+. Placements are arranged on a fix-it-yourself basis; volunteers should write 2-3 months in advance enclosing £5 or equivalent for a list of farms and further information. No wages paid, and volunteers must pay their own travel and insurance. Anti-tetanus vaccination recommended.

GENERAL

INVOLVEMENT VOLUNTEERS ASSOCIATION INC PO Box 218, Port Melbourne, Victoria 3207, Australia
✆/Fax Melbourne (3) 646 5504
A non-profitmaking organisation set up to find volunteer placements in Australia or countries en route such as New Zealand. Volunteers of all ages can take part in a variety of individual placements or team tasks including assisting teachers at special schools; acting as recreation officers at homes for older adults; farm tree planting programmes; researching, restoring or maintaining historic sites, gardens or covenanted areas; and developing National Parks.

Placements available all year. Discounted internal travel to placement sites or discounted Scuba diving courses on the Barrier Reef available. Volunteers must be able to speak English, arrange their own visitor visas, and organise their own international travel and insurance. Some itinerant paid work placements can be found for volunteers with suitable visas. Involvement Volunteers provides advice, placements, itinerary planning, meeting on arrival, initial accommodation, introductions to banking,

taxation and a communications base in Australia. Cost AU$300 (approx £125/$225/DM400). B D

In Europe, apply to Involvement Volunteers-Deutschland, Postfach 110224, W-3400 Göttingen, Germany ✆/Fax (551) 33 765.

In North America, apply to Involvement Corps Inc., 15515 Sunset Boulevard Suite 108, Pacific Palisades, California 90272, United States ✆/Fax (310) 459 1022.

NORTHERN IRELAND

INFORMATION

Tourist office
Northern Ireland Tourist Board, River House, 48 High Street, Belfast BT1 2DS ✆ Belfast (0232) 2315906 London office: 11 Berkeley Street, London W1X 6LN ✆ 071-493 0601

Youth hostels
YHA Northern Ireland, 56 Bradbury Place, Belfast BT7 1RU ✆ Belfast (0232) 324733

Youth & student information
USIT, Fountain Centre, Belfast BT1 6ET ✆ Belfast (0232) 324073

Entry regulations governing the employment of overseas workers in Northern Ireland are given under the **Great Britain** section.

CHILDREN'S PROJECTS

CHILDREN'S COMMUNITY HOLIDAYS PO Box 463, Belfast BT12 5HB ✆ Belfast (0232) 245650
Provides holidays in residential centres and converted schools throughout Northern Ireland for some 800 children aged 8-15 from all kinds of backgrounds, handicapped and able-bodied, Catholic and Protestant. All holidays include games, handicrafts, story-telling, music and exploring the countryside; some feature activities such as canoeing, horse riding, theme games and climbing. Volunteers are required to act as monitors, each taking responsibility for a group of 6-8 children. No experience is necessary as training is given; however applicants should have a strong interest in caring for children. Fluent English also required. Ages 17½+. Hours are as required during holidays; each holiday lasts 10 days, July-August, and is preceded by 7 day training course. Pocket money £25 per holiday. Full board accommodation, insurance and travel costs within Northern Ireland provided.

DUNCAIRN PLAYSCHEME 1-5 Albert Square, Belfast BT1 3EQ
Volunteers required to work on a summer scheme workcamp in the New Lodge and Tiger Bay estates of North Belfast, a deprived and

deeply segregated area. Ages 18+. 3 weeks, July and August. Volunteers receive accommodation and food but pay own travel costs. A few days are set aside before the camp begins for briefing and consultation. *Apply as early as possible.*

PAX CHRISTI 9 Henry Road, London N4 2LH
© 081-800 4612
An international Catholic movement for peace, founded at the end of the Second World War. Volunteers are needed to work on summer playschemes for Catholic and Protestant children and young people from housing estates, based at schools, community centres and youth clubs in Belfast, Dungannon and Antrim. The schemes aim to ease tension and promote integration by providing happy and creative play opportunities for those for whom there is otherwise very little provision. Each scheme has 6-20 volunteers and daily attracts up to 500 participants. Volunteers work in international teams and in close collaboration with the local community. Work involves helping to plan, organise and supervise indoor and outdoor activities including sports and team games, hiking, nature studies, drama, arts and crafts, discos, day trips, weekend camping trips, talent shows and fancy dress parades. Ages 18+. Experience with children desirable and volunteers must be self-disciplined, energetic, committed to community living, sensitive to the local situation, prepared to work together as an international team and to take considerable personal responsibility and initiative in planning, assessing and maintaining the schemes. Approx 30 hour, 5 day week, with some weekend work. 3-5 weeks, July/August. Self-catering accommodation in schools, empty houses, youth clubs, church halls or with families provided, plus food. Help may be given with travel costs if necessary. Volunteers arrange their own insurance. Essential that time is taken to study the history and current situation in Northern Ireland before arrival. Orientation weekend arranged, which volunteers are strongly urged to attend.

PHOENIX CENTRE 16 Alexander Square, Lurgan, Co Armagh BT66 6AT © Lurgan (0762) 325927
Volunteers are needed in Lurgan, helping to run constructive Catholic and Protestant playschemes for the children of the Shankhill,

Avenue Road and Wakehurst estates. Ages 18+. 3 weeks, July/August. Volunteers receive maintenance but pay own travel costs. A few days are set aside before the camp begins for briefing/consultation. *Apply by 1 April.*

COMMUNITY WORK

THE CORRYMEELA COMMUNITY
Volunteer Coordinator, Corrymeela Centre, 5 Drumaroan Road, Ballycastle BT54 6QU
© Ballycastle (026 57) 62626
An interdenominational Christian community working for reconciliation in Northern Ireland, and promoting a concern for issues of peace and justice in the wider world. Volunteers are recruited at the Community's ecumenical centre at Ballycastle on the north Antrim coast, to be with families who are there on holiday. Many of the families are under stress and from troubled areas. Volunteers must be prepared to spend 6 days living, working and playing with a group as one community in a residential setting. They should enjoy being with people of all ages and be prepared to help organise and be involved in activities for both parents and children. Ages 18+. 1-3 weeks, July and August. Cost £27, £18 unwaged, per week includes board and accommodation. Applicants are expected to attend a preparation weekend. PH *Apply by mid May. Overseas volunteers accepted.*

INTERNATIONAL VOLUNTARY SERVICE NORTHERN IRELAND 122 Great Victoria Street, Belfast BT2 7BG © Belfast (0232) 238147
The Northern Ireland branch of Service Civil International, which promotes international reconciliation through work projects. Volunteers are needed for community work on international workcamps. Recent projects have included running playschemes for children in Newry; helping to organise a community festival in Belfast; assisting in running a residential circus school in Newcastle, Co Down; and organising activities for patients in a psychiatric hospital in Antrim. Ages 18+. Overseas volunteers must speak at least basic English. Applicants should be prepared to work hard and contribute to team life. 35-40 hour week. 2-3 weeks, June-September, Christmas and Easter. Food, accommodation in schools,

hospitals or community centres with self-catering facilities, and insurance provided, but not travel. Membership fee £10 (£5 unwaged). Registration fee £10 (£5 unwaged) **B D PH** *Applicants in Northern Ireland should apply direct; applicants in the rest of the UK should apply to International Voluntary Service, Old Hall, East Bergholt, Colchester, Essex CO7 6TQ.*

Applications from outside the UK: please see information on page 30.

CONSERVATION

CONSERVATION VOLUNTEERS (NORTHERN IRELAND) 137 University Street, Belfast BT7 1HP
The Northern Ireland branch of the British Trust for Conservation Volunteers, a charity promoting practical conservation work by volunteers. Organises numerous projects on nature reserves, country estates, NT properties and country parks. Recent projects have included restoring the famous Brandy Pad smugglers' route in the Mourne Mountains; fencing and woodland management on Strangford Lough, County Down; drystone walling in the Fermanagh lakeland; and habitat management in an urban fringe woodland in Belfast. Practical conservation work can also be combined with other activities such as caving or canoeing on special interest holidays. Instruction given in the traditional techniques of drystone walling, fencing, coppicing, woodland and wetland management, and many other conservation skills. Approx 12 volunteers work on each task with an experienced leader; beginners welcome. Ages 16+. 7/8 hour day with 1 day off per week. 1+ weeks or weekends, all year. Food, insurance, accommodation in training centre, tents, youth hostels or cottages provided. Cost from £10, weekend breaks, £30 for 1 week. Tasks qualify under the Duke of Edinburgh's Award scheme. **B D PH W**

INTERNATIONAL VOLUNTARY SERVICE NORTHERN IRELAND 122 Great Victoria Street, Belfast BT2 7BG ✆ Belfast (0232) 238147
The Northern Ireland branch of Service Civil International, which promotes international reconciliation through work projects.

Volunteers are needed for conservation work on international projects. Recent projects have included clearing a nature walk and making paths alongside Carlingford Lough; carrying out a land use survey on the shores of Strangford Lough, an area rich in wildlife; and helping to re-lay the old railway line between Downpatrick and Ardglass to establish a permanent tourist attraction. Ages 18+. Applicants should be prepared to work hard and contribute to team life. 35-40 hour week. 2-4 weeks, June-September. Accommodation in schools or community centres, food, self-catering facilities and insurance provided, but not travel. Membership fee £10 (£5 unwaged). Registration fee £10 (£5 unwaged). **B D PH** *Applicants in Northern Ireland should apply direct; applicants in the rest of the UK should apply to International Voluntary Service, Old Hall, East Bergholt, Colchester, Essex CO7 6TQ.*

Applications from outside the UK: please see information on page 30.

NATIONAL TRUST NORTHERN IRELAND REGION Regional Volunteer Organiser, Rowallane House, Saintfield, Ballynahinch, Co Down BT24 7LH ✆ Saintfield (0238) 510721
A major conservation charity, organising several workcamps each year at its estate at Castle Ward on the shores of Strangford Lough. Typical projects include scrub clearance, fencing, conservation work and helping with the wildfowl collection. Ages 16+. July-August. Basecamp accommodation provided in stone houses. Participants should take sleeping bags.

DOMESTIC

THE CORRYMEELA COMMUNITY Volunteer Coordinator, Corrymeela Centre, 5 Drumaroan Road, Ballycastle BT54 6QU ✆ Ballycastle (026 57) 62626
An interdenominational Christian community working for reconciliation in Northern Ireland, and promoting a concern for issues of peace and justice in the wider world. Youth camps/projects and family weeks organised for children and families under stress and from troubled areas, at the Community's ecumenical centre at Ballycastle on the north Antrim coast.

Volunteers are recruited to supplement the resident domestic staff, assisting in the laundry, with general housework, in the kitchen, and in reception, receiving groups and visitors and performing routine administrative tasks. Ages 18+. Applicants must be able to cope with very hard and demanding work. 1-3 weeks, July and August. Full board accommodation provided. Applicants are expected to attend a preparation weekend. PH *Apply by mid May. Overseas volunteers accepted.*

MONITORS & INSTRUCTORS

THE CORRYMEELA COMMUNITY
Volunteer Coordinator, Corrymeela Centre, 5 Drumaroan Road, Ballycastle BT54 6QU
℗ **Ballycastle (026 57) 62626**
An interdenominational Christian community working for reconciliation in Northern Ireland, and promoting a concern for issues of peace and justice in the wider world. Youth camps/projects and family weeks are organised for children and families under stress and from troubled areas, at the Community's ecumenical centre on the north Antrim coast. Opportunities for volunteers to supplement the resident staff include assisting in drama and arts and crafts such as weaving, printing, macrame and candle making; organising and supervising recreational activities; and a music resource person to accompany singing at worship, barbecues and general sing songs. Ages 18+. Applicants must have relevant experience or skills and be able to cope with very hard and demanding work. 1-3 weeks, July and August. Full board accommodation provided. Applicants are expected to attend a preparation weekend. PH *Apply by mid May. Overseas volunteers accepted.*

GLEN RIVER YMCA National Centre, c/o 143 Central Promenade, Newcastle, Co Down BT33 0EU ℗ **Newcastle (039 67) 23172**
Offers a wide range of outdoor activities aiming to introduce young people to nature and improve their quality of life in a Christian atmosphere. Volunteers are needed to work as counsellors, instructors, domestic assistants and day camp leaders. Training given in basic activities such as ropes course, orienteering, archery, adventure and nature walks. Opportunities for canoeing, climbing, abseiling and bouldering as well as to participate in programmes/excursions with clients. All staff are expected to participate in domestic and other duties related to the running of the centre. Applicants should agree with the aims and purposes of the YMCA, be articulate, enjoy working with children and fit easily into the staff team. Ages 18+. Good knowledge of English required. 6 day week, June-August. £18 per week pocket money, accommodation, meals and public liability insurance provided. Participants pay own travel and insurance.

WORKCAMPS

INTERNATIONAL VOLUNTARY SERVICE NORTHERN IRELAND 122 Great Victoria Street, Belfast BT2 7BG ℗ **Belfast (0232) 238147**
The Northern Ireland branch of Service Civil International, which promotes international reconciliation through work projects. Volunteers are needed for manual work on international workcamps. Recent projects have included work at Glebe House, a children's holiday centre, and working farm near Strangford in Co Down; helping Tools for Self Reliance in refurbishing old tools for use in the Third World; building a community centre adventure playground in Bainbridge; helping with organic farming in Coleraine; and helping a community theatre group stage a play in Belfast's Botanic Gardens. Ages 18+. Applicants should be prepared to work hard and contribute to team life. 40 hour week. 2-3 weeks, June-September. Also a few camps at Christmas and Easter. Accommodation in community centres or schools, food, self-catering facilities and insurance provided, but not travel. Membership fee £10 (£5 unwaged). Registration fee £10 (£5 unwaged). B D PH *Applicants in Northern Ireland should apply direct; applicants in the rest of the UK should apply to International Voluntary Service, Old Hall, East Bergholt, Colchester, Essex CO7 6TQ.*

Applications from outside the UK: please see information on page 30.

INFORMATION

Royal Norwegian Embassy
25 Belgrave Square, London SW1X 8QD
☎ 071-235 7151

British Embassy
Thomas Heftyesgate 8, 0244 Oslo 2

Tourist office
Norwegian National Tourist Office, Charles
House, 5-11 Lower Regent Street, London SW1Y
4LR ☎ 071-839 6255

Youth hostels
Landslaget for Norske Ungdoms-herberger,
Dronningensgate 26, Oslo 1

Youth & student information
Universitetenes Reisebyra (Norwegian Student
Travel Office), Universitets-sentret, Blindern,
Boks 55, Oslo 3

Norwegian Foundation for Youth Exchange,
Rolf Hofmosgate 18, 0655 Oslo 6

Entry regulations A work permit is required
for all types of employment. This can only be
obtained before arrival in Norway, when a job
has been secured with an employer who has
been approved by the Norwegian labour
authorities to employ foreign personnel. An
Offer of Employment form must be completed
and signed by the employer before a work
permit can be applied for. A work permit is
very difficult to obtain and only people with
special skills are accepted, if a Norwegian
national cannot fill the job. The application will
be sent to the competent authorities in Norway,
who normally require 3-6 months for
investigations; in special cases and at peak
times the time required may be longer.
A current full passport is required; identity
cards or visitors' passports are not valid for
employment purposes. Applications for work
can be made under the International Clearing of
Vacancies scheme; for more details in the UK
contact the Training Agency. Because of the
labour situation, work permits will not usually
be given to foreign nationals seeking seasonal
employment. If a person has had an offer for

seasonal employment, they should apply for a work permit through the Consular Section of the Norwegian Embassy, see above, or to the Royal Norwegian Consulate General, 86 George Street, Edinburgh EH2 3BU ℗ 031-226 5701; Royal Norwegian Consulate, 2 Collingwood Street, Newcastle-upon-Tyne NE1 1JH ℗ 091-232 6358. Only in special cases, when the labour exchange has agreed to the job in question, is it advisable to go to Norway. Under the Norwegian Aliens Regulations applicants should not, in their own interest, enter the country during the period in which the application for a work permit is under consideration. These regulations may change as of January 1993 subject to the European Economic Space agreement, and a work permit may no longer be required by EC nationals.

Job advertising Frank L Crane (London) Ltd International Press Representation, 5/15 Cromer Street, Grays Inn Road, London WC1H 8LS ℗ 071-837 3330 can place job advertisements in daily newspapers.

Travel The Nordic Tourist Ticket entitles the holder to unlimited travel on trains in Norway, Denmark, Finland and Sweden, and is also valid on some inter-Scandinavian ferries. Valid for 21 days; cost £115, ages under 26, £155 ages over 26. Details from Norwegian State Railways, 21-24 Cockspur Street, London SW1Y 5DA ℗ 071-930 6666.

Campus Travel, 52 Grosvenor Gardens, London SW1W 0AG ℗ 071-730 3402 (offices throughout the UK) offers Eurotrain under 26 fares and youth/student flights to destinations in Norway.

Publications Lonely Planet's *Scandinavian and Baltic Europe on a Shoestring* £10.95 offers practical, down-to-earth information for the low-budget, independent traveller in Norway. *The Rough Guide to Scandinavia* £8.95 provides comprehensive background information on Norway plus details on getting around, places to explore and cheap places to stay. *Michael's Guide to Scandinavia* £10.95 is detailed and concise, providing invaluable practical advice for all kinds of travellers. Published by Inbal Travel. All the above are available from bookshops.

AU PAIR / CHILDCARE

ATLANTIS YOUTH EXCHANGE Rolf Hofmosgate 18, 0655 Oslo 6
Can place English-speaking au pairs in Norwegian families, to provide an experience of Norwegian culture. 9+ months. Ages 18-30. Board, lodging, health insurance and NKr2300 per month provided. Travel and language course fees paid by applicants. *Apply at least 4 months in advance of work period desired.*

COMMUNITY WORK

NANSEN INTERNASJONALE CENTER Barnegården Breivold, Nesset, 1400 Ski
Aims to help teenagers with social problems at a relief and activity centre in a renovated farm 25 km south of Oslo, based on total participation and involvement from the voluntary staff as well as the permanent staff and residents. Volunteers are needed to help with work ranging from cleaning and preparation tasks to creative work, hobbies, sports and the care of animals. The farm takes approx 10 children per week, aged 13+, and there are many opportunities to develop and use creative skills. The work is physically and mentally demanding, but rewarding. Ages 22+. Applicants should be mature, practical and have experience or strong motivation and commitment to work with children who are in need of care, and willing to take part in all activities. The staff is international and the working languages are English and Norwegian. Beginning June-mid August, and all year round. Long working hours on a rota basis, with approx 3 days free per fortnight. Board and lodging in barracks or houses, plus NKr450 per week pocket money and opportunities to travel in Norway. *Work permit required.*

CONSERVATION

BRITISH TRUST FOR CONSERVATION VOLUNTEERS Room IWH, 36 St Mary's Street, Wallingford, Oxfordshire OX10 0EU
The largest charitable organisation in Britain to involve people in practical conservation work. Following the success of the Natural Break

Programme in the UK, BTCV is now developing a series of international working holidays with the aim of introducing the volunteering ethic to communities abroad. It is hoped that British volunteers will adapt to and learn from local lifestyles as well as participate in the community. 2 weeks, July-August. Projects run in conjunction with the Nansen Society in Budor. Work involves footpath construction, restoration of traditional timber houses and the erection of bird boxes. Ages 18-70. Cost from £140 includes food and accommodation in log cabins. Everyone shares in domestic chores. Membership fee £12. No fares or wages paid.

FARMWORK

ATLANTIS YOUTH EXCHANGE Working Guest Programme, Rolf Hofmosgate 18, 0655 Oslo 6
Opportunities to stay on a farm as a working guest. The work involves haymaking, weeding, milking, picking fruit, berries and vegetables, tractor driving, feeding cattle, painting, housework and/or taking care of the children, combined with outdoor work. Most farmers and/or their children speak some English or German. Ages 18-30. Farming experience desirable but not essential; applicants must be willing to work hard. Up to 35 hour week, 1½+ consecutive free days. 4-12 weeks, all year. Board and lodging, health insurance and NKr500+ per week pocket money provided; work permits arranged. Participants pay their own travel costs. Registration fee NKr830; NKr700 refundable if the applicant is not placed. Some farms may accept 2 people who apply together. Applicants should receive job offers 4-6 weeks before their proposed date of arrival. *UK applicants should apply through Concordia (Youth Service Volunteers) Ltd, Recruitment Secretary, 8 Brunswick Place, Hove, Sussex BN3 1ET ✆ Brighton (0273) 772086. Administration fee £5.*

INTERNATIONAL FARM EXPERIENCE PROGRAMME YFC Centre, National Agricultural Centre, Kenilworth, Warwickshire CV8 2LG ✆ Coventry (0203) 696584
Provides assistance to young farmers and nurserymen by finding places in farms and nurseries abroad to enable them to broaden their knowledge of agricultural methods. Opportunities for practical horticultural or agricultural work, usually on mixed farms. Applicants live and work with a farmer and his family and the work is matched as far as possible with the applicant's requirements. The work can be strenuous. Girls should be prepared to work inside the home as well as outside. 2-3 months, May-September. Salary £30 per week; board and lodging provided. Ages 18-26. Applicants must have at least 2 years practical experience, 1 year of which may be at an agricultural college, and intend to make a career in agriculture or horticulture. Valid driving licence necessary. Applicants pay own fares. Registration fee £70. *UK nationals only.*

WORKCAMPS

INTERNASJONAL DUGNAD Langes Gate 6, 0165 Oslo 1
The Norwegian branch of Service Civil International, which promotes international reconciliation through work projects. Volunteers are invited to take part in international workcamps. Recent projects have included carrying out reconstruction work at an information centre for the peace movement in Kornhaug; painting a house and restoration work at a hill farm near Trondheim which acts as a community for young people with problems of drug and alcohol abuse; and making signposts for historical hiking paths through forests and mountains at Holtalen. Ages 18+. Applicants should by highly motivated and prepared to work hard as part of a team. 35-40 hour week. 2-4 weeks, June-September. Food, accommodation and insurance provided, but not travel. **B D PH W**

Apply through partner organisation in country of residence. In the UK: International Voluntary Service, Old Hall, East Bergholt, Colchester, Essex CO7 4TQ.

Outside the UK: please see information on page 30.

POLAND

INFORMATION

Polish Embassy
47 Portland Place, London W1N 3AG
℃ 071-580 4324/9

Visa Section: Consulate General, 73 New
Cavendish Street, London W1N 3AG
℃ 071-580 0476

British Embassy
Aleje Roz 1, 00-556 Warsaw

Tourist office
Polorbis Travel Ltd, 82 Mortimer Street,
London W1N 7DE ℃ 071-637 4971

Youth hostels
Polskie Towarzystwo Schronisk
Mlodziezowych, Chocimska 28, 00-791 Warsaw

Youth & student information
Almatur, Travel Bureau of the Polish Students'
Association, ul Kopernika 15, 00-364 Warsaw

Juventur Youth Travel Bureau, Gdanska 27/3,
01-633 Warsaw

Entry regulations UK nationals holding valid
passports may stay in Poland for up to 6
months without a visa. Nationals of most other
EC countries and the US do not require a visa
for stays of up to 90 days. Visa-free entry does
not apply to persons arriving to take up
employment in Poland, who should check
regulations governing visas and work permits
with the Polish Consulate General.

Travel Fregata Travel Ltd, 100 Dean Street,
London W1V 6AQ ℃ 071-734 5101 offers
express rail travel London-Poznan/Warsaw
from £155 return including couchettes, and a
coach service Manchester/Nottingham/
Birmingham-Poznan/Warsaw, from £119
return.

The Polrailpass entitles the holder to unlimited
travel on local and express trains. Valid for 8/
15/21/30 days, cost from £35. Available from
Polorbis Travel Ltd, 82 Mortimer Street,
London W1N 7DE ℃ 071-636 2217.

Campus Travel, 52 Grosvenor Gardens, London SW1W 0AG ✆ 071-730 3402 (offices throughout the UK) and Council Travel 28A Poland Street, London W1V 3DB ✆ 071-437 7767 (offices also in Paris, Lyon, Düsseldorf, Tokyo and throughout the US) offer Eurotrain under 26 fares and youth/student flights to destinations in Poland.

Publications Lonely Planet's *Eastern Europe on a Shoestring* £13.95, provides practical information on budget travel in Poland and many other east European countries.
Poland - A Travel Survival Kit £10.95 offers practical, down-to-earth information for independent travellers wanting to explore beyond the usual tourist routes.
The Rough Guide to Poland £7.99 provides comprehensive background information plus details on getting there, getting around, places to explore and cheap places to stay.
All the above are available from good bookshops.

Travellers Survival Kit Soviet Union & Eastern Europe £8.95 is a guide for travellers containing advice on where to go, travel bargains, budget accommodation and dealing with bureaucracy. Available from Vacation Work, 9 Park End Street, Oxford OX1 1HJ ✆ Oxford (0895) 241978.

FARMWORK

INTERNATIONAL FARM EXPERIENCE PROGRAMME YFC Centre, National Agricultural Centre, Stoneleigh Park, Kenilworth, Warwickshire CV8 2LG ✆ Coventry (0203) 696584
Provides assistance to young farmers and nurserymen by finding places on farms and nurseries, giving opportunities to live and work with local people. Placements provide a varied programme offering experience of private farms as well as state cooperatives. 3-12 months. Ages 18-26. Pocket money, some travel expenses, board and lodging provided. Applicants must have at least 2 years practical experience, 1 year of which may be at an agricultural college and intend to make a career in agriculture or horticulture. Registration fee £70. *UK nationals only.*

MONITORS & TEACHERS

ANGLO-POLISH ACADEMIC ASSOCIATION Secretariat, 93 Victoria Road, Leeds LS6 1DR ✆ Leeds (0532) 758121
Volunteers are required to teach English to Polish doctors, teachers and students. Ages 21-60. Applicants must have clear spoken English and legible handwriting. Teacher training or previous teaching experience desirable. 15 hours per week for 2-3 weeks, July-August; plus 1 week at end of stay to visit Poland. Full board university accommodation provided but volunteers pay own travel and insurance costs. Travel grant of up to 25% available. B D PH *Apply by mid April. UK nationals only.*

BRIT-POL HEALTH CARE FOUNDATION Gerrard House, Suite 14, Worthing Road, East Preston, West Sussex BN16 1AW ✆ (0903) 859222
Small number of teachers required to work on summer camps for children in Poland. Applicants must be of English mother tongue and have an ability to communicate with children. Ages 20-50. 20-25 hours per week, 3 weeks, July and August. Board and lodging provided in local family, or in self-contained flat with food allowance paid. Return travel provided but not insurance. Also opportunities for qualified and experienced teachers, ages 25+, to teach English, management or administration for 3+ months, all year. *Applications can take up to 3 months to process. UK nationals only.*

CENTRAL BUREAU FOR EDUCATIONAL VISITS & EXCHANGES Schools Unit, Seymour Mews House, Seymour Mews, London W1H 9PE ✆ 071-486 5101 ext 2411
Teachers and sixth formers are required at English language summer camps held concurrently at boarding schools at different venues in Poland, each accommodating approx 100 pupils from UNESCO Associated Schools which have specialised courses in foreign languages. The main objective is to provide Polish pupils aged 14-18 with the opportunity of practising English learnt in school, and by spending 4 weeks in the company of a group of British teachers and young people to acquire a deeper awareness of the British way of life.

Duties include assisting with the teaching of English as a foreign language, running conversation classes and organising sporting, musical and social activities. Ages up to 45. Applicants should be native English speakers, sixth formers willing to assist the staff; or teachers qualified in the teaching of any discipline: EFL or ESL qualifications an advantage.

Applicants should have a sense of responsibility, organisational skill, adaptability to new surroundings, a sociable nature and an interest in sports and/or drama and music, plus experience of working with or teaching children. Participants must fully commit themselves to the teaching of English and the organisation of various educational, outdoor and social activities. 4 weeks, July-August, including a 4 day trip to places of interest at the end. Board and accommodation provided, plus honorarium in Polish currency towards pocket money. Travel cost approx £220 including insurance and visa, paid by applicants. Organised by the Polish Ministry of Education and UNESCO. *Apply by mid April.*

WORKCAMPS

FOUNDATION FOR INTERNATIONAL YOUTH EXCHANGES (FIYE) Ul Grzybowska 79, 00-844 Warsaw
The Foundation for International Youth Exchange is a voluntary service organisation providing social services to disadvantaged groups and organising activities for young people. Volunteers are invited to take part in international workcamps. Recent projects have included building and repair work in a youth centre in Nowy Sacz; helping out with everyday duties on a state farm in Szczecin; and construction and renovation work at a holiday village for the rehabilitation of former drug addicts and alcoholics in Nonar. Educational, cultural and recreational activities arranged, including visits to national parks, sports activities and meeting local people. Ages 18+. Applicants should have previous workcamp experience and be fit, prepared to work hard and contribute to team life. 30-35 hour week. 2-4 weeks, June-August. Food and accommodation in schools, hostels, houses or under canvas provided.

Apply through partner organisation in country of residence. In the UK: International Voluntary Service, Old Hall, East Bergholt, Colchester, Essex CO7 6TQ or
Quaker International Social Projects, Friends House, Euston Road, London NW1 2BJ or
United Nations Association, International Youth Service, Temple of Peace, Cathays Park, Cardiff CF1 3AP ℂ Cardiff (0222) 223088.

Outside the UK: please see information on page 30.

GENERAL

POLISH JAZZ SOCIETY ul Mazowiecka 11, 00-052 Warsaw
Set up in 1959 to teach jazz and to organise festivals and charity concerts. Volunteers are needed to participate in the International Jazz Workshop at Chodziez, receiving training in different categories such as small groups, big bands, theory of improvisation and the history of jazz; with jazz sessions during the evenings. Classes are led by, amongst others, lecturers from the Berklee College of Music (USA), the Academy of Music in Graz (Austria) and the best jazz musicians from Poland and other countries. Participants must be able to read music fluently, and want to know more about jazz. They must submit a brief summary of their musical knowledge. 2 weeks, July, 10.00-21.00 with an evening jam session. Ages 16/17+. No wages paid but each participant is sponsored approx 40% of total cost, to cover the organisation of the workshop. Accommodation in youth hotels with meals; cost from US$250. Participants pay own travel costs. Open to those with a secondary school knowledge of music, professional musicians or amateurs with a recommendation from a qualified musician, music school or club. *All nationalities welcome; working languages English, German and Russian.* **B D PH**

When writing to any organisation it is essential to mention Working Holidays 1993 and enclose a large stamped, self-addressed envelope, or if overseas, a large addressed envelope and at least two International Reply Coupons.

INFORMATION

Portuguese Embassy
11 Belgrave Square, London SW1X 8PP
℡ 071-235 5331-4
Consular section: Silver City House,
62 Brompton Road, London SW3 1BJ
℡ 071-581 8722

British Embassy
35/37 Rua de S Domingos à Lapa, 1200 Lisbon

Tourist office
Portuguese National Tourist Office, 22/25a
Sackville Street, London W1X 1DE
℡ 071-494 1441

Youth hostels
Associacâo Portuguesa de Pousadas de
Juventude, Rua Andrade Corvo 46, 1000 Lisbon

Youth & student information
Associacâo de Turismo Estudantil e Juvenil, PO
Box 4586, 4009 Porto Cedex

Instituto da Juventude, Avenida da Liberdade
194, 1200 Lisbon

Turicoop, Turismo Social e Juvenil, Rua Pascoal
de Melo, 15-1, Dto, 1100 Lisbon

Entry regulations UK citizens intending to
work in Portugal should have a full passport.
EC nationals may stay for up to 3 months; those
wishing to stay longer must contact the local
office of the Serviço de Estrangeiros e
Fronteiras (SEF) to obtain a residence permit.
A list of SEF offices is available from the
Portuguese Consulate General. A work permit
and residence visa are required for non-EC
nationals wishing to work in Portugal. The
prospective employer applies for the work
permit through the local authorities;
applications for a residence visa should be
made to the Portuguese Consulate General at
least 6 months in advance. Volunteers on
workcamps do not require work permits.

*Portugal: a guide to employment and opportunities
for young people* offers advice and contacts for
those seeking long and short term teaching

posts, office employment, summer jobs and voluntary work. Available from the Hispanic and Luso Brazilian Council, Canning House, 2 Belgrave Square, London SW1X 8PJ ℗ 071-235 2303; price £2 (free to members).

Job advertising Publicitas Ltd, 525/527 Fulham Road, London SW6 1HD ℗ 071-385 7723 can place job advertisements in *Diario de Noticias* (Lisbon daily), *Journal de Noticias* (Oporto daily) and *Expresso* (business weekly).

Anglo-Portuguese News, Apartado 113, 2765 Estoril, Lisbon, can accept all kinds of job advertisements, especially for work in families as au pairs or domestics.

Travel STA Travel, 74 Old Brompton Road, London SW7 3LQ/117 Euston Road, London NW1 2SX ℗ 071-937 9921 (offices also in Birmingham, Bristol, Cambridge, Leeds, Manchester and Oxford) operates flexible low-cost flights between London and destinations throughout Portugal.

Campus Travel, 52 Grosvenor Gardens, London SW1W 0AG ℗ 071-730 3402 (offices throughout the UK) and Council Travel, 28A Poland Street, London W1V 3DB ℗ 071-437 7767 (offices also in Paris, Lyon, Düsseldorf, Tokyo and throughout the US) offer Eurotrain under 26 fares and youth/student flights to destinations in Portugal.

Publications The Portuguese National Tourist Office, see above, publish a brochure providing descriptions of regions, information on food, wines, folklore, handicrafts, fairs, festivals, travel, accommodation and other general information.

The Rough Guide to Portugal £7.99 provides comprehensive background information plus details on getting there, getting around, places to explore and cheap places to stay. Available from good bookshops.

Live and Work in Spain and Portugal £8.95 is a guide for those interested in finding temporary or permanent work, starting a business or buying a home in Iberia. Published by Vacation Work, 9 Park End Street, Oxford OX1 1HJ ℗ Oxford (0865) 241978.

Accommodation The Portuguese National Tourist Office, see above, can provide a brochure listing *pousadas* (state tourist inns) in historic houses, castles, palaces, convents and monasteries, situated in areas of natural beauty. Also publish a leaflet with a map showing campsites, with information on dates and facilities. Information sheet on accommodation for the disabled available. PH

Residência Universitária, Estrada da Costa, 1495 Cruz Quebrada, Lisbon has accommodation for students during August. 170 beds in double/triple rooms; cost Esc1500 per night. Meals available in restaurant; cost Esc400 each. Also offers discounts on train, boat and air travel. Further information from Servicos Socaiais da Universidade Técnica de Lisboa, Servico de Cultura e Turismo, Rua Goncalves Crespo 20, 1100 Lisbon.

Turicoop, Turismo Social e Juvenil, Rua Pascoal de Melo, 15-1, Dto, 1100 Lisbon can arrange cheap accommodation for young people in youth hostels, pensions and hotels. Also runs youth holiday centres and provides information on campsites.

ARCHAEOLOGY

INSTITUTO DA JUVENTUDE Avenida da Liberdade 194, 1200 Lisbon
Volunteers are invited to work on international workcamps assisting with archaeological digs aimed at discovering and preserving Portugal's heritage. Recent projects have included excavating, drawing, recording and cataloguing finds at prehistoric sites, Roman thermal baths, castles and other historic monuments in Beja, Braga, Braganca, Castelo Branco, Coimbra, Faro, Guarda, Leiria, Portalegre, Porto, Santarém, Setúbal and Viseu. Visits to local places of interest and sports activities arranged. Ages 18-25. 40 hour, 5 day week. 2 weeks, July-September. Food, accommodation in houses, schools or tents and insurance provided. Participants cook on a rota basis and must take a sleeping bag. Applicants pay their own travel.

Apply through partner organisation in country of residence. In the UK: Concordia (Youth Service Volunteers) Ltd, Recruitment Secretary,

8 Brunswick Place, Hove, East Sussex BN3 1ET
© Brighton (0273) 772086 or
International Voluntary Service, Old Hall, East
Bergholt, Colchester, Essex CO7 6TQ or
Quaker International Social Projects, Friends
House, Euston Road, London NW1 2BJ
(experienced volunteers only) or
United Nations Association, International Youth
Service, Temple of Peace, Cathays Park, Cardiff CF1
3AP © Cardiff (0222) 22308.

Outside the UK: please see information on page 30.

AU PAIR / CHILDCARE

**CENTRO DE INTERCAMBIO E TURISMO
UNIVERSITARIO avenida Defensores de
Chaves, 67-6, Dto, Lisbon**
Can provide information on au pair work.

**TURICOOP rua Pascoal de Melo, 15-1, Dto,
1100 Lisbon**
Can arrange au pair placements with families
during the summer, for girls aged 18+.

CONSERVATION

**INSTITUTO DA JUVENTUDE Avenida da
Liberdade 194, 1200 Lisbon**
Volunteers are invited to work on international
workcamps assisting with conservation
projects. Recent projects have included
restoring 16th-18th century ceramic tiles in
Beja; renovating an old watermill in Braga;
biological and geological studies in natural
caves in Portalegre; coastal protection work in
Setúbal; and renovating a Benedictine convent
in Serra da Arrabida. Visits to local places of
interest and sports activities arranged.
Ages 18-25. 40 hour, 5 day week. 2 weeks, July-
September. Food, accommodation in houses,
schools or tents and insurance provided;
participants cook on a rota basis and must take
a sleeping bag. Applicants pay their own travel.

*Apply through partner organisation in country of
residence. In the UK: Concordia (Youth Service
Volunteers) Ltd, Recruitment Secretary,
8 Brunswick Place, Hove, East Sussex BN3 1ET
© Brighton (0273) 772086 or
International Voluntary Service, Old Hall, East*

Bergholt, Colchester, Essex CO7 6TQ or
Quaker International Social Projects, Friends
House, Euston Road, London NW1 2BJ
(experienced volunteers only) or
United Nations Association, International Youth
Service, Temple of Peace, Cathays Park, Cardiff CF1
3AP © Cardiff (0222) 223088.

Outside the UK: please see information on page 30.

COURIERS / REPS

**SEASUN/TENTREK HOLIDAYS 71/72 East
Hill, Colchester, Essex CO1 2QW
© Colchester (0206) 861886**
Provides self catering family holidays in
apartments, mobile homes and tents plus
activity holidays for schools and groups.
Requires representatives for the summer
season, early April-mid November, in
Albuseira. 50/60 hour week. Ages 19+.
Applicants should be independent, resourceful
with commitment and good communication
skills. Knowledge of Portuguese an advantage.
Salary and subsistence £240 per month; £40 per
month extra paid on successful completion of
contract. Accommodation, travel, personal
insurance, training and partial uniform
provided. B D PH depending on ability.

WORKCAMPS

**ATEJ (Associacão de Turismo Estudantil e
Juvenil), Portuguese Youth & Student Travel
Association, PO Box 4586, 4009 Porto Cedex**
A non-profit association which organises a
variety of workcamps; volunteers are needed to
work in international teams. Recent projects
have included cleaning beaches, nature
protection, reconstructing monuments, and
constructing children's playgrounds. Previous
experience not necessary, but volunteers should
have a commitment to understanding and
learning about other cultures and nationalities.
Ages 16-30. Applicants should have a
knowledge of French, English, Spanish or
Portuguese. 5/6 hour day. June-September.
Accommodation and self-catering facilities in
youth hostels or camp sites and insurance
provided. Excursions arranged. Travel paid by
volunteers. Registration fee payable. PH

COMPANHEIROS CONSTRUTORES
Rua Pedro Monteiro 3-1, 3000 Coimbra
An international volunteers' association with
the aims of fighting misery and distress and
making a contribution towards a better
understanding between nations. Volunteers are
needed to work in international teams on behalf
of the socially, mentally, economically and
physically underprivileged. Recent projects
have included building and renovation work on
homes for the handicapped, the elderly, and
socially deprived families; in kindergartens,
children's villages and creches; on agricultural
cooperatives, roads and drainage systems; and
in social and cultural community centres. Ages
18+. 40 hour week. 3-4 weeks, July September.
Cost US$200 covers accident insurance, food
prepared by the volunteers, and tent, family or
centre accommodation; volunteers should take
a sleeping bag. Volunteers pay their own travel,
40% of which may be refunded. Also
opportunities for long-term volunteers on
development projects in rural areas, 1-12
months. *Apply 2 months in advance.*

INSTITUTO DA JUVENTUDE Avenida da Liberdade 194, 1200 Lisbon
Volunteers are invited to work on international
workcamps. Recent projects have included
renovating a youth hostel in Beja; restoring an
old castle in Portalegre; constructing kayaks in
Porto; preserving an abandoned village in
Viano do Castelo; studying and documenting
caves in Serra de Montejunio; and building a
children's playground and an open-air theatre
in Vila Real. Ages 18-25. 40 hour, 5 day week.
2 weeks, July-September. Food, accommodation
in houses, schools or tents and insurance
provided. Participants cook on a rota basis and
must take a sleeping bag. Applicants pay their
own travel.

*Apply through partner organisation in country of
residence. In the UK: Concordia (Youth Service
Volunteers) Ltd, Recruitment Secretary,
8 Brunswick Place, Hove, East Sussex BN3 1ET
© Brighton (0273) 772086 or
International Voluntary Service, Old Hall, East
Bergholt, Colchester, Essex CO7 6TQ or
Quaker International Social Projects, Friends
House, Euston Road, London NW1 2BJ
(experienced volunteers only) or
United Nations Association, International Youth*

*Service, Temple of Peace, Cathays Park, Cardiff CF1
3AP © (0222) 223088.*

Outside the UK: please see information on page 30.

MOVIMENTO CRISTAO PARA A PAZ (MCP)
**rua António José Almeida 210, Sub-Cave Esq,
3000 Coimbra ©/Fax Coimbra (39) 22303**
Volunteers are needed to work in international
teams on summer projects aimed at offering a
service in an area of need; promoting self-help
within the community; promoting international
understanding and the discussion of social
problems; and offering young people the chance
to live as a group and take these experiences
into the context of daily life. Recent projects
have included building and improving houses
near St Cruz; rebuilding houses damaged by
the weather for poor families; and helping to
build and set up a children's home with a
library and a garden. Ages 18+. Knowledge of
Portuguese or French useful. 6 hour day, 30
hour week for 2 weeks, July/August. Food,
accommodation and insurance provided, but
participants pay their own travel costs.

*Apply through partner organisation in country of
residence. In the UK: Christian Movement for
Peace, Bethnal Green United Reformed Church,
Pott Street, London E2 0EF*

Outside the UK: please see information on page 30.

GENERAL

**EUROYOUTH LTD 301 Westborough Road,
Westcliff, Southend-on-Sea Essex SS0 9PT
© Southend-on-Sea (0702) 341434**
Arranges stays where guests are offered board
and lodging in return for an agreed number of
hours English conversation with hosts or their
children. Time is also available for guests to
practise Portuguese. Mainly ages 15-25, but
there are sometimes opportunities for ages 13-
16 and for older applicants. The scheme is open
to British students interested in visiting
Portugal and living with a local family for a
short time. Compulsory language course.
2-3 weeks, June-August. Travel and insurance
paid by applicants. Registration fee approx £70.
*Apply at least 12 weeks prior to scheduled
departure date.*

INFORMATION

Romanian Embassy
4 Palace Green, London W8 4QD
℃ 071-937 9666/8
Visa Section: 071-937 9667

British Embassy
24 Strada Jules Michelet, 70154 Bucharest

Tourist Office
Romanian National Tourist Office,
17 Nottingham Place, London W1M 3FF
℃ 071-224 3692

Entry regulations Details of entry
requirements can be obtained from the Visa
Section of the Romanian Embassy. Employers/
workcamp organisers recruiting for work in
Romania will usually assist with arranging a
visa.

Travel Campus Travel, 52 Grosvenor Gardens,
London SW1W 0AG ℃ 071-730 3402 (offices
throughout the UK) and Council Travel, 28A
Poland Street, London W1V 3DB ℃ 071-437
7767 offer Eurotrain under 26 fares and youth/
student flights to Bucharest.

Publications Lonely Planet's *Eastern Europe on
a Shoestring* £13.95, provides practical
information on budget travel in Romania and
many other east European countries. Available
from good bookshops.

CONSERVATION

**BRITISH TRUST FOR CONSERVATION
VOLUNTEERS Room IWH, 36 St Mary's
Street, Wallingford, Oxfordshire OX10 0EU**
The largest charitable organisation in Britain to
involve people in practical conservation work.
Following the success of the Natural Break
Programme in the UK, BTCV is now developing
a series of international working holidays with
the aim of introducing the volunteering ethic to
communities abroad. It is hoped that British
volunteers will adapt to and learn from local
lifestyles as well as participate in the
community. Recent projects have included

repairing footpath erosion in the Jepilor Valley and fencing work in the dense woodland of the Danube Delta. 2-3 weeks, July-September. Ages 18-70. Cost from £110 includes transport from Bucharest Airport, food and basic accommodation, with everyone sharing in domestic chores. Membership fee £12. No fares or wages paid.

COURIERS/REPS

CRYSTAL HOLIDAYS Crystal House, The Courtyard, Arlington Road, Surbiton, Surrey KT6 6BW ✆ 081-390 8737
Tour operator arranging skiing holidays in Poiana Brasov and Sinaia. Representatives are required to meet and greet clients and look after their welfare during their holiday. Ski guides and chalet staff also required.
Ages 20-35. Previous experience and fluent Romanian desirable. Chalet staff must have catering qualifications and experience. Approx 60 hour, 6½ or 7 day week, December-April. Basic salary plus commission; board, lodging, insurance, travel costs and uniform provided. 1 week training seminar held at beginning of each season. *Apply April/May.*

APPLYING FOR A JOB

Before applying, read carefully all the information given. Unless otherwise indicated, applications should be made in writing. Check in particular:

✎ skills, qualifications or experience required

✎ the full period of employment expected

✎ any restrictions of age, sex or nationality

✎ application deadlines

✎ any other points, particularly details of insurance cover, and other costs you may have to bear such as travel and accommodation.

When writing to any organisation it is **essential** to mention **Working Holidays 1993** and to enclose a large, stamped, self-addressed envelope, or if overseas, a large addressed envelope and at least two International Reply Coupons (available at Post Offices). When applying be sure to include the following:

✎ name, address, date of birth, nationality, sex

✎ education, qualifications, relevant experience, skills, languages spoken

✎ period of availability

✎ a passport-size photo, particularly if you are to have contact with the public

✎ anything else asked for, eg a *cv*

SPAIN

INFORMATION

Spanish Embassy
16th Floor, Portland House, Stag Place, London
SW1E 5SE © 071-235 5555/6/7

Consular section: 20 Draycott Place, London
SW3 2RZ © 071-581 5921

British Embassy
Calle de Fernando el Santo 16, Madrid 4

Tourist office
Spanish National Tourist Office, 57/58 St
James's Street, London SW1A 1LB
© 071-499 0901

Youth hostels
Red Española de Albergues Juveniles, José
Ortega y Gasset 71, 28006 Madrid

Youth & student information
TIVE, Oficina Nacional de Intercambio y
Turismo de Jovenes y Estudiantes, José Ortega
y Gasset 71, 28006 Madrid

Entry regulations EC nationals are entitled to
take up employment in Spain without requiring
a visa or work permit. If they intend to stay in
Spain for over 3 months, a residence card or
Tarjeta Comunitaria Europea must be applied for.
These are obtainable from the *Comisaria de
Policia* or *Oficina Gubernativa de Extranjeros* in
the locality where the applicant intends to live
and work, upon presentation of a valid
passport or identity card and a photocopy of
the same, three passport-sized photographs, a
medical certificate and the contract or offer of
employment.

Non-EC nationals wishing to work in Spain
must apply in person for the appropriate visa
at the Spanish Consulate in their country of
residence. To do this they must present proof of
the offer of employment and complete four
application forms, one of which will be sent to
the future employer, who will take the
necessary steps with the Spanish employment
authorities. The Consulate will then notify the
applicant of the decision taken. In the UK, the
Consular fee is £39.36. Full details of the

regulations governing residence and employment in Spain are given on information sheets available from the Consular Section of the Spanish Embassy, see above.

Spain: a guide to employment and opportunities for young people offers advice and contacts for those seeking long and short term teaching posts, exchanges, office employment, summer jobs, voluntary work, au pair placements and travel. Available from the Hispanic & Luso Brazilian Council, Canning House, 2 Belgrave Square, London SW1X 8PJ © 071-235 2303; price £2 (free to members).

Job advertising Publicitas Ltd, 517/523 Fulham Road, London SW6 1HD © 071-385 7723 can place job advertisements in *El Pais* (leading national daily), *La Vanguardia* (leading Barcelona daily) and regional newspapers throughout Spain.

Travel Euro-Domino is a pass allowing 3, 5 or 10 days unlimited rail travel in 1 month on the railways of Spain. Cost from £76 (ages under 26) or £84 (ages 26+) for 3 days; £110 or £129 for 5 days; £176 or £207 for 10 days. Available from British Rail International Rail Centre, Victoria Station, London SW1V 1JY © 071-928 5151.

STA Travel, 74 Old Brompton Road, London SW7 3LQ/117 Euston Road, London NW1 2SX © 071-937 9921 (offices also in Birmingham, Bristol, Cambridge, Leeds, Manchester and Oxford) operates flexible, low-cost flights between London and destinations throughout Spain.

Campus Travel, 52 Grosvenor Gardens, London SW1W 0AG © 071-730 3402 (offices throughout the UK) and Council Travel, 28A Poland Street, London W1V 3DB & 071-437 7767 (offices also in Paris, Lyon, Düsseldorf, Tokyo and throughout the US) offer Eurotrain under 26 fares and low- cost student/youth airfares to destinations throughout Spain.

Publications *The Rough Guide to Spain* £8.99 and *The Rough Guide to Barcelona and Catalunya* £7.99 provide comprehensive background information plus details on getting there, getting around, places to explore and cheap places to stay. Available from good bookshops.

Live and Work in Spain and Portugal £8.95 is a guide for those interested in finding temporary or permanent work, starting a business or buying a home in Iberia. Published by Vacation Work, 9 Park End Street, Oxford OX1 1HJ © Oxford (0865) 241978.

ARCHAEOLOGY

INSTITUTO DE LA JUVENTUD Servicio Voluntario Internacional de España, José Ortega y Gasset 71, Madrid 28006
Volunteers with a genuine interest in archaeology are required to work on sites throughout Spain. Recent projects have included excavating a Bronze Age Agaric settlement in Murcia; excavating an 11th century castle in Toledo; documenting and cataloguing finds from a village dating back to the Celtic and Roman periods near Segovia; continuing excavations on an Iron Age site in Guipuzcoa; and excavating and cleaning mosaics in Sovia. Some of the projects include topographic studies, research, finds classification, lectures and discussions as well as excavation work. Cultural and sports activities and excursions arranged.
Ages usually 18-26; younger and older volunteers accepted on some camps. 40 hour week. 2/3 weeks, July and August. Food and accommodation in schools, youth hostels, centres or tents, and accident insurance provided. Participants pay own travel costs.

Apply through partner organisation in country of residence; in the UK: Quaker International Social Projects, Friends House, Euston Road, London NW1 2BJ (experienced volunteers only, ages 18+) or United Nations Association, International Youth Service, Temple of Peace, Cathays Park, Cardiff CF1 3AP © Cardiff (0222) 223088.

Outside the UK: please see information on page 30.

AU PAIR / CHILDCARE

In Spain, au pair posts are open to both males and females, ages 17-30. They are expected to work a maximum of 25 hours per week in return for board, lodging and at least Pt24000 per month pocket money; they should also take at least 10 hours of language classes per week. Where the au pair is not covered by the Spanish Social Security system, the host family must take out private medical insurance, paying at least half of the insurance premium. The bodies responsible for granting an au pair permit are the *Gobierno Civil* and the *Comisaria Provincial de Policia* in the area in which the prospective au pair will be resident.

ABOUT AU PAIRS 3 Garston Park, Godstone, Surrey RH9 8NE ℗ Godstone (0883) 743735
Can place au pairs. Single females only, ages 18-27. Pocket money £30 per week. Registration fee £25.

ACADEMY AU PAIR AGENCY LTD Glenlea, Dulwich Common, London SE21 7ES ℗ 081-299 4599
Can place au pairs. Ages 18-27. Some knowledge of Spanish essential. Pocket money approx £30-£35 per week. Administration charge £40. Positions as nannies and mothers' helps also available for those with qualifications/experience.

ANGLIA AGENCY 70 Southsea Avenue Leigh-on-Sea, Essex ℗ Southend-on-Sea (0702) 471648
Can place au pairs, mothers' helps and nannies. Ages 17+. Pocket money £30 per week. Service charge £40.

ANGLO PAIR AGENCY 40 Wavertree Road, Streatham Hill, London SW2 3SP ℗ 081-674 3605
Can place au pairs and au pairs plus. Ages 17-27. Pocket money £30-£50 per week. Also placements for experienced nannies and mothers' helps; salary up to £100 per week. Agency fee £40.

AVALON AGENCY Thursley House, 53 Station Road, Shalford, Guildford, Surrey GU4 8HA ℗ Guildford (0483) 63640
Can place au pairs. Ages 18-30. Basic knowledge of Spanish needed. Pocket money paid monthly. Service charge £40.

CENTROS EUROPEOS C/Principe 12, 6A, 28012 Madrid
Arranges au pair stays in Madrid, Bilbao, Asturias, Andalusia, Alicante, Valencia,

Zaragoza and Santander for girls aged 18+. Pocket money Pt6000 per week.

CLUB DE RELACIONES CULTURALES INTERNACIONALES Calle de Ferraz 82, 28008 Madrid ℗ Madrid (1) 541 7103
Can place au pairs in families all over Spain. Ages 18-28. Pocket money Pt6000-Pt7000 per week. Registration fee £25.

HELPING HANDS AU PAIR & DOMESTIC AGENCY 39 Rutland Avenue, Thorpe Bay, Essex SS1 2XJ ℗ Southend-on-Sea (0702) 602067
Can place au pairs mothers' helps. Ages 18-27. Pocket money approx £30 per week for au pairs, higher for mothers' helps. Introduction fee £40. *UK nationals only.*

HOME FROM HOME Walnut Orchard, Chearsley, Aylesbury, Buckinghamshire HP18 0DA ℗/Fax Aylesbury (0844) 208561
Can place au pairs in all areas of Spain. Ages 18+. Basic knowledge of Spanish preferable. Pocket money £25+ per week; Placement fee £40. *UK nationals only.*

JOLAINE AGENCY 18 Escot Way, Barnet, Hertfordshire EN5 3AN ℗ 081-449 1334
Can place au pairs and mothers' helps. Ages 17-27. Pocket money £25+ per week (au pairs) or £40+ (mothers' helps). Placement fee £40.

JUST THE JOB EMPLOYMENT AGENCY 8 Musters Road, West Bridgford, Nottingham NG2 6JA ℗ Nottingham (0602) 813224
Can place au pairs, mothers' helps and nannies. Ages 18+. Weekly pocket money £30-£40 (au pairs) or £75-£140 (other positions). *UK nationals only.*

LANGTRAIN INTERNATIONAL Torquay Road, Foxrock, Dublin, Ireland 18 ℗ Dublin (1) 289 3876
Can place au pairs in Spanish families. Ages 18+. Pocket money £25 per week. Placement fee £55.

PROBLEMS UNLIMITED AGENCY 86 Alexandra Road, Windsor, Berkshire SL4 1HU ℗ Windsor (0753) 830101
Can place au pairs. Ages 18-27. Pocket money £30-£35 per week. Service charge £40.

STUDENTS ABROAD LTD 11 Milton View, Hitchin, Hertfordshire SG4 0QD ℗ Hitchin (0462) 438909
Can place au pairs and mothers' helps on mainland and islands. Ages 18-30 for au pairs. Basic knowledge of Spanish useful. Pocket money from £30+ per week. Service charge £40. *Apply early for temporary summer positions.*

UNIVERSAL CARE Chester House, 9 Windsor End, Beaconsfield, Buckinghamshire HP9 2JJ ℗ Beaconsfield (0494) 678811
Can place au pairs in families in many areas of Spain. Some families visit the coast and the country during the summer holidays. Ages 17-27. Knowledge of Spanish desirable. Board and lodging provided. Salary approx Pt15000 per month. Service charge £47. *Apply 2 months before work period desired. EC nationals only.*

COMMUNITY WORK

SCI-SCCT CATALUNYA Rambla Catalunya, 5 pral 2na, 08007 Barcelona
Volunteers are needed to work in international teams on community service workcamps organised by SCI-SCCT, the Catalan branch of Service Civil International. Recent projects have included helping at a drug rehabilitation centre in Terrassa; organising leisure and festive activities with children and elderly people in a village in the pre-Pyrénées; and helping at institutes and homes which integrate people with disabilities in Barcelona, Tarragona and Girona.

Ages 18+. Applicants should be highly motivated and prepared to work hard as part of a team. Good knowledge of Spanish or Catalan essential for most camps. 35-40 hour week. 2-4 weeks, June-September. Food, accommodation and insurance provided, but no travel. **B D PH W**

Apply through partner organisation in country of residence. In the UK: International Voluntary Service, Old Hall, East Bergholt, Colchester, Essex CO7 6TQ.

Outside the UK: please see information on page 30.

CONSERVATION

INSTITUTO DE LA JUVENTUD Servicio Voluntario Internacional de España, José Ortega y Gasset 71, Madrid 28006
Volunteers are invited to work on voluntary conservation projects. Recent projects have included coastal protection work on Gran Canaria; cleaning the facade of a Renaissance church in Guipuzcoa; repairing forest pathways in Alicante; cleaning a river and creating a bathing pool in Asturias; painting and renovating churches and hermitages on Tenerife; planting trees in Castellon; restoring abandoned mountain villages using traditional techniques in Huesca; and conservation work in a seabird sanctuary on a river delta in Tarragona. Some of the projects include ecological studies and population surveys as well as conservation work. Cultural and sports activities and excursions arranged. Ages usually 18-26; older and younger volunteers accepted on some camps. 40 hour week. 2/3 weeks, July and August. Food, accommodation in schools, youth hostels, centres or tents and accident insurance provided. Participants pay own travel costs.

Apply through partner organisation in country of residence. In the UK: Quaker International Social Projects, Friends House, Euston Road, London NW1 2BJ (experienced volunteers only, ages 18+) or United Nations Association, International Youth Service, Temple of Peace, Cathays Park, Cardiff CF1 3AP ℗ Cardiff (0222) 223088.

Outside the UK: please see information on page 30.

LA SABRANENQUE CENTRE INTERNATIONAL rue de la Tour de l'Oume, 30290 Saint Victor la Coste, France
A small, non-profitmaking organisation that has been working since 1969 to preserve, restore and reconstruct abandoned rural sites, and bring them back to life. Aims to give volunteers the chance to discover the interest and pleasure of working directly on genuine rural restoration projects while being part of a cooperative international team. Helps to supervise a project in Ibort, a small village near the Pyrénées which was abandoned until several years ago. Volunteers work in small

teams, learning modern and traditional construction techniques on-the-job from experienced leaders. Work can include masonry, stone cutting, floor or roof tiling, interior restoration, drystone walling and path paving. Visits are made to the Pyrénées and nearby towns. No experience necessary. 2+ weeks, 1 July-30 August. Ages 18+. Cost Pt1500 per day includes full board dormitory accommodation in restored houses. Registration fee FF200.

SCI-SCCT CATALUNYA Rambla Catalunya, 5 pral 2na, 08007 Barcelona

Volunteers are needed to work in international teams on conservation projects in workcamps organised by SCI-SCCT, the Catalan branch of Service Civil International. Recent projects have included gardening and repairing houses in a half-abandoned village near Soria; improving the infrastructure of a nature reserve in Taradell, set up to protect endangered fauna; and restoring a mill in a village in the Pyrénées. Volunteers have the opportunity to participate in local festivals. Ages 18+. Applicants should be highly motivated, prepared to work hard as part of a team. Good knowledge of Spanish or Catalan essential on most camps. 35-40 hour week. 2-4 weeks, June-September. Food, accommodation and insurance provided, but not travel. B D PH W

Apply through partner organisation in country of residence. In the UK: International Voluntary Service Old Hall, East Bergholt, Colchester, Essex CO7 6TQ.

Outside the UK: please see information on page 30.

COURIERS / REPS

CANVAS HOLIDAYS LTD 12 Abbey Park Place, Dunfermline, Fife KY12 7PD

Resident couriers, children's couriers, nannies and watersports couriers are required to work on campsites for a holiday company providing accommodation for families in ready-erected fully equipped tents and cabins. The work involves a daily routine of tent cleaning as customers arrive and depart, providing information and advice on the local attractions and essential services, helping to sort out problems that might arise, and organising activities for the children and get-togethers for the families. 7 day week with no fixed hours; the workload varies from day to day. At the beginning and end of the season there is a period of physical work when tents are put up and prepared for the customers or taken down and stored for the winter. Other tasks include administration, book keeping and stock control. Working knowledge of Spanish essential.

Ages 18-25. Applicants are normally those with a year between school and further education, undergraduates or graduates. They need to be reliable, self-motivated, able to turn their hand to new and varied tasks, and with a sense of humour. 6 months, April-October. Return travel, dependent on successful completion of contract, and accommodation in frame tents provided. Salary £80 per week (1992). *UK nationals only; applications accepted any time, interviews commence early November.*

CLUB CANTABRICA HOLIDAYS LTD Overseas Department, Holiday House, 146-148 London Road, St Albans, Hertfordshire AL1 1PQ Ø St Albans (0727) 33141

Organises holidays providing fully equipped tents, caravans and mobile homes. Requires couriers and maintenance staff to work the whole summer season, mid May-early October. 6 day week. Ages 21+. Experience and good knowledge of Spanish an advantage. Wages from £45 per week, plus bonus at end of season. Self-catering accommodation in tents or caravans, travel costs from Watford and insurance provided. *EC nationals only. Apply enclosing cv and SAE/IRCs.*

EUROCAMP Summer Jobs, (Ref WH), PO Box 170, Liverpool L70 1ES

One of Europe's leading tour operators, specialising in providing quality camping and mobile home holidays for families throughout Europe. Campsite couriers are required: work involves cleaning tents and equipment prior to the arrival of new customers; checking, replacing and making repairs on equipment; replenishing gas supplies; keeping basic accounts and reporting on a weekly basis to England. Couriers are also expected to meet new arrivals and assist holidaymakers with any problems that arise; organise activities and parties; provide information on local tourist attractions and maintain an information noticeboard. At the beginning and end of the season couriers are also expected to help in erecting and dismantling tents. Couriers need to be flexible to meet the needs of customers and be on hand where necessary; they will be able to organise their own free time as the workload allows.

Ages 18+. Applicants should be independent, adaptable, reliable, physically fit, have plenty of initiative and relish a challenging and responsible position. Good working knowledge of Spanish also necessary. Preference given to those able to work the whole season, April-September/October; contracts also available for first half season, April-mid July and second half season, mid July-September/October.

Children's couriers are also required, with the energy and enthusiasm to organise a wide range of exciting activities for groups of children aged 4-13. Experience of working with children within this age range is essential, but language ability is not a requirement. Ages 20+. Children's couriers must be available for the whole season, May-September.

For both positions the salary is £91.50 per week. Training is provided together with accommodation in frame tent with cooking facilities, insurance and return travel.

UK/EC passport-holders only. Early application advisable; interviews start September/October.

HAVEN FRANCE & SPAIN Northney Marina, Northney Road, Hayling Island, Hampshire PO11 0NL
Tour operator organising self-drive package holidays, with accommodation in luxury mobile homes and tents. Seasonal park managers are required to work on sites on the Costa Brava. Work involves preparing accommodation, welcoming guests and sorting out any problems that may arise. Tiger Club couriers also required, to work with children and organise entertainment.
Ages 18+. Experience preferred but not essential, as training is given. Knowledge of Spanish essential. 40+ hour week, although hours vary. May-September. Salary approx £95 per week, but varies according to workload. Self-catering accommodation in mobile homes or tents, insurance and travel expenses provided. *UK nationals only.*

KEYCAMP HOLIDAYS 92-96 Lind Road, Sutton, Surrey SM1 4PL ✆ 081-395 8170
One of the UK's largest self-drive camping and mobile home tour operators, offering holidays on over 75 campsites in Europe. Campsite couriers are required to work for 3-6 months. Main duties include providing clients with information, organising social and sporting activities, cleaning mobile homes and tents, and providing activities for children. 3+ months, March-July or July-September. Knowledge of Spanish desirable. Ages 18+. Accommodation, uniform, training and competitive salary provided. *Applications welcome from September. Phone for application form.*

SCHOOL WORLD The Coach House, Tyn-y-Coed Place, Roath Park, Cardiff CF2 4TX ✆ Cardiff (0222) 470077
Organises skiing holidays for school groups at Arinsal in the Massana Valley, Andorra. Requires representatives to prepare for the groups' arrival, operate quality and safety control, deal with any problems, arrange après ski programmes and generally ensure that clients enjoy their holiday. Season lasts from late December-mid April depending on school holiday dates. Hours worked vary but representatives are on call at all times. Ages 19-30. Experience of working with the public and a good knowledge of Spanish essential; applicants must also be friendly and outgoing with a high level of common sense and personal organisation. Salary £35 per week, with a £15 bonus for each group looked after, depending on completion of contract. Full board accommodation, insurance and reasonable travel costs provided. 4-5 day residential training course held. Recruitment begins July for following winter season. *Applicants must have UK National Insurance number.*

SEASUN/TENTREK HOLIDAYS 71/72 East Hill, Colchester, Essex CO1 2QW ✆ (0206) Colchester 861886
Provides self-catering family holidays in apartments, mobile homes and tents plus

activity holidays for schools and groups. Requires representatives for the summer season, beginning April-mid November, in Castelli Montgri, Estartit and Lafosca. 50/60 hour week. Ages 19+. Applicants should be independent, resourceful and committed, with good communication skills. Knowledge of Spanish an advantage, but not essential. Salary and subsistence £240 per month; £40 per month extra paid on successful completion of contract. Accommodation, travel, personal insurance, training and partial uniform provided. B D PH depending on ability.

SOLAIRE INTERNATIONAL HOLIDAYS 1158 Stratford Road, Hall Green, Birmingham B28 8AF ✆ 021-778 5061
Organises camping and mobile home holidays at Salou on the Costa Dorada. Staff are required to prepare tents and mobile homes when the season begins in May and then close down at the end of the season in October. During the season staff act as couriers, ensuring the smooth running of the camps, and undertake some maintenance work. No fixed hours. Ages 18+. No previous experience necessary; foreign languages preferable but not essential. Wages £55-£75 per week, accommodation in tents or mobile homes, insurance and travel provided.

VENUE HOLIDAYS 21 Christchurch Road, Ashford, Kent TN23 1XD ✆ Ashford (0233) 642505
Small family company offering self-drive holidays with fully-equipped mobile homes at a campsite on the Costa Brava. Representatives are required to assist with montage and demontage, clean and maintain accommodation, sort out any problems and organise social events for adults and children. Average 50 hours per week with one day off, but daily workload varies considerably. Season lasts April-October, with a minimum requirement to work all of July and August.
Ages 18-30. Previous experience of working with the public desirable, as is a working knowledge of Spanish. Applicants should also be physically fit, able to work hard in hot conditions, mentally alert, with a pleasant, easygoing personality. Salary approx £45 per week, with possibility of bonus. Tented accommodation, communal meals, insurance and return fare provided.

LEADERS & GUIDES

CLUB DE RELACIONES CULTURALES INTERNACIONALES Calle de Ferraz 82, 28008 Madrid ✆ Madrid (1) 541 7103
Young people are required to work at hotels in coastal resorts, looking after children and arranging entertainments for them such as contests and parties. Full use of hotel facilities in spare time.

Ages 18-28. Applicants must have patience, imagination and experience of working with children. Knowledge of Spanish and other languages welcome. 4-6 hours per day. 1-3 months, April-September. Board, lodging, insurance and £40+ per week pocket money provided. Registration fee £25. *Apply January-March.*

MONITORS & INSTRUCTORS

ACORN VENTURE 137 Worcester Road, Hagley, Stourbridge, West Midlands DY9 0NW ✆ Hagley (0562) 882151
An activity holiday company catering for school groups at a centre in Cala Llevadó, north of Barcelona. Instructors required to supervise activities such as watersports, target sports, climbing, abseiling, orienteering, caving and gorge walking. Ages 18+. Previous experience and qualifications such as BCU/RYA essential. Fluency in Spanish a distinct advantage. 40-50 hour, 6 day week. Applicants are expected to work the full season, May-September. Salary approx £40-£45 per week. All meals and accommodation in tents, insurance and cost of return travel from ferry ports provided. *Apply in writing with cv by end January. If no reply within 28 days assume application unsuccessful.*

CLUB CANTABRICA HOLIDAYS LTD Overseas Department, Holiday House, 146-148 London Road, St Albans, Hertfordshire AL1 1PQ ✆ St Albans (0727) 833141
Organises camping holidays, providing fully equipped tents, caravans and mobile homes. Kiddies club staff are required to work the whole summer season, mid May-early October.

Ages 21+. Nursing, teaching or NNEB qualifications necessary. Salary from £45 per week, plus bonus at end of season. Self-catering accommodation in tents and caravans, travel from Watford and insurance provided. *Apply enclosing* cv. *EC nationals only.*

CLUB DE RELACIONES CULTURALES INTERNACIONALES Calle de Ferraz 82, 28008 Madrid ℗ Madrid (1) 541 7103

Young people are required to work as monitors on summer camps in Santander, Malaga, Segovia and Madrid. Work involves teaching English to the children and helping with sports, recreational and social activities. Some jobs involve working with mentally or physically handicapped children.

Ages 18+. Applicants with experience of working with children particularly welcome. July and August. Board and lodging, pocket money and a 4 day tour of Spain provided. Short and long-term teaching posts available throughout the year for young people with EFL experience.

Language helpers also needed to live with families and help with spoken English and children's homework. No housework or other duties involved. Ages 18-25. 5 hour day, 1-12 months, all year. Pocket money Pt2500 per week. Social service for all applicants, plus language programmes, weekend excursions and social club. Registration fee £25.

SEASUN/TENTREK HOLIDAYS 71/72 East Hill, Colchester, Essex CO1 2QW ℗ Colchester (0206) 861886

Provides self-catering family holidays in apartments, mobile homes and tents plus activity holidays for schools and groups. Requires qualified watersports instructors and senior instructors for the summer season, early April-mid November, in Estartit and La Fosca. 50/60 hour week.

Ages 19+. Applicants should be independent and resourceful with good communication skills and commitment. Knowledge of Spanish an advantage, but not essential. Training provided. Salary according to responsibility. Accommodation, travel, personal insurance and partial uniform provided.

TEACHERS

BRITISH COUNCIL ETRC Santa Barbara 10, 28004 Madrid

Can provide lists of English language establishments all over Spain where teachers can apply. Cost Pt1000.

CENTRO DE IDIOMAS LIVERPOOL Calle Libreros 11, 1ª, 28801 Alcala de Henares, Madrid ℗ Madrid (881) 3184

Small number of English teachers required by language school 30km from Madrid to teach at the school and at companies and schools in nearby towns.

Ages 22-30. Applicants must have an English degree, elementary Spanish, a recognised TEFL qualification and previous TEFL experience. 25 hour, 5 day week, mid-September-June. Salary Pt1,200 per hour; holidays are not paid. Insurance provided. Help given with finding accommodation. *Apply by July; interviews held in Britain during August. EC nationals only.*

CENTROS EUROPEOS English for Executives, C/Principe 12, 6 A, 28012 Madrid

Teachers with enthusiasm, imagination, and good communication skills are required to teach English, French, and occasionally German or Italian to small groups of mainly adult students. Classes take place within companies or privately.

Ages 20+. Applicants should have a university background and be reliable, conscientious and vivacious. Some experience preferred. Those without experience, but who have the necessary qualities and who attend an introductory course, may be accepted. Some knowledge of Spanish helpful but not essential. 15-25 hour week, October-June only; no summer positions. Pt2000 per hour. Accommodation can be arranged with families. Travel and insurance paid by applicants. PH *Native speakers only.*

ESCUELAS DE IDIOMAS BERLITZ DE ESPAÑA Ms Susan Taylor, Gran Via 80, 4ª, 28013 Madrid ℗ Madrid (1) 542 3586

Opportunities available for graduates of any discipline to teach English as a foreign/second language. Applicants will teach adult professionals at beginner through to advanced levels at language centres in Madrid, Barcelona, Bilbao, Sevila, Valencia and Palma de Mallorca. Also possibility of teaching English for Special Purposes in the areas of commerce, finance, science and engineering. The work may involve frequent travel within and around the city of allocation. Irregular timetable hours, 08.00-21.30, and Saturday mornings.

Ages 21+. Applicants should be mature, responsible, flexible regarding timetable, and have an outgoing personality. TEFL training/experience not necessary; full in-house training provided. 9 month contracts; details of salary on application.
Apply by mid April; applicants should send cv and recent photograph. Interviews held in the UK in September.

THE MANGOLD INSTITUTE Avda Marques de Sotelo 5, Pasaje Rex, Valencia 46002 ℂ Valencia (6) 352 7714/351 4556
Offers day and evening courses at all levels in languages, secretarial skills and computing. Languages taught include English, French, German, Italian, Russian, Arabic, and intensive summer courses in Spanish. EFL teachers and secretarial staff needed in Valencia and surrounding areas; native English speakers with knowledge of Spanish preferred.

Ages 25+. Teachers should have 1+ year's experience. 34 hour week. 9+ months, October onwards for teachers; April-June and October-December, secretarial staff. Wages approx Pt130000 per month, depending on qualifications. Accommodation approx Pt2000-Pt2500 per day, full board. Staff should allow Pt3500 per month, medical insurance.

WORKCAMPS

INSTITUTO DE LA JUVENTUD Servicio Voluntario Internacional de España, José Ortega y Gasset 71, Madrid 28006
Volunteers are invited to work in international workcamps on a variety of manual projects. Recent projects have included renovating an old youth hostel in Asturias; reconstructing a bridge and the city walls in Vallodolid; gardening in the grounds of a monastery in Madrid; renovating a Red Cross centre on

Tenerife; and reconstructing old houses in a village in Soria. Cultural and sports activities and excursions arranged.
Ages usually 18-26; older and younger applicants accepted on some camps. 2/3 weeks, July and August. Food, accommodation in schools, youth hostels, centres or tents, and accident insurance provided. Participants pay own travel costs.

Apply through partner organisation in country of residence. In the UK: Quaker International Social Projects, Friends House, Euston Road, London NW1 2BJ (experienced volunteers only, ages 18+) or United Nations Association, International Youth Service, Temple of Peace, Cathays Park, Cardiff CF1 3AP ℂ Cardiff (0222) 223088.

Outside the UK: please see information on page 30.

**SCI-SCCT CATALUNYA Rambla Catalunya, 5 pral 2na, 08007 Barcelona
SCI-MADRID Apdo 150086, 28020 Madrid**
Volunteers are needed to work in international teams on workcamps organised by SCI-SCCT, the Catalan branch of Service Civil International, and the local group based in Madrid. Recent projects organised by SCI-SCCT Catalunya have included restoring an old farm in the Serra Montsec National Park for use as a mountain refuge; and working alongside residents to clear gardens and put up fences at a centre for orphans and deprived children at Sant Feliu de Codines. Recent projects organised by SCI-Madrid have included building a greenhouse and nurseries near Villamalea to conserve rare Iberian plants in danger of extinction; and construction work and care of animals at a centre for injured wild animals in Majadahonda. Ages 18+. Applicants should be highly motivated and prepared to work hard as part of a team. Good knowledge of Spanish or Catalan essential on most camps. 40 hour week. 2-4 weeks, June-September. Food, accommodation and insurance provided, but no travel. B D PH W.

Apply through partner organisation in country of residence. In the UK: International Voluntary Service, Old Hall, East Bergholt, Colchester, Essex CO7 6TQ

Outside the UK: please see information on page 30.

GENERAL

ACORN VENTURE 137 Worcester Road, Hagley, Stourbridge, West Midlands DY9 0NW ✆ Hagley (0562) 882151
An activity holiday company catering for school groups at a centre in Cala Llevadó, north of Barcelona. Centre managers required to coordinate activities, organise evening entertainments and make sure groups have all they need. General maintenance staff also required.
Ages 18+. Applicants should have some previous experience and fluency in Spanish. 40-50 hour, 6 day week. Applicants are expected to work the full season, May-September. Salary approx £40-£45 per week. All meals and accommodation in tents, insurance and cost of return travel from ferry ports provided. *Apply in writing with cv by end January. If no reply within 28 days assume application unsuccessful.*

CANVAS HOLIDAYS LTD 12 Abbey Park Place, Dunfermline, Fife KY12 7PD
Provides ready-erected fully-equipped tents for family holidays, and requires a number of applicants to form flying squads, teams of 5/6 people who help set up and equip 200-250 6 berth frame tents in an area containing approx 12 campsites. Similar work also available dismantling tents and cleaning and storing equipment.
Ages 18-25. Knowledge of Spanish not required, but is an advantage as flying squad members sometimes have the opportunity to continue as couriers. Applicants must be sociable in order to work in a small community, fit and able to work hard for long hours under pressure, work without supervision and cope with living out of a rucksack. Driving licence an advantage. Early April-mid June, possibly longer to set up the tents, and September to dismantle them. Salary £80 per week, tented accommodation, self-catering facilities and outward travel provided. Return travel dependent on the completion of contract dates. *UK nationals only.*

EUROYOUTH LTD 301 Westborough Road, Westcliff, Southend-on-Sea Essex SSO 9PT ✆ Southend-on-Sea (0702) 341434
Arranges holiday guest stays where guests are offered board and lodging in return for an agreed number of hours English conversation with hosts or their children. Time is also available for guests to practise Spanish if desired. Mainly ages 15-25, but sometimes opportunities for older applicants. 2-3 weeks, and occasionally 1-2 months, mainly July and August. Travel and insurance arranged by applicants, but tickets at reduced rates can be obtained on request. Registration fee approx £70. *Apply at least 12 weeks prior to scheduled departure date. UK nationals only.*

INFORMATION

Swedish Embassy
11 Montagu Place, London W1H 2AL
✆ 071-724 2101
Consular Section: ✆ 071-724 6782

British Embassy
Skarpögatan 6-8/Box 27819, 115 93 Stockholm

Tourist office
Swedish National Tourist Office, 29/31 Oxford Street, London W1R 1RE ✆ 071-437 5816

Youth hostels
STS, Vasagatan 48, 101 20 Stockholm

Youth & student information
SFS Resor, Kungsgatan 4, 103 87 Stockholm

Östermahus Fritidsgard, Valhallavagen 142, 115 24 Stockholm

Entry regulations A work permit is required for all types of employment. Applications should be made to the Swedish Embassy or Consulate once an offer of employment has been secured. Work permits are issued for a specific job and period and applicants will be notified of the decision by the Embassy. An offer of employment is no guarantee that a work permit will be granted. Students should indicate their status when applying; vacation employment may cover a period of 3 months, 15 May-15 October. Opportunities extremely limited; students without a specific skill or knowledge of Swedish may have difficulty in obtaining a permit. Applications for work permits are not accepted from visitors already in Sweden; if an applicant enters Sweden before the work permit is granted, the permit will be refused. It usually takes 6-8 weeks to process an application. Applications for work can be made under the International Clearing of Vacancies scheme; for more details in the UK contact the Training Agency. Those intending to remain for more than 3 months will require a residence permit which must be issued before entering Sweden; if the period of work exceeds 3 months it is usually necessary to attend an interview at the Embassy.

These regulations may change as of January 1993 subject to the European Economic Space agreement, and a work permit may no longer be required by EC nationals.

Job advertising Frank L Crane (London) Ltd, International Press Representation, 5/15 Cromer Street, Grays Inn Road, London WC1H 8LS ✆ 071-837 3330 can place advertisements in *Svenska Dagbladet* (Stockholm), *Goteborgs-Posten* (Gothenburg), *Sydsvenska Dagbladet* (Malmö) and many other newspapers.

Travel Norwegian State Railways, 21/24 Cockspur Street, London SW1Y 5DA ✆ 071-930 6666 issues the Nordic Tourist Ticket which entitles the holder to unlimited travel on trains in Sweden, Norway, Denmark and Finland, and is also valid on some inter-Scandinavian ferry services. Valid 21 days; cost £115 for ages under 26, £155 for ages over 26.

Campus Travel, 52 Grosvenor Gardens, London SW1W 0AG ✆ 071-730 3402 (offices throughout the UK) and Council Travel, 28A Poland Street, London W1V 3DB ✆ 071-437 7767 (offices also in Paris, Lyon, Düsseldorf, Tokyo and the US) offer Eurotrain under 26 fares and competitive airfares to destinations in Sweden.

Publications Lonely Planet's *Scandinavian and Baltic Europe on a Shoestring* £10.95 offers practical, down-to-earth information for the low-budget, independent traveller in Sweden. *The Rough Guide to Scandinavia* £8.95 provides comprehensive background information on Sweden, with details on getting around, places to explore and cheap places to stay. *Michael's Guide to Scandinavia* £10.95 is detailed and concise, providing invaluable practical advice for all kinds of travellers. Published by Inbal Travel.
All the above are available from good bookshops.

Sweden Holiday Guide is a free magazine providing general information on travel to and around the country, places of interest, public services, medical treatment, eating, accommodation and outdoor activities, plus maps and colour photographs. Also *Holiday Guide for the Disabled*. Available from the Swedish National Tourist Office, see above. PH

FARMWORK

INTERNATIONAL FARM EXPERIENCE PROGRAMME YFC Centre, National Agricultural Centre, Stoneleigh Park, Kenilworth, Warwickshire CV8 2LG ✆ **Coventry (0203) 696584**
Provides assistance to young farmers and nurserymen by finding places in farms and nurseries abroad to enable them to broaden their knowledge of agricultural methods. Opportunities for practical horticultural or agricultural work, usually on mixed farms. Applicants live and work with a farmer and his family and the work is matched as far as possible with the applicant's requirements. 3-12 months, mostly spring and summer. Pocket money, board and lodging provided.

Ages 18-26. Applicants must have at least 2 years practical experience, 1 year of which may be at an agricultural college, and intend to make a career in agriculture or horticulture. Valid driving licence necessary. Applicants pay own fares. Registration fee £70. *UK applicants only; apply at least 3 months in advance.*

TEACHERS

FOLK UNIVERSITY OF SWEDEN The British Centre, c/o International Language Services (Scandinavia), 36 Fowlers Road, Salisbury, Wiltshire SP1 1ED ✆ **Salisbury (0722) 331011**
The British Centre is part of the Folk University, the only organisation concerned with promoting adult education in Sweden with no political, religious or sociological affiliations. The majority of English teachers are placed in Type B posts, in smaller towns, where they teach mainly general English at all levels for adults in study circles, plus some teaching in schools, with a limited number in Kursverksamheten (KVs), extra-mural departments of local universities. The largest KVs, in Gothenburg, Stockholm, Lund and Uppsala, employ teachers in Type A posts where work is of a more demanding nature.

Ages 22-40. Applicants must be British citizens and hold a university degree and/or qualified teacher status in the UK or recognised TEFL qualifications granted in the UK. For Type A posts 2+ years EFL experience and RSA TEFL Diploma or equivalent also required. Applicants must be in excellent health, sociable, adaptable and well informed; those with children will not be considered. Approx 26 academic hour week, September-May. Limited number of vacancies in January. Teachers must be prepared to work every weekday evening; some weekend work possible. Accommodation provided during initial training course. Salary approx Kr9500 per month, plus supplement of Kr1500-Kr2000 per month for Type A posts. Travel provided; teachers working 4+ terms receive contribution to return journey. Most teachers stay for at least 2 years. *Apply anytime; interviews held in spring, early summer and November.*

WORKCAMPS

INTERNATIONELLA ARBETSLAG (IAL)
Barnangsgatan 23, 11641 Stockholm
The Swedish branch of Service Civil International, which promotes international reconciliation through work projects. International teams of 8-10 volunteers live and work together on workcamps where the work may vary from manual labour to social activities or study. Recent projects have included planting, caring for animals and studying organic methods on a farm in Trollhätten; sorting and packing second-hand clothes and equipment to send to refugees at centres in Skane and Smaland; haymaking and building a barn at a collective set up to help drug abusers in Ramvik; and constructing turf houses using traditional Sami methods in a wildlife village in Solberget. Study themes are linked to the camps.
Ages 18+. Applicants should be highly motivated and prepared to work hard as part of a team. 35-40 hour week. 2 weeks, June-September. Food, accommodation and insurance provided, but not travel. **B D PH W**

Apply through partner organisation in country of residence. In the UK: International Voluntary Service, Old Hall, East Bergholt, Colchester, Essex CO7 6TQ.

Outside the UK: please see information on page 30.

SWITZERLAND

INFORMATION

Swiss Embassy
16-18 Montagu Place, London W1H 2BQ
℗ 071-723 0701
Consulate General: Sunley Building, 24th floor,
Piccadilly Plaza, Manchester M1 4BT
℗ 061-236 2933

British Embassy
Thunstraße 50, 3005 Bern

Tourist office
Swiss National Tourist Office, Swiss Centre,
Swiss Court, London W1V 8EE ℗ 071-734 1921

Youth hostels
Schweizerischer Bund für Jugendherbergen
(SJH), Postfach 265, Engelstraße 9, 3000 Bern 26

Youth & student information
Swiss Student Travel Office, SSR-Reisen,
Bäckerstraße 40, Postfach, 8026 Zürich

Entry regulations An *assurance of a residence
permit* is required for all types of employment;
this is a combination of both a residence and
work permit, entitling the holder to live in a
particular canton and work for a specified
employer. It should be obtained by the
prospective employer by applying to the
Cantonal Aliens Police before the applicant's
arrival in Switzerland. This procedure also
applies to au pairs and trainees.

The economic situation and quota restrictions
imposed by the Federal Government on the
granting of seasonal permits has resulted in a
considerable decrease in employment
opportunities for foreign nationals. The number
of permits granted is extremely limited and
only applicants offering specific skills or
qualifications are likely to succeed. As a rule,
only those who have been offered a job which
cannot be filled by a Swiss national have a
chance of receiving a permit.

The few jobs for which permits may be granted
are mainly in the hotel and catering trades, and
in shops and on farms. Seasonal permits are
granted to holders of assurance of a residence

permits after arrival in Switzerland for seasonal employment in the building, hotel and holiday industry for a period of 4/5-9 months; entry and exit dates must be strictly adhered to. Those married to Swiss women, and foreign children of a Swiss mother are not subject to the quota restrictions.

These regulations may change as of January 1993 subject to the European Economic Space agreement, and a work permit may no longer be required by EC nationals.

The Federal Office for Industry, Crafts and Labour in Bern publishes an informative booklet covering information on entry and residence, job availability, living and working conditions, wages, taxes and insurance schemes; available from the Swiss Embassy.

Job advertising Publicitas Ltd, 517/523 Fulham Road, London SW6 1HD ℂ 071-385 77 23 can place job advertisements in the *Basler Zeitung* (Basle daily), *Der Bund* (Bern daily), *Journal de Genève* (high class daily), *Neue Zürcher Zeitung* (leading high class daily), *La Suisse* (Geneva daily), *24 Heures* (Lausanne daily) and other newspapers.

Travel Euro-Domino is a pass allowing 5 days unlimited rail travel in 1 month on the railways of Switzerland, including most Swiss private railways. Cost (1992) from £64 (ages under 26) or £85 (ages 26+). Available from British Rail International Rail Centre, Victoria Station, London SW1V 1JY ℂ 071-928 5151.

STA Travel Ltd, 74 Old Brompton Road, London SW7 3LQ/117 Euston Road, London NW1 2SX ℂ 071-937 9921 (offices also in Birmingham, Bristol, Cambridge, Leeds, Manchester and Oxford) operates flexible, low-cost flights between London, Geneva and Zürich.

Campus Travel, 52 Grosvenor Gardens, London SW1W 0AG ℂ 071-730 3402 (offices throughout the UK) and Council Travel, 28A Poland Street, London W1V 3DB ℂ 071-437 7767 (offices also in Paris, Lyon, Düsseldorf, Tokyo and throughout the US) offer Eurotrain under 26 fares and charter flights to destinations in Switzerland.

Swiss National Tourist Office, Swiss Centre, Swiss Court, London W1V 8EE ℂ 071-734 1921 issues the Swiss Pass which gives unlimited travel on rail, boat and postbus routes, plus trams and buses in 24 towns, and reductions on mountain railways and cable cars. Cost £72-£144, 4-31 days.

Publications *Travel Tips for Switzerland* is a booklet containing information on travel formalities and facilities including accommodation, sports, culture and general information and advice. Available from the Swiss National Tourist Office, see above.

Michael's Guide to Switzerland £7.95 is detailed and concise, providing a invaluable practical advice for all kinds of travellers. Published by Inbal Travel and available from good bookshops.

Accommodation *Student Lodgings at University Cities in Switzerland* is a booklet giving the addresses of student accommodation. Available from the Swiss National Tourist Office, see above.

AU PAIR / CHILDCARE

HELPING HANDS AU PAIR & DOMESTIC AGENCY 39 Rutland Avenue, Thorpe Bay, Essex SS1 2XJ ℂ Southend-on-Sea (0702) 602067
Can place au pairs and mothers' helps. Ages 18-27. Pocket money approx £30 per week for au pairs, higher for mothers' helps. Introduction fee £40. *UK nationals only.*

HOME FROM HOME Walnut Orchard, Chearsley, Aylesbury, Buckinghamshire HP18 0DA ℂ/Fax Aylesbury (0844) 208561
Can place au pairs. Ages 18+. Reasonable level of French essential. Pocket money £25 per week. Placement fee £40. *UK nationals only.*

LANGTRAIN INTERNATIONAL Torquay Road, Foxrock, Dublin 18, Ireland ℂ Dublin (1) 289 3876
Can place au pairs with Swiss families. Ages 18+. Pocket money £25-£40 per week. Placement fee £55.

STUDENTS ABROAD LTD 11 Milton View, Hitchin, Hertfordshire SG4 0QD ✆ Hitchin (0462) 438909
Can place au pairs and occasionally nannies for 1 year stay. Ages 18-27 for au pairs. Knowledge of French, German or Italian helpful. Pocket money approx £30-£35 per week. Service charge £40.

UNIVERSAL CARE Chester House, 9 Windsor End, Beaconsfield, Buckinghamshire HP9 2JJ ✆ Beaconsfield (0494) 678811
Can place au pairs and mothers' helps. Ages 17-27. Pocket money usually £25 per week; higher for mothers' helps. Service charge £47. *Apply 2 months before work period desired. EC nationals only.*

COMMUNITY WORK

SERVICE CIVIL INTERNATIONAL Postfach 228, 3000 Bern 9
Service Civil International promotes international reconciliation through work projects. Volunteers are needed to work in international teams on community projects. Recent projects have included building a new school house at a Rudolf Steiner school in St Gallen; working on a holiday camp for handicapped and able-bodied children in Neuenberg; carrying out construction and agricultural work on a farm community in the canton of Bern for adults and children undergoing social therapy; and collecting information on museums, cinemas, restaurants and other public buildings in Basle, in order to update a guide for handicapped people.

Ages 18+. Applicants should be highly motivated and prepared to work hard as part of a team. Good knowledge of German needed on some camps. 35-40 hour week. 2-4 weeks, June-September. Food, accommodation and insurance provided, but not travel. B D PH W

Apply through partner organisation in country of residence. In the UK: International Voluntary Service, Old Hall, East Bergholt, Colchester, Essex CO7 6TQ.

Outside the UK: please see information on page 30.

CONSERVATION

INTERNATIONALE ARBEITSGEMEINSCHAFT für Wander, Ski-, Rad- and Rettungswesen (AWSR), Rosengartenstraße 17, 9000 St Gallen
Volunteers are needed for conservation work at international camps in Zermatt, Saas Fee, Sustenpass/Steingletscher and possibly Schwägalp. Small teams of volunteers go out from the basecamp to work on a variety of projects, which may include environmental protection on alpine roads and the shores of rivers and lakes; building footpaths and small bridges, clearing litter; or repairing damage caused by avalanches.

Ages 18-26. Knowledge of German required. 5-7 hour day, excluding travel to and from work place. 5 day week. 8-22 days; mid June-end August. Full board accommodation provided, plus SF6 per day pocket money. Volunteers must take mountain boots, warm clothes, rainwear, sleeping bag, first aid kit, pocket knife, torch, sunglasses and signal whistle; anyone arriving insufficiently equipped will not be accepted. Volunteers pay their own travel costs. Registration fee SF50. Families welcome. *Apply at least 4 weeks before intended date of arrival; applications confirmed 2+ weeks before starting date.*

INTERNATIONALE BEGEGNUNG IN GEMEINSCHAFTSDIENSTEN EV (IBG) Schlosserstraße 28, W-7000 Stuttgart 1, Germany
Founded by Scout leaders to organise work projects of benefit to the community and to promote better international understanding. Volunteers are needed on international workcamps; each camp is made up of 15-20 participants from 6-8 countries who work together on a common project. Recent projects have included forestry work at Olten; and renovating footpaths near Brig, Altdorf and Munster.
Ages 18-30. 30 hour week with weekends free. 3 weeks, August-September. Food, accommodation in youth hostels or schools with self catering facilities and insurance provided, but not travel. Volunteers should take a sleeping bag. Registration fee DM90.

Apply through partner organisation in country of residence; in the UK: United Nations Association, International Youth Service, Temple of Peace, Cathays Park, Cardiff CF1 3AP ☎ Cardiff (0222) 223088.

SERVICE CIVIL INTERNATIONAL Postfach 228, 3000 Bern 9

Service Civil International promotes international reconciliation through work projects. Volunteers are needed to work in international teams on conservation projects which have recently included restoring buildings and farmwork in an abandoned village in Ticino; clearing storm-damaged trees and repairing trails through alpine forests near Chur; rebuilding an ancient flight of steps leading along rocks in the canton of Grisons; and clearing alpine pastures in St Gallen, areas previously used for military exercises, in order to return them to their natural state.
Ages 18+. Knowledge of French or German useful. Applicants should be highly motivated and prepared to work hard as part of a team. 35-40 hour week. 2-4 weeks, June-September. Food, accommodation and insurance provided, but not travel. **B D PH W**

Apply through partner organisation in country of residence. In the UK: International Voluntary Service, Old Hall, East Bergholt, Colchester, Essex CO7 6TQ.

Outside the UK: please see information on page 30.

COURIERS / REPS

BLADON LINES Personnel Department, 56-58 Putney High Street, London SW15 1SF ☎ 081-785 2200

Opportunities for representatives to work in Swiss ski resorts. Work involves looking after guests, providing information, organising coach transfers and ensuring everything is running smoothly. Ages 24+. Relevant experience an advantage, and good spoken French or German essential. Applicants must be prepared to work hard but will get time to ski. December-May. Salary £50-£100, depending on the size of the resort. Board, lodging, return travel, insurance, ski pass, ski hire and company ski jacket provided. Training week

held in London before departure.
There are also a couple of places in each resort for ski guides who act as assistant representatives and whose work involves showing guests around the slopes, helping with coach transfers and organising *après ski*. Ages 22+ with good spoken French or German. Applicants should have good leadership qualities and be proficient skiers. Salary approx £50 per week. A week's training held in Val d'Isère before the season starts. PH depending on ability. *EC nationals only.*

CANVAS HOLIDAYS LTD 12 Abbey Park Place, Dunfermline, Fife KY12 7PD

Resident couriers, children's couriers, nannies and watersports couriers are required to work on campsites for a holiday company providing accommodation for families in ready-erected fully equipped tents and cabins. The work involves a daily routine of tent cleaning as customers arrive and depart, providing information and advice on the local attractions and essential services, helping to sort out problems that might arise and organising activities for the children and get-togethers for the families. 7 day week job with no fixed hours; the workload varies from day to day. At the beginning and end of the season there is a period of physical work when tents are put up and prepared for the customers or dismantled and stored for the winter. Other tasks include administration, book keeping and stock control. Working knowledge of French or German essential.
Ages 18-25. Applicants are normally those with a year between school and further education, undergraduates or graduates. They need to be reliable, self-motivated, able to turn their hand to new and varied tasks, and with a sense of humour. 6 months, April-October. Return travel, dependent on successful completion of contract, and accommodation in frame tents provided. Salary £80 per week (1992).
UK nationals only. Applications accepted any time; interviews commence early November.

CRYSTAL HOLIDAYS Crystal House, The Courtyard, Arlington Road, Surbiton, Surrey KT6 6BW ☎ 081-390 8737

Tour operator arranging air and self-drive holidays to Interlaken, Wengen and Grindelwald, and winter skiing holidays in

Château d'Oex, Davos/Klosters, Saas Fee, Verbier, Wengen and Zermatt. Representatives are required to meet and greet clients and be responsible for their welfare during their holiday. Ski guides also needed during winter season. Ages 20-35. Previous experience desirable and fluent German/French essential. Approx 60 hour, 7 day week, May-October and December-April. Basic salary plus commission; board, lodging, insurance, travel costs and uniform provided. 1 week training seminar held at beginning of each season. *Apply January/February for summer season, April/May for winter season.*

EUROCAMP Summer Jobs, (Ref WH), PO Box 170, Liverpool L70 1ES

One of Europe's leading tour operators, specialising in providing quality camping and mobile home holidays for families throughout Europe. Campsite couriers are required: work involves cleaning tents and equipment prior to the arrival of new customers; checking, replacing and making repairs on equipment; replenishing gas supplies; keeping basic accounts and reporting on a weekly basis to England. Couriers are also expected to meet new arrivals and assist holidaymakers with any problems that arise; organise activities and parties; provide information on local tourist attractions and maintain an information noticeboard. At the beginning and end of the season couriers are also expected to help in erecting and dismantling tents.

Couriers need to be flexible to meet the needs of customers and be on hand where necessary; they will be able to organise their own free time as the workload allows.

Ages 18+. Applicants should be independent, adaptable, reliable, physically fit, have plenty of initiative and relish a challenging and responsible position. Good working knowledge of French/German also necessary. Preference given to those able to work the whole season, April-September/October; contracts also available for first half season, April-mid July and second half season, mid July-September/October.

Children's couriers are also required, with the energy and enthusiasm to organise a wide range of exciting activities for groups of children aged 4-13. Experience of working with children within this age range is essential, but language ability is not a requirement. Ages 20+. Children's couriers must be available for the whole season, May-September.

For both positions the salary is £91.50 per week. Training is provided together with accommodation in frame tent with cooking facilities, insurance and return travel. *UK/EC passport-holders only. Early application advisable; interviews start September/October.*

LOTUS SUPERTRAVEL Alpine Operations Department, Mobbs Court, 2 Jacob Street, London SE1 2BT ✆ 071-962 9933

Arranges skiing holidays in the Swiss alpine resorts of Murren, Wengen, Zermatt and Verbier. Opportunities for resort representatives, responsible for looking after guests and supervising staff. Ages 24-30. Work involves travelling to the airport each weekend to welcome guests; organising their ski passes, ski hire and ski school; informing them of local events; overseeing the work of chalet girls and ensuring that chalets are kept in perfect running order. There are also opportunities for managers in jumbo chalets (24-60 beds) who are responsible for the smooth running of their chalets and, if not experienced in hotel work, should be experienced in managing others. Applicants should be used to working on their own initiative, often under pressure. Stamina, a sense of humour and fluent French or German essential. Applicants must be available for the whole season, early December-end April. Approx 40+ hours per week. Board, lodging, ski pass, ski and boot hire and return travel provided; also insurance in return for approx £35 contribution. Salary £55-£85 per week, paid in local currency. Training course held in London before departure, plus individual session to learn about the resort. *UK/EC passport-holders only.*

SCHOOL WORLD The Coach House, Tyn-y-Coed Place, Roath Park, Cardiff CF2 4TX ✆ Cardiff (0222) 470077

Organises skiing holidays for school groups at Château d'Oex and Les Diablarets. Requires representatives to prepare for the groups' arrival, operate quality and safety control, deal with any problems, arrange après ski programmes and generally ensure that clients enjoy their holiday. Season lasts from late December-mid April depending on school holiday dates. Hours worked vary but representatives are on call at all times. Ages 19-30. Experience of working with the public and a good knowledge of French essential; applicants must also be friendly and outgoing with a high level of common sense and personal organisation. Salary £35 per week, with a £15 bonus for each group looked after, depending on completion of contract. Full board accommodation, insurance and reasonable travel costs provided. 4-5 day residential training course held. Recruitment begins July for following winter season. *Applicants must have UK National Insurance number.*

VENTURE ABROAD Warren House, High Street, Cranleigh, Surrey GU6 8AJ ✆ Cranleigh (0483) 273027
Representatives are required by a tour operator specialising in European holidays for youth groups. The work involves assisting and advising groups staying in Adelboden, Grindelwald, Gstaad, Meiringen and Interlaken, all in the Bernese Oberland, helping to them to get the most out of their stay. Representatives meet groups on arrival, provide general local information, hire coaches, escort on excursions and act as guides to the surrounding countryside. Ages 19+. University students with knowledge of French or German and experience of working with youth groups preferred. 50 hour week, end June-end August. Salary £85 per week, self-catering accommodation, insurance, work permit and visa provided. Basic training given before departure. *Apply enclosing cv.*

DOMESTIC

BLADON LINES Personnel Department, 56-58 Putney High Street, London SW15 1SF ✆ 081-785 2200
Opportunities for cooks and cleaners to work in the ski resorts of Verbier, Crans Montana, Les Diablerets, Haute Nendaz, Saas Fee and Zermatt. Also opportunities for chalet girls, whose work involves cleaning chalets, making beds, caring for guests, shopping and preparing meals. Ages 20+. Experience and/or qualifications in catering or domestic work

essential. There are also positions for hostesses to work in the larger chalets, where no cooking experience is required. Hours are very variable; applicants must be prepared to work hard but will get time to ski. December-May. Salary approx £40 per week, ski pass, ski hire, company ski jacket, board, lodging, return travel and insurance provided. One day briefing in London before departure. *EC nationals only.* PH depending on ability.

CRYSTAL HOLIDAYS Crystal House, The Courtyard, Arlington Road, Surbiton, Surrey KT6 6BW ✆ 081-390 8737
Tour operator arranging skiing holidays in Château d'Oex, Davos/Klosters, Saas Fee, Verbier, Wengen and Zermatt. Chalet staff are required to cook daily breakfast, afternoon tea and 3-course evening meal for clients, and keep chalets clean and tidy. Ages 20-35. Catering qualifications, experience and fluent German essential. Approx 60 hour, 6½ day week, December-April. Basic salary plus commission; board, lodging, insurance, travel costs and uniform provided. 1 week training seminar held at beginning of season. *Apply April/May.*

JOBS IN THE ALPS AGENCY PO Box 388, London SW1X 8LX
Can provide work for hall and night porters, waiters, waitresses, and occasionally receptionists or barmaids, in hotels with international clientèle. Some 150 jobs are available each season. Good knowledge of French or German required. Limited number of other jobs such as chambermaids and kitchen helpers, and in mountain cafés, may be available for those with limited languages. Some jobs available for girls with a good knowledge of French in village cafés. Ages 18+. Applicants must be prepared to work hard and to a high standard, alongside an international workforce. 9 hour day with afternoons usually free. 2 days free per week, of which one may be paid in lieu during the high season. Jobs are for the whole season, December-April or June-September. Pay from approx £110 per week, board, lodging and insurance provided. Interview fee £1, plus £25 service charge and £15 per week levy depending on length of contract. *Closing dates for interviews: 30 September (winter) or 30 April (summer). EC nationals only.*

LOTUS SUPERTRAVEL Alpine Operations Department, Mobbs Court, 2 Jacob Street, London SE1 2BT ✆ 071-962 9933

Arranges skiing holidays in the alpine resorts of Zermatt and Verbier. Opportunities for chalet staff responsible for looking after guests and keeping chalet clean and tidy. Ages 21-30. Work involves cooking, cleaning, acting as hostess, sitting down to dinner with guests, advising them on skiing areas and keeping them up to date with events in the resort. Chalet staff must work to a budget and account for expenditure. Applicants must have cooking experience and preferably qualifications, be capable of running a chalet of approx 8 guests and have an outgoing and helpful personality. In the jumbo chalets (24-60 beds) there are opportunities for chalet girl helpers, whose duties are similar to the chalet staff but do not involve cooking, and also for chalet boy helpers, who look after the heavier duties such as cleaning of general areas, washing up, snow clearing, maintenance and sometimes bar work. Ages 20+. Applicants must be available for the whole season, early December-end April. Approx 40+ hours per week. Board, lodging, ski pass, ski and boot hire and return travel provided; also insurance in return for approx £35 contribution. Salary £45 per week, paid in local currency. Briefings held in London before departure. *UK/EC passport-holders only.*

VILLAGE CAMPS Chalet Seneca, 1854 Leysin

Organises a range of holidays in American-style camps for children aged 8-16 from the international business and diplomatic communities. Opportunities for chalet girls to work on winter ski camps in Anzere, Leysin and Morgins. Chalet girls are responsible for some kitchen work, dining room service, house cleaning and preparing the chalet for the weekly arrival of guests. Ages 21+. Applicants should be friendly and capable of dealing with groups of people of different ages and nationalities. English is the first language but priority consideration is given to applicants with French and German language skills. 45 hour week, December-Easter. Accommodation, ski pass, accident and liability insurance provided. Wages SF150 per week. Applicants pay their own travel costs. Compulsory pre-camp training course arranged.

FARMWORK

LANDDIENST-ZENTRALSTELLE Postfach 728, Mühlegasse 13, 8025 Zürich

Workers are required for agricultural and domestic work on small farms in French and German-speaking cantons. Work involves cleaning out cowstalls, haymaking, grass cutting, poultry feeding, transporting milk, manure spreading and spraying, vegetable and fruit picking, wood cutting, gardening and housework. Ages 17+. Basic knowledge of French or German essential. Maximum 48 hours per week, Sundays free. 3-8 weeks, March-October. Full board and lodging with the farmer's family, insurance and SF19+ per day pocket money provided. Applicants from western Europe can enter Switzerland under a global residence guarantee. It is not possible to place 2 people on the same farm. Applications should be made 4 weeks before intended date of arrival, and successful applicants will be sent details of arrangements before they are due to start work. *UK applicants may apply through Concordia (Youth Service Volunteers) Ltd, Recruitment Secretary, 8 Brunswick Place, Hove, Sussex BN3 1ET ✆ Brighton (0273) 772086. Registration fee £10, administration fee £15.*

WILLING WORKERS ON ORGANIC FARMS (WWOOF-CH) Patrick Bill, Speerstraße 7, 8305 Dietlikon ✆ 01-834 02 34

A non-profitmaking organisation which aims to help organic farmers and smallholders whose work is often labour-intensive as it does not rely on the use of artificial fertilisers or pesticides. Provides unskilled voluntary workers with first hand experience of organic farming and gardening and a chance to spend some time in the country. Places exist on some 80 farms throughout Switzerland. Members receive a quarterly newsletter which details farms needing help. Ages 16+. 30 hour week. 1-2+ weeks, all year. Full board and lodging provided in the farmhouse, tent or caravan; volunteers should take a sleeping bag. No wages paid, although long-term volunteers may receive small payment as arranged with host. Helpers pay own travel costs. Insurance and anti-tetanus vaccination recommended. Families welcome on some farms. Membership fee SF15 or US$15.

MONITORS & INSTRUCTORS

SKI EUROPE Brentham House, 45c High Street, Hampton Wick, Kingston-upon-Thames, Surrey KT1 4DG ℗ 081-977 7755
A company with its own ski school, operating holidays for groups and school parties. Part-time ski instructors are required for winter sports in the Bernese Oberland, Grisons and Valais regions. Work involves 6 hours teaching per day. BASI or full ASSI qualifications essential, together with a high level of teaching skill. Knowledge of foreign languages useful; fluent English a prerequisite. 1-4 week periods over Christmas, the New Year, February and April. Instructors receive full board accommodation and ski pass, plus travel expenses London/resort, and have access to the same facilities as the clients. Wages approx £75 per week, depending on qualifications. *Interviews held May-November.*

VILLAGE CAMPS Chalet Seneca, 1854 Leysin
Organises a range of holidays in American-style camps for children aged 8-16 from the international business and diplomatic communities. Opportunities for counsellors, special activity counsellors, programme leaders, special instructors, ski counsellors and nurses. Staff live, work and play with the children and are responsible for their safety, health and happiness.
Counsellors plan, organise and direct daytime and evening programmes, accompany campers on excursions and may be called upon to supervise other counsellors and take charge of a camper group. Evening activities include sports and games, films, competitions, fondues and discos. Special activity counsellors having a high degree of proficiency organise, execute and instruct specific programmes such as sports, arts and crafts, nature study and basic computer science. Counsellors with a substantial amount of leadership experience in recreational programmes can be appointed programme leaders, which includes running a camp programme and direction and supervision of adult counsellors. Assistant and junior counsellors are responsible for supporting counsellors in all activities and assisting with special activities at day camps as required. Specialist instructors should have 2 years training and experience and be able to instruct children of all ability levels; they are responsible for the concentrated teaching of their subject at a speciality camp such as football, golf, tennis, computer science or French and English language. Ski counsellors must be good parallel skiers, with a thorough understanding of mountain safety. Nurses are responsible for the general health and welfare of campers and counsellors, attending to accidents and maintaining an infirmary.

Compulsory pre-camp training course arranged for all staff. Summer camps are organised in Leysin; winter camps at Saas Fee, Anzere, Leysin, Saas Grund and Morgins. Ages 21+, 26+ for programme leaders. Applicants must have training and/or experience of working with children and have an interest in children from many ethnic and religious backgrounds. English is the first language, but priority consideration given to applicants with additional French, Italian or German language skills. For day camps preference is given to applicants living within commuting distance of the camp. 45 hour week.
Summer camps 1+ months, June-August; 1½ days plus 3 evenings free per 2 week session. Winter camps 1-4 weeks, December-Easter; 2 evenings free per week. Full board accommodation, accident and liability insurance provided, but not travel costs. Summer wages SF325 per two week session; winter wages SF100 per week plus ski pass for area worked. Wages for day camps are paid per 10 day session: counsellors, special activity counsellors and nurses SF275; assistant counsellors SF225; junior counsellors SF150.

TEACHERS

SWISS FEDERATION OF PRIVATE SCHOOLS Service Scolaire, rue du Mont-Blanc, PO Box 1488, 1211 Geneva 1
Publishes *Private Schools in Switzerland* (5 IRCs by surface mail, 10 IRCs by airmail), a booklet giving full details of schools to which teachers may apply, many international, from elementary to adult formation and including finishing schools. Many of them have English-

speaking sections which prepare for GCSE and A level exams, and include commercial, technical, secretarial, language and domestic branches with sports facilities. *Does not arrange individual placements; apply directly to the schools.*

SWISS NATIONAL TOURIST OFFICE Swiss Centre, Swiss Court, London W1V 8EE
✆ 071-734 1921
Can provide a booklet, *Switzerland - Country for Children*, published by the Association Suisse des Homes d'Enfants, which contains a large selection of schools and homes for children in the lowlands, mountains and towns to which teachers may apply. Some offer tutoring in English of American/English curricula.

WORKCAMPS

ATD QUART MONDE 1733 Treyvaux
Strives to protect and guarantee the fundamental rights of the most disadvantaged and excluded families to family life, education and representation. It is these families, being denied the means of being fully active members of society, who constitute the Fourth World in every country. Volunteers are invited to help in various tasks, including working weekends doing manual construction work at the organisation's two centres in Treyvaux and Geneva; helping to run street libraries in Freiburg, Geneva and Basle; and organising holiday activities for disadvantaged families at the Treyvaux centre. Applicants should be interested in better understanding the causes and effects of poverty and be willing to work hard with others as a team. Evening meetings and lectures focus on the concerns of the movement and are given by people working in the field. Ages 18+. No experience necessary. 2-3 weeks, July, and weekends at various times of year. Some insurance provided, but applicants pay their own travel, board and lodging expenses. B D PH

ECUMENICAL YOUTH COUNCIL IN EUROPE PO Box 464, Belfast BT4 2DE
✆ Belfast (0232) 651134
A fellowship of national ecumenical youth councils or denominational bodies dealing with church youth work. Offers young Christians from different countries and traditions the opportunity to meet and share their experiences and to discuss common issues and concerns. Promotes workcamps where international teams live and work together to serve the community on manual, social or study projects, offering an opportunity to share ideas on faith and life. Recent projects have included renovating a cabin used as a youth centre in the Alps; and assisting on a holiday camp for children from the poorer areas of Marseille. All camps include a relevant theme for study and discussion. Volunteers must be strongly motivated to contribute to the aims of the camp. Ages 18-30. 1-3 weeks, July-October. Board and lodging usually provided. Volunteers pay their own travel and insurance costs. *Apply by mid May.*

GRUPPO VOLUNTARI DELLA SVIZZERA ITALIANA CP 12, 6517 Arbedo
Based in Ticino in Italian-speaking Switzerland, exists to promote communal activity for the good of society and recruits volunteers to assist in reconstruction, maintenance and other essential work after natural disasters. Projects have included helping the inhabitants of Fusio which was struck by a flood; building river bridges in the Mogno region; operating schemes for young and handicapped people; excavating an aqueduct in Borgnone; and restoring a small church in Cess. Sports, social and cultural activities and excursions arranged.
Ages 18+. Applicants should enjoy living and working together and want to help the community in which they are based. No previous experience or special skills required. 4/6 hour day, 30 hour week. 1-3 weeks, July and August. Self-catering accommodation provided. Fee SF100.

SERVICE CIVIL INTERNATIONAL Postfach 228, 3000 Bern 9
Service Civil International promotes international reconciliation through work projects. Volunteers are needed to work in international teams on manual/social projects which have recently included building a pond and a space for animals to live on an organic farm near Aarau; renovating historical buildings in Grisons for use as holiday and course centres; building a greenhouse and a sports area at a Rudolf Steiner school in Solothurn; and laying a path at a peace centre

founded by a Franciscan friar near Lucerne.
Ages 18+. Applicants should be highly
motivated and prepared to work hard as part of
a team. Some camps require a knowledge of
French or German. 25–40 hour week. 2–4 weeks,
June-September. Food, accommodation and
insurance provided, but not travel. B D PH W

*Apply through partner organisation in country of
residence. In the UK: International Voluntary
Service, Old Hall, East Bergholt, Colchester, Essex
CO7 6TQ.*

Outside the UK: please see information on page 30.

GENERAL

**CANVAS HOLIDAYS LTD 12 Abbey Park
Place, Dunfermline, Fife KY12 7PD**
Provides ready-erected fully-equipped tents for
family holidays, and requires a number of
applicants to form flying squads, teams of 5/6
people who help set up and equip 200-250
6 berth frame tents in an area containing approx
12 campsites. Similar work also available
dismantling tents and cleaning and storing
equipment.
Ages 18-25. Knowledge of the native languages
not required, but is an advantage as flying
squad members sometimes have the
opportunity to continue as couriers. Applicants
must be sociable in order to work in a small
community, fit and able to work hard for long
hours under pressure, work without
supervision and cope with living out of a
rucksack. Driving licence an advantage. Early
April-mid June, possibly longer to set up the
tents, and September to dismantle them. Salary
£80 per week. Tented accommodation, self-
catering facilities and outward travel provided;
return travel dependent on the completion of
contract dates. *UK nationals only.*

**When writing to any organisation it is
essential to mention Working Holidays 1993
and enclose a large stamped, self-addressed
envelope, or if overseas a large addressed
envelope and at least two International Reply
Coupons.**

T U R K E Y

INFORMATION

Turkish Embassy
43 Belgrave Square, London SW1X 8PA
© 071-235 5252/3/4
Consulate General: Rutland Lodge, Rutland
Gardens, London SW7 1BW © 071-589 0360

British Embassy
Sehit Ersan Caddesi 46/A Cankaya, Ankara

Tourist office
Turkish Information Office, 1st Floor, 170-173
Piccadilly, London W1V 9DD © 071-734 8681

Youth & student information
Gençtur, Yerebatan Caddesi 15/3, Sultanahmet,
34410 Istanbul

Entry regulations A working visa is required
for all types of employment. This may be
applied for from the Consulate General once an
offer of work has been secured. Alternatively,
the prospective employer may make the
necessary application to the Turkish
authorities. In either case the applicant will be
informed of the decision by the Consulate.
Persons who enter Turkey as a tourist are not
permitted to take up employment.

Travel North-South Travel Ltd, Moulsham
Mill, Parkway, Chelmsford CM2 7PX
© Chelmsford (0425) 492882 arranges
competitively priced, reliably planned flights to
all parts of Turkey. Profits are paid into a trust
fund for the assignment of aid to projects in the
poorest parts of the South.

STA Travel, 74 Old Brompton Road, London
SW7 3LQ/117 Euston Road, London NW1 2SX
© 071-937 9921 (offices also in Birmingham,
Bristol, Cambridge, Leeds, Manchester and
Oxford) operates flexible low-cost flights
between London and destinations throughout
Turkey, and also offers accommodation and
tours.

Campus Travel, 52 Grosvenor Gardens, London
SW1W 0AG © 071-730 3402 (offices throughout
the UK) and Council Travel, 28A Poland Street,
London W1V 3DB © 071-437 7767 (offices also

in Paris, Lyon, Düsseldorf, Tokyo and throughout the US) offer Eurotrain under 26 fares to destinations in Turkey, and flexible low-cost youth/student charter flights to Turkey.

Publications Lonely Planet's *Turkey - A Travel Survival Kit* £8.95 offers practical, down-to-earth information for independent travellers wanting to explore beyond the usual tourist routes.
The Rough Guide to Turkey £8.99 provides comprehensive background information plus details on getting there, getting around, places to explore and cheap places to stay.
Michael's Guide to Turkey £7.95 is detailed and concise, providing invaluable practical advice for all kinds of travellers. Published by Inbal Travel.
All the above are available from good bookshops.

Turkey Holiday Guide is a booklet containing information, useful tips, addresses and maps. Available from the Turkish Information Office, see above.

AU PAIR / CHILDCARE

ANGLO PAIR AGENCY 40 Wavertree Road, Streatham Hill, London SW2 3SP © 081-674 3605
Can place au pairs and au pairs plus. Ages 17-27. Pocket money £30-£50 per week. Also placements for experienced nannies and mothers' helps; salary up to £100 per week. Agency fee £40.

COURIERS/REPS

SIMPLY TRAVEL LTD 8 Chiswick Terrace, Acton Lane, London W4 5LY © 081-995 3883
Specialist tour operator offering summer programmes in hotels and self-catering villas in the Bodrum, Marmaris and Fethiye areas of Turkey. Representatives are required to look after clients and ensure they have everything they need to enjoy their stay. Work also available for maids, watersports instructors, handymen, odd jobs people, cooks and operations staff. Season lasts from April-

October. 6 day week, with flexible hours. Ages 18+. Preference given to those with previous experience and the ability to speak Turkish. Salary £30-£200 per week, depending on job. Accommodation, insurance and travel costs provided. Training given before start of season.

MONITORS & TEACHERS

CENTRAL BUREAU FOR EDUCATIONAL VISITS & EXCHANGES Schools Unit, Seymour Mews House, Seymour Mews, London W1H 9PE © 071-486 5101 ext 2411
Teachers and sixth formers are required at two English language summer schools run under the auspices of the Turkish Ministry of Education, in the Mediterranean coastal town of Antalya, based at camping sites near the sea front. Schools are attended by approx 60 Turkish pupils and 7 Turkish staff. The main objective is to provide Turkish pupils aged 11-16 with the opportunity of practising English learnt in school, and by spending 3 weeks in the company of a group of British teachers and young people to acquire a deeper awareness of the British way of life.

Duties include assisting with the teaching of English as a foreign language, running conversation classes and organising sporting, musical and social activities. Ages up to 45. Applicants should be native English speakers, sixth formers willing to assist the staff; or teachers qualified in the teaching of any discipline: EFL or ESL qualifications an advantage. Applicants should have a sense of responsibility, organisational skill, adaptability to new surroundings, a sociable nature and an interest in sports and/or drama and music, plus experience of working with or teaching children. Participants must fully commit themselves to the teaching of English and the organisation of various educational, outdoor and social activities. 3 weeks, July-August, including excursions to places of interest and the opportunity to spend weekends with Turkish families. Board and accommodation provided, plus honorarium in Turkish currency towards pocket money (approx £50). Travel cost approx £230 including insurance, paid by applicants. *Apply by mid April.*

WORKCAMPS

GENÇTUR Yerebatan Caddesi 15/3, Sultanahmet, 34410 Istanbul ℗ **Istanbul (1) 526 5409/520 5274/5**
Volunteers are invited to participate on international workcamps, working in groups of 15-20 volunteers from 4-5 different countries in small villages throughout Turkey. Mainly environmental, social or manual projects such as forestry work, constructing schools, village centres and health care centres.
Also opportunities to work as monitors on children's camps.
Ages 18-35. 6-7 hour day, with 1 free day per week. 2 weeks, June-September. Working language is English. Accommodation provided in schools; volunteers should take a sleeping bag. Food supplied by the villagers or, occasionally, self-catering. Volunteers pay own travel expenses and insurance, and must attend an orientation meeting in Istanbul before each camp. **D**

Apply through partner organisation in country of residence. In the UK: Concordia (Youth Service Volunteers) Ltd, Recruitment Secretary, 8 Brunswick Place, Hove, Sussex BN3 1ET ℗ *Brighton (0273) 772086 or International Voluntary Service, Old Hall, East Bergholt, Colchester CO7 6TQ or Quaker International Social Projects, Friends House, Euston Road, London NW1 2BJ (experienced volunteers only) or United Nations Association, International Youth Service, Temple Of Peace, Cathays Park, Cardiff CF1 3AP* ℗ *Cardiff (0222) 223088*

Outside the UK: please see information on page 30.

GSM YOUTH ACTIVITIES SERVICE Yüksel Caddesi 44/6, 06420 Kizilay, Ankara ℗ **Ankara (4) 133 2200**
Requires volunteers for workcamps throughout Turkey. Recently, GSM has been working with local councils to develop green areas in town centres, including a natural recreation area along the banks of the river Kazilirmak in the town of Avanos, Central Anatolia; and transforming a derelict area into a public park in the historical town of Silifke on the Mediterranean. Tasks involve fencing, building paths and preparing the ground for planting. 5 hour day, weekends free. 2-3 weeks, July-September.

Ages 18-27. Excursions organised at weekends. Board and lodging provided in small hotels/ pensions. Volunteers pay their own travel costs and a registration fee.

Apply through partner organisation in country of residence. In the UK: United Nations Association, International Youth Service, Temple of Peace, Cathays Park, Cardiff CF1 3AP ℗ *Cardiff (0222) 223088.*

Outside the UK: please see information on page 30.

GENERAL

EUROYOUTH LTD 301 Westborough Road, Westcliff, Southend-on-Sea, Essex SS0 9PT ℗ **Southend-on-Sea (0702) 341434**
Holiday guest stays arranged where guests are offered board and lodging in return for an agreed number of hours English conversation with hosts or their children. Time also available for guests to practise the host language.
Mainly ages 17-25, but sometimes opportunities for older applicants. Open to anyone whose mother tongue is English, interested in visiting Turkey and living with a local family for a short time. 2-3 weeks, and occasionally 1-2 months, mainly July and August, but also during the year. Travel and insurance arranged by applicants, but tickets at reduced rates can be obtained on request. Registration fee approx £70. Apply at least 12 weeks prior to scheduled departure date.

SUNSAIL The Port House, Port Solent, Portsmouth, Hampshire PO6 4TH ℗ **Portsmouth (0705) 219847**
Crew members are required to work aboard cruising yachts sailing in flotillas off the Lycian coast. Vacancies for experienced skippers, responsible for the well-being of up to 13 yachts and 60 holidaymakers, giving daily briefings on navigation and providing sailing assistance where necessary. Applicants must have considerable sailing experience, be cheerful, hard working and able to deal with people of varying backgrounds and ages.

Ages 23-30. Also bosuns/mechanics needed, responsible for maintaining the marine diesel engines and repairing any other onboard items. Must have excellent knowledge of marine diesels and practical ability to cope with all sorts of breakdowns and repairs. Ages 22-30.

Hostesses required to look after laundry, accounting, cleaning of boats, advising holidaymakers on shops and restaurants, and organising social events and barbecues. Sailing experience useful; bright personality, patience and adaptability essential. Ages 22-30.

All staff should be prepared for very hard work and long hours. 12+ hour day. 1 day free per week. Knowledge of German useful but not essential. Staff must work the whole season, mid March-November. Wages approx £85 per week, paid monthly; return travel and medical insurance provided.

UNITED STATES

INFORMATION

US Embassy
24 Grosvenor Square, London W1A 1AE
© 071-499 9000
Visa section: 5 Upper Grosvenor Street, London
W1A 2JB © 0891-200290

British Embassy
3100 Massachusetts Avenue NW, Washington,
DC 20008

Tourist office
United States Travel and Tourism
Administration, PO Box 7EN, London W1A 7EN
© 071-439 7433

Youth hostels
American Youth Hostels Inc, 1332 1 Street NW,
Suite 800, Washington, DC 20005

Youth & student information
Council on International Educational Exchange
(CIEE), 205 East 42nd Street, New York, NY
10017

ISSTA, Suite 1204, 211 East 43rd Street, New
York, NY 10017

Student Travel Network, Suite 307, Geary
Street, San Francisco, CA 94108

Student Travel Network, Suite 728, 6151 West
Century Boulevard, Los Angeles, CA 90034

US-UK Educational Commission, 6 Porter
Street, London W1 © 071-486 1098

Entry regulations A visa is required for all
types of temporary employment. The applicant
must generally either be the beneficiary of a
petition approved by the US Immigration and
Naturalization Service or qualify as an
exchange visitor. Exchange Visitor Programmes
are operated from the UK by a number of
organisations; any young person wanting to
work in the US should check whether they
qualify under one of the programmes offered
and if so should apply as early as possible.
Once an application has been accepted, the
participant will receive form IAP-66 for a non-

immigrant Exchange Visitor Visa, which should be posted, with a completed Visa application (form OF-156) to the visa branch of the US Embassy, address above; or for residents of Northern Ireland to the American Consulate General, Queens House, 14 Queen Street, Belfast BT1 6EQ.

Holders of non-immigrant Exchange Visitor Visas may work in the US only under the terms of the programme and are not eligible to seek other employment while in the country. They are automatically exempt from paying social security and income tax. Participants should not plan to stay in the US longer than the duration of the programme, though the visa is valid for a period of travel, normally of 2/3 weeks, at the end of the programme. Changing to another visa is a difficult and complicated procedure, and there is no guarantee that it will be granted; full details available from the visa branch at the US Embassy. **B D PH W** Generally, physically or mentally handicapped people are not ineligible to receive visas.

Travel Campus Travel, 52 Grosvenor Gardens, London SW1W 0AG ℂ 071-730 8111 (offices throughout the UK) and Council Travel, 28A Poland Street, London W1V 3DB ℂ 071-437 7767 (offices also in Paris, Lyon, Düsseldorf, Tokyo and throughout the US) offer low cost student/youth airfares to destinations throughout the US.

Amtrak's National USA Pass offers unlimited travel on trains in the US; cost from $299 (45 days). Regional USA Pass offers unlimited travel on trains over key routes in 4 major regions. Cost from $175 (45 days). Bicycle boxes available. Details from Compass GSA, PO Box 113, Peterborough, Cambridgeshire PE1 1LE ℂ Peterborough (0733) 51780 or from Council Travel, see above.

Ameripass offers unlimited bus travel in the US, cost from £49 (4 days). **B D PH W** Helping Hand service enables a companion to travel free to assist a handicapped person who needs help in travelling on a bus. Certificate of eligibility required from a doctor; wheelchairs and other aids carried free. All tickets must be purchased in Britain. Details from Greyhound International Travel Inc, Sussex House, London

Road, East Grinstead, West Sussex RH19 1LD ℂ East Grinstead (0342) 317317, or from Campus Travel or Council Travel, see above.

North-South Travel Ltd, Moulsham Mill, Parkway, Chelmsford CM2 7PX ℂ Chelmsford (0425) 492882 arranges competitively priced, reliably planned flights to all parts of America. Profits are paid into a trust fund for the assignment of aid to projects in the poorest areas of the South.

STA Travel, 74 Old Brompton Road, London SW7 3LQ/117 Euston Road, London NW1 2SX ℂ 071-937 9971 (offices also in Birmingham, Bristol, Cambridge, Leeds, Manchester and Oxford) operates flexible low-cost flights with open-jaw facility - enter via one country and leave by another - between London and destinations throughout the US. Internal flights, accommodation, tours and air passes also available from STA offices in the US.

Publications *Rough Guides* provide comprehensive background information on cities and countries worldwide, plus details on getting there, getting around, places to explore and cheap places to stay. Titles include *USA* £12.99, *Florida* £6.99, *New York* £6.99 and *San Francisco* £5.99. *Culture Shock! USA* £6.95 introduces the reader to the people, customs, ceremonies, food and culture of the United States, with checklists of dos and don'ts. All the above are available from bookshops.

The Moneywise Guide to North America £8.85 including UK postage, provides information for anyone travelling on a budget in the US or Canada, with useful details on getting around, where to stay, what to eat and places to visit. Published by BUNAC, 16 Bowling Green Lane, London EC1R 0BD ℂ 071-251 3472.

Travellers Survival Kit USA & Canada £9.95, is a down-to-earth, entertaining guide for travellers to North America. Describes how to cope with the inhabitants, officialdom and way of life in the US and Canada. Published by Vacation Work, see below.

Summer Jobs USA 1993 £9.95, gives details of thousands of summer jobs for students in the United States and Canada, including work in ranches, summer camps, National Parks, theatres, resorts, restaurants and many more. Includes a section giving advice on legal requirements and visa procedure for non-US citizens.

Also *Internships USA 1993* £15.95, which lists career-oriented positions enabling students and graduates to train through a period of work with an established employer.

Both published by Peterson's Guides and available in the UK from Vacation Work, 9 Park End Street, Oxford OX1 1HJ ℗ Oxford (0865) 241978.

Accommodation The Council on International Educational Exchange (CIEE), 205 East 42nd Street, New York, NY 10017 publishes *Where to Stay USA 1991/92* $13.95 plus postage, a paperback listing over 1700 places to spend the night from $6, including hostels, motels, campsites and university halls of residence. Special section for foreign visitors included. Available in the UK from Council Travel, see above.

The YMCA of Greater New York operates the Ys Way International, 224 East 47th Street, New York, NY 10017. This programme offers inexpensive accommodation at YMCAs in New York City and other major cities from coast to coast in the US and Canada. Average cost per night is $30 including use of sports facilities. Details in the UK from Travel Cuts, 295A Regent Street, London W1R 7YA ℗ 071-637 3161.

ARCHAEOLOGY

Archaeological Fieldwork Opportunities Bulletin $12.50 plus $3.50 postage, lists archaeological sites throughout the US at which excavation and research work is being carried out. Details are given of staff needed at each site, with ages, experience required, board and lodging, wages, training and equipment provision, any costs involved and other conditions. Also lists archaeological field schools which provide practical training for students. Published annually in January by the Archaeological Institute of America, 675 Commonwealth Avenue, Department GG, Boston, Massachusetts 02215.

EARTHWATCH EUROPE Belsyre Court, 57 Woodstock Road, Oxford ℗ Oxford (0865) 311600
Aims to support field research in a wide range of disciplines including archaeology, ornithology, animal behaviour, nature conservation and ecology. Support is given to researchers as a grant and in the form of volunteer assistance. Recent projects have included excavating skeletons of bison killed by Native American hunters over 9,000 years ago in Nebraska; searching for surface features, food remains and artefacts on a civil war prison island in Lake Erie, Ohio; excavating slave cabins in Tennessee to uncover the lives of plantation slaves; and recording prehistoric petroglyphs at Mount Irish, Nebraska, one of the richest areas of rock art in North America.

Ages 16-80. No special skills are required, but each expedition may, because of its nature, demand some talent or quality of fitness. Volunteers should be generally fit, able to cope with new situations and work with people of different ages and backgrounds, and a sense of humour will help. 2-3 weeks, all year. Members share the costs of the project, from £500-£1200, which includes meals, transport and all necessary field equipment, but does not include the cost of travel to the staging area, although assistance may be given in arranging it. Membership fee £22 entitles members to join an expedition and receive magazines and newsletters providing the information necessary to choose a project. B D PH W depending on project.

FOUNDATION FOR FIELD RESEARCH PO Box 2010, Alpine, California 91903
A non-profitmaking organisation sponsoring research expeditions by finding volunteers to assist scientists in the field. Volunteers are required to help on archaeological projects, which have recently included an archaeological survey of a Zuni Indian pueblo in New Mexico; and recording the relationships between solar events and rock art features on the banks of the Gila river, Arizona.

Ages 14+. No special experience or skills required, but are always welcome. 20-25 hour week. 1-4 weeks, all year. Participants are given responsibilities to fulfil, so applicants should be willing to do their part to become active members of the research team. Members share the costs of the project, from $495 which includes transportation during the expedition, insurance, a preparatory booklet, most field gear, tent or dormitory accommodation and 3 meals per day. Travel to assembly point not provided. Scholarships available. **D PH** on certain expeditions. *Send 2 IRCs for a 40-page newspaper detailing current projects.*

LUBBOCK LAKE LANDMARK The Director, PO Box 4499, Lubbock, TX 79409
Volunteers are needed for research on Paleo-Indian, Archaic, Ceramic, Protohistoric and historic remains. Ages 18+. Applicants should be willing to work hard. 6+ weeks, June-August. Board and lodging, major equipment, instruction and training provided. Volunteers pay own fares, personal expenses and $40 for small equipment needs. Academic credit available. Sponsored by the Museum of Texas Tech University. **D PH W** *Apply by 1 May.*

MISSION SAN ANTONIO ARCHAEOLOGICAL SCHOOL Dr Robert Hoover, Social Sciences Department, California Polytechnic State University, San Luis Obispo, CA 93407
Volunteers are needed to assist in research into Spanish colonial archaeology at the Mission, one of the Franciscan establishments of Spanish California founded to convert the Indian population. Since 1976 the school has been excavating the 18th century site, including the Indian dormitories, the first brick and tile kiln excavated in Spanish California and the nearby barracks, and examining historical and cultural materials from the vine-grower's house to interpret the role of agriculture in educating the converts to the culture of 18th century Spain. Work involves excavating, recording and laboratory processing. Evening lectures and activities arranged; opportunities for weekend sightseeing.
Ages 18+. Applicants must be in good health. Interest and dedication essential; no experience necessary. Knowledge of English required. 35 hour, 5 day week. 3+ weeks, beginning mid June. Cost approx $100 per week, includes board and accommodation as guests of the Mission's Franciscan friars. Housekeeping chores are cooperative. No wages. Volunteers pay own insurance and travel costs.

MOUNT CLARE RESTORATION OFFICE Kristen L Stevens, Carroll Park, 1500 Washington Boulevard, Baltimore, MD 21230
Volunteers are needed to participate in a full range of archaeological activities involved in unearthing Baltimore's history and restoring the city's heritage. The excavation, entering its ninth year, seeks clues about this 18th century plantation's original appearance so that the entire landscape and numerous outbuildings may be reconstructed with as much care and accuracy as the main house. Areas scheduled for research are the parterre garden, kitchen garden, ice house, wash house, milk house and sheds. The work includes excavation and laboratory processing of artefacts, reconstruction of pots, historical research, surveying, analysis, report writing and acting as a tour guide for visitors. Ages 13+; those under 13 must be accompanied by an adult who will also dig. Applicants should have a desire to learn about and participate in archaeological activities. Previous experience not essential, but useful for certain tasks. Volunteers individually assigned to trained archaeologists. Up to 20 hour week, 10.00-16.00. Wednesday-Sunday, seasonal. Insurance provided, but volunteers must pay their own travel, board and accommodation costs. No wages paid.

PASSPORT IN TIME/USDA FOREST SERVICE Passport in Time Clearinghouse, PO Box 18364, Washington, DC 20036 ℂ (202) 293 0922
Provides opportunities for individuals and families to work under the supervision of professional archaeologists, historians and cultural resource managers on historic preservation projects. Work involves archaeological excavation, survey, analysis, research and interpretation. Projects take place in national forests throughout the US; recent projects have included recording and stabilising buildings at a mining ghost town in Arizona; cleaning and cataloguing finds at a bison kill site in Nebraska; locating and mapping Lt Col Custer's 1876 trail to Little Bighorn in North Dakota; excavating shell middens on the Oregon coast left by Native Americans thousands of years ago; and investigating construction camps used during the building of the Great Northern Railway in Washington State, to get a glimpse into the

daily lives of railway labourers.
Ages 18+ in most cases, unless accompanied by adult. No special skills or experience required but volunteers must have an interest in history, a willingness to learn and good spoken English. Usually 6 hours per day for 1 week, all year round. Basic training given in archaeological techniques. Campsites available near to projects; insurance cover provided. Volunteers are responsible for their own travel, food and incidental costs, although some projects provide up to $12 per day. Full details of all projects and application form provided in newsletter. **B D PH** at discretion of project leader.

UNIVERSITY RESEARCH EXPEDITIONS PROGRAM University of California, Desk M11, Berkeley, CA 94720
Volunteers are needed to assist on archaeological excavations. Recent projects have included excavating an early mammal site in Montana; researching the survival strategies of Anasazi Indians in New Mexico; and locating, mapping, drawing and photographing ancient Polynesian rock carvings on Hawaii. 2 weeks, June-September. Ages 16+. Applicants should be in good health, have a desire to learn, enthusiasm, a willingness to undertake rigourous but rewarding work, flexibility and sensitivity to other cultures. Skills such as surveying and photography, plus wilderness experience, some knowledge of archaeology, history, anthropology or geology useful. Contribution to costs from $865 covers research equipment and supplies, meals, accommodation, ground transportation and preparation materials. Travel to site not provided but route guidance given. *Partial scholarships available.*

AU PAIR / CHILDCARE

The au pair programme in the United States is open equally to males as well as females, with the emphasis as much on community involvement as on childcare. To be eligible you must be a citizen of a western European country with at least a fair degree of fluency in English. Character references and a medical certificate are required, and you will also need to have some childcare experience and,

particularly as some of the communities are rural, be able to drive. Most families prefer non-smokers. Au pairs work up to 45 hours per week spread over a maximum of 5½ days, with 1 full weekend free each month. Work involves active duties including feeding and playing with children, and passive supervision such as babysitting. Ages 18-25. The positions usually last 12 months (although there is also a 10 week summer programme available through Camp America, see below). The return flight plus approx $100 per week pocket money, board and accommodation, medical insurance, $300 for a course of study, 2 weeks holiday, and opportunities to travel are provided. Applicants are interviewed, and, if accepted, matched according to interests and experience with a selected host family and issued with a J-1 Exchange Visitor Visa authorised by the US Government. A short orientation programme is held on arrival in the US, and au pairs have access to a local counsellor during the length of their stay. Agencies will also require a good faith deposit of up to $500, refunded on completion of the programme.

The following agencies can arrange au pair placements on US Government authorised programmes:

ACADEMY AU PAIR AGENCY LTD Glenlea, Dulwich Common, London SE21 7ES ✆ 081-299 4599
12 month programme, as outlined above.

AMERICAN INSTITUTE FOR FOREIGN STUDY Au Pair in America Programme, 37 Queens Gate, London SW7 5HR ✆ 071-581 2730
12 month programme, as outlined above. Good faith deposit of $500 required, refundable upon successful completion of the placement and return to Europe. **B D PH W** applications considered from qualifying individuals who are able to perform household duties within the home.

AVALON AGENCY Thursley House, 53 Station Road, Shalford, Guildford, Surrey GU4 8HA ✆ Guildford (0483) 63640
12 month programme, as outlined above. Applicants must either be taking a year out before attending higher education, or

preferably be qualified in a childcare course (such as NNEB or BTEC) and seeking to gain experience for a career in childcare. Good faith deposit of £350 required, repaid on completion of contract.

CAMP AMERICA Dept ANRIIC, 37A Queens Gate, London SW7 5HR
An Exchange Visitor Programme offering a limited number of places for females as Family Companions in selected American families. Participants live as a member of the family, responsible for care and supervision of the children from 0-10 years of age, and undertake light household duties. 1½ days free per week.

Ages 18 (by 1 June)-24. Applicants must have a genuine love of children, enthusiasm to work and play with them in an imaginative manner, and the ability to adapt readily to different lifestyles. Driving licence preferred. The work is for 10 weeks, June-September. Pocket money $400. The programme includes return flight from London, orientation, sightseeing and accommodation in New York, and transfer. Applicants must have a willingness to work hard, be fit with a doctor's certification of good health, and speak good English. 1-8 weeks at the end of the programme for travel, the cost of which is not included. Deposit £50. Medical insurance fee £95. *Apply September-May. Interviews throughout Europe, Australia, India and Scandinavia.*

CBR AU PAIR 63 Foregate Street, Worcester WR1 1EE ✆ Worcester (0905) 26671
12 month programme, as outlined above. Good faith bond of £350, repaid when programme is successfully completed.

THE EXPERIMENT IN INTERNATIONAL LIVING Au Pair Homestay USA, Otesaga, West Malvern Road, Malvern, Worcestershire WR14 4EN ✆ Malvern (0684) 562577
A non-profitmaking organisation which aims to promote international understanding as a means of achieving world peace. Operates a 12 month au pair programme, as outlined above. £350 good faith bond, returnable at end of year; administration and orientation fee £150. *British nationals only; other EC nationals should apply to the EIL office in their own country.*

JUST THE JOB EMPLOYMENT AGENCY 8 Musters Road, West Bridgford, Nottingham NG2 5PL ✆ Nottingham (0602) 813224
12 month programme, as outlined above. *UK applicants only.*

STUDENTS ABROAD LTD 11 Milton View, Hitchin, Hertfordshire SG4 0QD ✆ Hitchin (0462) 438909
12 month programme, as outlined above. Good faith deposit of $500 refunded on successful completion of programme. *UK residents only.*

COMMUNITY WORK

BENEDICTINE LAY VOLUNTEERS Summer Experience Program, Mother of God Monastery, Box 254, Watertown, South Dakota 57201
The Program is designed for people interested in experiencing life in a monastic community, and is offered in the expectation that the volunteer might serve and at the same time grow spiritually. Volunteers serve primarily in South Dakota, in rural parishes, on summer day camp programmes, with Native American children, as well as in the monastery and the Harmony Hill Centre. Orientation provided to the monastery life and ministries. Sharing in the life of the religious community, such as reflection and days of prayer, is an important aspect of the programme. Ages 18+. 2-10 weeks, June-August. Board and lodging provided. Volunteers pay their own travel and insurance costs. *Apply by 1 May.*

SERVICE CIVIL INTERNATIONAL Route 2, Box 506, Crozet, Virginia 22932
Service Civil International promotes international reconciliation through work projects. Volunteers are needed to work on community projects. Recent projects have included reroofing a barn and cleaning the dairy at a Camphill community in New York State; playing games and reading with children at a centre for low-income black youth in Chicago; building work at a community in West Virginia providing free holistic health care; and hosting a camp for children with and without disabilities at a working community for the handicapped in the Blue Ridge Mountains. Ages 18+. Applicants should be highly

motivated and prepared to work hard as part of a team. 3-8 weeks, June-August. Food, accommodation and insurance provided, but not travel. B D PH some camps unsuitable for wheelchairs.

Apply through partner organisation in country of residence. In the UK: International Voluntary Service, Old Hall, East Bergholt, Colchester, Essex CO7 6TQ.

Outside the UK: please see information on page 30.

THE SIOUX INDIAN YMCA PO Box 218, Dupree, South Dakota 57623

The Sioux YMCAs were first founded in Dakota Territory in 1879 and today serve in 28 communities on 5 reservations in South Dakota, the only YMCAs operated by and serving primarily Indian people. Volunteers are required to live and work individually on small, remote reservation communities under the supervision of the YMCA. Projects may include developing recreational and children's activities; work in elementary and pre-schools; assisting with the nutrition program for the elderly; alcohol and drug abuse counselling; and developing libraries and health services. Time not spent in formally organised activity may be spent in a variety of counselling, recreation and community development activities, visiting homes, arts, crafts and sports, talking with children and getting to know the families and the communities. What is done largely depends on the volunteer's own abilities and the needs and supervision of the community and local YMCA. The personal relationships formed are at least as important as the specific activities carried out.

Ages 18+. Volunteers should speak good English, and preferably be skilled in recreation, leadership development, childcare and working with people. A love of children and people in general, and an ability to adapt to a different socio-economic and cultural setting are also necessary. Because of the poverty/alcohol syndrome on the reservation, volunteers are expected not to drink alcohol for the project period. Those from all religious faiths and commitments are accepted, but are expected to respect and participate in the Christian life of the community. 10 weeks, all year. Time

commitment should be to a 24 hour day, 7 day week. Full board and accommodation provided with families or in small community buildings, but volunteers must arrange own insurance and travel. Orientation and evaluation sessions arranged. Help given in obtaining a visa. PH depending on mobility and abilities.

VOLUNTEERS FOR PEACE INC 43 Tiffany Road, Belmont, Vermont 05730

Volunteers are invited to work on community projects organised by this independent, non-aligned, non-profit American organisation working for peace through youth exchanges and voluntary service. Recent projects have included building housing for low-income families and providing services for the homeless in Connecticut; providing support for wheelchair racers during their gruelling 9-day Midnite Sun marathon in Alaska; building a hiking and exercise trail at a youth ranch for abused boys in Maryland; and painting and carpentry at an HIV supportive community in Harlem. Ages 18-35. Applicants should preferably be already involved in the peace movement, as well as highly motivated, fit and prepared to work hard as part of a team. 2/3 weeks, June-August. Food, accommodation and insurance provided, but volunteers pay their own travel costs. B D PH but unsuitable for wheelchairs.

Apply through partner organisation in country of residence. In the UK: International Voluntary Service, Old Hall, East Bergholt, Colchester, Essex CO7 6TQ or
United Nations Association, International Youth Service, Temple Of Peace, Cathays Park, Cardiff CF1 3AP © Cardiff (0222) 223088.

Outside the UK: please see information on page 30.

WINANT-CLAYTON VOLUNTEERS ASSOCIATION The Coordinator, 38 Newark Street, London E1 2AA

A community service exchange scheme which aims to provide assistance to city community projects in the eastern states and to give volunteers an insight into a different culture. Volunteers are assigned to social work agencies, selected for their interest in the cultural exchange of young people. Projects include assisting at psychiatric rehabilitation centres and homes for emotionally disturbed children, working with the elderly and housebound, and helping organise day camps and centres for teenage groups and deprived children in the inner city. Ages 19+. Applicants should have some experience of work with children, youth and community work or other voluntary social work. They should be flexible, with a sense of humour and a real interest in people. Hours worked are comparable to full-time staff on the project. 3 months, June-September, including time for own travel. 2 days free per week. Board, accommodation and pocket money provided. Volunteers pay travel and insurance costs; small grants may be available. Participants should take enough money to support themselves during free time at the end of the project. Weekend orientation course organised. Registration fee £10. **B D PH W** depending on ability. *UK residents only; apply by mid January.*

CONSERVATION

Helping Out In The Outdoors $8 including postage is a directory listing hundreds of parks, forests and other public land agencies all over the United States where volunteers are required. Listings describe the park, agency and area, the types of volunteer positions available, job requirements and benefits available, followed by a contact address. Most of the positions are for campground hosts, trail maintenance crews and wilderness rangers. Published annually in November by the American Hiking Society, AHS Helping Out, PO Box 20160, Washington, DC 20041-2160 © (703) 385-3252.

AMERICAN HIKING SOCIETY Volunteer Vacations, Post Office Box 86, North Scituate, MA 02060 © Boston (617) 545-7019
Volunteers required for trail crews of 10-20 people working in national parks and forests, wilderness areas and state parks. These crews build and maintain trails and help with a variety of projects designed to make these areas safe, attractive and accessible. Recent projects have included cleaning and painting cabins on Hasselborg Lake in Alaska's Admiralty Island wilderness; converting the Galloping Goose

Trail from an abandoned railroad in Colorado's Uncompaghre National Forest; and fence maintenance work on an extinct volcano cone in Hawaii's Haleakala National Park. Volunteers should be experienced hikers who are in good physical condition, comfortable in remote, primitive settings and willing to work hard. Ages 16+. 2+ weeks, all year. Supervision, safety equipment, tools and food provided; volunteers should take their own sleeping bags and tents. Registration fee $40 payable after volunteer has accepted assignment. **D**

APPALACHIAN MOUNTAIN CLUB Volunteer Trails Conservation Corps, Box 298, Gorham, NH 03581 © (603) 466 2721
The AMC Trails Program maintains over 1,400 miles of trail in the north-eastern United States. Volunteers are invited to join the conservation corps and work in Trail Crews in the Berkshires, the Catskills and the White Mountains, building and maintaining shelters and trails, relocating sections and constructing new routes.

Ages 16+. Trail work experience helpful but not essential; more important are enthusiasm and willingness to learn and work to your best ability. Good health and backpacking experience also valuable; fluency in English essential. 1 week or 10 days, June-September. Approx 40 hours per week with weekends free. Full board and accommodation in basecamps or tents provided. Volunteers arrange own travel and insurance. Training provided in the use of handtools, safety procedures and maintenance techniques. Evening programmes of slide shows or talks arranged, plus options such as hiking or fishing in free time. Project fees $20-$60 for 1 week, $85-$175 for 10 days.

APPALACHIAN TRAIL CONFERENCE
PO Box 10, Newport, Virginia 24128 © (703) 544 7388
The Appalachian Trail is the world's longest continuously marked footpath, stretching for 2144 miles and following the Appalachian Mountains from Maine through Georgia. The trail has been maintained by ATC volunteers ever since its construction in the 1920s-30s as a place where workers in cities could go to take a break and learn about nature. Volunteers are invited to join teams of 6-8 people helping with

trail design, building and maintenance, shelter and bridge construction, rough carpentry, rehabilitation of eroded trail, clearing and open-areas management and a variety of other tasks. There are also a few paid positions for experienced trail crew leaders, camp coordinators and roving caretakers.

Ages 18+. No experience necessary for volunteer positions, as trail skills are taught by professionals. Applicants must be fit, enthusiastic, adaptable, willing to follow instructions and safety rules and happy to share in camp chores. 1-2+ weeks, May-October. Approx 40 hours per week, with 2 days off. Accommodation provided in tents or cabins, with time off spent at well-equipped base camp. All meals and insurance provided, but not travel costs. *Apply by 1 March.* B D depending on ability and project.

EARTHWATCH EUROPE Belsyre Court, 57 Woodstock Road, Oxford ✆ Oxford (0865) 311600
Aims to support field research in a wide range of disciplines including archaeology, ornithology, animal behaviour, nature conservation and ecology. Support is given to researchers as a grant and in the form of volunteer assistance. Recent projects have included tracking timber wolves in Minnesota to find out how roads, traffic and the presence of humans affects their behaviour; documenting the distribution of saltmarsh plants in Chesapeake Bay, Virginia, to see how they may survive a rise in global sea levels; working to save the dwindling bald eagle population in Michigan; and studying the feeding patterns of musk-oxen and caribou in Alaska in an attempt to boost their numbers.
Ages 16-80. No special skills are required, but each expedition may, because of its nature, demand some talent or quality of fitness. Volunteers should be generally fit, able to cope with new situations and work with people of different ages and backgrounds, and a sense of humour will help. 2-3 weeks, all year. Members share the costs of the project, from £500-£1200 which includes meals, transport and all necessary field equipment, but does not include the cost of travel to the staging area, although assistance may be given in arranging it. Membership fee £22 entitles members to join an expedition and receive magazines and newsletters providing all the information necessary to choose a project. B D PH W depending on project.

STUDENT CONSERVATION ASSOCIATION INC PO Box 550, Charlestown, NH 03603
Aims to provide resource management agencies with qualified and motivated volunteers, and to give volunteers educational opportunities and professional work experience in conservation and resource management in over 200 national parks, forests, wildlife refuges and similar areas throughout the US, including Hawaii, Alaska, Virgin Islands and Puerto Rico. Specific duties vary with location, but may include trail patrol, wildlife management, visitor contact, natural science interpretation, forestry, archaeological surveys or recreation management. Recent opportunities have included organising guided walks, hikes and cave tours around Mount Saint Helens, Washington; monitoring fledgling peregrine falcons in Glen Canyon, Utah; radio-tracking endangered red wolves in the Great Smokey Mountains, Tennessee; studying the effect of recent forest-fires upon elk behaviour in Yellowstone National Park, Wyoming; identifying and sampling marine fish, invertebrates and vegetation in the Everglades, Florida; conducting tours of a life saving station museum on Cape Cod, Massachusetts; monitoring Canada geese nesting in the Aleutian islands of the Alaskan Peninsula; and patrolling the remote wilderness areas of the Grand Canyon.
Ages 18+. Volunteers should have an interest in conservation or resource management. Some positions may require specific experience in public speaking, hiking or other outdoor activities, or in a particular academic field. Fluency in English essential; knowledge of other languages also helpful. 12+ weeks, all year. 40 hour week. Accommodation in apartment, trailer or ranger station, information and assistance with visas and partial travel reimbursement provided. Volunteers also receive $45-$90 per week, to cover food expenses, and a uniform allowance if required. Training, guidance and supervision provided by professional staff. Application fee $20. B D PH W depending on position and abilities. *Apply 2 months in advance.*

UNIVERSITY RESEARCH EXPEDITIONS PROGRAM University of California, Desk M11, Berkeley, CA 94720

Volunteers are needed to provide field assistance for research in the natural and social sciences. Projects include studying the endangered white pelican population in the Klamath Basin along the California-Oregon border; gathering information on the distribution and feeding patterns of seabirds in the Pribilof Islands of Alaska; and tracking elk and mule deer in the High Sierra of California, to determine if competition occurs in their activity and feeding patterns. Ages 16+. Applicants should be in good health, have a desire to learn, enthusiasm, a willingness to undertake rigourous but rewarding work, flexibility and sensitivity to other cultures. Skills such as surveying and photography, plus wilderness experience, some knowledge of botany, taxonomy and ecology useful. 2-3 weeks, all year. Contribution to costs from $800 covers research equipment, supplies, meals, accommodation, ground transportation and preparation materials. Travel to site not provided but route guidance given. *Partial scholarships available. Apply at least 2 months before session.*

VOLUNTEERS FOR PEACE INC 43 Tiffany Road, Belmont, Vermont 05730

Volunteers are invited to work in international teams on summer conservation projects organised by this independent, non-aligned, non-profit American organisation working for peace through youth exchanges and voluntary service. Recent projects have included erecting osprey nesting platforms and restoring historic buildings such as lighthouses at wildlife refuges on the coast of Maine; trail construction and maintenance alongside members of the US Forest Service in Alaska; and constructing solar-heated showers at an ecological farming and education centre in New Jersey. Ages 18+. Applicants should be highly motivated and prepared to work hard as part of a team. 6 hour day, 30-36 hour week. 2-3 weeks July-August. Food, accommodation and insurance provided, but volunteers pay their own travel costs. B D PH but unsuitable for wheelchairs.

Apply through partner organisation in country of residence. In the UK: International Voluntary Service, Old Hall, East Bergholt, Colchester, Essex CO7 6TQ or
United Nations Association, International Youth Service, Temple Of Peace, Cathays Park, Cardiff CF1 3AP ✆ Cardiff (0222) 223088.

Outside the UK: please see information on page 30.

DOMESTIC

BRITISH UNIVERSITIES NORTH AMERICA CLUB (BUNAC) 16 Bowling Green Lane, London EC1R 0BD ✆ 071-251 3472

Operates KAMP (Kitchen and Maintenance Programme), an Exchange Visitor Programme offering opportunities to work on children's summer camps in the US as domestic or maintenance staff. The camps are permanent sites catering for 40-600 children at one time. Camps can be organised privately, by the YMCA, Girl Scouts or Salvation Army, or they can be institutional camps for the physically, mentally or socially handicapped.
Vacancies for kitchen assistants, dining room staff, chambermaids, cleaners, laundry workers, dishwashers, assistant cooks and bakers, porters, janitors and nightwatchmen. Ground staff and general maintenance workers also required for mowing, weeding, plumbing, carpentry, electrical work, building, moving rubbish, painting, cleaning and repairing.
Vacancies for drivers (ages 21 + with full UK and international drivers licences) to transport children, staff and equipment. Relevant skills required for some jobs.
Ages 18+. Applicants must be full-time students studying at HND, 2 year BTEC or degree level in Britain, who like children and sports, and must be cooperative, energetic, sociable, conscientious, outgoing and cheerful. June-August. Hours vary from camp to camp, but can be long; the work is hard and often tedious and staff have to organise their own free time. Most camps allow staff to use recreational facilities. 8-10 hour day, 5½-6 day week. Contracts are for the full camp period, normally 9 weeks, but occasionally longer. Cost £59 (1992) towards flight to New York, transfer to camp, full board and basic accommodation in wooden cabins at camp, and visa charges. Insurance cost approx £84. Participants receive a salary of approx $500, at the end of the camp.

Approx 6 weeks are free at the end of the programme for independent travel; advice can be provided on onward travel. Friends can sometimes be placed on the same camp. Applicants will receive a list of jobs available, with details of size, type and location of camps, types of work available and any special facilities. Two references required of all applicants. Compulsory orientation programmes held at Easter throughout Britain. Membership fee £3. *Apply from October-November; directory available January/February.*

Irish applications to USIT, Aston Quay, O'Connell Bridge, Dublin 2 ✆ Dublin (1) 778117.

CAMP AMERICA Dept ANRIIC, 37A Queens Gate, London SW7 5HR
An Exchange Visitor Programme enabling young people to spend the summer in the US. Openings at summer camps in the US on the Campower programme, working in utility areas. Assignments include working with automatic washing and drying machines in the laundry; helping with food preparation, serving, dish and pot washing in the kitchen; dining room service; indoor and outdoor work, grass cutting, painting, moving and clearing rubbish, cleaning and general repair work; driving camp vehicles; and general secretarial work. Experienced cooks and bakers also required. On some camps workers are needed before camp opens, preparing the activity and living areas for the children. 10+ hour day. Students aged 18+. Pocket money $300. The programmes include return flight from London, orientation, sightseeing and accommodation in New York, transfer to camp, plus full board and lodging. Applicants must have a willingness to work hard, be fit, with a doctor's certification of good health, and speak good English. 1-6 weeks are left free at the end of the camp for travel, the cost of which is not included in the programme. Deposit £50; medical insurance £95. *Apply September-May.*

GOLDEN ACRES FARM & RANCH Box WH, Gilboa, New York 12076 ✆ (813) 786 2251 (2 December-14 April) or (607) 588 7329 (15 April-1 December)
A 600 acre farm and ranch resort in the Catskill Mountains of New York State. Requires waiting staff, chambermaids, cooks and dishwashers.

Ages 19+. Applicants must be English speaking and have previous experience of working with people. 40-55 hour, 6 day week, May-September. Wages $4.25 per hour, plus 2 bonuses of up to $40 per week upon successful completion of contract. Full board dormitory accommodation provided, cost $9.55 per day. All staff are given training and may use most of the resort facilities. Excursions organised to local places of interest. Staff must pay own travel and insurance costs, and organise own visa/work permit through an approved scheme operator. *Applications accepted 1 November-30 April.*

GRAND VIEW LODGE GOLF & TENNIS CLUB South 134 Nokomis Avenue, Nisswa, Minnesota 56468 ✆ (218) 963 2234
A luxury resort situated on the edge of Gull Lake in Minnesota, with guest cabins, a golf course, tennis courts and beach. Requires waiting staff, cooks, housekeepers, bartenders, clerks, beach attendants, shop staff and children's counsellors. Ages 18-28. Applicants must be English speaking; previous experience preferred. 35 hour, 5-6 day week, mid August-mid October. Wages $4.25 per hour, plus $0.25 per hour bonus paid on successful completion of contract. All staff must purchase uniforms on arrival. Full board accommodation provided in dormitories or cabins, cost $150 per month. Free use of resort facilities in spare time; occasional evening entertainments such as films, water skiing or bowling also organised. Staff must pay own travel and insurance costs, and organise own visa/work permit through an approved scheme operator. *Apply between 1 January and 15 April.*

FARMWORK

INTERNATIONAL AGRICULTURAL EXCHANGE ASSOCIATION YFC Centre, National Agricultural Centre, Stoneleigh Park, Kenilworth, Warwickshire CV8 2LG ✆ Coventry (0203) 696578
Operates opportunities for young people involved with agriculture, horticulture or home management to acquire practical work experience in the rural sector, and to strengthen and improve their knowledge and understanding of the way of life in other

countries. Participants are given an opportunity to study practical methods on approved training farms and work as trainees, gaining experience in their chosen field. Types of farm include cropping, dairy and mixed farms (crops plus dairy/beef) and a limited number of horticultural enterprises. Participants undertake paid work on the farm, approx 52 hours per week, and live as a member of the host family. Full board and lodging, insurance cover and a minimum net weekly wage of £50-£60 provided. All programmes include 3 weeks unpaid holiday. 3 day orientation seminar held at the beginning of each programme at agricultural colleges and universities throughout the United States. Stopovers (2-4 days) in Singapore/Thailand/Hawaii (for 14 month programme) arranged en route. Ages 18-30. Applicants should be single, and have good practical experience in the chosen training category, plus a valid driving licence. 7 months, (departing April); 14 months - 7 in Australia plus 7 in the US (departing September). Cost from £1725 covers airfare, work permit, administration fee, orientation courses seminar, information meetings, insurance, supervision, placement with a host family and travel costs to placement. £200 deposit payable. *Apply at least 4 months in advance. UK and Irish passport holders only.*

American applicants requiring an exchange should apply to IAEA, 1000 1st Avenue South, Great Falls, Montana 59401.

INTERNATIONAL FARM EXPERIENCE PROGRAMME YFC Centre, National Agricultural Centre, Stoneleigh Park, Kenilworth, Warwickshire CV8 2LG
℗ **Coventry (0203) 696584**
Provides assistance to young farmers and nurserymen by finding places in farms/nurseries abroad to enable them to broaden their knowledge of agricultural methods. Several schemes exist providing applicants with the opportunity to experience North American farm life. The University of Minnesota scheme involves 5-8 months on a farm/nursery followed by 3 months in the University. There are a variety of farms and the training is matched as far as possible with the applicants' requirements. Salary $300 per month including board and lodging. The Ohio

State University scheme involves 12 months practical training in nurseries, greenhouses, garden centres, landscaping projects, orchards and farms. Salary $4.25 per hour minimum. Also operates a combining scheme whereby trainees work on some of the large contract-combining crews. Crews generally leave Texas or Oklahoma in April or May, reach Canada in September, then head towards the Rockies and continue into Montana in October. Work involves combine and truck driving, and machinery maintenance. 12 months, starting March-May. Accommodation usually in mobile homes. Salary $4.25 per hour minimum, from which tax, board and lodging may be deducted. The National FFA Organization also offer agricultural and horticultural placements. 3, 6 or 12 months, beginning late March or late June. Salary from $3.35 per hour, from which tax, board and lodging are deducted. Programme fee $50 per month. 2 day orientation seminar arranged in Alexandria, Virginia before placements begin.

Ages 20-30. Applicants must have at least 2 years' practical experience, or at least 1 year at agricultural college and 1 year's practical experience, and intend to make a career in agriculture or horticulture. Valid driving licence necessary. Applicants pay own travel and insurance. Registration fee £160. *Apply early; EC nationals only.*

American applicants requiring an exchange should apply to one of the following: MAST/PART Program, Office of Special Programs, 405 Coffey Hall, 1420 Eckles Avenue, St Paul, Minnesota 55108; The Ohio State University, International Program in Agriculture, 113 Agricultural Admin Building, 2120 Fyffe Road, Columbus, Ohio 43210; National FFA Organization, PO Box 15160, Alexandria, Virginia 22309.

MONITORS & TEACHERS

AMERICAN CAMPING ASSOCIATION
5000 State Road 67 North, Martinsville, IN 46151-7902
Publishes *Guide to Accredited Camps* $15.95 including airmail postage, listing over 2,000 residential and day camps throughout the US. Written primarily for parents choosing a camp

for their children, it also includes a section on the camp job market which is estimated to provide more than 330,000 full-time posts. The majority of opportunities are for counsellors with skills in over 50 activity areas, including outdoor living, sports, climbing, horse riding, ocean biology projects, drama and music. The guide also gives details of practical job finding services operated by the American Camping Association. B D PH

BRITISH UNIVERSITIES NORTH AMERICA CLUB (BUNAC) 16 Bowling Green Lane, London EC1R 0BD © 071-251 3472
A non-profit, non-political educational student club which aims to encourage interest and understanding between students in Britain and North America. Operates opportunities for some 4,000 young people to work as counsellors on summer camps across the US, but mostly in the north east, upper mid west, south east and west coast. The camps are permanent sites and cater for 40-600 children at a time. Camps can be organised privately, by the YMCA, Girl Scouts, Salvation Army or they can be institutional camps for the physically, mentally or socially handicapped. Work involves living, working and playing with groups of 3-8 children aged 6-16. General counsellors are responsible for the full-time supervision of their group and ensure that the children follow the set routine, and should be able to provide counsel and friendship and must therefore have fairly general experience and aptitude in the handling of children. Specialist counsellors must have a sporting or craft interest, qualifications or skills plus ability and enthusiasm to organise or teach specific activities. These include sports, watersports, music, arts and crafts, science, pioneering, entertainments and dance. Staff with secretarial skills are needed for office work, and there are also vacancies for counsellors in institutional camps.

Ages 19½ (by 1 July)-35. Applicants must be resident in UK, single, hard working as hours are long, with a genuine love of children and relevant experience. They should be able to show firm, fair leadership and be flexible, cooperative, energetic, conscientious, cheerful, patient, positive and able to adapt to new situations, and to function enthusiastically in a structured setting. 8/9+ weeks, with 1 day off most weeks, mid June-end August, followed by 1-6 weeks free for travel after the camp. Return flight, overnight hostel accommodation, transfer to camp, orientation and training, guide to North America, plus board and lodging at the camp provided. Counsellors live with the children in log cabins or tents. Registration fee £50 (1992) Insurance fee approx £84. Salary approx £370; $430 for those aged 21+. Suitable for students, teachers, social workers and those with other relevant qualifications. Interviews held throughout the UK, mid November-early May. Compulsory orientation programme held at Easter. Membership fee £3. *Early application advisable.*

Irish applications to USIT, Aston Quay, O'Connell Bridge, Dublin 2 © Dublin (1) 778117.

CAMP AMERICA Dept ANRIIC, 37A Queens Gate, London SW7 5HR
An Exchange Visitor Programme which recruits young people to work as general or activities counsellors on summer camps in the US, mainly in New England, the middle Atlantic and mid-west states. Camps can be organised privately, by agencies such as the Boy Scouts, Jewish Youth Centres and YMCA, or they can be institutional, organised specially for the handicapped and the learning disabled. General counsellors will be responsible for the care and supervision of a group of 8-10 children aged 6-16. It involves working, playing and living with children 24 hours a day, and duties include supervising the camp and personal cleanliness, helping to maintain a high level of camp morale, ensuring that campers receive proper medical care, supervising rest hours, conducting activities and being on duty several nights a week. Specialist counsellors are responsible for instructing the children in specific activities such as sports, waterfront, sciences, arts and crafts, pioneering and performing arts. Other counsellors may be responsible for both activities and general work. Nurses and student nurses are also required as camp aides.

Ages 18 (by 1 June)-35. Applicants must be flexible, cooperative and adaptable, like and get on with children, prepared to work with young people intensively in an outdoor educational environment, and be willing to adjust to camp life. They must be fit, with a doctor's certification of good health, and speak good English. Applicants must be available June-September. The programme includes return flight, orientation in the US, transfer to camp, full board and lodging for 9 weeks at camp plus pocket money of $150-$450, according to age and experience. Up to 8 weeks are free at the end of the camp for travel, the cost of which is not included in the programme. Refundable deposit £50. Medical insurance fee £95. *Apply September-May.*

CAMP COUNSELORS USA (CCUSA)
27 Woodside Gardens, Musselburgh EH21 7LJ
✆ 031-665 5843
Recruits Counselors to work with children on American summer camps, usually instructing in a specific skill or sport area. Ages 19-28. Applicants must be fluent in English with previous experience of working with children and a recognised qualification in their particular skill or sport. 9+ weeks, June-September, with 1 day off per week. Full board accommodation provided in cabins or tents, return fare paid plus approx $300-$650 pocket money for 9 week work period. Orientation given in Britain and in the US before work begins. Cost (1992) £80 administration and £70 full insurance cover. *Apply by 1 April.*

THE SIOUX INDIAN YMCA PO Box 218, Dupree, South Dakota 57623
The Sioux YMCAs were first founded in Dakota Territory in 1879 and today serve in 28 communities on 5 reservations in South Dakota, and are the only YMCAs operated by and serving primarily Indian people. Volunteers are needed to work at a residential summer camp on the Oahe Reservoir of the Missouri River. Volunteers will provide partial leadership for a workcamp as it prepares the campground, and will assume staff responsibilities for four week-long camp sessions, plus shorter special camps for families, teenagers and canoeing. A camp director, head cook, nurse, waterfront director, maintenance person, crafts director and general counsellors are required. Staff live in teepees with campers, without electricity and running water; applicants should have skills suitable for primitive camping. Volunteers are also required to plan, organise and conduct 2-3

week day camps in small reservation communities at the request of, in cooperation with and under the direct supervision of the indigenous community YMCA. Camp activities may include basketball, volleyball, arts and crafts, storytelling, hiking, swimming, canoeing, baseball and group games. Time not spent in leadership of camps may be spent in a variety of counselling, recreation and community development activities and in just getting to know the families and the communities. Self-catering accommodation provided in one-room community buildings.

Ages 18+. Volunteers should be mature and committed, with definite camp skills, prepared to accept the disciplines of camp routine. They should be creative, responsible and flexible, speak good English, and be skilled in recreation, leadership development, childcare and working with people. A love of children and people in general, the ability to adapt to a different socio-economic setting and to relate meaningfully to other cultures are also necessary. Because of the poverty/alcohol syndrome on the reservation, volunteers are expected not to drink alcohol for the project period. Those from all religious faiths and commitments accepted, but are expected to respect and participate in the Christian life of the community. 10 weeks, summer. Commitment should be to a 24-hour day, 7-day week. Volunteers arrange own insurance and travel. Orientation and evaluation sessions arranged. Help given in obtaining a visa. PH depending on mobility and abilities.

WORKCAMPS

COUNCIL ON INTERNATIONAL EDUCATIONAL EXCHANGE (CIEE) 205 East 42nd Street, New York, NY 10017
Volunteers are invited to take part in international workcamps in various states including California, Florida, Idaho, Iowa, Kentucky, Maine, Montana and New York, organised by a non-governmental organisation seeking to promote international understanding and friendship. Recent projects have included site-mapping, artefact cleaning and record-keeping at an archaeological excavation of a prehistoric mound in Kentucky; digging a

trench to cook buffalo and acting as site-stewards at the National Indian Youth Council gathering in New Mexico; cleaning the shoreline, cabin maintenance and trail construction on Sitka Island, Alaska; improving facilities and assisting in recreational activities at a camp for children with disabilities in Iowa; and preserving historic fortifications on the Gulf Islands off the Florida coast. Ages 18+. Applicants should be highly motivated and prepared to work hard as part of a team. Approx 35 hours per week for 3 weeks, July-September. Food and self-catering accommodation provided. Participants should take work clothes and a sleeping bag and must pay their own travel costs. **B D PH W** depending on project.

Apply through partner organisation in country of residence. In the UK: United Nations Association, International Youth Service, Temple Of Peace, Cathays Park, Cardiff CF1 3AP © Cardiff (0222) 223088.

Outside the UK: please see information on page 30.

SERVICE CIVIL INTERNATIONAL Route 2, Box 506, Crozet, Virginia 22932

Service Civil International promotes international reconciliation through work projects. Volunteers are invited to work in international teams on workcamps. Recent projects have included digging to extend wolf enclosures and expand visitor areas at a mountain wolf sanctuary in Colorado; preparing and providing support for a Youth and Elders festival at an inter-tribal community college for Native Americans in California; and well-digging and irrigation at a centre for high-altitude sustainable farming in the Rockies. Ages 18+. Applicants should be highly motivated and prepared to work hard as part of a team. 30-40 hour week. 2-4 weeks, June-September. Food, accommodation and insurance provided, but not travel. **B D PH** some camps unsuitable for wheelchairs.

Apply through partner organisation in country of residence. In the UK: International Voluntary Service, Old Hall, East Bergholt, Colchester, Essex CO7 6TQ.

Outside the UK: please see information on page 30.

VOLUNTEERS FOR PEACE INC 43 Tiffany Road, Belmont, Vermont 05730

Volunteers are invited to work on international workcamps organised by this independent, non-aligned, non-profit American organisation working for peace through youth exchanges and voluntary service. Recent projects have included renovating a 100-year old railroad building for use as a cultural centre by Abenaki Native Americans in Vermont; working in a recycling centre and staffing a display of Third World crafts in Indiana; developing a nature trail and nursery at a community school in New Hampshire; and renovating a marionette theatre and taking part in its activities in Philadelphia. Opportunities for discussions, study groups, social and cultural activities, all linked to camp themes.

Ages 18-35. Applicants should preferably be already involved in the peace movement, and be highly motivated, fit and prepared to work hard as part of a team. 2/3 weeks, June-August. Food, accommodation and insurance provided, but volunteers pay their own travel costs. **B D PH** but unsuitable for wheelchairs.

Apply through partner organisation in country of residence. In the UK: International Voluntary Service, Old Hall, East Bergholt, Colchester, Essex CO7 6TQ or
United Nations Association, International Youth Service, Temple Of Peace, Cathays Park, Cardiff CF1 3AP © Cardiff (0222) 223088.

Outside the UK: please see information on page 30.

GENERAL

BRITISH UNIVERSITIES NORTH AMERICA CLUB (BUNAC) 16 Bowling Green Lane, London EC1R 0BD © 071-251 3472

A non-profit, non-political educational student club which aims to encourage interest and understanding between students in Britain and North America. Operates the Work America Programme, a general work and travel Exchange Visitor Program for full-time British college and university students aged 18+ who wish to work and travel in the US.

The Programme is sponsored in the UK by the Council on International Educational Exchange (CIEE). Participants can visit the US between 15

June-3 October, working for a maximum of 15 weeks; most work about 8 weeks and travel for 4. Members receive a handbook on how to get to the US, and a job directory which lists hundreds of jobs including hotel, restaurant and shop work, making and selling fudge, ice cream, sandwiches, soft drinks and fast food, laundry work, and helping in amusement parks. Alternatively members can go to the US on the basis of personal funds or on sponsorship and find a job once they are there. Compulsory orientation programmes held throughout Britain and upon arrival give advice on finding and choosing a job, obtaining a visa, income tax, accommodation, travel, food and budgeting. Flights arranged and include overnight accommodation in New York, cost £366 (1992); information also provided on onward travel, together with a guide to budget travel in North America and Mexico. Assistance provided by the summer office and by CIEE in New York. Cost £75 (1992) covers visa and administration costs. Insurance £84. Wages average $200+ per week. Participants can earn enough to cover the cost of the return flight, plus travel and all living expenses. Operates a loan scheme to help with flight costs. To qualify, participants must be able to provide evidence that they can support themselves during their stay, with between $300-$700 in travellers cheques, depending on whether they have a definite job offer, personal funds or individual sponsorship. Membership fee £3. *Apply for information in November.*

INTERNSHIP USA PROGRAMME Council on International Educational Exchange (CIEE), 33 Seymour Place, London W1H 6AT ℂ 071-706 3008 Fax 071-724 8468

Enables students to complete a period of work experience of up to 1 year in the United States, with optional travel period preceding or following placement. Ages 18+. Applicants must be enrolled in full time further or higher education (HND level or above) on a course where practical experience forms an integral part. They must find their own work placement and, either through payment from their employer or through other means, finance their own visit to the United States. Participants pay administration fee of £100 for a stay of up to 6 months or £125 for 6-12 months, and must have insurance cover for the length of their stay.

Official documentation and assistance with visa application provided, as are orientation materials covering issues such as Social Security, taxes, housing, American culture and transportation; plus 24 hour emergency assistance with any problems whilst in the United States. *Apply all year round, at least 2 months in advance.*

Applicants in France should apply to CIEE, 1 place de l'Odéon, 75006 Paris ℂ Paris (1) 46 34 16 10
Applicants in Germany should apply to CIEE, Thomas Mann Straße 33, W-5300 Bonn ℂ Bonn (0228) 6597 46/7

INVOLVEMENT CORPS INC 15515 Sunset Boulevard Suite 108, Pacific Palisades, California 90272 ℂ/Fax (310) 459 1022

Works in association with the Involvement Volunteers network to find volunteer placements in California and Hawaii. Volunteers of all ages can take part in individual placements or team tasks. Placements relate to conservation in urban or rural areas; farm programmes; sand dune restoration; bird observatory operations; developing nature reserves; and trail maintenance. Volunteers must be able to speak English, arrange their own visitor visas, and organise their own international travel and insurance. Involvement Volunteers provides advice on placements, itinerary planning, low cost accommodation, introductions to banking, and a communications base in the area of operations. Cost $225 (approx £125/DM400/AU$300). B D

In Europe, apply to Involvement Volunteers-Deutschland, Postfach 110224, W-3400 Göttingen, Germany ℂ/Fax (551) 33 765.
In Australia, New Zealand and Asia Pacific, apply to Involvement Volunteers Association Inc, PO Box 218, Port Melbourne, Victoria 3207, Australia ℂ/Fax Melbourne (3) 646 5504.

SANTA CRUZ SEASIDE COMPANY Employment Office, 400 Beach Road, Santa Cruz, California 95060 ℂ Santa Cruz (408) 427 1777

Santa Cruz Beach Boardwalk opened in 1907 and is classed as a State Historic Landmark. It is California's only seaside amusement park and features a variety of arcades, rides and food stops. Paid summer positions available in ride operations, food service, merchandise, arcades and ticket sales. Training given for all positions. Ages 18+. Applicants must speak English and be cheerful, cooperative, enjoy working with people in a tourist environment, and preferably have experience of customer service. 35 hour, 5-6 day week, May-September. Limited amount of dormitory accommodation available, cost approx $50-$60 per week. Staff must pay own travel costs and organise own visa/work permit through an approved scheme operator. *Application forms available at beginning of year, to be returned by 1 April.*

APPLYING FOR A JOB

Before applying, read carefully all the information given. Unless otherwise indicated, applications should be made in writing. Check in particular:

- skills, qualifications or experience required

- the full period of employment expected

- any restrictions of age, sex or nationality

- application deadlines

- any other points, particularly details of insurance cover, and other costs you may have to bear such as travel and accommodation.

When writing to any organisation it is **essential** to mention **Working Holidays 1993** and to enclose a large, stamped, self-addressed envelope, or if overseas, a large addressed envelope and at least two International Reply Coupons (available at Post Offices). When applying be sure to include the following:

- name, address, date of birth, nationality, sex

- education, qualifications, relevant experience, skills, languages spoken

- period of availability

- a passport-size photo, particularly if you are to have contact with the public

- anything else asked for, eg a *cv*

INFORMATION

Travel Eurolines, 23 Crawley Road, Luton LU1 1HX ✆ Luton (0582) 404511 or 071-730 0202 offers a wide range of coach services to over 200 destinations in mainland Europe, including daily services to Paris, Amsterdam, Brussels, Frankfurt and Cologne.

The British Rail International Rail Centre, Victoria Station, London SW1V 1JY ✆ 071-928 5151 can issue young people under 26 with Euro-Youth low-cost rail tickets to any one of 200 selected destinations in mainland Europe. Also issues Inter-Rail passes providing 15 days or 1 month's unlimited travel on the railways of 20 countries in Europe: cost £120 (ages under 26) or £160 (ages 26+) for 15 days; £160 or £230 for 1 month. European timetable booklets and assistance with journey planning also available.

Odyssey International, 21 Cambridge Road, Waterbeach, Cambridge CB4 9NJ ✆ Cambridge (0223) 861079 is a travel club which aims to match like-minded travelling partners.
An advice line is run by members who have just returned from abroad giving details of visa problems, vaccination requirements and employment prospects.
Publishes a quarterly newsletter detailing travel offers. Annual membership £20.
B D PH W welcome.

Exploring Europe £7.99 gives information on 22 countries, what to see, and background details about the people and way of life. Available from YHA shops or by post (add £1.21 to cover postage within the UK) from YHA Adventure Shops plc, 14 Southampton Street, London WC2E 7HY ✆ 071-836 8541.

Europe by Train 1993 £8.50 including UK postage, is a paperback guide for young European train travellers, giving advice on where to stay. Published annually in January. Also *Thomas Cook Rail Map of Europe* £4.40 including UK postage, shows passenger lines throughout Europe and in countries bordering the Mediterranean, including enlargements of 36 city plans.
Both available from Thomas Cook Publications, PO Box 227, Peterborough PE3 6SB.

Europe - A Manual for Hitch-hikers £3.95 gives country by country information on hitching techniques, route planning, entry procedures and attitudes towards hitch-hikers. Also includes an essential vocabulary in nine languages, advice on how to cross the channel cheaply and for free, how to read foreign number plates, addresses of hitch-hiking agencies, sources of free maps and how to get help with legal problems.

Travellers Survival Kit Europe £6.95, is a practical guide covering over 35 European countries, including details on the cost of food and accommodation, rules of the road, how the telephone systems work, car hire, health tips, public transport, shopping hours, Customs regulations, the law, where to get help and information and many useful addresses. Both available from Vacation Work Publications, 9 Park End Street, Oxford OX1 1HJ ℗ Oxford (0865) 241978.

The Traveller's Handbook £11.95 (£6.95 to members), is an 852 page reference and source book for the independent traveller, with chapters on travel, camping and backpacking, hitch-hiking, health, clothing, luggage and survival kits, where to stay, dealing with people when things go wrong, photography, choosing maps, passports, visas, permits, insurance, currency and Customs. Also includes special chapters for students, single women and the handicapped. Published by WEXAS International, 45-49 Brompton Road, London SW3 1DE ℗ 071-589 0500.

Accommodation The YMCA Inter-Point Programme offers low-cost accommodation for young travellers in various centres throughout Europe. All offer a warm welcome, advice and information. Available July-August/September. Cost from approx £4, bed and breakfast. Inter-Point card £2. Brochure giving full information available from National Council of YMCAs of Ireland Ltd, St George's Buildings, 37/41 High Street, Belfast BT1 2AB ℗ Belfast (0232) 327757.

YMCA World Directory £4 including UK postage, lists over 2,400 YMCA addresses in 90+ countries offering accommodation for men and women. *Pack for Europe* £2, post free, is a handbook containing addresses of hostels and

restaurants of the YMCA, YWCA and other recognised youth organisations, offering accommodation within a reasonable price range in Europe and the Middle East. Available from National Council of YMCAs, 640 Forest Road, London E17 3DZ ℗ 081-520 5599.

International Youth Hostel Handbook Vol I gives addresses and brief details of all the permanent hostels in Europe, North Africa and the Near East with the principal hostel regulations. Large folding map showing locations. Published annually in March.

International Youth Hostel Handbook Vol II details hostels in Australasia, America and Asia.

Price £5.99 each. Available from YHA shops or by post (add 56p per book for postage within the UK) from YHA Adventure Shops plc, 14 Southampton Street, London WC2E 7HY ℗ 071-836 8541.

Publications *Work Your Way Around the World* £8.95 is an informative book including firsthand accounts and details on preparation, working a free passage, opportunities in tourism, fruit picking, farming, teaching, domestic work, business and industry. Also contains details of areas of work and seasonal and temporary employment available.

Directory of Summer Jobs Abroad 1993 £7.95 including UK postage, details vacancies in over 40 countries, including information on jobs offered, wages given and addresses of employers.

Working in Ski Resorts - Europe £5.95 including UK postage, has information on finding work as a ski instructor, courier, chalet girl, teacher, au pair, ski technician, shop assistant, disc jockey, snow clearer, office worker or representative in a ski resort.

All available from Vacation Work Publications, 9 Park End Street, Oxford OX1 1HJ ℗ Oxford (0865) 241978.

A Place for You Overseas? In the Summer is a free leaflet containing addresses of organisations who can be contacted for details of workcamp, community and voluntary work opportunities for 1-3 months. Published by Christians Abroad, 1 Stockwell Green, London SW9 9HP ℗ 071-737 7811.

ARCHAEOLOGY

Archaeological Fieldwork Opportunities Bulletin US$12.50 + $3.50 postage, lists archaeological sites at which excavation and research work is being carried out. Details are given of staff and volunteers needed at each site, age/experience required, board and lodging, wages, training and equipment provision, any costs involved and other conditions. Also lists archaeological field schools which provide practical training. Published annually in January by the Archaeological Institute of America, 675 Commonwealth Avenue, Department GG, Boston, Massachusetts 02215, United States.

ARCHAEOLOGY ABROAD The Secretary, 31-34 Gordon Square, London WC1H 0PY Provides information on opportunities for archaeological fieldwork and excavations outside Britain. Three bulletins are published annually which provide details of digs, dates, the number of places offered, conditions of participation, details of board and lodging, and addresses of where to apply.

FOUNDATION FOR FIELD RESEARCH PO Box 2010, Alpine, California 91903, United States
A non-profitmaking organisation sponsoring research expeditions by finding volunteers to assist scientists in the field. Volunteers are required to help on archaeological projects which have recently included studies of textiles from pre-Columbian mummies in Peru; excavating a prehistoric cemetery and midden site in Grenada, to find out about the island's original inhabitants; and uncovering a 12th century motte and bailey castle in Wales. Ages 14+. Special experience or skills always welcome, but not essential. Participants are given responsibilities to fulfil, so applicants should be willing to do their part and become active members of the research team. Members share the costs of the project, from US$550-$1500 for 1-4 weeks, covering transportation during the expedition, preparatory booklet, most field gear, tent/dormitory accommodation and three meals a day. Travel to assembly point not provided. Scholarships available. D PH on certain expeditions. *Send 2 IRCs for a 40-page newspaper detailing current projects.*

COMMUNITY WORK

THE ACROSS TRUST Bridge House, 70/72 Bridge Road, East Molesey, Surrey KT8 9HF ✆ 081-783 1355
Set up in 1972 with the aim of taking bed-bound and severely handicapped people to Lourdes, the Trust now operates 15 Jumbulances - jumbo ambulances purpose built for the long-distance transportation of sick, handicapped and disabled people - on accompanied tours, holidays and pilgrimages across Europe. As well as Lourdes, destinations now include towns in Austria, Spain, Belgium, Switzerland, Germany, Israel, the Netherlands, Ireland, Poland and other eastern European countries. Qualified doctors and nurses, and unqualified helpers are needed to accompany tours, caring for, living, learning and laughing with the handicapped and sick throughout the journey. A willingness to help the *unable* is the most important requirement; muscle power is also helpful for pushing and lifting wheelchairs. The work can be demanding and tiring, requiring love, understanding and self-sacrifice. Satisfaction comes in knowing that the lives of those who suffer have been made happier and their courage renewed. Ages 16+. Most holidays last 10 days, March-November. Volunteers pay their own expenses and travel costs, from £350-£700, which also covers full board hotel accommodation and insurance.

ACTION D'URGENCE INTERNATIONALE (INTERNATIONAL EMERGENCY ACTION) Secrétariat International, rue Felix Ziem 10, 75018 Paris, France
A grouping of associations and volunteers who, conscious of the problems faced in time of natural disaster, wish to bring into being a supra-national structure for practical, humanitarian and environmental assistance, wholly unconcerned with political or territorial rivalries. Mobilises trained volunteers to go anywhere at any time in the event of a natural disaster. During the past years volunteers have been called for relief, rescue and reconstruction work after earthquakes in Algeria, Chile, Italy, Yugoslavia and Mexico; a volcanic eruption in Colombia; flooding in India and the north of England; a typhoon in the Dominican Republic; a tornado in France and a cyclone in the West

Indies. Tasks include setting up rescue services, procurement and distribution of vital supplies, provision of medical assistance, erection of temporary accommodation, repair of damaged property, restoration of transport and communication facilities, and helping survivors re-establish their lives and independence. Training courses held all year round introduce volunteers to the problems that go with natural disasters and give the basic skills needed for environmental and humanitarian development programmes as well as emergency actions. Membership fee FF120. B D PH W welcome to help with administrative work.

In the UK apply to Ms Gale Bennett, International Emergency Action, 8 Bartletts Row, Somerton, Somerset TA11 6QW℗ Somerton (0458) 72863/ 74747. Enclose A4 SAE.

ACTION HEALTH 2000 International Voluntary Health Association, The Director, The Bath House, Gwydir Street, Cambridge CB1 2LW ℗ Cambridge (0223) 460853
A voluntary charitable society concerned with health care issues in developing countries. Applications for a medical electives scheme are invited from medical school students in Britain; students from other European medical schools may also apply but must be prepared to travel to England to attend orientation course. Placements available in India, Bangladesh, China and East and Southern Africa. 6-8 weeks. Locations and type of work vary considerably, but personal interests are matched as far as possible. Participants are attached to the existing health team, often following a special programme. Returned elective students are encouraged to maintain links with the organisation and with the projects. The scheme operates on a non-profit basis; the fee of £62 covers selection, placement, orientation courses, practical help and advice with travel and insurance, and a support service during and after the placement. Participants also pay annual membership fee of £10, and approx £120 to cover hospital board and lodging. Applications considered throughout the year, but students are strongly advised to apply at least 6, and preferably 12 months before the elective date. Also operates short-term visitor and volunteer schemes for health professionals including doctors, dentists, physiotherapists, speech therapists, nurses, midwives and health visitors in India and Tanzania. Placements are in rural, semi-rural or deprived urban areas, often isolated, and may involve work in any area of primary health care. Positions may also be available in district general or specialist hospitals, teaching local health staff and passing on specific skills. 6+ months; may vary in special circumstances. Short-term visitors pay £90 fee to cover selection, placement, orientation courses and administrative costs. Board and lodging is provided but participants pay their own travel and insurance costs. PH

THE DISAWAY TRUST 2 Charles Road, Merton Park, London SW19 3BD ℗ 081-543 3431
Formed to enable physically disabled people to take holidays, the Trust needs able-bodied volunteers to look after disabled holiday-makers aged 16-80 on a 1:1 basis, helping with all their personal needs and ensuring that they gain the greatest possible enjoyment from their holiday. In 1992 holidays were arranged in Scotland and Florida. Ages 18+. Experience not necessary; volunteers who have never assisted disabled people before particularly welcome. 8-10 days, May-late September. Volunteers pay 50% towards the total cost of the holiday; from £185-£375 to cover transport, half board accommodation, excursions and insurance.

HELP THE HANDICAPPED HOLIDAY FUND (3Hs Fund), Holiday Organiser, 147A Camden Road, Tunbridge Wells, Kent TN1 2RA ℗ Tunbridge Wells (0892) 547474
Provides large group holidays for physically handicapped people from the age of 11 upwards. Able-bodied volunteers are required to care for the guests and help them enjoy their stay. Holiday venues have included Spain, Jersey, Swanage, Isle of Sheppey, Cliftonville and an adventure holiday in Cornwall. Ages 18+. No experience necessary. Tasks include washing, dressing, feeding and taking the guests on outings. Most holidays take place in the summer and last 1 week; volunteers have 1 afternoon off during the week. Full board accommodation in hotels/holiday camps, insurance and travel provided for UK venues. For continental holidays a nominal contribution is required to offset medical insurance and travel. *UK applicants preferred.*

PROJECT PHOENIX TRUST 56 Burnaby Road, Southend-on-Sea, Essex SS1 2TL
✆ **Southend-on-Sea (0702) 466412**
Runs overseas study tours and interest holidays for adults who would not be able to travel without physical assistance, or who are prepared to give such help as is needed in order that others may travel. Able-bodied helpers are needed to provide care for disabled adults. Holidays last 7-14 days, spring and September, and include Tunisia, Rome, Pompeii, Venice, Vienna, Florence, Andalucia, Bruges, Athens, Israel, Sweden and St Petersburg.
Ages 20+. Long hours and hard but rewarding work. Helpers should be strong and fit as tasks include pushing and lifting wheelchairs, and night attendance for turning patients in bed. Experience of caring for disabled people welcome, but not essential, providing there is genuine motivation to help. Accommodation in twin-bedded rooms shared by one handicapped and one able-bodied person. Volunteers are required to contribute 25% of the full costs, and organise their own insurance, pocket money and travel to and from London. *Apply well in advance; most places are allocated in January/February.*

YOUNG DISABLED ON HOLIDAY
33 Longfield Avenue, Heald Green, Cheadle, Cheshire SK8 3NH
Volunteers are needed to help on holidays abroad for young physically disabled people. Activities include sightseeing, theatre visits, discos, shopping expeditions and other adventure pastimes. Ages 18-35. Applicants should have a sense of fun and adventure. Each disabled person has at least 1 helper. 1 week, April-October. Volunteers are expected to contribute 40% of holiday costs.

CONSERVATION

EARTHWATCH EUROPE Belsyre Court, 57 Woodstock Road, Oxford ✆ Oxford (0865) 311600
Aims to support field research in a wide range of disciplines including archaeology, ornithology, animal behaviour, nature conservation and ecology. The support is given as a grant and in the form of volunteer assistance. Recent expeditions have included monitoring the feeding habits of baby lemurs in Madagascar; analysing water samples, flora and fauna in the fragile wetlands of Mallorca; saving the endangered leatherback turtle in the Virgin Islands; and examining coral communities in Fiji. Also supports projects run by scientists in eastern Europe, including studying the effects of acid rain on the forests of Bohemia, Czechoslovakia; reclaiming industrial wasteland in Bulgaria and monitoring the impact of wolves on Poland's red deer population.
Ages 16-75. No special skills required although each expedition may, because of its nature, demand some talent or quality of fitness. Volunteers should be generally fit, able to cope with new situations and work with people of different ages and backgrounds, and a sense of humour will help. 2-3 weeks, all year. Members share the costs of the expedition, from £500-£1200, which includes meals, transport and all necessary field equipment, but does not include the cost of travel to the staging area, although assistance may be given in arranging it. Membership fee £22 entitles members to receive magazines and newsletters providing all the information necessary to choose a project. B D PH W depending on project.

FOUNDATION FOR FIELD RESEARCH PO Box 2010, Alpine, California 91903, United States
A non-profitmaking organisation sponsoring research expeditions by finding volunteers to assist scientists in the field. Volunteers are required to help on conservation study projects, which have recently included monitoring the rate of rejuvenation of second-growth rainforest on the island of Grenada; studying the social structure of orca (killer whales) off the coast of Vancouver Island, Canada; helping to protect Mali's Gourma elephants, believed to be related to the ones that marched with Hannibal over the Alps; and patrolling a beach in Mexico where turtles lay their eggs.
Ages 14+. Special experience or skills always welcome, but not necessary. Participants are given responsibilities to fulfil, so applicants should be willing to become active members of the research team. Members share the costs of the project, from US$515-US$1285 for 1-4 weeks, depending on destination. This covers transportation during the expedition, a

preparatory booklet, most field gear, tent or dormitory accommodation and food. Travel to assembly point not provided. Scholarships available. D PH on certain expeditions. *Send 2 IRCs for a 40-page newspaper detailing current projects.*

UNIVERSITY RESEARCH EXPEDITIONS PROGRAM University of California, Desk M11, Berkeley, CA 94720, United States

Volunteers are needed to provide field assistance for research in the natural and social sciences. Recent projects have included collecting, photographing and sorting sponges and other marine animals from the reef environments of the Fiji Islands; studying the mother-pup interactions of sea-lions in Australia; and recording data on sheep flock numbers in Morocco. Ages 16+. Applicants should be in good health, have a desire to learn, enthusiasm, a willingness to undertake rigourous but rewarding work, flexibility and sensitivity to other cultures. Divers need SCUBA certification. Sailing and photographic skills desirable; background in marine biology, chemistry, ecology or natural history useful. 2-3 weeks, all year. Contribution to costs US$800-$1500 covers research equipment and supplies, meals, accommodation, ground transportation and preparation materials. Travel to site not provided but route guidance given. Partial scholarships available. *Apply at least 2 months before session.*

COURIERS / REPS

EF EDUCATIONAL TOURS EF House, Farman Street, Hove, Brighton, East Sussex BN3 1AL ✆ Brighton (0273) 727277/723651

Tour directors are required to lead educational tours of Europe made up of American and Canadian high school students and their teachers. Groups travel principally by coach, and tour directors have full responsibility for the group during the tour, supervising hotel check-ins and coach transfers, liaising with teachers, solving problems and providing commentaries during journeys. Applicants must have self-confidence and a good working knowledge of major European cities. Language skills an advantage. Ages 23+. Tours last 9-35 days and run during Easter and June-August.

Directors are continuously with the group throughout the tour. Salary under review. Full board hotel accommodation, travel expenses and insurance provided on tour. PH *Applications only accepted November-January.*

THOMSON HOLIDAYS Overseas Personnel Department, Greater London House, Hampstead Road, London NW1 7SD ✆ 071-387 3685

Britain's largest holiday company, operating throughout the world. Overseas representatives are required, meeting guests at the airport and transferring them by coach to their hotel, organising social occasions and generally giving assistance and advice on hotel and resort facilities. Representatives should be flexible and may be moved to different resorts during the season.

Ages 21-35. Applicants should be fluent in English and at least one of the following: Spanish, Italian, French, German, Greek, Portuguese, Serbo-Croat or Russian. The work involves close contact with guests and experience with the general public is desirable. No set working hours as representatives are expected to be on call to deal with any problems. Salary paid monthly in local currency with commission on excursion sales. Also work as youth representatives, which entails close contact with the younger guests, organising excursions, beach parties, outdoor sports and games to ensure they enjoy the holiday of a lifetime. Ages 21-30. Applicants should have a good working knowledge of Spanish or Greek, an extrovert but balanced personality and stamina as the job is very demanding. Children's representatives are also required, which involves organising activities, supervising meals, reading bedtime stories, evening patrolling services and ensuring the safety of the children is maintained at all times. Variable hours of work. Ages 18-28. Applicants must have childcare or nursing experience, should be friendly, and like children. Salary paid monthly in the UK. Accommodation, meals and uniform provided.

For all jobs applicants must have a high degree of patience, tact, strong sense of responsibility, a friendly, outgoing nature, and the ability to use their own initiative. Applicants must be available April-October, with the possibility of winter employment.

TRACKS EUROPE LTD The Flots, Brookland, Romney Marsh, Kent TN29 9TG ✆ Brookland (0797) 344343/344452
Couriers required by a coach/camping tour operator arranging tours of Europe, including Russia and Scandinavia, for groups of 35-45 people, mostly in the 18-35 age range.
Ages 25+. Applicants must be English speakers, prepared to work extremely hard for long hours to ensure the safety and comfort of passengers and deal with any contingencies that may arise. In return, they will have the opportunity to see many European and Scandinavian countries. Successful applicants attend a 4 week training trip around Europe and Scandinavia, departing in March. Participants pay £130 contribution to food kitty on the training trip, plus refundable bond of £250. Tours operate May-October. Trainee couriers receive £60 per week whilst on tour. Food and tent accommodation provided. *Applications accepted December-February only.*

TRAVELSPHERE LTD Compass House, Rockingham Road, Market Harborough, Leicestershire LE16 7QD ✆ Market Harborough (0858) 410456
Couriers required to escort groups of adult and elderly passengers on coaching holidays throughout Europe, including Austria, Belgium, Czechoslovakia, France, Germany, Hungary, Italy, the Netherlands, Russia, Spain and Switzerland. Work involves checking into accommodation, organising welcome meetings, guiding excursions and generally looking after passengers to ensure they have an enjoyable holiday.

Ages 20-35. Previous experience of courier work not essential but applicants must have a friendly, outgoing personality and an ability to deal with the general public. Experience of travelling in Europe useful. Good spoken English and one other European language required. 4 months, May-October. Couriers work long hours, but work is rewarding. Pay is at daily rate plus commission on sale of excursions. Half board accommodation generally provided, plus full insurance and travel costs. 3 day training course in the UK followed by additional training abroad. *Apply in writing between 1 November and 31 January enclosing a photograph.*

DOMESTIC

CLUB MEDITÉRRANÉE 106-110 Brompton Road, London SW3 1JJ ✆ 071-225 1066
Housekeepers, kitchen, laundry and bar staff, food buyers and chefs are required to work in holiday villages in Europe and north Africa. Applicants should be single, possess relevant qualifications and experience, must have minimum A level French, and, if possible, one other language. Ages 21-30. 6 months, May-October. It should be noted that applications cannot be made to work in a specific country; preference to work in a particular country can be indicated once applicants have worked for a few seasons. *Apply with cv, November-January. EC nationals only.*

TRACKS EUROPE LTD The Flots, Brookland, Romney Marsh, Kent TN29 9TG ✆ Brookland (0797) 344343/344452
Cooks required by a coach/camping tour operator arranging tours of Europe, including Russia and Scandinavia, for groups of 35-45 people, mostly in the 18-35 age range. Ages 25+. Applicants must be English speakers, with previous experience, prepared to work extremely hard for long hours. In return, they will have the opportunity to see many European and Scandinavian countries. Successful applicants attend a 4 week training trip around Europe and Scandinavia, departing in March. Participants pay £130 contribution to food kitty on the training trip, plus refundable bond of £250. Tours operate May-October. Trainee cooks receive £60 per week whilst on tour, and bonus on completion. Food and tent accommodation provided. *Applications accepted December-February only.*

FARMWORK

WILLING WORKERS ON ORGANIC FARMS (WWOOF) W Tree, Buchan, Victoria 3885, Australia
A non-profitmaking organisation which aims to provide voluntary help to organic farmers and smallholders whose work is often labour-intensive as it does not rely on the use of artificial fertilisers or pesticides. Publishes a list of 150 volunteer work opportunities,

including farmwork, available in 35 countries not yet served by a WWOOF group. Volunteers apply direct to organisations on the list. Cost £6 or £3 if ordered together with Australian WWOOF list.

MONITORS & INSTRUCTORS

CLUB MEDITÉRRANÉE 106-110 Brompton Road, London SW3 1JJ ✆ 071-225 1066
Qualified tennis, riding, golf, cycling, skiing, windsurfing, kayaking, swimming, archery, scuba diving, water skiing and sailing instructors, playgroup leaders, arts and crafts teachers, circus school instructors and children's activities monitors are required to work in holiday villages in Europe and north Africa. Applicants should be single, possess relevant qualifications and experience, must have minimum A level French, and, if possible, one other language such as German.
Ages 20-30. 5 months, May-October. It should be noted that applications cannot be made to work in a specific country; preference to work in a particular country can be indicated once applicants have worked for a few seasons. *Apply with cv, November-January. EC nationals only.*

TEACHERS

UNIVERSITIES' EDUCATIONAL FUND FOR PALESTINIAN REFUGEES (UNIPAL) 33A Islington Park Street, London N1 1QB ✆ 071-226 7997
Sends volunteers to work on short-term projects in the Israeli-occupied West Bank and Gaza Strip as well as with Palestinian communities in Israel and Jordan. Most projects involve teaching English or work with children. Ages 20-40. TEFL qualification, experience of teaching English or working with children essential. 3-8 weeks, July and August. Food and accommodation provided but volunteers pay their own travel and insurance costs. Long-term teaching opportunities also available. *Apply by end of March. Interviews in April; briefing in July for those selected.*

WORKCAMPS

ECUMENICAL YOUTH COUNCIL IN EUROPE PO Box 464, Belfast BT4 2DE ✆ **Belfast (0232) 651134**
A fellowship of national ecumenical youth councils or denominational bodies dealing with church youth work. Offers young Christians from different countries and traditions the opportunity to meet and share their experiences and to discuss common issues and concerns. Promotes international exchanges and seminars for young people; also workcamps where international teams live and work together to serve the community on manual, society or study projects, offering an opportunity to share ideas on faith and life. Recent projects have included cleaning up a centre for children with behavioural difficulties in Belgium; conservation and maintenance work at a former concentration camp in Germany; working in the garden, fields and kitchen of a monastery in Finland; and painting and carpentry in Cyprus. All camps include a relevant theme for study and discussion. Volunteers must be seriously motivated to contribute to the aims of the camp. Ages 18-30. 2-3 weeks, all year (mainly June-September. Board and lodging usually provided. Volunteers pay their own travel and insurance costs. *Apply by mid May. Applicants from outside Europe should enclose a letter of support from a church or ecumenical youth body in their region.*

WORLD COUNCIL OF CHURCHES Ecumenical Youth Action, 150 route de Ferney, PO Box 2100, 1211 Geneva 2, Switzerland ✆ **Geneva (22) 91 61 11**
Within the Ecumenical Youth Action programme there are opportunities for young people to participate in international workcamps, contributing to local and national development schemes. Recent workcamps have been held in Africa, Asia and the Middle East. Volunteers assist local groups in manual work such as agriculture, construction and renovation of buildings. The camps have theological reflections and discussions on vital issues affecting the local situation. Ages 18-30. 2-4 weeks, July and August. Volunteers pay travel and insurance costs and contribute approx $5 per day towards camp expenses.

GENERAL

CHRISTIAN SERVICE CENTRE Holloway Street West, Lower Gornal, West Midlands DY3 2DZ
Matches the personnel needs of missions and Christian organisations in Britain and abroad with the availability of those offering themselves for service, and also provides a counselling and advisory service for prospective workers. Both short and long-term paid and voluntary positions are available throughout the year in a wide variety of areas, ranging from pioneer missionary work, agriculture, community development and engineering, to jobs in the fields of radio, literacy, publicity, translation, accountancy and administration, and short-term work on summer camps and building projects. Vacancies in Britain also cover maintenance staff, cooks, housekeepers, social workers, secretaries and book-keepers in residential, rehabilitation or conference centres, and secretarial posts in mission offices. Experience/qualifications needed vary from post to post, as do hours, wages/pocket money, and provision of board, lodging and insurance cover. Ages 17+. Issues a *Job File* listing current vacancies in the UK, cost £15 for 8 issues, and *Time to Give*, a brochure listing short-term holiday opportunities, cost £1.50 including postage.

CLUB MEDITÉRRANÉE 106-110 Brompton Road, London SW3 1JJ ✆ 071-225 1066
Receptionists, secretaries, couriers, computer operators, book keepers, hostesses, cashiers, entertainment organisers and presenters, seamstresses, musicians, sound and lighting technicians, disc jockeys, administrative staff, boutique staff, hairdressers, electricians, plumbers, painters, mechanics, dressmakers, gardeners, laundry workers, doctors, dieticians, life-savers, and nurses are required to work in holiday villages in Europe and north Africa. Applicants should be single, possess relevant qualifications and experience, must speak fluent French, and, if possible, one other language such as German.
Ages 20-30. 6 months, April-October. It should be noted that applications cannot be made to work in a specific country; preference to work in a particular country can be indicated once

applicants have worked for a few seasons. *Apply with cv, November-January. EC nationals only.*

THE CRUISING ASSOCIATION Crewing Service, Ivory House, St Katharine Dock, London E1 9AT ✆ 071-481 0881
Maintains a register of people interested in crewing yachts, designed to put potential crews and skippers in contact. Applicants must be proficient sailors. None of the positions offered are paid, and skippers may expect a contribution towards expenses. Cost £14 to join the register.

INTERNATIONAL ASSOCIATION FOR THE EXCHANGE OF STUDENTS FOR TECHNICAL EXPERIENCE (IAESTE-UK) Seymour Mews House, Seymour Mews, London W1H 9PE ✆ 071-486 5101
The UK office of an international exchange scheme operating in 51 countries worldwide, and providing undergraduate students with course-related industrial, technical or commercial experience in another country. IAESTE covers a wide range of subject fields and operates in North and South America, Europe, the Middle East, Asia and Australia. Minimum 8-12 weeks during summer vacation, maximum 1 year. Students pay own travel expenses; a salary is paid by the firm. Accommodation arranged. Apply to own university or college, which normally must be affiliated to the national IAESTE office. Students should check application procedures with the IAESTE office in their own country. In the UK applications should be supported by the student's sponsoring company or by his/her university or college which should be affiliated to IAESTE-UK.

STABLE RELIEF SERVICE The Old Rectory, Belton-in-Rutland, Uppingham, Leicestershire ✆ Uppingham (0572) 86381
Arranges a variety of jobs working with horses throughout Britain, Europe, the Middle East, Japan, Australia, New Zealand and the United States. Work available throughout the year. Ages 18-30. Applicants must have experience of working with horses in a rural environment and be willing and helpful at all times. Good education required, and relevant qualifications a distinct advantage. Terms and conditions

vary depending on job: board and lodging generally provided, with £25-£50 pocket money per week for short stay periods. Higher wages and travel costs usually paid for stays of 3+ months. Training may be given. Agency can help with insurance and visas. Placement fee £40.

TRACKS EUROPE LTD The Flots, Brookland, Romney Marsh, Kent TN29 9TG ⊘ Brookland (0797) 344343/344452.
Drivers required by a coach/camping tour operator arranging tours of Europe, including Russia and Scandinavia for groups of 35-45 people, mostly in the 18-35 age range. Ages 25+. Experience of driving large vehicles preferred, and British PSV licence essential.
Applicants must be English speakers, prepared to work extremely hard. In return, they will have the opportunity to see many European and Scandinavian countries. Successful applicants attend a 4 week training trip around Europe and Scandinavia, departing in March. Participants pay £120 contribution to food kitty on the training trip, plus refundable bond of £200. Tours operate May-October. Trainee drivers receive £65 per week whilst on tour, and bonus on completion of each tour. Food and tent accommodation provided. *Applications accepted December-February only.*

A WORLD OF EXPERIENCE EQUESTRIAN EMPLOYMENT AGENCIES 36 The Street, Didmarton, Badminton, Avon GL9 1DS ⊘ Badminton (0454 238521
Agency arranging all types of work with horses throughout Europe and further afield. Work available all year round. Ages 17+. Applicants should have a responsible attitude and at least basic experience of equestrian work with a willingness to learn more. Conditions vary depending on job; board and lodging usually provided, wages range from £25-£180 per week. Some jobs offer training to BHS exams. Agency advises on travel and visas. Applicants pay own travel costs, which are generally reimbursed by employer. *Apply 4-6 weeks in advance.*

APPLYING FOR A JOB

Before applying, read carefully all the information given. Unless otherwise indicated, applications should be made in writing. Check in particular:

✎ skills, qualifications or experience required

✎ the full period of employment expected

✎ any restrictions of age, sex or nationality

✎ application deadlines

✎ any other points, particularly details of insurance cover, and other costs you may have to bear such as travel and accommodation.

When writing to any organisation it is **essential** to mention **Working Holidays 1993** and to enclose a large, stamped, self-addressed envelope, or if overseas, a large addressed envelope and at least two International Reply Coupons (available at Post Offices). When applying be sure to include the following:

✎ name, address, date of birth, nationality, sex

✎ education, qualifications, relevant experience, skills, languages spoken

✎ period of availability

✎ a passport-size photo, particularly if you are to have contact with the public

✎ anything else asked for, eg a *cv*

INDEX /
REPORT
FORM

REPORT FORM 1993

After you have been on a working holiday, we would appreciate it if you could answer the questions below and return this page to the Print & Marketing Unit, Central Bureau for Educational Visits and Exchanges, Seymour Mews House, Seymour Mews, London W1H 9PE. Up-to-date reports enable us to improve the accuracy and standard of information we provide. **All reports will be treated in strict confidence.**

Name and address of employing organisation(s)

Where work was undertaken

Period of work

Type of work

Ratio of work: free time

Salary/terms of employment

Food and accommodation provided? Yes [ ] No [ ]

Were you offered visits/excursions? Yes [ ] No [ ]

Age group of the other participants

PLEASE TURN OVER

Nationality of the other participants

Any other comments

Age

Occupation

Knowledge of foreign languages

Have you travelled overseas before? Yes [ ] No [ ]

If yes, which countries?

Have you been on a working holiday before? Yes [ ] No [ ]

Name

Address

Signed   Date